WHAT YOU SHOULD KNOW ABOUT THE
47 U.S. PRESIDENTS

BRUCE R. ELLIG

What You Should Know About the 47 U.S. Presidents

Copyright © 2025 by Bruce Ellig LLC

All rights reserved. No part of this book may be reprinted, reproduced, or utilized in any form or by any electronic, mechanical, or other means, now known or hereafter invented, including photocopying and recording, or in an information storage or retrieval system, without written permission in writing from the author of the book. The author can be reached at www.bruceelligauthor.com.

Printed in the USA. Second Printing.

ISBN: 979-8-9994314-0-0

Published by The Paper House

www.thepaperhousebooks.com

CONTENTS

ACKNOWLEDGMENTS v
DEDICATION vi
PREFACE vii
1. George Washington (1st President) 1
2. John Adams (2nd President)...25
3. Thomas Jefferson (3rd President) 34
4. James Madison (4th President)...47
5. James Monroe (5th President) 58
6. John Quincy Adams (6th President).................................66
7. Andrew Jackson (7th President) 73
8. Martin Van Buren (8th President) 83
9. William Henry Harrison (9th President)..........................90
10. John Tyler (10th President) 95
11. James K. Polk (11th President)...102
12. Zachary Taylor (12th President).......................................109
13. Millard Fillmore (13th President).....................................114
14. Franklin Pierce (14th President).......................................120
15. James Buchanan (15th President) 126
16. Abraham Lincoln (16th President)...................................133
17. Andrew Johnson (17th President) 152
18. Ulysses S. Grant (18th President) 158
19. Rutherford B. Hayes (19th President)..............................170
20. James A. Garfield (20th President)..................................177

21. Chester A. Arthur (21st President) 183
22. Grover Cleveland (22nd President) 191
23. Benjamin Harrison (23rd President) 198
24. Grover Cleveland (24th President) 205
25. William McKinley (25th President) 211
26. Theodore Roosevelt (26th President) 221
27. William Howard Taft (27th President) 234
28. Woodrow Wilson (28th President) 242
29. Warren G. Harding (29th President) 256
30. Calvin Coolidge (30th President) 263
31. Herbert Hoover (31st President) 273
32. Franklin D. Roosevelt (32nd President) 284
33. Harry S. Truman (33rd President) 308
34. Dwight D. Eisenhower (34th President) 325
35. John F. Kennedy (35th President) 346
36. Lyndon B. Johnson (36th President) 369
37. Richard M. Nixon (37th President) 387
38. Gerald R. Ford (38th President) 411
39. Jimmy Carter (39th President) 424
40. Ronald Reagan (40th President) 442
41. George H.W. Bush (41st President) 467
42. William J. Clinton (42nd President) 481
43. George W. Bush (43rd President) 502
44. Barack Obama (44th President) 527
45. Donald J. Trump (45th President) 560
46. Joseph R. Biden, Jr. (46th President) 593
47. Donald J. Trump (47th President) 643
APPENDIX A 660
APPENDIX B 669
APPENDIX C 688
APPENDIX D 704
APPENDIX E 714
APPENDIX F 797
INDEX 799

ACKNOWLEDGMENTS

First and foremost, I want to thank several people without whom this book would never have happened. I begin with McGraw-Hill and my first editor, **Mary Glenn**, for her initial support for my writing. Next is **Sandra Davidov** for her superb word-processing skills and for being a major contributor to my twelve books. Thanks to **Rachel Clarke** for researching the federal laws and the U.S. Supreme Court decisions in the book and for being helpful in numerous ways. To **Robert Hormats** for his presidential insights. To **Trang Mar** for publication research and analysis. To the **Library of Congress** for use of the presidents' photos. To **Mike Rizk** for making the book happen. To my copy editor, **Isabelle Steiger**, for her helpful assistance with the book's contents. To **Davia Temin** for her outstanding guidance in publishing and marketing the book. And to my extraordinary wife, **Janice**, for convincing me to write the book, as well as for coming up with the title.

Thank you all!

DEDICATION

I dedicate this book to my wife, Janice – lover, best friend, and soul mate. She takes such very good care of me in so many ways. In addition to all she does for me, she is the very successful owner of her own executive search firm, the Ellig Group.

PREFACE

Why did I write this book other than because I enjoy writing, and I enjoy research? I believe there is a need to better educate students and graduates about the history of our country and the presidents who held the top job in America. I wanted to write a book that would be a template for measuring the qualifications of future presidents. I wanted America to know why George Washington, Thomas Jefferson, and Abraham Lincoln were great presidents. What did they do that made them great? And why were James Buchanan, Andrew Johnson, and Warren Harding considered by many to be the worst of presidents? What did they do or not do to consider them failures? The reader is encouraged to make their own assessment and evaluation of each president.

There are at least three ways to read this book. The first is to start at the beginning and read to the end and then read the appendix on presidential highlights to refresh your memory. A second way is to read the appendix on presidential highlights and then go back and start to read with George Washington and read all forty-seven presidents in sequence. And the third way is to pick and choose what you want to read. I was tempted to start off the book with the highlights but decided, better to give the reader a choice. And although I made every attempt to be completely accurate in my writing, I apologize if there are errors. I hope you enjoy the book, and I hope it makes you a more informed voter.

Bruce R. Ellig

George Washington
(1st President)

April 30, 1789 – March 4, 1797

George Washington was born on February 22, 1732, to Augustine and Mary Ball Washington on their 1,000-acre farm in Westmoreland County, Virginia. Augustine had a daughter, Jane, and three sons, Butler (who died in infancy), Lawrence and Augustine Jr., from his first wife before she died. Augustine's second wife, Mary Ball Washington, gave birth to two daughters, Betty, and Mildred (who died in infancy), and four sons, George, who was the oldest, Samuel, John Augustine, and Charles. In addition to being a tobacco farmer, George's father was a justice of the peace.

George had an elementary education through tutoring. He memorized all 110 sayings of the **Rules of Civility and Decent**

Behavior in Company and Conversation and quoted them throughout his life. George's **father died** when George was eleven, and his half-brother Lawrence became George's **surrogate father**. George worked in the tobacco fields and later became a county land surveyor. Still later, he joined the Virginia militia.

As a result of cracking walnuts in his mouth, Washington had lost all his teeth except for one by age 19. He wore ill-fitting **dentures** made of slaves' teeth, causing him to use **laudanum** (a combination of alcohol and opium) to ease the pain. Naturally, he preferred soft foods, such as soup, cooked fish, mutton, and vegetables.

Lawrence and his wife died in 1752, leaving their **Mount Vernon** estate (built in 1734 by Augustine Sr.) and 4,500 acres to George. Also in 1752, George was commissioned a **lieutenant colonel** in the **Virginia militia**; he was denied a commission in the British army, as only men born in England could lead British troops. At 6'2", George was an imposing, majestic presence. It was said George was a graceful horseman and a sound decision-maker, with a **good mind** but a **quick temper**. At age 19, Washington came down with **smallpox**, giving him lifetime immunity to the disease, though it also probably made him **sterile**. It was believed half the population had contracted smallpox.

George's first exposure to battle was in 1754, when he represented Virginia and the King of England in the **French and Indian War**. George served as an aide to British **General Edward Braddock**, who was later killed in battle. The British suffered major losses because they marched in formation to fight, while the French and Indians fired their guns from behind rocks and trees.

At war's end, the British controlled everything east of the Mississippi River except for New Orleans. In 1755, George was commissioned a **full colonel** in the Virginia Regiment. George also became a member of the **Virginia legislature** in 1758 and resigned his commission.

In 1759, at age 27, George married the wealthy **Martha Dandridge Custis**, age 28. Martha's husband had died two years earlier. George and Martha would be married for 40 years. Apparently unable to conceive, George adopted Martha's two children, John and Martha, although both died at an early age. George also took responsibility for managing Martha's 17,000-acre estate. This, combined with his 5,000 acres made George one of **Virginia's wealthiest farmers**.

George called his wife "**Patsy**," and she called him "**the Old Man**," but when he headed the Continental Army, everyone called him "**General**." George bred hounds and held frequent **foxhunts**. He enjoyed Madeira wine, card games, and dancing the minuet. George and Martha lived in the Mount Vernon house. George, like other men of status, did not wear pants; **he wore breeches**, tight-fitting pantaloons cut off at the knees with the calves covered with knee-high stockings. Full-length pantaloons were worn by workers and soldiers. On formal occasions, George wore a powdered wig.

Before meeting Martha, George was very attracted to his 18-year-old neighbor, **Sally Fairfax**, who was married to George Fairfax. At one point, Washington wrote, "The world has no business to know the object of my love." But Sally and George supported the King and moved to England in 1752, ending Washington's hopes.

On October 25, 1760, King George II died, and his grandson became King George III.

On April 5, 1764, Parliament passed the **Sugar Act**, taxing molasses and sugar. On September 1, 1764, Parliament passed the **Currency Act**, prohibiting the colonies from issuing their own money. On March 22, 1765, Parliament passed the **Stamp Act**, imposing a tax on printed products. On March 24, 1765, Parliament passed the **Quartering Act**, requiring colonists to provide British soldiers with shelter and food. These acts led to protests that "**taxation without representation is tyranny.**"

On March 5, 1770, following a confrontation, British soldiers shot and killed five colonists in what was later called the **Boston Massacre**. On May 10, 1773, Parliament passed the **Tea Act**, requiring Americans to buy only British tea. In response to this action, in what was called the **Boston Tea Party**, on December 16, 1773, a group of colonists **dressed as Indians** threw cartons of tea into the Boston River. The British responded by closing Boston Harbor. In 1774, Washington was made Virginia's representative to the **First Continental Congress**. Representatives from the thirteen colonies convened in Philadelphia. Their focus was the various acts imposed on them by England.

On March 23, 1775, addressing the Virginia legislature, **Patrick Henry** stated, "Give me liberty or give me death." On April 18, 1775, **Paul Revere** and several others rode from Boston to Concord warning that the British were coming. The first battles of the Revolution were fought at **Concord** and **Lexington** on April 19, 1775, by **Massachusetts minutemen**, called that because they were ready to fight within a minute's notice. The militia's **minutemen** also fought the British on **Bunker Hill** with light casualties. John Adams stated, "Great Britain has at last driven

America to this last step, a complete separation from her, a **total absolute independence**, not only of her Parliament but of her Crown."

After his June 15, 1775 appointment as **Supreme Commander** of the Continental Army's 12,000 men, at no pay, Washington took personal charge of espionage. Referring to Washington's appointment, John Adams stated that "the liberties of America depend on him." Washington also created a small unit of bodyguards, called the **Life Guards**, to protect him.

On July 26, 1775, George Washington created a postal system for the country, naming **Benjamin Franklin** as its **first postmaster general**. Months later, Congress authorized the enlistment of riflemen (the birth of the **U.S. Army**), the construction of sailing vessels (the birth of the **U.S. Navy**), and the formation of a naval infantry (the birth of the **U.S. Marine Corps**).

Later in 1775, **Admiral Howe**, brother of General Howe**, landed 32,000 British troops** from 800 ships on Long Island. They headed for Brooklyn and Washington's 10,000 troops, but under cover of darkness and fog, Washington's troops escaped. In addition to having to fight the British, the Colonial Army had to fend off a **smallpox epidemic** that was raging through the colonies. Washington was immune to the disease because he had it in his youth.

On January 10, 1776, Thomas Paine published *Common Sense*, a rationale for American independence. Over 200,000 copies were reportedly distributed. Following the issuance of *Common Sense*, the Continental Congress met and created a **Committee of Five** to **draft a declaration of independence** from England. The members were: **John Adams** (Massachusetts), **Ben Franklin (Pennsylvania), **Thomas Jefferson** (Virginia), **Philip Livingston** (New York), and **Roger Sherman** (Connecticut). Jefferson was assigned to write the draft, upon the recommendation of John Adams. Jefferson's draft closely followed George Mason's Virginia Declaration of Rights and was a reference for similar declarations by seven states. With **John Hancock presiding**, the Continental Congress met and discussed the draft.

On **July 4, 1776**, the **Continental Congress** unanimously approved Thomas Jefferson's draft of the **Declaration of Independence** (see Appendix A). It separated America from England. This action was followed by **France** officially recognizing America's fight for independence and declaring war on England, in large part due to Ben Franklin's influence while in France.

In New York City, Mayor **Whitehead Hicks** and New York Governor **William Tryon** plotted the assassination of Washington. They approached members of **Washington's elite Life Guard** through intermediaries. One, Thomas Hickey, agreed to do the deed. But he was found out and hanged.

On September 22, 1776, **Nathan Hale**, a Washington spy, was captured by the British and hanged. On December 25, 1776, George Washington led his army across the Delaware River and routed a Hessian contingent in the **Battle of Trenton**.

In early 1777, the **Marquis de Lafayette**, age 19, arrived from France and was commissioned a major general in the Continental Army. Washington attempted to abolish slavery in 1777 but failed when several southern states threatened to leave the alliance and go to war with the North. Congress authorized the **American flag** with its stars and stripes on June 14, 1777. Later in 1777, some 11,000 Continental troops were defeated by

13,000 British troops at the **Battle of Brandywine**, but shortly after, British General Burgoyne surrendered his 6,000 troops in the **Battle of Saratoga** to American **General Horatio Gates**. Both had arrived to train the Continental troops.

A precursor to the Battle of Saratoga was the attack and capture of the British-held **Fort Ticonderoga**, along with its 60 cannons and plenty of ammunition, on **May 10, 1775**, by the Green Mountain Boys, led by Ethan Allen and Benedict Arnold. Months later, Colonel **Henry Knox** was put in charge by General Washington to bring those cannons and ammunition some 300 miles in the snow and mud to the hills overlooking Boston. Knox did so in 56 days. At that point, the **British** knew they were defeated, as their cannons could not reach the hills, and they **left Boston** for Halifax, Nova Scotia. In New York, on July 9, 1776, patriots toppled a statue of King George and melted it down for 40,000 balls of shot for their guns as a symbolic end to King George's tyrannical rule.

With the **Declaration of Independence** completed, the Continental Congress moved on to draft the **Articles of Confederation**, describing the relationship between the states and a new central government. After a discussion of a draft by **James Madison**, the Articles of Confederation were approved by Congress on November 15, 1777.

Beginning in 1777, Martha Washington joined and listened to the concerns of husband George for a week every winter, where she knitted socks for the troops. **Martha was George's helpmate**, and he was very dependent on her for help and advice. During the winter of 1777-78, 14,000 of Washington's troops, consisting of farmers and other non-professional fighters, wintered in **Valley Forge**. The camp was some 20 miles outside of British-held Philadelphia. During that winter, some 2,000 died from the cold, disease, and starvation.

In late 1780, **General Benedict Arnold** betrayed **West Point** to the British and was named a traitor. He then joined the British Army and was named a general. At about the same time, the British left New York City.

On March 1, 1781, all thirteen states ratified the **Articles of Confederation**, establishing the country as the **United States of America**. The states were united into one country under a **federal constitution**, but the central government lacked the power to print money and levy taxes. In late 1781, the states began printing their own money. That same year, at the Battle of Eutaw Springs, Francis **"Swamp Fox"** Marion and his guerilla style irregulars halted the British advance in the South. On October 19, 1781, General Cornwallis **surrendered Yorktown, as the French Navy blocked escape by sea**. The British defeat proved to be the final **decisive battle of the war**. Shortly after, **the British House of Commons** withdrew support for the war.

John Adams, Benjamin Franklin, and **John Jay** went to Paris and met with representatives from England to finalize the end of the **Revolutionary War**. The Result was the **Paris Peace Treaty**, signed September 3, 1783, recognizing American independence.

On November 3, 1783, Washington ordered that the army be disbanded. On December 4, he had a final meal with his officers at **Fraunces Tavern** in New York City. On December 23, **Washington resigned his commission**.

Afterward, he stated, "Having now finished the great work assigned to me, I retire from the theater of action." Washington returned to his home in Mount Vernon. There, his schedule was a 7:00am breakfast of fried cornmeal patties, followed by reading the papers. Then, it was time for horseback riding, checking his crops, and a late light lunch of soup at 3:00pm. This was followed by hunting with neighbors, then dinner at 7:00pm, featuring baked fish and cooked vegetables for his sensitive dentures along with plenty of Madeira wine.

GEORGE WASHINGTON (1ST PRESIDENT)

In 1784, Thomas Jefferson proposed banning slavery in the new territories, but nothing came of it.

In 1786, five states asked Congress to call a constitutional convention. From August 1786 to early 1787, **Daniel Shays** and other farmers, deeply in debt and unable to make payments, led **a rebellion** that was slow to be stopped because of a lack of federal troops. On May 25, 1787, a **constitutional convention** met in Philadelphia to firm up the **Articles of Confederation** by drafting a new **U.S. Constitution**. It was essentially **written by James Madison**, noted for his writing skills. George Washington presided over the convention.

On July 13, 1787, the Confederation Congress enacted the **1787 Northwest Ordinance Act** which banned slavery in the Northwest Territory and described the process by which a territory became a state. This was one of 129 acts passed by the Confederation Congress before they became the Federal Congress, which first met on March 4, 1789, and passed several key acts. The first act of the new Congress was **An Act to Regulate the Time and Manner of Administering Certain Oaths**, which described the procedure for administering oaths and was signed into law on June 1, 1789. Another, passed on July 31, 1789, was the **1789 Federal Customs Act**, which established the Customs Service.

The **U.S. Constitution** (see Appendix B) **was approved** by the Continental Congress by a vote of 52 to 3 on September 17, 1787. The three dissenters were **Elbridge Gerry** of Massachusetts and **George Mason** and **Edmund Randolph**, both of Virginia. Their objection was that the drafted constitution had **no guarantee of individual rights**. The draft now had to be ratified by at least nine of the thirteen states to become effective.

To convince the states that it was necessary to approve the newly drafted constitution, Alexander Hamilton, James Madison, and John Jay wrote 85 articles in support of the drafted constitution, describing the relationship between the states and the new central government. Hamilton wrote 51, Madison wrote 29, and Jay wrote 5. The articles were called the **Federalist Papers** and were distributed to the thirteen states.

On June 21, 1788, the **U.S. Constitution** was ratified by the required nine states. Delaware was the first state. New Hampshire was the ninth, preceded by Georgia, Connecticut, Massachusetts, Maryland, North Carolina, South Carolina, and Virginia. The last four states to ratify were New Jersey, New York, Pennsylvania, and Rhode Island.

Congress met in Federal Hall, New York City, on March 4, 1789, and declared the approved Constitution was now in effect.

Article I, Section 1 of the U.S. Constitution (see Appendix B) states that Congress shall consist of a **Senate** and a **House of Representatives**.

Article I, Section 2 of the U.S. Constitution (see Appendix B) states **each representative shall serve two years** and the number of representatives in a state "shall be determined by adding to the whole Number of free Persons, including those bound to Service for a Term of Years, and excluding Indians not taxed, three fifths of all other Persons." Since slaves were bound to service for life, not a "Term of Years," they fit in the "three-fifths" of all other persons. This was a big advantage for the southern states, which had the most of those "all other persons." In 1790, it was estimated there were 700,000 slaves in America, almost all in the southern states. Article I, Section 2 also stated, "The House of Representatives shall have the sole Power of Impeachment."

Article I, Section 3 of the U.S. Constitution (see Appendix B) states that the Senate shall consist of **two senators from each state, each serving six years, each senator having one vote**.

Congress decided that representatives and senators would be paid $6 for each day they were in session. Representatives and senators would be elected by the votes of those eligible.

Seeing the need for a process of requests for funds, Congress established the **House Ways and Means Committee**, which is provided for in **Article I, Section 7 of the U.S. Constitution** (see Appendix B).

Article II, Section 1 of the U.S. Constitution (see Appendix B) states, "The executive Power shall be vested in a **President** of the United States of America." He and a **vice president** shall hold office for **four years.**" **Article II, Section 1 of the U.S. Constitution** also states how the president and vice president are determined. Each state has a number of electors equal to the number of Senators and Representatives; the total constitutes the **electoral college**, and "no person except a natural born Citizen, or a Citizen of the United States, at the time of the Adoption of this Constitution, shall be eligible to the Office of the President, neither shall any person be eligible to that Office who shall not have attained to the Age of thirty five years and been fourteen Years a Resident within the United States."

It took considerable **convincing by** Washington's long-term friend **Alexander Hamilton** (who served with Washington in the Continental Army) for Washington to **run for president**. Washington simply wanted to stay retired on his Virginia farm. He had **deficient hearing** and an **unreliable memory**. Hamilton wrote to Washington that "on your acceptance of the office of President, having surrendered your commission, the success of the new government may materially depend." Washington relented and finally agreed to seek the nomination. On June 15, 1788, **Washington** was nominated by the Constitutional Convention, along with several others, with **New York City** serving as the **nation's capital**.

In the **election of 1789**, there were 69 electors in the electoral college. Each elector was to vote for two people for president. The person with the highest number of votes became the president. The person with the next highest number of votes became the vice president. The **1789 presidential** election took place on February 4, 1789, but the results were not known until April 10 due to travel limitations. **Washington** was voted president by all 69 electors and therefore **was unanimously named president**. **John Adams** came in second with 34 votes and **became vice president**. The remaining 35 votes went to other candidates. There was no popular vote. Adams believed that the voting confirmed that he was second only to Washington as a patriot.

John Adams was born on October 30, 1735, in Braintree, Massachusetts. He graduated from Harvard in 1755 and taught grammar school while studying law. He was admitted to the Massachusetts Bar in 1758, and in 1764 he married **Abigail Smith**. They had five children: Abigail Amelia, John Quincy (who became the sixth president), Susanna, Charles, and Thomas. Before serving as Washington's vice president, Adams was active in Massachusetts state politics. He also was a delegate to the First Continental Congress in 1774 and the Second in 1775. Adams later served sequentially as an ambassador to Great Britain, France, and the Netherlands.

Prior to Washington's presidency, the **first eleven states** entered the Union, in order: **Delaware, Pennsylvania**, and **New Jersey** in 1787; and **Georgia, Connecticut, Massachusetts, Maryland, South Carolina, New Hampshire, Virginia**, and **New York** in 1788. Others that followed during his presidency included North Carolina (1789), Rhode Island (1790), Vermont (1791), Kentucky (1792), and Tennessee (1796).

In a letter to Abigail, his wife, who was still in Massachusetts, Adams stated, "My country has in its wisdom contrived for me the most insignificant office that ever the invention of man contrived, or his imagination conceived." Lacking any executive powers except standing in line to be president, Adams remarked, "**I am Vice President. In this I am nothing, but I may be everything.**" Adams was referring to succeeding President Washington. **Article II, Section I of the U.S. Constitution** (see Appendix B) states, "In Case of the Removal of the President from Office or of his Death, Resignation, or Inability to discharge the Powers and Duties of said Office, the same shall devolve on the Vice President, and the Congress may by Law provide for the Case of Removal, Death, Resignation or Inability, both of the President and Vice President, declaring what Officer shall then act accordingly, until the Disability be removed or a President shall be elected." Barring this happening, the vice president serves as president of the Senate with the sole responsibility of breaking tie votes. Without this responsibility, the vice president has no job.

On April 30, 1789, Washington took the **oath of office** on the balcony of Federal Hall in **New York City** (the site of the first Congress), as described in **Article II, Section 1 of the U.S. Constitution** (see Appendix B): "I do solemnly swear (or affirm) that I will faithfully execute the Office of the President of the United States, and will to the best of my ability, preserve, protect, and defend the Constitution of the United States." **Washington added**, "That I take this obligation freely, without any mental reservation and that I will faithfully discharge the duties of the office on which I am about to enter. So help me God."

Congress decided that **future elections** would be in **November** (not February) because the harvest would have been completed. And **inauguration** was set at March 4th, as it provided the time needed to count the November votes and wait for winter to thaw.

Although Washington was the **first president to serve under the enacted U.S. Constitution,** he was not the first president of the country. In **1781, John Hanson** signed the ratified Articles of the Federation as "**President of the United States in Congress Assembled.**" Even General Washington addressed him as President of the United States. After discussion on how to address the president, it was decided the first officer should be called "**the President of the United States.**" This was reflected in **Article II, Section 1 of the U.S. Constitution** (see Appendix B). Thomas Paine was the first to suggest the title. He did so in his 1776 book, ***Common Sense.***

Washington was 57 years old at the time of his **inauguration**. Washington's **First Inaugural Address** was ten minutes long, and mainly about presidential duties and the consequences that would occur if he were to break them. Washington had a **barrel of rum** for his reception. He later stated, "To be prepared for war is one of the most effective means of preserving peace." While serving in the military, Washington received no salary, only money for expenses. Washington asked Congress to do the same while he was president. They refused and decided to pay him **$25,000** a year with no money for expenses. As vice president, John Adams was paid **$5,000** a year. These were very significant amounts of money, as laborers were paid $1 per week.

Article III, Section I of the U.S. Constitution (see Appendix B) provided for one **supreme court**, and the **1789 Judiciary Act** created federal trial courts in all thirteen states and stipulated the U.S. Supreme Court would consist of one Chief Justice and five Associate Justices. In 1789, Washington nominated **John Jay** as the **Chief Justice** of the Supreme Court and John Blair, William Cushing, James Iredell, John Rutledge, and James Wilson as the **Associate Justices**. The nominations were approved by the Senate. Congress approved annual salaries of $3,500 for the Associate Justices and $4,000 for the Chief Justice. The first case to reach the Court was **West vs Barnes** in 1791, involving a contract, debt, and a state statute. The court ruled on procedural issues, not the points of conflict. Washington later appointed three additional Associate Justices for a total of nine, a record that would stand for a long time.

New York received the moniker of "**Empire State**" from George Washington, who in **1789** identified it as the "**seat of the empire**." It was **Alexander Hamilton** who sponsored the move of the U.S. capital from New York to Philadelphia in 1789. Also in 1789, Congress created the Department of Foreign Affairs (and then changed it to the U.S. State Department), the Department of the Treasury, Department of War, and the Attorney General.

Article II, Section 2 of the U.S. Constitution (see Appendix B) states the president shall make treaties with the advice and consent of the Senate. The constitution mandates all treaties be **approved by two-thirds of the senators**. Washington negotiated **four treaties**: one with Great Britain that avoided a second war, another with Spain that allowed visitations of their territories, a third with Algiers that freed captured American seaman, and a fourth with England that settled British claims on America's unpaid debts to England.

Nothing in the U.S. Constitution gives the president authority to issue **executive orders** with the force of law, but Washington did just that when **he created the cabinet in 1789**. Since then, over 14,000 executive orders have been issued, in addition to some 20,000 laws.

The U.S. Constitution, U.S. Code of Laws, and the U.S. Supreme Court, namely, constitutional law, statutory law, and case law, are the foundations of the U.S. legal system. These actions were supplemented with executive orders by the president.

Washington selected his initial **cabinet**, consisting of **Vice President** John Adams, **Secretary of State** Thomas Jefferson, **Secretary of the Treasury** Alexander Hamilton, **Secretary of War** Henry Knox, **Attorney General** Edmund Randolph, and **Postmaster General** Samuel Osgood.

Congress decided to pay the Secretary of State an annual salary of $3,500, the Secretary of the Treasury $3,500, the Secretary of War $3,000, and the Attorney General $1,500. There is no record of pay for the Postmaster General, but it can be assumed it would have been at least $1,000. There is no record of the thought process behind the varied amounts. Given that the vice president and Associate Justices' salaries were set at $3,500 and the Chief Justice's at $4,000, one is left with questions about the differences and similarities in pay.

A **1789 Revenue Act** separated duty-free from taxed items.

On June 20, 1790, at a dinner hosted by Thomas Jefferson, bitter debates about Madison's **location of the federal government** and Hamilton's **taxation authority** were resolved. The nation's capital would be moved from New York to Philadelphia, and the federal government would be the country's major taxing authority. This was called the **Dinner Table Bargain** and was considered a major event in the history of the United States. It led to the **1790 Residence Act**, which established the **Executive Mansion** as the residence of the president in Virginia on the Potomac River and the **First Bank**.

The **1790 Federal Patent Act** established a registry of claims for investors; the **1790 Funding Act** stated the federal government would assume state debts of the Revolutionary War; the **1790 Tonnage Act** assessed duties on non-American items; the **1790 Naturalization Act** required two years' residency for citizenship; the **1791 Revenue Act** placed a tax on whiskey; and the **1791 Bank Legislation Act** chartered the **First Bank of the United States** in Philadelphia. With this act, Alexander Hamilton established the financial foundation permitting America to get foreign funds to pay for the Revolutionary War.

It was clear there were **significant policy differences** between Jefferson and Hamilton. **Jefferson supported farming; Hamilton supported manufacturing.** Jefferson supported the French Revolution; Hamilton did not support it.

Washington **read and responded to a limited number of letters he received each day**. Due to the lack of speedy mail service, there were significant delays between the receipt and the return of Washington's replies. This was the **start of an ongoing tradition** with succeeding presidents.

Washington was aware that every action, regardless of how minor, would become a **precedent** for future events. In his service as leader of the Continental Army, Washington developed **leadership skills** that aided him as President. He thought issues through before taking action and made effective use of the people under him. Issues would be forwarded to the appropriate cabinet member, who would prepare a draft reply for Washington's response.

In **1791**, George Washington and Thomas Jefferson hired **French architect Pierre L'Enfant** to design the new federal city (later called Washington) to feature thirteen broad diagonal avenues named after the original colonies.

The insistence of Gerry, Mason, and Randolph on the need to guarantee individual rights in the U.S. Constitution led James Madison to draft the first ten amendments named the **Bill of Rights** (see Appendix C). It guaranteed certain individual rights, including freedom of speech, freedom of religion, and freedom of the press. The amendments were ratified by the states on December 15, 1791.

Jefferson took the position that the federal government should pay for the state debts incurred during the revolution. Speculators made fortunes buying up what were thought to have been worthless state paper.

In **1792**, Congress passed the **Coinage Act**, which established the U.S. Mint in Philadelphia and authorized the minting of coins. The **first coins** minted were a **copper** half-cent and one cent with a liberty bust design. Other coins were based on the decimal system: ten pennies to a dime and ten dimes to a dollar. Congress approved a silver dollar (valued at a British pound) with the names of each of the thirteen colonies and a **$10 gold coin**, the equivalent of more than a week's pay for many workers. The **states** were issuing **paper** currency but no coins.

The **1792 Neutrality Act** banned U.S. citizens from military service in other countries and banned foreign warships in American ports, and the **1792 Presidential Succession Act** detailed the order of succession if both the president and vice president positions were open.

On October 13, 1792, George Washington laid the cornerstone of the **Executive Mansion**. Later, the capital moved to Virginia on the Potomac River, and it was named "**Federal City.**" Not controlled by any state, it would reside in the **District of Columbia**, named after Christopher Columbus. In 1792, President Washington moved from New York City to Philadelphia and then to Federal City in Virginia.

GEORGE WASHINGTON (1ST PRESIDENT)

Washington planned on serving **only one** term but was convinced by friends that there was still work to be done, so he agreed to a second term. In the **1792 election, Washington was reelected**, having received all of the 132 electoral votes, while John Adams, receiving 77 votes, was reelected vice president. **New York Governor George Clinton** received 50 votes. **Thomas Jefferson** received four votes, and **Aaron Burr** received one vote. Again, there was no popular vote.

Washington's March 4, **1793, inaugural speech** was the shortest on record. He said, "Fellow citizens. I am again called upon to be the voice of my country to execute the functions of the Chief Magistrate. When the occasion proper for it shall arrive, I shall endeavor to express the high sense I entertain of this distinguished honor, and of the confidence which has been reposed in me by the people of united America." Washington then fled to Mount Vernon. Later in 1793, **Jefferson** resigned as Secretary of State and **returned to Monticello**.

Washington's **cabinet** during his second term in office included **Vice President** John Adams, **Secretary of State** Edmund Randolph, **Secretary of the Treasury** Alexander Hamilton, **Secretary of War** Henry Knox, **Attorney General** William Bradford, and **Postmaster General** Timothy Pickering. Changes from the first cabinet were: Randolph replaced Jefferson, Bradford replaced Randolph, and Pickering replaced Osgood. During his second term, Adams's wife Abigail remained at the farm in Quincy, Massachusetts until late in his term.

After initially participating in the debates as he presided over the Senate, John Adams's sole responsibility was to break a tie vote, which he did 29 times. The senators ruled that Adams could not speak other than to break a tie. Due to his large stomach, some senators referred to Adams as "His Rotundity."

In **Chisholm vs Georgia** (1793), the U.S. Supreme Court ruled that federal courts have jurisdiction in suits "between a State and citizens of another State," where the state is a defendant.

In **1794**, Washington led troops to suppress the **Whiskey Rebellion**, consisting of farmers who distilled their own whiskey in Pennsylvania protesting a 1791 liquor tax. Washington later pardoned those arrested. The **1794 Revenue Act** imposed taxes on luxury purchases. And in **1794**, Alexander Hamilton created the **Federalist Party**, believers in a strong central government. Anti-federalist Thomas Jefferson created the **Democratic-Republican Party**, known as the **National Republicans**. They favored greater states' rights and smaller federal government along with lower taxes and fewer regulations. In 1820, it became the **Democratic Party**. But it is now known for more regulations, government control, government debt, and higher taxes. The current **Republican Party** was formed in 1854 in Ripon, Wisconsin.

In **Georgia vs Brailsford** (1794), the only jury trial in the Court's history, the U.S. Supreme Court ruled that state statutes sequestering debts do not vest those debts in the state.

Amendment XI to the U.S. Constitution (see Appendix C) specified that votes for the president and vice president would be separated. The amendment was approved February 7, 1795.

In **Talbot vs Janson** (1795), the U.S. Supreme Court ruled that the District Court has "clear jurisdiction" over a case involving an unlawful capture of a ship on the high seas by an American privateer.

The **1795 Naturalization Act** raised citizenship requirements to five years of residence from the earlier two-year requirement.

Communication was slow in Washington's time. A letter from Boston to New York took seven days to arrive, and one from America to England could take seven months. This meant that hostilities could continue for months after a treaty had been reached.

In **Ware vs Hylton** (1796), the U.S. Supreme Court, citing the Supremacy Clause, ruled that treaties are the "supreme law of the land" and overrule state laws.

Asked to serve a **third term**, Washington stated, "I decline being considered for nomination." He added that he looked forward to returning "to that retirement from which I had been reluctantly drawn," which he did in 1797. In his **farewell address**, Washington stated, "It was important to discharge the debts which unavoidable wars may have occasioned, not ungenerously throwing upon posterity the burden we ourselves ought to bear and to avoid entangling alliances and observe good faith and justice toward all nations."

In **Huger vs South Carolina** (1797), the U.S. Supreme Court ruled that in an equity suit against a state, showing the original subpoena to the secretary of state, delivering a copy to the attorney general, and leaving a copy at the governor's house is sufficient service of process.

George and Martha returned to Mount Vernon to enjoy a quiet life. **George died** on December 14, 1799, at the age of 67, of **pneumonia**. **Martha died** at age 70 in 1802, three years after George. Both were buried in the **Washingtons burial tomb** in Mount Vernon. At the time of his death, Washington **freed his slaves**. Washington's death was hastened by doctors drawing large quantities of his blood, further weakening him. His last words were, "'Tis well," though, fearing being buried alive, he added, "Have me decently buried and do not let my body be put into the vault in less than two days after I am dead." Upon his death, **Congress proclaimed** that Washington was "first in war, first in peace and first in the hearts of his countrymen." He is often called the "**father of our country**."

Washington's name is **honored in many ways**, starting with the changing of the **country's capital's name** from "Federal City" to "Washington" in the District of Columbia. Washington is also the name of one of the states and of numerous cities. Washington's face appears on the **quarter coin** and the **$1 bill**. In 1879, Washington's **birthday**, February 22, became a national holiday, celebrated on the third Monday in February; it is now known as **President's Day**. Additionally, a **555-foot monument in Washington, D.C.** was completed in 1885. Between October 4, 1927, and October 31, 1941, Gutzon Borglum and 400 workers sculpted the colossal 60-foot-high carvings of United States Presidents George **Washington**, Thomas **Jefferson**, Theodore **Roosevelt**, and Abraham **Lincoln** on **Mount Rushmore** in the Black Hills of South Dakota.

Washington not only led the Continental Army to **victory in the War for Independence**, he was judged by many as **second only to Abraham Lincoln as the country's greatest president**.

In 1976, President Ford posthumously awarded Washington the title of **General of the Armies** of the United States. General Pershing is the only other general to have held that title.

Key Events

Benjamin Franklin proved the existence of electricity with a kite in a storm and then invented the lightning rod (1752); South Carolina opened the first museum (1773); **Rhode Island** outlawed the importation of slaves (1774); a large fire in the city

GEORGE WASHINGTON (1ST PRESIDENT)

of New Orleans destroyed a large part of the city (1774); *The Wealth of Nations* was written by Adam Smith (1776); **Phi Beta Kappa** was founded in Virginia's College of William & Mary (1776); the **American flag** was created with thirteen stars and stripes (1777); France signed an aid treaty with the U.S. (1778); John Paul Jones on the *Bonhomme Richard* defeated the British warship *Serapis* (1779); the first daily newspaper, the ***Pennsylvania Evening Post***, was founded (1783); a congressional proposal to end slavery in new territories was narrowly defeated (1784); stagecoach service between New York and Philadelphia began (1785); Congress established the **U.S. Marshals Service** with the responsibility of protecting the federal judiciary and capturing fugitives – years later it became responsible for the witness protection program (1789); President Washington recommended November 26th be a public day of prayer and **thanksgiving** (1789); the **U.S. Coast Guard** was established (1790); the **U.S. population** was estimated to be 3.9 million people and Congress authorized a decennial U.S. census (1790); the **U.S. Patent Office** was created (1790); **Benjamin Franklin died** after a long and distinguished career in national government (1790); the **first stock exchange** opened in Philadelphia (1790); the **Buttonwood Agreement** was signed under a sycamore tree by 24 brokers agreeing to the purchase and sale of company stock – the origin of the **New York Stock Exchange** (1792); financier **William Duer** triggered America's first financial crash through reckless trading (1792); Congress authorized the use of **gold for currency** (1792); **Eli Whitney** invented the cotton gin, which separated cotton seeds from cotton fiber, creating the need for large land holdings and promoting the growth of slavery – slaves were expected to pick 200 pounds of cotton a day (1794); land speculation led to **financial panic** (1795); **Jim Beam** whiskey began operation (1795); the **University of North Carolina** became the first state university (1795); and the first gold coin, the **$5 Liberty Head gold coin**, entered into circulation (1795).

JOHN ADAMS
(2ND PRESIDENT)

MARCH 4, 1797 – MARCH 4, 1801

John Adams was born on October 30, 1735, to John Adams and Susanna Boylston Adams, in Braintree, Massachusetts. John had two younger brothers, **Elihu and Peter**. John Adams Sr. was a church deacon and a farmer. The three children grew up in a strictly disciplined Puritan household. Their parents' values guided John through life. John's cousin **Samuel Adams** became a member of the Continental Congress and a signer of the Declaration of Independence. In his youth, John Adams played a variation of baseball called "old cat." Although he hated school, John enjoyed studying government and the classical languages (Greek and Latin) and entered Harvard (the first President to do so) at age fifteen in 1751. He graduated **third in his class in**

1755 and went on to study law. Reportedly, Adams began each day with a tankard of hard cider and an explosive temper. **He was admitted to the Massachusetts Bar in 1758.**

In 1764, at age 29, Adams married the intelligent **Abigail Smith**, 20. They had **five children**, four of whom lived to adulthood: **Abigail, John Quincy** (who became the 6th president), **Susanna** (died at age 2), **Charles**, and **Thomas**. John stated, "Children should be educated and instructed in the principles of freedom." **Abigail** was very religious, an advocate for **women's rights**, and **opposed to slavery**. She and Martha Washington were close friends. John considered Abigail his **confidante** and **best advisor**. They exchanged **more than 3,000 letters** when he was in Washington and she in Massachusetts.

Adams became a significant opponent to England's **1765 Stamp Act**, which taxed various paper items. John's objection was that "taxation without representation is tyranny." Later, England repealed the Stamp Act.

In 1770, John defended the British soldiers who killed five colonists in the **Boston Massacre**. John was a delegate to the **First Continental Congress** in 1774, and the **Second Continental Congress** in 1776. The latter created the Continental army by combining state militias. Adams was a major force behind the **Declaration of Independence** since he selected Thomas Jefferson to write it. On **July 4, 1776**, it was approved by Congress. The **U.S. Constitution**, largely written by James Madison, was adopted by Congress on June 21, 1788, after being ratified by the states.

Working together on the **Declaration of Independence** and on the **U.S. Constitution**, Adams and Jefferson became **great friends**. But in 1783, Adams went off to become ambassador of England and Jefferson went off to Paris to become ambassador of France. **The French Revolution was a major disagreement** between Adams and Jefferson, and for years they did not speak to each other.

On April 30, 1789, Adams began two terms as George Washington's vice president, having come in second for the presidency. In the **1789 election, George Washington** got all 69 electoral votes, **John Adams** got 34 votes, **John Jay** got 9 votes, and 26 votes were spread between nine candidates. There was no popular vote. Based on the votes, **George Washington** was made president and **John Adams** was made vice president. In **the 1792 election, George Washington** received all 132 electoral votes, **John Adams** received a total of 77 votes, **George Clinton** received 50, and two other candidates received a total of 5 votes. Based on the votes, Washington was re-elected president, and Adams was re-elected vice president. **Adams** stated he would be "A Silent Spectator of the Silly and Wicked game," referring to the presidential election.

On December 15, 1791, Congress ratified **the first ten amendments to the U.S. Constitution** (see Appendix C). They are known as the **Bill of Rights**.

Federalist **John Adams** narrowly defeated Democratic-Republican **Thomas Jefferson** for the presidency in the **1796 election**, 71 to 68 electoral votes, automatically making Adams the president and Jefferson the vice president. There was no popular vote. Federalist **Thomas Pinckney** received 59 votes, Democratic-Republican **Aaron Burr** received 30 votes, and the remaining 48 votes were split among nine candidates. John Adams was the first **vice president** to become **president** and the first president to have graduated from **Harvard**. It was the first time in American history that the top two national offices were held by opposing parties – Federalist (Adams) and Democratic-Republican (Jefferson).

Thomas Jefferson was born on April 13, 1743, on his family's plantation in Albemarle County, located in Shadwell, Virginia. He was tutored in the classics and the sciences beginning at age five. He entered the **College of William & Mary** in 1762, graduated two years later, and served in Virginia's state politics. He married **Martha Wayles Skelton** in 1772 and had six children before she died in 1782. In 1776, he wrote the **Declaration of Independence**, then went to Europe for 14 years, returning to be Washington's **Secretary of State** from 1790 to 1793. Jefferson was a candidate for the presidency in 1796 but lost to John Adams and became his vice president. Jefferson was not a great public speaker, but he was a **brilliant thinker**. He and Adams had different views on government. **Federalist Adams** believed in a **strong central government**; Democratic-Republican **Jefferson** believed **states** should have more power than the federal government.

Upon being elected president, Adams requested that he be addressed as "His Highness, the President of the United States and Protector of the Rights of the same." In response, Congress said he would simply be addressed as "**President of the United States**," as that is how the position is named in **Article II of the U.S. Constitution** (see Appendix B). Others suggested he be called "His Rotundity" due to his portly shape.

In his March 4, **1797, inaugural address** in Philadelphia, Adams stated, "Liberty once lost, is lost forever." Adams was known for **strong moral values**. Not surprisingly, he refused bribes and political favoritism. Benjamin Franklin claimed that John Adams was "always an honest man, often a wise man." The **1797 transfer of power** from Washington to Adams was believed to be the first time in history that control of a major government by an incumbent party was transferred to its successor without violence.

As president, Adams's pay changed from $5,000 a year to $25,000 a year. Unlike Washington, Adams saved most of his presidential salary. He even did his own laundry, using the East Room. Adams was 61 at the time of his inauguration in 1797 and was living in Philadelphia. **Abigail Adams** was in Massachusetts. John had pleaded for Abigail to join him, stating, "I can do nothing without you." She joined him in Philadelphia in 1800. In that same year, on November 1st, they were the first to move into the **Executive Mansion** (with no heat), later to be called the **White House**, in Washington, D.C. The **nation's capital** was named after **George Washington,** and the **district** was named after **Christopher Columbus.**

Abigail and John were partners in everything. They hosted both lunches and dinners every week, serving New England courses of meat, vegetables, and puddings. Adams was **brilliant** but **stubborn and vain**; Abigail was a **great writer** and supporter of women, constantly reminding John to, "Remember the Ladies," and noting, "If man is Lord, woman is Lordess."

In **Hollingsworth vs Virginia** (1798), the U.S. Supreme Court ruled that the Eleventh Amendment was valid even without presidential approval. In **Bingham vs Cabot** (1798), the U.S. Supreme Court ruled it "necessary to set forth the citizenship" or alienage, if a foreigner, of the parties to be within the Circuit Court's jurisdiction.

There were **five key laws passed** in 1798 – four of which were known as the **Alien and Sedition Acts of 1798**. The **Alien Act** gave the president the authority to put in prison or deport aliens.

The **Alien Enemies Act** extended the president's authority over aliens during times of war. The **Naturalization Act** increased the residency requirement for citizenship to fourteen years, up from five years. The **Sedition Act** called for fines or imprisonment for those threatening the government. And the **Revenue Act** enacted a one percent estate and property tax.

In addition to **Vice President** Thomas Jefferson, the other members of John Adams's **first cabinet** were **Secretary of State** Timothy Pickering, **Secretary of the Treasury** Oliver Wolcott, **Secretary of War** James McHenry, **Attorney General** Charles Lee, **Secretary of the Navy** Benjamin Stoddert, and **Postmaster General** Joseph Habersham. The Secretary of the Navy was added to Washington's list of officials due to concern over naval attacks by other countries. Pickering was the **first cabinet member in history to be fired**.

In **Fowler vs Lindsey** (1799), the U.S. Supreme Court ruled that for the Court to have jurisdiction in cases where the state has an interest, the state must be a party.

Like George Washington, Adams had participated in the creation of the **Declaration of Independence**, believing that "Liberty, once lost, is lost forever." However, Thomas Jefferson was the true author of the document. Adams had not fought in the Revolution and was unpopular with the founders because he continually reminded them of their inadequacies. He said, "Facts are stubborn things and easily defeat lies." Adams also believed that "fear is the foundation of most governments and that men with power are a threat to the liberty of the public."

In **Mossman vs Higginson** (1800), the U.S. Supreme Court ruled that for federal courts to have jurisdiction, there must be a description of the parties. The **Slave Trade Act of 1800** imposed penalties on citizens or residents of the United States who held or had the rights to property in vessels employed in the slave trade. Also in 1800, the **U.S. population** was approximately 5.3 million people, 80% of whom lived on farms.

Adams sought a second term as a Federalist president in the 1800 presidential election, but he erred in spending too much time in Massachusetts and not enough in Washington, D.C. In 1800, the federal government moved from Philadelphia to Washington, D.C. And, while **articulate in the courtroom**, he did not use his verbal skills in communicating with the public, and he showed **little organizational ability**. In the **1800 election**, Adams was defeated in his bid for a second term, primarily because his own vice president, Thomas Jefferson, led a negative campaign against him. Jefferson said that Adams was "excessively distrustful, obstinate, excessively vain and takes no counsel from anyone." It was the **first negative presidential campaign**. Thomas Jefferson and Aaron Burr, both Democratic-Republicans, each received 73 electoral votes. Federalists John Adams, Charles Pinckney, and John Jay received 65, 64, and 1, respectively. Congress voted to decide the Jefferson-Burr tie and elected Jefferson president on the 36th ballot.

Congress made no pay changes during Adams's term of presidency.

Before leaving in 1801, Adams nominated **John Marshall** as Chief Justice for the U.S. Supreme Court. Marshall would go on to serve on the court for 34 years. Many would say he was the greatest justice of all time. Marshall's view was that Congress, and the president had broad powers while the states had limited authority. Adams also swore in dozens of new judges with Federalist beliefs, after they had been confirmed by Congress.

Adams and Abigail left at 4:00am on March 4, 1801, to return to their Massachusetts farm so they did not have to meet the incoming President Jefferson. A mutual friend to Adams and Jefferson, Benjamin Rush, convinced Adams to write a friendly note to Jefferson on New Year's Day in 1812. Over the following fourteen years, the two exchanged 158 letters, and the friendship was renewed.

Abigail contracted **typhoid fever** and died on October 28, 1818, at age 73. Adams saw his son **Quincy** sworn in as president in 1825. **John Adams died of heart failure** on July 4, 1826, at age 90. John's last words were, "Thomas Jefferson still survives," because he didn't know Jefferson (age 83) had died five hours earlier. Both died on July 4th, the 50th anniversary of the birth of the nation. John and Abigail were buried at the First Unitarian Church in Braintree, Massachusetts.

Most historians rank John Adams's performance as president **as more effective than most.**

Key Events

France attacked American ships because President Washington refused to aid France in its war against England, leading to a two-year quasi war with France (1797); the U.S. frigates *USS United States* and *USS Constitution* **(Old Ironsides)** were launched, and 365 privateer ships captured 84 French ships that had been raiding U.S. ports and ships (1797); three envoys from France demanded payment of a large sum and an apology from Adams for capturing French ships, but Adams declined and refused to identify the three, (this was known as the **XYZ Affair**) (1798); Adams stated one of his greatest achievements was avoiding war with France (1798); due to a yellow fever epidemic, thousands lost their lives on the East Coast (1798); Thomas Malthus published ***An Essay on the Principles of Population*** (1798); the **Bank of Manhattan** was formed (1799) (it would become the **Chase Manhattan Bank** in 1877); the **Pennsylvania Academy of Fine Arts** began in Philadelphia (1801); **John Marshall** was appointed the U.S. Supreme Court **Chief Justice** (1801); Marshall introduced the procedure where only one justice would give the opinion of the court rather than each justice writing their own opinion (1801); and, having signed 1,180 decisions and writing 549 himself, Marshall was recognized by most as the **Father of the American Justice System** (1801).

Thomas Jefferson
(3ʳᴅ President)

March 4, 1801 – March 4, 1809

Thomas Jefferson was born on April 13, 1743, in a log cabin (the first president so born) in Albemarle County, Virginia, to Peter and Jane Jefferson. His father was a farmer, judge, and land surveyor. Thomas had red hair and a face full of freckles. He was the eldest son and third oldest of **ten children**, eight of whom survived to adulthood, and began receiving private tutoring at five years of age, learning Greek and Latin and studying the natural sciences. He also enjoyed riding horses and playing the violin. Jefferson graduated in 1762 from the **College of William & Mary** and went on to practice law after passing the Virginia bar in 1767. After becoming certified as a lawyer, Jefferson kept detailed records of every aspect of his life. Jefferson

THOMAS JEFFERSON (3RD PRESIDENT)

was elected to the Virginia House of Burgesses in 1769. At age 29, he **married** his third cousin, **Martha Wayles Skelton** (age 24), on January 1, 1772. They had **six children**: an unnamed boy who died at birth, Elizabeth, Jane, Lucy, Mary (aka "Polly"), and Martha (aka "Patsy"). Only **Polly** and **Patsy** lived past three years of age. Martha was a **widow** who brought Jefferson the **wealth** he lacked; he used some of it to build a house on the thousand-plus acres of land he inherited from his father and named it **Monticello** ("little mountain" in Italian).

Jefferson and Martha were very happy together, and he was **devastated** when she died on September 6, 1782, at age 40, eighteen years before his presidency. Before she died, Martha made her husband promise that he **would never remarry**. She did not want another woman to bring up her children. He agreed and kept that promise. But Jefferson soon took up with his biracial slave, **Sally Hemings**, the half-sister of his dead wife Martha. Hemings had at least six children with Jefferson. She died in 1835.

In **1776**, Jefferson was called the **Father of the Declaration of Independence** (approved July 4th and signed August 2nd, 1776), since he wrote most of it, although it is very similar to Virginia's Declaration of Rights, written by George Mason (only weeks before Jefferson's work). Jefferson was also called the **Sage of Monticello**. He was a paradox: he declared all men were created equal, but he owned 600 slaves. He went on to state, "Equal laws must protect equal rights." He served as **Governor of Virginia** from 1779 to 1781.

In 1785, Jefferson served as minister to France, **taking Sally Hemings with him.** Jefferson and Hemings returned to America in 1789, and Jefferson became **Secretary of State** in 1790 under President Washington, serving until 1793.

In 1793, Jefferson and Madison formed the Democratic-Republican political party. It focused on limiting the federal government. Jefferson and Madison viewed the **Federalist Party** advocated by John Adams as giving the executive branch of the government more power than intended by the U.S. Constitution.

In the **1796 presidential election**, Federalist **John Adams** received 71 electoral votes, Democratic-Republican **Thomas Jefferson** received 68 votes, Federalist **Thomas Pinckney** received 59 votes, Democratic-Republican **Aaron Burr** received 30 votes, and the remaining 48 votes were scattered among nine other candidates. The public did not vote in this election. Having received a majority of the electoral votes, **John Adams** was elected **president**, and **Thomas Jefferson** having received the second-most votes, was named **vice president**. From 1797 to 1801, Jefferson served as **vice president** under President John Adams. During those years, Jefferson wrote *A Manual of Parliamentary Practice*, the rulebook of Congress.

In the **1800 presidential election**, **Thomas Jefferson** and **Aaron Burr**, both Democratic-Republicans, each received 73 electoral votes. Federalist **John Adams** received 65 votes, Federalist **Charles Pinckney** received 64, and Federalist **John Jay** received one vote. Since it was a tie, the election went to the House of Representatives, but the tie continued for thirty-five votes. On the thirty-sixth vote, **Jefferson won** by six votes and was named **president**, and Burr was named **vice president**.

Upon being elected president, Jefferson noted, "Every difference of opinion is not a difference of principle. We have been called by different names, brethren of the same principle. We are all Democrats, Republicans, and Federalists." Jefferson stated, "History cannot predict bad government, it can only report when it happened."

Federalist **Adams**, who received only 65 votes, **was so angry** at not being re-elected that he refused to attend the inauguration. Jefferson's election was called "the Revolution of the 1800s" because a Democratic-Republican won over the Federalists. Jefferson's Democratic-Republican (later changed to the Democratic Party) victory led to a reversal of Federalist policies on taxes and spending. Thomas Jefferson is the **second vice president** to later become president; John Adams was the first.

Aaron Burr was born on February 6, 1756, in Newark, New Jersey. His father was president of the College of New Jersey, later to become **Princeton University**. Burr served in the **Battle of the Revolution** in 1775 after graduating from college. He had a distinguished career serving under Washington as a **lieutenant colonel**. Burr resigned his commission in 1779 and moved to New York to study law. He was admitted to the bar in 1782, and he was appointed **attorney general of New York**. He later won a **Senate seat** and then ran for president in 1800 on the Democratic-Republican ticket, but he ended up second to Jefferson, thereby becoming Jefferson's vice president.

Jefferson was 57 years old on the day of his **1801 inauguration**, the first one in Washington, D.C. He **walked** from his boarding house because his new carriage had not arrived in time for the ceremony. In his March 4 **inaugural address**, Jefferson called for a "wise and frugal government" and stated, "That government is best which governs least." Jefferson was an **advocate of states' rights and common law**, or what many believed to be right. Jefferson also said, "A little rebellion now and then is a good thing; as necessary in the political world as storms in the physical world." Jefferson also stated the presidency was "a place of splendid misery" and "no man will bring out of the presidency the reputation which carries him into it."

In 1801, Jefferson installed the **first indoor bathroom** in the Executive Mansion. Also in 1801, there was one key law enacted: the **1801 Judiciary Act**, which reduced the number of Supreme Court Associate Justices to four, freed the justices from circuit duty, and stated the court would meet twice a year in two-week sessions from December to June. The **1802 Judiciary Act** which repealed the 1801 Act, closed the Supreme Court for two years, reduced the number of circuit courts to six, restored the need for Supreme Court Justices to do circuit court duty, eliminated one of the two-week sessions, and increased the number of Supreme Court Associate Justices to five.

In **1801, John Marshall** was named **Chief Justice** of the U.S. Supreme Court. Later, Marshall stated that President Thomas Jefferson wanted to have a judiciary, as well as a legislature, that would second the views of the executive.

President Jefferson chose his private secretary, **Meriwether Lewis**, to lead an expedition to explore lands up to the Pacific (Lewis asked **William Clark**, whom Jefferson had known through an earlier military campaign, to join him as a co-captain).

Jefferson's first **cabinet** included **Vice President** Aaron Burr, **Secretary of State** James Madison, **Secretary of the Treasury** Samuel Dexter, **Secretary of War** Henry Dearborn, **Attorney General** Levi Lincoln, **Secretary of the Navy** Benjamin Stoddert, and **Postmaster General** Joseph Habersham. Like Washington, Jefferson used his cabinet as a "sounding board" for reactions to various matters.

Jefferson's daughter, Patsy, took her mother's place at the White House, serving as hostess and running Monticello.

Jefferson was an outstanding writer and a great conversationalist with individuals and small groups, but he was a poor public speaker and a shy mumbler before large groups. Not surprisingly, with large groups, he **chose the written rather than the spoken word** in communication. It is believed that in his first term, he wrote over 600 letters. Jefferson **abolished state dinners** and separated political party representatives by inviting them to different dinners. He was interested in hearing shared views rather than conflicting debates. He enjoyed sparkling conversation around a round table. He also refused to give assigned seats, inviting guests to make their own selection. Those who wanted preferential treatment were not happy with this decree.

Jefferson **wore slippers and robes** in the Mansion, and **sometimes he opened the outside door himself**. And he never appeared in any clothing that appeared to reflect monarchy. He also preferred being addressed as **Mr. Jefferson** rather than Mr. President. He saw his role as **making recommendations** (via a written message not a personal appearance to Congress) and then executing the laws passed by Congress. His "hands off" style of government regarding legislation was deemed weak by many critics, but it seemed to work. Jefferson adopted a policy of not accepting a gift without paying for it out of his $25,000 annual salary. As a result, Jefferson's presidential salary did not cover his expenses, and he went further and further into debt. In addition to gifts, his **major expenses** were imported food delicacies and expensive wines from France for his daily luncheon and dinner guests. It is said that Jefferson introduced America to **French fries**, quite a departure from his usual delicacies.

In **Marbury vs Madison** (1803), the U.S. Supreme Court ruled that it can declare unconstitutional any Act of Congress that exceeds the Constitution. Upset with the apparent power of the U.S. Supreme Court, **President Jefferson** called for a constitutional amendment to make judgeships elective offices (1804). It received little support.

Wanting to acquire the city of **New Orleans**, Jefferson made an offer to Napoleon for the city in mid-1803 (Napoleon had acquired it from Spain). But instead of accepting the offer for New Orleans, Napoleon responded by offering the entire **Louisiana Territory** for $15 million. He needed more money to fight his wars. Jefferson accepted the offer, and on December 20, 1803, the **Louisiana Purchase** was finalized with Senate approval 24-7. For pennies per acre, the land of America doubled in size, with the addition of 827,000 square miles.

Based on a **strict construction interpretation**, Jefferson believed that Hamilton's **national bank** was not permitted under the U.S. Constitution. Hamilton argued that the right to coin money, levy taxes, and pay national debts was by definition a **bank**. And while Jefferson did not agree with many of Hamilton's recommendations, Jefferson did agree with Hamilton that the nation's security rested on the country's ability to borrow money.

As a Federalist, **John Adams** believed in a **strong federal government**; **Hamilton** did also. **Jefferson** was a **strict constructionist** of the Constitution and a believer in **states' rights**. He also believed that a **standing army** wasted taxpayer money and tempted those in power to use it for war.

Believing that former Secretary of the Treasury (under President Washington) Alexander Hamilton's critical comments about his character had cost him the New York gubernatorial election, **Aaron Burr challenged Hamilton to a duel**. They met on June 11, 1804, in Weehawken, New Jersey. Hamilton shot first and missed, allegedly on purpose. Burr shot and wounded Hamilton, who died in New York City the next day. Hamilton was buried at Trinity Church. Burr was charged with murder in both New Jersey and New York, but both charges were dropped. But Vice President Burr was dropped from the 1804 election ticket and was replaced with George Clinton. Burr's political career had ended.

Many thought Hamilton would be a good president. However, **Hamilton was born out of wedlock** on the isle of Nevis, and therefore many **thought him to be ineligible to be president**. However, **Article II, Section I** of the U.S. Constitution states, "No person except a natural born Citizen, or a Citizen of the United States, at time of the Adoption of this Constitution, shall be eligible to the Office of President; neither shall any Person be eligible to that Office who shall not have attained to the Age of thirty five Years, and been fourteen Years a Resident within the United States" (see Appendix B). While not a natural born citizen, **Hamilton was a citizen** at the time of the adoption of the Constitution. Therefore, he was eligible to be president. This has been verified by an expert on the Constitution.

During his first term, Jefferson reduced taxes and the national debt, along with reducing spending, primarily by reducing the size of the armed forces. But his greatest accomplishment was the **Louisiana Purchase**.

In **Faw vs Marsteller** (1804), the U.S. Supreme Court ruled that under Virginia's 1781 Act of Assembly, rent is to be paid at the date of the deed, "in specie" or "other money equivalent," and not reduced by the "scale of depreciation."

The **1804 election** was the **first presidential election** where each presidential candidate ran with his **own vice-presiden-**

tial candidate. Democratic-Republicans Thomas Jefferson and George Clinton defeated Federalists **Charles Pinckney** (for president) and **Rufus King** (for vice president), 162 to 14 electoral votes. **Thomas Jefferson** became president, and **George Clinton** became vice president. There was still no popular vote.

George Clinton was born on July 26, 1739, in Little Britain, New York. He served in the French and Indian War and was a hero of the American Revolution. He was a **brigadier general** in George Washington's army and also served in the Second Continental Congress in 1775. After many years of power in New York State, George Clinton replaced Aaron Burr on the Democratic-Republican ticket following Burr's killing of Alexander Hamilton. Clinton, a seven-term **governor of New York**, was a three-time loser for the presidency.

In his **second inaugural address** on March 4, 1805, Jefferson urged his fellow citizens to "unite with one heart and one mind, to restore to social intercourse that harmony and affection without which liberty and even life itself are but dreary things." He declared, "Confidence of my fellow citizens in my taking this office, inspires me to conduct myself as may satisfy their just expectations." and "Every difference of opinion is not a difference of principle." A believer in religious freedom, he also stated, "Another man's religious conviction neither picks my pocket nor breaks my leg."

In **United States vs Fisher** (1805), the U.S. Supreme Court ruled that in all cases of insolvency or bankruptcy of debtors, the United States has priority of payment.

When the **Barbary pirates** demanded **ransom** to stop attacking U.S. ships, Jefferson refused, leading to a series of naval battles resulting in the *USS Philadelphia* being captured in 1803. But on April 27, 1805, the U.S. Marines captured the port of **Tripoli**, leading to the **pirates' defeat** and a Tripoli addition to the **Marine Corps Hymn**.

Jefferson's **cabinet** during his second term of office included **Vice President** George Clinton, **Secretary of State** James Madison, **Secretary of the Treasury** Albert Gallatin, **Secretary of War** Henry Dearborn, **Attorney General** John Breckinridge, **Secretary of the Navy** Robert Smith, and **Postmaster General** Gideon Granger. Clinton replaced Burr, Gallatin replaced Dexter, Breckinridge replaced Lincoln, Smith replaced Stoddert, and Granger replaced Habersham.

Following the **Judiciary Acts of 1801 and 1802**, the **1807 Judiciary Act** increased the number of U.S. Supreme Court Associate Justices to six, and the **1807 Embargo Act** forbade American ships from leaving America. This backfired because it eliminated foreign trade. During his eight years in office, **Jefferson never vetoed any legislation**.

In 1807, **Aaron Burr was charged with treason** for attempting to take over the city of New Orleans with armed forces, then appointing himself governor of half of the Louisiana Territory. The case was a **jury trial** tried in a Virginia Circuit Court by U.S. Supreme Court Chief Justice John Marshall. The Supreme Court Justices traveled each year to preside over Circuit Courts. In **United States vs Burr** (1807), the U.S. Supreme Court ruled that the United States vice president is subject to the rule of law like every other citizen. Burr was found **not guilty, but his political career was over**.

Upon reflection, Jefferson once said, "I have sometimes asked myself whether my country is the better for my having lived at all." When asked about the future of America, Jefferson stated, "I carry with me the consolation of a firm persuasion that Heaven has in store for our beloved country, long ages to come of prosperity and happiness." Two of his more famous statements were, "Determine never to be idle," and "Diplomacy is the pest of the peace of the world."

Although he suffered from **headaches** throughout his life, he was an **avid reader** and collected many books. When the British burned the nation's capital in 1812, Jefferson sold some **10,000 of his books to the Library of Congress**. It not only replaced lost library books, it helped Jefferson pay some of his many debts. Jefferson stopped the reading of the **annual message to Congress** by the president, instead sending a written statement **by messenger**. This change continued until 1913, when Woodrow Wilson gave **the State of the Union Address** in person.

Jefferson was an **accomplished inventor, designer, and early adopter** of such things as a dumbwaiter, a duplicating machine, a folding ladder, a big clock, an improved plow, and a swivel chair. Jefferson was **also** an accomplished **architect, diplomat, educator, lawyer, musician, naturalist,** and **writer**. He was also considered to be **very smart** and accomplished in **Greek and Latin** languages. To reflect on Jefferson's talents, in 1963, at a dinner for **Nobel Prize winners**, President Kennedy remarked, "I think this is the most extraordinary collection of talent, of human knowledge, that has ever been gathered together at the White House, with the possible exception of when President Thomas Jefferson dined alone."

Although likely to win a third term, Jefferson declined to run. Like Washington and Adams, Jefferson believed in a maximum of two terms as president. In 1809, Jefferson left office and returned to **Monticello** along with his daughter **Patsy and her**

THOMAS JEFFERSON (3RD PRESIDENT)

eleven surviving children. Jefferson noted, "Never did a prisoner released from his chains feel such relief as I did on shaking off the shackles of power."

Congress made no pay changes during Jefferson's term of presidency.

In 1819, Jefferson **founded the University of Virginia**, which he could see from Monticello.

Jefferson was 83 years old when he **died** of kidney failure and pneumonia on July 4, 1826 – the same date that former President John Adams died, on the 50th anniversary of America's independence. **Jefferson's last words** were, "I have done for my country and for all mankind, all that I could do. And I now resign my soul, without fear, to my God, my daughter, and to my country." Jefferson and his wife were buried in the Monticello graveyard, in Charlottesville, Virginia. Due to his fondness for food and drink, he **died without any money**, forcing his heirs to sell his plantation to pay his debts. His philosophy: "It is neither wealth nor splendor but tranquility and occupation which gives happiness."

Jefferson's reputation suffered when it became clear that he asserted Blacks were inferior to whites, that he had fathered children with slaves, and that he made no provision in his will to free his slaves. And while he advocated frugality, he spent lavishly on food and wine.

Jefferson, like Washington, Lincoln, and Theodore Roosevelt, had his facial image engraved on **Mount Rushmore** in the Black Hills of South Dakota. Jefferson's image also appears on the **American nickel coin** and the **two-dollar bill**.

Many historians rank Jefferson below only Washington and Lincoln. The **epitaph** on his Monticello grave states, "Here was buried Thomas Jefferson, **author** of the Declaration of Independence, of the Virginia **statute** of religious freedom, and **father** of the University of Virginia." Not mentioned is that he was a **former president** of the United States.

KEY EVENTS

John Jacob Astor was worth a quarter of a million dollars from fur trades and had acquired significant property in Manhattan (1800); Jefferson ordered **200 cheap gunboats** to protect the American coast, causing critics to call him "**the First Admiral of American Gunboats**" (1801); Alexander Hamilton founded the *New York Evening Post*, known today as the *New York Post* (1801); **West Point Military Academy** was established (1802); **Ohio** joined the Union as the 17th state (1803); Jefferson **reduced the public debt to $45 million** (from $80 million) (1805); **Zebulon Pike** was hired by Jefferson to map the Louisiana Purchase (1805); **Lewis and Clark** returned after traveling more than 8,000 miles exploring the Northwest (1806); the 50-gun British warship *HMS Leopard* demanded a search of the battleship *USS Chesapeake* for deserted British sailors, guns were fired, and the *Chesapeake* limped to port (Americans called for revenge, but the military was not prepared to go to war) (1806); **Pike's Peak**, a 14,120-foot mountaintop, was named after the explorer Zebulon Pike (1806); and **Robert Fulton** launched the *Clermont* **steamboat** in the Hudson River. It was 150 feet long with a beam of 13 feet, and quickly became popular for moving goods and people, connecting Albany with New York City (1807).

JAMES MADISON
(4ᵀᴴ PRESIDENT)

MARCH 4, 1809 – MARCH 4, 1817

James Madison was born on March 16, 1751, in Port Conway, Virginia, to James and Eleanor Rose Conway Madison. They lived on the family 5,000-acre tobacco farm, which James later inherited from his father. It was called **Montpelier**. His father was a tobacco farmer and a colonel in the Virginia militia. James was the **oldest of twelve offspring**, six of whom survived to adulthood. He was **schooled at home** and studied history, mathematics, government, Greek, and Latin. Later, he studied law at the College of New Jersey, now named **Princeton University**. He graduated in 1771, returned to his farm, and became a lawyer after being admitted to the bar in New Jersey. In 1776, Madison became a member of the **Virginia Constitutional Convention**.

Although he never saw combat in the Revolutionary War due to ill health, he was commissioned a **colonel in Virginia's Orange County Militia**. In 1779, Madison was elected to the **Continental Congress**. At age 29, he was the youngest delegate. There, Madison worked on improving the **Articles of Confederation** which were adopted on March 1, 1781. They provided strong rights to the states and little to the central government. Madison knew other countries would not consider America seriously if it functioned as thirteen separate entities instead of one nation.

The first Continental Congress met at Federal Hall in New York City. But the **U.S. Constitution** was prepared at the Constitutional Convention in Philadelphia by delegates from the thirteen colonies. Madison went to work, converting the Articles of Confederation into a new constitution that was adopted on September 17, 1787. But Madison knew it had to be ratified by at least nine of the thirteen states. Knowing the states had to be convinced, Alexander Hamilton and James Madison started writing the **Federalist Papers**, laying out the reasons why the newly written constitution changing the power of the central government was needed. The shape of the federal government is described in the 85 articles in the **Federalist Papers**. In 1787, Alexander Hamilton wrote 51 articles, James Madison wrote 29 articles, and John Jay wrote 5 articles. The articles were first published in the newspapers in late 1787, and then in book form in 1788.

Madison realized the country had to have a **bicameral legislature**. **One section** would have a number of representatives **determined by the population**. This would be acceptable to the larger states. **Another section** would have **equal representation for all states**, which would be acceptable to the smaller states. Madison described this as the **House of Representatives** and the **Senate** in **Article I of the U.S. Constitution** (see Appendix B).

A key issue was the relationship between federal and state laws. Madison clarified the matter in **Article VI, Section 2 of the U.S. Constitution** (see Appendix B). It states, "This Constitution, and the Laws of the United States which shall be made in Pursuance thereof; and all Treaties made, or which shall be made, under the Authority of the United States, shall be the supreme Law of the Land; and the Judges in every State shall be bound thereby, any Thing in the Constitution or Laws of any State to the Contrary notwithstanding." This section of the constitution came to be called the **Supremacy Clause**, as it defined the relationship of federal and state laws. Namely, any action taken by Congress or federal officials that is consistent with the constitution is binding on the states.

The **U.S. Constitution** was ratified by the required nine states on September 17, 1787; the remaining states followed. The Constitution was adopted by Congress on March 4, 1789.

In 1789, Madison began an eight-year term in the **House of Representatives**. On September 15, 1794, at age 43, Madison married **Dolley Payne Todd**, age 26. She had been introduced to Madison by Aaron Burr. Dolley had two sons from an earlier marriage to **John Todd Jr.** John and his youngest son died from yellow fever in 1793. Madison adopted her 2-year-old son, **John Payne Todd**. John Payne, who was irresponsible and went to **debtor's prison** twice for failing to pay bills, survived his mother and step-father.

Madison would later be named the **Father of the Constitution**, as he had written most of it, just as Jefferson was named the **Father of the Declaration of Independence**.

Knowing that the Constitution had not clarified **individual rights**, Madison wrote the **Bill of Rights**. These are the **first ten amendments** to the U.S. Constitution (see Appendix C), which ensured the rights of ordinary people would be identified and protected. These rights included freedom to assemble, freedom of religion, and freedom to speak. These "great rights of mankind" were ratified by Congress on December 15, 1791.

In 1792, Madison and Jefferson created the **Democratic-Republican Party**, which would further evolve into the **Democratic Party**. The **Republican Party** would be formed in 1854.

From 1801 to 1809, Madison served as **Secretary of State** under Thomas Jefferson.

In 1807, Congress passed the **Embargo Act**, forbidding American trade with any port. This was in response to a fear that American trade would suffer from imports.

In the **1808 election**, Democratic-Republicans **James Madison** and **George Clinton** defeated Federalists **Charles Pinckney** and **Rufus King**, 122 electoral votes to 47. James Madison was elected president and George Clinton was elected vice president. There was no popular vote. Jefferson was pleased that a fellow Virginian and a critic of the Federalist philosophy succeeded him.

George Clinton was born on July 26, 1739, in Little Britain, New York, where his father was a successful land speculator and farmer. Clinton attended local schools and went on to serve as a lieutenant in the **French and Indian War**. After the war, he **studied law** in New York City and was admitted to the **New York bar** in 1764. Four years later, he was elected to the **New York State Assembly**, and in 1775 he became a delegate to the **Second Continental Congress**. On July 30, 1777, he took office as the **first governor of New York** while continuing to serve as an officer in General Washington's army. He won re-election as governor five times. Clinton was a staunch supporter of American independence, but he opposed ratification of the **Constitution**, as he felt it gave too much power to the federal government. Clinton was the **first vice president to hold the office under two presidents** (Jefferson and Madison). Clinton died in office on April 20, 1812, of a heart attack.

At the time of his election, weighing 100 pounds, at 5'4", Madison was the **shortest president**, and he was the first president to wear **full-length pants** rather than knee breeches. Madison was also the first president to show his **own hair** rather than wear a wig. He reportedly consumed a **pint of whiskey** daily.

In his March 4, **1809, inaugural address**, Madison stated that the United States would not tolerate foreign interference. That did not stop England and France from intercepting U.S. shipping and pressing American sailors into foreign service. Madison was the first president to have an **official inauguration ball**.

In **United States vs Peters** (1809), the U.S. Supreme Court ruled that the Court can declare state laws unconstitutional.

Madison's initial **cabinet** included **Vice President** George Clinton, **Secretary of State** Robert Smith, **Secretary of the Treasury** Albert Gallatin, **Secretary of War** William Eustis, **Attorney General** Caesar Rodney, **Secretary of the Navy** Paul Hamilton and **Postmaster General** Gideon Granger. Madison's cabinet was undistinguished until he convinced **James Monroe** to leave serving as the Virginia governor and join Madison's cabinet from 1811 to 1817 as Secretary of State. Monroe gained fame for writing the **Monroe Doctrine** in 1823, opposing European intervention in the Western Hemisphere. Except for Monroe, Madison appointed one of the weakest cabinets in history, basing his selections on Congressional accessibility rather than qualifications. And his **ineffective cabinet** had a high turnover.

Dolley Madison **used snuff tobacco and loved to party**, hosting sumptuous **dinners** every Wednesday for a variety of people. Madison had little interest in food or people. Dolley frequently posted **open invitations** in the newspaper. Called **Mrs. President**, Dolley was the first woman to create the role of **official hostess** and supportive wife that we now call the **First Lady**. She and Madison, whom she called "**Little Jamie**," had no children. James and Dolley were complete opposites. She was a **charismatic extrovert**; he was a **shy introvert**.

Madison's term of office was called the "**era of good feelings**." Madison stated, "Public opinion sets bounds to every government and is the sovereign in every free one." He also said, "The truth is that all men having power ought to be mistrusted."

When England and France started to stop American vessels to search for deserters, Congress passed the **1809 Intercourse Act**, prohibiting trade with England and France. That did not stop England or France from searching for deserters.

In **Fletcher vs Peck** (1810), the U.S. Supreme Court ruled that contracts between individuals or individuals and government cannot be voided by laws. An 1810 census of the United States revealed 1,191,364 of the total population of 7,239,988 were slaves.

In 1811, unconvinced of the need for its continuance, Congress failed to renew the charter of the **Bank of the United States**, and it went out of existence. Only state-chartered banks remained.

Vice President George Clinton died at age 72 from a heart attack on April 20, 1812. He was the **first vice president to die in office**.

JAMES MADISON (4TH PRESIDENT)

As there was no mechanism to select a replacement, Madison served the remainder of his term **without a vice president**.

In 1812, Madison asked Congress to **declare war on England** for its failure to stop harassing American ships, and Congress did so on June 18, 1812. It was the beginning of the **War of 1812**. At the time, England had over 400 warships and the U.S. fewer than ten, along with an almost non-existent army. Many called this **Madison's War**, since they thought it was foolish to declare war on England with a small army and navy. Madison believed he could call up military-age men when needed. In 1812, America's ability to borrow money to fight the war was dramatically affected by the failure of Congress to renew the charter of the **Bank of the United States** in 1811. Foreign funds were unavailable. Madison sent American troops into Canada, but the invasion failed except for the burning of York, later known as Toronto. The **1812 Tariff Act** increased taxes on imports.

In the **1812 election**, Democratic-Republicans **James Madison** and **Elbridge Gerry** defeated Federalists **DeWitt Clinton** and **Jared Ingersoll**, 128 electoral votes to 89. There was still no popular vote. Madison was 57 years old on the date of inauguration. In his March 4, **1813, inaugural address**, Madison stated, the War of 1812 "has been waged on our part…in a spirit of liberality which was never surpassed," and "[o]ur nation is…composed of a brave, a free, a virtuous, and an intelligent people." He added, "A general prosperity is visible in the public countenance." Not long after his inauguration, Madison remarked that, "The contest in which the United States are engaged appeals for its support to every motive that can animate an uncorrupted and enlightened people…."

Elbridge Gerry was born on July 17, 1744, in Marblehead, Massachusetts. He joined his wealthy merchant father in his business after graduating from Harvard in 1766. He later served two terms as governor of Massachusetts. He was also a signer of the **Declaration of Independence** as a member of the Continental Congress, as well as a delegate to the Constitutional Convention and a member of the first U.S. House of Representatives. His coming from a northern state continued the desired regional balance on the ticket. Gerry was a longtime supporter of Madison and had just been defeated for a third term as governor of Massachusetts. He died on November 23, 1814, at age 70.

Madison's second **cabinet** included **Vice President** Elbridge Gerry, **Secretary of State** James Monroe, **Secretary of the Treasury** Albert Gallatin, **Secretary of War** John Armstrong, **Attorney General** William Pinkney, **Secretary of the Navy** William Jones, and **Postmaster General** Gideon Granger. The changes from the first cabinet were: Gerry replaced Clinton, Monroe replaced Smith, Armstrong replaced Eustis, Pinkney replaced Rodney, and Jones replaced Hamilton.

The **1813 Civil Rights Act** established citizen property rights. On September 10, 1813, Commodore Oliver Perry defeated the British fleet at the **Battle of Lake Erie**. Also in 1813, General William Henry Harrison defeated Indian leader Tecumseh in the **Battle of the Thames**.

On March 19, 1814, the **Creek Nation** was forced to cede half its homeland (23 million acres) and move farther west after being defeated by Colonel Jackson.

When the **British troops landed** in Maryland on April 24, 1814, and proceeded to Washington, D.C., it was the first time since the Revolutionary War that the U.S. was invaded. President Madison fled for the Virginia forest, while Madison's wife,

Dolley, left the Executive Mansion with President **Washington's portrait** and a copy of the **Declaration of Independence** under her arm. Silverware and other valuables were put in bags and also removed from the Executive Mansion by servants. British **Admiral George Cockburn** ordered his troops to **set fire to the Capitol Building**, then went **to the Executive Mansion** on August 24, 1814, where they feasted on food and wine before setting it on fire and leaving the city. On September 13, 1814, watching the battle at nearby **Fort McHenry**, Baltimore, **Francis Scott Key** was inspired to write what would later be called "**The Star-Spangled Banner**." It became the **national anthem**.

Following the **War of 1812**, the nation began to shift away from an agricultural society as the Industrial Revolution began to take shape, affecting the shaping of tariffs in succeeding years.

On December 24, 1814, the **Treaty of Ghent** was signed ending the war between England and the United States, but the fighting continued. In early 1815, the frigate *USS Constitution* captured two Royal Navy frigates. And a British assault on **New Orleans** on January 8, 1815, was defeated by American troops led by **Andrew Jackson**. The British had more than 2,000 casualties; the Americans had less than 70. The War of 1812 finally came to an end in mid-June 1815. Also in 1815, Congress increased the pay of legislators to $1,500 a year (it had been $6 per day), but they made no more pay increases during Madison's term of presidency.

With the passage of the **1816 Bank Legislation Act**, Congress chartered the second Bank of the United States. The **1816 Tariff Act** placed a 25% tax on imports competing with U.S. goods. In **Martin vs Hunter's Lessee** (1816), the U.S. Supreme Court ruled that it can declare unconstitutional state court decisions.

Like Jefferson, Madison was an **ineffective public speaker**, but a **great writer** given his work on the U.S. Constitution and Bill of Rights. Madison was also **ineffective at dealing with Congress**, yielding to their wishes with little fight. His personality was bland, and he had a weakness for not standing up for his beliefs. Madison had a laidback personality; he was not a take-charge type of guy. And his strict interpretation of the U.S. Constitution kept him from abusing his presidential authority.

More is written about Madison's role in **framing the Constitution** and writing the **Bill of Rights** than his eight years as **president** because he was viewed as a better contributor than a leader. Madison stated that the beauty of the **U.S. Constitution** was that "every word decides a question between power and liberty." After his term of office, **Madison was sought** out by his successor, James Monroe, for **advice and counsel**. Madison also served as the **rector at the University of Virginia** during this period.

Madison was in ill health throughout his life and suffered from rheumatism and gall bladder attacks. His last six months of life were in bed. He **died** on June 28, 1836, at age 85, and his last words were, "Nothing more than a change of mind." He was buried in Montpelier, Virginia. Most historians give Madison a **significantly above average rating**. His wife, Dolley, died on June 12, 1849, at age 81, and was buried alongside her husband.

Key Events

The U.S. prohibited the **importation of slaves** (1808); Shawnee **Chief Tecumseh's** tribal forces, led by his brother Tenskwatawa ("The Prophet"), were defeated by William Henry Harrison's forces at the **Battle of Tippecanoe** (1811); Madison's image appeared briefly on a $5,000 bill before being withdrawn (1811); **Robert Fulton** launched a larger version of his **first steamboat** to traverse the Ohio and Mississippi Rivers (1811); **Lowell, Massachusetts** was named after the person who built the textile mills in the town, staffing them with women off the farm (1812); Massachusetts Governor Elbridge Gerry was credited with creating the political word "**gerrymandering**" – redefining voting districts to provide an electoral advantage (1812); the organization that later became Citigroup was formed (1812); three states, **Louisiana** (1812), **Indiana** (1816), and **Mississippi** (1817), joined the Union, making a total of 20 states; **Oberlin College** opened as the first co-education college (1814); the **Hartford Convention** ended the **Federalist Party** (1815); **Providence, Rhode Island** had more than 170 small factories (1815); **John Stevens** was the first to be given a state charter to build a railroad in New Jersey (1815); **Boston's Provident Institution for Savings** became the first chartered savings bank in the U.S. (1816); and the new **second National Bank of the United States** was established (1816).

JAMES MONROE (5ᵀᴴ PRESIDENT)

MARCH 4, 1817 – MARCH 4, 1825

James Monroe was born on April 28, 1758, to Spence and Elizabeth Monroe on a small family farm in Westmoreland County, Virginia. His father was both a carpenter and a farmer. James Monroe was the fourth of the first five presidents to come from Virginia; Adams had come from Massachusetts. James was the oldest of five children. He had a sister named Elizabeth and three brothers: Andrew, Joseph, and Spence Jr. James was initially homeschooled and then went to **Campbelltown Academy**. He entered the **College of William & Mary** in 1774, but he left a year later to fight in the **Revolutionary War** as a **lieutenant** in the **Third Virginia Infantry**. He later transferred to the **Continental Army** as a **captain**. Monroe was the first president who had been wounded in the Revolutionary War. The bullet was never removed from his shoulder. He left the army as a colonel. At age 28, he married **Elizabeth Kortright**, age 18, on February 16, 1786, while he was a delegate in the **Continental Congress**. They had three children together: **Eliza, James, and Maria**.

From 1780 to 1783, Monroe studied law under Thomas Jefferson. Having passed the Virginia bar, Monroe set up a practice in Fredericksburg, Virginia.

In 1787, Monroe voted against the approval of the Constitution, believing it gave the federal government too much power. However, he voted for its approval in 1788 after it was ratified by the states.

In 1790, Monroe was the first person to serve as a **U.S. senator** before becoming president. In 1794 he resigned the Senate and served as Minister to France; in 1799 he returned to the U.S. to become **governor of Virginia**; and in 1803 he returned to France to help negotiate the **Louisiana Purchase**. He subsequently spent three years as minister to England and in 1811 he served as **Secretary of State** for President Madison, a position he held until 1817. He was also Madison's **Secretary of War** from 1814-1815. **Monroe was the first president who previously had held two Cabinet positions simultaneously.**

In the **1816 election**, Democratic-Republicans **James Monroe** and **D.D. Tompkins** defeated Federalists **Rufus King** and **John Howard**, 183 electoral votes to 34. There was no popular vote. Monroe was 58 years old on the date of his inauguration. In his outdoor (the first) March 4, **1817, inaugural address** Monroe stated, "The heart of every citizen must expand with joy when he knows how near our Government has approached to perfection." (This optimism was tempered by the Panic of 1819, when the banks failed.) Monroe added, "National honor is a national priority of the highest value."

D.D. Tompkins was born on June 21, 1774, in Scarsdale, New York. His father was a tenant farmer and active in the local resistance during the American Revolution. Tompkins graduated first in his class at **Columbia University** in 1795. He was admitted to the **New York bar** two years later and practiced in New York City. In 1801 he won a seat in the New York Assembly, and in 1804 he was elected to the **House of Representatives** but resigned to take a seat on the **New York Supreme Court**. He served as the **governor of New York State** from 1807 to 1817. He unsuccessfully challenged Monroe for the position of the party's presidential candidate; but Monroe accepted him as his vice president to continue the regional balance of New York and Virginia. It was not a happy ending for Tompkins. He was unable to pay his bills because he personally funded the state militia during the War of 1812, and his poor health was compounded by a drinking problem. Tompkins died as a private citizen at age 50 in 1825, about three months after leaving office. He **died at an earlier age** than any other U.S. vice president. Many agreed that he had significant unrealized leadership potential.

Because of the devastation of the **War of 1812**, the Executive Mansion was still being refurbished in 1817, so the Monroes ordered 56 pieces of mahogany furniture and paid $1,500 for **Elizabeth's** gowns. Since no letters remain, little is known about Elizabeth other than that she was the Jacqueline Kennedy of her time. Supposedly, James shared his views with her. In his first term as president, Monroe was the last president to wear **buckled shoes**, **knee breeches**, **long white stockings**, and a **powdered wig**.

JAMES MONROE (5TH PRESIDENT)

In 1818, Monroe decreed that the **American flag** could have only **thirteen stripes** (honoring the thirteen original colonies) and the **number of stars was to equal the number of states**.

Monroe's first **cabinet** included **Vice President** Daniel Tompkins, **Secretary of State** John Quincy Adams, **Secretary of the Treasury** William Crawford, **Secretary of War** John Calhoun, **Attorney General** Richard Rush, **Secretary of the Navy** Benjamin Crowninshield, and **Postmaster General** R. Jonathan Meigs Jr. Monroe's Cabinet was **geographically diverse**, coming from the four corners of the nation that he visited in his 1818 goodwill tour. Monroe's Cabinet was not only very competent, it also had a low turnover. Four of the seven members served the full eight years. Crowninshield died in 1818. Also in 1818, Congress approved an increase in congressional pay to $8 per diem while in session.

In 1819, Congress approved several pay actions: $3,500 per annum for the attorney general, $4,000 per annum for the postmaster general, and $6,000 per annum for the other cabinet secretaries. Also in 1819, Congress approved an increase in annual pay for associate justices of the U.S. Supreme Court to $4,500 (up from 1789's $3,500) and an increase in the annual pay of the Chief Justice to $5,000 (up from 1789's $4,000).

In **McCulloch vs Maryland** (1819), the U.S. Supreme Court ruled that federal laws take precedence over state laws, and in **Dartmouth College vs Woodward** (1819), the U.S. Supreme Court ruled that arbitrary seizure by state or federal governments is unconstitutional.

Monroe's daughter Maria was the first president's daughter to be married in the Executive Mansion.

Monroe took the initiative in **proposing legislation to Congress** rather than waiting for their actions. He also built support with the voters by making several tours of the nation at his own expense. He was a **pragmatic** leader, focusing **on results rather than rhetoric**, after carefully considering alternatives. Monroe had an unrelenting capacity for **long hours of work**. While hardworking, Monroe lacked confidence and continually sought advice from Jefferson and Madison.

Two key laws were passed in 1820. The **Land Act** opened public lands to settlers for $1.25 an acre, with a minimum purchase of 80 acres. The **Missouri Compromise** brought in Missouri as a slave state and Maine as a free state, with a line drawn across the Louisiana Territory, north of which states would be admitted as **free states**, south of which states would be admitted as slave states. And states west of the Mississippi would also be admitted as free states.

In **Cohens vs Virginia** (1821), the U.S. Supreme Court ruled that the Court has appellate jurisdiction over state criminal cases as well as civil cases.

Monroe continued the pattern of a two-term presidency with elections in 1816 and 1820. In the **1820 election**, Democratic-Republicans **James Monroe** and **Daniel Tompkins** essentially ran unopposed, receiving 231 electoral votes. The Federalist Party had collapsed and elected no candidate, and Democratic-Republicans **John Quincy Adams** and **Richard Stockton** received one electoral vote from a New Hampshire voter who wanted George Washington to be the only president elected unanimously. There was no popular vote. On the Capitol steps, in his March 5, **1821, inaugural address**, Monroe stated, "We have shunned all the defects which unceasingly preyed on the vital and destroyed the ancient Republics."

JAMES MONROE (5TH PRESIDENT)

Following the 1820 election, the **"Era of Good Feelings"** was fading due to an economic downturn and the rising issue of slavery. Still, Monroe remained very popular. His policies continued to reflect a concern about Native Americans and African Americans.

The second Monroe **cabinet** included **Vice President** Daniel Tompkins, **Secretary of State** John Quincy Adams, **Secretary of the Treasury** William Crawford, **Secretary of War** John Calhoun, **Attorney General** William Wirt, **Secretary of the Navy** Smith Thompson, and **Postmaster General** Jonathan Meigs. The only changes from the initial cabinet were Wirt replaced Rush, and Thompson replaced Crowninshield. Tompkins, Adams, Calhoun, and Meigs served all eight years on Monroe's cabinet.

The most significant event during Monroe's term was the introduction of the **Monroe Doctrine**, essentially written by Secretary of State John Quincy Adams, thought by some to be the greatest ever to hold that position. Monroe announced it in his **1823 Annual Address** to Congress. It warned Europe to stay out of the Western Hemisphere. The U.S. sought to dominate the **Greater Caribbean** and did not want European countries reestablishing footholds in the region. An attempt to colonize the Western Hemisphere would be considered a direct threat to the United States. Monroe stated that **national honor** is a priority of the highest value. Somehow, he believed this was consistent with his support of the American Colonization Society and its goal of sending Black Americans back to Africa. Land was purchased in Africa and named **Liberia**; its **capital** was named **Monrovia** after **Monroe** (the first African city named for a U.S. president). But only about 15,000 of over 1.5 million Black Americans went to Liberia.

In **Gibbons vs Ogden** (1824), the U.S. Supreme Court ruled that Congress, not the states, is responsible for interstate commerce.

Monroe left the presidency in 1825 in **significant debt**, requiring him to sell his slaves. After leaving office, Monroe spent time on his estate, reading books from his 3,000-volume library. Unfortunately, Monroe had to sell many of his books to pay off his debts. He also spent considerable time with his friend, former President James Madison. And he took the time to write *The Political Writings of James Monroe*. Monroe following Presidents Jefferson and Madison meant that three Virginians held the presidency for twenty-four years. Monroe **died** on July 4, 1831, at age 73 of **heart failure**. Monroe's last words were, "I regret leaving this world." Like John Adams and Thomas Jefferson, Monroe died on Independence Day. Monroe was buried in Richmond, Virginia, along with his wife Elizabeth, who died on September 30, 1830, at age 62. Husband James had burned all of her letters except one. Most historians consider Monroe **one of the more effective presidents**.

KEY EVENTS

The first **free school for the deaf** was established in Hartford, Connecticut (1817); ***Principles of Political Economy*** was written by David Ricardo (1817); a seat on the New York Stock Exchange cost $25 (1817); pensions were approved for war veterans (1818); **four states joined the Union** during Monroe's presidency bringing the total to 24: **Illinois** (1818), **Alabama** (1819), **Maine** (1820), and **Missouri** (1821); America's oldest private military college, **Norwich University**, was founded in Norwich, Vermont (1819); the first major **Depression** hit the South and the West (1819); Washington Irving wrote *The Leg-*

end of Sleepy Hollow (1819); **Steamboat** *Savannah* crossed the Atlantic Ocean (1819); Washington Irving published *The Sketchbook* (1819); the first organized **immigration of Black Americans** from the U.S. departed for Sierra Leone (1820); the U.S. population was 9.6 million (1820); the **New York City population** was 60,000 (1821); **Troy Female Seminary** was the first women's college (1821); James Fenimore Cooper published the book *The Spy* (1821); yellow fever swept New York City, killing thousands (1821); **Yale College President Dwight** banned the playing of football as too violent, fining violators (1822); the **women weavers' strike** in Pawtucket, Rhode Island, was the first organized labor strike (1824); slavery was abolished in the state of Illinois (1824); the textile town of Lowell, Massachusetts, was the first large scale industrial **planned community**, with the following schedule: awake at 4:30am, at work by 5:00am, workday at 7:00am, and in bed by 10:00pm – a 12-hour day, six days a week (1824); and the organization that later became JPMorgan Chase was formed (1829).

John Quincy Adams
(6ᵗʰ President)

March 4, 1825 - March 4, 1829

John Quincy Adams, son of former President **John Adams**, was born on July 11, 1767, to John and Abigail Adams in Braintree, Massachusetts. John Quincy was named after his great-grandfather, John Quincy, who served in the Massachusetts Legislature for many years. John Quincy Adams had **two sisters**, Abigail and Susanna (who died as a child), and **two brothers**, Charles and Thomas. John Quincy was **home-taught** and read the Bible every day. Reportedly, John Quincy watched the Battle of Bunker Hill at age eight in 1775. At age eleven, John Quincy accompanied his father to France when Adams went as a special envoy. There, John Quincy went to a private school. Two years later, he and his father went to the Netherlands, then John Quincy went to Russia in 1781, when he was fourteen. They returned to America three years later, and John Quincy entered Harvard. He graduated from **Harvard** (second in his class of 51) at age 20 in 1787, and he went on to **practice law** in Boston. In 1797, at age 30, John Quincy married **Louisa Catherine Johnson**, age 22, having met her in London, England. They had four children: one daughter, Louisa, and three sons, Charles, John, and George Washington (who later took his own life).

In 1802, John Quincy Adams failed to win a seat in the U.S. House of Representatives. However, in 1803, he was elected to the **U.S. Senate**. While a Senator, Adams also taught at Harvard as a professor of rhetoric and oratory. In 1809, John Quincy served as a Minister to Russia. In 1811, John Quincy turned down an invitation from President Madison to sit on the **U.S. Supreme Court**; Adams had his eye on the presidency. In 1814, he served as a negotiator for the **Treaty of Ghent**, which ended the **War of 1812**. In 1817, Adams was appointed **Secretary of State** under President Monroe. Every president beginning with Jefferson was Secretary of State before becoming president. Quincy was the last to do so. While Secretary of State, John Quincy assisted with the **Treaty of 1818**, which set the boundaries for the United Kingdom and America's Northwest Territory. Adams also helped negotiate the **Transcontinental Treaty of 1819**, which set the western border of the Louisiana Purchase. In 1823, Adams helped President Monroe finalize the **Monroe Doctrine**, setting American foreign policy for the future.

In the **1824 election**, **John Quincy Adams**, **Henry Clay**, **William Crawford**, and **Andrew Jackson** (all running as Democratic-Republicans) each failed to get a majority of electoral votes as required by the Constitution. Adams received 84 votes,

Clay 37, Crawford 41, and Jackson 99. Lacking an electoral majority, the decision went to the House of Representatives. But before that happened, the Clay elector voters changed their vote to John Quincy Adams. This gave Adams a majority of 121 votes and the presidency. Democratic-Republican **John Calhoun** had run unopposed as **vice president**. He had been Monroe's Secretary of War. **John Calhoun** was born on March 18, 1782, in Abbeville, South Carolina. His father was a successful farmer and member of the South Carolina legislature. John graduated from **Yale University** in 1804, was admitted to the South Carolina bar in 1807, and began practicing **law** in his hometown. He was elected to the **state legislature** in 1805. Right after his election, he married his second cousin Florida Bonneau, and they had **ten children**. Two years later, he was elected to the **U.S. Senate**, where he was a champion for a national bank and improvements in canals and roads. In December 1817, he accepted the post of Monroe's **Secretary of War**. In 1824, Calhoun ran for president and lost but settled for **vice president** under John Quincy Adams. Calhoun died on March 30, 1850, in Washington, D.C., at age 68.

The **1824** election was the **first** where records exist on the **popular vote**: Adams received 108,240, Clay 46,618, Crawford 47,136, and Jackson 153,544. John Quincy Adams was the first person to win the electoral vote but lose the popular vote. Son, **John Quincy Adams** and father **John Adams were the first father and son presidential duo**. Later, George H.W. Bush the 41st president would be father to George W. Bush the 43rd.

In **United States vs The Antelope** (1825), the U.S. Supreme Court ruled that slaves aboard a ship could be lawfully carried by nations, such as Spain, that had not prohibited the practice.

In accordance with **Article II, Section I** of the U.S. Constitution (see Appendix B), the matter had to be sent to the House of Representatives to break the tie and elect a president. It was there that **Henry Clay**, Speaker of the House, swung his influence to have his voters vote for Adams, thereby electing him president. **Andrew Jackson** charged that the House election had been rigged and that there had been a **corrupt bargain**, and he called **Clay a scoundrel**. After Adams was elected, he made **Clay** his **Secretary of State**, reinforcing Jackson's claim. Because of the bizarre manner of his election, Adams was called by some the "**accidental president**." John Quincy Adams was the sixth president. Adams was 57 years old on the date of his inauguration. In his March 4, **1825, inaugural address**, Adams stated, "Ten years of peace at home and abroad, have assuaged the one minute of political contention." John Quincy believed in a strong central government; Jackson favored strong states' rights.

Adams's first **cabinet** included **Vice President** John Calhoun, **Secretary of State** Henry Clay, **Secretary of the Treasury** Richard Rush, **Secretary of War** James Barbour, **Attorney General** William Wirt, **Secretary of the Navy** Samuel Southard, and **Postmaster General** John McLean.

In 1827, the **Judiciary Act** increased the number of justices on the U.S. Supreme Court to nine, and in **Ogden vs Saunders** (1827), the U.S. Supreme Court ruled that New York's bankruptcy law did not violate the Constitution's Obligation of Contracts Clause. In 1828, the **Tariff Act** increased certain import duties.

During his four-year term, Adams had a difficult time. He was **constantly criticized** in the press as being an intellectual elitist. And although it was a period of prosperity, there were no major accomplishments by the Adams administration. He was unsuccessful in promoting the expansion of roads and canal improvements as the nation was on a westward move. He was criticized for supporting fairness toward Native Americans. When **he signed a treaty with the Muscogee** prior to the 1926 midterm elections, it brought more criticism of his administration. And his lack of security brought constant intrusions to the Executive Mansion. His **swimming** nude in the Potomac River did not go unnoticed, but few knew that Adams kept an **alligator** in the Executive Mansion's bathtub.

Adams stated, "May our country be always successful, but whether successful or otherwise, may it always be right." He also said, "Always vote for principle, though you may vote alone," and "Without balance of powers there can be no good government among mankind." Adams cautioned that "The indifference to all religion is not good" and believed "patience and perseverance have a magical effect before which obstacles vanish." His wife was a frequent entertainer. Born in England, Louisa was the **first foreign-born first lady**.

Congress made no pay changes during Adams's term of office.

In the **1828 presidential election**, National Republicans **John Quincy Adams** and **Richard Rush** lost to Democrats **Andrew Jackson** and **John Calhoun** 509,097 to 747,231 in the popular vote and 83 to 178 in the electoral vote.

John Quincy shared with his father the failure to win re-election, the only two of the first six presidents to so fail. And both father and son chose not to attend the inauguration of their successors.

In 1830, Adams was the first former president to be elected to the House of Representatives. No president had served as many years in public service as Adams, ending with nine consecutive terms in the **House of Representatives**.

John Quincy Adams (6th President)

In **1836**, a **Congressional "gag rule"** was instituted that limited debate. One of Adams's greatest achievements as a congressman was to fight for and win its repeal. Due to his oratory skills, he was nicknamed "Old Man Eloquent." He was an **outspoken opponent of slavery**. Not surprisingly, he defended before the U.S. Supreme Court 36 Africans sold as slaves who had rioted on the Spanish ship *Amistad*. In **1841**, the Court ruled in favor of the defendants.

Adams died on February 23, 1848, at the age 80 of a stroke while in the **Speaker's Room in the House of Representatives**. His last words were, "This is the last of Earth. But I am composed." His wife died of a heart attack on May 15, 1852, at age 77. Both were buried in the First Unitarian Church in Quincy, Massachusetts. The architect of the Monroe Doctrine, Adams smoothed over relations with England and arranged for the **purchase of Florida** while Secretary of State for Monroe but had few noteworthy events during his term as President. Most historians give John Adams an **average rating**.

Key Events

The **Smithsonian Institution** in Washington, D.C., opened (1825); the **Erie Canal** opened, linking the Hudson River with Lake Erie (1825); Jedediah Smith completed an expedition to California (1826); John Fenimore Cooper published *The Last of the Mohicans* (1826); the **Creek Nation** was relocated from Georgia to an area west of the Mississippi (1827); New York City abolished slavery (1827); Commodore Vanderbilt was worth over $100 million at the time of his death (1827); John Audubon published *Birds of America* (1827); the **United States and England agreed** to jointly occupy the Pacific Northwest (1827);

Massachusetts was the first state to provide tax dollars for public high schools (1827); the **Democratic Party** was formed, probably the most significant event during Adams's term (1828); work began on the **Baltimore and Ohio Railroad**, the nation's first passenger railroad (1828); and Noah Webster published the *American Dictionary of the English Language* (1828).

Andrew Jackson
(7th President)

March 4, 1829 – March 4, 1837

Andrew Jackson was born on March 15, 1767, to Andrew and Elizabeth Hutchinson Jackson in Waxhaw, South Carolina. His parents arrived from Ireland years earlier. Andrew's **father died** before Andrew was born. Andrew learned to read and write from frontier schools and at age 11 became a **reader of newspaper articles** for his neighbors in the Waxhaw River community. At age 13, Jackson joined the **South Carolina militia** and fought in the **American Revolution**.

Andrew had **two older brothers**, Hugh and Robert. Hugh served in the Revolutionary War and died in battle in 1779. Robert died of smallpox shortly after he was freed from a Southern British prison in 1781.

Andrew's **mother died** of cholera when Andrew was age 14. An orphan in 1781, Andrew refused to clean a British soldier's boots and was badly scarred by the soldier's sword and sent to a British prison. There Andrew contracted **smallpox**. After his release in 1792, Jackson moved to North Carolina and learned how to make a saddle and then **studied law**. Admitted to the bar in 1787, Jackson became a successful **lawyer** in Nashville, Tennessee, where he served as a **public prosecutor** and later a **judge** in a Tennessee court. Jackson had no **formal education** and stated, "It's a damn small mind that can think of only one way to spell a word." Harvard graduate John Quincy Adams said Jackson was "a barbarian who cannot write a sentence of grammar and can hardly spell his own name."

At age 24, Jackson married **Rachel Robards**, also age 24, in 1791. He had to marry her again in 1794 upon learning she had not been divorced before they married in 1791. Rachel Jackson was widely criticized for committing adultery and for smoking a pipe. They adopted her nephew and named him Andrew Jackson Donaldson. They had no children of their own, and either could have been sterile.

Jackson was elected to the **U.S. House of Representatives** in 1796, the year Tennessee became a state, and a year later he was elected to the **U.S. Senate** from Tennessee. In 1798, Jackson was appointed to the **Tennessee Supreme Court**, where he served until 1804. He was then promoted to **major general** in the Tennessee militia while continuing to practice law in Nashville. In 1814, Jackson's militia successfully fought in the **Creek War**, after which he took 2,500 volunteers to defend New Orleans. The **Battle of New Orleans** was actually fought after the War of 1812 ended in 1815, with 2,000 of the 14,000 British soldiers being killed or wounded and fewer than 100 American casualties. Jackson was a **national** hero and was dubbed "**Old Hickory**." In December 1817, General Jackson defeated the **Seminole Indians** by invading the Spanish territory called Florida. In 1821, he was the **governor of Florida** for two years. In 1824, he was again elected a U.S. senator from Tennessee.

Jackson lost the presidency to John Quincy Adams in the **1824 election**. Jackson won the popular vote, 153,544 to 108,740 for Adams, 47,136 for William Crawford, and 46,618 for Henry Clay. All four candidates were Democratic-Republicans. But Jackson received 99 electoral votes, Adams received 84, William Crawford received 41, and Henry Clay received 37. **Lacking an electoral majority**, the election had to be decided by the House of Representatives. There, Henry Clay supporters voted for Adams, who then won the election and became president. Jackson was angry, believing that Clay conspired to defeat him. This was confirmed when Adams selected Henry Clay to be his Secretary of State. Jackson distrusted the electoral college and believed elections should be determined by the popular vote.

Jackson was not subtle in communicating what he wanted; he was "crystal clear." He saw issues in black and white terms. His fiery personality meant using his temper to get his way. Due to that **explosive temper**, Jackson fought many duels, usually allowing the other combatant to fire first. In an 1806 duel, his opponent fired first, leaving a bullet so close to **Jackson's heart** that he carried it for the rest of his life. Then Jackson shot and killed his assailant. It was the only time Jackson killed a man in a duel. Jackson was in almost constant pain from dueling and war wounds, along with other ailments. And he needed a cane to walk.

In the **1828 election campaign**, Jackson's motto was, "I pledge to you all equal rights for all, special privileges for none." His opponents called Jackson a **jackass**. This apparently is the origin of the **Democratic mascot**. In the **1828 election**, Democrats President **Andrew Jackson** and Vice President **John Calhoun** defeated National Republicans **John Quincy Adams** and **Richard Rush** in both popular votes, 647,231 to 509,097, electoral votes, 178 to 83. John Calhoun was the first person to serve as **vice president under two different presidents** (John Quincy Adams and Andrew Jackson). Jackson's wife, Rachel, died of a heart attack on December 22, 1828, at age 67, and therefore she did not see her husband inaugurated. Rachel was buried in her inauguration gown.

John Calhoun was born on March 18, 1782, in Abbeville, South Carolina. His father was a successful farmer and member of the South Carolina legislature. John graduated from **Yale University** in 1804, was admitted to the South Carolina bar in 1807, and began practicing **law** in his hometown. He was elected to the **state legislature** in 1805. Right after his election, he married his second cousin Florida Bonneau, and they had **ten children**. Two years later, he was elected to the **U.S. Senate**, where he was a champion for a national bank and improvements in canals and roads. In December 1817, he accepted the post of Monroe's **Secretary of War**. In 1824, Calhoun ran for president and lost but settled for **vice president** under John Quincy Adams. In 1829, Calhoun served as **vice president** under Andrew Jackson for four years. Calhoun died on March 30, 1850, in Washington, D.C., at age 68.

Jackson was 61 years of age at the time of his first inauguration. It was the first inauguration to take place on the East Portico of the Capitol. In his March 4, **1829, inaugural address,** Jackson stated, "The bulwark of our defense is the national militia." His campaign slogans had been "Let the people rule." and "The great can protect themselves, but the poor and humble require the arm and shield of the law." He was considered the first **people's president**. Jackson called the presidency "dignified slavery." He promised to **limit government spending, reform a corrupt government**, and **eliminate government debt** by selling government land and getting France to pay for ships it destroyed during the Napoleonic Wars. He did all three, the **first president to fulfill all his campaign promises**. For the first time, the **government was free of debt**. But inflation lowered the value of the paper dollar from equity with gold to a ratio of 12 paper dollars to one dollar of gold.

Upon winning the election, Jackson invited all Tennesseans to the inauguration. Jackson preferred being addressed as "**General**," not "President." Reportedly, over 30,000 people came to the reception and were served Jackson's favorite drink, a very potent orange punch. During the partying, the attendees trashed the Executive Mansion, breaking china, furniture, and glassware. After repairing the party damage, Jackson later put twenty spittoons in the Executive Mansion to preserve the carpets. He also put in a pool table. With Jackson's wife, Rachel, dead, Jackson's niece, Emily Donaldson, became the White House hostess.

Jackson's first **cabinet** included **Vice President** John Calhoun, **Secretary of State** Martin Van Buren, **Secretary of the Treasury** Samuel Ingham, **Secretary of War** John Eaton, **Attorney General** John Berrien, **Secretary of the Navy** John Branch, and **Postmaster General** John McLean. Pay for the postmaster general was set at $4,000 a year and the other five secretaries' annual pay was set at $6,000 a year.

Andrew Jackson signed the **1830 Indian Removal Act**, which authorized Jackson to negotiate treaties with Indian tribes for their relocation from Georgia to western lands. Jackson believed whites and Indians could not live together. He informed Congress that the relocation of the tribes was a "benevolent ethnic cleansing."

In **1830**, the **U.S. population** stood at almost 13 million. That same year, another form of transportation was formed with the establishment of the **Underground Railroad**, helping African Americans escape to freedom in the north.

In **1831**, Jackson brought **running water** to the Executive Mansion.

There were three U.S. Supreme Court cases during Jackson's term. In **Cherokee Nation vs Georgia** (1831), the Supreme Court ruled that it lacked jurisdiction to upset the **Indian Removal Act of 1830**. In **Worcester vs Georgia** (1832), the U.S. Supreme Court ruled that federal troops may be employed to enforce Supreme Court decisions. And in **Barron vs Baltimore** (1833), the U.S. Supreme Court ruled that the Bill of Rights applies to the federal government, not state or local governments.

When Jackson supported the **extramarital affair** of Secretary Eaton, it split the Cabinet. Therefore, he asked for and got resignations from all of the Cabinet members. Jackson retained only Martin Van Buren as Secretary of State, then introduced the **spoils system** by giving cabinet jobs to his friends. Cabinet replacements were **Secretary of the Treasury** Louis McLane, **Secretary of War** Lewis Cass, **Attorney General** Roger Taney, **Secretary of the Navy** Lewis Woodbury, and **Postmaster General** William Barry.

ANDREW JACKSON (7TH PRESIDENT)

Jackson renewed the two-term presidency with his re-election. Because of Calhoun's feud with Jackson, Calhoun was dropped from the 1832 ticket and replaced by **Martin Van Buren**. Jackson had relied on Van Buren's counsel when he was Jackson's Secretary of State in 1829-1833. In the **1832** election, Democrats **Andrew Jackson** and **Martin Van Buren** received 687,507 of the popular votes vs 530,189 for National Republicans **Henry Clay** and **John Sergeant**. And Jackson-Van Buren received 219 electoral votes vs 49 for Clay-Sergeant and 18 for unknown others. Jackson was elected president, and Van Buren was elected vice president.

Martin Van Buren was born on December 5, 1782, in Old Kinderhook, New York. He went on to become a lawyer after graduating from the **Kinderhook Academy** in 1796. He practiced law and in 1813 was elected to the **New York Senate**. In 1815, he served as **attorney general of New York**, joined the **U.S. Senate** in 1821, and was elected **governor of New York** in 1828. Starting in 1829, he was **Secretary of State** under President Jackson for four years. As vice president, Van Buren presided over the U.S. Senate. He did so with two pistols strapped to his legs, ready for a fight. Van Buren died at age 79 in 1862 at his home in New York's Hudson Valley.

Jackson responded to South Carolina disqualifying the **1828 Tariff Act** by signing the **1832 Nullification Act**, nullifying the South Carolina law.

In his **1833 inaugural address**, Jackson stated, "Without the union our independence and liberty would never have been achieved."

Jackson's second term **cabinet** included **Vice President** Martin Van Buren, **Secretary of State** Louis McLane, **Secretary of the**

Treasury Roger Taney, **Secretary of War** Lewis Cass, **Attorney General** Benjamin Butler, **Secretary of the Navy** Levi Woodbury, and **Postmaster General** Amos Kendall.

In addition to his formal cabinet, President Jackson had an unofficial **kitchen cabinet**. The name suggested they came in through the kitchen, not the front door. They included Francis Blair (**newspaper editor**), Andrew Donaldson (**nephew**), Amos Kendall (**newspaper editor**), William Lewis (General Jackson's **former quartermaster**), John Overton (**friend** and **former business partner**), Roger Taney (**Attorney General**), and Martin Van Buren (former secretary of state and **current vice president**).

Jackson distrusted banks. He did not like the **second Bank of the United States**, which had been set up in 1816. It was a clearinghouse for payments on national debt, a source of credit for the federal government, and a depository for federal funds. In 1832, the bank asked that its charter be renewed. **Congress agreed, but Jackson vetoed the action**. President Jackson vetoed more Congressional actions than the previous six presidents combined. Jackson then **withdrew funds** from the **Bank of the United States** and **deposited** them in various **state banks**. This action led to a **joint resolution** of both the House and Senate to a **formal censure**. This was the **first time** that Congress formally censured a sitting president. Jackson responded, "The President is the direct representative of the American people." He claimed the president's responsibility is to carry out the will of the people and not that of Congress. Politicians and journalists called him **"King Andrew"** for his disregard for rules and regulations, but he was liked by and popular with the people. Jackson's enemies banded together and formed the **Whig Party**, named after the British political party.

ANDREW JACKSON (7TH PRESIDENT)

In January **1835**, Richard Lawrence, an unemployed, mentally ill house painter, shot at Jackson as he was leaving the funeral service of a congressman. Lawrence's gun misfired, and Jackson apprehended him with his cane. The man was ruled insane and never brought to trial. Jackson became the **first president** to successfully **avoid an assassination attempt**, the same year **Samuel Colt** invented his famed revolver, the first six shooter. In 1836, the Bank of the United States charter expired. That same year, a Mexican army of 10,000, led by **Santa Anna** was fought off for several days by 180 men at the **Alamo** in San Antonio in order to give **Sam Houston** time to raise an army to fight for Texas independence.

In his **farewell address**, Jackson stated, "Our Constitution is no longer a doubtful experiment and at the end of nearly a century, we find that it has preserved unimpaired the liberties for the people, secured the rights of property and that our country has improved and flourished." The **Panic of 1837** occurred the year Jackson left the presidency. It put Jackson heavily in debt, causing him to borrow extensively. nonetheless, he supported his vice president, Martin Van Buren, to succeed him and actively campaigned for him. And after President Harrison died, **Jackson supported President Polk** for election in 1841.

Congress made no pay changes during Jackson's term of presidency.

Jackson **died** on June 8, 1845, at age 78 of heart failure and tuberculosis at his estate, **the Hermitage**. His last words were, "Oh do not cry. Be good children, and we shall all meet in Heaven." He and his wife (who died in 1828) were buried in his Hermitage estate near Nashville, Tennessee. Most historians consider Jackson's presidency **more effective than most**.

WHAT YOU SHOULD KNOW ABOUT THE 47 U.S. PRESIDENTS

Key Events

Cornelius Vanderbilt acquired his own steamboat company (1829); the **New York City Working Man's** party began with 6,000 members (1829); the **Mormon Church** was established by Joseph Smith in Fayette, New York (1830); **South Texas** was ruled by 20,000 **Comanches** (1830); the **Baltimore and Ohio Railroad** began service as the first train to carry freight and passengers (1830); Senator Daniel Webster and Robert Hayne debated a state's right to nullify a federal law (1830); Virginia slave **Nat Turner** led an armed slave revolt in Virginia that killed over 50 whites within 24 hours before the army killed over 100 participants, and Turner was hanged (1831); thousands died in New York City from a **cholera epidemic** (1832); **New York City** became the first city with a streetcar (1832); the Democratic Party held the first national convention in Baltimore, Maryland (1833); **Oberlin College** became the first co-educational institution (1833); the area in New York City called **Five Points** contained a number of gangs operating out of the Old Brewery tenement (1834); frontiersman **Davy Crockett** moved from Tennessee to Texas (1834); **John Jacob Astor** sold the American Fur Company, America's first business monopoly (1834); **Cyrus McCormick** patented his farm implement reaper (1834); the **Liberty Bell** cracked when tolling the death of Chief Justice **John Marshall** (1835); **sleeping cars** were introduced on the Cumberland Valley Railroad (1835); freed slaves led to a race riot in Washington, D.C. (1835); the **Texas Rangers** were formed to protect the Mexican border (1836); Ralph Waldo Emerson published *Nature*, his philosophy of transcendentalism (1836); **John Deere** introduced the non-sticking steel plow (1836); former **President John Quincy Adams** was elected to the House of Representatives (1836); and two states joined the Union, **Arkansas** (1836) and **Michigan** (1837), bringing the total to 26.

MARTIN VAN BUREN
(8ᵗʰ PRESIDENT)

MARCH 4, 1837 – MARCH 4, 1841

Martin Van Buren was born on December 5, 1782, to Dutch parents, Abraham and Maria Hoes Van Buren, in Old Kinderhook, New York. Its abbreviation of "OK" brought "**okay**" into the English lexicon, meaning "correct." Martin was the first president whose **second language was English**; his first was Dutch. Van Buren was the **first president** born after the Revolution and the first president **born an American citizen**; the seven before him were British citizens. Martin's father was a **tavern keeper and farmer**. Martin had seven brothers and sisters, four full siblings, and three half-siblings. Maria's marriage to Abraham Van Buren was her second marriage.

Martin initially attended a **one-room schoolhouse** and later attended the **Kinderhook Academy** but had to leave at age 13 because of his family's financial problems. Van Buren worked in a Kinderhook law office for five years. In 1800, at the age of 18, Martin **campaigned for Thomas Jefferson** when he ran for president. Having passed the New York bar in 1803, Van Buren went on to become a **lawyer**, having set up his practice in **Kinderhook**. Van Buren signed all his memos, "OK," introducing it into the English lexicon.

Van Buren's nicknames included "**little squirt**" (as he was only 5'5") and "**the little magician**" (for his ability to rally political support and get things done). At age 25, Van Buren married first cousin and childhood friend, **Hannah Hoes,** age 24, in February 1807 and they had five children together: Abraham, John, Martin, Winfield (who died shortly after birth), and Smith Thompson.

In 1813, Martin was elected to the **New York Senate**, and in 1815 he became the **New York attorney general**, while still serving as a State Senator. As attorney general, Van Buren successfully tried General Hull for having surrendered the city of Detroit in 1812 to the British after little resistance. Hannah Van Buren died on February 5, 1819, at age 35 from tuberculosis, 18 years before Martin became president. Martin Van Buren never remarried. In 1821, Martin was elected a **U.S. senator** from New York, defeating incumbent Nathan Sanford, and in 1828 Van Buren was elected **governor of New York**. But he resigned within two months to join President Jackson's cabinet as **Secretary of State**, from 1829 to 1831. And when Senator **Rufus King** moved into a hotel with Cabinet Secretary Van Buren, rumors claimed that Van Buren was "wedded to Mr. King." Martin resigned his Secretary of State position, having been invited to be Andrew Jackson's vice president.

In 1832, Van Buren helped set up the **Democratic Party** from a disorganized Democratic-Republican Party. This was probably Van Buren's **greatest achievement**.

In the **1832 election**, Democrats **Andrew Jackson** and **Martin Van Buren** defeated National Republicans **Henry Clay** and **John Sergeant**, 687,507 to 530,189 in the popular vote and 219 to 49 in the electoral vote. The remaining 18 electoral votes were spread among several candidates. **Andrew Jackson** was elected president and **Martin Van Buren** was elected vice president. Martin served four years in that position. Vice President Van Buren and President Jackson both loved to ride horses together and to gamble on horseracing.

In the **1836 election**, the National Republican Party evolved into the Whig Party. Democrats **Martin Van Buren** and **Richard Johnson** received 762,678 popular votes to 550,816 for Whigs **William Henry Harrison** and **Francis Granger** and 170 electoral votes to 73. Van Buren was elected president and Johnson was elected vice president. Three other Whigs had 187,308 popular votes and 51 electoral votes. Van Buren was the last vice president **elected to succeed the president under whom he served** (Andrew Jackson) until George H.W. Bush was elected in 1988, having served as Ronald Reagan's vice president. Van Buren was also the **first president** to mention **slavery** in an **inaugural address**, stating he would oppose any attempt to abolish slavery. He was 54 years old on the day of his inauguration. That year, he also brought **central heating** to the Executive Mansion. Van Buren also announced he would continue Jackson's policies, including his cabinet.

Richard Johnson was born on October 17, 1780, in Beargrass, Kentucky. His father was one of the largest landowners in the state. Richard graduated from Transylvania University and was admitted to the Kentucky Bar in 1802. Johnson was elected to the **U.S. House of Representatives** in 1807 and served twelve years. He served and was a hero in the War of 1812 and claimed to have **killed Shawnee Chief Tecumseh** at the **Battle of the Thames** in 1813. Johnson then served in the **U.S. Senate** from 1819 until 1829 when he returned to the **U.S. House of Representatives**. Johnson retired after serving as Van Buren's vice president and died in his home in Frankfort on November 19, 1850.

Van Buren's first **cabinet** included **Vice President** Richard Johnson, **Secretary of State** John Forsyth, **Secretary of Treasury** Levi Woodbury, **Secretary of War** Joel Poinsett, **Attorney General** Benjamin Butler, **Secretary of the Navy** Mahlon Dickerson, and **Postmaster General** Amos Kendall. Poinsett introduced a number of tropical plants to the U.S. while serving as the Minister to Mexico under John Quincy Adams. One plant was given Poinsett's name, the **poinsettia**.

The **Panic of 1837** followed a period of inflation, bank failures, thousands of bankruptcies, and unemployment at 25%, resulting in a five-year period of depression that doomed Van Buren's chances of being re-elected. During the panic, Van Buren issued an **executive order** requiring the purchase of government land to be either in gold or silver. This was done to hinder land speculation.

There were two U.S. Supreme Court cases, and two significant laws passed during Van Buren's term of office. In **Sarchet vs United States** (1838), the U.S. Supreme Court ruled that "cases at law" can only be brought to the Court from the Circuit Court by writ of error, not by appeal. And in **United States vs Morris** (1840), the U.S. Supreme Court ruled that to constitute an offense under the Slave Trade Act of 1880, an actual transportation or carrying of slaves in a vessel was not necessary. **The Neutrality Act of 1838** expanded on the Act of 1818, increasing the government's authority to seize and detain any vessel or any arms or munitions of war illegally coming across the borders. And **the Independent Treasury Act of 1840** established an "independent treasury system," where the Treasurer would manage "all public moneys which shall come to his hands in the Treasury of the United States," not in commercial banks.

Van Buren was very **clothes-conscious**, always wearing the latest fashions. However, it was Martin's daughter-in-law, Angelica, who served as his **Executive Mansion hostess**. She did a fabulous job, but after returning from Europe, she remodeled the Executive Mansion, creating a European style that was not popular.

Van Buren introduced an **independent banking system** in 1839 to oversee the use of federal funds. Although short-lived, it was the model the Federal Reserve adopted under President Woodrow Wilson. As a Van Buren achievement, this banking action was second only to **setting up the Democratic Party**.

In the **1840 presidential election**, the Whig Party nominated **William Henry Harrison and Richard Johnson. Martin Van Buren** and **Richard Johnson** were unanimously elected by the **Democratic Party** but lost in the general election to Whig candidates **Harrison** and **Tyler**, who received 1,275,016 popular votes to 1,129,102 for Van Buren-Johnson. And Harrison-Tyler received 234 electoral votes to 60 for Van Buren-Johnson, thereby electing Harrison as president and Tyler as vice president. One of Van Buren's final acts as president was to sign an executive order limiting federal workers to a ten-hour day.

One of Van Buren's famous quotes was, "It is easier to do a job right than to explain why you didn't." He also said, "As to the Presidency, the two happiest days of my life were those of my entrance into office and my leaving it." After leaving office, Van Buren retired to **Lindenwold**, his estate in Kinderhook. There he took up writing his **memoirs** and occasionally **speaking** out on political issues. Van Buren was the first former U.S. president to tour Europe as a common man.

In spite of his losing the 1840 election, many thought Van Buren would be the Democratic nominee in the **1844 election**, but a virtual unknown, **James Polk**, became the **Democratic nominee**. Undaunted, **Van Buren** tried again in **1848**, this time as a nominee of the Free-Soil party. But he received only ten percent of the popular vote and no electoral votes.

Van Buren died on July 24, 1862, at age 79 of heart failure in Kinderhook. He allegedly said, "I am ready." Upon his death, **eighty carriages** accompanied the body, but no bells tolled because he had left specific instructions to that effect. He was buried in Kinderhook Cemetery in Kinderhook, New York, along with his wife. Most historians give Van Buren **an average rating**.

Key Events

During Van Buren's term a **lengthy depression** began shortly after his taking office, set off by a panic of business and financial uncertainty (1837); the organization that later became **Proctor**

& Gamble was formed (1837); **Charles Goodyear** received a patent to produce workable rubber (1837); the renewed and expanded **gag rule** prevented a slavery debate in Congress (1837); the **$10 Liberty Head Gold** coin was introduced (1838); **Henry David Thoreau** stated in his essay *Civil Disobedience*, "That government is best which governs least," reiterating the philosophy of Thomas Jefferson (1838); thousands of Indians died on the **"Trail of Tears"** to Oklahoma, including Cherokees, Creeks, and Seminoles, with more dying in Oklahoma, from cholera, influenza, malaria, and smallpox (1838); the **Atchison, Topeka and Santa Fe Railway** introduced private dining cars (1839); **Abner Doubleday** set down the rules of baseball in Cooperstown, New York (1839); the **U.S. population** was 17 million (1840); the **escalator** was introduced at **Coney Island Amusement Park** in Brooklyn, New York (1840); and **the American Medical Association** was formed in Philadelphia (1840).

WILLIAM HENRY HARRISON
(9ᵀᴴ PRESIDENT)

MARCH 4, 1841 - APRIL 4, 1841

William Henry Harrison was born on February 9, 1773, to Benjamin Harrison V and Elizabeth Bassett Harrison at Berkeley Plantation, Virginia. William was the **youngest** of seven children. His **father**, Benjamin Harrison V, was a farmer and politician. While he served as a member of the Second Constitutional Congress, he signed the **Declaration of Independence**. And Benjamin's **great-grandson**, also named Benjamin, was elected the 23rd U.S. president in 1888. Harrison had **private tutors** before attending **Hampden-Sydney College** and then going to **medical school**. In 1791, William dropped out of medical school when his father died. William then joined the **First Infantry Regiment**, serving under General Anthony Wayne.

In 1794, Harrison was cited for bravery in the **Battle of Fallen Timbers**.

At age 22, William Henry Harrison married **Anna Symmes**, age 20, on November 25, 1795. They had **ten children** together; four daughters, Anna, Elizabeth, Lucy, and Mary; and six sons, Benjamin, Carter, James, John Cleves, John Scott, and William. They also had **48 grandchildren** and **106 great-grandchildren**. Harrison was prolific, if not profound.

From 1798 to 1801, Harrison served as a **territorial delegate to Congress**. From 1801 to 1813, he served as **Territorial Governor of Indiana**. Then, serving as a **brigadier general**, Harrison defeated the **Shawnee Chief Tecumseh** in the **Battle of Tippecanoe**, Indiana, on November 11, 1811. Forever after, he was named "**Old Tippecanoe**." Following General Hull's surrender of **Fort Detroit**, General Harrison retook the Fort in 1813, chasing the British troops into Canada near Ontario, where Harrison defeated them at the **Battle of Thames River** on October 5, 1813. In 1816, he was elected to the **U.S. House of Representatives** from Ohio; in 1819, Harrison was elected an **Ohio state senator**; and in 1825 he was elected to serve as a **U.S. senator** from Ohio.

In the **1836 election**, Whig **William Henry Harrison** lost the U.S. presidential vote to Democrat **Martin Van Buren**, who had 762,678 popular votes to Harrison's 550,816. Van Buren also had 176 electoral votes to Harrison's 73. The other candidates received 187,308 popular votes and 51 electoral votes.

In the **1840 presidential campaign, William Henry Harrison** and his running mate, **John Tyler**, both Whigs, used the campaign slogan of "**Tippecanoe and Tyler Too**." Harrison portrayed himself as a man of the people. Cider was served at campaign rallies, along with short speeches by Harrison. Some of his favorite sayings were, "Times change and we change with them," and "I am just an ordinary man, not an elite like Van Buren."

In the **1840 election**, Whigs **William Henry Harrison and John Tyler** defeated Democratic President **Martin Van Buren** and Vice President **Richard Johnson**, 1,275,016 to 1,129,102 in the popular vote and 234 to 60 in the electoral vote. Harrison had been elected president and Tyler had been elected vice president. Both were helped in their election by the **Financial Crisis of 1837**, which saw banks fail and workers lose their jobs under Democrats Van Buren and Johnson.

John Tyler was born on March 29, 1790, on his family's plantation in Charles City, Virginia. His father was considered to be part of the Virginian aristocracy. Tyler graduated in 1807 from the **College of William & Mary** to practice law. He served in a local militia in the **War of 1812**. Later, he was elected to the **House of Representatives**; in 1825, he was elected governor of Virginia; and in 1827, he was **elected** to the U.S. Senate, representing Virginia.

Harrison was 68 years old on the date of his inauguration. He was the oldest elected president until Reagan, who was age 69 in 1989. Tyler was 50 years old. In his March 4, **1841, inaugural address**, Harrison stated, "The decent and manly examination of the acts of government should not only be tolerated, they should be encouraged." He also stated, "No other people have a government more of their respect." Harrison caught a cold during his one hour and 40-minute inaugural address, which he delivered in a driving rain without a hat or overcoat. His 8,445 words are the longest inaugural speech on record.

In **United States vs The Amistad** (1841), the U.S. Supreme Court ruled that 50 slaves on the ship *Amistad* accused of mutiny were not guilty.

Harrison **died** on April 4, 1841, at age 68 from pneumonia. He was the **first president to die in office**; his 32 days in office are the **shortest on record**. His last words were, "I wish you to understand the true principles of government. I wish them carried out. I ask nothing more." Wife Anna was still in Indiana, too ill to travel, when Harrison died, and therefore missed his inaugural and his funeral. She was the first president's widow to receive a pension – a lump sum of $25,000. She spent the shortest time as First Lady on record – one month. She died on February 25, 1864, at age 88. She and her husband were both buried in the William Henry Harrison Memorial State Park, in North Bend, Ohio.

Before his death, Harrison had elected a **cabinet**. They included **Vice President** John Tyler, **Secretary of State** Daniel Webster, **Secretary of the Treasury** Thomas Ewing, **Secretary of War** John Bell, **Attorney General** John Crittenden, **Secretary of the Navy** George Badger, and **Postmaster General** Francis Granger.

John Tyler served only 32 days as vice president before Harrison's death. Harrison's death led to a **Constitutional issue**. The Constitution said that in case of death, the vice president shall **act** as the president. It did not state that the vice president will **become** the president. It was expected the vice president would serve temporarily until Congress could agree on a successor or there was a new election. Meanwhile, Tyler had himself **sworn in as president**. The result: his relationship with Congress was badly damaged, and the beginning of the end of the **Whig Party** had begun.

Congress made no pay changes during Harrison's brief term of presidency.

Most historians agree that Harrison's term of office was **too short to rate.**

Key Events

Nothing of interest occurred during Harrison's one month of presidency.

John Tyler
(10ᵀᴴ President)

April 4, 1841 - March 4, 1845

John Tyler Jr. was born on March 29, 1790, to John Tyler Sr. and Mary Armstead Tyler on his family's plantation in Charles City, Virginia. His father was considered to be part of the **Virginian aristocracy**, having been a governor of Virginia and a Federal District Court Judge. John Jr. was an accomplished violin player. He was one of three sons, along with four sisters. John attended local schools before going to William and Mary Prep, then to the **College of William & Mary**, graduating in 1807 to practice **law** and enter **state politics**. In the **War of 1812**, Tyler commanded a local militia. At age 23, he married **Letitia Christian**, also age 23, in 1813. Letitia Tyler had **eight children** with John. There were five daughters, Alice, Ann, Elizabeth, Letitia, and Mary: along with three sons, John, Robert, and Tazewell. In 1816, Tyler was elected to the **House of Representatives**. In 1820 he returned to state politics. Tyler was elected the **governor of Virginia**, serving from 1825 to 1827, and in 1827 was elected to the **U.S. Senate** from Virginia. Refusing to overturn a Senate censure of President Jackson, Tyler resigned from the Senate in 1836. In 1839, Tyler was defeated in a Virginia election for state governor.

Tyler was an early supporter of the newly formed **Whig Party**. It was named after a political party in England in 1835. The Whig Party consisted of a diverse group of politicians who supported states' rights and were opposed to President Jackson. The **Whigs endorsed Tyler as a vice-presidential candidate** for William Henry Harrison's presidency. Tyler was selected as the vice-presidential candidate because of his recognition in the South, offsetting Harrison's strength in the North and West. **Harrison had the grandfather image; Tyler was the handsome statesman.** The **Whig presidential campaign** was one of parades, songs, and slogans. There was no political platform. Speeches were short and general in nature.

In the **1840 election, William Henry Harrison** and **John Tyler**, both Whigs, defeated Democrats **Martin Van Buren** and **Richard Johnson,** 234 electoral votes to 60 for Van Buren and Johnson and 1,275,016 to 1,129,102 in popular votes. William Henry Harrison was elected president and John Tyler was elected vice president.

After Harrison's death, **Tyler announced that the vice president became the president** upon the president's death or removal from office. The **Constitution was vague** on this point. The **Twelfth Amendment,** ratified on June 15, 1804, states, "The

JOHN TYLER (10TH PRESIDENT)

Vice President shall act as President as in the case of the death or other constitutional disability of the President." **It does not state that the vice president will become the president** (see Appendix C). Some believed the vice president was only an **acting president** until an election could be held. While Congress debated the issue, **Tyler had himself sworn in as president**. This infuriated Congress and was the beginning of a strenuous relationship. John Tyler was the first president to be elected to the **four federal offices**: representative, senator, vice president, and president.

Tyler was 51 years of age when inaugurated, the youngest president to date. At his April 6, **1841, inaugural address**, Tyler stated, "Patronage is the sword and cannon by which war may be made on the liberty of the human race." The year 1841 was the first time **three presidents served in the same year: Van Buren, Harrison, and Tyler**. There was no mechanism to replace Tyler as vice president, and he **refused to name a vice president**. Therefore, the position remained open. When some sent Tyler mail addressed to the "**Acting President**," Tyler returned it with the note, "Addressee Unknown." His other nicknames were **Accidental President** and **His Accidency**.

The Tyler administration began with the **same cabinet** President Harrison had selected, except for vice president: **Vice President** no one, **Secretary of State** Daniel Webster, **Secretary of the Treasury** Thomas Ewing, **Secretary of War** John Bell, **Attorney General** John Crittenden, **Secretary of the Navy** George Badger, and **Postmaster General** Francis Granger. Tyler announced to his Cabinet, "I shall be pleased to accept your counsel and advice. But I can never consent being dictated to. When you think otherwise, **your resignation will be accepted**." Badger, Bell, Crittenden, and Ewing were gone after the first year.

Tyler was **liked by the public**, but **not by politicians**, as he was an outspoken person on every issue and especially about the Democratic Party. Tyler later signed the **1841 Preemption Act**, giving squatters on government land the opportunity to buy 160 acres at an auction price, and the **1842 Webster-Ashburton Treaty**, which finalized the boundary between Canada and the United States.

In **Prigg vs Pennsylvania** (1842), the U.S. Supreme Court ruled that Pennsylvania's laws prohibiting the extradition of "any negro or mulatto" for the purpose of enslaving them violated Article IV, Section 2 of the Constitution and the Fugitive Slave Law of 1793, and that federal laws trump state laws, per the Supremacy Clause.

Letitia died of a massive stroke on September 10, 1842, at age 51, about sixteen months into her husband's term as president. They had little money but spent what they had on entertaining and fixing up the Executive Mansion.

When the House passed a bill re-chartering the **second national bank**, Tyler vetoed it. The House passed a repeat bill, and Tyler again vetoed it. The entire Cabinet then resigned, except for Daniel Webster. Tyler appointed replacements within two days in 1843 and set the record for the most cabinet secretaries in one year. The House then introduced a resolution to impeach Tyler, but it failed with a vote of 127 to 83.

In **Winston vs United States** (1844), the U.S. Supreme Court ruled that when the matter in dispute is below the amount necessary for the Court's jurisdiction, the writ of error must be dismissed.

After Letitia died, John married the "Rose of Long Island," actress **Julia Gardiner,** age 24 in 1844 (he was 54). Julia started to see John within months of Letitia's death. Julia's press agent

JOHN TYLER (10TH PRESIDENT)

came up with the title "The Lovely Lady Presidentress." Julia and John got married at the Church of the Ascension in New York. She is credited with starting the tradition of playing the music "**Hail to the Chief**" whenever the president appeared. They had seven children: two daughters, Julia and Pearl, along with five sons, David, John Jr., Lachlan, Lyon, and Robert. John Tyler Sr. became the father of **fifteen children** by two wives (a presidential record that may last a long time). John Tyler was the **first president to be married while president**. His children with Letitia were loyal to their mother, not Julia, who loved to entertain and introduced dancing to the Executive Mansion. Julia died on July 10, 1889, at age 69.

In **United States vs Freeman** (1845), the U.S. Supreme Court ruled that statutes *in pari materia* should all "be taken into consideration in construing any one of them," and "be taken together, as if they were one law." Where a statute's words are "doubtful or obscure," one must look to the legislature's intent to find its meaning.

Tyler vetoed the **1845 Tariff Act** which established new tariffs. But Congress overrode Tyler's veto on March 3, 1845, and the **1845 Tariff Act** became law. It was the **first such Congressional action** in history, and it came one day before the expiration of Tyler's presidency.

Tyler was a firm believer in **states' rights** but was opposed to secession. He also believed that "wealth can only be accumulated by the earnings of industry and the savings of frugality." Tyler also said, "Patronage attacks the liberty of the human race."

Congress made no pay changes during Tyler's term of presidency.

Tyler was **nominated** for reelection but **declined** and supported James Polk. Tyler retired to his Virginia plantation, Sherwood

Forest, where he planted crops. After his presidency, when his native state, Virginia, seceded in 1861, **Tyler** supported the action and was elected to the **Confederate Congress**, an act that labeled him a traitor to the U.S. government. He died on January 18, 1862, at age 71 from heart failure. His last words were, "Doctor, I am going. Perhaps it is best." He was buried in Richmond, Virginia, with a **Confederate flag-draped coffin**. He was the first president to **have his body exhumed** on the belief he might have been poisoned, but there was no evidence to support that possibility. Most historians give Tyler a **significantly below average rating**.

KEY EVENTS

Edgar Allan Poe published *The Murders in the Rue Morgue*, the first American detective story (1841); **Charles Fourier** established collectives (each about 1,500 persons) intended to be self-sustaining (1841); a wagon train left Independence, Missouri, and arrived in California six months later (1841); the first use of **ether gas anesthetic** was used in operations (1842); the magazine *Economist* was founded (1843); the second **Seminole War** in Florida ended (1843); the community organization B'nai B'rith was formed (1843); more than 1,000 settlers from Missouri arrived in Oregon after more than five months on the Oregon Trail (1843); the **Free-Soil** party was formed to support collectives (1844); a deck gun exploded on the *USS Princeton*, killing several, including the Secretary of State (Ewing), and the Secretary of the Navy (Badger) (1844); having received Congressional approval to build a **telegraph line** from Washington to Baltimore, **Samuel Morse** made distance shorter by sending the first telegraph message, "What Hath God Wrought," with his dots and dashes that made up the Morse code (1844); **Elias Howe** created the sewing machine (1844); **Lewis Tappan** introduced the credit rating system (1844); the state of Florida was admitted to the Union (1845); **Texas** was admitted into the Union (1845); and Edgar Allan Poe published the poem "**The Raven**" (1845).

James K. Polk
(11th President)

March 4, 1845 - March 4, 1849

James Knox Polk was born on November 2, 1795, in Pineville, North Carolina to Samuel and Jane Knox Polk. His father was a land surveyor and later a general store owner. James was the **oldest** of ten children. James had five brothers, Franklin, John, Marshall, Samuel, and William, and four sisters, Jane, Lydia, Naomi, and Ophelia. James suffered from poor health as a child, preventing him from going to school. At age 16, Polk had an **operation** for kidney stones without anesthesia. Following surgery, Polk attended a school in Mt. Zion, Tennessee, and then the Bradley Academy in Murfreesboro, Tennessee. He **did well academically** in both schools. Polk graduated from the **University of North Carolina** in 1818 and went on to study **law**, being admitted to the Tennessee bar in June 1820. He then served in a local militia, rising to the rank of colonel. From 1822 to 1824, Polk served in the **Tennessee House of Representatives**.

In January 1824, James married **Sarah Childress**, age 20. They had no children.

From 1825 to 1839, Polk served in the **U.S. House of Representatives**; Polk was also **Speaker of the House** from 1835 to 1839. Polk presided over a very divided House: 108 Democrats, 107 Whigs, and 24 members of other parties. Naturally, it was difficult to get anything done with such a split. In 1839, he was elected **governor of Tennessee**, but he was not reelected, losing two consecutive times.

Then, despite being a virtual unknown, Polk became the **Democratic candidate for president** in 1844. A two-thirds vote was required at the convention to become the nominee. Former President Martin Van Buren failed on the first seven ballots to secure the nomination, and Polk got it on the eighth ballot, primarily because Van Buren came out against annexing Texas, while Polk favored the annexing and expansion of the country. Polk also got President Jackson's endorsement.

Unlike Henry Clay and Theodore Frelinghuysen both abolitionists, Polk supported the **1820 Missouri Compromise** designating free and slave states.

In the **1844 election**, Democrats **James Polk** and **George Dallas** received 1,337,243 popular votes vs 1,299,062 for Whigs **Henry Clay** and **Theodore Frelinghuysen**. Polk-Dallas received 170 electoral votes vs 105 for Clay-Frelinghuysen. James Polk was elected president and George Dallas was elected vice president. Polk was the first elected president who **did not carry his own state**. Polk was also the **first former Speaker of the House of**

Representatives to become president. Polk was 49 years old on the day of his inauguration.

George Mifflin Dallas was born on July 10, 1792, in Philadelphia, Pennsylvania, and came from an affluent family. George was the second of six children born to Arabella Maria Smith Dallas and Alexander J. Dallas, who served as **Secretary of the Treasury** and **Interim Secretary of War** under James Madison. George was privately educated at Quaker-run preparatory schools and graduated with honors from what is now **Princeton University** in 1810. George studied law in his father's office and was admitted to the **Pennsylvania bar** in 1813. That same year, he became private secretary to **Secretary of the Treasury** Albert Gallatin and traveled to Russia and Britain with Gallatin on his mission to negotiate peace during the **War of 1812**. Dallas returned to the United States in 1814 and became counsel for the **Second Bank of the United States**. In 1816, he married Sophia Chew Nicklin. They went on to have eight children together. In 1817, he became **deputy attorney general of Pennsylvania** and then was elected **mayor of Philadelphia**. In 1831, he became the **senator from Pennsylvania**. In 1837, he was appointed by Martin Van Buren to serve as **minister to Russia**, a position he held until 1839. In 1844, the **Democratic Party** chose Dallas as the vice-presidential candidate to run with presidential candidate James K. Polk. Polk was elected president and Dallas was elected vice president. In 1849, he left office and resumed his legal practice. He served as **minister of Great Britain** from 1856 to 1861. And he died on December 31, 1864, of a heart attack. The cities of Dallas in Texas and Oregon are named in his honor.

In his March 4, **1845, inaugural address**, Polk stated, "Our union is a confederation of independent states whose policy is peace with each other and all the world."

In **United States vs Rogers** (1846), the U.S. Supreme Court ruled that even if he is a member of an Indian Tribe, a "white man" is not an "Indian" and is therefore not entitled to the jurisdictional exception in the Trade and Intercourse Act of 1834. (The case is notable for determining the criteria for who is an "Indian" under federal law.)

Sarah Polk was considered her husband's **political partner**, serving as his assistant, and actively participating in state dinner discussions. Sarah also shared a **sense of fashion** with **Dolley Madison**, with whom she was a close friend. Having no children, Sarah brought her nieces into the Executive Mansion to help with entertaining. A **devout Presbyterian**, Sarah did not approve of drinking or dancing.

In **United States vs Briggs** (1847), the U.S. Supreme Court ruled that for the Court to have jurisdiction in cases of division of opinion in the circuit court, the point upon which the judges differed must be stated and certified.

Polk expressed his frustration when he noted, "A president can only approve or veto laws, he cannot make laws." There were two significant laws enacted during Polk's term of office. The **Independent Treasury Act of 1848** established the Treasury as a "substantive treasury," with its own buildings, distinct from state or private banks. It would retain public revenues, and "all monies paid into the same shall be subject to the draft of the treasurer." The **Drug Importation Act of 1848** regulated the importation of "drugs, medicines, medicinal preparations, including medicinal essential oils, and chemical preparations used wholly or in part as medicine," into the U.S. and charged Customs with enforcement of the law, and appointed special examiners to check the "quality, purity, and fitness for medical purposes" of the imported drugs in the ports of New York, Boston, Philadelphia, Baltimore, Charleston, and New Orleans.

In **United States vs Yates** (1848), the U.S. Supreme Court ruled that the withdrawal of an attorney does not authorize a motion to dismiss for want of a citation, as long as the appeal is otherwise authorized, and doesn't preclude a party from moving to dismiss on other grounds.

Polk believed in **Manifest Destiny**, the supposed God-given right of white Americans to take over land not already in their control. When Mexico and the United States differed on the location of the border, Polk ordered **General Zachary Taylor** to set up camp along the Rio Grande. When the Mexicans attacked, Polk got Congress to **declare war** on Mexico on May 15, 1846. Illinois Congressman Abraham Lincoln questioned the action. But Mexico City fell in September 1847 to Taylor's troops. In the **1848 Treaty of Guadalupe Hidalgo**, Mexico ceded several states, including Arizona, California, New Mexico, and Texas, to the United States for $15 million, ending the war. California was added as a free state and Texas, was added as a slave state. Arizona and New Mexico were added as states later. The settlement of the **Oregon Territory** with Great Britain ended with the United States having control of the Pacific Northwest and Southwest territories, Mexico having been reduced to about half its former size. The nation had fulfilled much of Polk's "Manifest Destiny" objective, having added more than one million square miles.

Polk's first **cabinet** included **Vice President** George Dallas, **Secretary of State** James Buchanan, **Secretary of the Treasury** Robert Walker, **Secretary of War** Robert Marcy, **Attorney General** John Mason, **Secretary of the Navy** George Bancroft, and **Postmaster General** Cave Johnson. The latter was the first to authorize the use of American postage instead of British.

Polk allegedly **did not stop working** until everything on his desk had been completed. It helped that in 1848, Polk introduced **gas**

JAMES K. POLK (11TH PRESIDENT)

lighting to the Executive Mansion. Not surprisingly, he worked ten or twelve hours at least six days a week. He claimed that "No President who performs his duties faithfully and conscientiously can have any leisure." He finally took a month off in his fourth year.

Polk was among the first presidents to have **delivered on all of his campaign promises**: acquire California, settle the Oregon dispute, and serve only four years. He did it **without delegating any work** to others because of his **lack of trust**! That same distrust applied to banks. He carried his money in a suitcase.

Congress made no pay changes during Polk's term of presidency.

Polk looked forward to leaving; he stated, "I heartily rejoice that my term is so near its close. I will soon cease to be a servant and will become a sovereign." Before he died, Polk left word that after he and his wife died, their slaves should be freed. **Polk died on June 15, 1849**, at age 53 of cholera complications, months after leaving the presidency. Polk reportedly said on his deathbed, "I love you Sarah for all eternity." He was buried on State Capital Grounds in Nashville, Tennessee. Upon her husband's death, Sarah wore only mourning clothes until the time of her own death. She died on **August 14, 1891**, at age 87. She was buried with her husband. Most historians give Polk a **somewhat above average rating**.

KEY EVENTS

The **U.S. Naval Academy** was established in Annapolis, Maryland (1845); a unit of 30 **Texas Rangers** crossed into Mexico and arrested 300 cattle rustlers (1845); due to the **Irish Potato Famine**, millions immigrated to Boston and New York (1845);

former slave **Frederick Douglass** published *Narrative of the Life of Frederick Douglass* (1845); the **first baseball game** was played in Hoboken, New Jersey (1846); the **Smithsonian Institution** opened (1846); **George Donner** led a wagon train of some 90 people west only to be trapped in a **vicious winter**, with the seven survivors resorting to cannibalism (1846); a **group of Mormons** followed the Donner Trail and founded Salt Lake City (1847); the 5¢ (Ben Franklin) and 10¢ (George Washington) **adhesive postage stamps** were approved by Congress (1847); at a convention in Seneca, New York, **women demanded** the right to vote (1848); **Cyrus McCormick** attempted to renew his patent for the Reaper but was unsuccessful (1848); the **Chicago-New York telegraph line** was completed (1848); the **Chicago Board of Trade** was established (1848); **four more states** entered the Union, raising the total to 30: **Florida** (1845), **Texas** (1845), **Iowa** (1846), and **Wisconsin** (1848); **Texas statehood** resulted in a war (1846-1848) with Mexico that ended with the Southwest ceded to the United States (1848); Polk laid the cornerstone for the **Washington Monument** (1848), although it would not be completed until 1888; the giant pharmaceutical company to-be **Pfizer** began as a small chemical firm in Brooklyn (1849); **gold was discovered** in California (1848); and those seeking gold were called **49ers** because of the year in which they arrived (1849).

Zachary Taylor
(12th President)

March 4, 1849 - July 9, 1850

Zachary Taylor was born on November 24, 1784, in Orange County, Virginia, to Richard and Sarah Taylor. Zachary's father was a farmer and justice of the peace. He also served as an officer in the Revolutionary War. Zachary had four brothers, George, Hancock, Joseph, and William, and three sisters, Elizabeth, Emily, and Sarah. Zachary received an education from **private tutors** and then joined the **Kentucky Militia** in 1808, rising through the ranks. As a captain, Taylor helped defend **Fort Harrison** from an Indian attack commanded by Tecumseh during the **War of 1812**. As a major, he fought in the **Black Hawk War** of 1832 and the **Seminole War** of 1837. As a general, Taylor drove the Mexican army from Texas in 1846, and **defeated Santa Anna's army** in the **Mexican War** in 1847. It was this victory that brought him to national attention. Taylor had made his career in the army. His nickname was "**Old Rough and Ready**" because he wore old, ragged clothes and was always ready to fight. Having fought in many wars and defeated Mexican General Santa Anna, Taylor was well liked by his men. And Taylor knew it was easier to form an army than to pay for it.

He married **Margaret Mackall Smith** on June 21, 1810, and they had **six children** together: Ann, Sarah, Octavia, Margaret, Mary, and Richard. Sarah would later marry Jefferson Davis, who had served under Zachary Taylor when Zachary was a general. Mrs. Taylor traveled with her husband during the many years he spent in the military.

At the **Whig** Convention, Zachary Taylor was nominated for president and Millard Fillmore was nominated for vice president. In the **election of 1848**, Whigs "Old Zack" Taylor and **Millard Fillmore** defeated Democrats **Lewis Cass** and **William Butler** 1,360,099 to 1,220,644 in the popular vote and 163 to 127 in the electoral vote. Free Soil candidates **Martin Van Buren** and **Charles Adams** received 291,263 popular votes but no electoral votes. Zachary Taylor was elected president and Millard Fillmore was elected vice president. **Taylor and Fillmore first met only days before the election.** Taylor was victorious because the North formed the anti-slavery **Free Soil Party**, which took enough votes away from **Lewis Cass**, the Democratic nominee, to tilt the scale. James Polk stated Taylor was "giddy with the idea of Presidency." **Taylor was the first president whose party lacked a majority in either house throughout his term of office.**

Millard Fillmore was born on January 7, 1800, the second of nine children, in Summerhill, New York. He was raised in extreme **poverty** on a farm. His only education was learning how to read and write during breaks at the **textile mill** where he was working. At age 14, he enrolled in the **New Hope Academy**. His favorite teacher was Abigail Powers. He was admitted to the **New York Bar** in 1824. He was an **impeccable dresser**. Millard married his teacher, **Abigail Powers**, (age 28) in 1826. She continued teaching for several years. They moved to Buffalo in 1830 when he got interested in state politics and became a member of the **Whig Party**. Beginning in 1833, he served four terms in the **U.S. House of Representatives**. He lost the bid to become a **vice-presidential candidate** in 1844 and for **New York governor** that same year.

Taylor was 64 years old on the day of his inauguration, which was on Monday, March 5th, because the March 4th inauguration date fell on a Sunday and Taylor refused to do it on Sunday because of his religion. In his March 5, **1849, inaugural address**, Taylor stated, "We are warned by the admonitions of history and the voice of our own beloved Washington to abstain from entangling alliances with foreign nations." He was the first president to have been elected **without** having been **previously elected** to any office. He himself had **never voted** before being elected president. But he was proud of his country, stating, "For more than half a century during which kingdoms and empires have fallen, this Union has stood unshaken."

Margaret **was not at ease with being the first lady** and enjoyed her six children more than the demands of her social life. **Unwilling to preside over social events, Margaret turned them over to her 23-year-old daughter**, Elizabeth. Margaret disliked the **smell of tobacco** and refused to have **her picture taken**.

Taylor's **cabinet** included **Vice President** Millard Fillmore, **Secretary of State** John Clayton, **Secretary of the Treasury** William Meredith, **Secretary of War** George Crawford, **Attorney**

General Reverdy Johnson, **Secretary of the Navy** William Preston, **Postmaster General** Jacob Collamer, and **Secretary of the Interior** Thomas Ewing. The newly added Interior position was responsible for the government pension system, Indian affairs, the patent office, and public land. The incumbent, Thomas Ewing, had served as treasury secretary under both the Harrison and Tyler administrations. Like the other cabinet secretaries, Ewing was paid $6,000 a year.

Congress made no other pay changes during Taylor's term of office.

In **United States vs Staats** (1849), the U.S. Supreme Court ruled that an indictment under an 1823 punishment for fraud's statute only requires the act be done "with intent to defraud the United States" and does not require "felonious intent." In **Sheldon vs Sill** (1850), the U.S. Supreme Court ruled that an act of Congress can limit a circuit court's jurisdiction and preclude them from hearing cases, such as those involving assignees of a "chose in action."

In his address to Congress in 1850, Taylor stated he would not permit slavery to spread into new territories, whereas Lewis Cass believed the residents of the territory should decide the issue. When Southern leaders protested Taylor's position, he vowed he would lead the Army against those dissenters and hang anyone who rebelled against the Union. Taylor also believed in **Manifest Destiny**, namely that God wanted the United States to expand its borders. Taylor opposed the **Compromise of 1850** and said he would veto it if Congress passed it, but Taylor died before its passage and his successor, Millard Fillmore, signed the Act.

Taylor died on July 9, 1850, at age 65 from **cholera or typhoid fever**, after a July 4th celebration only 16 months into his Presidency. His last words were, "I am about to die. I expect the summons very soon. I have tried to discharge all my duties faithfully. I regret nothing, but I am sorry that I am about to leave my friends." **Abraham Lincoln** delivered the eulogy. Taylor was buried in the **family burial grounds** in Louisville, Kentucky. When her husband died, Margaret was devastated. She died on August 14, 1852, at the age of 63 and was buried with her husband. With some believing Taylor had been poisoned, his body was exhumed and tissue samples were taken in 1991. The results were inconsistent with poisoning.

Most historians give Taylor a **below average rating**.

KEY EVENTS

The famed **Gold Rush of 1849** resulted in the first $1 and $20 gold pieces (1849); **stagecoaches to California** followed the 1848 discovery of gold (1849); blue jeans were introduced by Levi Strauss (1850); the **U.S. population** was at 23 million (which included the addition of 2.5 million immigrants in 20 years) (1850); and *The Scarlet Letter* was published by Nathaniel Hawthorne (1850).

Millard Fillmore
(13ᵀᴴ President)

July 9, 1850 - March 4, 1853

Millard Fillmore was born into poverty on January 7, 1800, in Locke, New York, to Nathaniel and Phoebe Fillmore. They had three daughters, Julia, Olive, and Phoebe, and six sons, Almon, Calvin, Charles, Cyrus, Darius, and Millard. At first, Millard was **home-taught**, then at age 14 he began work as a **clothing apprentice**. At age 17, he attended **New Hope Academy**. In 1818, Fillmore began studying law. In 1823, he passed the **New York bar exam** and began practicing law near Buffalo, New York. At age 26, he **married** his high school teacher, **Abigail Powers**, age 27, on February 5, 1826. They spent their early years of marriage in a log cabin. They had two children, Millard Jr. and Mary. Fillmore was elected to the **New York State**

Assembly in 1828. In 1833, he was elected to the **U.S. House of Representatives** as a member of the Whig Party. After serving three terms, he ran for governor of New York in 1844 but was defeated. In 1849, Fillmore served as **vice president** under Zachary Taylor. A year later, he turned down an honorary degree from Oxford, stating he was not worthy of it. Fillmore did not smoke, drink alcohol, or have any apparent vices.

Millard Fillmore was 50 years old on July 9, 1850, the day of his inauguration as president after Zachary Taylor's death at age 65. Fillmore was the **fifth** vice president to become president (John Adams, Thomas Jefferson, Martin Van Buren, and John Tyler preceded him). Millard Fillmore was the **second** vice president to assume the presidency upon the death of his president (John Tyler was the first). In his March 4, **1851, inaugural** address, Fillmore stated, "Although we may sympathize with the unfortunate in their struggles for freedom, our principles forbid us from taking part in foreign contests."

Upon becoming president, Fillmore decided to replace the president's carriage. The best he could find was a used one. He asked the salesman if it was appropriate for the president to have a second-hand carriage. The salesman replied, "Why not? You are a **second-hand president**."

When Fillmore became president, he asked for and got the resignation of Taylor's **cabinet** and then appointed his own: **Secretary of State** Daniel Webster, **Secretary of the Treasury** William Meredith, **Secretary of War** John Crawford, **Attorney General** Reverdy Johnson, **Secretary of the Navy** William Preston, **Postmaster General** Jacob Collamer, and **Secretary of the Interior** Thomas Ewing.

Abigail Fillmore, a former teacher who **loved books**, established the **first White House library** in an oval shaped room that later became the **Oval Office**. Abigail planned and presided over an almost endless list of receptions, dinners, and parties. Her wit and expensive dresses made her a welcome companion to her husband. However, their **ban on smoking and drinking alcohol** curtailed social events.

A series of laws were passed during Fillmore's term of office as part of the **Compromise of 1850**. Most notably, it admitted California to enter the Union as a free state, and, most controversially, it increased regulations with the **Fugitive Slave Act of 1850**, requiring local marshals to pursue, apprehend, and return escaped slaves to their owners. Failure to do so incurred a $1,000 fine. Rewards for the returns ranged from $10 to $100. This was the last act signed by a Whig president.

Fillmore was interested in preserving the Union. He said, "May God save the country, for it is evident that the people will not." On September 7th, Congress passed the **Compromise of 1850**. It admitted **California** as a free state, amended the **Fugitive Slave Act**, compensated **Texas** for its loss of territory to New Mexico, decreed **New Mexico** and **Utah** would decide slave or free-state status for themselves, and abolished the slave trade in the nation's capital. In response to the Compromise, the **Underground Railroad** was created to help slaves escape to freedom (it is estimated as many as 40,000 escaped). Some believe there were some three million slaves and 400,000 freed slaves at the time.

The Fugitive Slave Act and the publication of Harriet Beecher Stowe's book *Uncle Tom's Cabin* in 1852 increased the tension between proslavery advocates and abolitionists.

As for his accomplishments, other than the **Compromise of 1850**, which delayed the Civil War a decade, Fillmore can take credit for expanding rail service throughout the country.

In **United States vs Guillem** (1851), the U.S. Supreme Court ruled that a neutral citizen leaving a country engaged in war has the rights of a neutral for himself and his property the moment he leaves port, and confiscation of his property on board an enemy's vessel is prohibited, unless he is aware of the vessel's "guilt."

In **United States vs Reid** (1852), the U.S. Supreme Court ruled that state law determines the admissibility of testimony in criminal cases. In **Cooley vs Board of Wardens** (1852), the U.S. Supreme Court ruled that states can regulate interstate commerce as long as those regulations don't conflict with federal law.

Fillmore decided to run in the **1852 presidential election,** but the **Fugitive Slave Act of 1850** made him unpopular within the Whig Party, and he was opposed by **General Winfield Scott**. It took 53 ballots before Scott was elected the Whig candidate. But Scott lost to Democrat **Franklin Pierce** in the general election.

In 1853, Fillmore acquired the **first stove** for the Executive Mansion, ending the practice of preparing food over an open fire.

Congress made no pay changes during Fillmore's term of presidency.

Following his loss on the Whig presidential ticket, Fillmore retired to Buffalo where he was appointed **chancellor** to the **University of Buffalo**, which he founded. In the 1850s, the slavery issue tore apart the Whig Party. The southerners joined the Democratic Party; the northerners joined the Republican Party. After his wife died in 1853 and his daughter in 1854, Fillmore spent time in Europe. He returned to the United States in 1856 and accepted the presidential nomination of the **American Party**, better known as the **Know Nothing Party**. He received 874,534 popular votes and only 8 electoral votes in the 1856 general election. Fillmore once said, "An honorable defeat is better than a dishonorable victory." In 1858, Fillmore **married** the wealthy widow, **Catherine McIntosh**. Millard Fillmore had no children with his second wife.

Fillmore died on March 8, 1874, at age 74 from a stroke. As he was dying, Fillmore allegedly said, "I am going without regrets." His papers were burned by his son after his death, leaving little known about Fillmore's character and thoughts other than that he believed slavery was protected by the U.S. Constitution. He was buried in Buffalo's Forest Lawn Cemetery. Abigail was buried with her husband. Most historians give Fillmore a **significantly below average rating**.

Key Events

Herman Melville published *Moby Dick* (1851); Allan **Pinkerton** set up the Pinkerton Detective Agency (1851); the **Y.M.C.A. of the USA** began (1851); the *New York Times* **newspaper** began (1851); **Wells Fargo and Company** used stagecoaches to provide banking and mail services (1852); **Lynn, Massachusetts** became the shoemaking capital of the country (1852); England delivered the **Liberty Bell to Philadelphia** (1852); a compulsory school attendance law was adopted in Massachusetts (1852); **Robert Morris** was America's first **Black judge** having been appointed to the magistrate's court in Boston (1852); Harriet Beecher Stowe published *Uncle Tom's Cabin* with **Simon Legree**, further splitting the North and South on slavery (1852); escaped slave **Frederick Douglass** wrote the fictional novella

The Heroic Slave (1852); the Apaches led by **Geronimo** roamed the lower Southwest (1852); New York City's Crystal Palace was the site of the first **World's Fair** (1853); and Stephen Foster published *My Old Kentucky Home* (1853).

Franklin Pierce
(14th President)

March 4, 1853 – March 4, 1857

Franklin Pierce was born on November 23, 1804, in Hillsborough, New Hampshire, to Benjamin Sr. and Anna Pierce. Pierce had four brothers: Benjamin Jr., Charles, John, and Henry, and three sisters, Charlotte, Harriet, and Nancy. His father was a farmer, saw action at the **Battle of Bunker Hill**, and served as **New Hampshire governor** for two terms. After attending a schoolhouse, Franklin attended Hancock Academy and the Francistown Academy. He then went to **Bowdoin College**, graduating in 1824. Pierce studied law, was admitted to the New Hampshire bar in 1827, and then set up a private practice in Hillsborough. Pierce was elected to the **New Hampshire House of Representatives** in 1829 and went on to become Speaker of the House. In 1832, at the age of 28, Pierce was elected to the **U.S. House of Representatives**. On November 19, 1834, at age 30, Franklin married **Jane Appleton**, age 28, a woman Pierce had courted for years. They had **three children**, Benjamin, Franklin Jr., and Frank. In 1836, Franklin was elected to the **U.S. Senate**, and in 1842, he returned to New Hampshire to resume his law practice. In 1847, Pierce declined President Polk's offer to become his attorney general and instead enlisted in the **U.S. Army**, where he would be commissioned a **brigadier general** while fighting in the **Mexican-American War**.

Franklin Pierce was elected as a "dark horse" choice on the 50th ballot at the Democratic Convention. Pierce's campaign slogan was, "We Polked you in '44, and we shall Pierce you in '52." In the **1852 election**, Democrats **Franklin Pierce and William King** received 1,601,474 popular votes to 1,386,942 for Whigs **Winfield Scott** and **William Graham** and 254 electoral votes versus 42 for **Scott-Graham**. Pierce was elected president and King was elected vice president.

Franklin's son Benjamin was killed in a train accident two months before Pierce's inauguration, both parents were heartbroken. Pierce was 48 years old on **March 4, 1853**, the date of his inauguration. Pierce swore his oath on a law book. He **memorized** his 3,319-word **inaugural address**, in which he stated, "I believe that involuntary servitude as it exists in different states of this Confederacy, is recognized by the Constitution."

William King was born on April 7, 1786, to a wealthy family in Sampson, North Carolina. He graduated from the **University of North Carolina** in 1803 and was admitted to the **North Carolina bar** in 1806. He was elected to the House of Representatives in 1810 and later became one of **Alabama's first** two senators on

December 14, 1819, the date of its statehood. After more than 24 years in the U.S. Senate, in 1844 he accepted the position of **U.S. Minister to France**. In 1850, he filled a vacant U.S. Senate seat and resigned in 1852 to accept the position of vice president under President Pierce. King served as president pro tempore of the Senate, but he **died of tuberculosis** 25 days after being elected and was the **first unmarried vice president**.

Jane Pierce was still in mourning when Franklin was elected president, as all three of her sons had died. A strict **Calvinist**, Jane consulted with a medium and declined to appear at receptions or receive guests. The mourning bunting lasted for two years in the Executive Mansion. Jane's official duties were taken over by others as she spent her time on the second floor of the Executive Mansion. She hated politics and often reacted to confrontation by fainting.

Pierce's first **cabinet** included **Vice President** William King, **Secretary of State** William Marcy, **Secretary of the Treasury** James Guthrie, **Secretary of War** Jefferson Davis, **Attorney General** Caleb Cushing, **Secretary of the Navy** James Dobbin, **Postmaster General** James Campbell, and **Secretary of the Interior** Robert McClelland. Pierce had convinced **Jefferson Davis** to become his **Secretary of War** and make the army more efficient. Jefferson did, and four years later, he fought that army during the Civil War.

Pierce referred to the **U.S. Constitution** as "the unshaken rock." He was the first president to put up a **Christmas tree** in the Executive Mansion and starting in 1853, also the first to have a full-time **bodyguard**. His nickname was "**Handsome Frank**." After Commodore Perry landed in Japan in 1853, a trade treaty was shortly enacted, opening Japan to U.S. ships. Pierce also signed a treaty with Canada and approved the **1854 Gadsden Purchase** with Mexico. The **1854 Kansas-Nebraska Act** repealed the Missouri Compromise on slavery and allowed Kansas and Nebraska the right to choose to be either free or slave states. Pro-slavery and anti-slavery advocates fought over the issue, bringing the country closer to a civil war. And the **1857 Tariff Act** increased duties on all imports.

In **United States vs Fremont** (1856), the U.S. Supreme Court ruled that if the appellant doesn't file the record and docket the case in the time prescribed by the Court, and the appellee files a copy, the appeal will be dismissed upon the appellee's motion.

In **United States vs Booth** (1856), the U.S. Supreme Court ruled that if a state supreme court clerk "neglects or refuses" to return a writ of error issued under the 25th section of the Judiciary Act, the Court can order him to do so or show cause why it has not been done.

In **United States vs Le Baron** (1856), the U.S. Supreme Court ruled that a deed "speaks" on the day of delivery, not the day it is dated.

The pay actions approved by Congress during Pierce's term of office were: in 1853, all cabinet secretaries salaries were increased to an annual pay of $6,000 (up from 1819's $4,500); in 1855, legislators were paid $3,000 per annum (up from 1819's $8 per day), associate justices of the U.S. Supreme Court were paid $6,000 per annum (up from 1819's $4,500), and the Chief Justice was paid $6,500 per annum (up from 1819's $5,000). **These were the only pay changes made by Congress during Pierce's term of presidency.**

When his party refused to nominate him for a second term, Pierce declared, "There's nothing left but to get drunk," and he retired from public life. **Pierce died** on October 8, 1869, at the age of 65 from heart failure and stomach inflammation caused by years of alcohol abuse. His wife, Jane, preceded him, dying on December 2, 1863, at age 57 of tuberculosis. Both were buried in Old North Cemetery, in Concord, New Hampshire. The day before he died, Pierce stated, "History will vindicate my memory." Unlikely, since he, Harrison, and Buchanan are considered by many to be the least effective presidents. Because of a lack of significant accomplishments, he is essentially a forgotten president.

Most historians give Pierce a **significantly below average rating**.

KEY EVENTS

An attempt by Mormon Brigham Young to defy federal laws in Utah Territory was suppressed (1853); the **Republican Party** was founded in Ripon, Wisconsin, by northern Whigs who left the Democratic Party (1854); the business world was advanced with the invention of the **safety elevator** by Elisha Otis (1854); **Henry David Thoreau** described the serenity of living in nature apart from society in *Walden* (1854); **Walt Whitman** celebrated democracy and individualism in his publication of *Leaves of Grass* (1855); the **adding machine** was invented by John Burroughs (1855); the **Mississippi River** was crossed by the first railroad train (1855); the **Bessemer** process for converting iron to steel in open blast furnaces was developed (1855); the **first kindergarten** opened in Watertown, Wisconsin (1856); **abolitionist John Brown** led anti-slavery protests in Lawrence, Kansas (1856); **Isaac Singer** patented the affordable sewing machine (1856); New York to St. Louis **rail service** began (1856); for those on the move **boarding houses** charged $5 to $10 a week, hotels half that because they didn't serve meals (1856); and lithographers **Currier and Ives** issued their first print (1857).

James Buchanan
(15th President)

March 4, 1857 – March 4, 1861

James Buchanan was born on April 23, 1791, to James Sr. and Elizabeth Buchanan in Cove Gap, Pennsylvania. James was the **last president** born in the 1700s. James had **four brothers**, Edward, George, John, and William, and **six sisters**, Elizabeth, Elizabeth Jane, Maria, Mary, Sarah, and Harriet. Buchanan went to school at Old Stone Academy and then to **Dickinson College**, where he studied law and graduated in two years in 1809. Buchanan was admitted to the Pennsylvania bar in 1813 and went on to practice law in Lancaster, Pennsylvania. During the **War of 1812**, Buchanan fought with the Pennsylvania militia and is the first president who **never served as an officer**. In 1814, Buchanan began a two-year term in the Pennsylvania state legislature and then returned to his law practice. In 1819, Buchanan was briefly engaged to Anne Coleman, but the engagement broke off, and he was the first president who never got married. **Originally a Federalist, Buchanan became a Democrat** in 1821 and was elected to the **U.S. House of Representatives**. In 1831, he served three years as **U.S. Minister to Russia**. In 1834, Buchanan was elected to the **U.S. Senate**, serving until 1845. After losing the presidential nomination to James Polk in 1845, he served as **Secretary of State** to President Polk. In 1853, he began a three-year term as **U.S. Minister to England**.

Buchanan failed in his attempts to be nominated for president in 1844, 1848, and 1852. But he was nominated in 1856, and in the **1856 presidential election**, Democrats **James Buchanan** and **John Breckinridge** defeated Republicans **John C. Frémont** and **William Dayton**. Reportedly, Abraham Lincoln gave over 50 speeches in support of Frémont before the election, but it did little good. Buchanan and Breckinridge received 1,838,167 popular votes vs 1,341,264 for **Frémont** and **Dayton**. Buchanan and Breckinridge received 174 electoral votes vs 114 for Frémont and Dayton. The result: **James Buchanan** was elected president and **John Breckinridge** was elected vice president. Millard Fillmore and Andrew Donaldson of the American Party received 874,534 popular votes and 8 electoral votes.

John Cabell Breckinridge was born on January 16, 1821, on his family's estate near Lexington, Kentucky. He was the fourth of six children, and the only son, born to Mary Clay Smith Breckinridge and Joseph Cabell Breckinridge, a lawyer and politician. His father died in 1823, and John and his sisters were raised by their mother and grandmother. He graduated from **Centre College** in Danville, Kentucky, in 1838 and studied law at what is now **Princeton University**. He was admitted to the bar in 1841.

After practicing law in Iowa for a couple of years, he returned to Kentucky, where he met Mary Cyrene Burch. They were married in December of 1843, settled in Georgetown, Kentucky, and had six children. In 1847, he was appointed a major of the **Third Kentucky Infantry Regiment** to fight in the Mexican-American War. In 1849, he formed a new law partnership and co-founded a newspaper, the **Kentucky Statesman**. He served two terms as a **congressman** from 1851 to 1855. At the end of his term, he returned to practice law in Lexington. In 1856, he won the Democratic nomination for vice presidential candidate to James Buchanan, and on March 4, 1857, at the age of 36, he became the **youngest vice president** in U.S. history. He died in Lexington on May 17, 1875, at the age of 54.

Buchanan was 65 years old on the day of his inauguration. In his March 4, **1857, inaugural address**, James Buchanan stated that the **slavery** issue should be **settled in the courts** or by the states. Two days after this speech, in **Dred Scott vs Sandford** (1857), the U.S. Supreme Court ruled that **slavery was permitted in all U.S. territories**. The court also ruled that slaves were not citizens and had no right to sue in court. In 1857, Congress gave Buchanan $25,000 to buy portraits of five past presidents, and Buchanan signed the **1857 Tariff Act**, which increased duties on all imports.

Buchanan's first **cabinet** included **Vice President** John Breckinridge, **Secretary of State** Lewis Cass, **Secretary of the Treasury** Howell Cobb, **Secretary of War** John Floyd, **Attorney General** Jeremiah Black, **Secretary of the Navy** Isaac Toucey, **Postmaster General** Aaron Brown, and **Secretary of the Interior** Jacob Thompson.

Buchanan had to deal with three major issues: (1) the **financial panic of 1857** and the resulting **depression** (2) the fallout of the **Dred Scott** case; and (3) fighting over slavery after the

1854 Kansas-Nebraska Act repealed the **1820 Missouri Compromise Act**. In 1859, **abolitionist John Brown** and twenty-one men raided the U.S. armory in **Harper's Ferry Virginia**; six were hanged for treason. Harper's Ferry became a rallying cry for **slavery abolishment**.

As Buchanan was the first, and only lifelong, **bachelor president**, **Harriet Lane**, his niece served as **hostess** of the **Executive Mansion**. She was quite good at it and was well-liked. Buchanan once complained, "I have gone a wooing to several gentlemen but have not succeeded with any one of them." He did live with **Rufus King**, another bachelor, for some twenty years, causing Andrew Jackson to call them "Aunt Nancy and Miss Fancy." Reportedly, Buchanan was **bisexual**. But Buchanan also had an eagle and elephant as pets for companionship.

In **Land Warrant Titles** (1858), the U.S. Supreme Court ruled that titles to land warrants vest to the widow, or if there is no widow, to his legacies or claimants.

In **Abelman vs Booth** (1859), the U.S. Supreme Court ruled that federal courts have supremacy over cases involving federal law and state courts lack authority to issue rulings that conflict with decisions made by federal courts. The **Pacific Telegraph Act of 1860** authorized the Secretary of the Treasury to seek bids and the U.S. Government to fund, up to a specific amount, the construction and maintenance of a transcontinental telegraph line.

Buchanan was a **serious drinker**, able to consume two or three bottles of liquor in a sitting, reportedly without a hangover. But he did suffer from **gout** due to his drinking. Buchanan stated, "All agree that under the Constitution, slavery in the United States is beyond the reach of any human power except that of the States themselves wherein it exists." But he **denied the right of states to secede from the Union**, adding, "What is right and what is practical are two different things."

With his **December 1860 address to Congress**, Buchanan tried to save the Union as southern states threatened to secede noting that, "Interference of the Northern people with the question of slavery in the Southern States has at length produced its natural effects." **Buchanan** was a **strong supporter of slavery** but argued that states should be able to "enter the Union **with or without slavery**, as their constitutions should prescribe," and that neither Congress nor the president has the power to prevent a state from leaving the Union. Within two weeks of his speech, **South Carolina seceded from the Union**. Buchanan's inability to address the slavery issue and his lack of good judgment and courage to do the right thing fueled the **fires of civil war over slavery**. His admission of **Kansas** as a slave state in 1861 (the 34th state overall) was a major example. By the time Buchanan's term had expired, seven states had seceded and formed the **Confederate States of America**. In defiance, Buchanan refused to turn over Union forts in the seceded states. Oddly enough, Buchanan bought slaves with his own money and set them free. He added, "The ballot box is the surest arbiter of disputes among freemen. There is nothing stable but Heaven and the Constitution."

Congress made no pay changes during Buchanan's term of presidency.

After serving four years as Buchanan's **vice president**, John Breckinridge ran for president in **1860** with Joseph Lane as his running mate as the Democratic Southerners Party. They received 847,953 popular votes and 72 electoral votes. Stephen Douglas and Herschel Johnson of the Democratic Northerners

Party received 1,375,157 popular votes and 12 electoral votes, and John Bell and Edward Everett of the Constitutional Union Party received 590,631 popular votes and 39 electoral votes. But the **winners were Republicans Abraham Lincoln and Hannibal Hamlin**, with 1,866,452 popular votes and 180 electoral votes. Since 180 votes were more than half of the total 303 electoral votes cast, Lincoln was declared president and Hamlin was declared vice president. Lincoln was married to Breckinridge's cousin, Mary Todd. Following the **1860 election** of Abraham Lincoln and believing the Southern states would break up the Union, President Buchanan announced, "I am the last elected President of the United States." Late in his term, Buchanan stated, "Whatever the result may be, I shall carry to my grave that at least I meant well for my country."

After losing the presidential vote, Breckinridge was appointed to the **U.S. Senate** by the Kentucky legislature. But he was **expelled in 1861** when he **joined the Confederate Army**, serving as a brigadier general. Having risen to the rank of Major General, he fought against the Union Army in **Shiloh, Chickamauga**, and **Lynchburg**. In 1865, **Jefferson Davis** appointed Breckinridge **Secretary of War** of the Confederacy. When the war ended in 1865, Breckinridge fled to England to avoid being arrested for treason. He returned in 1869 when **pardoned by President Andrew Jackson** and resumed his law practice in Lexington, Kentucky. Breckinridge died on May 17, 1875, in Lexington from pneumonia.

Due to his indecisiveness, lack of action, and poor decisions, **many historians blame Buchanan** for the onset of the **Civil War**. Essentially politically powerless, Buchanan watched the country disintegrate as his term of office ended on March 4, 1861. Upon leaving the presidency, he told Lincoln, "If you are as happy in coming to the presidency as I am in leaving it, then you are a happy man."

Buchanan died on June 1, 1868, at age 77 of **pneumonia** in Lancaster, Pennsylvania. On his deathbed he reiterated the statement made by President Pierce, "History will vindicate my memory." Not true: most historians consider him among the **worst of all presidents**. He was buried in Woodward Cemetery, Lancaster, Pennsylvania.

Key Events

Daniel Adams codified the **rules of baseball**, years before Alexander Cartwright was given credit for creating the game (1857); a great riot occurred in Five Points, New York City (1857); the **National Association of Baseball Players** was formed (1858); gold was discovered in **Pike's Peak, Colorado**, causing New York Tribune editor **Horace Greeley** to cry, "Go West, young man" (1858); the **Lincoln-Douglas** debates took place (1858); **George Pullman** converted sleeping cars into sleeping at night and seated during the day (1858); the first **Atlantic cable** was completed (1858); the **first commercial oil well** began operation in Titusville, Pennsylvania (1858); the **eraser-topped** lead pencil was patented (1858); the **Comstock Silver Mines** were established in western Utah (1859); the **combine harvester** was introduced (1859); **Brink's** armored car service began operation (1860); the **Pony Express** began business, with riders covering 250 miles a day (1860); **Andrew Carnegie** built large steel mills (1860); **Jay Gould** made a fortune by "watering stock" (issuing huge numbers of new shares) (1860); **Tammany Hall** flourished in New York with Irish immigrants (1860s); the **U.S. population** reached 31 million (1860); and the states that entered the Union during Buchanan's presidency were **Minnesota** (32nd – 1858), **Oregon** (33rd – 1859), and **Kansas** (34th – 1861).

Abraham Lincoln
(16ᵀᴴ President)

March 4, 1861 – April 15, 1865

Abraham Lincoln was born on February 12, 1809, to Thomas and Nancy Lincoln in a **one-room cabin** built by his Baptist father in Hodgenville, Kentucky. The Lincolns had **three children**, Sarah, born two years before Abraham, and Thomas, who died in infancy.

In 1816, the family moved to Spencer County, Indiana where Thomas built a slightly larger log cabin. There, their mother helped both children learn to read and write. They were **essentially self-taught**, as neither attended school. While Abraham had a good relationship with his mother, his father considered him lazy, in spite of the fact that Abraham **worked ten hours a**

day for his father or a neighbor, clearing fields or helping with carpentry. Abe also learned how to turn corn into whiskey.

Nancy Lincoln died during childbirth at age 34, as did the child, when Abraham was nine years old. Later, his sister, Sarah, also died during childbirth. Thomas Lincoln married Sarah Bush Johnston several years after Nancy's death. They had three children, John, Matilda, and Elizabeth.

In 1830, the family moved back to Macon County, Illinois. Although he had **no formal education, Abraham liked to read** and went on to become a **lawyer** after being admitted to the bar in Springfield, Illinois in 1837. Before teaching himself law, he had been a **blacksmith, rail splitter, store clerk, bartender, ferryboat captain, surveyor,** and **postmaster**. After his first love, Anne Rutledge, died of typhoid in 1835, Lincoln was despondent for several years. At age 33, he married **Mary Todd**, age 23, in 1842. They went on to have **four children**: Robert Todd, Edward Baker, William Wallace, and Thomas Todd. Amid their **stormy relationship**, Lincoln said, "I fell in love with her and what is more, I have never fallen out."

From 1834 to 1836, Lincoln served in the **Illinois state legislature**, after which he practiced law in Springfield, Illinois. In 1846, Lincoln was elected to the **U.S. House of Representatives**, where he served until 1849 and then returned to his law practice. In 1854, Lincoln stated, "No man is good to govern another without that man's consent." Lincoln was a member of the **Whig Party**, but when the **Kansas-Nebraska Act of 1854** permitted slavery in the territories, the Whig Party fell apart and many members, including Lincoln, switched to the **Republican Party**, which was founded that year in Ripon, Wisconsin.

Typically, **Lincoln got up at 5:00am every** day and quickly went to work. Several hours later, he had a light breakfast of an egg, a slice of toast, and black coffee. Midday he would have a biscuit and a glass of milk. In the afternoon, he would snack on fresh fruits. And for dinner, his favorites were possum stew, squirrel dip, and corn cakes.

In August 1858, the **Republicans nominated Lincoln** for an Illinois seat in the **U.S. Senate** held by **Democratic Senator Stephen Douglas**. The outcome of the senatorial election was especially important because of the 31 states, 15 were slave states containing around **500,000 slaves,** and the other 16 were **free states**. Illinois was a slave-free state.

Lincoln and **Douglas** engaged in **seven three-hour historic debates** that drew as many as 15,000 people. The two candidates for the U.S. Senate for Illinois were in sharp contrast to each other. **Stephen Douglas** was 5'4" and was known as the **Little Giant**. **Abraham Lincoln** was a **gawky giant of 6'4"**. The **fiery words** of Douglas contrasted with the **quiet words** of Lincoln. Lincoln quoted from the Bible, "A house divided against itself cannot stand," referring to the northern-southern split on the issue of slavery. **Opinions varied** as to **who was the better debater**; Lincoln drew very favorable reviews, but the Democrats held the **state legislature**, which controlled the election outcome. It **chose Douglas, who then won the Senate election**. Asked how he felt about the loss, Lincoln replied, "It hurts too much to laugh, and I am too old to cry." But then he added, "The **ballot box** is the surest arbitrator of disputes among free men." Some questioned Lincoln's veracity, saying he was **two-faced**. His reply: "If I had two faces, why would I wear this one?"

When the Republicans gained seats in the **1858 midterm election**, Congress was deadlocked over the slavery issue. The **Democratic Party** was split into Northern and Southern portions, resulting in neither a platform nor a standard bearer and **leaving the Republican candidate, Abraham Lincoln, a clear path**

to the presidency. Southern states stated that if he won, they would leave the Union.

Lincoln got the Republican nomination for the presidential election on November 6, 1860, in a four-way race. **Abraham Lincoln** and **Hannibal Hamlin** drew 1,866,452 of the 4,680,193 popular votes, and the other 2,873,741 were split among three Democratic nominees, **Stephen Douglas, John Bell,** and **John Breckinridge.** Lincoln-Hamlin were not on the ballot in 10 southern states, but they took 180 of the 303 electoral votes and won the election. The other 123 electoral votes were split among the three Democrats. Lincoln was elected president and Hamlin was elected vice president, much to the unhappiness of Southern slave owners.

Hannibal Hamlin was born on August 27, 1809, in Paris, Massachusetts. He was named after the famed Carthaginian General Hannibal who marched his elephants across the Pyrenees. After attending local schools, he studied law and set up a practice in Hamden, Maine. He was elected to Maine's **House of Representatives** in 1836 and then became Speaker in 1837. He was unsuccessful in his 1840 bid for the **U.S. House of Representatives** but was elected in 1842 and then won a **U.S. Senate** seat in 1848. In 1856, he left the **Democratic Party,** then joined the **Republican Party** in 1857 and was elected **Governor of Maine.** But he resigned later that year and was **re-elected to the U.S. Senate.** He was still in the Senate when he was put on Lincoln's ballot and elected vice president. Hamlin died in Bangor, Maine, on July 4, 1891, at age 81.

The **abolitionist Lincoln** was unacceptable to the southern states, and a number of anti-Lincoln groups were formed. They included the **Knights of the Golden Circle,** the **National Volunteers,** and the **Palmetto Group.** Members of these **white supremacist** organizations carried weapons and used codes and hand signals to recognize each other. When it was learned that Lincoln would travel through Baltimore to get to Washington for his inauguration, the groups began making **plans to kill Lincoln** while he was in Baltimore.

While working for several railroad companies concerned about sabotage in Baltimore, **Allan Pinkerton** learned of an 1860 plot in Baltimore to assassinate Lincoln on his way to Washington, D.C. Pinkerton made himself available to Lincoln, promising to get him safely there. Allan Pinkerton was the founder of the Pinkerton National Detective Agency. Pinkerton made history in 1856 by hiring Kate Warren as the first female detective. Pinkerton's ads included an open eye, leading to an investigator being called a **private eye**.

Pinkerton sent six agents to Baltimore posing as Southerners. They infiltrated the elite of Baltimore gaining more knowledge of the white supremacist, pro-slavery groups, and their secret plans to assassinate Lincoln.

On February 11, 1861, **Lincoln**, along with his family and a small protection detail **left Springfield, Illinois**, bound for Washington, D.C. and Lincoln's inauguration as president. It would take two weeks for Lincoln's train to reach Washington from Illinois due to the many stops. Along the way, they had to change trains frequently and were always met by large unruly crowds wanting to see and hear the president-elect. At one stop, Lincoln met with the little girl, **Grace Bedell**, who wrote to him in 1860 saying **he would look better with a beard. He agreed** and grew a beard. When he saw Grace, Lincoln shook her hand and thanked her for the advice. In Buffalo, New York, Lincoln was greeted by former **President Fillmore**; both were surrounded by a company of armed soldiers for protection.

When Pinkerton learned that **Lincoln had to not only change trains in Baltimore, but also change stations** that were 30 minutes apart, Pinkerton decided to make a **change of plans**. Lincoln would get to Baltimore late at night the day before (not early in the afternoon the next day). Wearing a long black coat, a muffler, and a soft hat (not his famed stovepipe), Lincoln was accompanied by Kate Warren and two other Pinkerton agents. Telegraph lines were cut between Philly and Baltimore to keep the scheduled changes unknown. In Philadelphia, Lincoln's party took a sleeping car arriving in Baltimore at 11:00pm, then changed to a different train leaving at 3:00am for Washington. **Lincoln posed as a disabled brother** to Warren, and his disguise fooled everyone. The group changed trains and successfully got to Washington, D.C. unnoticed.

In Baltimore, on February 22, some 10,000 people were waiting, ready to stop Lincoln's carriage as it took him from the arriving station to the departing station. Once stopped, six men would storm Lincoln's carriage and shoot him. They were disappointed to learn Lincoln was already on his way to Washington.

Amid **fears of assassination** upon his arrival in Washington, on February 23, 1861, Lincoln was hustled into the capital by agent Allan Pinkerton and lodged in the Willard Hotel. Lincoln had given his personal black bag containing **his inaugural address to his son Todd**, who had been told to hold onto it. Instead, he gave it to a hotel attendant. Fortunately, Lincoln found the bag. On March 4, 1861, Abe asked his son to read the speech aloud and made a few changes.

On March 14, 1861, following a lunch of mock turtle soup, corned beef, and cabbage, Mr. and Mrs. Lincoln went to the **Executive Mansion** and were greeted by outgoing **President**

Buchanan and his orphaned niece, who served as presidential hostess. Buchanan commented that he was happy to be leaving the presidency. The Lincolns then took a **carriage to the Capitol** along a route lined with soldiers with fixed bayonets and thousands of people.

Lincoln took off his **stovepipe hat** and handed it to Senator Douglas, who held it during the **oath of office**. Lincoln took the oath on a borrowed bible, as his family bible was still in Springfield. Lincoln was 52 years of age at the time of his inauguration and the first president born outside of the original thirteen colonies. He gave his **inaugural address** while Allan Pinkerton watched, stating, "**The Union will endure forever**, it being impossible to destroy itself except by some action not provided for in the instrument itself. The minority does not have the right to break up the government. Secession is possible only if all states agree to it. I warn European governments to remain neutral during the civil war." He added, "I have no purpose to interfere with the institution of slavery in the States where it exists. We are not enemies but friends." **The slavery issue had split the Democratic Party**, ensuring a Lincoln victory. Lincoln stated, "Whenever a person argues for slavery, ask him if he would like to try it personally." As Lincoln was being inaugurated, **Jefferson Davis** was appointed president of the Confederacy in the confederate capital, Richmond, Virginia.

Mary Todd Lincoln added some polish to her unpolished husband. He, on the other hand, said of her family, "God only needed one 'd' but the Todds of Kentucky needed two." He also said he and his wife were the long and short of it, since he was six-foot-four (he was one of the **tallest presidents**) and she was five-foot-two. When Lincoln wore his **stove-pipe hat**, he was over seven-feet tall. When asked why he wore the hat, he replied, "Because I like to carry things in it." Very intelligent and from a good family, Mary Todd took her **Executive Mansion hostess** responsibilities very seriously. She always addressed her husband as **Mr. Lincoln**. She did not like the name Abraham, and he did not like being called **Abe**. She loved entertaining, having as many as 800 guests for dinner. And she enjoyed **her four sons**, all born before the presidency, but she was in mourning for a year after Willie died in 1862.

During **1861, three key laws** were enacted: the **Conscription Act**, which identified Confederates as traitors, had their properties legally confiscated, and drafted 75,000 men between the ages of 18 and 35 for 90 days of military service; the **National Banking Act**, which created nationally chartered banks and gave them authority to issue paper money backed by government bonds; and the **Revenue Act**, which was the first federal income tax, established to help finance the Civil War with a flat tax of 3 percent on annual income in excess of $800.

Lincoln's first **cabinet** included **Vice President** Hannibal Hamlin, **Secretary of State** William Seward, **Secretary of the Treasury** Salmon Chase, **Secretary of War** Simon Cameron, **Attorney General** Edward Bates, **Secretary of the Navy** Gideon Welles, **Secretary of the Interior** Caleb Smith, and **Postmaster General** Horatio King. Cameron got his position due to his support for Lincoln's candidacy, but Lincoln was unaware of the promise, though he made good on it. When Cameron started to make sweetheart deals with friends, Lincoln removed him from the cabinet and appointed him Minister to Russia, keeping him far away from his D.C. friends.

Lincoln blockaded the southern ports in 1861 to prevent the exporting of goods and the importing of war supplies. On April 12, 1861, a little over a month since Lincoln's inauguration, Jefferson Davis, president of the Confederate States of America,

ABRAHAM LINCOLN (16TH PRESIDENT)

consisting of the seven southern states which left the union; Alabama, Florida, Georgia, Louisiana, Mississippi, South Carolina, and Texas, ordered troops to fire on the Union's **Fort Sumter** in Charleston, South Carolina. The **Civil War** had begun. The period prior to the Civil War is called the **Antebellum**. After 33 hours of bombardment in which 10,000 rebel troops attacked the 68 federal troops, the fort surrendered. Before the Civil War began, Lincoln stated, "Both parties considered war, but one of them would make war rather than let the nation survive, and the other would accept war rather than let it perish."

Lincoln called for **75,000 volunteers** to fight. When insufficient numbers responded, Lincoln signed into law the **first Conscription Act** in 1861, an involuntary drafting of 75,000 men between the ages of 18 and 35 for 90 days of military service. **Andrew Carnegie, James Mellon, J.P. Morgan,** and **John D. Rockefeller**, among others, reportedly escaped military service by paying $300 for a substitute to take their place. In New York City and elsewhere, **mobs rioted in protest. Confederates were identified as traitors**, and the property of such traitors, including slaves, was confiscated.

Lincoln's objective was to preserve the Union. During the Civil War, New York sent 365,000 men to fight; over 50,000 were killed, and half of those under age 30 were Black Americans. Among those who fought was the famed **Irish Brigade**, consisting mainly of Irish immigrants. Lincoln used **Allan Pinkerton**, founder of the **Pinkerton Detective Agency**, for intelligence during the Civil War.

Harriet Beecher Stowe's ***Uncle Tom's Cabin*** (1851) bolstered the anti-slavery movement, and on meeting her, Lincoln said, "So you're the little lady who started the Civil War."

During the 1860s, the Apaches led by **Cochise, Victorio**, and **Geronimo** harassed settlers in the Southwest. **General George Crooks** took charge of troops fighting the Apaches. Armed with repeating rifles and carbines, stripped down to minimum clothing, with good horses, the Apaches could cover 60 to 80 miles in 24 hours.

Mathew Brady accompanied and photographed the Union Army in 1861. There were a number of famous battles from 1861 through 1865 between the **Confederate's Johnny Reb and the Union's Billy Yank**, beginning with the first **Battle of Bull Run** (there were two), fought in Virginia. The South, led by P.G.T. Beauregard, defeated the Union forces led by General Winfield Scott (1861). The second **Battle of Bull Run** (1862) was again fought in Virginia and again won by the South, who were led by General Robert E. Lee. The North was led by General John Pope. In the **Battle of Shiloh**, Tennessee, (place of peace) the North, led by General Grant, defeated General Beauregard (1862). Unhappy with George McClellan's performance as general of the army, Lincoln replaced him with General Ambrose Burnside, who was replaced by General Joseph Hooker, who was replaced by McClellan, who defeated General Robert E. Lee in the **Battle of Antietam** (1862) in Maryland. Each side lost 2,000 men in the one-day battle.

In **United States vs Jackalow** (1862), the U.S. Supreme Court ruled that for a circuit court to have jurisdiction over an offense not committed within its district, the accused must have been apprehended in the district and the offense must not have been committed in another state's jurisdiction or in another district in the United States. In **United States vs Knight's Administrator** (1862), the U.S. Supreme Court ruled that once a case has been decided, the Court will not hear a motion to change the decision based on facts not in the record.

During **1862, three key laws** were enacted: the **Legal Tender Act**, which authorized paper money (called greenbacks) as legal tender; the **Revenue Act**, which introduced a tax of 3 percent on income over $500 but less than $10,000 and a tax of 5 percent on income over $10,000; and the **Railway Act**, which provided funds to build a railway from California to Missouri. Later in 1862, Congress created the **Medal of Honor**.

In 1862, the federal government introduced **fractional currency** (paper money with values of less than one dollar), a practice that continued for over ten years. Also in 1862, the Department of Agriculture was established, which Lincoln called the **People's Department**. It reflected the importance of farming in the country.

The first ironclad ships, the Confederate *Merrimac* and the Union *Monitor*, fought to a draw in 1862. Later in 1862, in the **Battle of Mobile**, Union Admiral **David Farragut** led 18 ships through a minefield, shouting, "Damn the torpedoes, full speed ahead." This was followed by the **Battle of Vicksburg** in Mississippi won by the Northern army and General Ulysses Grant, who succeeded McClellan. He defeated the South's General John Pemberton (1863).

When told he **should fire General Grant for his drinking**, Lincoln replied, "Tell me the brand of whiskey he drinks, and I will send a case to my other generals. Grant is my man, and I am his." Grant added the middle initial "S" to his name. He became Ulysses S. Grant. His nickname was **U.S. Grant**, and then **Uncle Sam Grant**, a moniker that lasted long after his death.

Union Chief Medical Officer Jonathan Letterman introduced the **triage of wounds**, an organized ambulance corps and effective field hospital care, saving the lives of thousands (1863).

On January 1, 1863, President Lincoln issued the **Emancipation Proclamation** freeing all slaves, stating, "That on the last day of January, A.D. 1863, all persons held as slaves within any State or designated part of a State the people whereof shall then be in rebellion against the United States shall be then, thenceforward, and forever free; and the executive government of the United States, including military and naval authority thereof will recognize and maintain the freedom of such persons and will do not act or acts to repress such persons, or any of them, in any efforts they may make for their actual freedom." Based on this action, Lincoln became known as "**the Great Emancipator**." He stated "Gentlemen, I never, in my life, felt more certain that I was doing right than in signing this paper," and "If slavery is not wrong, nothing is wrong." Lincoln believed his greatest accomplishment was the **1863 Emancipation Proclamation**. Unfortunately, the **Proclamation** exceeded presidential authority because the **Constitution** protected slavery and the **Fifth Amendment**, ratified on December 15, 1791, prohibited depriving a citizen of property without due process of law. Southerners ignored the Proclamation.

In **United States vs The Schooner Brilliante** (1863), the U.S. Supreme Court ruled that the president of the United States is authorized to use military force against "insurrection or invasion" by hostile parties, whether or not they are foreigners, even without a formal declaration of war by Congress.

During **1863**, the **Homestead Act** allowed settlers to claim 160 acres of public land, and at the **Battle of Gettysburg**, Pennsylvania, led by Generals Grant and Lee, 150,000 Union soldiers fought 50,000 Confederates. On November 19, 1863, upon dedicating the Gettysburg cemetery, Lincoln delivered the famous **Gettysburg Address**, apparently written on the back of an envelope in his office (not while riding the train to the cemetery as some claimed): "Four score and seven years ago our fathers brought forth on this continent, a new nation, conceived in Liberty, and dedicated to the proposition that all men are created equal. Now we are engaged in a great civil war, testing whether that nation, or any nation so conceived and so dedicated, can long endure. We are met on a great battlefield of that war. We have come to dedicate a portion of that field as a final resting place for those who here gave their lives that that nation might live. It is altogether fitting and proper that we should do this. But, in a larger sense, we cannot dedicate – we cannot consecrate – we can not hallow – this ground. The brave men, living and dead, who struggled here, have consecrated it, far above our poor power to add or detract. The world will little note, nor long remember what we say here, but it can never forget what they did here. It is for us the living, rather, to be dedicated here to the unfinished work which they who fought here have thus far so nobly advanced. It is rather for us to be here dedicated to the great task remaining before us – that from these honored dead we take increased devotion to that cause for which they gave the last full measure of devotion – that we here highly resolve that these dead shall not have died in vain – that this nation, under God, shall have a new birth of freedom – and that government of the people, by the people, for the people, shall not perish from the earth." Also, in **1863**, Confederate Major General "**Stonewall**" Jackson died in the Chancellorsville battle with General "**Fighting Joe**" Hooker.

Lincoln believed his greatest accomplishment was the **1863 Emancipation Proclamation**, which gave Black Americans equal rights to public accommodations and injury. The slavery issue was an economic, oral, and political matter, and therefore could be attacked or defended in a number of different ways.

In 1864, **General Ulysses Grant** was put in charge of all Union forces as General William **Tecumseh Sherman** marched his troops through Georgia, setting Atlanta aflame. **General Lee** added 300,000 slaves to his army, promising their emancipation.

West Virginia (1863) and Nevada (1864) entered the Union, raising the total number of states to 36.

During **1864**, another **Revenue Act** was enacted. It provided for a tax of 5 percent on income up to $5,000; a tax of 7.5 percent on income between $5,000 and $10,000; and a tax of 10 percent on income over $10,000. All income taxes were repealed in 1872. Also in 1864, **William Tweed** became boss of Tammany Hall and would for eight years of plunder in New York City amass a great fortune.

In **Ex Parte Vallandigham** (1864), the U.S. Supreme Court ruled that the Court's appellate powers are governed by Congress, and therefore it has no power to hear appeals from military tribunals.

As the war neared an end, **Lincoln replaced Hamlin with Andrew Johnson** as his vice president during his second term because Johnson was a War Democrat, former governor, and senator from Tennessee, who supported the Union even though his state seceded from it. **Johnson was the only Southern senator to oppose the Confederacy.**

In the **1864 election**, Republican Lincoln's campaign slogan was, "Don't swap horses in midstream." **Abraham Lincoln** and **Andrew Johnson** received 2,213,635 popular votes to 1,805,237 for Democrats **George McClellan** and **George Pendleton**. Lincoln-Johnson received 213 electoral votes to 21 for **McClellan** and **Pendleton**. Lincoln was elected president and Johnson was elected vice president. Not voting were the seven Confederate states, representing 80 electoral votes. Prophetically, that year Lincoln stated, "If it is God's will that I must die at the hands of an assassin, I must be resigned to do my duty as I see it and leave the rest with God." He also said, "It has been my experience that folks who have no vices generally have very few virtues," and "The country will never be destroyed by others, it can only be destroyed by ourselves."

Andrew Johnson was born on December 29, 1808, in a **log cabin** in Raleigh, North Carolina. He grew up in poverty, never attended school, and was essentially illiterate until his wife, Eliza McCardle, began tutoring him. He served as a **tailor's apprentice** and then ran away to Greeneville, Tennessee. There he worked as a tailor and met Eliza. He rose through local politics, serving in the **House of Representatives** from 1843 to 1855 and in the U.S. Senate from 1857 to 1862. He was elected for two terms as **governor of Tennessee**, then to the **U.S. Senate** in 1857. He opposed seceding from the Union and was the only Southern senator to remain in the U.S. Senate during the Civil War.

In Lincoln's March 4, **1865, inaugural address**, he urged, "With malice toward none, with charity for all let us achieve a just and lasting peace among ourselves and with all nations." This was the first inauguration **captured on film**. Following Lincoln's **second inauguration**, hundreds of people attended a White House reception. Two days later, the Lincolns hosted their second inauguration ball, attended by over 4,000 people. At midnight, long tables of food arrived, featuring various meats, stews, and pastries.

Lincoln's **cabinet** in his second term of office included **Vice President** Andrew Johnson, **Secretary of the Treasury** Hugh McCulloch, **Secretary of War** Edwin Stanton, **Attorney General** James Speed, **Postmaster General** William Dennison, and **Secretary of the Interior** John Usher. Changes in the cabinet included: Johnson replaced Hamlin, McCulloch replaced Chase, Stanton replaced Cameron, Speed replaced Bates, Dennison replaced King, and Usher replaced Smith.

General Lee surrendered 27,000 sick and starving Confederate troops to **General Grant** at **Appomattox**, Virginia, after Union **General George Meade** defeated Confederate **General George Pickett** in the **Battle of Appomattox Court House** on April 19, 1865. With General Lee's surrender, some 175,000 confederate soldiers returned home to their families. It is believed the **Civil War** destroyed over **$5 billion in property** and took over **600,000 lives**, which included over 50,000 war prisoners. General Robert E. Lee died at home in 1870 at age 63.

The **period of Reconstruction** (laws giving former slaves their Constitutional rights) began with the end of the war, as corruption based on opportunism became rampant. Among the worst were **carpetbaggers** (named after their tapestry luggage) from the North who got involved in business and government. Anyone who supported the North's reconstruction efforts was known as a "**Scalawag.**" Black voters were disenfranchised. Federal troops sent to enforce the laws were completely gone by 1877.

Congress made no other pay changes during Lincoln's term of presidency other than increasing the legislative pay to $5,000 a year in 1865 (up from $3,000), that of the annual associate justices of the U.S. Supreme Court to $39,500 a year, and the Chief Justice's to $40,000 a year.

ABRAHAM LINCOLN (16TH PRESIDENT)

Only 41 days after being re-elected and five days after the surrender at Appomattox, **Lincoln was shot** in the back of the head at age 56 by racist **actor John Wilkes Booth** while Lincoln and Mary were **watching a theatrical performance** of "Our American Cousin" at Ford's Theater in Washington, D.C. on Good Friday, April 14, 1865. General Grant and his wife had been invited to join the Lincolns, but they declined. Lincoln died the following day. He was the **first assassinated president**. Mary was not at her husband's bedside when he died. Earlier, Lincoln had dreamed he would be killed during this second term.

Booth was the first person to assassinate a president of the United States. **He was an actor** from a very famous acting family. He reportedly earned $20,000 a year, while a typical family earned $300 per annum. **Booth was upset with Lincoln** and believed Lincoln would destroy the South and slavery. Booth's initial plan was to kidnap Lincoln and exchange him for Confederate soldiers. But the elaborate plans failed, and he decided instead to kill Lincoln, which he did with a .44 caliber derringer pistol at the time of the audience's laughter. **Booth** jumped onto the stage and escaped, but he was cornered in Maryland by federal troops and was **shot and killed. His four co-conspirators were hanged on July 7, 1865.**

Lincoln had authorized the approval of the **Secret Service**, which was to begin within a week after what would be his assassination date. It would be a division in the U.S. Treasury, but its **mission was financial crimes**. It was not until 1901 that congress gave it the responsibility of protecting the president and other designated persons.

After lying in state on a catafalque in the Capitol Rotunda, **Lincoln's body** was placed on an **eight-coach train** for a cross-country trip and burial in **Springfield, Illinois**. The Lincoln Catafalque** has been used for every following dead president in the Capitol Rotunda.

Lincoln's wife, **Mary Todd**, remained in the White House for four months before returning to Springfield. The death of three of her children (only Robert Todd lived a full life) and the 1865 assassination of her husband were too much for her fragile emotional state, and **she was committed to an asylum**. She died at age 65 on July 16, 1882, and was buried with her husband.

Lincoln's images appear on the **penny** and the **$5 bill**. And the **Lincoln Memorial**, featuring a **seated Lincoln**, appears at the **head of the Reflecting Pool** in Washington, D.C. In the White House, there is the **Lincoln Sitting Room** and the **Lincoln Bedroom**. The latter is available for distinguished visitors of the president of the United States. And many cities bear Lincoln's name.

Lincoln, like Thomas Jefferson, Teddy Roosevelt, and George Washington, had his facial image engraved on **Mount Rushmore** in the Black Hills of South Dakota.

Most historians agree that Lincoln was the **greatest of all presidents**.

Key Events

The **Confederate States of America** formed with **seven southern states** and Jefferson Davis as president (1861); the **Civil War** began with the Confederates firing on Fort Sumter in Charleston, South Carolina (1861); **Elisha Otis** received a patent for his **lifting device** called an elevator (1861); the first transcontinental **telegraph** line opened (1861); **John D. Rockefeller** entered the kerosene business, buying half-interest in a large oil refinery

(1861); with the end of the war, **steel mills** replaced iron factories, **breweries** emerged in Milwaukee and St. Louis because of German populations, and meat packing in Chicago expanded (1861); **George Pullman**, "inventor of railroad comfort," introduced a swing-down upper berth along with a lower berth sleeping car (1862); **elevated railways** began replacing horsedrawn vehicles (1862); Macy's put **Santa Claus** in its department store (1862); a group of Irish mine workers calling themselves the **Molly Maguires** beat up a group of scab replacement workers (1862); bank robber **Jesse James** was shot in the back and killed by **Robert Ford** in St. Joseph, Missouri (1862); **trains** started to **replace the stagecoach** (1863); and the famed feud between the Kentucky **Hatfield and McCoy families** began with the murder of a Union McCoy soldier by a Confederate Hatfield (1865).

Andrew Johnson
(17th President)

April 15, 1865 – March 4, 1869

Andrew Johnson was born on December 29, 1808, in Raleigh, North Carolina, to Jacob and Mary Johnson. Andrew had one older brother, William. Jacob Johnson died when Andrew was three years old, while attempting to save a person from drowning. **Andrew grew up in poverty**, never attending school. Andrew served as a tailor's apprentice and then ran away to Greeneville, Tennessee, where he **worked as a tailor** and made his own clothes. In Greeneville, he met **Eliza McCardle**, and they married in 1827, when she was 16 and he was 18. She began tutoring him in reading and writing. They had five children: **Andrew, Charles, Martha, Mary,** and **Robert**. Andrew served as mayor of Greeneville in 1833 and state legislator in 1835 before serving in the **U.S. House of Representatives** from 1843 to 1853 (his nickname was the **Tennessee Tailor**) and in the U.S. **Senate** from 1857 to 1862. In 1861, President Lincoln appointed Johnson **military governor of Tennessee**. Johnson **disagreed with seceding from the Union** and was the only Southern senator to remain in the U.S. Senate when the Confederacy was founded. Therefore, he was hated in the South and liked in the North.

Johnson was 56 years old at the time of his inauguration on April 15, 1865, following Lincoln's death (Johnson served only six weeks as vice president). Andrew Johnson was the **third vice president** to assume the presidency upon the death of his president (John Tyler and Millard Fillmore preceded him). He was the **sixth vice president** to become president (John Adams, Thomas Jefferson, Martin Van Buren, John Tyler, and Millard Fillmore preceded him) and the **second president** to be elected to the four federal offices, representative, senator, vice president, and president (John Tyler preceded him). Johnson served his term of office without a vice president. He was a **heavy drinker** and reportedly got so drunk at Lincoln's inauguration that he was too drunk to swear in the incoming senators. Eliza brought two daughters and five grandchildren with her to the Executive Mansion, which was in disrepair. She got it cleaned up. Eliza was well read and expressed different viewpoints to her husband. One of their daughters, Martha, served as the official hostess.

Johnson's initial **cabinet** included **Secretary of State** William Seward, **Secretary of the Treasury** Hugh McCulloch, **Secretary of War** Edwin Stanton, **Attorney General** James Speed, **Secretary of the Navy** Gideon Welles, **Postmaster General** William Dennison, and **Secretary of the Interior** John Usher. He also hired the first official **presidential doctor**; previous doctors were private physicians.

The **13th Amendment to the U.S. Constitution** was ratified on December 6, 1865. It stated that neither slavery nor involuntary servitude shall exist within the United States (see Appendix C). Later in 1865, **Congress increased the salaries** for congressmen to $5,000 a year, up from $3,000 beginning ten years earlier. **Congress made no other pay changes during Johnson's term of presidency.**

In 1866, the **Judicial Circuits Act** became law. It drew the boundaries of the judicial circuits. That year, Johnson vetoed the **1866 Civil Rights Act**, which declared all persons born in the United States, excluding Indians, were citizens of the United States. The Act also gave ex-slaves the right to own property and enforce contracts. Congress overrode the veto and the Act was passed into law.

In **Ex parte Milligan** (1866), the U.S. Supreme Court ruled that when civilian courts are in operation, it is unconstitutional to try citizens by military commissions. And in **Mississippi vs Johnson** (1867), the U.S. Supreme Court ruled that the Court does not have "jurisdiction of a bill to enjoin the President in the performance of his office duties."

In 1868, the **Reconstruction Act** was made law. It declared all elections were to be decided by a majority of the votes actually cast. And the **Expatriation Act of 1868** declared that expatriation is a natural and inherent right of all people.

Northerners believed Johnson did not seek enough retribution from the South for leaving the Union. He even welcomed Confederate soldiers back into the Union. In February 1868, while president, **Johnson was impeached** by the House and **came within one vote of being convicted** by the Senate for violating the Tenure of Office Act by firing Secretary of War Edwin Stanton without Senate approval. According to **Article II, Section 4 of the U.S. Constitution** (see Appendix B), "a federal officer can be **impeached** for treason, bribery, a high crime or a misdemeanor." A simple majority of the House of Representatives is **sufficient to impeach**, and 2/3 of the seated Senate is necessary **to convict**. At the time there were 54 senators; 36 had to vote guilty for removal. The final vote was 35 guilty, 19 not guilty. Verdict: not guilty. In spite of all this, Johnson stated, "If a man does not disgrace his profession, it never disgraces him." Did he not consider himself disgraced? He was the first president to be impeached.

On July 9, 1868, the **14th Amendment to the U.S. Constitution** was ratified. It stated that persons born in the United States are citizens, and no state shall deprive them of life, liberty, or property without due process of law (see Appendix C).

Johnson was a **slave owner**, an avowed **racist**, a **white supremacist**, and an **arrogant bigot**, but he was a **staunch Unionist**. On July 28, 1868, the **Burlingame Treaty of 1868** was signed, which protected commerce, eased immigration restrictions, and gave China "most favored nation" status.

He was called "**King Andy**." His **favorite pets** were white mice. He once stated that God had Lincoln killed so that he, Johnson, could become president. Upon becoming president, he said, "This is a country for white men, and by God, as long as I am president, it shall be a government for white men."

When his term of office ended, he returned to Tennessee to state politics and won back much of the respect he had lost earlier. In 1875, Johnson became the first **former president to be elected to serve in the U.S. Senate**. He served four months before his death on July 31, 1875, at the age of 67. His **final words** were,

"Oh do not cry. Be good. Are the doctors here? I need no doctor." His wife **Eliza died** on January 15, 1876, at age 65. Both were buried in the **Andrew Johnson National Cemetery** in Greeneville, Tennessee.

Before he died, Johnson said, "I was not fit for this office." **Many historians agree that Johnson was second only to Buchanan as the worst president of the United States.**

Key Events

The **coffee percolator** was invented (1865); Johnson proclaimed **amnesty** for the **Confederate** rebels declaring allegiance to the Union (1865); newly freed Black slaves from the south drifted into Washington, D.C., resulting in a **race riot** (1865); hundreds of **whites rampaged through Memphis**, Tennessee, destroying churches and schools and resulting in many deaths and injuries (1866); the **Ku Klux Klan** was formed from **former Confederate soldiers** in Pulaski, Tennessee, who sought to assert white supremacy and curb free Black activities (1866); the **bicycle** was invented (1866); a **telegraph cable** linked the United States and England (1866); **Coca-Cola** was introduced (1866); Congress authorized the **five-cent coin**, called the **nickel** for its nickel content (1866); **Nebraska** entered the Union as the 37th state (1867); **Alaska** was purchased from Russia for $7.2 million, or about 2¢ an acre (1867); the **Pullman Car Company** began (1867); some **Confederate soldiers**, as well as **former slaves**, headed west and **became cowboys** to help herd and protect cows from rustlers (1867); trapper and scout **Kit Carson** died of an aneurysm at age 59 (1868); **Buffalo Bill Cody** reportedly got his name after **killing hundreds of buffalo** in a single day, as 60 million roamed the plains (1868); **Louisa May Alcott** published *Little*

Women (1868); **barbed wire** was invented (1868); **tobacco** was introduced (1868); the first reported **World Almanac** appeared (1868); and news of England's 1862 Companies Act creating a **limited liability equity organization** was of particular interest to sole proprietorships and partnerships that sought protection of their personal assets in the United States (1868).

Ulysses S. Grant
(18ᵀᴴ President)

March 4, 1869 - March 4, 1877

Hiram Ulysses Grant was born on April 27, 1822, in Point Pleasant, Ohio, to Jesse Root Grant and Hannah Simpson Grant. He was named Hiram after his maternal grandfather. Grant had two brothers, Samuel and Orvil, and three sisters, Clara, Mary, and Virginia. His father was a farmer and a leather tanner. Grant excelled at riding and training horses on the family farm. He also worked in his father's tannery. Grant attended local schools until entering the Presbyterian Academy, graduating at age 17. He then attended the **U.S. Military Academy** at **West Point**, New York, in 1839 on the recommendation of Congressman Thomas Hamer. Hamer misidentified Grant as **Ulysses Simpson Grant**, a name that Grant adopted. But Grant's

ULYSSES S. GRANT (18TH PRESIDENT)

maternal grandfather nicknamed him "Useless." Ulysses was an unimposing man of 5'7" and 175 pounds.

Grant graduated from the **U.S. Military Academy** in 1843, twenty-first in his class of thirty-nine cadets. He was commissioned a second lieutenant in September 1843, in the Fourth U.S. Infantry in the Jefferson Barracks in Missouri, near St. Louis. While stationed in Missouri, Grant spent time with the family of his West Point roommate **Frederick Dent**. He spent even more time with Dent's sister, Julia. Grant went off to fight in the **Mexican-American War** in 1846, where he was cited for **bravery** and promoted to **first lieutenant**. He returned to **marry Julia** on August 22, 1848. In 1854, after six years of various assignments in the United States and now having four children (Ellen, Frederick, Jesse, and Ulysses Jr.), Grant **resigned** from the army. For the next seven years, he went from job to job. Julia Grant was outspoken and might argue with her husband, but she was very supportive and managed the money while also being a good mother to four children. They were a close family who enjoyed each other.

When the Civil War began in 1861, Grant accepted command of an Illinois company of volunteers and rose to the rank of brigadier general. Grant earned the **nickname "Unconditional Surrender"** (matching his U.S. initials) for his significant victories. This led to Lincoln promoting Grant to major general. In 1862, he suffered heavy losses in the **Battle of Shiloh** but followed with key victories in the **Battle of Vicksburg** and the **Battle of Chattanooga** in 1863. In 1864, Lincoln appointed Grant lieutenant general in charge of all Union armies.

On April 9, 1865, Grant accepted the surrender of General Lee and the Confederate Army at **Appomattox, Virginia**. For his role in ending the Civil War, Grant was showered with many gifts, ranging from cigars to thousands of dollars. Asked about the art of war, Grant replied, "It is simple enough. Find out where your enemy is. Get at him as soon as you can. Strike him as hard as you can and keep moving on."

When President Lincoln was killed on April 15, 1865, by John Wilkes Booth, **Vice President Andrew Johnson was sworn in as president.** When President Johnson fired Secretary of War Edwin Stanton, without approval by Congress, it led to **Johnson's impeachment,** which he survived by one vote in the Senate. **Grant** was appointed by President Johnson as **Stanton's replacement.** After serving a year, Grant quit, and in 1868 he was named the Republican candidate for the presidency. Asked if he wanted to be president, Grant replied, "I suppose so if I am nominated and elected." He claimed, "This office comes to me unsought." His **campaign slogan** was "Vote as You Shot." He also stated, "I have never advocated war except as a means to peace."

In the **1868 election,** Republicans **Ulysses Grant** and his vice president **Schuyler Colfax** defeated Democrats **Horatio Seymour** and **Francis Blair**, 3,012,833 to 2,703,249 in the popular vote and 214 to 80 in electoral votes. Grant was elected president and Colfax was elected vice president.

Schuyler Colfax was born on March 23, 1823, in New York City. He was named after his grandmother, Hester Schuyler. His grandfather, William Colfax, served under George Washington. After Schuyler's father died before Schuyler's birth, his mother remarried, and the family moved to South Bend, Indiana. Schuyler developed an interest in journalism and politics. In 1842, he was **named editor of the** *South Bend Free Press*, and three years later he purchased the newspaper and renamed it the *St. Joseph Valley Register*. The editor of the New York Tribune, **Horace Greeley**, published Colfax's reports. Colfax was the delegate to the Indiana Convention that drafted the Indiana Constitution in 1849. After several unsuccessful attempts at a House seat, he ran as a Republication in 1854 and won. He remained a **congressman for 14 years** before becoming vice president under Grant. Schuyler married Ellen Wade shortly after being elected Grant's vice president. Schuyler's **reputation was ruined** when he was involved in the **Crédit Mobilier** scandal. Grant was not implicated in the scandal. Schuyler declined to run for public office again and returned to South Bend, Indiana. He died on January 13, 1885, of a heart attack in Mankato, Minnesota, and was buried in South Bend.

Grant was 46 years old on the day of his inauguration. Canaries were supposed to sing at his inauguration, but they all froze to death. **Grant was the first president to graduate from West Point**. In his March 4, **1869, inaugural speech**, Grant called for an end to regional divisiveness. Grant also pledged for a reform of policy with Native Americans and that all government debts would be paid in gold. Several thousand attended the inaugural ball at the Treasury building.

The **Executive Mansion was in disrepair,** and Julia Grant refused to move in until it was repaired. It was the first renovation since the British burned it in 1814. Ulysses liked the billiard room, where he smoked up to 20 cigars a day with friends.

Grant was not as effective in politics as he was at winning the war. He was not diplomatic and showed poor judgement by appointing friends rather than qualified candidates to his cabinet. The initial **cabinet** included **Vice President** Schuyler Colfax,

Secretary of State Elihu Washburne, **Secretary of the Treasury** Alexander Stewart, **Secretary of War** John Rawlins, **Attorney General** Ebenezer Hoar, **Secretary of the Navy** Adolph Borie, **Postmaster General** John Creswell, and **Secretary of the Interior** Jacob Cox. Senator James Garfield challenged the appointments of the cabinet, stating that Grant chose them based on personal relations, not professional qualification.

Government scandals and swindles plagued the Grant administration, fueled by the patronage of a **spoils system**. Appointments were based on support for an elected official, rather than the competence of the person. Scandals happened during Grant's presidency but he himself did not seem to be guilty of corruption, only of appointing the incompetent. In response, Grant made changes in the Justice Department and established a **Civil Service Commission**. And in response to criticism, Grant replied, "My failures have been errors in judgement. Not intent."

A major issue facing Grant was **greenbacks**, government printed money from the Civil War that was not backed by gold. In 1869, when the **Wall Street speculators** Abel Corbin, Jim Fisk, and Jay Gould bought huge amounts of gold, it drove down the value of the greenbacks, leading to a crisis and financially ruining hundreds of people on September 24, 1869, **Black Friday**, when the stock market crashed. Grant released gold reserves to settle the crisis. Julia defended Grant in the **Black Friday** gold scandal.

The **1869 Judiciary Act** increased the number of Associate Justices of the U.S. Supreme Court to eight.

In **Texas vs White** (1869), the U.S. Supreme Court ruled that, once admitted to the Union, there is an "indissoluble relation," and states cannot unilaterally secede. In **Ex Parte McCardle** (1869), the U.S. Supreme Court ruled that while the Constitution confers appellate jurisdiction, Article III Section 2's Exception Clause gives Congress the authority to withdraw appellate jurisdiction at any time.

The **15th Amendment to the U.S. Constitution** (see Appendix C) was ratified by Congress on February 3, 1870. It stated that the right to vote could not be denied "on account of race, color, or previous servitude."

Three key laws were the focus of **Reconstruction** in the South. Unhappy with the progress of Reconstruction, Grant ensured that the **1870 Enforcement Act**, which authorized federal troops to enforce the 15th Amendment, was enacted. The **1870 Civil Rights Act** gave citizens the right to enter into and enforce contracts. The **1871 Civil Rights Act** outlawed the Ku Klux Klan. In **Collector vs Day** (1871), the U.S. Supreme Court ruled that under the Constitution, Congress does not have the right to impose a tax on the salary of a state judicial officer.

In 1871, Congress increased the annual salary for a congressman to $7,500 (up from 1865's $5,000), and for the associate justices of the U.S. Supreme Court, pay was increased to $8,000 a year (up from 1855's $6,000). The Chief Justice's salary was increased to $8,500 a year (up from 1855's $6,500).

In 1872, stockholders of the Union Pacific Railroad changed its name to **Crédit Mobilier of America**. The Union Pacific had awarded large amounts of government money to itself. Construction costs for building a railroad from the Midwest to the Pacific were doubled. As a result, the stockholders got very rich. To stop a government investigation, bribes of over $33 million were paid. These amounts were even more generous with the enactment of the **1872 Revenue Act** which terminated personal income tax. Grant was not implicated in the scandal. Grant's problems did not stop Congress from increasing his annual pay to $50,000 in 1873, the first change since Washington's $25,000 in 1789. With worker pay reportedly at about $400 a year, this resulted in a pay ratio of 125:1, significantly higher than Washington's 80:1. The vice president's salary was increased to $10,000 (up from $5,000) per annum, also the first change since 1789.

Resentful Southerners called Northerners who came south to enforce the Reconstruction **carpetbaggers**, describing them by their luggage. The **1872 Amnesty Act** restored civil rights to the citizens of the South.

In the **1872 election**, Republicans **Ulysses Grant** and **Henry Wilson** defeated Democrats **Horace Greeley** and **Benjamin Brown**, 3,597,132 to 2,834,079 in the **popular vote** and 286 to 0 in the **electoral vote**. Because Horace Greeley died shortly after the election, his electoral votes were distributed to four other candidates.

Henry Wilson served as Grant's second **vice president**. He was born Jeremiah Jones Colbath on February 16, 1892, in Farmington, New Hampshire. His hard-drinking father named his son after a wealthy neighbor, hoping to profit from the action. He did not. Colbath changed his name on his 21st birthday. Wilson grew up as an uneducated, troublemaking field hand in Massachusetts. He learned to be a shoe cobbler. Wilson identified with the plight of the disadvantaged and poor. In 1840, he married Harriet Howe Henry. Wilson was elected to the State Senate in 1844 at age 28 and moved from the **State Senate** to the **U.S. Senate** in 1854. Wilson was an **abolitionist**. He traveled 10,000 miles and gave 96 speeches after being nominated vice president. Wilson suffered a stroke shortly after being elected that affected his speech and caused partial paralysis. Wilson died on November 22, 1875, at age 63 from a fatal stroke.

In his March 4, **1873, inaugural address**, Grant stated, "The freed slave is not possessed of the civil rights which citizenship should carry with it. This is wrong and should be corrected." Grant was the **last president to own slaves**.

Grant's initial **cabinet** in his second term of office was a complete change from his first cabinet. It included **Vice President** Henry Wilson, **Secretary of State** Hamilton Fish, **Secretary of the Treasury** William Richardson, **Secretary of War** William Belknap, **Attorney General** George Williams, **Secretary of the Navy** George Robeson, **Postmaster General** John Creswell, and **Secretary of the Interior** Columbus Delano. Wilson replaced Colfax, Fish replaced Washburne, Richardson replaced Stewart, Belknap replaced Rawlins, Williams replaced Hoar, Robeson replaced Borie, and Delano replaced Cox.

The **1873 Coinage Act** stopped the production of silver coinage. And in 1873, Congress increased the annual salary of the associate justices of the U.S. Supreme Court to $10,000 (up from 1871's $8,000) and the chief justice's annual salary to $10,500 (up from 1871's $8,500).

In 1874, Congress increased the pay of legislators to $6,000 per annum (up from 1865's $5,000). **Congress made no other pay changes during Grant's term of presidency**.

Julia Grant enjoyed hosting Executive Mansion dinners. Grant's first state dinner was on December 12, 1874, for the King of Hawaii, who brought a food taster because he feared being poisoned. When not entertaining, the Grants were up at 7:00am, had breakfast at 8:30am, lunch at noon, and dinner at 5:00pm. They preferred simple food. President Grant looked forward to a favorite meal of bacon, broiled fish, and fried apples. The White House chef was a former army quartermaster who believed quantity was more important than variety and regularly served roast beef, turkey, and apple pie with cheese.

The **1875 Bland Silver Act** restored the silver dollar to legal currency, and the **1875 Specie Resumption Act** returned America to the gold standard. In **Munn vs Illinois** (1877), the U.S. Supreme Court ruled that private companies that operate for public interest are subject to public regulation.

After **leaving office** in March 1877, Grant and his wife went on an extended **world tour**. She was disappointed Grant did not seek a third term. Julia often said her eight years in the Executive Mansion were the best years of her life. They were the third couple to take a world tour; the Van Burens and the Fillmores did it earlier. Abroad, the Grants met with dignitaries and world leaders, returning months later to New York City.

When Grant retired, he did not have much money. What he had, he invested with his son, Ulysses Jr., who had gone into investment banking. Ulysses Sr. even borrowed from William Vanderbilt. His **son's firm went bankrupt** three years later after Jr. invested in a Ponzi scheme, and Grant went into debt, forcing him to sell his war souvenirs. **Dying from throat cancer** from smoking a dozen or more cigars every day, Grant took the recommendation of author Mark Twain and began writing his memoirs. Grant finished the book in June 1885 and **died** on July 23, 1885, at the age of 63. The book *The Personal Memoirs of U.S. Grant*, was very successful. It paid off the Ponzi scheme **debts**. The book is considered to be one of the best **military autobiographies** ever written. Before dying, Grant said, "The two happiest days of my life were when I graduated from West Point and when I left the Presidency."

After Grant died, donations of over $600,000 paid to build a 150-foot-tall marble **mausoleum** in New York City, the tallest mausoleum in the U.S. It overlooks the Hudson River. The mausoleum bears the inscription, "**Let us have peace**." When **Julia died** on December 14, 1902, her body was placed alongside that of her husband in the mausoleum.

Due to economic hardships, government scandals, and regional diversity, most historians rank Grant's term **somewhat below the average of other presidents**.

Key Events

The **Central Pacific** and **Union Pacific** railroads met at Promontory Summit, Utah with a golden spike in the tracks linking the East and West (1869); **coast-to-coast travel**, previously twenty-six days, became coast-to-coast rail service of three and a half days (1869); **Goldman Sachs** began (1869); the collapse of the **Avondale coal mine** killed 179 miners (1869); a financial panic followed **Jay Gould** and **James Fisk's** attempt to corner the gold market, which led to financial **Black Friday** (1869); **Cornelius Vanderbilt** stopped the Wall Street panic by buying millions of dollars of failing company stock (1869); **George Westinghouse** introduced **air brakes** (1869); **chewing gum** and **vacuum cleaners** were patented (1869); **Wyoming** was the first state to give women the right to vote (1869); the first **U.S. Post Card** was issued (1869); an **earthquake** devastated San Francisco and killed over 6,000 people (1869); gambling was legalized in Nevada (1869); the **U.S. population** reached almost 40 million, led by New York City with one million (1870); the **Atlantic City Boardwalk** was completed in New Jersey (1870); former Confederate states required African Americans to take literacy tests, effectively eliminating their voting rights (1870); **Jonathan Wright** was the **first Black judge** added to a **state**

Supreme Court (South Carolina) (1870); **Hiram Revels** (from Mississippi) was the **first Black man** elected to the **U.S. Senate** (1870); South Carolina elected **Joseph Rainey** as the **first Black congressman** to the **House of Representatives** (1870); the **Library of Congress** was given responsibility for copyrights (1870); the **U.S. Weather Bureau** was founded (1870); John D. Rockefeller set up **Standard Oil** of Ohio, later to become **Exxon** (1870); the **Metropolitan Museum of New York City** opened (1870); **Thomas Edison** invented the electric typewriter (1870); **Macy's** hired its **first Santa** (1870); **corrugated paper** was patented (1871); the **National Rifle Association** was founded (1871); a **smallpox epidemic** in New York and Philadelphia killed thousands (1871); the **Great Chicago Fire** occurred, killing over 300 people, leaving some 100,000 homeless, and destroying over 17,000 buildings (1871); **Yellowstone National Park** was created by Congress (1872); **Montgomery Ward** opened the first department store in Chicago (1872); the **stock ticker tape** was invented by Thomas Edison (1873); **cable-drawn cars** replaced horses in San Francisco (1873); a **major silver lode** in Wyoming was discovered (1873); **Jacob and Levi Strauss** received the patent on workingmen's pants they called "waist high overalls" – later called jeans (1873); **Pabst** and **Schlitz** led **Milwaukee brewers,** producing over 250,000 barrels a year (1873); **Tammany Hall's Boss Tweed** was convicted of stealing $50 million of New York public funds (1873); the Get-Rich-Quick Greedy were described in Mark Twain's *The Gilded Age* (1873); **Jesse James** and his gang began operation (1873); using long-range rifles, twenty-eight buffalo hunters drove back 700 Commanches at **Adobe Walls**, Texas (1874); the first **public zoo** opened in Philadelphia (1874); Philip Armour patented the disassembly line of separating cattle parts and shipping them off in refrigerated cars (1874); the **Remington typewriter** was introduced (1874); **Bank of America** began operation (1874); railroads started selling off unneeded land as cattle drives from Texas to the midlands expanded (1875); **mining for silver** in Nevada was introduced (1875); **Andrew Carnegie** opened the Bessemer steel mill in Pittsburgh, Pennsylvania, beginning the **Steel Age** (1875); the first **Kentucky Derby** was held (1875); **Custer** and 264 men of the 7th Cavalry were massacred by Sioux warriors at the **Little Big Horn River** in Montana (1876); Marshall "**Wild Bill**" Hickok was shot and killed by **Jack McCall** at age 39 holding a "**dead man's hand**" – aces and eights (1876); the **Greenback Party** called for the issuance of paper money backed by government gold and silver (1876); Robert's *Rules of Order* was published (1876); the **World's Fair** opened in Philadelphia (1876); Mescalero **Apache** leader **Victorio** and half of his followers were killed (1876); ten **Molly Maguires** were hanged in Pottsville for murder and arson (1876); *The Adventures of Tom Sawyer* was published by Mark Twain (1876); **Marshall Wyatt Earp** and **Bat Masterson** kept law and order in Dodge City, Kansas (1876); the **Anheuser-Busch** company was formed and **Heinz Ketchup** was introduced (1876); the Wall Street financial firm **Drexel Burnham and Lambert** began (1876); Alexander Graham Bell invented the **telephone**, successfully relaying the words, "Mr. Watson, come here – I want to see you." (1876); and **Colorado** was admitted as a state (1876).

Rutherford B. Hayes (19ᵀᴴ President)

March 4, 1877 – March 4, 1881

Rutherford Birchard Hayes was born on October 4, 1822, in Delaware, Ohio, to Sophia and Rutherford Hayes. They had two sons, Lorenzo and Rutherford, and a daughter named Fanny. His father died of malaria two months before Rutherford was born. Rutherford was one of three presidents who was born after his father died (the other two were Andrew Jackson and Bill Clinton). Due to a wealthy uncle, Rutherford attended private schools. As a young boy, Hayes suffered from the **fear of going insane**. However, he went on to graduate from **Kenyon College** in 1842 and **Harvard Law School** in 1845. Hayes was admitted to the Ohio bar in 1847 and set up a law practice in Cincinnati. At the age of 30, he married **Lucy Ware Webb**, age 21 in

1852. They had **eight children**: one daughter, Francis, and seven sons, James, Joseph, George, Manning, Rutherford Jr., Sardis, and Scott. Joseph, George, and Manning died as infants. Lucy was a devout Methodist and graduated from Wesleyan Female College in 1838. She traveled with her husband during the Civil War and was called "**Mother Lucy**" by the soldiers she tended to.

In 1861, Hayes was commissioned a **major** in the 23rd Ohio Volunteer **Infantry**. Hayes served throughout the **Civil War** (one of seven presidents to do so) fighting in many major battles and rising to the rank of **major general**. Hayes was wounded five times in the Civil War. Hayes was elected to the **U.S. House of Representatives** in 1864 but did not take his seat until the war was over in 1865. Hayes then served three terms as **governor of Ohio** (1868-1872 and 1875-1876). Hayes said, "**He serves his party best who serves his country best**," and "**Nothing brings out the lower traits of human nature like office-seeking.**"

In 1876, Republicans **Rutherford Hayes** and **William Wheeler** received 4,036,298 popular votes, and Democrats New York Governor **Samuel Tilden** and **Thomas Hendricks** received 4,300,590. But **Hayes** and **Wheeler** received **185 electoral votes vs 184** for Tilden and Hendricks. This was only after 20 disputed votes from Florida, Louisiana, and South Carolina. The results were challenged because of possible voter irregularities in the three states and the matter was referred to Congress, who appointed a bipartisan commission, that upheld the election results. Hayes was named president, and Wheeler was named vice president. Some referred to Hayes as "**His Fraudulency**." Hayes was the **second president to win the electoral college but lose the popular vote** (John Quincy Adams was the first) and the third president to have a **law degree from Harvard**

(John Adams was the first and his son John Quincy was the second).

William Wheeler was born on June 30, 1819, in Malone, New York, near the Canadian border. His father died in debt shortly thereafter. Wheeler and his younger brother helped their mother, who took in boarders and helped with farm work. He scraped up enough money to attend the **state college** for two years but then had to quit and studied law under a local attorney. In 1845, he was admitted to the New York bar and became interested in local and state politics. In 1867, he was elected to the **U.S. Senate**. He caught Hayes's eye and was put on his ticket and elected. But Wheeler wanted to go back to the Senate because as vice president he had little responsibility. Wheeler died at the end of his term on June 4, 1887, at age 68 in his hometown.

Lucy Hayes arrived in D.C. with her husband following the very close and controversial election. Hayes stated, "I regret I was nominated. You know I did not want the position. I am not fit to be president." Hayes was 54 years of age on the date of his inauguration and was sworn in on a Sunday in the Executive Mansion because Grant's term expired on a Sunday, and it was feared the Democrats might try to swear in Tilden. In his March 4, **1877, inaugural address**, Hayes stated, "I will put forth my best efforts to forever wipe out the color line and the distinction between North and South." At his inauguration, Hayes was protected by six Secret Service agents, **the first president protected during their inauguration**, except for an informal appearance by Allan Pinkerton at Lincoln's inauguration.

A **Union general** during the Civil War, one of Hayes's first acts as president was to **remove federal troops from the South, ending Reconstruction**, returning self-determination to the southern states (1877). However, he had to use troops to restore order during the **Great Railroad Strike** (1877) when workers seized trains and stations in response to reductions in pay.

Lucy was a gracious hostess, but she **forbade alcohol** in the Executive Mansion. Her nickname was **Lemonade Lucy**. She supported women's education and women's suffrage.

Hayes's **cabinet** included **Vice President** William Wheeler, **Secretary of State** William Evarts, **Secretary of the Treasury** John Sherman, **Secretary of War** George W. McCrary, **Attorney General** Charles Devens, **Secretary of the Navy** Richard Thompson, **Postmaster General** David Key, and **Secretary of the Interior** Carl Schurz.

In **Munn vs Illinois** (1877), the U.S. Supreme Court ruled that private companies that operate for public interest are subject to public regulation. And in **United States vs Fox** (1877), the U.S. Supreme Court ruled that an act is only an offense at the time which it is committed.

Hayes was opposed to **patronage** and always went with the most qualified candidate, which caused him some problems with influential congressmen. One example was his appointment of **Frederick Douglass**, probably America's most prominent African American, to serve as Marshal for the District of Columbia (1877). Hayes went on to require competitive examinations of candidates for **civil service positions** before hiring them.

Unfortunately, despite Hayes's efforts to ensure Native Americans were treated fairly, there were a number of uprisings as various **Indian Nations** rebelled against relocation and other mistreatments. But unlike General Grant's term as president, Hayes's term of office was not rocked with scandals. He was generally recognized as **honest and not tolerant of corruption or patronage**. Hayes insisted appointments be based on merit, not personal reasons. But he was unable to get much done with Congress due to the closeness of the election vote. Hayes had Alexander Graham Bell install the first **Executive Mansion telephone** (1877).

Three laws were enacted in 1878. The **National Quarantine Act** shifted quarantine authority from the states to the federal government. The **Posse Comitatus Act of 1878** prohibited the federal government's "willful use" of the U.S. Army to "execute the laws" unless expressly authorized by the Constitution or an act of Congress. And the **Bland-Allison Act** required the U.S. Treasury to purchase between $2 and $4 million of silver each month and coin it into legal tender.

In **Reynolds vs United States** (1879), the U.S. Supreme Court ruled that a federal statute prohibiting polygamy did not violate the First Amendment's Free Exercise Clause.

In **Strauder vs West Virginia** (1880), the U.S. Supreme Court ruled that a state statute that denies citizens the right to serve on a jury due to their race is discrimination, which is prohibited by the Fourteenth Amendment.

Hayes installed **indoor plumbing** in 1880. And he was also the first president to set aside and protect his papers for posterity. Hayes introduced the **typewriter** to the Executive Mansion, as well as the **Easter Egg Hunt**. The **Resolute Desk** in the Oval Room was given to President Hayes by Queen Victoria in 1880. It was carved from the timbers of the British ship H.M.S. *Resolute*. It has been the president's desk ever since.

Congress made no pay changes during Hayes's term of presidency.

Leaving as promised after one term, **Hayes died** on January 17, 1893, at age 70 of heart failure in Fremont, Ohio. Rutherford's last words were, "I am going to be with Lucy." **Lucy died** on June 22, 1889, at age 57. They were both buried in Spiegel Grove State Park in Fremont, Ohio.

Most historians agree Hayes was **somewhat below average as a president**.

Key Events

Cornelius Vanderbilt was prominent in railroads and steamships (1877); the **Bell Telephone Company** was formed (1877); Thomas Edison demonstrated the invention of the **phonograph** by recording the words "Mary had a little lamb" (1877); **Andrew Carnegie** formed his steel company with Henry Frick in charge (1877); over 500,000 heads of cattle were driven to Dodge City, Kansas (1877); the **Molly Maguires** terrorist mining group was broken up by the hanging of eleven of its leaders (1877); the **yellow fever** epidemic almost wiped out Memphis, Tennessee (1878); Tombstone, Arizona's **Boot Hill** opened (1878); the first telephone exchange opened in New Haven, Connecticut (1878); the first **Morgan silver dollar** was minted in Philadelphia (1878); **Thomas Alva Edison** invented the incandescent **light bulb**, the first of 1,092 other Edison patents (1879); Edison formed the Edison Electric Light Company (1879); **cash registers** were patented (1879); **Frank Woolworth** opened the first five and dime store in Lancaster, Pennsylvania (1879); soap-maker James Gamble and candle-maker William Procter formed **Procter & Gamble** (1879); the first **Madison Square Garden** in New York City was built by J.P. Morgan (1879); **St. Patrick's Cathedral** opened in New York City (1879); Cleveland, Ohio was the first city to install electric lighting (1879);

the **Salvation Army** was founded (1879); actress **Sarah Bernhardt** made her debut (1879); although **gold** was discovered on his land, **John Sutter** died a pauper at age 77 (1880); **Irish gangs** were rampant in lower New York City (1880); the United States **population** exceeded 50 million for the first time (1880); former slave **Booker T. Washington** was selected to head up a new Black school in **Tuskegee**, Alabama (1881); and the Earp brothers and rustlers fought at the **O.K. Corral** in Tombstone, Arizona (1881).

James A. Garfield
(20th President)

March 4, 1881 – September 19, 1881

James Abram Garfield was born on November 19, 1831, in a log cabin near Cleveland, Ohio, to Abram and Eliza Garfield. James was the youngest of five children. He had three brothers, James, Mehetable, and Thomas, and one sister, Mary. His father died when James was two years old, and his mother went to work to support the family. In 1842, Eliza married Alfred Belden. The children divided their time between work and school. James enjoyed hunting and reading. As a teenager, he **worked on barges** and **tugboats** until he contracted malaria. Garfield became a traveling preacher for the Disciples of Christ after he graduated from **Hiram College** in 1854 and **Williams College** in 1856. He went on to become a **Classics professor** at Hiram College. At age 26, he served as **president of Hiram College**.

There he published a proof of the **Pythagorean Theorem** and could **write Latin** with one hand and **Greek** with the other. At age 27, Garfield married schoolteacher **Lucretia Rudolph** age 26, in 1858. They had **seven children** together all before his presidency: five sons, Abram, Edward, Harry, Irvin, and James, and two daughters, Eliza and Mary.

In 1859, Garfield was elected an Ohio state senator, during which time he studied law and was elected to the Ohio bar in 1861. That year, Garfield joined the **Union Army** and was quickly promoted to **Colonel**. He fought at **Shiloh** (1862) and **Chickamauga** (1863). And he was a **major general** in 1863 when Lincoln persuaded him to take a seat in the **U.S. House of Representatives** while still in the army. James Garfield noted that Lincoln was "distressedly homely" but had a "look of transparent, genuine goodness that makes you trust and love him." As Chair of the Military Affairs Committee, Garfield proposed legislation to establish the precursor to the Reserve Officer Training Corps **(ROTC)** on college campuses. He went on to become **House Minority Leader**. He supported **hard currency** (money based on the gold standard). He also served on the House commission to decide the disputed 1876 presidential election.

In 1880, after serving **eighteen years** in Congress, Garfield was a **senator-elect** when he became the **Republican nominee** for president. When the Republican Party met to select a presidential candidate, they discovered they could not agree. Some chose President Grant for a third term; others wanted Maine legislator James Blaine. The **convention voted thirty-five times** without a final candidate. Garfield won on the next ballot because Blaine dropped out and gave his votes to Garfield. **Chester Arthur** was chosen as the vice-presidential candidate, as he was a strong political leader and a powerful customs collector from New

JAMES A. GARFIELD (20TH PRESIDENT)

York. Arthur stated that "such an honor and opportunity comes to very few of the millions of Americans and to that man but once. No man can refuse it, and I will not."

In the **1880 election**, Republicans **James Garfield** and **Chester Arthur** received 4,454,416 popular votes vs 4,444,952 for Democrats **Winfield Hancock** and **William English**. And Garfield and Arthur received 214 electoral votes vs 155 for Hancock and English. New York's electoral votes were the difference. Garfield was elected president and Chester Arthur was elected vice president. **James Garfield** was the first seated **House Republican member** to be elected president.

Chester Arthur was born on October 5, 1829, in Fairfield, Vermont. His father was a Baptist minister, and Arthur was the fifth of eight children. Arthur became a **lawyer** after graduating from **Union College** in 1851. At age 30 he married **Ellen Herndon**, age 22, in 1859; they had **three children** together, all before Garfield's presidency. Ellen Arthur came from a wealthy family and was very supportive of her husband's career. Unfortunately, Ellen died on January 12, 1880, at age 42 of pneumonia. She died a year and a half before Garfield's presidency.

Garfield was 49 years old on the rainy date of his inauguration. In his March 4, **1881, inaugural address**, held in the Senate Chamber, Garfield stated, "The elevation of the negro race from slavery to the full rights of citizenship is the most important political change we know since the doctrine of the U.S. Constitution in 1788." Garfield was the third **Civil War general** in a row to become president, following Grant and Hayes. He was the **first ordained preacher** ever to be elected president of the United States, and his mother was the first mother to attend her son's inauguration. His nickname was "**the Preacher President." His notable sayings include, "The truth will set you free, but first it will make you miserable," **"We cannot overestimate the fervent love of liberty,"** and **"Pluck is better than luck."** For his support of Garfield, New York Senator Conkling received Garfield's promise to appoint several of the senator's favorites to key federal jobs.

Garfield's initial **cabinet** included **Vice President** Chester Arthur, **Secretary of State** James Blaine, **Secretary of the Treasury** William Windom, **Secretary of War** Robert Todd Lincoln, **Attorney General** Isaac Wayne MacVeagh, **Secretary of the Navy** William Hunt, **Postmaster General** Thomas James, and **Secretary of the Interior** Samuel Kirkwood. It included none of U.S. Senator Roscoe Conkling's candidates, breaking Garfield's promise.

Two **major** issues faced the new president. One was the **Star Route** scandal, in which western postal officials and stagecoach operations agreed to steal tax collections. The second was the **patronage system,** which overlooked men of merit for those with political contacts. Garfield solved neither before he was assassinated, but he initiated an investigation into the first. Congress later passed the **1883 Pendleton Civil Service Reform Act**, which mandated competition for civil service jobs.

Charles Guiteau shot Garfield in a Washington, D.C. train station on July 2, 1881. With Garfield was **Robert Todd Lincoln,** President Lincoln's son, who was **Garfield's Secretary of War**. Garfield said, "He must have been insane to shoot me." Garfield was placed on a mattress, taken by an ambulance, and driven to the Executive Mansion, where he was carried up to his bedroom. Independence Day was cancelled for the first time.

Charles Guiteau was sexually frustrated because he was unable to find a lover in the Oneida utopian community. He went to Chicago as a traveling preacher, where he contracted **syphi-**

lis after frequent use of prostitutes. This may have led him to believe he deserved a political appointment, and he went to the White House and told Garfield of this view. Garfield turned the matter over to James Blaine, his Secretary of State. After months of daily visits to Blaine's office in the White House, Guiteau decided Garfield was the problem and had to be eliminated, so he bought a handgun. Guiteau stated, "Killing the president was a **political necessity.**" Guiteau was arrested and confessed that he shot Garfield.

Congress made no pay changes during Garfield's brief period of presidency.

For weeks, Garfield seemed to be recovering, but then in mid-August his condition worsened, and minor improvements were followed by setbacks. Before dying, Garfield stated, "We cannot overestimate the fervent love of liberty, the intelligent courage, and the sum of common sense with which our fathers made the great experiment of self-government." On September 19, 1881, **Garfield died** at age 49, having lost 80 pounds due to blood poisoning from several surgeries performed with unsterilized instruments and unwashed hands. One of the doctors was **Alexander Graham Bell**, whose electrical device was unable to find the bullet while Garfield screamed, "Can't you stop the pain?" Garfield was two months short of age 50 at the time of his death, was the second president to be assassinated (Abraham Lincoln was the first). Guiteau was found guilty, and when about to be hanged, he stated, "I am going to the Lordy. I am so glad."

Garfield was buried in Lake View Cemetery in Cleveland, Ohio. Garfield had been in office only 199 days, the second fewest after Harrison's 32 days. Given his brief time in office, historians agree not to rate Garfield's performance as president. With Garfield's death, Chester Arthur became president.

Lucretia Garfield contracted **malaria** following her husband's inauguration and almost died. Following her husband's death, she received an **annual presidential widow's** pension ($5,000). Earlier widows also then received the same pension. Several former first ladies reached out to Lucretia as members of the sorority of surviving presidential spouses. Lucretia died on March 14, 1918, at age 85, and she was buried alongside her husband.

Key Events

Due to the brief period of his presidency, only the opening of **Marshall Field's** department stores (1881); the formation of the **Barnum & Bailey Circus** (1881); and Clara Barton's founding of the **Red Cross** (1881) happened during Garfield's term of office.

Chester A. Arthur
(21st President)

September 19, 1881 – March 4, 1885

Chester Alan Arthur was born on October 5, 1829, in Fairfield, Vermont, to Malvina and Reverend William Arthur. Chester's father taught school in Quebec, Canada, then eloped with Malvina Stone to Vermont. In 1828, he became a Baptist. Arthur was the fifth of eight children. He had six sisters, Almeda, Ann Eliza, Jane, Malvina, Mary, and Regina, and one brother, William. Arthur was homeschooled before going to a school in Schenectady, where he edited the school's newspaper.

After high school, Chester, now known as "Chet," enrolled in the Lyceum in Schenectady, New York, but after a year he switched to the men-only **Union College** in the same city. It was a prestigious institution of some 300 students. Chet opted for a classical curriculum and later a course on independent thinking. He did well in school and was liked by his classmates. He was also president of a debating society and edited the school's newspaper. Chet graduated **Phi Beta Kappa** in 1851 and took a job as a teacher. He then went on to study **law**, was admitted to the New York bar in 1854, and began his law practice in **New York City**. Arthur became interested in politics and the antics of publisher Boss Tweed, head of the New York Democratic Party. Tweed could get a person select jobs.

At age 30 he married **Ellen Herndon**, age 22, in 1859. They had **three children** together, all before his presidency: **Ellen, William,** and **Chester Jr**. Ellen Herndon came from a wealthy family and was very supportive of her husband's career.

In 1859, Arthur joined the New York State militia. When the **Civil War** started, Arthur enlisted and served as **quarter master general** of New York State in Albany, New York, providing supplies to the troops and eventually rising to the rank of **brigadier general**. He returned to New York City to resume practicing law in 1863 and became a strong anti-slavery advocate, supporting both Lincoln and Grant. The latter named Arthur **Customs Collector of the Port of New York** in 1871. The Custom House collected over 75% of America's import taxes. As Customs Collector in 1873, Arthur was paid $50,000 a year (the same as the U.S. President). Members of Congress were paid $5,000 a year, Supreme Court Associate Justices were paid $10,000 a year, and Chief Justice was paid $10,500 a year. President Hayes removed Arthur from the Customs Collector position in an attempt to end the spoils system. Although a believer in the spoils system, Hayes was considered honest in business dealings.

Ellen Arthur died of pneumonia on January 12, 1880. She was 42 years old.

CHESTER A. ARTHUR (21ST PRESIDENT)

In 1880, the Republican Party named Chester Arthur to be the running mate of James Garfield. In the 1880 election, **James Garfield** and **Chester Arthur** defeated Democrats **Winfield Scott Hancock** and **William H. English** in both the electoral and popular votes. Garfield had been elected president and Arthur had been election vice president.

In mid-1881, unmarried 31-year-old **Julia Sand** sent a letter to Vice President Arthur telling him that "the hours of Garfield's life are numbered, and you are his successor." As Garfield's vice president, Arthur ascended to the presidency at the time of Garfield's death, September 19, 1881. It was the second ascension following a presidential assassination (Johnson was the first), and Arthur went into a closet and cried.

Arthur was 51 years old on the date of his inauguration, which he held in New York City, the first to do so since George Washington. Arthur added, "**so help me God**" to the **oath of office** in 1881. In his September 19, **1881, inaugural address**, Arthur stated, "Men may die, but the fabrics of our free institutions remain unshaken." No one held the position of vice president during Arthur's presidency.

Chester Arthur is the fourth vice president (Tyler, Fillmore, and Johnson preceded him) to assume the presidency upon the death of his president (James Garfield). Chester Arthur was the seventh vice president to become President (John Adams, Thomas Jefferson, Martin Van Buren, John Tyler, Millard Fillmore, and Andrew Johnson preceded him).

Arthur's initial **cabinet** was a holdover of Garfield's appointments. It included **Secretary of State** James Blaine, **Secretary of the Treasury** William Windom, **Secretary of War** Robert Todd Lincoln, **Attorney General** Isaac Wayne MacVeagh, **Secretary of the Navy** William Hunt, **Postmaster General** Thomas James, and **Secretary of the Interior** Samuel Kirkwood.

Believing the Executive Mansion was shabby, Arthur refused to move in until all 132 rooms had been completely renovated by designer Louis Tiffany, son of the famous jeweler. Before that could begin, Arthur auctioned off 24 wagonloads of Executive Mansion items and had an **elevator installed**. The work was completed in late March 1882. **New china** for fourteen-course state dinners had been added, in addition to a **new bathroom** with new plumbing.

Arthur was the **perfect host** and loved entertaining. He brought his **butler** and **personal chef** with him, providing the best food and liquors. The **receptions** and **dinners** were the best Washington had seen in years. Unfortunately, Arthur had to do it all without his wife, who died a year before he became president. In honor of his wife, the place next to him on his left at dinner was always kept vacant. Arthur ordered fresh flowers every day and placed them by a photo of his late wife. Arthur asked his **sister**, Mary McElroy, to serve as **hostess** for Executive Mansion events.

Arthur took pride in his personal appearance and was **fashionably attired**. He spent considerable money on clothes (including 80 pairs of pants) and changed clothes several times during the day. He was known as "**Elegant Arthur**." He also had impeccable manners.

Julia Sand's letters to Arthur resumed, critiquing his performance, and giving him recommendations. Her health deteriorated, and she became an invalid. In 1882, she went to Saratoga Springs, New York, for the mineral springs. Before leaving, she wrote a letter telling him to veto the **Chinese Exclusion Act** (which prohibited Chinese immigration for ten years), which he did (but Congress overrode his veto). On the night of August 20, 1882, the president made a surprise visit to Ms. Sand while her brothers, mother, and a sister were with her. After an hour, he graciously left. Julia Sand died at age 83 in 1933, never disclosing the input she gave to President Arthur.

In return for Roscoe Conkling's support, in September 1882 Arthur nominated Conkling for the U.S. Supreme Court. It was confirmed, but Conkling refused the offer. After years of being New York State's Republican leader, Conkling died at age 59 on April 18, 1888.

As president, Arthur based his **appointments** on skill and experience. In December 1882, Arthur delivered his second annual message to Congress; he urged the passage of the **Pendleton Act,** which required competitive examinations for civil service jobs. They passed the act, and Arthur signed it into law on January 16, 1883. But the **1883 Pendleton Act** only applied to federal jobs in Washington, custom houses, and post offices with more than 50 employees. These were only about 10% of all federal government jobs. In **United States vs Harris** (1883), the U.S. Supreme Court ruled that Section 2 of the 1970 Enforcement Act was unconstitutional; the Fourteenth Amendment applies to state actions, and individual actions; and state governments have the power to penalize crimes, such as assault or murder. The **1883 Mongrel Tariff Act** reduced tariffs and tax rates by less than two percent on a wide variety of items.

Arthur vetoed a number of appropriations bills attempting to keep the government out of debt, but he supported building new **naval steel ships** and was called the "**Father of the Steel Navy**," making the country a major naval power. In March of 1883, Arthur got Congress to pass legislation requiring the retirement of any navy vessel with repair costs exceeding 20% of its original expense.

Arthur once said, "**Fame is a bubble that bursts too soon.**" In late 1883, Arthur spent three weeks in Yellowstone National Park. Stopping in Chicago on the way back to the White House, Arthur was met by some 10,000 people who wanted to shake his hand.

Arthur reportedly stated, "**I may be president of the United States, but my private life is nobody's damned business.**" This degree of independence lasted until after JFK's presidency. Arthur stated, "I believe reporters would rather invent a story rather than report actual information."

In **Ex parte Yarbrough** (1884), the U.S. Supreme Court ruled that under the Constitution's Article I, Section 4, the Necessary and Proper Clause of Article I, Section 8, and the Fifteenth Amendment, Congress had the authority to regulate federal elections and to pass the Enforcement Act of 1870.

After a vacation in Florida in mid-1884, President Arthur had an acute stomachache on his return to Washington. It was diagnosed as the **onset of Bright's Disease**, a chronic blood vessel inflammation of the kidneys. It caused depression, lethargy, pain, and nausea. Arthur was not nominated by the Republican party to run for re-election in 1884. He did not want it to be known to the public, but his illness was the reason he made a half-hearted attempt to compete for a second-term nomination. James Blaine won the nomination on the fourth ballot. Blaine was defeated by Democrat Grover Cleveland in the **1884 presidential election** due to Arthur's illness and waning support for the Republican Party.

Congress made no pay changes during Arthur's term of presidency.

On March 4, 1885, President Arthur watched as President-elect Grover Cleveland took the oath of office before a crowd of

CHESTER A. ARTHUR (21ST PRESIDENT)

50,000. Arthur's last official act as president was the February 21st, 1885 dedication of the Washington Monument. After leaving Washington, he returned to New York and his law practice.

Arthur died on Thursday, November 18, 1886, at age 59, in the bed he shared with his wife Ellen, who preceded him in death by nine years. His last words were, "It is time to go." Before his death, Arthur bundled up his letters and papers and burned them. President Cleveland and his cabinet arrived to pay their respects as the body laid in state at Arthur's home. The hearse made its way through 1,000 policemen and hundreds of army, marine, and navy troops on the way to the Park Avenue Church, then traveled in Cornelius Vanderbilt's private railcar to the Albany Rural Cemetery and the family plot, where he was buried alongside his wife.

The *New York Times* stated Arthur's performance "has unquestionably been more satisfactory than was expected." Others have added that Arthur proved to be an able, fair, and respected administrator. Still others give Arthur a **somewhat below average rating**.

In June 1899, a statue of Chester Arthur was placed in Madison Square, New York City.

KEY EVENTS

John D. Rockefeller's **Standard Oil Company controlled 90% of the petroleum industry**, with 40 allied companies included in the famous Standard Oil Trust (1881); J.P. Morgan stated, "If you have to ask the price of a yacht, you cannot afford it" (1881); William Bonner (aka **Billy the Kid**) was shot and killed at age 22 by **Sheriff Pat Garrett** (1881); **Billy Clanton** and the **McLaury**

brothers were shot and killed by **Doc Holliday** and the **Earp brothers** at the **OK Corral** in Tombstone, Arizona (1881); bank robber **Jesse James**, age 35, was shot in the back and killed by **Bob Ford** (1882); cattle rustler **Johnny Ringo** age 32 was shot and killed by **Doc Holliday** (1882); the return of business prosperity also led to a tripling of annual **immigrant arrivals** to about 800,000 (1882); New York City introduced the **first electric power station** (1882); the **electric fan** was invented (1882); **Northern Pacific Railroad** was operational (1882); the **financial markets** crashed (1883); **Thomas Edison** put in underground transmission in lower Manhattan for 50 customers (1883); **telephone service** began between Chicago and New York (1883); the **U.S. Mint** opened in Carson City, Nevada, to take advantage of recently discovered **Comstock Lode** in the state (1883); **Buffalo Bill Cody** opened his Wild West Show featuring cowboys and Indians, including Sioux **Chief Sitting Bull** (1883); **Bat Masterson** and **Wyatt Earp** returned to Dodge City to restore peace (1883); the **Brooklyn Bridge** opened (1883); **Jay Gould** sold the *New York World* to **Joseph Pulitzer** (1883); **standard time zones** were established in the U.S. (1883); **Vaudeville** was introduced with the opening of the **Boston Gaiety Theatre** (1883); **Geronimo** and his **Chiricahua Apaches** were defeated (1883); **Daimler** introduced the **motorcycle** (1884); Lewis Waterman patented a **pen with an ink supply** (1884); **John Patterson** set up the **National Cash Register** Company (1884); the **Ringling Brothers Circus** gave their first performance (1884); **telephone service** began **between New York and Boston** (1884); the famed **Dakota apartment building** opened in New York City (1884); the first amusement park **roller coaster** opened in Coney Island, New York (1884); and Mark Twain wrote, *The Adventures of Huckleberry Finn* (1884).

GROVER CLEVELAND
(22ND PRESIDENT)

MARCH 4, 1885 – MARCH 4, 1889

Grover Cleveland was born on March 18, 1837, in Caldwell, New Jersey, to Ann and Richard Falley Cleveland. Grover was one of nine children. He had three brothers, Lewis, Richard, and William, and five sisters, Ann, Mary, Margaret, Susan, and Rose. His father was a **Presbyterian minister** whose death in 1853 ended Grover's college plans. With little formal education, Grover studied law and passed the New York bar in 1859, setting up a law practice. Grover avoided being drafted in the Civil War by paying an immigrant $150 to take his place. He is the fourth president to have **no military service**. In 1870, he served as a **sheriff** in Erie County, New York, during which time he hung two criminals. In 1874, Grover Cleveland met **Maria Halpin**. She recognized the county sheriff and allowed him to take her home, where he allegedly raped her.

After serving as sheriff, Cleveland returned to his law practice and was elected **mayor of Buffalo** in 1881. He was nicknamed "the veto mayor" for exposing graft and saving the city more than $1 million in his first year in office. In 1883, he was elected governor of New York. In 1884, the Democrats selected Cleveland as their presidential candidate, largely because of his New York politics. Thomas Hendricks was selected as his running mate, primarily because of his several unsuccessful attempts at running for president.

Having fathered an **illegitimate child** ten years earlier, Cleveland had to overcome a Republican Blaine campaign attack of "Ma, ma, where's my pa? Gone to the Executive Mansion, ha, ha, ha." Cleveland admitted to having the child. His campaign response was "Above all tell the truth." This seemed to blunt Blaine's attack. **Cleveland's presidential campaign** slogan was, "**Public office is a public trust.**"

In the **1884 election**, Democrats **Grover Cleveland** and **Thomas Hendricks** received 4,874,986 popular votes vs 4,851,981 for Republicans **James Blaine** and **John Logan**. Cleveland and Hendricks received 219 electoral votes to 182 for Blaine and Logan. The victory was due in large part to New York's giving Cleveland 36 of its 37 electoral votes. If women could have voted, the outcome might have been different, given Cleveland's illegitimate child. Ohio Senator Allen Thurman was selected by Cleveland to be vice president when Thomas Hendricks died in his first year of office.

Thomas Hendricks was born on September 7, 1819, in Zanesville, Ohio, but soon after the family moved to Indiana, where they worked on a farm. Thomas attended local schools and then went to the Indiana College of Hanover. After graduation, he studied **law** under an uncle in Pennsylvania, then returned to practice law in Shelbyville, Indiana, in 1843. Thomas got interested in politics and was elected to the **Indiana House of Representatives** in 1848 and two years later to the **U.S. House of Representatives** as a Democrat. He lost his bid for re-election because he believed states should determine if slavery should be permitted. In 1855, he accepted a position in President Pierce's Interior Department. In 1859, he ran unsuccessfully for governor of Indiana, but in 1862 he was selected by the Indiana legislature to fill an open **U.S. Senate** position. He lost the 1868 presidential nomination and returned to practice **law** in Indiana. He was elected **Governor** in 1872 and again in 1880, and in 1884 he was selected to be the running mate of Grover Cleveland. But within nine months of the election, he died in his sleep on November 25, 1885.

Cleveland was **47 years of age** on the date of his inauguration. He was the first Democrat elected president since Buchanan in 1856. In his March 4, **1885, inaugural speech**, Cleveland stated, "Every citizen owes to the country a vigilant watch and close scrutiny of its public servants," adding "The ship of democracy may sink through the mutiny of those on board." Cleveland also said, "Though the people support the government, the **government should not support the people**."

Grover's first **cabinet** included **Vice President** Thomas Hendricks, **Secretary of State** Thomas Bayard, **Secretary of the Treasury** Daniel Manning, **Secretary of War** William Endicott,

Attorney General Augustus Garland, **Secretary of the Navy** William Whitney, **Postmaster General** William Vilas, **Secretary of the Interior** Lucius Lamar, and **Secretary of Agriculture** Norman Colman. Cleveland **added the agriculture post** due to the importance of food to the economy and the fact that farmers were struggling to survive.

Grover Cleveland met **Frances Folsom** when she was nine years old. Asked if he would ever marry, he replied, "I am only waiting for my wife to grow up." Grover was a friend and law partner of Frances' father, Oscar Folsom. In 1886, they married when she was 21 and he was 49. He was the first, and only, president to be married in the Executive Mansion, although John Tyler was the first to marry while in office. The Clevelands went on to have **five children**: Esther, Francis Grover, Marion, Richard, and Ruth. Mrs. Cleveland said, "I can wish the women of our country no greater blessing than that their husbands may be as kind, attentive, considerate and affectionate as mine."

The First Lady loved to entertain. She held **two receptions** in the Executive Mansion **every week**. One was on Saturday, when women who had to work, could attend. The other was early in the week. Although Frances took a temperance vow at age 14, she served alcohol in the Executive Mansion.

On October 28, 1886, Cleveland dedicated the **Statue of Liberty** in New York Harbor.

Grover was very fond of **good bourbon**. He also **loved to eat**, earning him the nickname "**Uncle Jumbo**." Grover personally answered the **phone** in the Executive Mansion. During his first term, he **vetoed 414 pieces of legislation**, more than his 21 predecessors combined. This earned him the nickname "the veto president."

In **Santa Clara County vs Southern Pacific Railroad Co.** (1886), the U.S. Supreme Court ruled that corporations are "persons" under the Fourteenth Amendment's Equal Protection Clause and are entitled to its protections.

The **1886 Presidential Succession Act** removed the candidates from the 1792 Act, inserting four Cabinet secretaries in the following order: State, Treasury, War, and Attorney General; the **1887 Interstate Commerce Act** created the Interstate Commerce Commission, the first federal regulatory agency; and the **1887 Dawes Act** allowed Native Americans to buy lots on tribal lands. The intent was to encourage them to move from tribal culture to private citizenship.

In **Kidd vs Pearson** (1888), the U.S. Supreme Court ruled that state statutes that concern manufacturing and that do not conflict with Congress's power to regulate commerce between the states are valid.

In the **1888 presidential election**, Democrats **Grover Cleveland** and **Allen Thurman** won the **popular vote** over Republicans **Benjamin Harrison** and **Levi Morton**, 5,540,309 to 5,444,337, but lost the **electoral vote**, 233 to 168. Therefore, Harrison not Cleveland, was elected president. Tariffs were the major issue. Harrison was for them; Cleveland was not. In the Executive Mansion after the 1888 loss, Mrs. Cleveland told the Executive Mansion staff, "**I want you to take care of all the furniture. I want to find everything just as it is now when we come back again.**" They came back in 1892, when Cleveland won re-election. Meanwhile he resumed his law practice in Buffalo. Grover also **liked to smoke**. This resulted in a **malignant tumor** in his mouth requiring the removal of a portion of his upper jaw in 1893.

Congress made no pay changes during Cleveland's term of presidency.

Most historians give Cleveland **an average rating**.

KEY EVENTS

France showed its desire to remain friends with the United States by sending it the **Statue of Liberty for the New York Harbor** (1885); Chicago's 10-floor **Home Insurance Company** was considered the first skyscraper (1885); the **American Telephone and Telegraph** was formed as a subsidiary of Bell Telephone Company (1885); the **National Cash Register** Company began business (1885); **Honeywell** opened (1885); **Philip Morris** began (1885); about 70 percent of U.S. oil was exported (1885); the **linotype machine** was invented (1885); the Apache leader **Geronimo** was captured and sent to live in Florida (1886); the weather-predicting groundhog **Punxsutawney Phil** made his first appearance (1886); **Coca-Cola** was started (1886); the **motion picture film** was developed (1886); **Johnson & Johnson** began business (1886); the cosmetics company **Avon** was formed (1886); the **tuxedo** was named after Tuxedo Park, NY, where it was introduced (1886); the price of oil fell from $27 to $10 a barrel (1886); New York City held its **first tickertape parade**, celebrating the arrival of the **Statue of Liberty** (1886); President Cleveland reclaimed over **80 million acres of unused railroad land** (1887); the **electric trolley** was introduced in Richmond, Virginia (1887); what would become **Bristol-Myers Squibb** started (1887); dentist, gambler, and gunfighter **Doc Holliday** died of tuberculosis at age 36 (1887); the **Baby Ruth** candy bar was introduced, named after either the baseball player Babe Ruth or President Cleveland's daughter (1887); the **Great**

Blizzard struck the Eastern United States causing great damage and over 400 deaths (1888); **Ernest Thayer** published the poem "**Casey at the Bat**" (1888); what would become **Abbott Laboratories** was formed (1888); the **National Geographic Society** was formed (1888); George Eastman introduced the **Kodak Camera** and formed the Eastman Kodak Company (1888); and **Edison General Electric Company** was formed from the **Edison Electric Light** Company, with **Thomas Edison** holding only 10% of the equity (the rest was held by **J.P. Morgan's** Drexel, Morgan and Villard) (1888).

Benjamin Harrison (23ʳᴰ President)

March 4, 1889 – March 4, 1893

Benjamin Harrison was born on August 20, 1833, in North Bend, Ohio on a modest farm, to John Scott and Elizabeth Irwin Harrison. Harrison was one of 13 children. Harrison's **great-grandfather** signed the Declaration of Independence, his **grandfather** was the ninth president of the United States, and his **father** worked on a farm and was a two-term congressman. Benjamin worked on the farm, enjoyed hunting and swimming, and was tutored at home. After a brief period at **Farmers College**, Harrison moved to **Miami University** in Oxford, Ohio. He enjoyed debates and was an excellent student, graduating third in his class in 1852. At age 20 he married **Caroline Scott**, age 20, in 1853. They met while he was taking a mathematics course from her father at Miami University. They had three children, Russell, Mary, and one who died at birth. He went on to become a **lawyer** after being admitted to the Ohio bar in 1854. In 1862, he formed a company of volunteer **infantrymen** to fight in the Civil War. He was **commissioned** a colonel in the army and left a brigadier general when the war ended. Harrison returned to his **law practice** in Indianapolis and became a Republican. He ran for governor of Indiana in 1876 but lost the election. But in 1880, he won a seat in the **U.S. Senate**, where he championed the rights of Civil War veterans, homesteaders, and Native Americans.

Harrison received the Republican nomination for president and Levi Morton received the nomination for vice president. Harrison's campaign was built around **tariffs** designed to protect American farmers and manufacturing. He also advocated for **pensions** for war veterans. Believing it unhealthy, Benjamin **refused to shake hands**, and he was known as the "**human iceberg**" for his behavior in social settings and his lack of charisma. In the **1888 election**, Republicans **Benjamin Harrison** and **Levi Morton** received 5,444,337 popular votes vs 5,540,309 for Democrats President **Grover Cleveland** and **Allen Thurman**. Harrison and Morton received 233 electoral votes to 168 for incumbents Cleveland and Thurman. Harrison was elected president and Morton was elected vice president. Harrison was the last bearded president.

Levi Morton was born on May 16, 1824, in Shoreham, Vermont. He attended local schools, but his parents were unable to afford college, so Levi **worked in stores** and became a **schoolteacher**. He went on to become an **importer** for the New England textile industry in 1854. In 1863, he opened a **banking house** on Wall Street. By the early 1870's, with the opening of another banking house in London, he became one of America's **wealthiest** and most influential businessmen. In 1876, he became the Financial Chairman of the Republican Party. During his four-year term as vice president, Morton was often at odds with President Harrison; he therefore dropped from the 1892 ticket and went on to become governor of New York from 1895 to 1897. He then returned to the banking business and merged his company with **J.P. Morgan**. Morton died on May 16, 1920, at the age of 96. He was the first vice president to **die on his birthday** and was buried in Rhinebeck, New York.

Harrison was 55 years old when inaugurated. In his March 4, **1889, inaugural address**, he stated that "an unlawful expedient cannot become a permanent condition of government" and "the bud of victory is always the truth." The 23rd president also stated, "The decent and manly examination of the acts of government should not only be tolerated but encouraged."

Harrison's initial **cabinet** included **Vice President** Levi Morton, **Secretary of State** James Blaine, **Secretary of the Treasury** William Windom, **Secretary of War** Redfield Proctor, **Attorney General** William Miller, **Secretary of the Navy** Benjamin Tracy, **Postmaster General** John Wanamaker, **Secretary of the Interior** John Noble, and **Secretary of Agriculture** Jeremiah Rusk.

Harrison had many **nicknames**. Because he was only 5 and a half feet tall, he was called **"Little Ben"** in the Civil War. In politics, he was called **"Kid Gloves"** for his mild manners and the **"Centennial President"** for taking office 100 years after George Washington.

On May 31, 1889, the Capital was flooded with sewage from the **Johnstown Flood** and some 2,200 lost their lives. Also in

1889, Harrison was the first president to have a **recording made of his voice**. It was made while he attended the Pan-American Congress.

At the Executive Mansion, Caroline enjoyed **entertaining**, which included bringing back dancing, banned since the Polks, and **redecorating** the building. **Electric lights** were installed in the Executive Mansion in 1889. But President Harrison and his wife were afraid of being electrocuted by the new electrical wiring and had the servants turn the lights on and off.

In 1890, Harrison gave 140 speeches in a month's time. Also in 1890, in **Davis vs Beacon**, the U.S. Supreme Court ruled that federal laws that ban polygamy do not violate the right to free exercise of religion under the First Amendment's Free Exercise Clause.

Three key laws were enacted in **1890**: the **Dependent Pension Act**, which provided monthly payments to honorably discharged veterans, their spouse, and their children; the **Sherman Anti-Trust Act**, which prohibited commercial monopolies; and the **McKinley Act**, which increased duties on over 100 items. One law was enacted in 1891, the **National Reserve Act**, which set up national parks. Although Harrison's term of office was in peacetime, he oversaw over a billion dollars in spending, which included twenty new naval ships.

In the **1892 election**, Republicans **Benjamin Harrison** and **Whitelaw Reid** received 5,176,108 popular votes to 5,556,918 for Democrats **Grover Cleveland** and **Adlai Stevenson**. And Cleveland and Stevenson received 277 electoral votes to 145 for Harrison and Reid. Populists James Weaver and James Field received 1,041,028 popular votes and 22 electoral votes. Harrison had been defeated; Cleveland had been re-elected president. After losing the presidency, Harrison returned to his law practice and wrote several books.

He **married** Caroline's niece, **Mary Dimmick** (25 years his junior), in 1896 after Caroline's death, in 1892. Mary and Benjamin had one child, Elizabeth. Benjamin and Mary enjoyed codfish balls, flapjacks, fried steak, and other simple foods.

Congress made no pay changes during Harrison's term of presidency.

Before **Harrison died** on March 13, 1901, at age 67 from pneumonia, he said, "Are there any doctors here?" He was buried in Indianapolis. Mary died on January 5, 1948, at age 89 and was buried with her husband.

Most historians give Harrison an **average rating**.

Key Events

The **Tower Building** in New York City qualified as the first true skyscraper (1889); the **Wall Street Journal** began publication (1889); **Berkshire Hathaway** was formed (1889); the **Oklahoma Territories** were opened to settlers, with those who entered early illegally called "**sooners**" (1889); six **states were admitted to the Union**, raising the total to 44: **North Dakota** (1889), **South Dakota** (1889), **Montana** (1889), **Washington** (1889), **Idaho** (1890), and **Wyoming** (1890); through patronage, the Irish began to dominate civil service jobs (1890); in Topeka, Kansas, the **People's Party** (aka the Populist Party) was formed with the intention of freeing the industrial class from abuses by corporations headed by greedy capitalists (1890); Harrison's

Congress was the first to spend more than $1 billion; **J.P. Morgan** dominated the insurance industry by owning several large companies (1890); **American Tobacco** and **Caterpillar** were formed (1890); **peanut butter** was developed (1890); **Yosemite National Park** was created (1890); the Battle at **Wounded Knee** reservation, resulting in over 350 Lakota dead, along with 25 U.S. soldiers, was the last major battle between U.S. troops and Native Americans (1890); the **Church of Latter Day Saints** outlawed plural marriages (1890); iron ore deposits were discovered in Mesabi Range, Minnesota (1890); the **first recording studio** opened in New York City (1890); **Emily Dickinson's** poems were published (1890); the **U.S. population** reached almost 63 million (1890); Sicilian gangs in New York called themselves **Cosa Nostra** ("our thing") (1890); sharpshooter **Annie Oakley** joined the Buffalo Bill Cody Wild West Show (1891); **Carnegie Hall** opened in New York City (1891); **Madison Square Garden** opened as a sports arena in New York City (1891); **Leland Stanford** founded a university in his name in California (1891); the **riverboat *General Slocum*** caught fire on the East River in New York City, killing over 1,000 people (1891); the **Merck** Company and **Wm. Wrigley** started up (1891); **Rockefeller's Standard Oil** Company controlled 70% of the world oil market (1891); the first electric car was introduced (1891); **James Naismith** invented basketball in Springfield, Massachusetts, using a peach basket (1892); what would become **CVS Caremark** started up (1892); **Willis Carrier** invented air conditioning (1892); toothpaste in a tube was patented (1892); the **gas-powered automobile** was invented (1892); **General Electric** was founded from the former Edison Company with **Charles Coffin** as president, a position he held for some 35 years (1892); a flood of **immi-**

grants since 1880 resulted in a 50% increase in the population (1892); twenty-seven million attended the **Chicago World's Fair,** known as the Columbian Exposition to celebrate **Columbus's discovery of America** (1892); **Ellis Island** was opened in New York City to process immigrants (1892); the **Dalton gang** was killed while robbing a Kansas City bank (1892); an average worker's pay was $10 a week, while **J.D. Rockefeller** made $10 million a year, a multiple of about 20,000 to 1 (1892); Andrew Carnegie's endowment created over 3,000 public libraries in addition to the **Carnegie Music Hall** in New York City (1892); James Corbett defeated John L. Sullivan to become the world's **first heavyweight boxing champion** (1892); **President Harrison** was the first president to attend a professional **baseball game**, watching the Cincinnati Reds defeat the Washington Senators, 7 runs to 4 (1892); the **nationwide unemployment** rose to 4 million (1893); and falling steel prices combined with a declining agricultural output led to a drop in the stock market and the onset of the **Panic of 1893.**

Grover Cleveland
(24th President)

March 4, 1893 – March 4, 1897

In the **1888 presidential election**, Democrats **Grover Cleveland** and **Allen Thurman** won the popular vote over Republicans **Benjamin Harrison** and **Levi Morton** (5,540,309 to 5,444,337) but lost the electoral vote (233 to 168). Therefore, Harrison, not Cleveland, was elected president and Morton was elected vice president. Following his defeat in the **1888 presidential election**, as they were leaving the Executive Mansion, Grover's wife, Frances said, "We'll be back in four years so keep everything in good shape." Grover and Frances moved to New York City, where he practiced law and stayed active in Democratic politics. Grover was also very critical of President Harrison's actions.

In the **1892 presidential election**, Democrats **Grover Cleveland** and **Adlai Stevenson** defeated Republicans President **Benjamin Harrison** and Vice President **Whitelaw Reid** 277 to 145 in the electoral college. Thereby making Cleveland the 23rd individual becoming the 24th president. Cleveland and Vice President Adlai Stevenson received 5,556,918 popular votes, and President Harrison and Whitelaw Reid received 5,176,108 popular votes. Populist James Weaver and James Field received 1,041,022 popular votes and 22 electoral votes. Cleveland is the **first president to serve two non-consecutive terms of office**. He served as the 22nd president from 1885 to 1889 and the 24th from 1893 to 1897. Cleveland was 55 years old on the date of his second inauguration. In his March 4, **1893, inaugural address**, Cleveland stated, "Nothing is more vital to our supremacy as a nation and to the beneficent purposes of our Government than a sound and stable currency," and "Above all, tell the truth."

Adlai Stevenson was born on October 23, 1835, on his family's **tobacco farm** in Christian County, Kentucky. The family moved in 1852 to Bloomington, Illinois, where they ran a small mill. After graduating from **Centre College**, Adlai studied law and was admitted to the **Illinois** bar in 1858. In 1874, Stevenson was elected to the **U.S. House of Representatives** from Illinois. After two years, he was appointed to the powerful position of **Assistant U.S. Postmaster,** where he hired 50,000 Democrats to replace the Republican previous job holders to reward them for supporting Cleveland's presidential campaign. When Cleveland was again nominated for the Democratic presidential position in 1891, Grover nominated Stevenson for his running mate. Later, Cleveland and Stevenson disagreed on many issues. In 1900, Stevenson received the vice-presidential nomination alongside presidential nominee William Jennings Bryan, but they lost to

William McKinley and Theodore Roosevelt. At age 73, Stevenson ran for Illinois governor and lost. He died on June 14, 1914, in Chicago, where he was buried. His **grandson**, also named Adlai, was the unsuccessful Democratic presidential candidate in 1952 and 1956, losing both times to Dwight D. Eisenhower.

In 1893, Cleveland repealed the **Sherman Silver Purchase Act** that put America on a **silver standard** with the issuance of certificates rather than coins. The act led to the **Panic of 1893** due to the drop in the value of the dollar and set off a stock market crash throwing the country into a **major** depression. Over 20% of the U.S.'s 15 million workers lost their jobs in 1894, leading to a **march on the Capitol** by the unemployed. With **20% unemployment** and **hundreds of failed banks**, the country would not recover for seven years. The financial crisis caused a heavy drain on the Treasury's gold reserves, prompting many to argue for the use of silver. When the U.S. Treasury gold reserves fell to $10 million, J.P. Morgan sent in $65 million in exchange for government bonds, saving the banks from further major withdrawals.

Cleveland's **initial cabinet in his second term** of office included **Vice President** Adlai Stevenson, **Secretary of State** Walter Grisham, **Secretary of the Treasury** John Carlisle, **Secretary of War** Daniel Lamont, **Attorney General** Richard Olney, **Secretary of the Navy** Hilary Herbert, **Postmaster General** Wilson Bissel, **Secretary of the Interior** Hoke Smith, and **Secretary of Agriculture** Julius Morton.

Probably Cleveland's **greatest achievement** was breaking the Pullman railroad strike in 1894 by sending federal troops to Chicago, however the move was very unpopular with the working class. That same year, he created **Labor Day** as a federal holiday to appease the unions.

The **1894 Revenue Act** restored a federal income tax of 2% on income over $2,000 a year. In **Pollock vs Farmers Loan & Trust** (1895), the U.S. Supreme Court ruled that the **1894 Tax Act** was unconstitutional. In the **United States vs E.C. Knight Co** (1895), the U.S. Supreme Court ruled that the **1890 Sherman Antitrust Act** applied only to actual interstate commerce. In **Plessy vs Fergusson** (1896), the U.S. Supreme Court ruled that equal but separate accommodations did not violate the **14th Amendment**.

In 1895, Cleveland's portrait was put on a **$1,000 Federal Reserve Note** used in banking transactions rather than in general circulation. Cleveland was affectionately known as **Uncle Jumbo** due to his weight, caused by lots of beer and rich food.

The **Dow Jones Industrial Average (DJIA)** was established by **Charles Dow** and **Edward Jones** in 1896. It used **12 stocks** to give investors an indication of what was happening in the stock market. Those companies were American Cotton Oil, American Sugar, American Tobacco, Chicago Gas, Distilling and Cattle Feeding, General Electric, Laclede Gas, National Lead, North American Co., Tennessee Coal & Iron, U.S. Leather, and U.S. Rubber. In 1916, it expanded to 20 companies and in 1928 it expanded to 30 where it remains. **DJIA is price weighted**. A stock selling at $80 a share will have twice the weight of a share selling at $40.

Congress made no pay changes during Cleveland's term of presidency.

Grover sought a third term, but the **Panic of 1893** and two recessions defeated his attempt. When the Democrats nominated **William Jennings Bryan** for the **1896 election** instead of Grover, he and his wife retired to their Princeton, New Jersey home and he became a trustee of Princeton University. Grover also remained outspoken on political issues. Cleveland **died of a heart attack** on June 24, 1908, at age 71. His last words were, "**I have tried so hard to do right.**" Grover was buried in Princeton Cemetery in Princeton, New Jersey. Five years after Grover's death, Frances married a Princeton archeology professor. She died at age 83 in 1947.

Most historians gave Cleveland an **average performance rating**.

Key Events

Richard Sears and Alvah Roebuck formed **Sears, Roebuck & Company** (1893); the zipper was patented (1893); with the **United States Treasury** facing a drain on gold supplies, billionaire **J.P. Morgan** bailed them out (1893); the **Mormon Temple** was dedicated in Salt Lake City (1893); an army of unemployed workers led by Jacob Coxey marched on Washington, D.C. (1894); the telephone patent expired (1894); Marconi invented the **wireless telegraph** including the radio (1894); Kellogg introduced cold **cereal flakes** (1894); the **United States Golf Association** was formed (1894); **Fredericka Mandelbaum**, reportedly, the first organized crime boss in New York City, died at age 68 (1894); Milton Hershey started the **Hershey Chocolate Company** (1894); Thomas Edison revealed the **motion picture kinetoscope** invention (1894); the **National Association of Manufacturers** was formed, favoring the "**open shop**" where unions could not force union membership, unlike the "**closed shop**" (1895); **Frederick Taylor** introduced "**scientific management**," stating that time and motion studies would benefit both worker and company (1895); Stephen Crane published *The Red Badge of Courage* (1895); Ford built the **first automobile**, "the quadrangle" (1896); Samuel Insell introduced the **first hydroelectric generator** to produce alternating-current electricity (1896); a major **gold discovery in Alaska** helped neutralize those who advocated unlimited silver coinage to solve the country's problems (1896); **Utah** was admitted as the 45th state (1896); the *New York Times* was purchased by publisher Adolph Ochs (1896); **Mount Denali** ("Great One") was renamed **Mt McKinley** (1896); **Butch Cassidy** and the **Sundance Kid** formed the **Wild Bunch** group of bank robbers and rail train highwaymen (1896); John Phillip Sousa composed "**The Stars and Stripes Forever**" (1896); the **DJIA** closed at 40.46 (1896); the first **Boston Marathon** was won by John McDermott (1897); and **business leaders** during the period were Andrew Carnegie (steel and libraries), J.P. Morgan (banking), and J.D. Rockefeller (oil) (1897).

William McKinley
(25ᵀᴴ President)

March 4, 1897 – September 14, 1901

William McKinley was born on January 29, 1843, in Niles, Ohio, to William Sr. and Nancy Allison McKinley. William's father ran an iron foundry, and both of his grandfathers fought in the Civil War. William was the seventh of nine children. He had three brothers, Abner, David, and James, and five sisters, Abigail, Anna, Helen, Mary, and Sarah. William was **homeschooled** and was responsible for taking care of the family cattle. Later he attended the **Poland Academy**, where he became president of the school's debate team. Later still, he attended **Allegheny College** but dropped out because of poor health. When the **Civil War** broke out, William enlisted as a private in the **Union Army** in 1861 and fought in a number of battles.

He served under **Colonel Rutherford B. Hayes**, the future 19th president of the United States. By the end of the war, McKinley had reached the rank of major. McKinley left the service and enrolled in the **Albany Law School**, passed the bar exam in 1867 (aided by a photographic memory), and practiced law in Canton, Ohio until being elected to the **U.S. House of Representatives** in 1877, where he served fourteen years. McKinley gained a reputation as a champion of individual rights and protected American businesses through tariffs. He was elected to **governor of Ohio** in 1892 and served two terms before becoming president of the United States.

At age 28, he married **Ida Saxton**, age 23 in 1871. They had **two daughters** together, **Katherine** and **Ida**; unfortunately, both died before age five. William and Ida met while she was working at a bank where he had an account. Ida McKinley was an **epileptic**. When she had a seizure, her husband draped a handkerchief over her face. Additionally, she had a compromised immune system and nerve damage to her left leg. Ida caused the **egret** to be listed as an endangered species because she used the feathers for her boas and her fashion choice was copied by thousands of women, resulting in the endangered listing.

William Jennings Bryan addressed the **1896 Democratic convention** with the words, "We will answer their demands for a **gold standard** by saying to them: You shall not press down upon the brow of labor this **crown of thorns**; you shall not crucify mankind upon a cross of gold." In 1896, **Republican McKinley** and his vice-presidential candidate **Garret Hobart**, had never met before becoming running partners. They were the first to use **campaign buttons**. McKinley had **three campaign slogans**: "Let Well Enough Alone," "Patriotism, Protection and Prosperity," and "Four More Years of the Full Dinner Pail." McKinley did little campaign travel, instead inviting Americans to his home in Canton, Ohio, where he campaigned from his front porch. McKinley was quite popular, especially in his home state of Ohio. Hobart convinced McKinley to **defend the gold standard**. This was a major factor in defeating William Jennings Bryan.

In the **1896 election**, Republicans **William McKinley and Garret Hobart** received 7,104,779 popular votes vs 6,509,052 for Democrats **William Jennings Bryan** and **Arthur Sewall**. McKinley and Hobart also received 271 electoral votes vs 176 for Bryan and Sewall. McKinley was elected president and Hobart was elected vice president. Upon being elected, Hobart said he would be very active as president of the Senate and would not resign from his corporate boards.

Garret Hobart was born on June 3, 1844, in Long Branch, New Jersey. He did not serve in the Civil War; instead, he graduated with honors from **Rutgers University**. He was then tutored in law and married his tutor's daughter, Jenny, in 1869. They went on to have two children. He was admitted to the bar in 1866 and entered politics to become **mayor of Paterson**, New Jersey, and later the **Speaker of the New Jersey Assembly**. Active in Republican affairs, he attended every national convention beginning in 1876. His legal work centered around railroad bankruptcies. He turned down several opportunities to run for governor, but in 1896 he was nominated to be the Republican candidate for vice president, joining presidential candidate William McKinley.

McKinley rode to his inauguration in an automobile. He was the **first president to ride in a car** to his inauguration. When McKinley took the oath of office, the economic depression that began with the **Panic of 1893** had passed and the country was on the path to prosperity. Unlike his immediate predecessors, McKinley benefitted from a period of growth and prosperity that came to be called the **Gilded Age**. The Republicans had control of both the House and the Senate.

McKinley was 54 years old on the date of his inauguration. In his March 4, **1897, inaugural address**, he stated, "We want no wars of conquest; we must avoid the temptation of territorial aggression." It was the **first inauguration recorded by a motion picture camera**. Then McKinley added, "War should never be entered upon until every agency of peace has failed." He was the last president to serve in the **Civil War**.

The initial McKinley **cabinet** included **Vice President** Garret Hobart, **Secretary of State** John Sherman, **Secretary of the Treasury** Lyman Gage, **Secretary of War** Russell Alger, **Attorney General** Joseph McKenna, **Secretary of the Navy** John Long, **Postmaster General** James Gary, **Secretary of the Interior** Cornelius Bliss, and **Secretary of Agriculture** James Wilson.

Hobart and his wife hosted many state dinners; his wife also assisted in many Executive Mansion events because McKinley's wife suffered from epilepsy. McKinley relied on Hobart's advice in domestic matters. But Hobart's health was failing, and he died on November 21st, fifteen months before the end of his term in office. His open position was not filled.

The **1897 Revenue Act** established a 20% tax on imported art. A year later, Congress approved the annexation of Hawaii. In **United States vs Trans-Missouri Freight Association** (1897), the U.S. Supreme Court ruled that the Sherman Antitrust

WILLIAM MCKINLEY (25TH PRESIDENT)

Act of 1890 applies to "common carriers by railroads." The **Olney-Pauncefote Treaty** with England gave both countries the opportunity to settle disputes (1897).

The **defining event** of McKinley's presidency was the sinking of the **battleship *Maine*** in Cuba's Havana Harbor, killing 266 Americans on February 15, 1898. Believing Spain was responsible, the U.S. declared war on Spain on April 24, 1898. Congress passed the **1898 Volunteer Army Act**, which called for the organization of a First Volunteer Cavalry – a "cowboy cavalry" that the press would christen "Rough Riders." Resigning his post as assistant secretary of the navy, Theodore Roosevelt took a commission as lieutenant colonel of the brigade. The **Rough Riders**, led by Teddy Roosevelt, took San Juan Hill. President Clinton awarded Roosevelt the first Medal of Honor (posthumously). **Commodore Dewey** destroyed six warships of the **Spanish fleet** in Manila Bay on May 1, 1898. The **Treaty of Paris** ended the war, and the United States acquired Cuba, Guam, the Philippines, Puerto Rico, and Wake Isle.

McKinley supported free trade, not isolation. Moving from isolationism, the country became a world military power and economic leader. He supported economic competition, believed in the gold standard, and was a champion of individual rights vs private interests. Additionally, he was a protector of American business by supporting tariffs on imported goods.

In **United States vs Wong Kim Ark** (1898), the U.S. Supreme Court ruled that the Citizenship Clause of the Fourteenth Amendment to the Constitution grants citizenship to all persons born in the United States no matter their "race or color," and includes children born to resident aliens (with a few exceptions).

McKinley reportedly could **shake 2,500 hands** in an hour with the famous McKinley grip, shaking hands with his right while his left hand took the person's elbow, pushing the person along. He noted, "Unlike any other nation, here the people rule and their will is the supreme law." He also said, "In the time of darkest defeat, victory may be nearest."

McKinley was the one of the **best-dressed** presidents, changing clothes several times a day, always with a red carnation in his lapel. And he enjoyed listening to his parrot whistle the tune "Yankee Doodle Dandy." Formalizing a tradition started by President Washington, McKinley replied to a number of letters he received, establishing the **Office of Presidential Correspondence** in 1900.

In 1899, McKinley announced his **open-door policy**, declaring China was an open international market, and advising Japan and Europe to keep their hands off China. When the **Boxer Rebellion** erupted in North China as a nationalist group formed to keep foreigners out, McKinley sent in American troops to restore order. Also in 1899, the United States acquired the **Samoan Islands** from Germany and England.

The **1900 Gold Standards Act** declared gold was the only backing of the U.S. dollar. That same year, Hawaii and Puerto Rico were approved as U.S. territories. In the *Paquete Habana* (1900), the U.S. Supreme Court ruled that "customary" international law can be used by federal courts, as "[i]nternational law is part of our law."

McKinley was confirmed at the **Republican presidential convention** with acclamation, and in the **1900 election, McKinley** and Vice President **Theodore Roosevelt** (Hobart had died) received 7,207,923 popular votes vs 6,358,134 for Democrats **William J. Bryan** and **Adlai Stevenson**. In the electoral college,

McKinley-Roosevelt received 292 votes vs 155 for Bryan-Stevenson. McKinley was elected president and Roosevelt was elected vice president. In his March 4, **1901, inaugural address**, McKinley stated, "We face at this moment a most important question – that of the future relations of the United States and Cuba." He later added, "Unlike any other nation, here the people rule and their will is the supreme law." The Republicans controlled the Senate 56-32 and the House 200-151.

Theodore Roosevelt was born on October 27, 1858, into a wealthy family in New York City, the grandson of a New York real estate millionaire and the son of a prominent philanthropist. He was a near-sighted and sickly child but grew into a strong and vigorous man. He loved physical exercise and outdoor life. He was taught at home by tutors, and in 1877, at the age of 19, he published the first of 30 books. Roosevelt graduated from **Harvard** in 1880, **married** Alice Hathaway Lee, and entered **state politics** in 1882. In 1889, he served four years on the U.S. Civil Supreme Court. In 1892, he served in the **Spanish American War** in Cuba with the "**Rough Riders**." In 1895, he was appointed **police commissioner** of New York City, where he stated, "**Speak softly and carry a big stick**." In 1897, Roosevelt served as Assistant Secretary of the Navy. While governor of New York in 1899, he had to be convinced to accept the vice-presidency in 1901. Teddy once stated that McKinley had "a backbone like a chocolate éclair." Apparently, he changed his view after being selected as McKinley's running mate. Theodore Roosevelt was known to have proclaimed, "I would a great deal rather be anything, say professor of history, than vice president."

The initial **cabinet** during McKinley's second term of office included **Vice President** Theodore Roosevelt, **Secretary of State** John Hay, **Secretary of the Treasury** Lyman Gage, **Secretary of War** Elihu Root, **Attorney General** Philander Knox,

Secretary of the Navy John Long, **Postmaster General** Charles Smith, **Secretary of the Interior** Ethan Hitchcock, and **Secretary of Agriculture** James Wilson. Only Gage, Long, and Wilson remained from the first term Cabinet.

Congress made no pay changes during McKinley's term of presidency.

McKinley was shot twice on September 6, 1901, by **anarchist Leon Czolgosz** with a .32-caliber pistol wrapped in a handkerchief while they were shaking hands at the Pan-American Exposition in Buffalo, New York. As the crowd attacked the assassin, McKinley shouted out, "Don't let them harm him." The president was rushed to the hospital and seemed to be recovering, but gangrene set in, and he died on September 14, 1901, at age 58, six months into his second term. His last words were, "Good-bye. Good-bye to all. It is God's will. His will be done." A new **bulletproof vest** would have awaited McKinley on his return to the capital. McKinley once stated, "That's all a man can hope for during his lifetime – to set an example – and when he is dead, to be an inspiration for history."

Upon learning of her husband's death in 1901, Ida never again set foot in the Executive Mansion, nor did she attend his funeral.

McKinley was the **third president** to be assassinated (Abraham Lincoln and James Garfield preceded him). McKinley's vice president, Theodore Roosevelt, became the 26th president on September 14, 1901. And **Czolgosz was executed** a speedy 45 days after McKinley's death by the electric chair in New York.

Roosevelt was the **eighth vice president** to directly follow his president. Adams, Jefferson, Van Buren, Tyler, Fillmore, Johnson, and Arthur preceded him. Roosevelt was also the **fifth vice**

president to assume the presidency after the death of the president. Tyler, Fillmore, Johnson, and Arthur preceded him.

At the time, some considered McKinley the greatest president since Lincoln, as he had gotten the country out of the greatest depression in its history. Most historians consider McKinley a **somewhat more effective than average president**. McKinley was buried in the McKinley National Memorial at West Lawn Cemetery in Canton, Ohio. Ida died on May 26, 1907, at age 59, six years after McKinley's assassination, and she was buried alongside her husband.

Key Events

The first subway service in America began in Boston, Massachusetts (1897); **Bob Fitzsimmons** knocked out Jim Corbett in the 24th round to win the **world heavyweight title** (1897); the **California Klondike Alaska gold** rush was in full swing (1897); **George Washington Carver** developed crop rotation to replenish depleted soil (1897); **General Motors** opened (1897); the **DJIA** closed at 49.41, up 22.2% (1897); the **five boroughs of New York City** were created (1898); **electric trolleys** replaced old-fashioned horsecars (1898); the **DJIA** closed at 69.52, up 22.5% (1898); **Kresge** opened its first store (in Detroit) (1899); **Delaware** became the first state to enact a law enabling companies to incorporate in the state (1899); the **first pay phone** appeared in New York City (1899); the **DJIA** closed at 66.08, up 9.2% (1899); the New York City newsboys' strike hurt newspaper owners Randolph Hearst and Joseph Pulitzer (1899); *The Theory of the Leisure Class* was published by Thorstein Veblen (1899); *The Distribution of Wealth* was written by John Clark (1899); a category 4 **hurricane** left over 2,000 dead in **Galves-**

ton, Texas (1900); temperance leader **Carrie Nation** began attacking saloons while brandishing a hatchet (1900); there were reportedly **300,000 saloons** in the U.S., up from 100,000, thirty years earlier (1900); the United States population rose to over 75 million (1900); Kodak introduced the **Brownie camera**, named after the inventor Frank Brownell (1900); Henry Flagler built the **Breakers Hotel** in Palm Beach, Florida (1900); the **DJIA** closed 70.71, up 7.0% (1900); the first significant **oil well** was discovered in Spindletop, near Beaumont, Texas (1901); the new century was marked by trains, streetcars, and steamships as the country moved forward into the industrial age, tractors and cars replacing the horse (1901); Congress assigned the protection of the president to the Secret Service, in addition to its investigation of financial crimes (1901); and Booker T. Washington published *Up From Slavery* (1901).

THEODORE ROOSEVELT
(26ᵀᴴ PRESIDENT)

SEPTEMBER 14, 1901 – MARCH 4, 1909

Theodore Roosevelt was born on October 27, 1858, to Theodore Roosevelt Sr. and Martha Bulloch Roosevelt, the second of four offspring, in New York City, New York. He and his **wealthy family** lived in New York City, where he was **homeschooled** by tutors. He loved physical exercise and grew into a strong and athletic man as his **asthma attacks** became less frequent. He also suffered from nearsightedness and a weak heart. He was known as **Ted** to family, **TR** to friends, but **never Teddy** (a nickname he loathed). In 1876, Roosevelt left for **Harvard** with these words from his father: "Take care of your morals first, then your health and finally your studies." His father died during TR's second year at Harvard. By 1877, he had published his first of 30 books, as well as countless articles, letters, and speeches. He was also a voracious reader, reading a book a day. Aided by a **photographic memory** and his father's admonition, he graduated in 1880. Within months of graduating Harvard, at age 22, TR married **Alice Hathaway Lee**, age 25, in 1880.

In 1882, Roosevelt began a two-year term as a New York **State assemblyman**. On February 14, 1884, both Roosevelt's **wife** and **mother died**. Alice died during the birth of their daughter, also named Alice. TR was devastated and sought solitude at his Dakota ranch on the Elkhorn River. After two years, he married **Edith Carow**, a woman he had known for years. They honeymooned in England and then returned to New York City. They had five children together. She was the strict parent; he was the indulgent one. She impressed everyone with her charm and intelligence. He impressed everyone with his knowledge.

From 1889 to 1895, Roosevelt served on the U.S. **Civil Service Commission**. TR then went on to serve as the New York City **police commissioner** for two years. In 1897, TR served as assistant secretary to the **Navy**. In 1898, Roosevelt volunteered to fight in the **Spanish American War** as a lieutenant colonel. He formed a unit he called the "**Rough Riders**," made up of cowboys. For his bravery, he reportedly should have received the **Medal of Honor**, but he didn't because he was critical of President McKinley. But President Clinton awarded the **Medal of Honor** to TR posthumously in January 2001. From 1899 to 1900, TR served as **governor of New York State**. And in 1901, Roosevelt served as William McKinley's vice president.

As vice president, **Roosevelt** said the following about foreign policy: "**Speak softly and carry a big stick.**" His meaning: exercise intelligent foresight and decisive action sufficiently far in advance of any likely crisis. He also made use of the **bully pul-**

pit, publicly stating his views. He called his policies a "**Square Deal**," referring to the average American. He also coined the words "**lunatic fringe**," referring to persons on the sleazy side of life. TR considered himself not simply the **Chief Executive**; he also thought he was the **chief legislator** and called for a comprehensive legislative agenda. Also, he did not agree with the U.S. Supreme Court that the Constitution applied only to interstate commerce and not intrastate commerce.

Only **six months into his term** as vice president, Roosevelt became president upon McKinley's assassination in 1901. At age 42, Roosevelt was the **youngest ever** at that date to assume the presidency. John Kennedy, at age 43, would become the youngest elected president. Theodore Roosevelt was the **fifth vice president** to assume the presidency (Tyler, Fillmore, Johnson, and Arthur preceded him) with the death of his president (William McKinley). Theodore Roosevelt was the **eighth vice president** to become president (John Adams, Thomas Jefferson, Martin Van Buren, John Tyler, Millard Fillmore, Andrew Johnson, and Chester Arthur preceded him).

After Theodore's elevation to the presidency, Edith renovated the **Executive Mansion**, making the upstairs for the family and the downstairs for business and the public. In 1901, Roosevelt officially changed the name of the **Executive Mansion** to the **White House**. Also in 1901, TR invited **Booker T. Washington** to a White House dinner following the publication of his autobiography, *Up From Slavery*. Roosevelt wanted to get talented Black Americans into his administration and believed Washington would be a good source. After dinner, the two adjourned to discuss the matter. Washington followed up with reference letters. Some progress was made, but not as much as the president wanted.

Roosevelt's initial **cabinet** included **Secretary of State** John Hay, **Secretary of the Treasury** Lyman Gage, **Secretary of War** Elihu Root, **Attorney General** Philander Knox, **Secretary of the Navy** John Long, **Postmaster General** Charles Smith, **Secretary of the Interior** Ethan Hitchcock, **Secretary of Agriculture** James Wilson, and **Secretary of Commerce and Labor** George Cortelyou. Roosevelt **added the last position** due to his view of the importance of the interaction of business and labor. The dominant voices in business were J.P. Morgan and J.D. Rockefeller. The Industrial Workers of the World headed the labor movement.

After the 1902 midterm elections, the GOP controlled the Senate 57-33 and the House 201-176. Also in 1902, Roosevelt appointed **Oliver Wendell Holmes** to the U.S. Supreme Court. Holmes went on to be a very good justice for 30 years. He was known for his eloquent language and independent views, earning him the title of the **Great Dissenter.**

In 1904, Roosevelt updated the Monroe Doctrine, stating that America was free to intervene in any affairs in the Western Hemisphere. He called this the **Roosevelt Corollary** stating, "The United States would interfere with them (the peoples of the Greater Caribbean) only in the last resort, and then only if it became evident that their inability or unwillingness to do justice at home and abroad had violated the rights of the United States or had invited foreign aggression to the detriment of the entire body of the American Nations." Helping Panama free itself from Colombia was the first action the U.S. took under the Roosevelt Corollary.

Roosevelt was an **avid hunter,** and among the animals he had in the White House were a **badger** (named Josiah), a **bear cub** (named Teddy Bear), a **snake** (named Emily Spinach), and a one-legged **rooster** (named Holiday). He probably had **more pets** than any previous president. Not surprisingly, he bought and stuffed a dead seal as a boy. On one of his hunts in 1902, Roosevelt refused to shoot a small tied-up bear. This inspired candy store owners Rose and Morris Michtom to create a small stuffed bear and send it to the president, calling it **Teddy's Bear**. TR's daughter, Alice, renamed the toy **Teddybear**. It went on to become a children's favorite for decades to come.

Ted and his wife enjoyed "coarse food and plenty of it." He enjoyed the fish he caught, the game he shot, and greens from his farm, along with most fruits. But he also enjoyed beans and pork. At breakfast, he would have a dozen hardboiled eggs with homemade rolls. At lunch it was bread, fruits, and various meats. At dinner it was fried chicken, grilled steak, and wild game or fish. He enjoyed coffee with sugar (no cream), but he drank no alcohol except for a spritzer of white wine. TR used his dinners to test policies and discuss various topics and he wore out his stenographers with long and frequent letters to colleagues, friends, and the press.

Roosevelt was also a **sports enthusiast**. He played **tennis** on a court he built at the White House, **jogged** around the Washington Monument, and even **fought** a professional boxer, suffering a detached retina and a blind left eye. He also insisted **college football** be made safer or he would ban the game. To make himself safer, he **carried a gun** in the White House. Like John Quincy Adams, Teddy **enjoyed skinny-dipping** in the Potomac River; however, he had to be more careful than Adams because photography had been invented. He said, "No president has ever enjoyed himself as much as I," and "Let us run the risk of wearing out rather than rusting out."

In **Lone Wolf vs Hitchcock** (1903), the U.S. Supreme Court ruled that the plenary authority of Congress gave it the power to unilaterally abrogate the provisions of treaties, such as the Medicine Lodge Treaty of 1867, between the United States and Indian tribes. Also in 1903, Congress increased the annual pay of the associate justices of the U.S. Supreme Court to $12,500 (up from 1873's $10,000) and that of the Chief Justice to $13,000 (up from 1873's $10,500).

Roosevelt's **greatest accomplishment** was the purchase of the French-abandoned rights to the **Panama Canal** property from Colombia in **1903** for $40 million dollars. A treaty gave the U.S. rights to a six-mile-wide zone to use for 100 years. America would pay $10 million up front, followed by $250,000 a year. But when Colombia demanded more, America supported a Panamanian independence revolution. America immediately recognized the country's independence and negotiated a treaty similar to the one rejected by Colombia, except this one was for a nine-mile zone. Construction proceeded, and the **first ship** went through the Canal on August 15, 1914, connecting the two oceans.

In the **1904 election**, Republicans **Theodore Roosevelt** and **Charles Fairbanks** crushed Democrats **Alton Parker** and **Henry G. Davis**, receiving 7,623,468 popular votes to 5,077,911 for Parker and David and 336 of the 476 electoral votes.

Charles Fairbanks was born in a log cabin in Unionville, Ohio, on May 11, 1852. His parents were abolitionists. Their farm was a safe haven for runaway slaves. Fairbanks graduated from **Ohio Wesleyan University** and went on to study law. He was admitted to the Indiana bar and was recognized for his skill in representing bankrupt railroads, from which he became quite rich. He used some of his money to purchase a majority interest in *Indianapolis News*. As a Republican, Fairbanks developed a personal friendship with Ohio Governor William McKinley. Having lost an 1893 attempt at a U.S. Senate seat, Fairbanks was a keynote speaker at the 1896 Presidential convention, where he supported William McKinley. Fairbanks was considered by many old guard Republicans to be a conservative in the McKinley style. In 1897, Fairbanks was elected to the **U.S. Senate**. In 1904, Fairbanks was chosen to be Roosevelt's running mate. As president of the U.S. Senate, Fairbanks was the first vice president to serve his full four-year term and **never cast a tie-breaking vote**. In 1908, Fairbanks lost the presidential nomination to William Taft and after losing again in 1916, he resumed his law practice in Indianapolis. He died at age 66 on June 4, 1918.

In **Northern Securities vs United States** (1904), the U.S. Supreme Court upheld the breakup of the Great Northern and Northern Pacific Railroads.

In Roosevelt's March 4, **1905, inaugural address,** a speech of over a thousand words, he never once used the word "I." Roosevelt stated, "Knowing what's right doesn't mean much unless you do what is right." He explained that meant "do what you can with what you have." He then stated, "The credit of the government, the integrity and the invisibility of its obligations must be preserved." The GOP continued to hold both Houses: Senate 68-32 and House 251-135.

The **cabinet** during Roosevelt's **second term** included **Vice President** Charles Fairbanks, **Secretary of State** Elihu Root, **Secretary of the Treasury** Leslie Shaw, **Secretary of War** William Taft, **Attorney General** William Moody, **Secretary of the Navy** Paul Morton, **Postmaster General** Robert Wynne, **Secretary of the Interior** James Garfield, **Secretary of Agriculture** James Wilson, and **Secretary of Commerce and Labor** Oscar Straus.

In **Swift & Co. vs United States** (1905), the U.S. Supreme Court ruled that under the Commerce Clause, Congress can regulate local business activities that are a part of a "current of commerce among the States."

In 1905, Roosevelt promised to **fight large businesses** that monopolized free trade and to create a fair playing field for business and workers. He also promised the **square deal**, stating, "We must treat each man of his worth and merits as a man. We must see that each man is given a square deal because he is entitled to no more and should receive no less."

An advocate for open lands available to all, Roosevelt established a number of **national parks** protecting millions of wilderness areas.

Upton Sinclair's exposure of unsanitary meat-packing working conditions in his book *The Jungle* in 1906 led to the adoption of the **1906 Pure Food and Drug Act**, which made it illegal to mislabel drugs and the **1906 Meat Inspection Act**, which prohibited the sale of unsafe meat. Also in 1906, the **Hepburn Act**, and the **Railroad Regulation Act** were enacted. The first regulated railroads, and the second stated a worker strike was a strike against free enterprise.

In 1906, Roosevelt used the **Sherman Antitrust Act of 1890** to break up some 44 companies including American Tobacco, DuPont Chemical, and Standard Oil. These actions earned him the nickname of **trustbuster** for attacking trusts that reduced competition and controlled prices. He also intervened in strikes, forcing both sides to come to some agreement. TR stated, "Is there a difference between gambling at the racetrack and gambling in the stock market?" He did not think there was a difference.

THEODORE ROOSEVELT (26TH PRESIDENT)

In 1906, the annual pay of the vice president was increased to $12,000 (up from 1878's $10,000).

In the **1906 midterm elections**, little changed in Congress. The GOP held the Senate 61-31 and the House 223-167. As for his view of the importance of the founding fathers, TR stated, "I do not for a moment believe that the America of today should be a mere submission to the American ideals of the period of the Declaration of Independence." In 1906, TR was the first U.S. president to win the **Nobel Peace Prize**, given for his role in ending the Russo-Japanese War.

At a White House function on New Year's Day in 1907, TR reportedly set a record for handshakes by a head of state – over 8,000. (Although President McKinley could supposedly shake 2,500 hands an hour.) In 1907, to demonstrate to the world America's military might, Roosevelt sent the **Great White Fleet** of 16 battleships around the world. Also in 1907, an **Immigration Act** limited arrivals to the U.S.

In 1907, the annual pay of legislators went up to $7,500 (from 1865's $6,000), and the annual pay of cabinet secretaries went up to $12,000 a year (from 1853's $8,000). These were the last pay changes made during Roosevelt's term of presidency.

In **Adair vs United States** (1908), the U.S. Supreme Court struck down yellow-dog contracts, which stipulated a person could not join a labor union.

Second only to the **Panama Canal**, if not an even greater accomplishment, was that during Roosevelt's seven years in office, **not one shot was fired** from or to a foreign country. America was at peace with the world.

Upon **leaving** office, TR stated, "No president has ever enjoyed himself as much as I." Following his presidency, over a two-year period (1909-10), Roosevelt led an expedition into central Africa and reportedly killed some 10,000 creatures that were preserved, mounted, and sent to museums in the United States.

Roosevelt died at his Elkhorn ranch on January 6, 1919, at age 60, of a coronary embolism in his sleep. Before he went to sleep, his last words were, "Please put out the lights." He is buried in Young's Memorial Cemetery in Oyster Bay, New York. His wife **Edith died** at age 87 on September 30, 1948, and was buried with her husband.

Many historians consider Roosevelt **one of the most effective presidents**.

Between October 4, 1927, and October 31, 1941, Gutzon Borglum and 400 workers sculpted the colossal 60-foot-high carvings of United States Presidents George Washington, Thomas Jefferson, **Theodore Roosevelt**, and Abraham Lincoln on **Mount Rushmore** in the Black Hills of South Dakota. In 2022, a statue of TR was removed from the front of the American Museum of Natural History because he portrayed Black and other Indigenous persons as racially inferior.

Key Events

The **standard of living was rising**: water and sewage systems were improved, electricity was having an impact, and gas was replacing coal (1901); **New York City** was now recognized as the nation's financial capital (1901); **Andrew Carnegie** sold his steel company for $250 million to **J.P. Morgan**, who formed U.S. Steel Co. and went on to create over 3,000 public libraries (1901); **Walgreens** opened its first drug store (1901); **Henry**

Ford received a patent on motor carriages (1901); the **paper clip** was invented (1901); a **Texas oil boom** began and J.D. **Rockefeller** controlled 90% of U.S. oil refineries (1901); Cuba became independent as U.S. troops withdrew (1901); **Butch Cassidy and the Sundance Kid** left for South America (1901) only to be killed seven years later in Bolivia; the **DJIA** closed at 64.56 at year-end, down 8.7 percent (1901); **Maryland** became the first state with a workers' compensation plan (1902); the **Bureau of the Census** was established (1902); the **Twentieth Century Limited** train began a 65-year career connecting New York City and Chicago (1902); Joseph Horn and Frank Hardart invented the **automat** (1902); **Macy's** department stores opened in New York City (1902); Minnesota Mining and Manufacturing (**3M**) was formed (1902); **Thomas Edison** invented the battery (1902); **JCPenney's first store** was open for business (1902); **Bethlehem Steel** set up an annual **cash bonus plan** for its top executives (1902); sharpshooter and army scout **Calamity Jane**, age 51, died of pneumonia and was buried next to her lover "**Wild Bill Hickok**" (1902); Roosevelt broke up **a coal miner strike** (1902); the **DJIA** closed at 64.29 at year-end, down 0.4 percent (1902); a **financial crisis** triggered by overextended banks caused the DJIA to lose a fourth of its value in a day before the government deposited $12 million in gold in New York banks (1903); U.S. Steel hired **Price, Waterhouse & Co.** to certify the accuracy of what is considered to be the first annual report (1903); **Ford Motor Company** and **International Harvester** were formed (1903); the **Flatiron 21 Story Building** opened in New York City (so-called because it resembles a laundry iron) (1903); **Wilbur and Orville Wright** flew their motorized glider plane in Kitty Hawk, North Carolina (1903); the **safety razor** was patented (1903); the New York Yankees began operation (1903); singer **Enrico Caruso** made his American debut at the

Metropolitan Opera House (1903); the **DJIA** closed at 49.11 at year-end, down 23.0 percent (1903); Amadeo Giannini opened the **Bank of Italy**, later to become the **Bank of America** (1904); Edward Francis Hutton founded the **E.F. Hutton** brokerage house (1904); **Long Acre Square** was renamed **Times Square** after the location of the *New York Times* at 42nd Street and Broadway (1904); the **first subway** system opened in New York City (1904); *The Protestant Ethic and the Spirit of Capitalism* was published by Max Weber (1904); the **DJIA** closed at 69.61 at year-end, up 41.7 percent (1904); Edison sold his electric patents to **General Electric** (1905); **Albert Einstein** described the **theory of relativity** (1905); **Henry Flagler** (age 75), co-founder of Standard Oil with John D. Rockefeller, left the company to build a **railroad to Key West, Florida** (1905); **TIAA-CREF** was established with $10 million from **Andrew Carnegie** (1905); the **Pierpont Morgan Library** was completed in New York City (1905); the **St. Regis** Hotel opened in New York City (1905); the **Industrial Workers of the World** (known as the Wobblies) was formed from 34 labor unions advocating **Marxism** (1905); the **Rotary Club** was founded in Chicago (1905); the **DJIA** closed at 95.20 at year-end, up 38.2 percent (1905); San Francisco suffered a major **earthquake**, killing some 3,000, leaving 300,000 homeless, and destroying 30,000 buildings (1906); the **National Collegiate Athletic Association** (NCAA) was formed (1906); TR briefly outlawed football as a dangerous sport (1906); the U.S. Mint opened in Denver, Colorado (1906); the **DJIA** closed at 94.35 at year–end, down 1.9 percent (1906); **Oklahoma** was admitted as the 46th state (1907); Leo Baekeland created plastic, which he named **Bakelite** (1907); excessive speculation in copper triggered a **crash of the stock market**, but the crisis passed when pledges by the banks kept the NYSE open (1907); **J.P. Morgan** rescued the United States Treasury with an infusion of $100 million (1907); **Alfred Vanderbilt** paid $10,000 for a year's lease of a suite in the just opened **Plaza Hotel** in New

York City (1907); **taximeter cabs** replaced hansom cabs in New York City (1907); the **Dictaphone** replaced shorthand stenographers (1907); the **Maytag washing** machine was invented in Newton, Ohio (1907); the **United Parcel Service** began operation (1907); the **DJIA** closed at 58.75 at year–end, down 37.7 percent (1907); the Bureau of Investigation (later to become the **FBI**) was established (1908); **Thomas J. Watson** wrote the word "THINK" on a presentation (1908); the **New York Central Railroad** connected New York City and New Haven with electric train service (1908); a newly designed production line produced the **Ford Model T**, which sold for $500 (1908); **William Durant** founded what would become General Motors (GM), with Buick as its sole product (1908); **Howard Hughes's** father invented the drill bit used to cut through bedrock to get to oil (1908); **Thomas Edison** created the Motion Picture Patents Company to protect his patents (1908); the **DJIA** closed at 86.1 at year-end, up 46.6 percent (1908); the classification job evaluation method was developed by E.O. Griffenhagen (1909); and **hurricanes** destroyed much of the work on Flagler's railroad in Florida (1909).

WILLIAM HOWARD TAFT (27ᵀᴴ PRESIDENT)

MARCH 4, 1909 - MARCH 4, 1913

William Howard Taft was born on September 15, 1857, in Cincinnati, Ohio, to Alphonso Taft and Louisa Maria Torrey Taft. Alphonso was a **judge** and had been President Grant's **Secretary of War** in 1876 and **Attorney General** in 1876-1877. William had two half-brothers, Charles and Peter, from Alphonso's first marriage. William also had three full siblings: Frances, Henry, and Horace. **William went to public schools**, receiving a diploma in 1874. He was always overweight and was nicknamed "**Big Bill**" and "**Big Lub**." He attended **Yale** and graduated in 1878, second in his class of 132. Then he went to the University of Cincinnati Law School. After being admitted to the Ohio bar in 1880, he practiced **law** in Cincinnati and became a judge in the **Supreme Court of Ohio** in 1887, **Solicitor General** in 1890, and then civil **governor of the Philippines** in 1901. He was **Secretary of War** from 1904-1908 under Theodore Roosevelt. At age 29, he married **Helen "Nellie" Herron**, age 25, in 1886. They had three children together, all before his presidency: Charles, Helen, and Robert.

Taft's goal was to get on the U.S. Supreme Court, not to win the presidency, but family and friends, especially FDR, convinced Taft to go for the presidency. With FDR's support, Taft won the Republican nomination for president. He said that was a great mistake. But in the **1908 election**, Republicans **William Howard Taft** and **James Sherman** soundly defeated Democrats **William Jennings Bryan** and **John Kern**, 7,678,908 to 6,409,104 in the popular vote and 321 to 162 in the electoral vote. The **GOP** continued to hold Congress, Senate 60-32 and House 219-172.

James Sherman was born on October 24, 1855, into a **well-to-do family** in Utica, New York. His father owned a food-canning company and a newspaper. James graduated from **Hamilton College** in 1878, was admitted to the **New York bar** in 1880, and then practiced law in Utica. Although his father was a Democrat, **James became a Republican** and was elected **mayor of Utica**. Sherman was elected to the **House of Representatives** in 1886 and re-elected in 1888. He lost in 1890 but then won again in 1892. Politically, Sherman was known for his common sense, **upbeat demeanor**, and ability to make political deals. For this he was known as "**Sunny Jimmy**."

Taft was 51 years old on the date of his inauguration. In his March 4, **1909, inaugural address**, Taft stated, "The progress which the Negro has made in the last fifty years from slavery is marvelous and furnishes hope in the next twenty five years that a still greater improvement will be made." The media said that T.A.F.T. stood for "**Take advice from Theodore**." But unlike

Roosevelt, Taft refused to accept **political** contributions from corporate officers and directors. Upon his inauguration, Congress increased **Taft's pay to $75,000 a year**, up from $50,000 in 1873 for President Grant.

Taft's **cabinet** included **Vice President** James Sherman, **Secretary of State** Philander Knox, **Secretary of the Treasury** Franklin MacVeagh, **Secretary of War** Jacob Dickinson, **Attorney General** George Wickersham, **Secretary of the Navy** George Meyer, **Postmaster General** Frank Hitchcock, **Secretary of the Interior** Richard Ballinger, **Secretary of Agriculture** James Wilson and **Secretary of Commerce and Labor** Charles Nagel.

Taft was the first president to have **two cows** in the White House. They were working animals, not pets, and provided fresh milk, since refrigeration had not been invented. And he is credited with being the first president to throw out the pitch to **begin the baseball season** in 1909. Taft is also credited with initiating the **seventh inning stretch** that same year. Uncomfortable at the game, he got up to stretch. Seeing the president rise, everyone else did so as well out of respect for his office.

Taft's primary area of interest was tariff reform. The public wanted to lower consumer prices by lowering tariff rates on imported goods. Taft got the **1909 Payne-Aldrich Tariff Act** passed. It lowered tariffs on 650 items. But big business was not happy with the act because it also introduced the **initial corporate income tax**. Any business with more than $5,000 in revenue would have to pay 1% of that excess, though the act also stated that an employer's cost for employee term life insurance was tax deductible. The **1910 Mann-Elkins Act** extended the authority of the Interstate Commerce Commission.

Business was also unhappy with President Taft when he announced he would continue the efforts of former President

Roosevelt as a **trustbuster**. Both presidents were against big trusts because large companies got together in the late 19th century and formed those trusts with the intent of driving out smaller companies, so that the trust would be able to raise prices. This led to the **1890 Sherman Antitrust Act**, but the law was ineffective. Taft wanted to change this. Taft told Attorney General George Wickersham to go after the largest trust of them all, Standard Oil Company, owned by **John D. Rockefeller**. In 1911, Wickersham took the case to the **U.S. Supreme Court** and won. The U.S. Supreme Court in **Standard Oil of New Jersey vs United States** (1911) ruled that only unreasonable monopolies (such as Standard Oil of New Jersey) are counter to public interest. The result was the breakup of John D. Rockefeller's Standard Oil Company. This led Rockefeller's philanthropic organization to begin dispensing his $500 million dollars in trusts. And in the **United States vs American Tobacco Company** (1911), the Court broke up the tobacco company, following the same logic as the Standard Oil case.

Nellie Taft played the piano and read the classics. She also enjoyed drinking alcohol, smoking and playing bridge for money. While Nellie was very happy living in the White House, her husband considered it a prison. He suffered from **sleep apnea** and often fell asleep during cabinet meetings.

In the 1910 midterms, the **Democrats** gained strength: the GOP still held the Senate, 52-44, but the **Democrats** took the House 230-162. Taft said, "Congress is more interested in passing laws than in examining their results."

Taft loved to eat, evidenced by his weight of over 350 pounds, making him the heaviest president to date. Taft liked almost every kind of food, except eggs, and plenty of it. He especially liked a thick steak for breakfast along with coffee, orange juice, and toast. Steak was also common at lunch and dinner. Both meals also featured various forms of seafood, especially mussel soup. To satisfy her husband's tastes, Nellie replaced the male cooks with three Irish women and installed the first White House **housekeeper**. Nellie also took responsibility for landscaping the Washington Mall and **planting over 3,000 cherry trees** donated by Japan in 1912. An additional 3,000 trees were donated by Japan and planted by Lady Bird Johnson in 1965.

In 1911, **Congress increased the pay** of associate justices of the U.S. Supreme Court to $14,500 a year (up from 1903's $12,500) and the pay for the chief justice to $15,000 (up from 1903's $13,000). **Congress made no other pay changes during Taft's term of presidency.**

Following the admission of **Arizona** and **New Mexico** as states in 1912, Taft became the first U.S. president to rule over the "**lower 48.**"

The **16th Amendment to the U.S. Constitution** (see Appendix C) was ratified on February 3, 1913, removing the earlier restriction on imposing other than a flat personal income tax.

Theodore Roosevelt had considerable support to return to the presidency, but when he did not get the Republican nomination, he set up the **Progressive Bull Moose Party**. The 1912 election results were split in the popular vote between Taft (3,484,980), Roosevelt (4,119,538), and Woodrow Wilson (6,293,454), with the latter winning only 42% of the popular vote but 435 of the electoral votes vs. 88 for Roosevelt and 8 for Taft. Wilson was elected president and Thomas Marshall was elected vice president. Taft noted, "The intoxication of power rapidly sobers one in the knowledge of its restrictions."

The **17th Amendment to the U.S. Constitution** (see Appendix C) was ratified on April 8, 1913, stating that each state would have two senators, and each would be elected for six years.

After Taft's defeat in 1912 to Woodrow Wilson, Nellie Taft proved to be a careful manager of the family money, as they left the White House with $100,000 in the bank. Taft became a **law professor at Yale** and was later appointed **Chief Justice of the United States Supreme Court** by President Warren Harding in 1921. Taft considered this his greatest achievement. He served as Chief Justice until he died in 1930. Taft had always aspired to become a member of the Supreme Court, not president of the U.S. Taft lost 70 pounds during his first year in office as Chief Justice of the Supreme Court.

Taft is the **first person** to have been **both a U.S. president and a Supreme Court Chief Justice**. He is also the **first** president to be buried in **Arlington National Cemetery**, having died on March 8, 1930, at age 73 of heart failure in Washington, D.C. His last words were, "It was a good life." Nellie suffered several strokes and died on May 22, 1943, at age 81. She is the first First Lady buried at **Arlington National Cemetery** (Jackie Kennedy is the second).

Most historians consider Taft an **average president**.

KEY EVENTS

Admiral Robert Peary planted the American flag at the North Pole (1909); the **McGraw-Hill** Book Publishing company was formed by James McGraw and John Hill (1909); the **National Association for the Advancement of Colored People** (NAACP) was formed by W.E.B. Dubois in New York City (1909); the **DJIA** closed at 99.05 at year-end, up 15.0 percent (1909); bartender **Mickey Finn** developed a drink with a knockout powder that was named after him (1910); the foundation for what would become the **Federal Reserve System** was created by powerful bankers in 1910 to make it appear to be part of the federal government, which it was not (in spite of the words on paper money stating, "**Federal Reserve Note**," the U.S. Treasurer has no say in how many bills are printed); Taft put the **Interstate Commerce Commission** in charge of the emerging telephone and telegraph industry, largely controlled by American Telephone and Telegraph (**AT&T**) (1910); **Pancho Villa** invaded Texas and was rebuffed by **General John "Black Jack" Pershing** and 20,000 soldiers (1910); the Glacier National Park was created (1910); the **electric washing machine** was invented (1910); the **DJIA** closed at 81.36 at year-end, down 17.9 percent (1910); the **Boy Scouts** and the Camp Fire Girls, later changed to the **Girl Scouts**, were founded (1910); the U.S. population reached almost 92 million (1910); Wisconsin Senator **Robert La Follette** set up the National Progressive Republican League and unsuccessfully ran for president (1911); the **American Stock Exchange** opened (1911); the **National Industrial Conference Board** began (1911); the **Triangle Shirtwaist Company** in NYC caught fire, killing 146 women because the exit doors were locked (1911); the first **transcontinental airplane flight** took 82 hours (1911); the **DJIA** closed at 81.68 at year end, up .04 percent (1911); hatchet-wielding temperance leader **Carrie Nation** died at age 65 of natural causes (1911); **Ronald Amundsen** discovered the South Pole (1911); the **U.S. Chamber of Commerce** was formed (1912); the **Indianapolis 500-Mile** auto race began (1912); U.S. military muscle was flexed, with **troops** sent to Cuba, Honduras, Nicaragua, and Santa Domingo (1912); Vincent Astor inherited $87 million following death of his father, **John Jacob Astor** (1912); the first **Horn & Hardart Automat** opened in New York City (1912); New York State passed the **1912 Sullivan Act** restricting access and use of guns by private citizens (1912); **Flagler** completed a **railroad** from

Jacksonville to Key West – 500 miles (1912); the ruthless nature of business was described in Theodore Dreiser's ***The Financier*** (1912); **Fenway Park** opened for the Boston Red Sox baseball team (1912); the **DJIA** closed at 87.87 at year end, up 7.6 percent (1912); **Buffalo Bill Cody** closed his show after a run of 30 years (1913); and **Grand Central Terminal** opened in New York City for train service (1913).

WOODROW WILSON
(28ᵀᴴ PRESIDENT)

MARCH 4, 1913 – MARCH 4, 1921

Woodrow Wilson was born on December 28, 1856, in Staunton, Virginia, to Janet and Joseph Wilson. His father was a Presbyterian minister, and shortly after Woodrow's birth, he moved the family to Augusta, Georgia. Woodrow had three siblings, Ann, Joseph, and Marion. When the Civil War broke out, his father served the Confederacy as a minister. After the war, he moved the family to Columbia, South Carolina, where he became a professor at Columbia Theological Seminary.

During his childhood, Wilson had difficulty learning to read, as he suffered from **dyslexia**, but he taught himself **shorthand**. He also had difficulty breathing and poor blood circulation. In

1873, Wilson entered **Davidson College**, where his father was a trustee, but later he transferred to and graduated from the **College of New Jersey** (later to become Princeton University) in 1879. After a brief career practicing law in New Jersey, Wilson enrolled in **Johns Hopkins University** in 1883, focusing on history and political science. Wilson **authored many books** on American history, his first in 1885.

At age 29, Wilson married **Ellen Louise Axson**, age 25, on June 24, 1885, after he returned from Johns Hopkins University with a **PhD**. She met Woodrow when he came to the church where her father was preaching in New York. They had three children: Eleanor, James, and Margaret. He moved on to teach at **Wesleyan College** in 1888, then to **Princeton** in 1890 as a professor and administrator. As an academic, he was getting a reputation as both a speaker and a writer. He later went on to become **President of Princeton** from 1902 until 1910. Wilson was a devoted father and husband, although it is believed he had at least one **extramarital affair** while he was president of Princeton University. He was elected **governor of New Jersey** in 1911.

In the **1912 presidential election**, Democrats **Woodrow Wilson and Thomas Marshall won** the president and vice president positions, respectively, defeating Progressive Party candidates **Theodore Roosevelt** and **Hiram Johnson**. The Democrats received 6,293,454 popular votes to 4,119,538 for the Progressive candidates. Wilson and Marshall received 435 electoral votes to 88 for Roosevelt and Johnson. Wilson was the **first president with a PhD** (from Johns Hopkins). Republican candidates William Taft and James Sheridan received 3,484,980 popular votes and 8 electoral votes. The Democrats took control of both Houses: Senate 51-44 and House 291-134.

Thomas Marshall was born on March 14, 1854, in North Manchester, Indiana. At age four, his father took him to the Abraham Lincoln-Stephen Douglas debate. Marshall graduated from **Wabash College** and, after studying law, was admitted to the Indiana Bar in 1875. After several years, he ran for district attorney as a Democrat, but he was unsuccessful and went back to his law practice. In 1882, he met Lois Kimsey, and they were married in 1895. She was almost twenty years younger than he was. Marshall's **law practice** was very successful, and he became quite wealthy and very active in his community of Columbus City. Although considered as a candidate for the U.S. Senate, Marshall chose to run for **governor of Indiana** in 1908 and was successful. He went on to become a high-ranking Freemason. The National Democratic Party liked his progressive agenda and made him a candidate for the presidency, but Woodrow Wilson won the nomination and selected Marshall as his running mate. They won in a landslide. In 1920, Marshall returned to Indiana and his law practice. He died on June 1, 1925, of a heart attack in Washington, D.C.

Wilson rode in a horse and carriage to the inauguration. In his March 4, **1913, inaugural address**, Wilson stated, "Our life contains every great thing, and contains it in rich abundance." He also stated, "America is not anything if it consists of each of us. It is something only if it consists of all of us." Wilson added, "Men of ordinary physiques and discretion cannot be president and live."

The **17th Amendment to the U.S. Constitution**, ratified on April 8, 1913, defined the number of senators (two from each state) and the term of office is six years (see Appendix C). Also in **1913**, Wilson signed into law the **Underwood-Simmons Tariff Act**, which introduced a graduated personal income tax, beginning at one percent for income over $20,000 and ending with a six percent tax on income over $500,000. The **Federal Reserve Act** created the Federal Reserve System, America's central national bank, and the **Webb-Kenyon Interstate Liquor Shipments Act** barred the transportation of liquor into dry states.

On March 1, 1914, some 358,000 **Americans filed tax returns for the first time**. Those with annual income of several thousand dollars felt good; they could afford a car, a dishwasher, a radio, and a refrigerator. The false sense of security this provided was described by Sinclair Lewis in his book *Babbitt*.

In **Weeks vs United States** (1914), the U.S. Supreme Court ruled that the unwarranted seizure of private documents and letters from a citizen's home violates their Fourth Amendment rights against unreasonable searches and seizures, and evidence obtained in this manner cannot be used by courts against the accused in criminal prosecutions.

Woodrow insisted wife Ellen precede him into a room. Wilson also broke precedent by not naming his cabinet until after his first presidential luncheon.

Wilson's initial **cabinet** included **Vice President** Thomas Marshall, **Secretary of State** William Jennings Bryan, **Secretary of the Treasury** William McAdoo, **Secretary of War** Lindley Garrison, **Attorney General** James McReynolds, **Secretary of the Navy** Josephus Daniels, **Postmaster General** Albert Burleson, **Secretary of the Interior** Franklin Lane, **Secretary of Agriculture** David Houston, **Secretary of Labor** William Wilson, and **Secretary of Commerce** William Redford. Wilson made one major **cabinet** move. He separated **Labor** and **Commerce**, believing each department would be better represented under separate secretaries.

World War I began in June of 1914 when a young Bosnian radical shot and killed Archduke Franz Ferdinand and his wife in Sarajevo, the capital of Bosnia. The deaths caused Russia to mobilize, followed by Germany, fearing the Russian action. Germany's action caused the French to mobilize. It was not long before armed intervention took place. From 1915-17, the Germans and Russians fought each other, with the Germans doing the most damage. The French also suffered heavy losses from the Germans. This caused England to enter the war on behalf of the French. **Ellen** came down with kidney trouble and **died on August 6, 1914**, at the age of 54 of Bright's disease in the White House. On May 7, 1915, a German submarine sank the British Cunard liner *Lusitania* and over 1,000 were killed, many of them Americans.

On October 15, Wilson signed the **1914 Clayton Anti-Trust Act** identifying various unfair trade practices and limiting injunctions in labor disputes. In the **1914** midterms, the **Democrats retained control of Congress**: Senate 56-40 and House 230-196.

Wilson considered himself **chief legislator**, and he was the first president since John Adams to personally appear before Congress to present his State of the Union rather than sending it in writing. He believed that as the political leader of the nation, it was appropriate that he infused his personal beliefs into the legislative process.

Wilson said, "The role of government is to separate the common interests from the special interests and liberty comes only with the limitation of government power, not with the increase of its powers." He also said, "If you want to make enemies, try to change something."

Woodrow Wilson suffered from **chronic indigestion, constipation, heartburn, and hypertension** and therefore preferred bland food; pancakes were his favorite. He also liked buttermilk, chicken salad, clear soup, country ham, eggs, homemade ice cream, and plain white cake. At virtually every breakfast, President Wilson had two raw eggs in a glass of orange juice alongside oatmeal.

Wilson argued that the president should be more like a prime minister, and that is how he governed. He was "**Dictator Wilson**," a term he actually took a shine to. He believed that states could not be trusted "to move the political process…only the central government, top down worked." Wilson did not defend the Constitution. He stated, "**The Constitution has become outdated** and ill equipped to handle the problems of the Modern Age."

Edith Bolling met Woodrow through his doctor. They were **married** on December 18, 1915 (a little more than a year after Ellen's death). Edith was age 42 and a widow with no children; he was age 58. She was an accomplished painter and an advocate of equal rights for Black people and women. She preferred small receptions to big parties. She was liked by the press and the public. His three daughters were happy for him.

In **Brushaber vs Union Pacific Railroad** (1916), the U.S. Supreme Court ruled that the Sixteenth Amendment authorizes Congress to levy an income tax, direct or indirect, that is not subject to apportionment "applicable to all other direct taxes."

In the **1916 presidential election**, Democrats **Woodrow Wilson** and **Thomas Marshall** won the president and vice president positions, respectively, **defeating** Republican Party candidates **Charles Hughes** and **Charles Fairbanks**. Wilson-Marshall received 9,129,606 popular votes to 8,538,221 for Hughes-Fairbanks. Wilson and Marshall received 277 electoral votes to 254 for Hughes and Fairbanks. Wilson was elected president and Marshall was elected vice president.

Wilson was the last president to take a **horse and carriage** ride to his inauguration. In his **inaugural address**, Wilson stated, "I would rather belong to a poor nation that was free, than to a rich nation that had ceased to be in love with liberty." The Democrats retained control of the Senate, 54-42, and the House was a narrow victory for the GOP, 215-214. Republican Jeannette Rankin from Montana was elected to the U.S. House of Representatives. She was the **first woman elected to Congress**.

Wilson's **cabinet** in his second term had seven holdovers and three new members (Lansing, Baker, and Gregory): **Vice President** Thomas Marshall, **Secretary of State** Robert Lansing, **Secretary of the Treasury** William McAdoo, **Secretary of War** Newton Baker, **Attorney General** Thomas Gregory, **Secretary of the Navy** Josephus Daniels, **Postmaster General** Albert Burleson, **Secretary of the Interior** Franklin Lane, **Secretary of Agriculture** David Houston, **Secretary of Labor** William Wilson, and **Secretary of Commerce** William Redford.

A German telegram to Mexico asking them to join the war against the United States was enough for **America to enter the war against Germany**. The Americans also believed Germany had to be punished for the sinking of the *Lusitania*. On February 3, 1917, America cut diplomatic ties with Germany, and on **April 6, 1917, the U.S. declared war on Germany**. To make a personal contribution to the World War I effort, President Wilson kept a flock of sheep on the White House lawn for their wool. The first American troops arrived in Europe on June 26, 1917. More than two million American **"doughboys"** crossed the Atlantic to serve in the American Expeditionary Force. Led by General John "Black Jack" Pershing, the American forces prevailed killing over 50,000. In total, more than 8 million lost their lives in the war.

Wilson appointed **Herbert Hoover** to lead the Food Administration program to persuade Americans to eat less, grow more food, and donate food to others. **German food was renamed**; frankfurters became Liberty Sausages and sauerkraut became Liberty Cabbage. And more than five million gardens produced over one billion dollars of food.

In **1917**, Wilson signed **five key pieces of legislation** into law. The **Conscription Act** required aliens to register for the military draft. The **Selective Service Act** required men between the ages of 21 and 32 to register for military service. The **Espionage Act** prohibited false statements that might impede military success. The **Revenue Act** introduced a 67% tax on incomes over $2 million. And the **War Risk Act** provided life insurance for those serving in the military.

In **1918**, Wilson signed **three key acts**: the **Pittman Act** sanctioned the melting of 350 million of the 657 million silver dollars in existence; the **Revenue Act** provided funds to pay WWI war bills; and the **Sedition Act** stated that disloyal acts or language about the flag or the government were punishable with time in prison. In the **1918** midterms, the GOP took control of both Houses: Senate 49-47 and House 240-192. **World War I ended on November 11, 1918**.

During his life, Wilson **gave many speeches**. When asked how long it took him to prepare, he stated, "If I am to speak for ten minutes, I need a week for preparation; if fifteen minutes, three days; if half an hour, two days; if an hour, I am ready now."

The **18th Amendment to the U.S. Constitution** was ratified on January 16, 1919. (It was repealed in 1933.) It banned the manufacture, sale, or transportation of intoxicating liquors within the United States and marked the start date of prohibition (see Appendix C). Later in **1919**, in **Dodge vs Ford Motor Company**, the U.S. Supreme Court ruled that a "business corporation is organized and carried on primarily for the profit of the shareholders." In **Schenck vs United States** (1919) the U.S. Supreme Court ruled that the First Amendment does not protect speech that creates a "clear and present danger." A good example is yelling "fire" in a crowded theater when there is no fire.

In **1919**, Wilson suffered a **severe stroke**. Partially paralyzed, he retreated to his bedroom and existed on bouillon, bread, and water for several months. Following the stroke, his wife assumed some of his presidential duties. During that time, Edith met with the Cabinet, took their questions, and returned with answers. Were they hers or Woodrow's? Either way, Edith was probably the most **important First Lady**, at least to that date. She represented her husband, and the public was not informed of Wilson's stroke.

Following the end of World War I, Wilson was a strong advocate for the **League of Nations** but after his stroke he was too weak to counter the negative lobbying against it by Senator Henry Cabot Lodge. Wilson was also unable to convince the Senate to approve the **Treaty of Versailles** ending the war. Nonetheless, in 1920, Wilson was the second President to win the **Nobel Peace Prize**; Theodore Roosevelt was the first.

In **United States vs United States Steel Corp.** (1920), the U.S. Supreme Court ruled that the "combinations" under the control of the United States Steel Corporation were combinations "in restraint of trade" in violation of Section I of the Sherman Antitrust Act of 1890.

In **1920**, Wilson signed into law the **Volstead Act**, which provided reinforcement provisions for the **18th Amendment**, and the **Revenue Act**, which scaled back annual income over $500,000 to a max tax of 50%. The **19th Amendment to the U.S. Constitution** was ratified on August 18, 1920, and stated the right to vote did not depend on a person's sex, giving women the right to vote (see Appendix C). And the **1918 Sedition Act** was repealed.

Congress made no pay changes during Wilson's term of presidency.

When he left the presidency in 1921, Wilson remained in Washington, where he set up a law practice after being elected to the bar. Wilson **died** at age 67 on February 3, 1924. His **last words** were, "I am a broken piece of machinery. I am ready." He was buried in the National Cathedral in Washington, D.C. Edith died on December 28, 1961, at age 89 and was buried with her husband.

Even given his wife's role after the stroke, most historians consider Wilson one of the **most effective presidents**.

Key Events

The skyscraper was introduced in New York City when the **Woolworth Building's** 57 floors rose 792 feet above street level (1913); Charles Merrill and Edmund Lynch formed **Merrill Lynch** brokerage (1913); **Prentice-Hall** began publications (1913); the **Actors Equity Association** was formed (1913); **Ebbets Field** opened for the Brooklyn Dodgers baseball team (1913);

Thomas Watson left the National Cash Register Company and set up the Computer-Tabulating-Recording Company (1913), later to become International Business Machines (**IBM**) (1913); Ford reversed the meat-packing disassembly line, making it his **assembly line** for cars (1913); AT&T became a government-approved monopoly (1913); the **zipper** was invented (1913); the parcel-post service began (1913); the **Consumer Price Index** was created (1913); the **DJIA** closed at 78.78 at year-end, down 10.3 percent (1913); Garrett Morgan received the patent for traffic signals (1914); the **Dodge** brothers introduced their automobile (1914); intelligence testing by the U.S. Army began (1914); the **Biltmore Hotel** opened in New York City (1914); **Wrigley Field** opened for the Chicago Cubs baseball team (1914); the Federal Trade Commission was established (1914); to defend American interests, Marines were sent into Mexico (1914); when war broke out in Europe, Wilson urged neutrality (1914); the **Panama Canal** opened connecting the Atlantic and Pacific Oceans (1914); the **DJIA** closed at 54.58 at year-end, down 30.7 percent (1914); stagecoach service was phased out at the **San Francisco World's Fair** (1915); coast-to-coast (New York to San Francisco) long distance telephone service was introduced (1915); to defend American interests, Marines were sent to Haiti (1915); the dramatic movie *The Birth of a Nation* appeared, featuring white supremacy and the demonization of Black people (1915); the **DJIA** closed at 99.15 at year-end, up 81.7 percent (1915); having donated millions for libraries **Andrew Carnegie** wrote that a man who dies rich dies disgraced (1916); **Piggly Wiggly** opened the first self-serve grocery store (1916); Garrett Augustus Morgan invented the **gas mask** (1916); the National Industrial Conference Board (later known as the **Conference Board**) was formed (1916); **Aero Products** (later to become

Boeing Company) was founded in Seattle, Washington (1916); **General Motors** was incorporated, having acquired 25 companies (1916); the **American Tobacco Company** introduced Lucky Strike cigarettes (1916); Jeannette Rankin was the **first woman to serve in Congress** – four years before women won the right to vote (1916); **Pancho Villa** was chased back into Mexico by General Pershing for raiding U.S. borders (1916); federal funding of roads began (1916); the **DJIA** closed at 95.00 at year-end, down 4.2 percent (1916); the **Katherine Gibbs** secretarial school opened (1917); the **Spanish Flu** killed 700,000 in America (1917); **air mail** service began between New York and Washington, D.C. (1917); **Barnes & Noble** opened its first retail book store in New York (1917); Puerto Rico was made a U.S. territory and its inhabitants became U.S. citizens (1917); the U.S. purchased the Virgin Islands from Denmark for $25 million (1917); **Al Capone** received facial scars in a bar fight, giving him the nickname "Scarface" (1917); the **DJIA** closed at 78.38 percent at year-end, down 21.7 percent (1917); the **Lions Club** was formed (1917); fewer than 1,000 people owned all of General Motors' stock (1918); the **tin can** was introduced (1918); unemployment dropped to 1.4% (1918); the **Frigidaire Company** was formed, transforming iceboxes into refrigerators (1918); the **Ford Model T** sold for $450, equal to a year of worker's pay (1918); **daylight savings time** was established (1918); the *New York Times* received its first **Pulitzer Prize** in journalism (1918); the **DJIA** closed at 82.20 at year-end, up 10.5 percent (1918); **rotary dial telephones** went into use (1919); the Radio Corporation of America (RCA) was formed by **General Electric** (1919); the **League of Women Voters** was formed (1919); **Andrew Carnegie** died, having given away over 90% of his estate ($350 million) to build more than 2,800 public libraries and other buildings (1919); thirty-six **package bombs** from an anarchist were intercepted before being delivered to key business and government leaders (1919); New York City gave **General John "Black Jack" Pershing** a ticker tape parade (1919); Wilson was the first president to regularly schedule **press conferences** (1919); the **strike by Boston police** was the first strike by government employees (1919); the **Grand Canyon** National Park opened (1919); a violent race riot in Chicago began when Black swimmers strayed over an imaginary racial divider (1919); twenty-four year old attorney **J. Edgar Hoover** headed up the Radical Division within the FBI (1919); John Maynard Keynes published *The Economic Consequences of Peace* (1919); the newspaper *New York Daily News* was founded (1919); the **DJIA** closed at 107.23 at year-end, up 30.5 percent (1919); regular **radio broadcasts** began in Pittsburgh (1920); more than 500 company coal-towns existed (1920); a bombing on Wall Street in front of the J.P. Morgan building killed 30 and injured more than 200 (1920); the **American Civil Liberties Union** was founded (1920); half of the states had put in place worker's compensation laws (1920); **Charles Ponzi** promised investors a 50 percent return in 90 days, thereby becoming the poster boy for swindlers promising outlandish returns (1920); Clarence Darrow and William Jennings Bryan faced off in the **Scopes evolution trial** (1920); the United States population topped 105 million (1920); Susan B. Anthony published *History of Woman Suffrage*, campaigning for the right of women to vote, but it did not happen until the 19th Amendment to the U.S. Constitution was ratified on August 18, 1920 (1920); **anarchists planted bombs** that exploded at noon on Wall Street, killing 50 people (1920); **German spies** blew up a warehouse in New Jersey loaded with ammunition that had been headed for the war in Europe (1920); the **DJIA** closed at 71.95 at year-end, down 32.90 percent (1920); the legendary lawman and professional gambler **Bat Masterson** died of a heart attack at age 66 in New York City (1921); FDR contracted polio at age 39 (1921); hundreds were killed in the **Tulsa Massacre** (1921); and Congress set a **national quota system** for immigration (1921). The 1920s were marked by a number of significant writings: *Main Street*, *Babbitt*, *Arrowsmith*, *Elmer Gantry*, and *Dodsworth* by Sinclair Lewis, *An American Tragedy* by Theodore Dreiser, and *The Bridge of San Luis Rey* by Thornton Wilder.

Warren G. Harding
(29th President)

March 4, 1921 – August 2, 1923

Warren Gamaliel Harding (**WG was his nickname**) was born on November 2, 1865, to George Tryon Harding and Phoebe Elizabeth Harding on a farm near Blooming Grove, Ohio. Harding was the oldest of eight children, but only five of his siblings lived beyond childhood: Abigail, Charity, George, Mary, and Phoebe (Eleanor and Charles died in childhood). Warren's **father was a farmer** who became a physician, his mother was a midwife. He also had the **nickname** Big Foot, as he wore a size 14 shoe. Harding's mother nicknamed him "Winnie" because she had wanted his name to be Winfield, but her husband had said no" His father told him, "Warren, it's a good thing you wasn't born a gal because you'd be in the family way all the time. **You can't say no.**"

Warren went to a one-room schoolhouse and later graduated in 1882 from **Ohio Central College**. He went on to **newspaper work**, being a reporter, an editor, and later a publisher. In 1884, having **bought the *Marion Daily Star*** for $300, he drove the other two local newspapers out of business. Warren did well.

Warren liked young, beautiful women, and they liked him. His favorite pastimes were drinking, poker, and sex. **Florence King** met Warren when she went to his house to teach piano to his sister. Florence avidly pursued Warren, and he saw that Florence could help him with his business and political career. They got married on July 8, 1891, but they had no children. Florence proclaimed she would get Warren elected president of the country. She made his **newspaper** a big success, but Harding did not like her bossy style and called her "**Duchess.**" After over a year of marriage, Warren was depressed after several nervous breakdowns and admitted himself to the **Battle Creek Sanitarium**, run by Dr. **Kellogg**, inventor of **corn flakes**, which he claimed would cure depression.

In 1894, Warren resumed chasing women and got one of Florence's friends pregnant. But Warren gave her child support. Then he met **Carrie Phillips**, and they began an affair. Florence knew of Warren's affairs but supported his business and political careers. And although he loved many women, he would not divorce Florence. He liked having sex with other women, but he also liked his business partnership with Florence. Then in 1895, Warren lost his bid for **county auditor**, in 1899 began four years in the **Ohio State Senate**, followed by two years as **lieutenant governor of Ohio**. Warren was recognized as a prominent Republican, and he gave the nominating address for William Taft at the **1912 party convention**. In 1915, Harding was elected to the **U.S. Senate**. Then, Harding chaired the **1916 Republican Convention** and delivered the keynote address.

In the **1920 Republican Convention**, although a frontrunner, Harding did not get the nomination until the 10th ballot. Harding chose Calvin Coolidge to be his running mate. In the **1920 presidential** election, Republicans **Warren Harding** and **Calvin Coolidge** defeated the Democratic team of **James Cox** and **Franklin Roosevelt**, 16,152,200 to 9,147,353 in the popular vote and 404 to 127 in the electoral vote. Cox was the son-in-law of the outgoing president, Woodrow Wilson. Harding was 55 years old on the date of his inauguration. In his March 4, **1921, inaugural address**, Harding stated, "A world of super government is contrary to everything we cherish and can have no sanction by our Republic." He also said, "America's present need is not heroics, but healing: not nostrums, but healing." The Republicans took firm control of Congress, Senate 59-37 and House 302-131. Harding was elected president and Coolidge was elected vice president. Harding was the first person to be elected president while serving in the U.S. Senate.

Calvin Coolidge was born on July 4, 1872, on a farm in Plymouth, Vermont. He graduated from **Amherst College** in 1895 and was admitted to the Massachusetts Bar in 1897. After ten years of private practice, he served in the Massachusetts State House, then as mayor of Northampton (1910-1911), **state senate** (1912-1915), **lieutenant governor** (1916-1918), and **governor of Massachusetts** (1919-1920). When Labor Leader **Samuel Gompers** tried to convince Coolidge he was wrong to fire police officers in Boston for going on strike, Coolidge replied, "There is no right to strike against the public safety by anybody, anywhere, anytime." This got him on Harding's ticket in 1920. Known as "**Silent Cal**," Coolidge regularly attended cabinet meetings (the first vice president to do so), but he made few contributions at the meetings.

The **1921 Revenue Act** introduced favorable capital gains and permitted companies to take a tax deduction for profit sharing and stock bonus plans at the time of contribution, whereas employees would not be taxed until paid.

As first lady, Florence spent considerable time with the press, developing a friendly relationship. She posed for photos and maintained a private life while continuing a public one.

Harding's **cabinet** included **Vice President** Calvin Coolidge, **Secretary of State** Charles Hughes, **Secretary of the Treasury** Andrew Mellon, **Secretary of War** John Weeks, **Attorney General** Harry Daugherty, **Secretary of the Navy** Edwin Denby, **Postmaster General** William Hays, **Secretary of the Interior** Albert Fall, **Secretary of Agriculture** Henry Wallace, **Secretary of Labor** James Davis and **Secretary of Commerce** Herbert Hoover. And for some reason Harding gave his dog a chair in the Cabinet Room.

Harding was a hard-drinking, avid gambler, once losing the White House china in a poker game. He was also the **first president to broadcast** a speech over the radio, which he did from the White House in 1922. In **Leser vs Garnett** (1922), the U.S. Supreme Court ruled that the Nineteenth Amendment, which prohibited the federal government and states from denying citizens the right to vote on the basis of sex, was a valid part of the

Constitution. In the 1922 midterm elections, the Republicans still controlled Congress, but their margins were lowered: Senate 53-42 and House 225-207.

Harding stated that "collecting more taxes than needed is robbery." Harding also said, "Ambition is a commendable attribute without which no man succeeds, only inconsiderate ambition imperils." He notoriously proclaimed, "Let the Black man vote when he is fit to vote, prohibit the white man voting when he is unfit to vote." It is not surprising, then, that Harding was accused of being inducted into the **Ku Klux Klan** in a 1922 White House ceremony. Appropriately, Harding once stated, "I am not fit for this office and never should have been elected." Many agreed years later. Harding also said, "The presidency is hell! No other word can describe it." Also in 1922, the **Cable Act** stated that citizenship is not automatically granted by marrying a citizen.

Harding was also not a great grammatician. The poet E.E. Cummings wrote that Harding was "**the only man, woman or child who wrote a simple declarative sentence with seven grammatical errors.**" Woodrow Wilson said, "Harding is incapable of thoughts because he has nothing to think with."

In **Adkins vs Children's Hospital of D.C.** (1923), the U.S. Supreme Court ruled, citing Lochner vs New York, that D.C.'s September 19, 1918, minimum wage law for women and children was unconstitutional, as it interfered with the "freedom of contract" right under the Due Process Clause of the Fifth Amendment.

The Harding administration was rocked with **scandals**, ranging from Harding's **philandering** to government officials taking **kickbacks**, but the worst was probably the **Teapot Dome**

Conspiracy. Interior Secretary Albert Fall took $400,000 from oil executives in exchange for illegally leasing oil reserves in the Teapot Dome. Fall was sentenced to a year in jail and a fine of $100,000. As the story broke, Harding and his wife left town and traveled to **Alaska** (making him the first president to visit that territory – it became a state in 1959). Harding died of a heart attack on this trip, on August 2, 1923, at age 57, making Calvin Coolidge the 30th president.

Congress made no pay changes during Harding's term of presidency.

His last words were, "I expect to be well remembered." He was not. Many historians consider Harding among the **worst presidents** alongside James Buchanan and Andrew Johnson. A funeral train took the body from San Francisco to Washington. The rumor was that his **wife had poisoned him**, retaliating for his years of cheating and womanizing. Since she refused an autopsy, this could not be confirmed. Upon Harding's death, Florence destroyed the majority of his papers to shield his affairs and corruption from discovery. Harding was buried in the Marion Cemetery in Marion, Ohio. Florence died on November 21, 1924, at age 64 of kidney failure and was buried next to her husband.

Key Events

New Jersey and New York formed the **Port Authority of New York** (1921); the last **Morgan silver dollar** was minted in Denver, Colorado (it was the **Peace Dollar**, commemorating the end of World War I) (1921); an **Unknown Soldier of World War I** was buried in **Arlington National** Cemetery, creating the **Tomb** of the **Unknown Soldier** (1921); Harding's term saw the beginning of a **two-year recession** (1921); **Ida Rosenthal** introduced the **Maidenform Bra** (1921); **Johnson & Johnson** introduced **Band-Aids** (1921); **Sardi's** Restaurant opened in New York City (1921); **Filene** opened the first credit union (1921); the **DJIA** closed at 81.10 at year-end, up 12.7 percent (1921); a variety of **international treaties** to promote peace and reduce tensions were put in place (1922); Congress authorized each **Supreme Court Justice** to hire **one law clerk** at $3,600 (1922); Georgia resident **Rebecca Felton** became the **first woman** elected to the U.S. Senate (1922); Congress passed a resolution favoring a **Jewish homeland** in Palestine (1922); *Reader's Digest* began publication (1922); a nationwide **coal strike** curtailed production (1922); **Sinclair Lewis's** novel *Babbitt*, depicting a crass, materialistic real estate agent, was seen by some as descriptive of business at the time (1922); the name "**bootlegger**" was coined from legging a bottle of booze in a boot (1922); Charles Walgreen introduced the malted milk shake at his drug store (1922); **T.S. Eliot** published *The Wasteland* (1922); **John Thompson** developed the **.45-caliber machine gun** (1922); **skill-based pay** was introduced by the **Franklin Company** (1922); the **DJIA** closed at 98.73 at year-end, up 21.7 percent (1922); **Alfred Sloan** succeeded Pierre DuPont at General Motors and introduced **decentralization**, as opposed to Ford's **central control** (1923); and the **DJIA** closed at 95.52 at year-end, down 2.70 percent (1923).

Calvin Coolidge
(30ᵗʰ President)

August 2, 1923 - March 4, 1929

John Calvin Coolidge Jr. was born on July 4, 1872, in Plymouth, Vermont, on a farm to John and Victoria Coolidge. Calvin was the first president **born on the Fourth of July**. He was **sickly** and suffered from asthma. He was devastated when his mother died when he was 12 years old. Calvin had one sister, Abigail, and she died when he was 18. Schooling consisted of elementary school, then the Black River Academy, and St. Johnsbury Academy followed by **Amherst College**. He graduated from Amherst in 1895 and went on to practice **law**, having been admitted to the Massachusetts bar in 1897. He married **Grace Goodhue** in 1905. They had two children: John and Calvin Jr.

In 1907, Calvin began serving in the Massachusetts House of Representatives for two years. This was followed by two years as **mayor** of Northampton. In 1911, he began four years as a **state senator**. This was followed by two years as **lieutenant governor** of Massachusetts and then two years as **governor**. Calvin then served as **President Harding's vice president**. When the latter died on August 2, 1923, Coolidge became the 30th president. This happened while he was vacationing in Vermont with his father, who, being a notary public, swore his son into office. Coolidge was the **first president not sworn in at the nation's capital** by a U.S. Supreme Court Justice.

Coolidge was the **sixth vice president to become president** due to his president's death (Tyler, Fillmore, Johnson, Arthur, and Roosevelt preceded him). He also became the ninth vice president to become president (John Adams, Thomas Jefferson, Martin Van Buren, John Tyler, Millard Fillmore, Andrew Johnson, Chester Arthur, and Theodore Roosevelt preceded him).

His 1923 year-end address to Congress was the first radio broadcast of the president's annual speech.

Coolidge's first **cabinet** was a continuation of Harding's last cabinet. Coolidge's first term cabinet included **Secretary of State** Charles Hughes, **Secretary of the Treasury** Andrew Mellon, **Secretary of War** John Weeks, **Attorney General** Harry Daugherty, **Secretary of the Navy** Edwin Denby, **Postmaster General** Harry New, **Secretary of the Interior** Hubert Work, **Secretary of Agriculture** Henry Wallace, **Secretary of Labor** James Davis and **Secretary of Commerce** Herbert Hoover.

Calvin's sixteen-year-old son, Calvin Jr., died from an infection during the summer his father was nominated for a full term in

1924. Coolidge's presidential campaign slogan was "Keep Cool and Keep Coolidge." In the **1924 presidential election**, Republican **Calvin Coolidge** and his running mate **Charles Dawes** received 15,725,016 popular votes to 8,386,508 for Democrats **John Davis** and **Charles W. Bryan**. Coolidge and Dawes received 382 electoral votes; Davis and Bryan received 136. Progressive candidates Robert La Follette and his running mate received 4,822,856 popular votes and 13 electoral votes. All the electoral votes were from La Follette's home state of Wisconsin. Calvin Coolidge was elected president and Charles Dawes was elected vice president. The Republicans continued to control Congress, Senate 54-41 and House 247-18. In 1924, Nellie Taylor Ross from Wyoming and Miriam Ferguson from Texas were the first female elected governors.

Charles Gates Dawes was born on August 27, 1865, in Marietta, Ohio. His father represented the North in the Civil War and was subsequently elected to the U.S. House of Representatives. Charles' childhood and educational history are a mystery, but he did become a lawyer and a bank director in Lincoln, Nebraska. When the financial Panic of 1893 happened, Dawes moved to Chicago and became a leader in the utilities industry, and in 1896, he managed Ohio Governor William McKinley's successful presidential campaign in Illinois. After being elected, McKinley appointed Dawes U.S. Controller of the Currency, where he reformed banking practices. Following McKinley's assassination in 1901, Dawes ran unsuccessfully for the U.S. Senate and then founded the Central Trust Company. In 1917, he joined the army and rose to become a highly decorated brigadier general. After the war, President Harding appointed Dawes the first Director of the U.S. Bureau of the Budget, where he streamlined the budgetary procedures and received the **Nobel**

Peace Prize for the Dawes Plan. After Dawes was elected vice president, he told future Vice President Alben Barkley, "This is a hell of a job. I look at newspapers every morning to see how the president's health is." Later, President Hoover appointed Dawes the U.S. Ambassador to Great Britain in 1929. In 1932, he resumed his banking career, and he died on April 23, 1951, at age 85 in Evanston, Illinois.

In his March 4, **1924, inaugural address**, Coolidge stated, "The method of raising revenue ought not to impede the transaction of business; it ought to encourage it. I am opposed to extremely high rates because they produce little or no revenue. It was the **first inauguration broadcast nationally on radio**. Coolidge was 46 years old on the date of his inauguration.

Coolidge's second-term **cabinet** included **Vice President** Charles Dawes, **Secretary of State** Frank Kellogg, **Secretary of the Treasury** Andrew Mellon, **Secretary of War** Dwight Davis, **Attorney General** John Sargent, **Secretary of the Navy** Curtis Wilbur, **Postmaster General** Harry New, **Secretary of the Interior** Hubert Work, **Secretary of Agriculture** William Jardine, **Secretary of Labor** James Davis and **Secretary of Commerce** Herbert Hoover. Coolidge replaced half of his original cabinet: Hughes, Weeks, Daugherty, Denby, and Wallace were gone.

Coolidge said, "Nothing is easier than spending public money; nothing is harder than to resist doing it." Coolidge **quickly restored faith** in a government shaken by scandals and graft by cleaning house of corrupt officials. He shook hundreds of visitors' hands each day. Announcing that "the business of America is business," he ushered in a period of prosperity sometimes called the "**Roaring Twenties**", although he was frugal and conservative. The automobile was well established, shrinking distance.

The **1924 Immigration Act** put in place a quota system regarding immigration. In **Barnes vs Andrews** (1924), the U.S. Supreme Court ruled that a director's inattentive behavior must be proved the reason for company loss in order for a shareholder to bring a successful court action.

The **1925 Certiorari Act** stated the U.S. Supreme Court would review only those cases it wanted to review, and they would be granted a certiorari petition. In 1925, Congress increased the pay of legislators to $8,000 per annum (up from 1907's $7,500).

Three key laws were enacted in **1926**: the **Revenue Act**, which reduced income and excise taxes; the **Air Commerce Act**, which created government agencies to control airports; and the **Railway Act**, which safeguarded railway unions. In **Myers vs United States** (1926), the U.S. Supreme Court ruled that the president has the "exclusive power" to remove executive officers appointed by him, and removal does not need to be done "with the advice and consent of the Senate."

In **Nixon vs Herndon** (1927), the U.S. Supreme Court ruled that a 1923 Texas statute denying Black citizens from voting in the Democratic Party primary in Texas violated the Equal Protection Clause of the Fourteenth Amendment. In 1927, Congress increased the pay of the associate justices of the U.S. Supreme Court to $20,000 (up from 1911's $14,500), and the chief justice's pay was increased to $25,000 (from 1911's $15,000). **Congress made no other pay changes during Coolidge's term of presidency.** In 1927, Charles Lindbergh completed a solo nonstop flight from New York to Paris.

In **Olmstead vs United States** (1928), the U.S. Supreme Court ruled that illegal wiretaps by the government of incriminating private telephone conversations to be used as evidence in a criminal trial in federal court did not violate the Fourth Amendment's protection from unreasonable search and seizure.

Coolidge was a **man of few words**. Once told by a woman that she made a bet she could get him to say more than two words, he responded, "You lose." Reportedly, the president and First Lady visited a farm, and the First Lady was told by the farmer that a rooster had sex several times a day. She said, "Tell that to Mr. Coolidge." He did, and the president asked, "With the same hen?" The farmer said no. Coolidge said, "Tell that to Mrs. Coolidge." His nickname was "**Silent Cal.**" Nonetheless, he held over 500 press conferences. Calvin was **taciturn** and said to be **silent in five languages**.

Grace Coolidge charmed the public and was a vibrant White House hostess. While Calvin was **aloof**, Grace was **outgoing and charming**. Both were animal lovers. They had a pet raccoon, a pygmy hippopotamus, two lions, and a white collie. That collie sitting alongside First Lady Grace was the **first portrait of a dog** in the White House. Grace considered the White House a museum, so she went about redecorating the building. Her favorite **charity** was the **Clarke School for the Deaf**, where **she taught**. It was important to her that she was both a good wife and a good mother. Some said she "had taught the deaf to hear; now she might be able to teach the mute to speak," an obvious reference to Silent Cal. As First Lady, Grace welcomed the role of entertainer. Deaf and blind disability advocate **Helen Keller** was a frequent White House guest.

Coolidge was known for **tax cutting, frugality**, and an **unwillingness** to spend federal dollars on local issues. He stated, "There is no dignity quite so impressive and no independence quite so important, as living within your means." Coolidge preferred a "hands-off approach of government intervention in business or people's lives." He believed in **local self-government** not federal-dollar bailouts. He also believed in the **Constitution** and used his veto as a check on unconstitutional legislation, expecting Congress to work things out. His firm **religious beliefs** guided his domestic and foreign policies.

The Coolidges hosted dinners aboard the *Mayflower*, the presidential yacht. Typical dinners included boiled ham, chicken chop suey, corn muffins, roast beef, soft-shelled crabs, and veal curry. Calvin called every meal "supper" and preferred to either eat alone or with his wife.

Cal stated, "I have never been hurt by anything I didn't say." As he was leaving office, he stated, "Perhaps one of the most important accomplishments of my administration has been minding my own business." He went on to add, "If the federal government should go out of existence, the common man would not detect the difference in affairs of their daily life for a considerable length of time." Rather lengthy for a man of few words.

When Secretary of Commerce Herbert Hoover announced, he was going to run for the 31st presidency, Cal stated, "That man has offered me unsolicited advice for six years, all of it bad." Calvin declined to run for a second full term in 1928. In 1929, several months after Cal left office, the stock market crashed.

Calvin died on January 5, 1933, of a **coronary** at age 60 while working on a George Washington jigsaw puzzle. Before dying, he stated, "I feel I no longer fit in with these times." In his **twenty-three words will**, he gave everything to his wife. He was buried in Plymouth North Cemetery in Plymouth, Vermont. His wife, Grace, died on July 8, 1957, at age 78 and was buried with her husband.

Most historians give Coolidge a somewhat **below average rating**.

Key Events

Bootlegger Owney Madden opened the **Cotton Club** speakeasy in Black Harlem (1923); the famed New York restaurant **Delmonico's** closed (1923); *New Yorker* magazine began publication (1923); Henry Ford published *My Life and Work* (1923); Walt and Roy Disney formed the **Disney Company** (1923); **J. Edgar Hoover** became head of the FBI (1923); the **Thompson submachine gun**, invented in World War I, was nicknamed the "tommy gun" or "Chicago typewriter," as it was favored by bootleggers (1923); *Time Magazine* appeared on newsstands (1923); the **American Management Association** was formed (1923); the **DJIA** closed at 95.52 at year-end, down 2.70 percent (1923); the film company **Metro-Goldwyn-Mayer** began (1924); Charles Birdseye invented **frozen foods** (1924); Congress created the **Border Patrol** to curtail the flow of illegal alcohol from Canada during Prohibition (1924); a four-year period of war began between **Al Capone** and the Irish O'Bannion Mob, resulting in 200 gang killings (1924); after North Side Chicago bootlegger **Dion O'Bannion** was killed in his florist shop, the funeral was attended by 10,000 people with 26 truckloads of flowers (1924); **Johnny Torrio** bought out O'Bannion's bootlegging business for $500,000 (1924); **Elinor Smith** became the first licensed airplane pilot (1924); George Gershwin penned *Rhapsody in Blue* (1924); **Max Weber** published *The Theory of Social and Economic Organization* (1924); the **DJIA** closed at 120.51 at year end, up 26.2 percent (1924); A. Philip Randolph organized the **Brotherhood of Sleeping Pullmans**, the first African-American labor union (1925); Walter Chrysler founded the **Chrysler** automotive company (1925); **Bell Laboratories** was founded (1925); thirty-thousand **Ku Klux Klansmen** marched on Washington, D.C. (1925); installment **plans** for purchasing consumer goods were introduced (1925): the first **Grand Ole Opry** was broadcast (1925); F. Scott Fitzgerald published *The Great Gatsby*, a novel depicting the life of a decadent multi-millionaire (1925); **radar** was invented (1925); Theodore Dreiser's *An American Tragedy* focused on the unconventional morality of the time (1925); gangster **Frankie Yale's** silver coffin was accompanied by 200 limousines (1925); Columbia University and the Presbyterian Hospital created the **Columbia Presbyterian Hospital** (1925); the **DJIA** closed at 156.66 at year-end, up 30.0 percent (1925); **Wheaties** cereal aired the first singing commercial on radio (1926); the **Industrial Relations Counselors** (predecessor to Organizational Resources Counselors) began (1926); **Alfred Sloan** reorganized General Motors succeeding William Durant (1926); **Hammacher Schlemmer** opened in New York City (1926); the **National Broadcasting System** (NBC) was founded by David Sarnoff (1926); the **Book-of-the-Month Club** was founded (1926); Dr. Robert Goddard created the **first liquid fuel rocket** (1926); the U.S. Treasury ruled that exercise of an **employee stock option** for less than fair market value generated taxable income (1926); it became known that **Al Capone** was not Sicilian and therefore technically not **mafia** (1926); it was estimated **bootleg liquor sales** exceeded $3.5 billion a year (1926); **Ernest Hemingway** published *The Sun Also Rises* (1926); the **DJIA** closed at 157.20 at year-end, up 0.3 percent (1926); the **Bank of America** was created from Amadeo Giannini's Italian Bank (1927); **Juan Trippe** formed the **Pan American World Airways**, carrying mail and passengers to South America (1927); **Henry Ford** shut down production for six months to make the switch from the **Model T** to the **Model A** car (1927); **Philo Farnsworth** introduced **television** (1927); **Christ Cella** opened in New York City as a **speakeasy restaurant** (1927); the **electric chair** replaced the hangman's noose in Illinois (1927); **Sinclair Lewis** illustrated the importance of self-promotion in *Elmer Gantry* (1927); the first full-length talking picture, *The Jazz Singer*, opened with **Al Jolson** (1927); the **Mississippi Great Flood** left 100,000 homeless (1927); the **DJIA** closed at 202.40 at year-end, up 28.8 percent (1927); **Edwin Armstrong** began experimenting with wideband frequency modulation (**FM**) (1928); the **Columbia Broadcasting System** (CBS) was founded by **William Haley** with 47 stations (1928); the **DJIA** closed at 300.00 at year-end, up 48.2 percent (1928); anthropologist **Margaret Meade** published *Coming of Age in Samoa* (1928); **Mickey Mouse** was created by **Walt Disney in** *Steamboat Willie* (1928); one **Texas Ranger** was sent in response to a request to stop a riot in Austin, Texas (when asked why only one Ranger?, the response was, "You only said there was one riot.") (1928); **Amelia Earhart** became the first woman to fly across the Atlantic Ocean (1928); the airship *Graf Zeppelin* crossed the Atlantic (1928); and George Eastman introduced the colored motion picture film (1928).

Herbert Hoover (31ˢᵗ President)

March 4, 1929 – March 4, 1933

Herbert Hoover was born on August 10, 1874, to Quakers Jesse Clark Hoover and Huldah Randall Hoover in West Branch, Iowa. His father was a Quaker blacksmith and died six years later. Herbert had two siblings, Mary and Theodore. Herbert was born between the two. The Quaker philosophy of co-operation, hard work, nonviolence, and spirituality influenced Hoover deeply. His mother died when Herbert was nine years old. An uncle took him to Oregon. As a young boy, Hoover was paid $1 for every 100 bags he picked of potatoes. Except for mathematics, Hoover performed below average in school. Nevertheless, he was the **first student** to be enrolled in **Stanford University**, California, in 1891. To pay his expenses, Hoover did typing and student laundry, as well as manage the school's baseball and football teams. He also assisted in geological surveys. Herbert graduated with a degree in **geology** in 1895 and went to work as a **mining engineer** in Africa, Australia, China, and Europe.

In 1898, he proposed by telegram to his college girlfriend, Lou Henry, a geology student, and she accepted. Lou's father gave her the name Lou because he wanted a son, and he raised her as a tomboy. They were **married** on February 10, 1899, both age 25. They later had two children, Allen and Herbert Jr. Lou was fascinated with the outdoors and was one of the first women to get a degree in geology from Stanford University where she met Herbert. They traveled extensively. While they were in China, the **1900 Boxer Rebellion** placed them under siege. Lou took to helping the sick and injured. Both learned Chinese. Later, they moved to London and worked for British mining companies. Herbert was a **millionaire** by age 40, using his engineering degree to **locate gold mines** around the world. His nickname was the "great engineer." But the Great Depression put a great stress on their relationship.

When World War I broke out, Lou sought to help relief efforts. Herbert headed up the **U.S. Food Administration** from 1915 to 1919 and worked with war relief agencies. General Pershing called Hoover "the food regulator of the world," and the press called him "America's Food Czar." Hoover's work earned him a place on a list of the **ten greatest living Americans** published by the *New York Times* at war's end. In 1920, FDR thought Hoover would make a great U.S. president, but Hoover could not be convinced to join the Democratic Party. From 1921 to 1923, Hoover served as **Secretary of Commerce** under President Harding, during which time he headed an effort to alleviate the famine raging in Russia. He joined Harding's cabinet, earning an annual pay of $15,000, turning down an annual income of $500,000 from the Guggenheim family. Hoover was also considered to be the undersecretary of everything else by Harding. From 1922 to 1925, Lou served as **president of the Girl Scouts** and from 1923 to 1928, Herbert served as Secretary of Commerce under President Coolidge. His nickname was "chief of the leadership and organization skills."

When Calvin Coolidge decided not to run for re-election, Secretary of Commerce Herbert Hoover launched an isolationist, pro-business, and prohibition-tolerant campaign for the presidency.

The **Republican presidential convention** was held in Kansas City and lasted four days. Before it even opened, Hoover had 476 of the 545 delegate votes needed. He also had backing from President Coolidge. Hoover's advisors, believing Hoover's image was that of a strict businessman, had pictures taken of him smiling with his dog. **Hoover accepted the nomination** by telegram. In his campaign, he promised, "A chicken in every pot, and a car in every garage."

In the **1928 election**, Republicans **Herbert Hoover** and **Charles Curtis** received 21,392,190 of the popular votes, **crushing** Democrats **Alfred Smith** and **Joseph Robinson** who received 15,016,443 popular votes. Hoover and Curtis took the electoral college 444 to 87. GOP control of Congress was strengthened: Senate 56-39 and House 270-164.

Charles Curtis was born on January 25, 1860, in Topeka, Kansas. His mother was a Native American; his father was European. Charles grew up on the **Kaw Reservation** near Topeka. He operated a horse-drawn taxi service and studied law. Having passed the Kansas bar in 1881, he went on to become a **prosecuting attorney** from 1885 to 1889. In 1893 he was elected to the House of Representatives, where he served from 1907 until 1913. In 1915, he was again elected to the U.S. Senate, and he served until 1929, when he was elected vice president. Following his term of office, he stayed in Washington, D.C., where he practiced law until he died of a heart attack at age 76 on February 8, 1936. He was buried on a reservation in Topeka, Kansas.

The swearing-in by **Chief Justice William Taft** on March 4, 1929, was the first inauguration covered by a **talking newsreel**. Taft is the only person to have served as **both as a president** (the 27th) and a **chief justice**. Hoover was 54 years old on the date of his inauguration. In his **March 4, 1929, inaugural address**, Hoover stated, "Our whole system of self-government will crumble if officials elect what laws they will enforce or citizens elect what laws they will support." Hoover was the last president to **write his own acceptance speech**.

Hoover's **cabinet** included **Vice President** Charles Curtis, **Secretary of State** Henry Stimson, **Secretary of the Treasury** Andrew Mellon, **Secretary of War** James W. Good, **Attorney General** William Mitchell, **Secretary of the Navy** Charles Adams, **Postmaster General** Walter Brown, **Secretary of the Interior** Ray Lyman Wilbur, **Secretary of Agriculture** Arthur Hyde, **Secretary of Labor** James Davis and **Secretary of Commerce** Robert Lamont.

Lou Henry was the first first lady to make a national radio address encouraging volunteerism to help others. Although Herbert promised "a chicken in every pot, and a car in every garage," the **1929 Wall Street crash** on Black Thursday, October 24th, and Black Tuesday, October 29th, made that promise unachievable. **Easy credit** allowing investors to buy stock on the margin and an **agricultural drought** were the two conditions that led to the **stock market crash**. Within weeks, the market lost **over $25 billion**, some 1,300 banks had closed, and millions had lost their jobs. But with unemployment soaring, Herbert did get $116 million for public works projects.

The crash had been preceded by a dramatic drop in farm prices due to foreign competition a year earlier. The decade ended in 1929 with an orgy of self-indulgence, along with a decade of astronomical productivity increases. Months before the crash, Merrill Lynch founder Charles Merrill advised clients to take advantage of high stock prices and rebalance their asset portfolios. With the stock market collapse, fortunes were wiped out and individuals who bought on margin were thrown into bankruptcy when they could not cover the margin calls. Thousands of **banks failed**, and millions were quickly **unemployed**.

With a booming stock market, many companies had moved to various types of stock award and stock purchase plans in the 1920s, but following the stock market crash in 1929, not only were few new benefit plans introduced, many were suspended or terminated because of company financial woes. With **unemployment at 25%**, workers were happy to have a job. Since they had demonstrated an inability to guarantee employment, union membership was down to 10% of the workforce, half that of a decade earlier.

In **The Pocket Veto Case** (1929), the U.S. Supreme Court upheld the "pocket veto" and ruled that, under the second clause in Section 7 of Article 1 of the Constitution, the president can constitutionally veto a bill by not signing and returning it to Congress "within ten Days (Sundays excepted) after it shall have been presented to him."

In 1930, **Babe Ruth** was asked to justify being paid $80,000 a year when President Hoover made $75,000. Ruth replied, "I had a better year."

In the 1930 midterms, the GOP margins were reduced: Senate 48-47 and House 218-216.

The **1930 Smoot-Hawley Tariff Act** raised tariffs on a wide range of imports by 20% to protect American industry. Prompt retaliatory tariff action by foreign companies contributed to the start of the Great Depression. The **Great Depression** followed the **stock market crash**. The stock market would not reach its 1929 peak for more than 25 years. Its low of 85 was reached in late 1932. Hoover believed private enterprises and local entities should be the ones to focus on the problem of the economy. He noted, "About the time we think we can make ends meet, somebody changes the ends." Terms such as **"Hoover Hotel"** for a cardboard shack and **"Hooverville"** for a town of such shacks were common. However, Hoover did his bit by **donating his $75,000 salary to charity**. JFK would later do the same. Over seventy percent of U.S. family income was below the $2,500 annual income considered standard for decent living. Hoover said, "Being a politician is a poor profession. Being a public servant is a noble one."

Herbert Hoover was a very **private person**. In the White House, he used Woodrow Wilson's desk and replaced his one secretary with three. The White House servants were expected to disappear when he entered a room. And when discussing confidential topics, he and his wife conversed in **Mandarin** for fear of being overheard.

Hoover sent Congress a written copy of his **1930 State of the Union Address** rather than deliver it in person.

The **1931 Revenue Act** established a 1.75% corporate income tax and a 45% tax on estates in excess of $10 million. The **1931 Davis-Bacon Act** required area-comparable pay for those working on federal contracts. In **Near vs Minnesota** (1931), the U.S. Supreme Court ruled that Minnesota's 1925 Public Nuisance Law, which censored information prior to publication, was unconstitutional.

After a game with a six-pound **medicine ball** on the White House lawn with friends, Hoover would get into a **formal dinner jacket** and have a seven-course meal featuring an appetizer, soup, salad, meat, fish, dessert, and coffee, along with a Cuban cigar. A quick eater, he had to slow down when guests were present. Husband and wife dined alone only once a year, February 10th, the date of their anniversary. Those meals consisted of imported delicacies and salmon.

The **1932 Federal Kidnapping Act** made kidnapping a felony. This was known as the **Lindbergh Law**, as it followed the kidnapping and murder of aviator Charles Lindbergh's son. In **Powell vs Alabama** (1932), the U.S. Supreme Court ruled that under the Due Process Clause of the Fourteenth Amendment, in capital cases, the accused has the right to the effective aid of counsel.

In the **1932 presidential election**, Democrats **Franklin Roosevelt** and his vice-presidential candidate **John Nance Garner** easily defeated the Republicans, President **Herbert Hoover** and **Charles Curtis**, 22,821,857 to 15,761,845 in the popular vote and 472 to 59 in the electoral vote. Roosevelt was elected president and Garner was elected vice president. The Democrats took over Congress: Senate 59-36 and House 313-103.

In 1932, Congress increased the legislative salaries to $8,000 a year (up from 1907's $7,500). **The only pay change made by Congress during Hoover's term of presidency**.

The **20th Amendment to the U.S. Constitution**, ratified on January 23, 1933, stated the terms of office of the president, vice president, senators, and representatives (see Appendix C).

During the 1930s, he traveled through Europe, even meeting Hitler and Chamberlain. Hoover wanted America to stay neutral in international conflict. Hoover **failed at attempts to be the Republican nominee** for president in 1936, 1940, and 1944. The **Hoover Dam** was named after President Hoover while he was still in office.

Hoover once stated, "Let us remember that the great human advances have not been brought about by mediocre men and women. They were brought about by distinctly uncommon men and women with vital sparks of leadership." Hoover also said, "The sole function of government is the beneficial development of private enterprise." He is also credited with the phrase, "Blessed are the young for they shall inherit the national debt."

By 1951, according to the Gallup pollster, Hoover was the **fifth most admired man** in his country. When asked why, he stated, "I outlived the negative voters."

Hoover died on October 20, 1964, at 90 of intestinal cancer and was buried in the Herbert Hoover National Historic Site in West Branch, Iowa. His last words were, "Good night." His wife died of a heart attack on January 7, 1944, at age 69 and was buried next to him.

Historians rate Hoover's performance as **significantly below average**.

Key Events

Edwin Land developed a machine to produce **Polaroid** strips (1929); the **flight simulator** was introduced (1929); the **Yuengling Brewery** opened in Pottsville, Pennsylvania (1929); following a financial disaster, **Goldman Sachs** became a private partnership (1929); nearly half of American industry was controlled by 200 companies (1929); Ford introduced its Model A **station wagon** (1929); **former Interior Secretary Albert Fall** was convicted of accepting bribes in leasing the **Teapot Dome** naval oil reserve (1929); the **New York Yankees** became the first team to put numbers on player uniforms (1929); the **Museum of Modern Art** opened in New York City (1929); gangster "**Bugs**" Moran escaped being killed in the Al Capone-ordered Chicago **St. Valentine's Day massacre** in which seven died, a sign of Capone's control over Chicago (1929); while **prohibition** was in effect, bootlegging was in vogue, and gangsters were killing each other, so **Lucky Luciano** called for a three-day conference of top gang leaders in Atlantic City (1929); a **national syndicate**, which was to operate as a business corporation, with grievances brought before the board for resolution, where necessary – the ruling council, called "**The Commission**," gave permission to murder someone (**Louis Lepke Buchalter** was put in charge of **Murder** Inc., the execution arm of the Syndicate) (1929); ex-bootlegger **Sherman Billingsley** opened the **Stork Club** speakeasy (one of 25,000 in New York City) (1929); federal agent **Eliot Ness** formed his team of **Untouchables** to battle bootleggers (1929); a fictional General Motors was described in *Dodsworth* by Sinclair Lewis (1929); William Faulkner published *The Sound and the Fury* (1929); the **DJIA** closed at 248.48 at year-end, down 18.8 percent (1929); Salvatore Maranzano (**capo di tutti capo** – boss of all bosses) set up the Five Families of New York City, headed by **Luciano** (later Genovese), Joseph

Profaci (later Joseph Columbo), Tommaso **Gagliano** (later Gaetano Lucchese), Vincent **Mangano**, and Joseph **Maranzano** (later Joseph Bonanno) (1930); horse **Gallant Fox** was the Triple Crown winner (1930); **Sinclair Lewis** was the first American to win the **Nobel Prize for Literature** (1930); the 77-floor **Chrysler Building** opened in New York City as the tallest in the world (1930); the **Communist Party** held a demonstration of 100,000 in New York (1930); the U.S. population was over 122 million (1930); **Jack Kriendler** and **Charlie Berns** opened the speakeasy **"21" Club**, disguised as a tearoom in New York, on New Year's Day (1930); **Kohler Plumbing** opened in Wisconsin (1930); Philo Farnsworth received the **television** system patent (1930); **Juan Trippe** completed the first round-trip across the Atlantic, later forming **Pan American Airways** (1930); 3M introduced **Scotch tape** (1930); the **Chase Manhattan Bank** was formed (1930); the **George Washington Bridge** opened, connecting New Jersey and New York (1930); the hotels **Carlyle and Pierre** opened in New York City (1930); the **Whitney Museum** opened in Greenwich Village, New York (1930); the **McCann-Erickson** advertising firm was formed (1930); shack towns were called **Hoovervilles**, named after the President (1930); the **DJIA** closed at 164.58 at year-end, down 33.8 percent (1930); **Leonarde Keeler** patented the **polygraph** (1931); the **Empire State Building** opened, passing the Chrysler Building as the as the world's tallest building (1931); the new **Waldorf-Astoria** opened on Park Avenue, NYC (1931); **Al Capone** was convicted of income tax evasion (1931); Joseph Maranzano, age 45, was killed by Meyer Lansky and Bugsy Siegel on orders from Luciano (1931); "The Star Spangled Banner" became the national anthem (1931); the *Ziegfeld Follies* gave its last performance (1931); **Nevada legalized gambling** (1931); a **corporate income tax** of 1.75 percent was established (1931); **gangster-based movies** were popular, including ***Little Caesar*** with Edward G. Robinson and ***Public Enemy*** with James Cagney (1931); the **DJIA** closed at 77.90 at year-end, down 52.8 percent (1931); Congress put in place the **Reconstruction Finance Corporation** (1932); a "**Bonus Army**" of some 12,000 veterans marched on Washington demanding they be paid (1932); unemployment reached over **12 million** (1932); **Ellis Island** was converted from an immigration entry to a detention center (1932); the **Radio City Music Hall** opened in New York City (1932); gangster "**Mad Dog**" Coll was gunned down in Chicago (1932); **Bruno Hauptmann** was found guilty for kidnapping and killing Charles Lindbergh's child (1932); in the **Hawthorne Telephone Company** studies, Elton Mayo observed that production improved in response to workers being noticed (1932); multi-millionaire **Pierre du Pont** financed the Prohibition Repeal Movement, believing the tax on liquor would lower income tax (1932); **Hattie Wyatt Caraway** (Wyoming) became the first woman elected to the U.S. Senate (1932); **Rensis Likert** developed **attitude measurements** (1932); and the **DJIA** closed at 59.93 at year-end, down 23.1 percent, as the stock market bottomed out to about 20% of its pre-crash high (1932).

Franklin D. Roosevelt (32ND President)

March 4, 1933 – April 12, 1945

Franklin Delano Roosevelt was born on January 30, 1882, to James Roosevelt and Sara Delano Roosevelt in Hyde Park, New York. Franklin was named after his first great-grandfather and his mother. Franklin had a half-brother from James' first marriage. He quickly got the nickname **FDR**. Delano was his **mother's maiden name**. She was from a wealthy family. Franklin's father headed a successful coal and transportation business. President Theodore Roosevelt was a fifth cousin.

Franklin's wealthy parents sent him to **private schools**, where he learned to speak French and German, and provided him with a **governess** who watched over him. He enjoyed traveling with his parents in the United States and Europe. His lifelong hobby was **stamp collecting**, and he reportedly amassed over 25,000 of them. He was also a **triskaidekaphobic**: one who fears the number thirteen. He once stated, "Happiness lies in the joy of achievement and the thrill of creative effort." FDR went on to graduate from **Harvard College** in 1903 and then to **Columbia Law School**. There he met **Anna Eleanor Roosevelt**, daughter of Theodore Roosevelt's brother. She did not use the name Anna. She was orphaned at age ten. FDR and Eleanor were **married** on March 17, 1905. President Theodore Roosevelt walked her down the aisle. They would have **six children** together. The five who lived past childhood were Anna, Elliott, Franklin Jr., James, and John. In 1907, FDR passed the **New York bar exam** and began practicing law. To help him with his correspondence, FDR hired Marguerite LeHand, known as **Missy**. She was efficient but not very attractive.

In 1910, FDR began an affair with **Lucy Mercer**, Eleanor's private secretary. It would continue until his death. During World War I, Eleanor volunteered to work with the **Red Cross**. After the war, she began campaigning for **women's rights**. Later, as FDR's First Lady, she pressured him to place women in federal jobs. The results were more **women were put in government jobs** than under all the previous presidents combined. Eleanor wrote a **daily column** for many years, and during World War II, she co-authored the **Office of Civil Defense**. Eleanor became more active in support of a number of social issues, and FDR appreciated her work with the less fortunate.

FDR used the **Roosevelt name** to be elected a **New York state senator** in 1910 and backed Woodrow Wilson's presidency in 1912. FDR **became Assistant Secretary of the U.S. Navy** in 1913, a position he held through World War I (1914-1918). He failed to get the Democratic nomination for the U.S. Senate in 1914. But in 1920, he was chosen as the vice-presidential **running mate of Ohio Governor James Cox** for president. They were **defeated** by Warren Harding and Calvin Coolidge in the **1920 presidential election**. The following year, while traveling in Canada, FDR **contracted polio** and was paralyzed from the waist down. He could only walk with heavy metal braces, or he needed a wheelchair. However, since he was rarely photographed with either, **few knew of his paralysis**. When behind a podium, he needed to hold on with both hands to prevent himself from falling. His philosophy on public speaking was, "Be sincere, be brief, be seated." In his case, this meant a wheelchair.

In 1923, FDR moved to **Florida** and lived on a houseboat. Eleanor did not join him, but Missy did. Then he bought a run-down hotel in Georgia and named it **Warm Springs** for its thermal pools. Meanwhile, Eleanor made friends with **lesbians** Nancy Cook and Marion Dickerman. In 1927, FDR left the South and entered politics. In 1928, he ran for **governor of New York** and was elected.

With unemployment at 25% of the workforce and widespread dissatisfaction with how President Hoover was handling the economy following the stock market crash in 1929, FDR accepted the Democratic **nomination for president** on July 2, 1932. FDR stated, "I promise a **new deal** for the American people by creation of jobs, pension for workers and regulation of the stock exchange." These promises far exceeded the cautious approach of President Hoover in solving the great depression facing the nation. FDR got the nomination only after House Speaker John Nance Garner, also a candidate, freed his delegates, and threw his support to FDR.

In the **1932 presidential election**, Democrats **Franklin Roosevelt** and his vice-presidential candidate **John Nance Garner** easily defeated the Republicans, President **Herbert Hoover** and

FRANKLIN D. ROOSEVELT (32ND PRESIDENT)

Charles Curtis, 22,821,857 to 15,761,845 in the popular vote and 472 to 59 in the electoral vote. The Democrats took over Congress: Senate 59-36 and House 313-103.

John Nance Garner was born on November 22, 1868, in a **log cabin** in Detroit, Texas, the son of a Confederate military officer. He had to walk three miles each way to go to a schoolhouse. Later, he was only able to afford one semester at Vanderbilt University in Tennessee. Returning to Texas, he worked for an attorney and learned enough to pass the **Texas bar exam** in 1889 at age 21. He practiced law and then served as **county judge** from 1883 to 1889. From 1892 to 1902, he served in the **Texas House of Representatives**, followed by his election to the **U.S. House of Representatives**, where he was reelected 14 times. He was **Speaker of the House** in 1931. FDR named John Nance Garner his vice-presidential candidate. After being elected, Vice President Garner stated his **job "was not worth a bucket of warm piss."** Having resigned as Speaker of the House, Garner considered the **vice presidency a demotion**, adding, "It was the worst damn fool mistake I ever made." After serving a second term and having not been nominated for a third, Garner and his wife, Ettie, returned to Texas. They celebrated their 50th wedding anniversary in 1945. Ettie died three years later, and John died on November 7, 1967.

One month before the inauguration, **anarchist Giuseppe Zangara** shot five times at FDR, missing him but hitting Chicago Mayor Anton Cermak. In his **1933 inaugural address**, FDR gave his famous speech, "So, first of all, let me assert my firm belief the **only thing we have to fear is fear itself.**"

FDR's initial **cabinet** included **Vice President** John Nance Garner, **Secretary of State** Cordell Hull, **Secretary of the Treasury**

William Woodin, **Secretary of War** George Dern, **Attorney General** Homer Cummings, **Secretary of the Navy** Claude Swanson, **Postmaster General** James Farley, **Secretary of the Interior** Harold Ickes, **Secretary of Agriculture** Henry Wallace, **Secretary of Commerce** Daniel Roper, and **Secretary of Labor** Frances Perkins. Perkins was the first woman appointed to the Presidential Cabinet.

FDR spent more time with Lucy and less with Missy, to the satisfaction of the first and unhappiness of the second. Upon moving into the White House, FDR instructed the switchboard to accept calls from a "Mrs. Johnson," the **code name for Lucy Mercer**. Learning that Lucy was back in FDR's life, Eleanor took up with journalist **Lorena Hickok**, nicknamed "Hick," who, when off the job, wore men's clothing. Eleanor and Lorena exchanged many love letters. Eleanor gave Hick a bedroom in the White House. And FDR gave Missy a bedroom next to his bedroom.

On March 12, 1933, in FDR's first of 30 **fireside chats** on the radio, he explained his actions to the public. FDR stated, "I can assure you that it is safer to keep your money in a reopened bank than under the mattress." This followed his reopening of banks with Treasury Department licenses. He also addressed the issue of farm mortgages, allocating $2 billion for refinancing.

In **Rogers vs Hill** (1933), the U.S. Supreme Court ruled that payments unrelated to services rendered constitute a waste of corporate assets and may be actionable by the shareholder.

FDR's first 100 days were focused on government intervention to put the 12 million unemployed to work, aid the sick and elderly, and assist in the recovery of banking, business, and farming. These were the focal points of FDR's **New Deal**. FDR rammed his New Deal through Congress with personal zeal, leading his detractors to name him "**King Franklin**." Based on constitutional criteria alone, Roosevelt would fall below only Washington and Lincoln to among the bottom three: Buchanan, Johnson, and Harding. FDR created an **alphabet soup of agencies** without congressional approval. The agencies included the Federal Deposit Insurance Corporation, the Federal Housing Administration, the Public Works Administration, the Tennessee Valley Authority, the Securities Exchange Commission, and the Social Security Administration. And he issued more executive orders than all previous presidents combined.

With the country still recovering from the **Great Depression**, FDR saw the need to reduce the time between the election and the inauguration so that the government could act sooner on voters' choices. With that in mind, FDR got Section 1 of the **20th Amendment to the U.S. Constitution** (see Appendix C) changed to state, "The terms of the President and Vice President shall end at noon on the 20th day of January." This change was ratified on January 23, 1933. Previously, the terms ended on March 4th. The election was held in November.

In **1933**, FDR got **four key laws** passed: the **1933 National Industrial Recovery Act** helped to restore jobs and gave workers the right to collectively bargain for wages and work conditions; the **1933 Revenue Act** established the 3rd national bank; the **1933 Glass-Steagall Act** prohibited banks from underwriting bonds and stocks; and the **1933 Securities Act** instituted disclosure requirements when offering company securities for sale to the public. Also, the **1933 Federal Deposit Insurance Corporation (FDIC)** was established, protecting up to $5,000 of customer deposits. And funding for **the Reconstruction Finance Corporation** was increased to stimulate banking and business.

In 1933, Congress increased the pay of legislators to $8,500 a year (up from 1932's $8,000), in 1934 to $9,000, and in 1935 to $10,000. **Congress made no other pay changes during Roosevelt's term of presidency.**

The **Twenty-First Amendment to the U.S. Constitution** (see Appendix C), ratified on December 5, 1933, repealed the **Eighteenth Amendment** and prohibition.

In 1934, FDR put a **heated swimming pool** in the White House, which he used daily. A special stop put on the rail tracks allowed FDR to take an elevator into the Waldorf Astoria Hotel without being seen when he arrived in New York City from the White House.

In **1934**, FDR got **five more key laws passed**, starting with the **1934 Securities Exchange Act**, which limited the actions of insiders and stated reporting requirements, as well as creating the Securities and Exchange Commission to protect investors and prevent fraud. Joseph Kennedy served as the first SEC Commissioner. The **1934 Copeland Act** prohibited kick¬backs on wages paid while working on government contracts. The **1934 Revenue Act** declared personal income tax data was public information. The **1934 Gold Reserve Act** transferred all gold from the Federal Reserve to the U.S. Treasury and made the private holding of gold illegal. The **1934 National Housing Act** established the Federal Housing Administration, with responsibility for middle-class loans. And the **Works Progress Administration (WPA)** created jobs for public projects.

In **1935**, FDR got **four more key laws** passed: the **1935 Banking Act** gave the Federal Reserve control; the **1935 Federal Insurance Contribution Act** established a payroll tax to assist in the funding of Social Security benefits; the **1935 Social Security Act** which established old age, survivors and disability insurance, as well as the federal/state unemployment system; the **1935 National Labor Relations Act** (sponsored by Senator Robert Wagner) – **aka the Wagner Act** established, the National Labor Relations Board and officially recognized the right of employees to form a union and bargain collectively.

In **A.L.A. Schechter Poultry Corp. vs United States** (1935), the U.S. Supreme Court ruled that Section 3 of the National Industrial Recovery Act of 1933, the "Live Poultry Code," was unconstitutional.

In his **1936 presidential campaign**, FDR's campaign motto was "Remember Hoover!" FDR also stated, "The lessons of history, confirmed by the evidence immediately before me, show conclusively that **continued dependence upon relief** induces a spiritual disintegration fundamentally destructive of the national fiber." A 1936 Gallup poll indicated that 96% of Americans wanted to stay out of a war in Europe.

In the **1936 presidential election**, the country was convinced that President Roosevelt was leading the country out of its **major depression** by implementing many new social programs. Democratic candidates FDR and John Nance Garner received 27,476,673 popular votes vs 16,679,583 for Republican candidates Alfred Landon and Frank Knox and 449 electoral votes vs 82 for Landon and Knox. Roosevelt was re-elected president, and Garner was re-elected vice president. The Democrats retained strong control of Congress: Senate 76-16 and House 334-91.

In 1936, FDR **proposed reorganizing the Supreme Court** by adding one associate (up to a maximum total of 15) for every justice over age 70 who had not retired. This attempt to "pack the court" failed, but in his twelve years as president, FDR was still able to appoint eight associate justices.

The **1936 Walsh-Healey Workers Contract Act** established minimum wages and overtime requirements for those working more than 40 hours a week on federal contracts. In **Ashwander vs Tennessee Valley Authority** (1935), the U.S. Supreme Court ruled that Congress had the authority under the War Powers Clause and the Commerce Clause to construct a dam "for the purposes of national defense and the improvement of navigation."

FDR's second term **cabinet** included **Vice President** John Nance Garner, **Secretary of State** Cordell Hull, **Secretary of the Treasury** Henry Morgenthau, **Secretary of War** Harry Woodring, **Attorney General** Homer Cummings, **Secretary of the Navy** Claude Swanson, **Postmaster General** James Farley, **Secretary of the Interior** Harold Ickes, **Secretary of Agriculture** Henry Wallace, **Secretary of Commerce** Daniel Roper, and **Secretary of Labor** Frances Perkins.

The **1937 Bankhead-Jones Farm Tenant Act** authorized a modest credit program to assist tenant farmers in purchasing land. In **National Labor Relations Board vs Laughlin Steel Corp.** (1937), the U.S. Supreme Court ruled that unfair labor practices were barred in companies engaged in interstate commerce.

FDR enjoyed eating. One of his favorite dishes was terrapin turtle soup, but wife Eleanor thought it was an elitist meal. FDR might have herring for breakfast, gumbo soup for lunch (which he called dinner), and buffalo tongue, frogs, and oyster crabs for dinner (which he called supper). And FDR enjoyed his "**reverse martini**" – one part gin and three parts dry vermouth. He also enjoyed culinary gifts from around the world. Eleanor preferred meals as a source of calories, not epicurean delights. Her tastes took over, and the president began complaining about the redundancy of plain meals. It became common knowledge for guests to eat before they dined at the White House because the uninspired meals were poorly prepared.

In **Erie Railroad Co. vs Tompkins** (1938), the U.S. Supreme Court overturned *Swift vs Tyson* and ruled that, in diversity jurisdiction cases, federal courts must apply state law "as declared by the highest state court," except in matters "governed by the Federal Constitution or by Acts of Congress," as there is no federal common law.

After the 1938 midterms, the Democrats were still in significant control in both the House and the Senate.

The **1938 Revenue Act** stipulated that an employer's contribution to a retirement plan must be irrevocable; and the **1938 Fair Labor Standards Act** established a minimum wage of 25 cents per hour and time and one-half overtime pay for all hours worked in excess of 40 in the week (except for categories exempt from overtime) for those engaged in interstate commerce.

In **National Labor Relations Board vs Fansteel Metallurgical Corp.** (1939), the U.S. Supreme Court ruled that NLRB had no authority to order employers to reinstate workers fired after a sit-down strike.

The **1939 Revenue Act** excluded payments for injuries or illness to employees from taxable income; the **1939 Hatch Act** forbid government employees from engaging in political activity; and a **1939 Internal Revenue Service Ruling** revisited the issue of stock options and changed its longtime view that the spread between fair market value and exercise cost on date of purchase constituted income to the optionee. Instead, the IRS decided to look to intent. If it was not intended to be compensation (but rather an investment), the spread would not be considered taxable income.

When **King George VI and Queen Elizabeth** visited Washington in June 1939, FDR invited them to Hyde Park for a hot dog and beer picnic. When the King eyed the hot dog, he was unsure of what to do. FDR quipped, "Put it in your mouth and keep chewing until you finish it." The King enjoyed it so much, he had a second and washed it down with beer. In private, FDR promised to support England in the war. The event was called "the picnic that won the war."

Every president dating back to George Washington received a daily summary of key events affecting America. This came to be called the **President's Daily Briefing (PDB)**. Starting with FDR, the PDB was prepared by the early version of the CIA.

Believing that FDR needed additional companionship, in early 1940 a cousin of his gave him a black Scottish terrier that he named **Fala**. Fala accompanied FDR everywhere.

Breaking the tradition of a maximum of two terms, FDR decided he wanted to go for a **third term** in the **1940 election**. He wanted Secretary of State Hull to be his running mate, but he declined, so FDR decided on Secretary of Agriculture **Henry Wallace**. When FDR was told the convention might not like Wallace, FDR replied, "They will go for Wallace or I won't run, and you can jolly well tell them so."

In the **1940 presidential election**, with war raging in Europe and the U.S. and the economy continuing to improve, Democrats **FDR** and his vice president, **Henry Wallace**, received 27,243,466 popular votes vs 22,304,755 for Republicans **Wendell Willkie** and **Charles McNary** whose motto was "work and Willkie." There were 449 electoral votes for FDR and Wallace vs 82 for Willkie and McNary. The **Democrats controlled Congress** by a significant margin: Senate 66-28 and House 167-162. In his third **inaugural address**, FDR stated, "We Americans of today are passing through a period of supreme test."

Henry A. Wallace was born on October 7, 1888, in Orient, Iowa. Henry's father was Secretary of Agriculture under both Presidents Warren Harding and Calvin Coolidge. Henry graduated from **Iowa State University** in 1910 and worked on his father's agricultural journal for ten years, then created a **hybrid corn**, leading to the founding of the Hi-Bred Corn Company in 1926. Based on his writing and hybrid corn development, Henry had considerable influence in the farming community, which led to his being active in politics. He was a supporter of FDR and his policies. FDR asked Wallace for help in getting the farm vote, and he obliged. When FDR won, he named Wallace his Secretary of Agriculture in both his first and second cabinets and then as his vice president in his third term, but he was not considered a strong vice president. Wallace was the first vice president to have **never held an elected office**. Wallace died on November 18, 1965, in Danbury, Connecticut, of Lou Gehrig's disease.

A **1940 National Labor Relations Board** ruled that bonuses, holidays, and vacations were subject to collective bargaining; the **1940 Investment Company Act** regulated mutual funds and other security trading; the **1940 Investment Advisors Act** required the registration of such advisors with the SEC; the **1940 Selection Service Act** required males to register for the draft; and the **1940 Smith Act** stated that overthrowing the government by force was a crime punishable with prison time.

In a **1940 fireside chat**, FDR stated, "The U.S. must be the great arsenal of democracy, but a good leader must not get too far ahead of its follower." Germany had invaded Poland and France, Great Britain and Russia had declared war on Germany, and Hitler and Mussolini announced a formal alliance.

In FDR's third term of office his **cabinet** included **Vice President** Henry Wallace, **Secretary of State** Edward Stettinius, **Secretary of the Treasury** Henry Morgenthau, **Secretary of War** Henry Stimson, **Attorney General** Francis Biddle, **Secretary of the Navy** William Knox, **Postmaster General** Francis Walker, **Secretary of the Interior** Harold Ickes, **Secretary of Agriculture** Claude Wickard, **Secretary of Commerce** Jesse Jones, and **Secretary of Labor** Frances Perkins.

U.S. entry into **World War II** began with FDR's December 8, 1941 address to Congress: "Yesterday, December 7, 1941 – **a date which will live in infamy** – the United States of America was suddenly and deliberately attacked by naval and air forces of the Empire of Japan." Nineteen navy ships (including the Battleship *USS Arizona*) were sunk, over 200 airplanes were destroyed, and 2,400 Americans were killed. That same day, **Congress declared war** on Japan.

When Germany and Italy declared war on America, Congress declared war on both countries on December 11, 1941. Following the declaration of war on Japan, Germany, and Italy, FDR stated, "I honestly feel that it would be best for the country to keep baseball going in spite of many men called up in the draft." **War bonds** not only helped finance the war, but also removed money from consumer spending, helping to control inflation. FDR established the **Office of Strategic Services**, the first foreign intelligence agency, in 1941 under William "Wild Bill" Donovan.

When **Winston Churchill** arrived in Washington on December 22, 1941, he and FDR dined well on a dinner of chicken noodle soup, roast beef, broccoli, potatoes, salad, cream pie, and coffee, followed by brandy. Then they discussed war plans.

In his **1942 State of the Union Address**, FDR declared there were **four basic freedoms**: speech, religion, from want, and from fear. Congress passed the **1942 Wage Stabilization Act**, which froze wages but permitted fringe benefit increases; the **1942 Revenue Act**, which changed tax rates on income and lump sum distributions; and the **1942 Victory Tax**, which added a 5% tax on top of all income taxes.

In **Betts vs Brady** (1942), the U.S. Supreme Court ruled that the Due Process Clause of the Fourteenth Amendment does not incorporate the Sixth Amendment right to assistance of counsel in all criminal cases. And in **Korematsu vs United States** (1944), the U.S. Supreme Court upheld the validity of a Civilian Exclusion Order.

In the **1942 Battle of Midway**, American aircraft carriers gave Japan its first major defeat. The Americans sank three Japanese aircraft carriers while losing only one of their own, the *Yorktown*, thus turning the tide in the Pacific Ocean in favor of America. This was followed by **Colonel Jimmy Doolittle** leading a flight of 16 B-25s taking off from the aircraft carrier ***Hornet*** later in 1942, marking the first bombing assault on Tokyo. Also in 1942, upon leaving Russia, Germany had racked up casualties of almost two million.

In the 1942 midterm elections, the margins were reduced, but the Democrats still controlled Congress: Senate 57-38 and House 222-209.

The **1943 Lend Lease Act** permitted allies to buy American arms and supplies with cash, and the **1943 Current Tax Payment Act** established paycheck income tax withholding, introduced standard deductions on income taxes, and recognized healthcare benefits as a tax-free form of pay. Perhaps the biggest "**abuse of power** during World War II was the 1943 creation of concentration camps for Japanese Americans."

In 1943, allied forces captured Sicily. FDR's 1943 campaign slogan was "We are going to win this war and the peace that follows." Also in 1943, FDR created the **War Production Board** to mobilize the mass production of war arms. After initial setbacks in the Far East, America started to gain the upper hand. That same year, the **Pentagon** building was completed in D.C. Later in 1943, **Churchill, FDR, and Stalin** had summit meetings in **Tehran**, Iran, to discuss war efforts. FDR hosted the first night with steak and potatoes. The second night, Stalin hosted with Caviar and sturgeon. The third night was hosted by Churchill on his 69th birthday and they were served soup, salmon, cheese soufflé, wine, along with a cake with 69 candles. At the meeting's conclusion, the Big Three agreed to cooperate on troop movements and the postwar order. Churchill noted that "the stomach governs the world."

In his **1944 State of the Union Address**, FDR outlined his "**Second Bill of Rights**," including the "right" to a job, food, clothing, recreation, a home, medical care, and education, as well as freedom from the "fear of unemployment, old age, and sickness." The **1944 G.I. Bill of Rights** provided education and medical benefits for war veterans; the **1944 Victory Tax Act** raised the maximum tax to 94% on annual income over $200,000 while allowing a 25% tax on capital gains; and the minimum federal wage received its third adjustment, raising it to 40 cents per hour. Also in 1944, following massive bombing of Germany, a number of the islands Japan had captured were retaken. **General MacArthur** kept his promise to return to the Philippines when he returned with troops to liberate the Philippines from the Japanese. On June 6th, 1944 (D-Day), 175,000 American, British, and Canadian troops landed on the **beaches of Normandy**, France, as part of **Operation Overlord**. The last altercation was the **Battle of the Bulge**, December 18, 1945, Germany's last failed counteroffensive. More than **12 million men and women** were in the **armed forces** of America.

Having broken tradition with a third term, FDR decided to go for a **fourth term**. With the wars in Europe and Asia winding down, FDR's chief political advisors convinced him that Wallace should be removed from the ticket. FDR was convinced that the only person acceptable to the Senate was Missouri New Deal Senator **Harry Truman**. Henry Wallace was dropped from the ticket and replaced by Truman.

In the **1944 presidential election**, Democrats **FDR** and **Harry S. Truman** received 25,602,505 popular votes and 432 electoral votes vs 22,006,505 and 99 for Republicans **Thomas E. Dewey** and **John Bricker**. FDR returned to office for an unprecedented fourth term. FDR was **the only president to have been elected four times. Democrats still controlled Congress**: Senate 57-38 and House 242-191.

Harry S. Truman was born on May 8, 1884, in Lamar, Missouri, to John and Martha Truman. The letter "S" is not an abbreviation; it represents no name. In 1900, Truman applied to West Point but was rejected due to poor eyesight, so he stayed to work on his father's farm. When World War I came, he entered the **army**, and even with poor eyesight he was accepted and rose to the rank of first lieutenant in a **field artillery unit** (apparently poor eyesight was not excusable for rejection). Within a year, he was promoted to captain, and by the time he was discharged, he was a major. He then **married Elizabeth "Bess" Virginia**, a woman he had known for years. They had one child, Mary Margeret. Truman opened a men's **clothing store** and later was elected county judge for ten years. In 1934, he was elected a **U.S. senator**. He was a solid supporter of FDR and his policies.

In FDR's January 20, **1944, inaugural address**, which was only fifteen minutes long (the second shortest after Washington's second inaugural), FDR stated, "Today, in this year of war, we have learned lessons at a fearful price and we shall profit by them. We have learned that we cannot live alone at peace, that our own well-being is dependent on the well-being of other nations."

FDR's fourth-term **cabinet** included **Vice President** Harry Truman, **Secretary of State** Edward Stettinius, **Secretary of the Treasury** Henry Morgenthau, **Secretary of War** Henry Stimson, **Attorney General** Francis Biddle, **Secretary of the Navy** James Forrestal, **Postmaster General** Francis Walker, **Secretary of the Interior** Harold Ickes, **Secretary of Agriculture** Claude Wickard, **Secretary of Commerce** Jesse Holmes, and **Secretary**

of Labor Frances Perkins. Harold Ickes and Frances Perkins are the only cabinet members who served on all four cabinets.

On February 4, 1945, the **Big Three** (Churchill, FDR, and Stalin) met in **Yalta** to discuss the Allied country's occupation of Germany. FDR stated, "The Conference ought to spell the end of unilateral action, the exclusive alliance spheres of influence and the balances of power."

In 1945, the IRS returned to its 1920 position that all stock options were to be taxed at the time of exercise, regardless of their intent, thus reversing its 1939 position.

While in **Warm Springs** to relax and have his portrait painted, FDR said to Lucy Mercer, "I have a terrific pain in the back of my head," and then **died of a massive stroke** at 3:35pm on April 12, 1945. He was 62 years old. **Germany surrendered on May 7, 1945**. Upon FDR's death, Eleanor was appointed the U.S. **delegate to the United Nations**. She died on November 7, 1962, at the age of 78, and was buried in Hyde Park, New York. Eleanor and FDR were both buried in the family plot in New Hyde, New York. Lucy Mercer died on July 17, 1948, at age 57.

Roosevelt was well liked, as evidenced by his having been elected four times. When he entered office, the country was immersed in what would be called **the Great Depression**. In order to tackle massive unemployment, he spent his first 100 days in office putting the country back to work. His **fireside chats** explained to his audience how his **New Deal policies** were focused on this issue. As employment was improving, he then had to lead the country's response to Japan and Germany's aggressions, which ended the Great Depression because factories needed to respond to and produce needed war material.

Many historians consider FDR **one of the best presidents, below only Lincoln and Washington.**

KEY EVENTS

By FDR's executive order, the U.S. **banned private ownership of gold** and abandoned the gold standard it established in 1879 in backing government securities, and the **Federal Deposit Insurance Corporation** was formed in response to bank failures (1933); **National Bank Notes** were replaced with Federal Reserve Notes (1933); **Fiorello** (Little Flower) **LaGuardia** began a 12-year term as **mayor of New York City** (1933); about 2 million workers, or about 6% of the **total workforce**, were labor union members vs about 12% in 1920 (1933); the **unemployment rate** was about 25% (1933); about 11,000 banks **had failed** since 1929 (1933); **IBM** entered the **typewriter business** (1933); somewhere between one-third and one-half of the **workforce had no job** (1933); the **Dun & Bradstreet** ratings firm was created by merger (1933); the airship *USS Akron* crashed into the Atlantic Ocean, killing nearly everyone on board (1933); **Rockefeller Center** in New York City put up the first **Christmas Tree** (1933); the **DJIA** closed at 99.90 at year-end, up 66.7 percent (1933); with **national prohibition** coming to an end with the repeal of the 18th Amendment (1933), the gangster era was winding down, and **gangsters killed** during the period (1934-1935) included **Charles (Pretty Boy) Floyd**, age 30, **George (Baby Face) Nelson**, age 25, **Bonnie Parker**, age 24, and **Clyde Barrow**, age 25, **Arthur (Dutch Schultz) Flegenheimer**, age 33, and **John Dillinger**, age 32; the United States issued a **$100,000 Federal Reserve Note** with President Wilson on its face, primarily for the transfer of large amounts of cash between banks

(1934); the alleged stock manipulator and prohibition whiskey baron **Joseph Kennedy** (father of President JFK) became the **first Chairman of the Securities Exchange Commission** (1934); the **International Longshoremen's Association**, led by organizer **Harry Bridges**, went on strike, tying up ports from Oregon to California, but after four days the **ILA agreed to arbitration** ending the hiring hall system (1934); **General Motors** was among the first to appoint a **head of industrial relations** to deal with unions (1934); **Bill Wilson** created the **Alcoholics Anonymous** twelve-step program (1934); the **DJIA** closed at 104.04 at year-end, up 4.1 percent (1934); President Roosevelt created the **National Labor Relations Board** to enforce collective bargaining (1935); a **DuPont** chemist created nylon (1935); the last **Peace Silver Dollar** was minted (1935); the first **Gallup poll** was held (1935); J.P. Morgan Bank split off from **Morgan Stanley brokerage** (1935); **Boulder Dam** was completed (1935); the **Federal Bureau of Investigation** (FBI) was created, superseding its predecessor formed in 1908, the Bureau of Investigation (1935); FDR announced a "**Second New Deal**," often called the second 100 days (1935); the **SEC** published insider stock transactions (1935); the **American Institute of Accountants** was formed (1935); the **DJIA** closed at 144.13 at year-end, up 38.5 percent (1935); the U.S. declared neutrality in the **Spanish Civil War** (1936); **John Maynard Keynes** gave credence to FDR's approach to government spending, stating business would not take this action in his book, *The General Theory of Employment, Interest and Money* (1936); **Fort Knox, Kentucky** was built to hold U.S. gold (1936); the **first Social Security checks** were mailed (1936); the **Triborough Bridge** opened connecting the Bronx, Queens and Manhattan (1936); **Bruno**

Hauptmann was executed for kidnapping and killing **Charles Lindbergh Jr.** (1936); *Life* magazine began publication (1936); the **DC-3 airplane** made its first flight (1936); **Margaret Mitchell** published *Gone with the Wind* and won a Pulitzer Prize (1936); the **DJIA** closed at 179.90 at year-end, up 24.8 percent (1936); the **airship** *Hindenburg* exploded in New Jersey, killing over 20 people (1937); the **shareholder protection formula** was developed by General Electric (1937); the **Lincoln Tunnel** opened, connecting Manhattan with New Jersey (1937); the **unemployment rate was 14%** (1937); the financial giants **John D. Rockefeller** and **Andrew Mellon** died (1937); **Edwin Land** founded **Polaroid** (1937); **Al Wonderlic** created his **cognitive ability test** (1937); **Columbus Day** (October 22nd) was proclaimed a federal holiday by Roosevelt (1937); pilot **Amelia Earhart** disappeared in the Pacific Ocean (1937); the **Golden Gate Bridge** opened in San Francisco (1937); **Dale Carnegie's** book *How to Win Friends and Influence People* sold over 750,000 in its first year (1937); the horse **War Admiral** won the Triple Crown in racing (1937); the **National Basketball League** was established (1937); **Joe Louis** knocked out **James Braddock** to become the world heavyweight champion (1937); the **DJIA** closed at 120.85 at year-end, up 32.8 percent (1937); **DuPont** introduced **Teflon** (1938); **Hewlett-Packard** was formed (1938); filmmaker **Howard Hughes** set the **around-the-world flight** record of just under four days and received a **New York tickertape parade** (1938); **Cincinnati baseball pitcher Johnny Vander Meer** pitched two consecutive no-hitters (1938); **Thornton Wilder** wrote *Our Town* (1938); **Orson Welles** produced *War of the Worlds* (1938); **Seabiscuit** beat War Admiral in horse racing (1938); **Joe Louis** defeated **German Max Schmeling** for the heavyweight boxing title (1938); "**Wrong Way**" Corrigan landed in Ireland instead of California (1938); *The Functions of the Executive* was written by Chester Bernard (1938); the **DJIA** closed at 154.75 at year-end, down 28.1 percent (1938); **LaGuardia Airport** (named after the New York City mayor) opened in New York (1939); the **Bronx-Whitestone Bridge** opened, connecting the Bronx with Queens (1939); **Charles Goodyear** invented the vulcanization of **rubber** (1939); **Al Capone** was released from prison after serving time for income tax evasion (1939); the movie *The Roaring Twenties* featuring **Humphrey Bogart** and **James Cagney**, put gangsters on the silver screen (1939); New York Yankee **Lou Gehrig** retired from baseball after playing 2,130 straight games and was the **first player in sports to have his number (4) retired** (1939); the **Brooklyn Dodgers** defeated the **Philadelphia Eagles** 23-14 at Brooklyn's Ebbets Field in the **first NFL televised game** (1939); John Steinbeck's *The Grapes of Wrath* described a farm family's hardships during the Great Depression (1939); the movie *The Wizard of Oz* was released (1939); **Nile Kinnick** (University of Iowa) won the **Heisman Trophy** and was the first winner to have the school's football stadium named after him (1939); singer **Marian Anderson** performed before 75,000 at the Lincoln Memorial (1939); the **World's Fair** opened in New York City (1939); the **Federal Security Agency** was created (1939); the **DJIA** closed at 150.24 at year-end, down 2.9 percent (1939); the **Queens Midtown Tunnel** opened, connecting Manhattan with Queens (1940); Charles Merrill formed the investment firm **Merrill Lynch** (1940); the **Oldsmobile** was the first car with an automatic transmission (1940); the **American Bantam Car** introduced the **Jeep** to the U.S. Army (1940); the peacetime military draft was enacted following the creation of the **Selective Service System** (1940); **Thurgood Marshall** founded the **Legal Defense Fund** (1940); the **New York Copacabana nightclub**, owned by gangsters Frank Costello and Albert Anastasi, opened (1940); in the most legendary game in football history, the **Chicago Bears** defeated the Washington Redskins 73-0 in the **championship football game** (1940); the U.S. population was over 131 million (1940); the **International Longshoreman's Association** had 40,000 members in New York and 100,000 nationwide (1940); the **DJIA** closed at 131.13 at year-end, down 12.7 percent (1940); the word "**teenager**" was introduced by *Popular Science* magazine (1941); the **Velcro** fastener was created (1941); President Roosevelt got a pledge from unions and companies that there would be **no lockouts or strikes** during the war (1941); by late in the year there were fewer than **1 million unemployed**, or about 10% of the workforce, versus 8 million a year earlier (1941); **Pfizer** was the first company to mass produce **penicillin** (1941); FDR implemented a **lend-lease** of equipment to England (1941); the **New Deal** was outlasted by the **Great Depression** as 775,000 WPA workers were dismissed (1941); when African American worker discontent threatened the war effort, **FDR banned racist employment practices** (1941); the horse **Whirlaway** was the Triple Crown winner (1941); the **USO** was formed and **Bob Hope** made the first USO appearance (1941); **Orson Wells** appeared in *Citizen Kane* (1941); the **DJIA** closed at 110.96 at year-end, down 15.4 percent (1941); **General Motors had 102 plants** in the United States (1942); New York City **Mayor Fiorello LaGuardia** was the first mayor to live in **Archibald Gracie's mansion** which dates back to the early 1800s (1942); the **Voice of America** began the first broadcast to Europe (1942); FDR issued an executive order relocating some **200,000 West Coast Japanese Americans** into **detention camps** (1942); Physicist **Enrico Fermi** achieved a **nuclear chain reaction** beneath the football stadium at the University of Chicago (1942); the famed **Latin Quarter in New York City**, founded by Barbara Walters' father,

Lou, replaced the Times Square **Cotton Club nightclub** (1942); a **German spy-ring** in New York had been in operation for two years before its 32 members were arrested by the FBI (1942); the movie *Casablanca*, with Humphrey Bogart and Ingrid Bergman, appeared in theaters (1942); the **luxury liner *Normandy*** caught fire and capsized in New York Harbor (1942); the **DJIA** closed at 119.40 at year-end, up 7.6 percent (1942); the **aerosol spray** can was invented (1943); *A Theory of Human Motivation* was published by **A.H. Maslow** (1943); the **DJIA** closed at 135.89 at year-end, up 13.8 percent (1943); the **Mark I** (reportedly the world's **first computer**) was built at Harvard (1944): the **International Monetary Fund** was created by 44 countries with representatives meeting in Bretton Woods, New Hampshire (1944); Hollywood stars who got on the **FDR bandwagon** included Humphrey Bogart, Bette Davis, Rita Hayworth, Danny Kaye, Edward G. Robinson, Frank Sinatra, and Orson Welles (1944); and the **DJIA** closed at 152.32 at year-end, up 12.1 percent (1944).

Harry S. Truman
(33ᴿᴰ President)

April 12, 1945 – January 20, 1953

Harry S. Truman was born on May 8, 1884, in Lamar, Missouri, to John and Martha Truman. Harry was the first president born in Missouri. The initial "S" was not the first letter of a name; the letter was a compromise honoring his grandfathers, Anderson Shipp, and Solomon Young. Harry had a brother, John, and a sister, Mary Jane. Harry worked on his **father's farm** and then as a bank clerk. He attended the University of Missouri and Kansas City **Law School** but graduated from neither. **He was the first 20th century president who did not have a college degree.** He tried to get into West Point, but 20/400 in his left eye prevented that from happening. But he was admitted to the Missouri **National Guard** after memorizing the eye chart and rose to the rank of lieutenant. When America entered World War I in 1917, Truman was promoted to **captain** of an artillery unit. By the time the war ended, he was a major.

Returning to Missouri at age 35, he married his longtime friend **Elizabeth "Bess" Wallace**, age 34, on June 28, 1919. They went on to have **one child**, Margaret. Harry started a **haberdashery** business, but it failed. Then he was introduced to Tom Pendergast, head of the Kansas City Democratic Party. Tom's nephew served under Truman in the war. With Pendergast's support, Truman was elected to public office in 1922. Truman served as supervisor of buildings and roads in Jackson County, Missouri. Working his way up the ranks, Truman was elected to the **U.S. Senate** in 1934. Following his re-election, Truman headed a number of Congressional committees. In 1944, FDR asked Truman to be his vice president. Harry asked Bess what he should do. She said, "Go ahead." Harry asked her opinion on everything. While vice president, at a **National Press** Club session, Harry was joined by a leggy **Lauren Bacall**, who sat on top of the piano. Bess was not thrilled. With FDR's death on April 12, 1945, Harry Truman became president. Bess said that first and foremost she was the wife of the president and secondly, she was the First Lady. Bess was a very private person, but the Trumans entertained extensively.

On April 12, 1945, Harry Truman was having a bourbon and water in the Senate cloakroom when he got a call to immediately go to the White House. There he was told that **FDR was dead** and Harry was the new president. Truman had only met FDR twice. Learning of FDR's death, Truman cancelled his upcoming weekly poker game.

Eighty-two days after his election as vice president, Truman became president when FDR died. After FDR's death, Truman asked Eleanor, "Is there anything I can do for you?" She replied, "Is there anything I can do for you. You are the one in trouble."

Harry Truman became the **tenth vice president** to become president (John Adams, Thomas Jefferson, Martin Van Buren, John Tyler, Millard Fillmore, Andrew Johnson, Chester Arthur, Theodore Roosevelt, and Calvin Coolidge preceded him). Harry Truman was the **seventh vice president** (Tyler, Fillmore, Johnson, Arthur, Roosevelt, and Coolidge preceded him) to assume the presidency upon the death of his president (Franklin Roosevelt). When asked about being president, he responded, "Being president is like riding a tiger. You have to keep riding or be swallowed."

Truman's initial cabinet included **Secretary of State** Edward Stettinius, **Secretary of the Treasury** Henry Morgenthau, **Secretary of War** Henry Stimson, **Attorney General** Francis Biddle, no **Secretary of Defense**, **Secretary of the Navy** James Forrestal, **Secretary of the Interior** Harold Ickes, **Secretary of Agriculture** Claude Wickard, **Secretary of Commerce** Henry Wallce, and **Secretary of Labor** Francis Perkins.

On May 8th, 1945, Truman celebrated his 61st birthday as **Germany** signed an unconditional surrender, a day earlier. On July 17, 1945, at the **Potsdam Conference**, Britain, the Soviet Union, and the United States agreed on Germany's disarmament, occupation zones, and war crimes trials.

Following the death of FDR, Truman was **briefed on the planned attack of Japan**. Japan was to be attacked by air and by land. It was estimated that 500,000 Americans would be lost. Truman decided to use the **atomic bomb** in order to save American lives and end the war sooner. On August 6, 1945, the **B-29 Enola**

Gay dropped **Big Boy** on **Hiroshima's** 345,000-person population, killing some 75,000. When the Japanese did not agree to surrender, on August 9, 1945, the **B-29 Bock's Car** dropped **Fat Man** over **Nagasaki's** 200,000-person population, killing some 40,000. **The Japanese surrendered on September 2nd** on the battleship *Missouri*. General Douglas MacArthur moved to Tokyo and took control of the government. Following the end of the war, the combined American military forces were down to 1.5 million, from 12 million at the war's peak.

At war's end, England's Winston Churchill told Truman, "You more than any other man have saved Western civilization." **After the war**, Truman supported the start of the United Nations and the improvement of civil rights.

The **1945 Employment Act** focused on postwar job development and permitted government seizure of coal mines and railroads during lengthy union strikes. In anticipation of a strike by workers, Truman seized the steel companies.

In late January 1946, after a four-week strike, some 750,000 steel workers settled for more pay in a month; and some 400,000 coal mine workers involuntarily settled a strike in two months for more pay after the government seized the coal mines.

In **Morgan vs Virginia** (1946), the U.S. Supreme Court ruled a Virginia statute that mandates segregation of passengers on interstate buses violates the Commerce Clause, as it "unlawfully burdens interstate commerce" where "uniformity is essential."

In 1946, British Prime Minister Winston Churchill coined the phrase "Iron Curtain" for the Russian occupation of Eastern Europe.

In the 1946 **midterm elections**, the Republicans took control of Congress, Senate 51-45 and House 246-188.

In 1946, **Congress increased the pay** of the associate justices of the Supreme Court to $25,000 per annum (from 1927's $20,000), and the chief justice's to $25,500 per annum (from 1927's $20,500). In 1947, Congress increased the pay of the cabinet officers to $15,000 per annum (from 1907's $12,000) and the pay of congressmen to $12,500 per annum (from 1935's $10,000). And in 1949, Congress raised the pay of the president to $100,000 per annum (from 1909's $75,000) and the vice president's pay to $30,000 per annum (from 1946's $20,000). **Congress made no other pay changes during Truman's term of presidency.**

Truman believed he needed someone to manage the flow of people into his office and give him honest advice on issues. Truman selected a person he knew when he was in the Senate. That person was **John Steelman**, who took the title of **Assistant to the President of the United States**. Steelman took the job on December 12, 1946, and held it until Truman left office on January 20, 1953. Steelman holds the record for the longest time in the job, which was renamed **Chief of Staff** by Sherman Adams during Eisenhower's presidency.

In **United States vs Silk** (1947), the U.S. Supreme Court ruled that in determining whether workers are independent contractors or employees under the Social Security Act of 1935 a multi-factor "economic realities" test should be used. And in **SEC vs Transamerica** (1947), the Court ruled that shareholder resolutions dealing with governance actions cannot be excluded from the proxy by management.

Truman convinced Congress to give **aid to Greece and Turkey**, both threatened by a Communist takeover. They did so, and the motive for the 1947 aid was called the **Truman Doctrine**. Also in 1947, Secretary of State George Marshall proposed aid to war stricken countries; and Congress approved $12 billion for U.S. aid to European countries. Truman insisted it be called the **Marshall Plan**. Truman changed the Office of Strategic Services to the **Central Intelligence Group** (CIG). This later morphed into the Central Intelligence Agency **(CIA)**. The **1947 National Security Act** created the **National Security Council** and the **Joint Chiefs of Staff**. President Truman vetoed the **1947 Taft-Hartley Labor Act**, as it restricted labor union power, but Congress overrode the veto, and the act became law. President Truman raised the **federal minimum wage** from 40¢ an hour to 75¢. The **1947 Portal-to-Portal Act** limited paid time to time worked, not simply time on the worksite. Also in 1947, the **Presidential Succession Act** was passed, placing the Speaker of the House and the Senate President pro tem ahead of the cabinet members.

In 1947, Truman installed a **bowling alley** in the West Wing. Every morning Harry took a **long walk, swam laps in the White House pool, used a sauna**, and spent time on the **exercise machine**. He also **played the piano** for two hours every morning in the White House, before the official day began. When Bess was away, Harry dined alone. His favorite foods were fried chicken with cream gravy, buttered asparagus, hot biscuits, shoestring potatoes, and vanilla ice cream.

In response to Russia closing the access to Berlin in June 1948, America began airlifting supplies into the city until it stopped in September after the blockade ended.

Without a vice president for three and a half years, Truman selected a long-time senator from Kentucky, **Alben Barkley**, after being nominated by acclamation at the **1948 Democratic**

Convention. But the party was split into the **right** (former Republican Henry Wallace), the **center** (Truman), and the **left** (Democratic Governor Strom Thurmond). Truman and Barkley won the nomination. The **Republicans**, believing they would take the presidency in 1948, chose New York Governor **Thomas E. Dewey** over Ohio Senator **Robert Taft**, son of President William Howard Taft. Reportedly, gangster **Dutch Schultz** put out a $10,000 contract to kill Dewey, but he was himself killed. Dewey later died at age 68 on March 16, 1971, of a heart attack. The **1948 Revenue Act** scaled back taxes on annual income over $400,000.

In his pre-election campaign, **Truman traveled across the country** on a train covering 30 states. His slogan was "I'm just wild about Harry." At a rally, a supporter yelled, "Give 'em hell, Harry," and Truman adopted the slogan. It also became his nickname. Prior to the election, Russia stopped all surface travel into Berlin; Truman's response was the authorization of **airlifts of supplies** until the blockade ended four months later.

In 1948, Truman recognized the **State of Israel**. This was in spite of the fact that the Arab states' population numbered some 30 million to Israel's two million. Secretary of State **George Marshall** was recognized for his brilliance in winning World War II and for being a great statesman after the war rebuilding Europe.

In the **1948 presidential election**, Democrats **Harry Truman** and **Alben Barkley** were elected, receiving 24,105,695 popular votes to 21,969,171 for Republicans **Thomas Dewey** and **Earl Warren** and 1,169,021 for **Strom Thurmond** and **Fielding Wright**. The electoral votes were 303, 189, and 39, respectively. All nine Gallup polls predicted that Dewey would win by a landslide as the Democrats were split into three groups. Even before all votes were counted, the *Chicago Tribune* published a paper with the headline "**Dewey Defeats Truman.**" But in the biggest presidential election upset to date, **Truman won**. And Truman waved the erroneous headline in the paper to the public. Margaret Chase Smith was the first woman to have served in both houses of Congress.

Alben William Barkley was born on November 24, 1877, in a log cabin in Lowes, Kentucky. He grew up and worked on his father's tobacco farm. He graduated from **Marvin College** in 1898 and then went to the **University of Virginia Law School** and was admitted to the Kentucky bar in 1901. Shortly after, he met his wife-to-be. They were married in Paducah, Kentucky, where he practiced law. In 1905, he was elected prosecuting attorney for McCracken County. This led to county judge in 1910, in 1912 he was elected to the **House of Representatives**, and in 1927 he was elected to the **U.S. Senate**. In 1923, he ran for governor of Kentucky and lost; it was his only election loss. He was well respected and considered for the vice-presidential nomination in 1928, 1940, and 1944. He was Senate **Majority Leader** in 1937 and met regularly with President Roosevelt. When elected vice president, Barkley was the **oldest VP** at the time of inauguration and the last vice president born in the 1800s. Shortly after entering office, he married his second wife; the first had in died in 1947. In 1950, President Truman gave Barkley the **Congressional Gold Medal** for years of distinguished service. When his tenure in office expired, Barkley returned to Kentucky and in 1954 was **elected U.S. senator**. He died in office on April 30, 1956, and was buried in Paducah, Kentucky.

After the election, the **Cold War** (a term created by Winston Churchill) heated up. **Writer Whittaker Chambers** admitted before Richard Nixon's committee that in the 1920s and 1930s, he had been a **communist**. Also in 1949, former State Department officer Alger Hiss was found guilty of perjury in a spying case when he lied about passing secret documents to the Soviets.

Truman was 60 years old on the date of his **inauguration**. His 1949 swearing-in was the **first covered by television**. In his January 20, **1949, inaugural address**, Truman stated, "We need not fear the expression of ideas – we do need to fear their suppression." The Democrats regained control of the Senate (54 to 42) and the House (263-171). After being sworn in as president, Truman met with FDR's cabinet and asked them all to stay on. They did for a year or two before departures began.

When the White House groaned and creaked, Truman believed the building was haunted. Due to neglect, the building was a rickety firetrap. After his 1949 inauguration, the **Trumans vacated the building** and moved across the street to the **Blair House**. The White House was completely rebuilt over two years at a cost of close to $6 million. The 62 rooms had been expanded to 132. The family quarters now included 43 rooms and sixteen baths.

Truman's **cabinet** after his 1948 election included **Vice President** Alben Barkley, **Secretary of State** Dean Acheson, **Secretary of the Treasury** John Snyder, **Attorney General** James McGrath, **Secretary of Defense** James Forrestal, **Secretary of the Interior** Oscar Chapman, **Secretary of Agriculture** Charles Brannan, **Secretary of Commerce** Charles Sawyer, and **Secretary of Labor** Maurice Tobin. Truman combined the Navy and War Departments into the **Defense Department**. Forrestal moved from the Navy Department to the new Defense Department, and Patterson left the cabinet. Truman also relied very much on the opinion of Special Counsel Dwight Clifford, who reported directly to him.

There were two notable U.S. Supreme Court cases decided during Truman's second term. In **Inland Steel vs United Steel Workers** (1949), the U.S. Supreme Court ruled that companies must bargain for employee benefits with unions. In **Youngstown Sheet & Tube Company vs Sawyer** (1952), the U.S. Supreme Court ruled that the president does not have the authority to issue an executive order to seize and operate private property.

Two Puerto Rican nationalists were unsuccessful in **attempting to assassinate President Truman** in the Blair House on November 1,1950. Also in 1950, Wisconsin **Senator Joseph McCarthy** charged that the State Department had knowingly hired communists. Numbers varied over time, but the charge was constant. Truman responded that the "greatest asset the Kremlin has is Senator McCarthy." Congress passed, over Truman's veto, the **1950 McCarthy Act** which required all communist organizations to register with the government, and members would be jailed in times of national emergency and prohibited their working in defense companies. Also in 1950, the **Defense Production Act** was passed.

The **1950 Revenue Act** introduced the essential features of statutory stock options, i.e.: (1) option price could be as low as 85% of fair market value at time of grant; (2) if stock were held more than six months after exercise and more than two years from date of grant, the gain would be taxed at 25% as capital gain; and (3) the option grant could be as long as ten years. The act also introduced a maximum tax of 91% on income over $400,000. The **1950 Defense Production Act** created the Wage Stabilization Board with authority to limit pay increases and increases in fringe benefits.

The **Korean War** began on June 25, 1950, when 90,000 North Korean troops crossed the 38th parallel and attacked South Korea. President Truman responded within days, sending troops to South Korea with Congressional approval and calling it a **police action,** not a war. An amphibious landing at Inchon by **General Douglas MacArthur** turned the tide in favor of America. Then Chinese troops entered the action on October 25, 1950. MacArthur wanted to chase the Chinese troops into China, but Truman said no. When MacArthur refused Truman's order to stop at the China border, Truman fired him.

The 1950 U.S. population exceeded 150 million.

In the **1950 midterm elections**, the margins between parties were narrowed. The Senate was 49-47 and the House 235-199, both in favor of the **Democrats.**

The **22nd Amendment to the U.S. Constitution** limited presidents to two four-year terms in office (see Appendix C). It was ratified on February 7, 1951.

Truman had a number of notable statements. He had a **sign on his desk** with a Mark Twain quote: "Always do right. This will gratify some people and astonish the rest." He also said, "If you can't stand the heat, get out of the kitchen." Also on his desk was a sign stating, "**The buck stops here**." And he once said, "I want a one-armed economist so that the guy can never make a statement and then say, on the other hand…!" and "If you want a friend in Washington, get yourself a dog." Additionally, he said, "It's amazing what you can accomplish if you don't care who gets the credit." He also said, "A statesman is a politician who's been dead 10 or 15 years." Additionally, he stated, "If you cannot convince them, confuse them."

HARRY S. TRUMAN (33RD PRESIDENT)

Truman was an **avid reader**. Referencing the U.S. Constitution, he stated, "Read it one hundred times, and you will always find something new," but he sometimes took exception to the language. For example, he was **against term limits**. He also stated, "It is the historic background of our ideals and institutions that will prevent dictatorship, not the Twenty-Second Amendment."

In the summer of 1952, President Truman announced that he **would not seek another term** of office. He had served for three years and then for a four-year term, but he could have run again because he was grandfathered from the 22nd Amendment to the Constitution which set a two-term limit. The reasons given for his decision were the loss of the New Hampshire Senate seat to Senator Estes Kefauver and an approval rating of 22%.

In 1952, House Speaker Sam Rayburn stated, "Truman was right on all the big things and wrong on all the little things."

Upon retirement on January 20, 1953, President Truman stated, "Long ago I learned to gather all the facts and the best opinions and then made my decision. If I made a wrong decision, I made another to correct it." In addition to revenue from speeches and a book, Truman reportedly received over three million dollars as a former president. But he did not allow his name to be used in any way for the profit of others. And he refused to accept consulting fees.

Truman died on December 26, 1972, at age 88 of **heart failure** and is buried with his wife (who died on October 18, 1982, at age 97) at the Truman Library and Museum in Independence, Missouri. His last words were, "I gave it my best."

Many historians rank Truman's performance **as only below** that of Lincoln, Washington, FDR, Jefferson, and Theodore Roosevelt.

Key Events

Congress officially recognized the **Pledge of Allegiance** (1945); the **federal budget deficit** rocketed up to 30 percent of the GDP from 4 percent in 1940 (1945); the IRS determined that all **stock options**, regardless of intent, would be considered compensation when exercised (1945); Congress decided **Father's Day** would be celebrated on the third Sunday in June (1945); the **U.S. Naval Academy** was established in Annapolis, Maryland (1945); **Reynolds's ballpoint pen** went on sale (1945); the **National Hockey League Hall of Fame** opened in Toronto with 14 initial inductees (1945); the **United Nations** was established with an initial meeting of representatives from 46 countries in San Francisco (1945); a U.S. Army bomber struck the **Empire State Building**, killing 14 people (1945); *The Catcher in the Rye* was written by J.D. Salinger (1945); the **Sloan-Kettering Cancer Research Center** was set up, adding the name of GM research head Charles Kettering to GM President Alfred Sloan (1945); the **DJIA** closed at 182.91 at year-end, up 26.6 percent (1945); **Truman** issued an executive order ordering the **end of wage and price controls** (except for rent) (1946); **JFK** was elected to **two House terms** because his father bought off the competition (1946); **Operation Paperclip** brought more than a dozen top German scientists into America (1946); ten left-leaning **movie directors and writers were imprisoned and blacklisted** for refusing to testify to the House of Un-American Activities Committee (1946); the **Atomic Energy Commission** was created (1946); the first **Teflon™** products were commercially sold (1946); the **mobile telephone** went into service (1946); the Electronic Numerical Integrator and Computer (**ENIAC**) was created using 18,000 vacuum tubes (1946); **Levittown** opened, consisting of 7,500 Cape Cod houses in Hempstead, Long Island

(1946); **Bell Labs** invented the **transistor** (1946); **Estée Lauder** launched her cosmetic company (1946); the **Ford Modeling Agency** was founded in New York City (1946); **Dr. Benjamin Spock** published *Baby and Child Care* (1946); after helping in the war effort, **"Lucky" Luciano** was released from prison and deported to Italy (1946); the **color barrier** was broken in **professional football** by Marion Motley, Woody Strode, Kenny Washington, and Bill Willis (1946); the **American Theatre Wing** established the **Tony Award** to honor outstanding Broadway contributors (1946); **Peter Drucker's** book *Concept of the Corporation* was based on General Motors (1946); the horse **Assault** was the Triple Crown winner (1946); the **DJIA** closed at 177.20 at year-end, down 8.1 percent (1946); the **Central Intelligence Agency** (CIA) was created by President Truman from the former Office of Strategic Services (OSS) (1947); the **Cold War** with Russia began (1947); the **Federal Mediation and Conciliation Service** was formed (1947); General Georges Doriot launched a **venture capital company** (1947); the TV program *Meet the Press* went on the air (1947); the **microwave oven** was invented by Raytheon (1947); the **Metropolitan Life Insurance Company** financed the construction of **Peter Cooper Village** (9,000 apartments) and **Stuyvesant Town** (11,000 apartments) in New York City (1947); **Bugsy Siegel** was killed by the mob after opening the **Flamingo Casino** in Las Vegas (1947); **Jackie Robinson** integrated professional baseball joining the Brooklyn Dodgers (1947); Air Force Captain **Chuck Yeager** broke 760 mph and the sound barrier in a rocket plane (1947); an **alien spaceship** allegedly fell on the town of **Roswell, New Mexico** (1947); the **DJIA** closed at 181.18 at year-end, up 2.2 percent (1947); the United States recognized the state of **Israel** (1948); thousands of **Japanese Americans** who had been interred in Crystal City, Texas, during the war were released (1948); **military segregation** was stopped by President Truman's executive order (1948); President Truman introduced the name **Air Force One,** to be used only when the President is aboard an airplane (1948); a U.S. Court of Appeals ruled that the **collective bargaining process** must include wages, hours, and other conditions of employment, with the latter bringing the various insurance programs for the benefit of employees to the bargaining table (1948); concerned about receiving his pension, a Brooklyn rabbi established a non-funded trust known today as a **rabbi trust** (1948); **Lee Coleman** was the first Black man to clerk at the U.S. Supreme Court (1948); the first **McDonald's restaurant** opened (1948); the advertising agency **Doyle Dane Bernbach** was started (1948); CBS introduced a **record with 33** revolutions per minute (replacing the 78) (1948); Edwin Land created the **Polaroid instant camera** (1948); the temporary service company **Manpower** started up (1948); supplemental unemployment benefits were added to Ford's contract with the UAW (1948); **General Motors** introduced a **cost-of-living wage escalator** in a UAW contract (1948); because of the increased interest in "fringe benefits" following World War II, the U.S. Chamber of Commerce initiated a survey of the subject (1948); **unemployment benefits** were introduced by **Ford and the UAW** (1948); **Idlewild Airport** (later to become JFK) opened in New York City (1948); entertainers **Dean Martin and Jerry Lewis** became a featured couple in Las Vegas (1948); the published **Kinsey Report** described human male sexuality (1948); the horse **Citation** was the Triple Crown winner (1948); the **DJIA** closed at 177.30 at year-end, down 2.1 percent (1948); the **North Atlantic Treaty Organization** (NATO), consisting of 12 countries, stated an attack on one was an attack on all (1949);

the hedge fund created by **Alfred Winslow Jones** was believed to be the first of its kind (1949); the **National Basketball Association** (NBA) was formed from the merger of the National Basketball League (NBL) and the Basketball Association of America (BAA) (1949); the DJIA closed at 200.13 at year-end, up 13 percent (1949); **Senator Estes Kefauver** led a 12-month **investigation of organized crime** in 14 cities (1950); **Truman sent 35 advisors to Vietnam** (1950); **Eugene Stoner** developed the **M-16 rifle** for the U.S. army (1950); **Diners Club** introduced the restaurant credit card (1950); the **Rainbow Room** opened in New York City (1950); the importance of trade unions in determining wage levels was recorded by **John Dunlop** in *Wage Determination Under Trade Unions* (1950); seven Boston hoods broke into a **Brinks** armored car service storage facility and made off with **$2.7 million** in cash and securities (1950); the **MIT Sloan School of Management** was created with a $5 million gift from Alfred Sloan (1950); the **DJIA** closed at 235.41 at year-end, up 17.6 percent (1950); **Julius and Ethel Rosenberg** were executed for giving atomic bomb secrets to Russia (1951); the **color TV** was introduced in the U.S. (1951); **direct dial long distance** service was made available (1951); **Remington Rand** introduced the **(UNIVAC)** Universal Automatic Computer (1951); **Connie Mack** retired from coaching baseball after winning 3,731 games over 53 years, always wearing a suit, never a uniform (1951); the **DJIA** closed at 269.23 at year-end, up 14.4 percent (1951); **Senator Joseph McCarthy** and lead counsel **Roy Cohn** looked for communists in the government (1952); **Puerto Rico** became a U.S. commonwealth (1952); **GM President Charles Wilson** told Congress, "What is good for America is good for GM, and what is good for GM is good for America." (1952); the textile maker **Textron's** decision to buy companies in unrelated industries was seen by some as the beginning of **conglomerate companies** (1952); the **productivity guru Deming** published his 14 points of quality, which was adopted by Japanese manufacturers (1952); the **United Nations building** opened in New York City (1952); **Malcom X** joined U.S. Black Muslim leader **Elijah Muhammad** (1952); Dave Beck became president of the **Teamsters** (1952); the **DJIA** closed at 291.90 at year-end, up 8.4 percent (1952); **Governor Earl Warren** was sworn in as Chief Justice of the U.S. Supreme Court (1953); **Hugh Hefner** published the first issue of *Playboy* magazine (1953); and unemployment was at 2.9 percent (1953).

Dwight D. Eisenhower
(34th President)

January 20, 1953 – January 20, 1961

David Dwight Eisenhower was born on October 14, 1890, to David and Ida Eisenhower in Denison, Texas. He had six brothers: Arthur, Earl, Edgar, Milton, Roy, and Paul (who died in childhood). David, called Dwight from a young age and nicknamed "Little Ike," grew up in Abilene, Kansas, where he attended public schools. His mother was warm and supportive, while his father was the stern disciplinarian.

Dwight's mother insisted that her sons learn how to cook, sew, and wash. When his mother had to tend to one of his brothers who had come down with scarlet fever, Dwight became the family cook and learned how to prepare simple meals. Two of his favorites while young were squirrel stew and two-day vegetable soup.

The family was **tight knit**. Dwight enjoyed school, especially learning about ancient Greek and Roman battles. He was **active in sports** while also working with his father in his store. A sports injury in his freshman year of high school required him to repeat his freshman year. While considering college, Dwight saw a military academy as a way to get a free college education. He applied to both Annapolis and West Point, having passed regional exams. But the extra year in school disqualified him for Annapolis, so he joined the class of 1915 of **West Point** in 1911, which would produce sixty generals. Born David Dwight Eisenhower, he legally **changed his name** to Dwight David before entering **West Point** in 1911, although his nickname, "Ike," stuck. He did well in sports, especially football. But he was mischievous with a sense of humor. When ordered to report to an officer wearing his dress coat, he did, but he wore only the coat.

In 1915, Ike graduated 61st out of a class of 164. Commissioned a second lieutenant, he reported to Fort Sam Houston in Texas, where he served as a training instructor. World War I ended before he had to go overseas. However, in 1916, Ike met **Mary "Mamie" Doud**. They were married on July 1st of that year. He was 25 and she was 19. They had a son, Doud Dwight, in 1917, who died from scarlet fever at age three, and a second son, John, in 1922.

In 1919, Ike was sent to the Army's Transcontinental Motor Convoy, which was assigned to study the nation's highways. After a tour in the Panama Canal Zone for several years, he secured a spot in the **general staff school** in Leavenworth, Kansas, where he flourished, graduating first in his class. He next worked several years under five-star **General John Pershing** before being assigned to Army Chief of Staff five-star **General Douglas MacArthur** in 1930. When he left MacArthur in 1939, MacArthur reported Ike was the best officer he had ever met. Ike was next assigned to five-star Army Chief of Staff **George C. Marshall**, who asked him to develop a strategy to defeat the Japanese following their 1941 attack on Pearl Harbor. He did, and it was accepted. He was then **promoted** to a one-star general and Chief of Staff to the Third Army. Marshall was so impressed that he put Ike in charge of the War Plans Division and promoted him to a two-star general.

Placed in charge of **Operation Overlord**, the landing plan of Europe, and Ike was transferred with his staff to London, England. There he was given a **personal driver**, former model and ambulance driver **Kay Summersby**. Since all the street signs had been removed in anticipation of German troops, ambulance drivers had to know the streets from memory. Working long hours, Kay and Ike shared a mutual respect that later turned to love. Assigned to the fashionable Claridge's Hotel, which he disliked, Ike moved his staff to a five-bedroom house in a large park. It provided comfort and privacy.

Although Ike and Kay loved each other, due to war stress and lack of Viagra, two attempts at sexual satisfaction failed. Ike took Kay with him to Africa. Not ready for a full attack on German troops in Europe, Ike landed 100,000 troops in Algeria on November 8, 1942, in **Operation Torch** and defeated the Germans on May 8, 1943. Ike then returned to England. With the operation's success, Ike was **promoted** to five-star general and named **Supreme Commander** of all the Allied Forces in Europe and **General of the Army**. When the **war was over**, Ike was appointed **military commander** of the American occupation zone, where he promoted Private Summersby to a first lieutenant. Since only privates were drivers, Summersby became Ike's assistant. Ike told her he would bring her to America and divorce Mamie. But when he told General of the Army Marshall of his plans, Marshall told Ike, "I will kick you out of the army if you divorce Mamie." Ike returned to America without Summersby, where New York City gave Ike a ticker-tape parade. After three years as Chief of Staff of the Army, Ike left the Army and in 1948 became **president of Columbia University**. Kay followed Ike's career until his death. Her own death came in January 1975 at the age of 66.

Impressed with Ike, Truman asked him to run for president as a Democrat. Ike declined and accepted **command of NATO** in 1950. Also in 1950, the Eisenhowers bought a 189-acre farm near the Gettysburg battlefield. In 1952, Ike accepted an invitation to run for **president as a Republican, with Richard Nixon** as his vice president. Ike won the nomination over Senator Robert Taft and California Governor Earl Warren. Truman was so upset he did not speak to Ike until JFK's death.

Ike was enraged when Nixon refused to return gifts he had received after winning the vice-presidential nomination, including a dog named **Checkers** that his daughter loved. In his **Checkers speech** in 1952, Nixon asserted he did nothing wrong. Ike decided to leave Nixon on his presidential ticket. Nixon did not share a warm relationship with Ike while serving as his vice president. Asked about Nixon's contribution to his presidency, Ike replied, "Give me a week, I might think of one."

Referring to Ike's accomplishments, Nixon replied that a record "is not something to stand on, but something to build on, and building on this great record of this Administration, we shall build a better America." Ike stated, "Leadership is the art of getting someone else to do something you want done because he wants to do it." He added, "Patronage is the enemy of democracy. But sometimes a president must be a dictator."

A joke popular with the Democrats at the time was "How does an Eisenhower doll work? You wind it up and it does nothing for years." Meanwhile, Republicans labeled Democrat Adlai Stevenson as an eloquent, liberal "egghead." Stevenson's presidential campaign message was, "Let's talk sense to the American people. Let's tell them the truth, that there are no gains without pains."

In the **1952 presidential election**, Republicans **Dwight D. Eisenhower** and **Richard M. Nixon** defeated Democrats **Adlai E. Stevenson** and **John J. Sparkman,** 33,778,964 to 27,314,992 in the popular vote and 442 to 89 in the electoral vote. Dwight Eisenhower was the second president to graduate from West Point; Ulysses Grant was the first. The GOP also took control of both houses: Senate 48-47 and House 221-213.

Ike was the **last president** to have been **born in the 19th century** and the first to be president of all 50 states.

Richard Milhous Nixon was born on January 9, 1913, in Yorba Linda, California, and was raised in a poor, devout **Quaker** household. Richard was one of five sons who worked in his father's roadside farm stand and gas station. Richard **did well in school** and was an accomplished piano and violin player. Upon graduation, he was accepted into Harvard, but his family couldn't afford the tuition, so he attended nearby **Whittier College** and worked his way through, graduating in 1934. He then received a scholarship to **Duke University Law School**, graduating third in his class in 1937. He went on to practice law after being admitted to the bar. Nixon met and married Thelma (nicknamed Pat) Ryan in June 1940. They went on to have two daughters, Julie and Tricia. Nixon joined the **U.S. Navy** in August 1942. After rising to the rank of **lieutenant commander**, he left the Navy in 1946. That same year, he entered the **U.S. House of Representatives**, and in 1950, the **U.S. Senate** after he defeated Helen Douglas, who labeled him "**Tricky Dick**." Nixon's strong anti-communist position, including his investigation of Alger Hiss, led him to be Ike's candidate for the vice presidency in 1952 and 1956.

On January 20, 1953, Eisenhower was 62 years old on the date of his inauguration and Mamie was 56. The White House was their 36th residence and the first they would live in for more than one year. In his January 20, **1953, inaugural address**, Ike stated, "God help the nation when it has a president who does not know as much about the military as I do." He later stated, "So long as we govern our nation by the letter and spirit of the Bill of Rights, we can be sure that our nation will grow in strength and wisdom and freedom."

Ike continued the **New Deal** and **Fair Deal** policies of FDR and Truman. And Eisenhower formed a partnership with Speaker of the House Sam Rayburn and Senate Majority Leader Lyndon Johnson to shape legislation during this period. Ike began two terms as president at a time of growing concern of **nuclear war** with Russia.

During Ike's presidential campaign, **Bess Truman** and **Mamie Eisenhower** became good friends, in spite of the problems between Harry and Ike. **Mamie** was skeptical of the press but enjoyed interaction with the public and responded personally to thousands of letters. Mamie loved being the **First Lady**. She loved entertaining. She held daily conferences with the chief usher responsible for social events, the housekeeper for the building upkeep, and the maître'd for butler and kitchen duties. Mamie took personal responsibility for approving all menus. But she kept her distance from her husband's office. She stated she had been in the Oval Office only four times during the eight years of Ike's presidency and she was invited each time. The *Washington Post* labeled Mamie as a career woman: her career was Ike. Mamie stuck with Ike even though there were rumors that he had had an affair with his driver, former model and U.S. Army private, Kay Summersby, who Ike nicknamed **Private Parts**.

Ike is credited with being the first president to create the position of **Chief of Staff**. **Sherman Adams** was President Eisenhower's first Chief of Staff, serving until partway into his second term. Secretary of the Interior Adams came to the job after having served as **governor of New Hampshire**.

Ike's initial **cabinet** after his 1952 election included **Vice President** Richard Nixon, **Secretary of State** John Dulles, **Secretary of the Treasury** George Humphrey, **Attorney General** Herbert Brownell, **Postmaster General** Arthur Summerfield, **Secretary of the Interior** Douglas McKay, **Secretary of Agriculture** Ezra Benson, **Secretary of Labor** Martin Durkin, **Secretary of Commerce** Sinclair Weeks, **Secretary of Defense** Charles Wilson, and **Secretary of Health, Education and Welfare**, Oveta Culp Hobby. Ike added the last position because he saw the needs of an expanding aging population. Ike trusted his cabinet to do the right thing and was annoyed if they came to him for advice.

In **United States vs Reynolds** (1953), the U.S. Supreme Court ruled that the government may invoke privilege and refuse to produce documents in civil cases if the privilege is valid, such as for national security, if there is a sufficient showing of privilege, and if the privilege outweighs the necessity for production.

Eisenhower was easily the **best cook** among the list of presidents to date. For breakfast, after rising at 6:00am, he had a four-ounce rib steak, followed by staff meetings. Then for lunch, a six-ounce hamburger, followed by more meetings and a little time on the **putting green** (which he installed in 1953) outside the office or maybe a quick round at a nearby course. President Eisenhower **played golf** almost every day, and on at least one occasion played Augusta National (home of the **Masters**) twelve days in a row. He was the first president to have a **hole-in-one**. Ike grilled a very thick porterhouse steak medium rare with a baked potato and salad and had dinner with Mamie at 8:00pm in front of the television set. But both also liked Chinese take-out.

Both Ike and Mamie liked **state dinners** and had over 500 during the first year of Ike's presidency. Ike also liked occasional **stag dinners** with a dozen or more successful business leaders and/or key political figures. Ike used their dinners to gain different viewpoints on various issues. For private time, Ike played bridge, while Mamie liked canasta.

And on July 27, 1953, Ike fulfilled a pre-election promise: seeing an armistice ending the war in Korea, which began three years earlier. Also in 1953, Ike issued the **Eisenhower Doctrine**, stating the United States would provide aid to any Middle Eastern country threatened by communists. And the **1953 Refugee Relief Act** permits 214,000 additional immigrants over existing quotas from European countries between 1953 and 1956.

In 1954, Ike signed a **Revenue Act** which was a major rewrite of the Internal Revenue Code, including that contributions to employee health plans were tax deductible to the employer but not taxable income to the employee. In 1954, the U.S. Supreme Court in **Brown vs Board of Education of Topeka** ordered the desegregation of public schools. Also in 1954, Eisenhower changed the name of the Presidential retreat from **Shangri-La**, the name given by FDR, to **Camp David** to honor the name of his father and grandson. Ike and Mamie used the **presidential yacht**, named *Barbara Anne* after their granddaughter, only occasionally. While not a churchgoer, in 1954, on **Flag Day**, Ike approved "**One Nation Under God**" in the Pledge of Allegiance and "**In God We Trust**" on U.S. currency.

Ike was a very **likeable extrovert** with a quick smile, but he also had a **quick temper**. Nonetheless, although he was a demanding boss, he gained **respect and loyalty** because he was **open and honest**. And he was always **clear and direct** in what he wanted. He also urged his staff and cabinet to disagree with the execution of an assigned task when warranted. He was very **organized** in everything he did stating the goal was to "simplify, clarify, coordinate and expedite." He preferred conversations to reports but, nonetheless, was a voracious reader. Contrary to what John Adams said, "The middle way is no way." Ike noted, "The middle way is the right way, extremes do not work."

Eisenhower relied on **detailed intelligence reports** from the Pentagon and the State Department to guide his decision-making. This was an extension of Ike's information-gathering while Commander in Chief during World War II.

Ike's **domestic agenda** included extending statehood to Alaska and Hawaii, expanding Social Security, expanding the space program, developing an Interstate Highway System, and retaining the Taft-Hartley Labor Law. He was successful on all five, while balancing the budget in all eight years of his office. He was also successful in getting **Earl Warren** appointed Chief Justice of the U.S. Supreme Court in 1953, following the retirement of Fred Vinson.

Ike's **international agenda** included not sending troops to Indonesia, getting a peace agreement in Korea, (the **Korean War** ended on July 27, 1953, after more than 36,000 Americans were killed), supporting NATO, and seeking better relations with Russia since Stalin died shortly after Ike entered office.

Following the belief of George Marshall, author of the Marshall Plan who said, "Hunger and insecurity are the worst enemies of peace." Ike signed the 1954 Agricultural Trade Development and Assistance Act, better known as **The Food for Peace Act**, providing humanitarian assistance. It was a powerful foreign policy. America has shipped food abroad since 1812 when President Madison sent aid to Venezuela.

In January 1955, Ike held the **first televised press conference**. He sat in front of the **Resolute Desk** given to President Rutherford Hayes in 1890. In that same year, Ike suffered a heart attack. While recovering, he was told to keep his temper and blood pressure under control.

In 1955, Congress increased the annual pay for the legislators to $22,500 (up from 1947's $12,500), for the associate justices of the U.S. Supreme Court to $35,000 (up from 1946's $25,000), and for the chief justice to $35,500 (up from 1946's $25,500). In 1956, Congress increased the annual pay for the cabinet officers to $25,000 (up from 1949's $22,500). Congress made no other pay changes during Eisenhower's term of presidency.

Ike's four years can be summed up with three words: peace, prosperity, and golf. **Peace** came about eight months into his first term when the Korean War was settled. **Prosperity** was exemplified by low unemployment and modest inflation. **Golf** was a game; he played virtually every day.

In the **1956 presidential election**, Republicans **Dwight D. Eisenhower** and **Richard M. Nixon** defeated Democrats **Adlai E. Stevenson** and **Estes Kefauver**, 35,581,003 to 25,738,765 in the popular vote and 457 to 73 in the electoral vote.

The **1956 Federal Highway Act** created the inter-state highway system and converted more than 40,000 miles to four-lane and eight-lane highways.

In **Commissioner vs LoBue** (1956), the U.S. Supreme Court ruled that unless otherwise covered by the Internal Revenue Code, the difference between exercise price and fair market value will be ordinary income on date of exercise of an employee stock option.

In his January 20, **1957, inaugural address**, Ike stated, "The unity of all who dwell in freedom is their only sure defense. The supreme quality of leadership is integrity." Also in 1957, the **Civil Rights Act** was signed. It protected voting rights and created the **1957 Civil Rights Commission**.

The initial **cabinet** members of Eisenhower's **second term** included **Vice President**, Richard Nixon, **Secretary of State** John Dulles, **Secretary of the Treasury** George Humphrey, **Attorney General** Herbert Brownell, **Postmaster General** Arthur Summerfield, **Secretary of the Interior** Frederick Seaton, **Secretary of Agriculture** Ezra Benson, **Secretary of Labor** Jane Mitchell, **Secretary of Commerce** Frederick Mueller, **Secretary of Defense** Charles Wilson, and **Secretary of Health, Education and Welfare** Marion Folsom. Winston Churchill once said of Secretary of State John Foster Dulles, "Dull, Duller, Dullest," reflecting on his quiet and cautious behavior.

The **1957 Civil Rights Act** created the U.S. Commission on Civil Rights with authority to investigate incidences of discrimination and the Act established the Civil Rights section in the Justice Department with authority to prosecute those interfering with citizens right to vote. In that same year, Ike had another minor stroke. In **Reid vs Covert** (1957), the U.S. Supreme Court ruled that civilian United States citizens abroad retain their Article 3, Section 2, Fifth and Sixth Amendment protections, and courts of law, not military tribunals, have the power to try civilians.

The **1958 Former Presidents Act** provided lifetime Secret Service protection for former presidents' families, a pension equal to a Cabinet Secretary's, transition funding, and lifetime medical coverage in military hospitals. The **1958 National Aeronautics and Space Act** created the National Aeronautics and Space Administration with the responsibility for research into problems of flight inside and outside the earth's atmosphere.

In **Cooper vs Aaron** (1958), the U.S. Supreme Court ruled that states are bound by the Supreme Court's decisions, even if there are state laws to the contrary, as Article 6 made the Constitution the "supreme Law of the Land" and *Marbury vs Madison* made the federal judiciary the "supreme" interpreters of the "law of the Constitution," therefore the Court's interpretation of the Fourteenth Amendment in *Brown vs Board of Education* is binding on the states and cannot be nullified by "state legislators or state executive or judicial officers."

The **1959 Labor-Management Reporting and Disclosure Act** regulates labor unions and their relationship with members. The act also establishes reporting requirements, standards and safeguards while barring Communist Party members from holding office. The Act is also called the **Landrum-Griffin Act**.

On September 22, 1958, Chief of Staff **Sherman Adams** resigned for taking bribes. **Wilson Persons** followed Adams and served for the remainder of Eisenhower's second term of office. He had served in the army during both World War I and II. In the latter, he was a special assistant to Ike when he was the **Supreme Commander of the Allied Forces**. In the 1958 midterm election, the Democrats strengthened their hold in both Houses: Senate 65-35 and House 283-153. Eisenhower stated, "America is best described by one word, **freedom**."

With the March 5, 1959, death of Soviet dictator **Joseph Stalin**, tensions between America and Russia eased slightly. Ike invited Soviet Leader **Nikita Khrushchev** and his family to the White House. On a tour of Russia, on July 24, 1959, Vice President Nixon engaged in a **"kitchen debate"** at a U.S. exhibit with Premier Khrushchev. On December 5, 1959, Ike stated, "There can be no second-class citizens in this country."

The **1960 Pension Act** stated employer and employee rights in 401(k) plans. Also in 1960, the U.S. Supreme Court in **Commissioner vs Duberstein** ruled that in determining what constitutes a "gift," excludable from gross income under the Internal Revenue Code, the transferor's intention is the "most critical consideration," and questions of fact must be determined on a "case-by-case basis."

On May 1, 1960, the Russians shot down the **American U-2 spy plane** and captured its pilot, **Gary Powers**. Ike was furious because the Russians canceled the upcoming Paris Summit between the two countries. Ike's approval rating dropped from 77% to 50% after the spy plane incident. Powers was later released in exchange for a Russian spy. But Ike refused to "pass the buck," announcing, "If anyone should be punished, they should punish me."

In **Boynton vs Virginia** (1960), the U.S. Supreme Court ruled that the Interstate Commerce Act of 1887, which forbids discrimination by any interstate common carrier by motor vehicle, extends its prohibitions against racial segregation to bus terminals and restaurants in the terminal where they "operate as an integral part of the bus carrier's transportation service for interstate passengers."

Ike was disappointed that Nixon lost and frustrated that Kennedy won in the **1960 presidential election**. Ike not only thought JFK was not prepared for the job, but he was also still angry with how JFK had repeatedly stated Ike's administration did a very poor job. And Ike believed JFK would use every opportunity to take credit for what Ike had done and again point out where he had failed. Nonetheless, Ike had to prepare for an **orderly transition**. Ike appointed staff assistant Wilton Parsons to be his point of contact; JFK appointed lawyer Clark Clifford to be his representative. The two would handle the details of the January 20th inauguration. Ike was president until then, JFK after that date. Ike and JFK agreed to meet at 9am on December 6, 1960, to discuss the transition.

Since there had been no progress in the **nuclear arms** talks, on December 5th, Ike suspended the talks. It would be left to JFK to restart the talks, which began in October 1958. In late December 1960, the Army returned Ike to the **rank of general**. Returning to his rank of five-star general gave him the use of documents for his library. And as an outgoing president, he would receive a $25,000 presidential pension and $25,000 for office expenses.

The Augusta National Golf Club indicated he would also have an office when he visited. Ike noted, "One leaves the presidency with less reputation and few friends."

On January 3, 1961, **Ike terminated diplomatic relations with Cuba**, after disputes over naturalization of US firms had been unacceptable. Ike briefed JFK on the situation. Meanwhile, the **CIA trained Cuban exiles** for an invasion.

On January 9, 1961, Ike attended Nixon's 48th birthday celebration and said he was grateful to him for his loyalty and absolute readiness to undertake any chore. On January 17, 1961, Ike gave a **farewell speech** to the public on TV. Among the words on his 26-page script was a warning, "We must guard against the acquisitions of unwanted influence by the military industrial complex." and he closed by thanking the American people for giving him the presidency. Ike's final press conference (his 93rd), on January 18th, lasted 30 minutes, and he got a standing ovation.

Ike, JFK, and their wives met on the morning of January 20th in the White House for coffee and then proceeded to the Capitol Building for the inauguration. After JFK was sworn in, he stated, "Ask not what your country can do for you, ask what you can do for your country." **The baton had been passed**. Ike and Mamie left to settle down on their farm near Gettysburg.

After leaving the presidency, Ike received offers of a free car, a board seat, and many other items. He declined everything, saying he had **never allowed his name to be used**, except for charitable purposes. And following tradition, Ike and other cabinet members purchased their meeting chair for $88. In retirement, Ike continued to paint; he was a talented artist who created more than 400 paintings.

In the four years following Ike's retirement, Gallup polls identified him as the "**most admired man in America,**" and he **was respected globally** for being the architect of winning the war in Germany. He had a heart attack in 1965 and two in 1968. He died on March 28, 1969, at age 78 of congestive heart failure in Walter Reed Medical Center. His last words were to his son, John: "I want to go. God take me." He was buried in the Eisenhower Presidential Library in Abilene, Kansas, on April 2, 1969. Mamie died on November 1, 1979, of a stroke at age 82. She was buried with her husband.

Ratings of the presidential performance of Eisenhower have varied. A 1962 poll of historians rated Eisenhower 28th of the 33 presidents rated – a low average. But a 2017 poll of historians rated him 5th, behind only Abraham Lincoln, George Washington, Franklin Roosevelt and Theodore Roosevelt. The passage of time and different historians have yielded significantly different interpretations. Kennedy was ranked 8th in the 2017 poll.

Key Events

The **U.S. Weather Bureau** began to name hurricanes (1953); **Ralph Ellison** won a National Book Award for *Invisible Man* (1953); Swanson introduced **TV dinners** (1953); the lifting of wage and price control impacted pay and benefits during the period (1953); the molecular biologists Francis Crick and James Watson discovered Deoxyribonucleic Acid, the **DNA** molecule (1953); **Julius and Ethel Rosenberg** died in Sing Sing's electric chair for selling America's atomic bomb secrets to Russia (1953); the **DJIA** closed at 280.90 at year-end, down 3.8 percent (1953); the first computer (**UNIVAC-1**) was sold to General Electric (1954); **Citibank** was created from the merger of National City

Bank and the First National Bank of New York (1954); **Chase Manhattan Bank** was created from the merger of Chase National Bank and the Bank of the Manhattan Company (1954); **Ellis Island** was boarded up (1954); *Sports Illustrated* began publication (1954); Zenith Electronics introduced the **TV remote control** (1954); **Elvis Presley** launched a singing career and the Beatles landed in New York (1954); the labor participation rate was at 58.1% (1954); stocks returned to the 1929 levels (1954); the first **United States nuclear submarine**, *USS Nautilus*, was launched (1954); **Veterans Day** became a national holiday by act of Congress (1954); the Air Force Academy began operation (1954); **U.S. Senator Joseph McCarthy** charged the U.S. government with concealing the names of communists in the federal government, and he was then censured by the U.S. Senate for his communist allegations (1954); Bobby Kennedy became the chief counsel of Senator McClellan's committee investigating **organized crime** – over 1,500 witnesses and 20,000 pages of testimony (1954); the **DJIA** average exceeded its previous high of 346 in 1929 (1954); the New York Curb Exchange became the **American Stock Exchange** or AMEX (1954); Congress changed the tax filing date from March 15 to April 15 (1954); actress **Marilyn Monroe** married former New York Yankees baseball star **Joe DiMaggio** (1954); the movie *On the Waterfront* starring Marlon Brando, showed corruption in the longshoremen's union (1954); mafia boss **Sam Giancana** held a meeting of about 100 gangsters in the Appalachian, New York, an event that did not go unnoticed by the police (1954); the **DJIA** closed at 404.39 at year-end, up 44 percent (1954); **Disneyland** opened in Anaheim, California (1955); *Fortune* **magazine** published its first 500 largest company list, headed by General Motors, Standard Oil of New Jersey, U.S. Steel, and General Electric (1955); **Jonas Salk** developed a cure for polio (1955); Sony introduced Japan's first transistor radio (1955); **AFL and CIO merged** with George Meany as president and Walter Reuther in charge of industrial unions (1955); *Money and Motivation* was written by W.F. Whyte (1955); in the United States, the issue of **civil rights** was gaining much greater awareness among the public, and a movement began to grow as **Rosa Parks** was arrested in Montgomery, Alabama, for refusing to give up her bus seat to a white man (1955); the Interstate Commerce Commission ordered the **desegregation** of public transportation (1955); the **DJIA** closed at 488.40 at year-end, up 20.8 percent (1955); Malcolm McLean launched the **first container ship** (1956); William Whyte published *The Organization Man* (1956); the **transatlantic cable** began operation (1956); **Ford Motor Company** went public (1956); actress **Marilyn Monroe** married playwright Arthur Miller (1956); New York Yankees pitcher **Don Larsen** recorded a perfect game in the World Series against the Brooklyn Dodgers (1956); the **DJIA** closed at 499.47 at year-end, up 2.3 percent (1956); **IBM** moved its headquarters to Armonk, New York, and **Pepsi** moved its headquarters to Purchase, New York (1957); Jack Kilby and Robert Noyce developed the **first microchip** (1957); baseball teams the **Brooklyn Dodgers** and the **New York Giants** moved to California (1957); teamster boss **Jimmy Hoffa** was investigated by the senate's **McClellan Committee**, but he had a convenient memory loss (1957); the American Institute of Accountants became the **American Institute of Certified Public Accountants** (AICPA) (1957); **Arkansas Governor Faubus** called in the National Guard to prevent the schools from being integrated, but President Eisenhower sent federal troops to enforce the integration (1957); the surgeon general stated there was a direct link between cancer and smoking (1957); the **DJIA** closed at 435.69 at year-end, down 12.8

percent (1957); the **teamsters** were booted out of the AFL-CIO (1957); the **National Basketball Hall of Fame** opened in Springfield, Massachusetts and the first inductees were Luther Gulick, Ed Hickox, Ralph Morgan, James Naismith, Harold Olson, and Amos Alonzo Stagg (1957); Albert (Lord High Executioner) Anastasi of **Murder Inc.** was killed at age 54 (1957); actress **Ava Gardner** divorced Frank Sinatra and would never marry again (1957); **National Airlines** initiated **jet passenger service** between Miami and New York (1958); American Express introduced **credit cards** (1958); Harry Winston donated the 44.5 carat **Hope Diamond** to the Smithsonian Institute (1958); the **U.S. Marines** were sent to Lebanon to avoid an overthrow of the government (1958); Fairchild Semiconductor and Texas Instruments created the integrated circuit or **microchip** (1958); the Baltimore Colts defeated the New York Giants in an overtime game, labeled "**the greatest football game ever played**" (1958); the **DJIA** closed at 583.65 at year-end, up 34.0 percent (1958); Robert Noyce helped invent the microchip and found **Intel** (1959); Xerox introduced the **914 copier** – called that because it copied on nine by fourteen inch paper (1959); the **Duane Reade** drugstore chain opened on the corner of Duane and Reade in New York City (1959); Samuel Bronfman opened the **Seagram Building** on Park Avenue in New York City with the Four Seasons restaurant in the building (1959); **Motown Records** was founded by Berry Gordy (1959); the **Barbie doll** made an appearance (1959); **Harold Geneen** became the CEO of International Telephone and Telegraph, which he would turn into a major diversified conglomerate (1959); the **St. Lawrence Seaway** opened, linking the Great Lakes with the Atlantic Ocean (1959); the movie *Ben Hur* received 11 Academy Awards (1959);

the U.S. Commission on Civil Rights was formed in 1954 to enforce the Supreme Court order in **Brown vs Board of Education of Topeka** to desegregate public schools (1959); **Alaska** was admitted as the 49th state (1959); **Hawaii** was admitted as the 50th state (1959); the U.S. launched its first satellite (1959); Ike issued an injunction, upheld by the U.S. Supreme Court, that ended a **116-day steel strike** (1959); **Joe Kennedy** met with Chicago mafia head Sam Giancana asking for help to elect son JFK, stating, "Any administration led by the Kennedy family will be good for your people." (1959); the **DJIA** closed at 679.36 at year-end, up 16.4 percent (1959); **IBM's System 360** established the common computer language (1960); Brooklyn's **Ebbets Field** was demolished to make way for apartment buildings (1960); U.S. imposed a **trade embargo on Cuba** (1960); the **oral contraceptive** was introduced (1960); the U.S. **population** approached **180 million** (1960); a pizza slice sold for 15¢ in New York City (1960); a midair collision of TWA flight 266 and United Flight 826 over New York City killed 134 people (1960); Alfred Hitchcock released the movie *Psycho* (1960); the largest employers were **General Motors** (595,000 employees) and **Bell System** (580,000) employees (1960); **Sinatra formed the Rat Pack** (Joey Bishop, Sammy Davis Jr., Peter Lawford, and Dean Martin) (1960); **Soviet Premier Nikita Khrushchev** banged a shoe on the desk for attention at the United Nations (1960); House Representative **Adam Clayton Powell** stated that the mafia was in complete control of Harlem (1960); the first birth-control pill was approved by the Federal Drug Administration (1960); the nuclear submarine *Nautilus* made the first undersea crossing of the North Pole (1960); the National Labor Relations Board (NLRB) ruled that the Kohler Company owed its employees $4.5 million in back wages (1960); four Black college students did a sit-in at a Woolworth lunch counter when denied service (1960); the **American Football League** began with eight teams: the Boston Patriots, the Buffalo Bulls, the Dallas Texans, the Denver Broncos, the Houston Oilers, the Kansas City Chief, the Los Angeles Chargers, and the New York Titans (1960); Pete Rozelle became Commissioner of the NFL (1960); track star **Wilma Rudolph** was the first American woman to win three gold medals at one Olympics (1960); the Winter Olympics featured an American hockey "**miracle on ice**" gold medal victory (1960); heavyweight **boxer Floyd Patterson** regained the title, knocking out Ingemar Johansson (1960); racial justice sit-ins that began in 1960 had over 70,000 participants in a ten-year period (1960); the first expansion of the **National Hockey League** since its 1917 formation added the California Seals, the Los Angeles Kings, the Minnesota North Stars, the Philadelphia Flyers, the Pittsburgh Penguins, and the St. Louis Blues (1960); starting salaries for college graduates ranged from $4,500 to $7,000 a year, while baseball star **Stan Musial's** $80,000 salary led the league (1960); the **DJIA** closed at 613.89 at year-end, down 9.3 percent (1960); and on New Year's Day, Fidel Castro took control of Cuba (1961).

John F. Kennedy
(35ᵗʰ President)

January 20, 1961 – November 22, 1963

John Fitzgerald Kennedy was born on May 29, 1917, in Brookline, Massachusetts, to Joseph and Rose Kennedy. John (known to his friends as either Jack or JFK) was the second of nine children born into a **powerful and wealthy Irish Catholic family**. JFK had three brothers: Edward, Joseph Jr. (the oldest), and Robert. JFK also had five sisters: Eunice, Jean, Kathleen, Patricia, and Rosemary. JFK's roots date back to Irish great-grandparents whose grandchildren, Rose Fitzgerald and Joseph Kennedy, got married. Mother Rose was the daughter of Boston Mayor John Francis "**Honey Fitz**" Fitzgerald. Joe Sr. instilled in his children that **nothing was more important than family**.

Among the mantras of the patriarch, Joe Kennedy's were, "Win at all costs," "Complaining is strictly prohibited," and "To whom much is given, much is expected." The family moved to different homes around Boston, finally settling in **Hyannis Port** on Cape Cod, Massachusetts.

John Kennedy was educated in **private schools** and then entered **Harvard** in 1936. Kennedy was quickly **known as Jack** to his friends and later as JFK. He was an **excellent athlete** and both a sailor and a swimmer. But a **football injury** to his spinal cord while at Harvard gave him back pain for the rest of his life. He graduated from Harvard in 1940. JFK was a **speed-reader**, capable of reading an 80,000-word book in an hour. He was also diagnosed with **Addison's Disease**, which added to his back pain. Jack was **sick most of his life**. He had chicken pox, measles, scarlet fever, and whooping cough. Throughout his life there were few days when he was not in pain.

Joe Kennedy Sr. went to Hollywood, **made a fortune in films**, and had affairs with several actresses. Later he left Hollywood and returned to New York, where he had made a **fortune investing in the stock market** before the 1929 crash. He turned to **bootlegging** during Prohibition, and when it ended, he invested in the Seagram Company and real estate. In 1934, he served as the first **Chairman of the Securities and Exchange Commission** under FDR.

On January 8, 1938, Joseph Kennedy was named **Ambassador to Great Britain** whereupon Joe Sr. moved his family to London. While the rest of the family was in Washington, D.C., JFK was in London, England. JFK wrote the book *While England Slept*, describing its role in the upcoming war with Germany, while attending the London School of Economics in 1935.

When Germany declared war on the United States, Joe Kennedy Sr. sent his family back to America, all that is, except "special needs" Rosemary, who Joe kept with him to have a lobotomy. It left her functioning equivalent as a two-year old. In a November 11, 1940 interview with a **Boston Globe** reporter, Ambassador Kennedy stated, "Democracy is finished in England." When that appeared in print, President Roosevelt asked for and received Kennedy's resignation.

Of the four brothers, the father was grooming Joe Jr. for a major role in politics. But that vanished when **Joe Jr., a pilot, was killed** at the beginning of the Second World War. In 1941, Jack tried to enlist and was rejected twice by the army and the navy; but he ended up in the Naval Reserve, where he was "called up" and put in charge of the patrol boat **PT-109** in the Pacific in August 1943. It was cut in half by a Japanese destroyer. Jack floated for two days before being rescued and returned home with **malaria**. In 1945, Jack was awarded the **Marine Corps Medal** and the **Purple Heart**. He is the only president to date to receive a **Purple Heart** for being wounded in action.

With his father's money to pay for his campaign expenses, Jack was elected to the **U.S. House of Representatives** at age 29 in 1946, 1948, and again in 1950. Richard Nixon was also a freshman **Congressman** in 1946. In 1951, JFK was interviewed by **Jacqueline** (Jackie) **Bouvier** who was working for the *Washington Times Herald*. Like Jack, Jacqueline also was from a very wealthy family. **JFK was fascinated by Jackie.** She was beautiful and brilliant. They had long talks and long walks. They exchanged books. He gave her books on America; she gave him books on France. She had gone to Vassar but transferred to and graduated from **George Washington University** with a degree in French literature. She worked briefly for ***Vogue*** magazine but then transferred to the ***Washington Times Herald*** and became a reporter. JFK once asked her, "A penny for your thoughts." She replied, "If I told them to you, they would no longer be mine, would they?" JFK's back pain meant he had to use crutches.

JFK and Jackie were married on September 12, 1953, in Newport, Rhode Island, by Cardinal Cushing before 600 people. Jackie's nickname for Kennedy was **Magic**. On October 21, 1954, JFK had back surgery – a metal plate was bolted into his backbone. While recovering from his operation, he began writing his book, ***Profiles in Courage***, featuring profiles of eight senators and their courage to take significant risks. On February 5, 1955, JFK had another back operation to remove the steel plate and replace it with a bone graft. On August 15, 1956, at the **Democratic Convention** for the presidency, JFK gave the nominating address for Senator Kefauver as the running mate for Governor Adlai Stevenson. Following that convention, JFK decided he would run for the **1960 presidential election**.

JFK and Jackie had three children **Caroline** in 1957, **John Jr.** in 1960, and **Patrick** in 1963, who died shortly after birth, after several miscarriages. Jackie had little interest in politics, but she was very helpful in JFK's campaign for the U.S. Senate, as she was especially good at assessing people.

In 1952, JFK was elected to the **U.S. Senate**, defeating Henry Cabot Lodge Jr. Back pain and Addison's Disease contributed to a poor Senate attendance record. JFK was hospitalized nine times for back and other problems between 1955 and 1957. Recovering from back surgery, JFK made the **nomination speech** for Adlai Stevenson at the **1956 Democratic Convention** for president. The good-looking millionaire, who was also a very good speaker, almost got himself nominated as Stevenson's vice-presidential candidate at age 39.

In 1957, JFK became the first **president-to-be** to be awarded a **Pulitzer Prize**. It was for his book, *Profiles in Courage*. In 1958, JFK was re-elected to the **U.S. Senate**. But the close loss in the 1956 convention catapulted JFK to be the party's favorite for the **1960 presidential race**. And he was nominated at the 1960 convention with Senate Majority Leader Lyndon Johnson as his running mate. JFK was surprised when Johnson agreed to the vice presidency. But LBJ knew that one of every four presidents to date had died in office, and he liked the odds.

Kennedy entered the primaries with **two disadvantages**: his youthful age of 43 and his catholic religion. His response was, "I will be older when elected," and "I am not the Catholic candidate for president, I am the Democratic Party candidate who happens to be Catholic." JFK overcame the odds and won both the Wisconsin and West Virginia primaries. Campaigning in West Virginia, JFK learned that it was legal to pay money to voters for their ballot. Before both elections, Joe Sr. sent JFK a telegram stating, "Do not buy one more vote than you need. I'll be damned to pay for a landslide." Preparing for JFK's political rise, Joe Kennedy met with former Capone triggerman and current Chicago mob boss Sam Giancana to get Chicago's votes.

JFK knew he had a tough race for the presidency, realizing the Republican candidate, **Richard Nixon**, President Eisenhower's vice president, was an attractive candidate. So **JFK focused on Nixon** and **Eisenhower's administration as boring, dull, inept, lethargic, and listless**. He claimed that it had lost its energy and purpose. **Ike was furious** that his administration was so charged. JFK also stated that "America is losing its global power to be a greater country, and it is a powerful country, but I think it could be a more powerful country."

There were **four televised presidential debates** between Democrat John Kennedy and Republican Richard Nixon. The first debate was held on September 26, 1960, in Chicago, Illinois. The second debate was held on October 7, 1960, in Washington, D.C. The third debate was held on October 13, 1960, with Kennedy in New York and Nixon in Los Angeles. And the last debate was held on October 21, 1960, in New York City with both candidates present. There was no vice presidential debate between candidates Democrat Lyndon Johnson and Republican Henry Cabot Lodge Jr. in 1960.

Most agreed that Kennedy had won the four debates. He was calm, charming, good-looking, and organized. The known-to-be disorganized, indecisive JFK did not appear on TV. Nixon appeared uncomfortable and uneasy on TV. But **on radio**, where these features were unknown, many believed Nixon had won the debates because of what he said and how he said it. At the time, JFK made wardrobe changes up to four times a day, each time with a back brace to help with the pain.

In the **1960 election**, Democrats **John F. Kennedy** and **Lyndon B. Johnson** won the popular vote by a close margin vs Republicans **Richard M. Nixon** and **Henry Cabot Lodge**, 34,227,096 to 34,107,647. The same outcome was more dramatic in the electoral votes, 303 to 219. Kennedy was elected president and Johnson was elected vice president.

Lyndon Baines Johnson was born on August 27, 1908, in Stonewall, Texas. He was the first of five children. His grandparents were among the first settlers in Texas and started a cattle ranch. His father had been a state legislator for five terms. After working odd jobs, LBJ graduated from **Southwest Texas**

Teachers College in 1930 and went on to teach in local schools before attending **Georgetown University Law School** in 1934. That year, LBJ married Claudia (Lady Bird) Johnson. They went on to have two children, Lynda Bird and Luci Baines. He served six terms in the **U.S. House of Representatives**, with a leave of absence during **World War II** where he served as a naval officer and received the Silver Star. He then won a **Senate** seat in 1948 and 1954 before being elected vice president in 1960. He was the Senate minority leader in 1953 and the Senate majority leader in 1955.

At age 43, JFK was the **first Roman Catholic president**, the **youngest elected president**, and the **first president born** in the **20th century**. After his defeat, Nixon said to the press, "You won't have Nixon to kick around anymore." But eight years later, Nixon again ran for the presidency and was elected.

JFK was helped by Lyndon Johnson's delivery of the South. Some believed that Frank Sinatra's connection with mob boss Sam Giancana delivered a lot of Chicago votes as well, but because of Sinatra's mob contact, JFK's brother, Attorney General Bobby, cut off all contact between Sinatra and JFK. And in 1962, the U.S. Justice Department opened a formal investigation of Sinatra's ties to organized crime.

After the **1960 election**, the Democrats controlled Congress: Senate 64-36 and House 263-174. JFK knew the election results were not final until the Electoral College voted on December 19th, but he could not wait until then to begin planning for the inaugural, which would occur at noon on January 20th. JFK had to start thinking about who he should be, what he wanted to accomplish, and who he was going to hire. Among the cabinet officers, the most important were Secretary of State, Secretary of Defense, Secretary of the Treasury, and Attorney General. To staff these top four positions, JFK selected **Dean Rusk**, president of the Rockefeller Foundation, for **Secretary of State**, **Robert McNamara**, president of Ford Motors, for **Secretary of Defense**, **Douglas Dillon**, Under Secretary of State for Eisenhower, for **Secretary of the Treasury**. And **for Attorney General**, JFK selected his **brother Robert** over objections by many but strongly supported by their father. In response to the criticism of Robert Kennedy as Attorney General, JFK retorted, "I can't see that it is wrong to give him a little legal experience before he goes out to practice law." Bobby said, "I don't care if anybody likes me, as long as they like Jack." Reportedly, Bobby had his father's characteristics. Both were caustic, defiant, ferocious, and relentless. This was the first tier of selections and would be finalized before the end of the year.

The **second** tier of some 500 appointments were those who ran various divisions and departments including cabinet officers. This would be accomplished before the inauguration. And finally, there was a **third** tier of over 1,000 support positions. JFK had taken responsibility for tier one, and he gave the responsibility for tiers two and three to his brother-in-law **Sargent Shriver**, assisted by **Lawrence O'Brien**. They were to find the motivated best who would work hard and stay out of the press.

The final decision for JFK's **cabinet** included **Vice President** Lyndon B. Johnson, **Secretary of State** Dean Rusk, **Secretary of the Treasury** Douglas Dillon, **Attorney General** Robert Kennedy, **Postmaster General** Edward Day, **Secretary of the Interior** Stewart Udall, **Secretary of Agriculture** Orville Freeman, **Secretary of Labor** Arthur Goldberg, **Secretary of Commerce** Luther Hodges, **Secretary of Defense** Robert McNamara, and

Secretary of Health, Education and Welfare Abraham Ribicoff. Kennedy deleted the **Postmaster General** from his cabinet, a position that dated back to George Washington. The reason he gave was that the U.S. mail was now only one of various ways in which material was being forwarded. The other carriers, such as Amazon, were all publicly owned.

To ensure the transition from the Eisenhower administration to the Kennedy administration went smoothly, JFK appointed longtime friend **Clark Clifford** to work with **Wilton Parsons**, Ike's last Chief of Staff. Their first meeting was on November 14th in the White House. It would be the first of many meetings.

President-elect JFK named Kenneth O'Donnell (age 34) his **chief of staff**, Allen Dulles (age 67) his **director of the Central Intelligence Agency**, J. Edgar Hoover (age 65) his **director of the Federal Bureau of Intelligence**, Pierre Salinger (age 35) his **press secretary**, and Ted Sorensen (age 32) his **political advisor.**

With Clifford heading the **transition** and Shriver and O'Brien responsible for **finding the people**, **Ted Sorenson** was assigned by Kennedy to develop JFK's **policy agenda**. First, he had to look at what JFK had promised the public during the campaign: there were eighty-one promises. Next, Sorenson reviewed the list of expiring laws and then the short-term requirements and longer-term issues. The three facets were put together in a report along with recommendations and given to Kennedy for review, discussion, and determination.

Kennedy's **initial list of priorities** included the defense budget, economic recovery, fiscal policy, foreign aid, gold and the balance of payments, health and hospital care, the Peace Corps, laws, regulations, and taxation. This led to more than 300 requests to Congress for legislation.

JOHN F. KENNEDY (35TH PRESIDENT)

Ike was disappointed that Nixon had lost and frustrated that Kennedy had won. Ike believed it was a voter referendum on Ike's terms in office. Ike not only thought JFK was not prepared for the job, he was also still angry with how JFK had repeatedly stated Ike's administration did a very poor job. And Ike believed JFK would use every opportunity to take credit for what Ike had done well and again point out where Ike had failed. Nonetheless, Ike had to prepare for an orderly transition. Ike appointed staff assistant **Wilton Parsons** to be Ike's point of contact; JFK appointed lawyer **Clark Clifford** to be his representative. The two would settle the details of the January 20th inauguration. Ike was president until that action, JFK after that date.

Kennedy and Eisenhower first met on December 6th in the Oval Office to discuss transition issues. Their second meeting was on January 19th, one day before the inauguration, to discuss White House emergency issues. They and their wives would meet the next morning for coffee and go to the inauguration on the east front of the Capitol Building.

Eisenhower and Kennedy were different. One was the last president born in the nineteenth century, while the other was the first born in the twentieth century. Eisenhower was a highly organized extrovert; Kennedy was a disorganized, indecisive introvert. Eisenhower grew up in the Midwest in a family of modest means; Kennedy grew up in the East in a wealthy family. Eisenhower was the oldest serving president at age 70 when he left the presidency to Kennedy, who was the youngest incoming president at age 44.

After JFK was sworn into the office of president on January 20, 1961, on the Capitol steps by Chief Justice Earl Warren, Robert Frost read a poem. JFK then delivered his **memorable speech**,

"Let the word go forth from this time and place to friend and foe alike, the torch has been passed to a new generation of Americans – born in this century, tempered by war, disciplined by a hard and bitter peace, proud of our ancient heritage – and unwilling to witness or permit the slow undoing of those human rights to which this Nation has always been committed; and to which we are committed today, at home and around the world. Let every nation know, whether it wishes well or ill, that we shall pay any price, bear any burden, meet any hardship, support any friend, oppose any foe to assure the survival and success of liberty. And to my fellow Americans, ask not what your country can do for you – ask what you can do for your country." He also stated, "Mankind must put an end to war or war will put an end to mankind." Ike and JFK shook hands and departed. The baton had been passed.

The **inauguration had been jeopardized** because of a nine-inch snowfall the night before the event, but workers cleaned the snow. The inauguration was followed by a parade of over 30,000 marchers, and that evening a ball for some 25,000 spread over five hotels. Father Joe Kennedy's Palm Beach residence became the **Winter White House**, and his Hyannis Port house became the **Summer White House**.

Words from his inaugural speech formed the **Kennedy Doctrine**: "Let every nation know, whether it wishes us well or ill, that we shall pay any price, bear any burden, meet any hardship, support any friend, oppose any foe, in order to assure the survival and success of liberty." Following the inauguration, Kennedy gave his first **presidential press conference**, it was the first to be televised live.

Chief of Staff Kenneth O'Donnell and assistant **Larry O'Brien**, along with **David Powers**, became known as the **Irish Mafia**.

At staff meetings, JFK liked to doodle; his favorite subject was sailboats.

On March 29, 1961, Congress ratified the **23rd Amendment to the U.S. Constitution** (see Appendix C) establishing that the District of Columbia is to have the same number of electors to the electoral college as if it was a state.

On April 17, 1961, an attempt was made to overthrow Cuba's leader Fidel Castro (who had taken control of Cuba on New Year's Day in 1961) with 1,500 CIA-trained Cuban exiles. They failed in the disastrous **Bay of Pigs**. The exiles were either captured or killed. JFK stated, "How could I have been so stupid, to let them go ahead?" When Khrushchev threatened the U.S. after the 1961 botched **Bay of Pigs** fiasco, JFK covered up the U.S. involvement and said, "I have previously stated and I repeat now, that the United States intends no military intervention in Cuba."

In **Mapp vs Ohio** (1961), the U.S. Supreme Court ruled that all evidence obtained by a search and seizure that violates the Fourth Amendment's prohibition against unreasonable search and seizure, applicable to the States through the Due Process Clause of the Fourteenth Amendment, is inadmissible in State court.

JFK was always late for everything, even though he drove his car very fast. Almost every noon, JFK had a swim in the White House pool and then lunch with his family, followed by a 45-minute nap. JFK said, "Some days I get more information from the *New York Times* than I get from my intelligence reports." JFK had high approval ratings; the highest was in April 1961 when it reached 83%.

Kennedy had an active **international travel** schedule in 1961. First, he **visited** Argentina, Colombia, and Mexico. This was followed by visits to England, France, Germany, and Ireland. In Germany, JFK announced, "Ich bin ein Berliner," not knowing that what he said was, "I am a pastry." So much attention was paid to his **wife Jacqueline** in France that JFK quipped, "I am the man who accompanied Jacqueline Kennedy to Paris, and I enjoyed myself."

In a **September 1961 speech** at the United Nations, JFK stated, "The weapons of war must be abolished before they abolish us." After a 1961 five-hour summit meeting with Russian leader Khrushchev, JFK announced, "We are determined to resist aggression, whatever and wherever it takes place."

Asked to describe the **benefits of being president**, JFK responded, "The **pay is good** and I can **walk to work**." JFK was the second president to **donate** his full salary ($100,000) to **charity**; Hoover was the first. Asked about his **favorite song**, JFK replied, "It was from the play *Camelot*. Don't let it be forgot, that there once was a spot for a brief shining moment that was known as Camelot." Jackie added that JFK frequently listened to that recording. She believed that **Camelot** described her husband's presidency: "There will be great presidents again, but there will never be another Camelot."

Jackie enjoyed being **First Lady**, but she was an **introvert** and preferred playing tennis, reading books, riding horses, and shopping. And she took to overhauling the White House's 132 rooms. She said she was **not redecorating** the building; she was **restoring** it. And everything in it had to have a reason for being there. She reduced the five-course dinners to four: soup, salad, entrée, and dessert. JFK's favorites were patterned after Manhattan's **La Caravelle** (named after Columbus's ship) in Manhattan. Among these were pasta with lobster sauce and several dishes he grew up on: baked beans, chowder, and corn muffins. Jackie said, "JFK likes everything." Jackie Kennedy believed it was very important to always have **good food**, as it led to **good conversations** and **good politics**. Jackie's favorites included: orange juice and toast for breakfast, broth, and a sandwich for lunch, and poached salmon, lamb, string beans, and ice cream for dinner. The government expense accounts were for official entertainment, but private entertaining was covered by JFK or his father.

In February 1962, **John Glenn** became the **first American** to make three orbits around the earth. JFK stated, "We set sail on this new sea because there is new knowledge to be gained and new rights to be won." Later he stated that America would put a man on the moon before the end of the decade.

The **1962 Manpower Development and Training Act** became law; it provided $35 million to help technologically displaced persons find work. And the **1962 Self-Employed Individuals Tax Retirement Act** established Keogh plans.

While hosting a White House dinner for **Nobel Prize winners**, JFK remarked, "I think this is the most extraordinary collection of talent, of human knowledge, that has ever been gathered in the White House, with the possible exception of when Thomas Jefferson dined alone." JFK was the first president to receive the award, for ***Profiles in Courage***.

In April 1962, JFK announced a new **LASER** (Light Amplification by Stimulated Emission of Radiation) spear weapon. A month later, America dropped an H-bomb near Christmas Island in the Pacific.

On May 29, 1962, on JFK's 45th birthday, which he celebrated with 15,000 people at Madison Square Garden, **Marilyn Monroe** sang, "Happy Birthday, Mr. President." Later, Ripley's reportedly paid five million dollars for Marilyn's gold-rhinestone dress. Monroe died shortly after the event from an apparent suicide. JFK reportedly strayed with Monroe, as well as with the mistress of Mafia boss Sam Giancana. A classic Casanova, Jack almost always had sex on his mind. JFK once said, "If I don't have sex for three days I get terrible migraines." **JFK reportedly had numerous affairs**, including with strippers Blaze Starr and Tempest Storm and with actresses Angie Dickenson, Jayne Mansfield, Marilyn Monroe, and Zsa Zsa Gabor, along with hundreds of other lesser-knowns. He seemed to be a **sex addict without any self-restraint**. On at least one occasion, Jackie found evidence of these flings when she found a bra under her pillow and gave it to Jack, saying, "it's not my size."

In **Baker vs Carr** (1962), the U.S. Supreme Court ruled that federal courts have subject matter jurisdiction over redistricting cases, and these cases have a justiciable cause of action under the Fourteenth Amendment's Equal Protection Clause.

On October 16, 1962, a U.S. **U-2 spy plane over Cuba** revealed the **Russians were building nuclear missile facilities**. This occurred while Castro had agreed to release the captured 1,000 plus Bay of Pigs prisoners in exchange for America's promise not to invade Cuba and some $50 million in food and medical supplies. JFK invoked the **Monroe Doctrine** and demanded the immediate removal of the facilities. JFK announced a naval blockade to prevent offensive weapons from reaching Cuba. Also, that month, JFK ordered Russia to dismantle their rocket base in Cuba and send the missiles back to Russia. After six days, the missiles were removed, and war was averted. Upon inspection of ships leaving Cuba, the **U.S. Navy** confirmed forty missiles were headed back to Russia. JFK said, "Forgive your enemies, but don't forget their names." JFK added that, as head of the government, he was responsible for everything: "Victory has one hundred fathers, but defeat is an orphan."

In the mid-term **November 1962 election**, the Democrats secured a 68-32 lead in the U.S. Senate and a 259-176 majority in the House. JFK's brother Ted was elected to the U.S. Senate, representing Massachusetts.

In early 1963, **Joe Kennedy** suffered a paralytic stroke, rendering him speechless and confined to a wheelchair. In August of 1963, America and England signed a **Nuclear Test Ban** on atomic weapons on the sea or in the air, but not on underground testing.

The **1963 Equal Pay Act** became law. It required men and women be paid equally for work requiring equal effort, responsibility, and skill. It also codified the principle of equal costs or equal benefits.

Later in 1963, President Kennedy by executive order renamed the **Medal of Freedom** the **Presidential Medal of Freedom**, the highest civilian award. JFK cited the basis for the award was "any person who has made an especially meritorious contribution to (1) the security or national interests of the United States or (2) world peace, or (3) cultural or other significant, public or private endeavors." **The first awardees were** Marian Anderson and Ralph Bunche.

Tensions were high in the Cold War due to the U-2 spy plane incident and the Bay of Pigs fiasco, leading to the Russians building a wall to separate East and West Germany in early 1963. But President de Gaulle, recognizing an opportunity to improve relations with America, agreed to JFK's request to put the **Mona Lisa** on loan at the National Gallery on January 8, 1963. It was the first time the painting had left France.

Riots followed the **May 1963 March for Civil Rights** in Birmingham, which led to the desegregation of the University of Alabama in spite of **Governor Wallace's efforts** on June 11, 1963. Also, on June 11th in a televised report to the nation, President Kennedy promised legislation to ensure Blacks received treatment equal to that of whites. **Martin Luther King Jr.** called the speech a "clear cry for black justice." It was the beginning of a lasting relationship between the two which led to the **1964 Civil Rights Act** prohibiting pay and other actions based on color, national origin, race, religion, and sex. The act also created the **Equal Employment Opportunity Commission**. The **Civil Rights Act** was followed by the **1965 Voting Rights Act**, which protected African American's right to vote.

Later in June 1963, following the assassination of Medgar Evars, 250,000 marched on Washington to hear Martin Luther King proclaim, "**I have a dream**" on August 28, 1963, on the steps of the Lincoln Memorial. In **Gideon vs Wainwright** (1963), the U.S. Supreme Court ruled that the Sixth Amendment's right to counsel is a "fundamental right" in accordance with the Due Process Clause of the Fourteenth Amendment.

As if **predicting his future**, while leaving for Dallas, JFK stated, "If anybody really wants to shoot the president of the United States, it is not a very difficult job. All one has to do is get into a high building with a telescopic rifle and there is nothing anybody can do to defend against such an attempt." On **November 22, 1963,**

JOHN F. KENNEDY (35TH PRESIDENT)

JFK and his wife were greeted by a large crowd in Dallas. They rode with **Texas Governor John John Connally** and his wife, who told JFK, "You can't say Dallas does not love you." With that, **three shots** rang out. JFK was shot once in the throat and once in the back of the head, and Connally was wounded. The event was recorded by **Abraham Zapruder** on 16mm film, for which he was paid $16 million by the U.S. government.

Ex-Marine sniper **Lee Harvey Oswald** was seen holding a rifle from a warehouse window facing the motorcade. Police entered the building, but Oswald was gone. However, his rifle was found in the warehouse with three empty cartridges nearby. Both victims were rushed to a hospital five minutes away. At 1:00pm, 25 minutes after he was shot, **JFK was pronounced dead**. At the hospital, Jackie said, "They have shot my husband. I have his brains in my hand." Jackie took her wedding ring off and put it on Jack's finger. John Kennedy was the **fourth president to be assassinated** (Lincoln, Garfield, and McKinley preceded him). Kennedy died at an earlier age than any other president. He was 46 years old. He never recovered from the shooting for any last words. **Camelot** had been snuffed out.

After JFK was assassinated, Queen Elizabeth had **Big Ben** chimed every minute for one hour. The **lights of Piccadilly** in London were out for three hours after the announcement of JFK's death, and **Moscow played organ music** on television.

The **Kennedy children** were having **upcoming birthdays** without their father: John, Jr., three, and Caroline, six. Earlier in 1963, their third child, Patrick, died hours after birth.

Lee Harvey Oswald shot and killed police officer Tippet, and a half an hour later Oswald was captured in a movie house. While being moved from the jail in City Hall to the county jail, Oswald was **shot and killed** by night club owner **Jack Ruby**, who the police thought to be a detective.

The president's body was placed in a bronze coffin and put on **Air Force One**, where it was joined by Vice President Lyndon Johnson; JFK's brother Bobby, the Attorney General; and Jackie. Jackie's role shifted from **First Lady** to **First Widow** as she watched while LBJ was sworn in as president by District Judge Sarah Tilghman aboard Air Force One, which was taking them and JFK's body back to Washington. This was only the second time a president **was not sworn in by a U.S. Supreme Court Justice; Calvin Coolidge** was the first in 1923. Landing in Washington, President Johnson said, "This is a sad time for all people. We have suffered a loss that cannot be weighed. I will do my best – that is all I can do."

Before his death, **JFK profoundly predicted**, "A nation reveals itself not only by the men it produces but also by the men it honors, the men it remembers." JFK's "New Frontier" social programs were stalled in Congress at the time of his assassination. Congress made no pay changes during Kennedy's term of presidency.

JFK's body was taken to the East Room in the **White House**. The next morning, it was taken to **Boston**, where Cardinal Cushing, who had married Jack and Jackie, said the mourning mass. Following the mass, the body was flown back to Washington and taken to the **Capitol Rotunda**, where JFK's body rested on the **catafalque used for President Lincoln**. Representatives from **ninety-two countries**, along with **thousands of others**, paid their respects as they passed the **closed casket**.

After the viewing, the coffin was placed on Lincoln's gun carriage and towed by six grey horses, preceded by a riderless Black horse with stirrups in reversed cavalry boots, noting a dead warrior. **Millions watched on television** as kings, princes, and world leaders walked behind the horses on the two-mile trip to the **Arlington Military Cemetery** where Jackie lit the **Eternal Flame** over JFK's grave. Fifty jet planes flew overhead with the lead plane missing. Riflemen gave a 21-gun salute, and a bugler blew "Taps." Shortly after, in 1963, JFK received the first **Presidential Medal of Freedom**, posthumously from President Johnson.

The **1963 Transition Act** became law. It stipulated government payments associated with the cost of transition from one president to another.

On September 24, 1964, the **Warren Commission**, named after U.S. Supreme Court Justice Earl Warren, having interviewed more than 500 witnesses, reported that **Lee Harvey Oswald was the lone assassin**: three shots, six seconds, and one gunman? Upon learning of the report, former President Eisenhower stated, "**Appointing Earl Warren as Chief Justice** to the U.S. Supreme Court on October 5, 1953, was the worst decision I ever made." The position had opened up with the death of Chief Justice Fred Vinson earlier in 1953.

Some believed JFK was killed by the CIA, the mafia, or both. Among others doubting the Warren Report was **New Orleans District Attorney Jim Garrison** who believed the assassination was planned in New Orleans with focus on businessman **Clay Shaw** for his alleged involvement. Some wondered why Secret Service agents were not riding on the car's running boards.

Most historians consider JFK **one of the most effective presidents**.

After JFK's assassination, **Ted Sorenson** and **Arthur Schlesinger** raced to get out books on the Kennedy administration. Sorenson got his out first, but Schlesinger got his second **Pulitzer Prize**.

On the Greek Island of Scorpios, on October 21, 1968, Jackie Kennedy married 62-year-old long-time friend and billionaire **Aristotle Onassis**. Jackie died on May 19, 1994, at age 64 of cancer in New York City.

Key Events

New York Yankee **Roger Maris** hit his 61st home run, eclipsing Babe Ruth's 34-year single-season record (1961); JFK got two airmen, who had been shot down by the Russians in the Artic Circle the previous year, released (1961); JFK coined the phrase "**affirmative action**" (1961); Ray Kroc purchased the **McDonald** name from two brothers for $2.7 million, launching the hamburger giant (1961); **Procter & Gamble** marketed **Pampers** (1961); the Kennedys were the first presidential couple to dine in **Buckingham Palace** since the Wilsons in 1918 (1961); the **Throgs Neck Bridge** opened, connecting the Bronx and Queens (1961); Russian astronaut **Yuri Gagarin** was the first man to circle the earth (1961); **Alan Shepard** was America's first man in space, 120 miles from Earth (1961); **Lutece** and **Sylvia** opened restaurants in New York City (1961); **Robert Noyce** received a patent on the **semi-conductor** (1961); IBM introduced the **Selectric typewriter** (1961); JFK created the **Peace Corps**, a program that trained volunteers for humanitarian and social service in underdeveloped countries (1961); the **Playboy Club**

JOHN F. KENNEDY (35TH PRESIDENT)

opened in New York City (1961); British-born **Peter Lawford**, JFK's brother-in-law, became a U.S. citizen (1961); Consolidated Edison opened a **nuclear-powered plant** at Indian Point on the Hudson River (1961); **freedom riders** went into the South to protest inter-state segregation (1961); JFK introduced a Marshall Plan lookalike, which he called the **Alliance for Progress**, to help Latin American countries (1961); **Joseph Heller** published *Catch 22* (1961); **Hurricane Donna** devastated the East Coast (1961); the **Seton Hall** basketball team was charged with shaving points (1961); the **DJIA** closed at 731.14 at year-end, up 18.7 percent (1961); **Nike** began operations (1962); **Sam Walton** opened his first discount store, which later became **Walmart** (1962); **Cesar Chavez** set up the National Farm Workers Association, leading to a **walkout of grape workers** for increased wages using nonviolent civil disobedience (1962); **Rachel Carson's** *Silent Spring* exposed the dangers of pesticides (1962); **the Gateway Arch** opened in St. Louis (1962); **James Meredith** became the first Black student to register at the University of Mississippi (1962); boxer **Sonny Liston** knocked out **Floyd Patterson** for the heavyweight title (1962); the **Beach Boys** and the **Rolling Stones** began performing (1962); basketball star **Wilt Chamberlain** scored 100 points against the New York Knicks (1962); *Dr. No*, starring Sean Connery, was the first **James Bond** movie (1962); JFK's brother **Ted was elected to the U.S. Senate**, representing Massachusetts (1962); JFK got **steel companies** to not raise prices (1962); some **1,800 U.S. Marines** landed in Siam to protect it from communists (1962); Russia released captured U-2 pilot **Francis Gary Powers** in exchange for the captured Soviet spy **Rudolph Abel** (1962); **Arthur Goldberg** was appointed an Associate Justice to the U.S. Supreme Court, the first Jewish appointee to the court (1962); the **DJIA** closed at 652.10 at year-end, down 10.8 percent (1962); **Jan Nidetch** incorporated "**Weight Watchers**" (1963); the **Idlewild Airport** in New York was renamed the **JFK Airport,** honoring John F. Kennedy (1963); *A Business and its Beliefs: The Ideas That Helped Built IBM* was written by **Thomas Watson** (1963); JFK publicly endorsed the **Keynesian approach** of tax cuts to stimulate demand (1963); America withdrew support from **South Vietnam**, and President Ngo Ninh Diem was assassinated (1963); England's **Winston Churchill** was made an honorary U.S. citizen (1963); President Kennedy ordered National Guard soldiers to not interfere with **desegregating Alabama schools** in spite of **Governor George Wallace** (1963); Black leader **Medgar Evars** was shot and killed by a sniper in Mississippi (1963); *My Years with General Motors* was published by **Alfred Sloan** (1963); the **National Football Hall of Fame** opened in Canton, Ohio, with its **first inductees**: Sammy Baugh, Bert Bell, Joseph Carr, Dutch Clark, Red Grange, George Halas, Mel Hein, Pete Henry, Cal Hubbard, Don Hutson, Curly Lambeau, Tim Mara, George Preston Marshall, John "Blood" McNally, Bronko Nagurski, Ernie Nevers, and Tim Thorpe (1963); Attorney General Bobby Kennedy brought **Joe Valachi** before a Senate hearing where he described the inner workings of the **Cosa Nostra** (1963); and the **U.S. population was over 200 million** (1963).

Lyndon B. Johnson
(36th President)

November 22, 1963 – January 20, 1969

Lyndon Baines Johnson, the first of five children, was born on August 27, 1908, to Samuel and Rebekah Baines Johnson in a farmhouse in Stonewall, Texas. He was known by his initials "**LBJ**." His grandparents were early Texas settlers and built a large cattle ranch. Lyndon had one brother, Sam, and three sisters: Rebekah, Josefa and Lucia. Lyndon's father was a state legislator for five terms before returning to cattle ranching. Johnson grew up on the family Texas farm. Graduating from high school at age 15 in 1924, he held a **number of jobs**, including shining shoes, washing dishes, collecting trash, and picking crops, before going to college. He graduated from **Texas State Teach-**

ers College in 1930 and attended **Georgetown University Law School** in 1934. Also that year, at age 26, he married Claudia **"Lady Bird"** Taylor, age 21, two months after meeting her. He saw her as ambitious, determined, and focused. He called her the **Steel Magnolia**. The Kennedys called the two **Uncle Capone** and his **Little Pork Chop**. The Johnsons had **two children**, both daughters: Lynda Bird and Luci Baines.

"Lady Bird" carefully reported what she did each day in a diary. Shortly after her marriage, she was introduced to the nation's capitol since Lyndon was a Congressional aide. Except for a brief absence from military service during World War II, Lyndon and Lady Bird rarely left Washington. She was the quintessential Washington **political wife**. In 1951, **LBJ** and Lady Bird bought a ranch in central Texas. It later became the **Texas White House**. LBJ loved to host a Texas barbecue of beans, corn bread, and ribs, with a lot of beer. Lady Bird was the first woman to campaign with her husband, traveling in her railroad car, the **Lady Bird Special**. At first, she was seemingly **oblivious to his extramarital affairs**.

Lyndon served as the Texas Director of the **National Youth Administration** for several years and in 1937 won a special election to the **House of Representatives** with the backing of fellow Texan and House Majority **Leader Sam Rayburn**. Following the Pearl Harbor attack, LBJ was among the first congressmen who enlisted for **military duty**. He was awarded the **Silver Star** while serving as a **naval officer**. After the war, he returned to his seat in the **House**. Following service in the House, LBJ moved on to the **U.S. Senate**, where he served from 1949 to 1960. The last five of those years, he was the **majority leader**. He had a big ego, crude humor, distrust of others, and steely determination. Known for a wheeling-dealing philosophy, he caused some to say, "You know LBJ is lying when he moves his lips." The **LBJ Treatment** cycled through accusation, cajolery, compliance, exuberance, scorn, supplication, tears, and threats, all one after the other, virtually hypnotizing the person. And while LBJ got good ratings for human rights, animal rights activists were incensed when he would pick up his pet beagles by their ears.

Accepting JFK's invitation, LBJ joined JFK on the presidential ticket. **Johnson assumed the presidency with the death of JFK** on November 22, 1963. LBJ was reportedly drunk on the morning of his inauguration. Johnson was 55 years old on the date of his inauguration. He was sworn in on Air Force One with widow Jacqueline Kennedy at his side, by the U.S. District Judge Sarah Hughes. No Supreme Court justice was available. Hughes is the **only woman to have sworn in a president**. LBJ stated, "For me, it is a deep, personal tragedy. I know the world shares the sorrow that Mrs. Kennedy and family will bear. I will do my best. That is all I can do. I ask for your help and for God's." LBJ was the **fourth president to come into office following the assassination** of a president (Lincoln, Garfield, and McKinley were the previous three). Lyndon Johnson was the **eighth vice president** (Tyler, Fillmore, Johnson, Arthur, Roosevelt, Coolidge, and Truman preceded him) to assume the presidency with the death of his president (John Kennedy). Johnson was the **ninth vice president to ascend to the presidency** because the president did not serve out his term. These presidents included William Henry Harrison, Zachary Taylor, Abraham Lincoln, James Garfield, William McKinley, Warren Harding, Franklin Roosevelt, and John Kennedy. And Lyndon B. Johnson was the **thirteenth vice president** to become president (John Adams, Thomas Jefferson, Martin Van Buren, John Tyler, Millard Fillmore, Andrew Johnson, Chester Arthur, Theodore Roosevelt,

Calvin Coolidge, Harry Truman, Richard Nixon, and Gerald Ford preceded him). Johnson is **one of three presidents** who served in the four elected federal offices, namely representative, senator, vice president, and president (**John Tyler** and **Andrew Johnson** were the other two).

On Wednesday, November 27th, LBJ addressed the nation before a joint session of Congress: "All I have, I would have given gladly not to be standing here today. The greatest leader of our time has been struck down by the foulest deed of our time. No words are sad enough to express our sense of loss. No words are strong enough to express our determination to continue the forward thrust of America that he began." Johnson vowed to continue President Kennedy's cause by announcing a "war on poverty." He also noted that "The separation of church and state is a source of strength." Shortly after, in a joint session of Congress, LBJ stated, "An assassin's bullet has thrust upon me the awesome burden of the presidency."

Shortly after JFK's death, LBJ told JFK's staff that he wanted them to stay. He needed them because he did not know how the White House presidential staff worked. He kept the cabinet intact without change for 13 months.

The initial **cabinet** for Johnson included **Secretary of State** Dean Rusk, **Secretary of the Treasury** Douglas Dillon, **Attorney General** Robert Kennedy, **Secretary of the Interior** Stewart Udall, **Secretary of Agriculture** Orville Freeman, **Secretary of Labor** Willard Wirtz, **Secretary of Commerce** Luther Hodges, **Secretary of Defense** Robert McNamara, and **Secretary of Health, Education and Welfare** Anthony Celebrezze. LBJ added the positions of Housing and Urban Development and the Secretary of Transportation. LBJ and Bobby Kennedy had a mutual distrust, which made a working relationship very difficult. Bobby quit in 1964 when he decided to run for president.

The **1963 Transition Act** was passed. It approved government payment for the cost of the transition from one president to another.

Walter Jenkins was a longtime aide of Johnson's before serving as his Chief of Staff for about a year. His service ended after he was arrested with another man in a public restroom for **disorderly conduct**. Journalist **Bill Moyers** was the next Chief of Staff, following many years in public broadcasting. After just short of a year of service, Moyers was succeeded by lobbyist and longtime President of the Motion Picture Association of America **Jack Valenti**. After just short of a year of service, Valenti was in turn succeeded by **Marvin Watson**, who also served about a year and then went on to become Postmaster General. The fifth and last Chief of Staff to President Johnson was **James Jones**, who was a former Congressman and would go on to become Ambassador to Mexico under President Clinton.

In 1962, Arthur Goldberg was appointed to the U.S. Supreme Court.

LBJ later proclaimed, "**I will not be defeated in Vietnam.**" When LBJ and Secretary of Defense McNamara's view differed, LBJ replaced him with Clark Clifford and appointed McNamara President of the World Bank in 1967. Johnson inherited Vietnam involvement, but he expanded our role, making it worse without a congressional declaration of war.

At the time of the **inauguration**, it is estimated that some 50 million living in America were hungry and some 35 million were living in poverty. This led to LBJ's call for "an unconditional **war on poverty**" in his first state of the union address. He was committed to finishing FDR's **New Deal** and Truman's **Fair Deal**. He stated, "The richest nation on Earth can afford to win it. We cannot afford to lose it."

LBJ had two goals: **eliminating poverty** and **establishing a great society**. The former meant medical coverage for poor Americans. The latter meant civil rights, environmental protection, publicly funded education, medical coverage for retired Americans, and voting rights. He believed that the Great Society would result in a larger economy with everyone benefiting. He had a notable list of domestic achievements, but on the international scene, Vietnam was still unsolved. When LBJ left office, the number of soldiers that had died in Vietnam had risen to over 15,000. By the time the last American troop left the country in 1973, that number would rise to over 57,000.

Lyndon **typically got up at 7:00am.** LBJ's favorite breakfast was cured bacon, brownies, grits, peach chili preserves, popovers, scrambled eggs, and coffee. He typically worked in his pajamas throughout the day. Dinner was chili shrimp curry, cooked custard, fried chicken, fruit, steak, ribs, and homemade ice cream. LBJ said he liked his wife's chili best, made with venison, not beef. He went to sleep late, after midnight. LBJ was known for **working long hours** and expecting his staff to do the same. But a close LBJ aide said he never saw LBJ read a book. Wife Lady Bird said her husband did not like being alone. He reportedly said, "An eight-hour man ain't worth a damn to me." LBJ was constantly testing others to determine **who could be trusted**. His behavior could be described as belittling, demanding, and mistrusting, often accompanied by cursing. It was difficult to give him unwelcome but necessary information. LBJ's ego and crude manners led to his **bullying** many of his staff members. After dressing down an aide for poor performance, LBJ added, "If I don't bawl you out every once in a while, you ain't part of the family."

The **President's Daily Briefing** (PDB) was introduced under President Lyndon Johnson. It contained highly classified material prepared by the CIA. Johnson liked his delivered at night for bedtime reading. It was given each working day. LBJ spent about a third of his time at his ranch.

LBJ was known to have **sex with women** in the White House and on the presidential yacht. Lady Bird even caught him in the act several times. LBJ reminded the press that his **personal life** was none of their business. He was the last president whose **infidelities** were kept from the public.

The **24th Amendment to the U.S. Constitution** was ratified on January 23, 1964, and stated the right to vote cannot be denied by any tax.

In September 1964, a commission headed by **Chief Justice Earl Warren** reported that President Kennedy **was killed** by **Lee Harvey Oswald, firing three shots from one gun**. This did not stop speculations that the CIA, Fidel Castro, and/or the mafia was involved.

In his **1964 State of the Union Address**, President Johnson outlined his Great Society and War on Poverty Programs.

For the **1964 election**, LBJ had to choose a vice president. Not wanting Bobby Kennedy (who was the attorney general) in the wings, LBJ announced that Kennedy cabinet members were ineligible for 1964 vice-presidential consideration. Secretary of Defense Robert McNamara and Senator Gene McCarthy were offered the post and declined. That left Minnesota **Senator Hubert Humphrey** as the prime contender. LBJ chose Humphrey for having successfully passed the Civil Rights legislation in the Senate. LBJ told Hubert that the relationship between president and vice president "Is like a marriage with no chance of divorce." Humphrey had been a senator since 1948 and an **unsuccessful presidential candidate** in 1960.

Hubert Humphrey was born on May 27, 1911, in Wallace, South Dakota, and lived in Dust Bowl poverty, helping his father run a pharmacy. He graduated from the Capital College of Pharmacy in 1932 and was a **druggist** from 1933 to 1936. In 1937, he **married Muriel Buck**. He then went to the University of Minnesota, receiving a **Bachelor of Arts degree** in 1939 and a **master's degree in political science** from Louisiana State in 1940. When the war came, Hubert tried to enlist but was rejected due to being **color blind**. From 1941 to 1945, he served in **various public service jobs**, including assistant director of the **War Manpower Commission** and state director of war production training. In 1945, he was elected **Mayor of Minneapolis**, and he was reelected in 1947. He then served as **U.S. senator** for Minnesota from 1949 to 1965. After Lyndon Johnson selected him as his running mate, Humphrey was elected vice president in 1964. After completing his term, he was selected at the **1968 Democratic Convention** to be their presidential candidate and lost to Republican Richard Nixon. Hubert returned to Minnesota and became a **professor** of public affairs at the University of Minnesota. He was elected a **U.S. senator** in 1970 and re-elected in 1976. Hubert Humphrey was known as the "**happy warrior**." He died of cancer on January 14, 1978. After Hubert's death,

Minnesota Governor Rudy Perpich appointed Humphrey's widow, Muriel, to his Senate seat to serve out Hubert's term of office. Hubert received two major awards: the **Congressional Gold Medal** in 1979 and the **Presidential Medal of Freedom** in 1980.

There was **no televised presidential debate** before the 1964 November election between Democratic candidates Lyndon Johnson and Republican Barry Goldwater. The presidential candidates refused to debate. Also, there was **no vice presidential debate** between Democratic candidate Hubert Humphrey and Republican William Miller.

In the **1964 election**, Democrats Lyndon **Johnson** and Hubert **Humphrey** defeated Republicans Barry **Goldwater** and William **Miller** receiving 43,167,895 popular votes to 27,175,770 and 486 to 52 electoral votes. Johnson was elected president and Humphrey was elected vice president. When Hubert Humphrey became LBJ's vice president, LBJ treated him the way he had been treated by JFK: he was essentially ignored.

The **1964 Revenue Act** scaled back maximum taxes and introduced a new form of a statutory stock option and a statutory stock purchase plan. The **1964 Civil Rights Act** prohibited pay and other actions based on race, color, sex, religion, and national origin, as well as creating the Equal Opportunity Commission.

There were two U.S. Supreme Court cases of interest in 1964. In **New York Times vs Sullivan**, the U.S. Supreme Court ruled that the First Amendment protection extended to the press when writing about public officials. In **J.I. Case vs Borak**, the U.S. Supreme Court ruled that in addition to the SEC enforcement of its rules, shareholders are also permitted to bring civil charges.

Johnson's **cabinet** after his 1964 election included **Vice President** Hubert Humphrey, **Secretary of State** Dean Rusk, **Secretary of the Treasury** Henry Fowler, **Attorney General** Nicholas Katzenbach, **Postmaster General** Lawrence O'Brien, **Secretary of the Interior** Stewart Udall, **Secretary of Agriculture** Orville Freeman, **Secretary of Labor** William Wirtz, **Secretary of Commerce** John Connor, **Secretary of Defense** Robert McNamara, **Secretary of Health, Education and Welfare** John Gardner, **Secretary of Housing and Urban Development** Robert Weaver, LBJ added this cabinet post believing the growth of the cities' needs to address housing and related issues, and **Secretary of Transportation** Alan Boyd. The latter position was an existing governmental agency raised to cabinet level.

For his **1965 inauguration**, LBJ rode two miles from the Capitol Building to the White House **in the same car JFK rode when assassinated**. In his **January 20, 1965, inaugural address**, LBJ stated, "I do not believe the **Great Society** is the ordered, changeless and sterile battalion of ants." The Democrats increased their **control of Congress**: Senate 68-32 and House 259-176. LBJ was a **domestic issues president** with success in civil rights and Medicare, but he was a **military neophyte**, which was reflected in his Vietnam decisions.

In his **1965 State of the Union Address**, President Johnson outlined his **Great Society** and **War on Poverty Programs** which included anti-poverty, civil rights, and healthcare legislation. Two major areas of debate during LBJ's presidency were **military and government programs** to support his Great Society. Less controversial were his confident leadership and civil rights support. LBJ was the first president since John Quincy Adams to propose federal aid for the arts. And his civil rights legislation required a constitutional amendment.

The **1965 Immigration and Nationality Act** eliminated national origin quotas in effect since 1902. The **1965 Tax Reform Act** scaled back the maximum tax of 70% on income over $200,000. The **1965 Social Security Amendments** introduced Medicare and Medicaid. Known as the **1965 Medicare and Medicaid Act**, it provided healthcare coverage for disabled and retired employees. And the **1965 Voting Rights Act** provided African Americans the right to vote.

In 1965, America reportedly had over **29,000 missiles** and Russia had over **5,000** and **Operation Rolling Thunder**, the sustained bombing of North Vietnam and South Vietnam began. By year-end, there were 200,000 troops in Vietnam.

In 1966, in **Miranda vs Arizona**, the U.S. Supreme Court ruled that criminal suspects must be informed of their rights before being questioned by the police.

LBJ continued the **unconstitutional expansion** of the executive branch. Johnson proposed to provide federal funding for virtually every aspect of American life, thereby alleviating, if not eliminating, poverty in America. This was the **Great Society**. This included the introduction of **Medicare** (medical coverage for retired workers) and **Medicaid** (medical coverage for poor Americans). Both were unconstitutional, as was environmental legislation.

In the 1966 **midterms**, the results were similar: Senate 64-36 and House 247-187 in favor of the Democrats.

The **1967 Age Discrimination in Employment Act** prohibited employment discrimination against those over 40. Also in 1967, the **25th Amendment to the U.S. Constitution** was ratified on February 10, 1967, it detailed what should happen if there is vacancy in the presidency. And in **Loving vs Virginia** (1967), the U.S. Supreme Court ruled that Virginia's anti-miscegenation statutes which prevented marriages between persons solely on the basis of race, violated the Equal Protection and Due Process Clauses of the Fourteenth Amendment.

An **aircraft carrier** that had been authorized by JFK was named the *USS John F. Kennedy* by LBJ in 1967. Also in 1967, President Johnson and **Russian Premier Alexei Kosygin** had peace talks in New Jersey, where LBJ stated the government did not have solutions for all of the nation's problems, but they would be wrong if they did not address the issues. Not happy with reporters, LBJ once said, "If I walked across the Potomac River, the newspapers would claim the president can't swim." Johnson did not like FBI head Hoover, but he once said, "It is better to have Hoover inside the tent pissing out than have him outside the tent pissing in."

At a March 31, 1968 televised presentation, President Lyndon Johnson talked about the war in Vietnam and then stated, "I shall not seek, and I will not accept, the nomination of my party for another term as your president." It is believed this decision was due to a combination of reasons: frustrated with the ongoing Vietnam war, another heart attack, pending competition from Senator Eugene McCarthy and JFK's younger brother, Bobby Kennedy, an approval rating of 36% and the pressure of the office. He added, "The magnitude of the job dwarfs every man who aspires to it." Days later, on April 4, 1968, **Martin Luther King Jr.** was assassinated in Memphis, Tennessee. And a month later, on June 5, 1968, **Robert Kennedy** was assassinated in Los Angeles while campaigning for the Presidency.

When the last American troops left Vietnam in 1975, over 58,000 Americans had died.

LYNDON B. JOHNSON (36TH PRESIDENT)

The **1968 Williams Act** required those attaining five percent or more of a company to disclose details of the action to the SEC. The **1968 Civil Rights Act** identified federally protected activities and the penalties for violators. The **1968 Omnibus Crime Control Act** introduced the witness protection program. The **1968 Revenue & Expenditure Act** added a 10% tax surcharge on personal income.

Leaving office after thirty-nine years, LBJ retired to his ranch and returned to smoking five cigarette packs a day, drinking too much, and gaining weight. **LBJ died** on January 22, 1973, at age 64 of **cardiac arrest** at his Stonewall ranch and was buried in the family cemetery at the Lyndon B. Johnson National Historical Park in Johnson City, Texas. President Carter posthumously awarded the **Presidential Medal of Freedom** in 1980 to LBJ. There is **no record of any last words**. Lady Bird died on July 11, 2007, at age 94 and was buried with her husband.

Most historians consider LBJ to be **one of the most effective presidents**.

Key Events

The **March for Civil Rights** in Birmingham, Alabama, ended in violence (1963); National Guard troops forced **Alabama Governor George Wallace** to permit minority students to enter the University of Alabama (1963); Civil Rights leader **Medgar Evers** was assassinated (1963); over 200,000 joined **Martin Luther King Jr.** on the Equal Rights March on Washington, prompting his "**I Have a Dream**" speech (1963); Alfred Sloan published *My Years with General Motors* (1963); Betty Friedman published *Feminine Mystic* (1963); labor leader A. Phillip Randolph organized a **March on Washington** of some 200,000-300,000 jobs for Black Americans (1963); **NFL Pro Football Hall of Fame** opened in Canton, Ohio initial inductees included Samuel Baugh, Bert Bell, Joe Carr, Earl (Dutch) Clark, Harold (Red) Grange, George Halas, Mel Hein, Wilbur (Pete) Henry, Robert (Cal) Hubbard, Don Hutson, Earl (Curly) Lambeau, Tim Mara, George Preston Marshall, John (Blood) McNally, Bronko Nagurski, Ernie Nevers, and Jim Thorpe (1963); the **DJIA** closed at 762.95 at year-end, up 17.0 percent (1963); Elaine Kaufman opened **Elaine's** restaurant in New York City (1964); **IBM** introduced the early mainframe computer, System 360 (1964); Ford introduced the **Mustang** (1964); the bodies of three civil rights workers were found in Mississippi, seven were convicted of the slayings (1964); Bobby Kennedy won a New York U.S. Senate seat (1964); the House of Representatives challenged tobacco executives' claims that **cigarettes were not harmful** to health (1964); Speaker of the House John McCormick introduced the **Christmas tree lighting** at the White House (1964); New York's Idlewild International Airport was renamed **John F. Kennedy International Airport** (1964); the **Gulf of Tonkin Resolution** allowed Vietnam escalation (1964); **Beatles** landed at JFK and performed at Carnegie Hall and the Ed Sullivan Show in New York City (1964); **World's Fair** opened in New York City, it closed two years later (1964); U.S. Olympic Hockey team defeated Russia for **Olympic gold medal** (1964); **Verrazano Narrows Bridge** opened in New York City connecting Brooklyn and Staten Island (1964); a major earthquake occurred in Anchorage, Alaska (1964); the **New York Mets baseball team** moved to newly opened **Shea Stadium** from the Polo Grounds (1964); **Pete Gogolak** signed by the Buffalo Bills was the first soccer-style kicker in the NFL (1964); the boxing heavyweight champion announced he would no longer be known by his birth name of Cassius Clay; as a member of the Nation of Islam he was now **Muhammad Ali** (1964); two White and one Black civil right workers were shot and killed by the **Ku Klux Klan** and police in Mississippi as they were registering Black people to vote (1964); LBJ awarded the **Presidential Medal of Freedom** posthumous to President John F. Kennedy and to his Holiness, Pope John XXIII (1964); the **DJIA** closed at 874.13 at year-end, up 14.6 percent (1964); Warren Buffet took control of **Berkshire Hathaway** (1965); **major power blackout** in Northeast (1965); DuPont developed **Kevlar** (1965); Ralph Nader's "**Unsafe at any Speed**" exposed the safety risks of automobiles (1965); **Studebaker auto plant closed**, after 63 years of production, thousand lost their jobs and became a focal point for the **1973 Employment Retirement Security Act (ERISA)** (1965); President Johnson convinced **Arthur Goldberg** to resign from the U.S. Supreme Court and become the U.S. Ambassador to the United Nations (1965); **Abe Fortas** became an Associate Justice of the U.S. Supreme Court (1965); after singing at a White House event, **Sarah Vaughn** cried, stating, "Twenty years ago I could not even get a hotel room in DC and tonight I sang for the President of the United States." (1965); Bobby Kennedy climbed to the highest unnamed peak in North America and planted President Kennedy's family flag, naming it **Mount Kennedy** (1965); Martin Luther King led a **Black Voting Rights** demand in a Selma to Montgomery, Alabama march (1965); power outage resulted in **major blackout** in most of northeastern US (1965); silver was eliminated from dimes and quarters and was reduced in half dollar coins to 40 percent (1965); precipitated by arrest of Black motorist, **Rodney King**, by white policeman, **Los Angeles Watts** riot marked wave of ghetto riots (1965); **Malcolm X** was assassinated by Nation of Islam members (1965); U.S. troops landed in **Vietnam** (1965); more than 50,000 packed Shea Stadium to hear the Beatles (1965); **Andy Warhol** created the famous "Campbell's Tomato Soup" painting (1965); Chicago Bear running back **Gail Sayers** scored a record 22 touchdowns during the season (1965); **NFL Films** began under Ed Sabol (1965); the **DJIA** closed at 969.26 at year-end, up 10.9 percent (1965); **Cesar Chavez** led strike against California wine growers (1966); **National Organization of Women** (NOW) was formed (1966); **Digital Equipment Corp** (DEC) went public (1966); **Howard Hughes** was forced to sell his majority share in Trans World Airlines for $1.5 billion and became the richest man in the U.S. (1966); over **300,000 anti-war** demonstrators marched to the United Nations (1966); Edward Brooke, Republican from Maine, was the **first elected Black senator** in 85 years (1966); **John Lindsay** became first Republican New York Mayor since Fiorello LaGuardia (1966); Cleveland running back **Jim Brown** retired at age 30 with 12,312 yards (1966); **American Football League and National Football League** agreed to merge (1966); **Charles Whitman** shot 46 people from an Austin, Texas town (1966); "**Black Power**" slogan came into being (1966); Baltimore Orioles outfielder **Frank Robinson** was named the American League Most Valuable Player; he received the same award in 1961 while playing with the Cincinnati Reds, making him the first to receive the most valuable player award in both the National and American league (1966); the **DJIA** closed at 785.69 at year-end, down 18.9 percent (1966); **George Doriot** started first venture capital company (1967); **Texas Instruments** introduced the handheld calculator (1967); **New York Lottery** was introduced to compete with illegal number games (1967); **Muriel Siebert** became the first woman with a seat on NYSE at a cost close to $500,000 (1967); **Shirley Chisholm** was the first Black woman elected to the House of Representatives for New York City (1967); hundreds of thousands anti-war protestors marched on Washington, D.C. (1967); race riots took place in Detroit and Newark that killed close to 100 and wounded over 1,000 (1967); creation of the **Corporation for Public Broadcasting and National Public Radio** (1967); the Green Bay Packers defeated the Kansas City Chiefs 35-10 in the **first Super Bowl** (1967); three astronauts died in **Apollo 1** fire during preflight testing (1967); boxer **Muhammad Ali** refused to serve in the U.S. Army and was sentenced to five years in prison and stripped of his boxing title. Three and a half years later the U.S. Supreme Court overturned his conviction (1967); the **DJIA** closed at 905.11 at year-end, up 15.2 percent (1967); the new **Madison Square Garden** opened replacing the one built in 1925 (1968); "**Bunkie**" Knudson left GM and became president of Ford at $600,000 salary (1968); **Intel** (Integrated Electronics) was founded (1968); **Fannie Mae** became a publicly traded company (1968); North Korea captured and then released the ship *USS Pueblo* and its 82 man crew (1968); **antiwar protestors** at the Democratic National Convention in **Chicago** required 29,000 police and National Guard soldiers to keep order (1968); the **Tet Offensive** in Vietnam began; during the cease fire, Defense Secretary McNamara resigned and Senator Robert F. Kennedy announced he would be campaigning for the Democratic nomination for president (1968); "**Hong Kong flu**" killed 100,000 people in U.S. (1968); **Apollo 7** – 3 astronauts were 22 days in space (1968); **Apollo 8**, in a five-day mission, orbited the moon 10 times (1968); Jackie Kennedy married Greek shipping millionaire **Aristotle Onassis** in October (1968); the **first Special Olympic** games were launched in Chicago

(1968); Houston University defeated UCLA basketball team 71-69, **ending 47-game winning streak** (1968); Oakland Raiders defeated New York Jets 43-32 but the last minute of the game was preempted by showing the **Heidi** movie, forever after named the **Heidi Game** (1968); Lt. **William Calley** led 200 soldiers who slaughtered hundreds of My Lai villagers in Vietnam (1968); **Martin Luther King Jr.** was assassinated in Memphis, Tennessee by James Earl Ray (1968); **Senator Robert Kennedy** was assassinated in Los Angeles by Sirhan Sirhan while campaigning for the presidential nomination (1968); looking at **Bobby Kennedy's** flag draped coffin, Ted Kennedy reflected that all three of his brothers have died while serving their country (1968); the **DJIA** closed at 943.76 at year-end, up 4.3 percent (1968); a number of conglomerates and their CEOs rose to prominence: ITT (**Harold Geneen**); Ling-Temco-Vaught (**James Ling**); Litton (**Roy Ash**) and Textron (**William Miller**) (1968); **Joseph Kennedy** died of a stroke; he had been a big time bootlegger and the force behind JFK's presidency; he was also FDR's first SEC Commissioner (1969); and former secretary to Bobby Kennedy, Mary Jo Kopechne died from a car accident while in Senator Edward Kennedy's car on Martha's Vineyard (1969).

RICHARD M. NIXON
(37ᵀᴴ PRESIDENT)

JANUARY 20, 1969 – AUGUST 9, 1974

Richard Milhous Nixon was born on January 9, 1913, to Frank and Hannah Nixon in Yorba Linda, California, and was raised in a poor, devout **Quaker** household. Frank Nixon was a farmer before working in the oil fields and at a combination convenience store and gas station. Richard was one of five sons, and with his brothers Arthur, Edward, Francis, and Harold, who all worked in their father's roadside **farm stand** and **gas station**. Richard did well in school, graduating first in his high school class, and was an accomplished piano and violin player. He was also quiet and serious. Upon graduation, he was accepted into Harvard, but there was no money to pay the tuition, so he attended nearby **Whittier College** and worked his way through, graduating second in a class of eighty-five in 1934. He then received a scholarship to **Duke University Law School**, graduating third in his class of twenty-five in 1937. While at Duke, he befriended a disabled student, carrying him up the steps to class every day. Nixon was admitted to the California bar in 1937 and opened a law practice.

At age 27, Richard married former model **Thelma "Patricia" Ryan**, age 28, in 1940. They had **two daughters**, Tricia and Julie. Tricia went on to marry Ed Cox, and Julie went on to marry David Eisenhower (Ike's grandson). Nixon practiced law before joining the **U.S. Navy** in August 1942, rising to the rank of **lieutenant commander** (earning two battle ribbons). He left the Navy at the end of the war and in the same year was elected to the **U.S. House of Representatives**. Nixon was a member of the **House Un-American Activities Committee** that investigated those who conspired against the government. With that responsibility, Nixon led the investigation into **Alger Hiss**, a State Department official. Writer **Whittaker Chambers** testified that when he was a communist in the 1930s, Hiss passed him secret information to pass on to Russia. Hiss denied the charges but was convicted of **perjury**. This gave Nixon national recognition, leading to a **Senate** seat in 1950 where he defeated Californian Helen Douglas, who labeled him "**Tricky Dick**." In 1952, Nixon was the running mate of Eisenhower. When newspapers revealed he had received funds from businessmen who expected **political favors**, Nixon gave an **impassioned speech** on television. He denied the allegations, stating he received only one gift, a little dog that Nixon's six-year-old daughter Julie, named **Checkers**. Ike had been thinking of dropping Nixon from the ticket, but after hearing the positive response to Nixon's speech, Ike kept him on the ticket.

In the **1952 presidential election**, Republicans **Dwight D. Eisenhower** and **Richard M. Nixon** received 33,378,964 popular votes to 27,314,993 for Democrats **Adlai E. Stevenson** and **John J. Sparkman**. Eisenhower-Nixon received 442 electoral votes to 89 for Stevenson-Sparkman. Eisenhower was elected president and Nixon was elected vice president.

Pat Nixon continued the work of Jackie Kennedy by continuing to add **antique furnishings** to the White House while Nixon was the vice president.

In 1953, Julius and Ethel Rosenberg died in a Sing Sing electric chair for selling America's bomb secrets to Russia. In 1954, Citibank and Chase Manhattan Bank were created by mergers and Ellis Island was boarded up. Senator Joseph McCarthy charged the government with concealing the names of communists in the federal government. For his allegations, McCarthy was censured by the Senate. President Eisenhower added "under God" to the Pledge of Allegiance. And Congress changed the tax filing date from March 15 to April 15.

The **1954 Internal Revenue Act** was a major rewrite of the 1939 Internal Revenue Act that removed out-of-date portions, and the 1956 Federal Highways Act created the inter-state highway system, with more than 40,000 miles of four-lane highways. In 1954, the U.S. Supreme Court in **Brown vs Board of Education Topeka** ordered the desegregation of public schools. In **Commissioner vs LoBue** (1956) the U.S. Supreme Court ruled that unless otherwise covered by the Internal Revenue Code, the difference between exercise price and fair market value will be ordinary income on the date of exercise of an employee stock option.

In 1955, the AFL and CIO merged with George Meany as president. Rosa Parks was arrested for not giving up her bus seat to a white man, and the Interstate Commerce Commission ordered the desegregation of public transportation.

In the **1956 presidential election**, Republicans **Dwight D. Eisenhower** and **Richard M. Nixon** received 35,581,003 popular votes to 25,738,765 for Democrats **Adlai E. Stevenson** and **C. Estes Kefauver**. And Eisenhower-Nixon received 457 electoral votes vs 73 for Stevenson-Kefauver. Eisenhower was re-elected president, and Nixon was re-elected vice president.

In 1957, teamster boss Jimmy Hoffa was investigated by the Senate McClellan Committee, but he had convenient memory loss. The American Institute of Accountants became the American Institute of Public Accountants. Arkansas Governor Faubus called in the National Guard to prevent schools from being integrated, and the Surgeon General stated there was a direct link between smoking cigarettes and cancer.

The **1958 Federal Welfare and Protection Disclosure Act** became law. It required information to be provided to plan participants upon request and that an annual report be filed with the government.

There were **four televised presidential debates** between Democrat John Kennedy and Republican Richard Nixon. The first debate was held on September 26, 1960, in Chicago, Illinois. The second debate was held on October 7, 1960, in Washington, D.C. The third debate was held on October 13, 1960, with Kennedy in New York and Nixon in Los Angeles. And the last debate was held on October 21, 1960, in New York City with both candidates present. There was no vice presidential debate between candidates Democrat Lyndon Johnson and Republican Henry Cabot Lodge Jr. in 1960.

The pundits stated that Nixon won the pre-election debates on the **radio** but lost the **TV** debates because Kennedy's lively personality and good looks contrasted with Nixon's dull, tired, uncomfortable appearance.

In the **1960 presidential election**, Republicans **Richard Nixon** and his running mate **Henry Cabot Lodge** lost to Democrats **John F. Kennedy** and **Lyndon Johnson**. The popular vote was very close, 34,227,096 to 34,107,647, but the electoral vote was not that close, 303 to 219.

Patricia was a big supporter of her husband and was very disappointed when he lost the 1960 election. She became very involved in volunteerism, spending time with the volunteers and the people they were helping. Her husband praised her, stating she was "at her very best when the going was the toughest." She was his rock, believing he was thinking about the country and not himself.

Disappointed by the loss to Kennedy, Nixon **returned to California** and decided to run for state **governor** as a Republican. But his charge that Governor Brown was "soft on crime and communism" was not enough, and Nixon **lost to Democrat Edmund Brown**. Unhappy with the result, in his post-election comments, Nixon told the attendees he was through with politics and "you won't have Nixon to kick around anymore." Then he moved to New York City, passed the bar, and **set up a law practice**. He reinstated his support for the Republican Party and joined the campaigns of various persons. Now considered a moderate candidate, candidate Nixon went to the **1968 Repub-**

lican National Convention in Miami. The year was marked with **numerous race riots** and featured the **assassinations** of both Martin Luther King and Robert Kennedy.

Based on support for Nixon's view of the need for **law and order**, Nixon received and **accepted the Republican nomination for president**, stating in reference to Lincoln's nomination, "The question then was **freedom** for slaves and the survival of the Nation. The question now is freedom for all mankind and the survival of civilization." Later, Nixon stated, "**We must move forward** – better jobs, better living conditions, better security for all our old people. We must move forward, as well in providing better schools, better hospitals, all the things that speak progress." Spiro Agnew received the nomination for vice president.

Believing he would appeal to Southern Democrats; Nixon had selected Maryland Governor **Spiro Agnew** as his running mate. **Nixon liked Agnew** for his views on domestic and racial violence. He also believed Agnew would be a good **hatchet man** and attack Democratic candidate **Hubert Humphrey**. But the polls showed Nixon did not need anyone on his ticket to get elected. As for the threat of assassination, Nixon said, "Who in his right mind would kill me and make Agnew President?"

J.R. Haldeman joined the Nixon campaign in 1968; he was the head of the LA office of the J. Walter Thompson advertising company. Nixon was one of the **most qualified** candidates to serve as president due to his experience in both the legislative and executive branches of government, having served in the House of Representatives, the Senate, and as vice president. But he **distrusted others** due to his humble upbringing and wanted to control all decision-making. Nixon's campaign slogan was,

"This time, vote like your whole world depended on it." In addition to the two assassinations, this was a time when there were significant demonstrations, protests, and riots. In response, Nixon portrayed himself as the **law-and-order candidate**. Paraphrasing JFK, Nixon stated, "Ask not what government will do for me, ask what can I do for myself."

There was **no televised presidential debate** between Democrat Hubert Humprey, Republican Richard Nixon, and Independent George Wallace in **1968**. And there was **no televised vice presidential debate** between Republican Spiro Agnew and Democrat Edmund Muskie.

In the **1968 presidential election,** Republicans **Richard Nixon** and **Spiro Agnew** received 31,710,470 popular votes to 31,209,677 for Democrats **Hubert Humphrey** and **Edmund Muskie**. Nixon and Agnew received 301 electoral votes to 191 for Humphrey and Muskie. Nixon was the first vice president who later became president but did not go directly from vice president to president. Independent Party candidates **George Wallace** and **Curtis LeMay** received 9,893,952 popular votes and 46 electoral votes.

Spiro Theodore Agnew (birth name Spiro Theodore Anagnostopoulos) was born on November 9, 1918, in an apartment above a flower shop in Baltimore, Maryland, the son of a Greek immigrant. He was an average student but well-liked and a good piano player. He went to the **University of Baltimore**, taking law courses after taking chemistry courses at **Johns Hopkins University**. He was **drafted into the U.S. Army** at the start of World War II, shortly after meeting his wife to-be. He received the **Bronze Star** for his role in **the Battle of the Bulge** in 1944. Agnew was in Germany when it surrendered in 1945. Shortly thereafter, he was discharged and returned to Baltimore to get his **law degree** in 1947. In 1951, Agnew was called back into the army due to the outbreak of the **Korean War**. Back in the U.S. in 1960, he **ran for circuit judge** and lost, but in 1962 he was elected Baltimore County Executive. In 1966, Agnew was elected **governor of Maryland** as a Republican and worked on ending school segregation and employment and housing issues.

Richard Nixon was the **twelfth vice president** to become president (John Adams, Thomas Jefferson, Martin Van Buren, John Tyler, Millard Fillmore, Andrew Johnson, Chester Arthur, Theodore Roosevelt, Calvin Coolidge, Harry Truman, and Lyndon B. Johnson preceded him). Richard Nixon was the **fourth president** to be elected to the **four federal offices**: representative, senator, vice president, and president (John Tyler, Andrew Johnson, and Lyndon Johnson preceded him).

Nixon was 56 years old on the **date of his inauguration**. Nixon's election after losing to JFK in 1960 was a reminder of Grover Cleveland's return to defeat Benjamin Harrison in 1892 after losing to him in 1888. The **Democrats still controlled Congress**, Senate 57-43 and House 243-192. In the 1970 midterms, the results were similar: Senate 54-44 and House 225-180.

In 1969, Nixon was the recipient of an increase in **presidential pay** to $200,000 per annum (up from 1949's $100,000), and the **vice president's salary** was increased to $62,500 per annum (up from 1964's $43,000). Nixon was asked by the press why he paid less than $1,000 in federal income taxes in both 1970 and 1971. He said he had donated his vice-presidential papers, and his tax accountants valued them at $500,000. Some interpreted this as an **I am not a crook statement**. Also in 1969, the **pay of Congress** was set at $42,500 per annum (up from 1965's $30,000).

The annual pay for the **associate justices** of the U.S. Supreme Court was set at $60,000 (up from 1964's $39,500), and the **chief justice's** pay was increased to $62,500 (up from 1964's $40,000). Congress made no other pay changes during Nixon's term of presidency.

The initial **cabinet** in Nixon's **first term** included **Vice President** Spiro Agnew, **Secretary of State** William Rogers, **Secretary of the Treasury** David Kennedy, **Attorney General** John Mitchell, **Postmaster General** Winton Blount, **Secretary of the Interior** Walter Hickel, **Secretary of Agriculture** Clifford Hardin, **Secretary of Labor** George Schultz, **Secretary of Commerce** Maurice Stans, **Secretary of Defense** George Melvin Laird, **Secretary of Health, Education and Welfare** Robert Finch, **Secretary of Housing and Urban Development** George Romney and **Secretary of Transportation** John Volpe. Nixon added the last position due to the increased needs of transportation in the country.

In **Tinker vs Des Moines** (1969), the U.S. Supreme Court ruled that to prohibit free speech under the First and Fourteenth Amendments, speech must substantially interfere with the rights of others.

During his first year in office, Nixon signed into law two acts that significantly changed income taxes: the **1969 Personal Income Tax Act** distinguished between personal service income and ordinary income for tax purposes, and the **1969 Tax Reform Act** scaled back the maximum tax rate to 50% of income over $200,000 (it had been 90%) and introduced tax preference income with a minimum tax of 10% on income.

On December 26, 1969, President Nixon released the **Nixon Doctrine**: Asian nations need to develop economically and self-sufficiently without relying on the United States.

In 1970, Nixon signed into law **five acts** of Congress: the **1970 Federal Pay Comparability Act**, which reported that federal employees were to be paid the same as private sector workers for comparable jobs; the **1970 Economic Stabilization Act**, which gave the president authority to establish price and wage control; the **1970 Occupational Safety and Health Act**, which mandated employee safety in the workplace; the **1970 Securities Investor Protection Act**, which focused on safeguarding investment accounts; and the **1970 Clean Air Act**, which limited emissions from both stationary (industrial) and mobile sources.

Nixon's White House had a number of bitter **power feuds**. The worst was probably between National Security Advisor **Henry Kissinger** and Secretary of State **William Rodgers**, a Harvard professor vs a cabinet secretary. Kissinger had the advantage that Nixon wanted foreign policy to run out of the White House, not Foggy Bottom. It was Nixon's chief of staff, H.R. Haldeman, who made sure that cabinet officers executed policy rather than deciding it.

The Nixon-Kissinger National Security Council and Charles Colson, Nixon's Assistant to the President for Domestic Affairs, are good examples of a controlling centralized management control system. They both **disempowered the cabinet system**. Kissinger's hard-driving manner resulted in rapid turnover of assistants and submissive behavior from others. Kissinger was not liked by Nixon's cabinet. Secretary of Defense McNamara once quipped, "How do you deal with a four-year old genius?"

Nixon considered the **CIA** a "group of Ivy League liberals" and instead relied on Henry **Kissinger** and Attorney General John **Mitchell**. Nixon wanted **facts separated from opinions** in his Daily Presidential Brief. Nixon's DPB was screened by Kissinger before being given to the president, who liked his DPB first thing in the morning.

In **New York Times Company vs United States** (1971), the U.S. Supreme Court ruled that government didn't meet its "heavy burden of showing justification" for preventing the publication of classified documents by the press sufficient to overcome their First-Amendment rights. The **26th Amendment to the U.S. Constitution** (see Appendix C) was ratified by Congress on July 1, 1971; it gave all citizens aged 18 and above the **right to vote**. It had been age 21 and above.

Nixon's response to inflation took place on August 15, 1971, when, using the authorization of the **1970 Economic Stabilization Act**, he imposed a 90-day freeze on prices and wages. This was followed by a maximum pay increase of 5.5% in pay and a .7% increase in benefits.

The **1972 Civil Rights Act** gave the Equal Employment Opportunity Commission (EEOC) enforcement authority over civil rights legislation. And the **1972 Clean Air Act** established the Environmental Protection Agency. In **United States vs United States District Court** (1972), the U.S. Supreme Court ruled that the government's warrantless domestic electronic surveillance of a domestic threat violated the Fourth Amendment.

When longtime friend **John Mitchell** left his position as Attorney General to head up Nixon's reelection campaign, **Richard Kleindienst** replaced him. During his 1972 election campaign, Nixon pledged he would visit all the states, and he did, logging some 65,500 miles, while appearing in 188 cities and giving innumerable speeches before an estimated 10 million people.

Two national holidays were added in 1972 by Congress: **President's Day**, the third Monday in February, replaced Lincoln's

Birthday on February 12th and Washington's Birthday on February 22nd, and **Memorial Day,** on the last Monday in May, standardized a day of recognition dating back to the Civil War.

On the **foreign front,** Nixon was the first American president to enter China, establishing diplomatic relations in 1972. He also signed **the Anti-Ballistic Missile (ABM) Treaty** and held **the Strategic Arms Limitation Talks** (SALT) with Russia.

At the **1972 National Republican Convention**, Nixon and Agnew were renominated for president and vice president. At the **1972 National Democratic Convention**, George McGovern was nominated for president and Sargent Shriver was nominated for vice president.

There **was no televised presidential debate** between Democrat George McGovern and Republican Richard Nixon in **1972**. And there **was no televised vice presidential debate** between Republican Spiro Agnew and Democrat Sargent Shriver.

In the **1972 presidential election**, Republicans **Richard Nixon** and **Spiro Agnew** received 47,168,710 popular votes vs 29,173,222 popular votes for Democrats **George McGovern** and **Sargent Shriver**. Nixon and Agnew received 520 electoral votes vs 17 for McGovern and Shriver. Nixon won every state except Massachusetts. Senator **Thomas Eagleton** had been selected as McGovern's running mate, but 18 days later, he admitted to having received electric shock therapy for depression. Party pressure pushed him off the ticket, and he was replaced by Sargent Shriver, a former ambassador to France and a member of the extended JFK family. The Democrats still controlled Congress: Senate 56-42 and House 242-192. In his January 20, **1973, inaugural address,** Nixon stated, "At every turn we have been beset by those who find everything wrong with America and little that is right." When Nixon took office in 1973, he had a **67 percent approval rating**.

Shortly after being elected, Nixon had a **one-lane bowling alley** put in under the driveway of the White House. He loved baseball; Hank Aaron once stated that "Nixon knew more about baseball than some of the people in the game." After taking office, Nixon had the **uniformed Secret Service** detail wear tunics and hats. That didn't last long, and the uniforms were given to a school's marching band.

Nixon vowed, "**I will not be the first American president to lose a war.**" He was referring to **Vietnam**; not surprisingly he stepped up American involvement. This led to anti-war protests and a response from **Senator Kennedy**: "I feel it is both senseless and irresponsible to continue to send our young men to their deaths to capture hills and positions that have no relation to ending this conflict." Nixon stated, "No event in American history is more misunderstood than the Vietnam war." Nonetheless, he also stated, "Always give your best, never get discouraged," and "History depends on who writes it." When Nixon was elected, there were half a million American troops in Vietnam; by mid-1973 there were none.

The **initial cabinet** in Nixon's **second** term included **Vice President** Spiro Agnew (followed by Gerald Ford) **Secretary of State** Henry Kissinger, **Secretary of the Treasury** George Schultz, **Attorney General** Elliot Richardson, **Postmaster General** Winton Blount, **Secretary of the Interior** Walter Hickel, **Secretary of Agriculture** Rogers Morton, **Secretary of Labor** Peter Brennan, **Secretary of Commerce** Frederick Dent, **Secretary of Defense** James Schlesinger, **Secretary of Health, Education** and **Welfare** Caspar Weinberger, **Secretary of Housing and Urban Development** James Lynn, and **Secretary of Transportation** Charles Brinegar.

It has been said that Nixon sought to make the **executive branch** the overwhelming dominant force in government, with unconstitutional agencies given a greater role in healthcare and social schemes, mostly by way of executive orders. Nixon was not the first to take this action, nor was he the last. Nothing in the U.S. Constitution gives the president the authority to issue **executive orders** with the force of law. Yet in **1789**, President Washington was the first to do so, authorizing Treasury Secretary Hamilton to borrow and spend funds without Congressional approval.

Leaks of information were used by both parties to strengthen their political positions. Nixon created the **Plumbers Unit** to find the leakers and stop the leaks. Wanting information on the Democratic plans for the upcoming election, Nixon told Attorney General Mitchell to send the plumbers over to the **Watergate** building complex, where the Democratic National Headquarters was based, to **break in** and get the information. This happened on **June 17, 1972**, and the plumbers were caught. That year, prior to the event, a Gallup poll reported a **53.7% approval rating** for Nixon.

In **Roe vs Wade** on January 22, 1973, the U.S. Supreme Court ruled that women had the right to an abortion. Also in January 1973, a peace treaty was signed with **Vietnam** and the military draft was ended. In February 1973, the Senate established a special subcommittee, headed by special prosecutor **Archibald Cox**, to investigate the Watergate break-in and learn what Nixon knew and when he knew it. Nixon denied prior knowledge of the break-in at Watergate. Then presidential aide **Alex-**

ander **Butterfield** revealed a taping system was in place at the White House. Nixon said the tapes were under **executive privilege**. But when asked by Nixon to intervene in the Watergate break-in, Attorney General **Richard Kleindienst** resigned and was replaced by **Elliott Richardson**. In June 1973, White House Counsel **John Dean** testified before the Senate Watergate Committee that Nixon knew about the Watergate break-in. **Archibald Cox** ordered Nixon to turn over the White House tapes. Nixon refused. When he ordered Eliott Richardson's second-in-command, **William Ruckelshaus**, to fire Cox, Richardson refused and resigned. Acting on Nixon's orders, Acting Attorney General **Robert Bork** fired Cox. Then Nixon appointed **Leon Jaworski** to replace Cox. These October 20, 1973 actions were labeled the **Saturday Night Massacre**. *Washington Post* reporters Carl **Bernstein** and Robert **Woodward** covered Watergate in their book *All the President's Men*.

In the summer of 1973, Nixon signed into law **two acts**: the **1973 Health Maintenance Organization Act**, requiring employers to offer qualified HMOs to employees, and the **1973 War Powers Act**, requiring Congressional approval of the use of armed forces in combat for more than 60 days.

In early October 1973, on the Jewish holiday **Yom Kippur**, Egyptian and Syrian forces attacked Israel. With a request for help from Israel's prime minister, Golda Meir, America put **Operation Nickel** into effect, sending over **500 air supply missions** with military supplies to Israel. The war lasted over three weeks, with thousands killed on both sides before **Israel won**. **Saudi Arabia** was not happy with America's intervention in the Middle East war, and they **shut down exports of oil to America**. The result was a big increase in the price of gasoline and long lines at gas stations. The embargo was lifted in March 1974.

On October 10, 1973, Spiro **Agnew resigned**, pleading "no contest" to tax evasion while governor of Maryland. Agnew was **the first vice president to resign because of criminal charges**. Agnew had to pay a $10,000 fine and serve three years on probation. Nixon lost no time in selecting a **replacement** in accordance with the **25th Amendment to the U.S. Constitution** (see Appendix C), which states, "The President shall nominate a Vice President who shall take office upon confirmation by a majority vote of both houses." Nixon decided he wanted Congressman **Gerald Ford**, a man he had worked with and liked. Nixon nominated Ford and Ford was approved by a majority vote in Congress on December 6, 1973. He said he was "a Ford, not a Lincoln."

At birth **Gerald Ford** was named **Leslie Lynch King**. But his mother got a divorce later that year and in 1919 married Gerald Rudolph Ford. Leslie was given his **new father's name**. Ford graduated from the University of Michigan, where he played football, in 1935. Ford went on to graduate from **Yale University Law School** in 1941. He then practiced law in Grand Rapids, Michigan. During the war, Ford served in the **U.S. Navy**. Returning home in 1943, he resumed his law practice. At age 35, he **married Elizabeth "Betty" Bloomer Warren**, age 30, in 1948 after she divorced William Warren. The Fords had four children together: Michael, John, Steven, and Susan. Betty was candid about her personal struggles, including **breast cancer**. A lot of her challenges bonded her with many women having similar issues. She developed **drug and alcohol dependencies** because of arthritis. It was more of a problem before and after, not during, the White House period. After leaving the White House, Betty entered a treatment facility, and in 1982 she founded the **Betty Ford Clinic** for those chemically dependent. In 1949, Ford was elected to the **U.S. House of Representatives**. From 1965 until his appointment as vice president on December 6, 1973, Ford served as **Minority Leader** of the House. During that period, he moved for the impeachment of Supreme Court Justice William Douglas for his ties to a private foundation. When asked for the definition of an **impeachable offense**, Ford replied, "An impeachable offense is whatever the House of Representatives considers it to be at a given moment in history."

On January 30, 1974, **Nixon addressed the nation** on television. He said, "I believe the time has come to end that investigation and other investigations of this matter. One year of Watergate is enough." At the end of February 1974, a **federal grand jury** that had been hearing evidence for almost a year handed down **indictments** of Chuck Colson, John Ehrlichman, H.R. Haldeman, John Mitchell, and others. Nixon was named "an unindicted co-conspirator." Top aides John Ehrlichman, H.R. Haldeman, Charles Colson, and John Mitchell resigned for their part in the Watergate break-in, and John Dean was fired by Nixon. **Impeachment** was on the minds of many, especially since it was believed such actions were exempt from claims of executive privilege. Nixon's approval rating had **dropped to a low of 24 percent** in a Gallup poll in July 1974.

In May 1974, the **House of Representatives** prepared articles of **impeachment** (for obstruction of justice) and sent them to the Senate for conviction.

In **United States vs Nixon**, on July 24, 1974, the U.S. Supreme Court ordered Nixon to turn over the **64 audio tapes** he had made of White House conversations but left open the question of **presidential immunity**. When the White House tapes were released, it was noted there was a gap of almost 20 minutes at a critical point. President Nixon's secretary, Rose Mary Woods, said she did it accidentally. Elsewhere, the tapes revealed that Nixon knew his associates were involved in the Watergate break-ins. Hearing this, Nixon stated, "It is not illegal if the president does it." But he had violated his oath to defend the Constitution and was **impeachable** under the requirement of "high crimes and misdemeanors." Nixon hired attorney **James St Clair** to represent him in the Watergate matter. Nixon's critics included former Presidents Carter and Truman. Carter said, "I believe he disgraced the presidency," and Truman said, "Richard Nixon is a no-good lying bastard."

In 1974, there were **three new laws** enacted: the **1974 Gold Act**, which reversed a 1933 executive order banning the private holding of gold; the **1974 Vietnam Veterans Reemployment Rights Act**, which provided Vietnam war vets with discrimination protection; and the **1974 Employee Retirement Income Security Act (ERISA)**, which established minimum pension standards for participation, vesting accruals funding, and disclosure, and established individual retirement (IRA) annuity accounts for those not covered by an employee pension plan.

Faced with being the first president to be impeached and removed from office, **Nixon decided to resign**. On August 8, 1974, in a prime-time TV address, Nixon said, "By taking this action, I hope that I will have hastened the start of that process of healing which is so desperately needed in America." On August 9, 1974, Nixon became the **first president to resign from office**. Before leaving to board the helicopter, Nixon said, "I have never been a quitter, but as president, I must put the interests of America first." Boarding his helicopter, he raised his arms in his famous victory salute. Nixon, Pat, daughter Tricia, and son-in-law Edward Cox took the copter to Andrews Air Force Base, where a large crowd had gathered, some cheered, while others yelled, "Jail to the Chief." Nixon and the others boarded a plane, now no longer Air Force One, and **flew** to La Casa Pacifica, San Clemente, California.

Also on August 9, 1974, after Nixon's resignation, **Gerald R. Ford** took office as the thirty-eighth president. Upon being sworn in, he stated, "Our long national nightmare is over." Ford became the ninth vice president to become president when Nixon resigned while president. The others who became president when the president left office were Tyler, Fillmore, Johnson, Arthur, Coolidge, Roosevelt, Truman, and Johnson. Ford appointed **Nelson Rockefeller** vice president, who was then approved by Congress. Not wanting the country to go through any more of Nixon's problems, President Ford granted ex-President Richard Nixon "a full and free absolute pardon" on September 8, 1974. Not everyone was happy with this decision.

Not long after his resignation, **Nixon's phlebitis** flared up, threatening his life, but he recovered. He was then faced with hundreds of thousands of dollars in charges for **hospital and legal expenses**, in addition to taxes. Later, Nixon stated, "The way I tried to deal with Watergate was the wrong way. It is a burden I shall bear for every day of the life that is left to me." **Deep in debt**, Nixon agreed to four interviews with **David Frost** for $600,000 and a $2.5 million **royalty advance** for his memoirs. In a 1977 David Frost interview, Nixon stated, "I brought myself down." He knew **he had destroyed his career** with a pointless, stupid act. Richard and Pat **sold their California home** for $1,000,000 and **moved** to a townhouse in **New York City**. Nixon took and passed the **New York bar**.

Some twenty years after resigning the presidency, Nixon decided to make the most of his time with Pat and to **focus on world** events. He **wrote eight books** and traveled to China and Moscow, meeting with their leaders. In 1979, President Carter **invited Nixon to a state dinner** at the White House, where he talked foreign policy with **Carter advisors**. Nixon later said Carter could not focus on strategy because he spent too much time on small details. Later still, Nixon was an advisor to President Reagan. Nixon told Pat, "I just get up every morning to confound my enemies," and "the general rule should be reward your friends and ignore your enemies."

Pat Nixon had a stroke and died at age 81 in New York City on June 22, 1993. **Richard Nixon also died of a stroke** in New York City on April 22, 1994. They were both **buried at the Nixon Library Grounds**, Yorba Linda, California. One of Nixon's last quotes was, "Remember Lot's wife, don't look back." His tombstone simply says, "Richard Nixon 1913-1994. The greatest honor history can bestow is that of peacemaker."

At the time of Nixon's death, **President Clinton** stated, "He suffered defeat that would have ended most political careers, yet he won stunning victories that many of the world's most popular leaders have failed to attain." President Clinton's words are on the Nixon Library wall: "May the day of judging President Nixon on anything less than his entire life and career come to a close."

Most historians rate Nixon's performance as **below average**, significantly impacted by the Watergate issue. The combination of a high inflation rate and a declining stock market was a reversal of the period 1952 through 1960.

RICHARD M. NIXON (37TH PRESIDENT)

Key Events

At the cost of $24 billion, **Apollo 11** landed on the moon; astronauts **Neil Armstrong** and **Buzz Aldrin** were the first to walk on the moon while **Michael Collins** remained in orbit (1969); the official use of the **$1,000 bill** and those of higher denominations was ended due to the fear of counterfeiting and the introduction of **wire transfers** (1969); the **Concorde** (first supersonic transport) flew between Paris and New York (1969); **Frank Sinatra** was denied credit at Caesar's Palace in Las Vegas because of never paying his debts, while always collecting his winnings (1969); *Sesame Street* debuted (1969); Mafia boss **Vito Genovese** died of a heart attack at age 72 (1969); union organizer **Walter Reuther** died in a plane crash (1969); the price of **oil** was $2 a barrel (1969); a crowd of 400,000 gathered in rural Bethal, New York, for the **Woodstock Festival** – three days of music, drugs and sex (1969); the **AFL and NFL** merger took effect, forming a new **National Football League** (1969); for the first time in history, **one city (New York) had three** major champions: baseball (Mets), basketball (Knicks), and football (Jets) (1969); St. Louis Cardinals outfielder **Curt Flood** challenged **baseball's reserve clause** in his contract (1969); the father of JFK, **Joe Kennedy Sr.** died, leaving a $500 million estate (1969); the **DJIA** closed at 800.36 at year-end, down 15.2 percent (1969); Corning developed **optical fibers** (1970); **Penn-Central Railroad** went bankrupt (1970); **One World Trade Center** opened in New York City (1970); the **securitization** of U.S. mortgages began (1970); **five mafia families ruled** New York City: Bonanno, Columbo, Gambino, Genovese, and Lucchese (1970); reportedly, America had over 26,000 missiles, while Russia had over 11,000 (1970); 400,000 workers went on strike at **General Motors** for 67 days (1970); the NFL approved player names on their jerseys

(1970); **Monday Night Football** started with **Howard Cosell, Keith Jackson,** and **Don Meredith** (1970); nationwide protests increased with the escalation of **war in Vietnam** (1970); **Betty Friedan** organized an abortion rights march (1970); the **DJIA** closed at 838.92 at year-end, up 4.8 percent (1970); the **second World Trade Center** opened in New York City (1971); **Raymond Damadian** introduced the **MRI** scanner (1971); **Federal Express** began service (1971); **Starbucks** began operation in Seattle (1971); **Intel** produced the first microprocessor chip and went public (1971); Wall Street's Over-the-Counter Market became **NASDAQ** (National Association of Securities Dealers Automated Quotation System) (1971); New York City was given the name "**Big Apple**" by the New York Convention and Visitors Bureau (1971); stock broker **Merrill Lynch** went public (1971); IBM introduced the **floppy disc** (1971); **Lockheed Aircraft** received $250 million in federally backed loans to save jobs (1971); the **Advanced Research Projects Agency Network** sent the **first email** (1971); **Nixon commuted the prison sentence of teamster boss Jimmy Hoffa** (1971); the *New York Times* published the "**Pentagon Papers**," detailing the Vietnam War and the government's duplicity as outlined by analyst **Daniel Ellsberg** (1971); the Eisenhower **silver dollar** was introduced (1971); the American **Viking spacecraft** landed on Mars for photos (1971); **Apollo 13** went to the moon and back (1971); **Apollo 14** went to the moon and back (1971); **Apollo 15** was the first to use the "moon buggy" (1971); **Apollo 16** landed on the moon and returned (1971); **Charles Manson** and three others were found guilty of first degree murder of **actress Sharon Tate** and six others (1971); Gary Kildall, the "**Edison of Computers**," signed with **Bill Gates** (not IBM) to develop personal computer technology (1971); **Apple Computer** founders **Steve Jobs** and

Steve Wozniak were introduced to one another (1971); Intel created the **micro-processing chip** (1971); **heavyweight boxer Joe Frazier** defeated previously undefeated **Muhammad Ali** in the **Fight of the Century** (1971); a **major earthquake** rocked Southern California (1971); the television program *All in the Family* starring Carroll O'Connor as Archie Bunker, premiered (1971); a man **hijacked a commercial** airline for $200,000 and then parachuted from the plane – the man and money were never found (1971); the **Washington Senators** baseball team left DC and became the **Texas Rangers** (1971); **Walt Disney World** opened in Florida (1971); **Evel Knievel** jumped 13 cars with his motorcycle (1971); the **DJIA** closed at 890.20 at year-end, up 6.1 percent (1971); **Robert Irsay** bought the Los Angeles Rams and traded them to **Carroll Rosenbloom** for the Baltimore Colts (1972); **Robert Vesco** paid close to **$400 million to settle SEC** charges of defrauding the mutual company **Investors Overseas Services** (1972); **Apollo 17** was the last of 75 lunar missions (1972); the teamsters endorsed Nixon for president (1972); FBI agent Mark Felt was the "**Deep Throat**" in the Watergate Democratic Headquarters break-in (1972); Nixon became the **first president** to visit China and Russia (1972); Nixon's visit to China led to full diplomatic relations in 1978 (1972); Alabama Governor **George Wallace** was shot and wounded by **Arthur Bremer** in a shopping center (1972); the **Confederate Memorial** opened in Stone Mountain, Georgia (1972); the **Miami Dolphins** were the first NFL football team to go **undefeated** (1972); swimmer **Mark Spitz** won seven gold medals at the Olympics (1972); gangster "**Crazy Joey**" **Gallo** was killed in New York City's Umberto Clam House restaurant (1972); Academy Awards winning movie *The Godfather* gave new meaning to the word **family** (1972); the **DJIA** closed at 1,020.02 at year-end, up 14.6 percent (1972); **bar codes** for identifying products were introduced (1973); the **Chicago Board Options Exchange** (CBOE) opened (1973); CBS **sold the New York Yankees to George Steinbrenner** for $10 million (1973); a Native American uprising took place at **Wounded Knee**, South Dakota (1973); the horse Secretariat was a **Triple Crown** winner (1973); in the "Battle of the Sexes," **Billie Jean King** defeated **Bobby Riggs** in tennis (1973); oil prices skyrocketed to $12 a barrel due to an oil embargo following U.S. aid to Israel (1973); the **DJIA** closed at 850.85 at year-end, down 16.6 percent (1973); the **cellular** telephone came into being (1974); the **Sears Tower** opened in Chicago (1974); safety risks were identified at the **Kerr-McGee nuclear plant** (1974); and **conglomerate companies** fell into disfavor with investors, who chose to build their own conglomerates by buying individual stocks (1974).

Gerald R. Ford
(38th President)

August 9, 1974 – January 20, 1977

Gerald Rudolph Ford was born on July 14, 1913, to Leslie Lynch King, Sr. and Dorothy Gardner King in Omaha, Nebraska. He had three younger half-brothers: James, Richard, and Thomas. At birth, Ford was named **Leslie Lynch King**. But his mother got divorced later that year and in 1919 married Gerald Rudolph Ford. Leslie was given his new father's names, becoming **Gerald Rudolph Ford Jr**. He enjoyed sports and was a boy scout in 1924 and the first **Eagle Scout** to become president. Ford graduated from the **University of Michigan**, where he was the center and linebacker of the 1932 and 1933 undefeated national championship **football teams**. In 1974, the university retired Ford's football uniform, number 24. After graduation in 1935, Ford went to **Yale University Law School**. At Yale, he coached boxing and football. He graduated in 1941 and was offered tryouts with the Green Bay Packers and the Pittsburgh Steelers, but he chose **male modeling** and was on the cover of *Cosmopolitan* magazine. Gerald Ford was the **first president** to graduate from Yale Law School.

At the beginning of **World War II**, Ford enlisted in the **U.S. Navy**. He became an officer and received a number of awards and medals while serving in the Pacific. At the end of the war, he returned home and practiced law in Grand Rapids, Michigan, after being admitted to the Michigan bar. Shortly after, he met **Elizabeth "Betty" Bloomer Warren**, and they were married on October 15, 1948. They had **four children**: Michael, John, Steven, and Susan. Betty was later candid about her struggles with **breast cancer**. Her health problem bonded her with other women. Supporting the **1973 Roe vs Wade** decision, Betty said it was time to bring abortion out of the backwoods and put it in hospitals where it belonged. She also said, "Being ladylike does not require silence." She developed **drug and alcohol dependencies** because of arthritis. It was more of a problem before and after, not during her stay in the White House. After leaving the White House, she entered a treatment facility, and in 1982 she founded the **Betty Ford Clinic** for those chemically dependent. She also was known for her work fighting breast cancer.

In 1949, Ford was elected to the **U.S. House of Representatives** and went on to be re-elected 12 times. Ford was known for leading bipartisan compromises with Democratic leaders. In Congress, Ford was known as a **consensus builder**. As House **Minority Leader**, Ford challenged President Johnson's Great Society programs. He also served on the **Warren Commission** that investigated the assassination of President Kennedy.

Additionally, Ford moved for the **impeachment of Supreme Court Justice William Douglas** for his ties to a private foundation. When asked for the definition of an impeachable offense, Ford replied, "An **impeachable offense** is whatever the House of Representatives considers it to be at a given moment in history." Ford once noted, "Truth is the glue that holds government together; compromise is the oil that makes government run." Ford was selected by President Nixon to replace the departed Spiro Agnew, who resigned due to criminal activities.

President Nixon announced his **resignation** at noon on August 8, 1974, in accordance with the **25th Amendment to the U.S. Constitution** (see Appendix C), which stated, "In the case of the removal of the President from office or of his death or resignation, the Vice President shall become President." Ford once said, "The constitution is the bedrock of all our freedoms." With Nixon's resignation, Ford became president at age 61. Ford was the **first person** to have served as both the **vice president and the president without having been elected to either position**; some refer to him as the **accidental president.** Gerald Ford was the twelfth vice president to become president (John Adams, Thomas Jefferson, Martin Van Buren, John Tyler, Millard Fillmore, Andrew Johnson, Chester Arthur, Theodore Roosevelt, Calvin Coolidge, Harry Truman, and Richard Nixon preceded him). Gerald Ford was the ninth vice president (Tyler, Fillmore, Johnson, Arthur, Roosevelt, Coolidge, Truman, and Johnson preceded him) to assume the presidency with the departure of his president.

Upon taking the **oath of office** on August 9, 1974, Ford stated, "I assume the Presidency under extraordinary circumstances. This is an hour of history that troubles our minds and hurts our hearts. My fellow Americans, our long national nightmare is over. I am acutely aware that you have not elected me as your president by your ballots. So, I ask that you confirm me as your president with your prayers. I have not sought this enormous responsibility, but I will not shrink from it."

On September 8, 1974, Ford issued a **pardon to Nixon** for any federal crimes he may have committed as president. Ford stated it was time to close the wound. With the pardon, Ford's popularity fell because many believed that Nixon should have been impeached, not pardoned.

Rumors circulated that Nixon had agreed to resign if Ford would pardon him. At his inauguration, Ford addressed this rumor when he stated, "I am indebted to no man and only one woman, my wife." He also told the House Judiciary Committee, "There was no deal, period, under no circumstances."

The Nixon-to-Ford transition was not easy. One day, Ford was vice president and the next day he was president. Although Ford initially made no changes in his supporting staff, within three months Nixon's people were gone. One who remained was the former four-star general and Nixon's chief of staff, Alexander Haig. Haig eventually left, replaced by Donald Rumsfeld. Haig and Ford's longtime friend, journalist Robert Hartmann, hated each other. Haig called Hartmann "the fat Kraut" and an "SOB," which Hartmann said meant "Sweet Old Bob."

The initial **cabinet** during Ford's period of appointed office included **Vice President** Nelson Rockefeller, **Secretary of State** Henry Kissinger, **Secretary of the Treasury** William Simon, **Attorney General** William Saxbe, **Secretary of the Interior** Rogers Morton, **Secretary of Agriculture** Earl Butz, **Secretary of Labor** Paul Brennan, **Secretary of Commerce** Frederick Dent, **Secretary of Defense** James Schlesinger, **Secretary of Health, Education and Welfare** Caspar Weinberger, **Secretary of Housing and Urban Development** James Flynn and **Secretary of Transportation** Claude Brinegar.

Shortly after assuming the presidency, Ford appointed Nelson Rockefeller as his vice president. **Nelson Aldrich Rockefeller** was born on July 8, 1908, in Bar Harbor, Maine, into a family made wealthy by their inheritance from his grandfather, **John D. Rockefeller Sr.**, co-founder of Standard Oil. Nelson majored in economics at Dartmouth University. In 1930, he married Philadelphia socialite Mary Todhunter Clark. In 1938, he became president of the New York Rockefeller Center. In 1944, Nelson was active in the formation of the United Nations and got his grandfather **to donate the land for the United Nations building**. In 1953, Nelson was the first **undersecretary** of the new Department of Health, Education and Welfare. Rockefeller was elected **governor of New York** in 1958 and was re-elected in 1962, 1966, and 1970. But in 1961, Nelson divorced his wife Mary and married Margaret "Happy" Murphy, in 1963. The remarriage cost Nelson three failed attempts at the presidency. On August 29, 1974, Ford appointed Nelson **vice president** the position Ford had just vacated. Nelson's swearing-in was the first television broadcast from the Senate Chambers. When asked about his duties as vice president, Rockefeller quipped, "I go to earthquakes." When Ford ran for election in 1976, he replaced Nelson with **Bob Dole** as his vice president. In 1977, Ford gave Nelson the **Presidential Medal of Freedom**. After leaving office, Nelson returned to New York and died on January 26, 1979.

Ford had to contend with two pieces of recent legislation that limited his authority: the **1972 War Powers Act**, which required the president to get congressional approval before sending troops into combat, and the **1974 Reform Act**, which limited presidential impact on federal spending.

When Queen Elizabeth visited President Ford during a Fourth of July celebration, she noted that she was a direct descendant of George III, the last sovereign to have ruled America. She noted that the founding fathers taught England a valuable lesson: "We lost the American colonies because we lacked the statesmanship to know the right time, and the manner of yielding. And what is important to keep." Ford's response: "The United States has never forgotten its British heritage."

Several key legislative actions impacted compensation and benefits in 1974. They were: the **1974 Employee Retirement Income Security Act (ERISA)**, which dramatically overhauled company pension plan requirements, establishing minimum standards for participation, vesting, accruals, funding, and disclosure requirements, as well as creating IRAs (this coming as a response to the failure of the Studebaker pension plan in the early 1960s) and introducing the Pension Benefit Guaranty Corporation (PBGC), a federally controlled agency to assume responsibility for paying benefits of terminated defined-benefit pension plans from monies collected from employers; the **1974 Vietnam Era Veterans Reemployment Act**, which provided vets with discrimination protection; the **1974 Gold Act**, which reversed a 1933 executive order banning private holding of gold; and the **1974 Commodity Futures Trading Commission Act**, which established the Commodity Futures Trading Commission.

For **breakfast**, Ford enjoyed oatmeal and coffee; for **lunch**, cottage cheese, A-1 sauce, an onion, a quarter of a tomato, and a scoop of ice cream; for **dinner**, cooked vegetables, potatoes, prime ribs, spareribs with sauerkraut, stuffed cabbage, salad, or tuna fish casserole; and for dessert, pecan ice cream or chocolate angel food cake. Thanksgiving usually included a giant turkey, a roast pig, avocados, spinach, potatoes, and rice, along with ice cream and apple and mince pies. As for alcohol, Ford stated, "The three-martini lunch is the linchpin of business."

Ford enjoyed sports and once said, "I enjoy watching the Detroit Tigers on the radio." Really? How can you do that?

Ford took a controversial action by offering clemency to Vietnam draft dodgers. Then, in an attempt to warm up the **Cold War**, Ford met with Russian Party Head Leonid Brezhnev in Vladivostok in 1974, with little effect.

A year later, the **1975 Security Act Amendments** established electronic links with eight markets; and the **1975 Tax Reduction Act** introduced the tax favored employee stock ownership plan. Also in 1975, Congress increased the pay of legislators to $44,600 per annum (up from 1969's $42,500), the pay of the associate justices of the U.S. Supreme Court to $63,000 per annum (up from 1969's $60,000), the pay of the chief justice to $65,600 per annum (up from 1960's $62,500), and the annual pay of the cabinet secretaries to $63,000 per annum (up from 1964's $35,000).

Secret Service protection was increased when Ford was **almost assassinated twice** in September 1975, once by **Lynette "Squeaky" Fromme**, a Charles Manson follower, and two weeks later by radical **Sara Jane Moore**. Both women were sentenced to life in prison. Ford began wearing a bulletproof vest soon after.

Plagued by inflation, Ford tried to keep rising inflation under control, and he introduced the **Whip Inflation Now** (WIN) program. But since it called on Americans to tighten their belts and scrimp on purchases, it failed. He also vetoed some three-dozen government spending bills. But that did not stop him from authorizing millions of dollars to stop an uprising in Angola. In 1975 with New York City on the verge of bankruptcy, Ford authorized a $2.3 billion short-term loan for the city.

In **Taylor vs Louisiana** (1975), the U.S. Supreme Court ruled that the "selection of a petit jury from a representative cross section of the community is an essential component" of a criminal defendant's Sixth Amendment right to an impartial jury trial. And in **Goss vs Lopez** (1975), the U.S. Supreme Court ruled that a state statute that permits public schools to suspend students for misconduct for up to 10 days without a hearing violates their Due Process rights under the Fourteenth Amendment.

In late November 1975, the Ford administration experienced the **Halloween Massacre**. James Schlesinger was replaced by Donald Rumsfeld as secretary of defense, Richard Cheney replaced Rumsfeld as chief of staff, and George H.W. Bush replaced William Colby as director of the CIA. Ford later admitted it was too much too soon: "It was the biggest **political mistake** of my life." It was not an easy presidency for Ford, having to deal with an assassination attempt, an economic recession, an energy crisis, a Nixon pardon, and the Cold War.

Deciding he wanted to be elected for a full term as president, Ford got the Republican nomination, but only after being challenged by Ronald Reagan. **Ford won the nomination** after agreeing to take Nelson Rockefeller off the ticket and replacing him with **Kansas Senator Bob Dole**. The Democrats nominated Georgia Governor **Jimmy Carter**, who pledged, "I will never lie to you."

In April 1976, **Operation Freedom Wind** resulted in over 600 helicopter flights taking Americans out of Saigon as communist troops took over Vietnam. Also in 1976, Congress increased the pay of the associate justices of the U.S. Supreme Court to $65,000 per annum (up from 1975's $63,000) and of the chief justice to $68,800 per annum (up from 1975's $65,600). Congress made no other pay changes during Ford's term of presidency.

In 1976, the **July 4th Bicentennial** took place; and the **1976 Tax Reform Act** eliminated statutory stock options by 1981, introduced tax-favored legal service plans, and increased the alternative minimum tax on tax preference income to 15 percent. Also in 1976, the U.S. Supreme Court ruled in **Gregg vs State of Georgia** that the death penalty is constitutional.

There were **three televised presidential debates** between Republican President Gerald Ford and Democrat Jimmy Carter. They were held on September 23, 1976, in Philadelphia, Pennsylvania, on October 6, 1976, in San Francisco, California, and on October 22, 1976, in Williamsburg, Virginia. There was **one televised vice presidential** debate between Republican vice-presidential candidate Bob Dole and Democrat Walter Mondale on October 15, 1976, in Houston, Texas.

In the **1976 presidential election**, Republicans **Gerald Ford** and **Robert Dole** received 39,422,671 popular votes to 40,977,147 for Democrats **Jimmy Carter** and **Walter Mondale**. And Ford and Dole received 240 electoral votes to 297 for Carter and Mondale. Carter was elected president and Mondale was elected vice president.

Robert "Bob" Dole was born on July 22, 1923, in Russell, Kansas, where his father had a roadside stand selling eggs and vegetables. His mother was a traveling saleswoman who sold sewing machines and vacuum cleaners. Bob had one brother and two sisters. His parents instilled in Bob the value of hard work and strong religious beliefs. He was taught to trust in God, not government, and not to confuse the two. He was a **boy scout** and a soda jerk. After high school he went to the **University of Kansas**, but the war interrupted his education. He enlisted in 1942 and became a combat military officer. He was **severely wounded** and almost died. He was left with a paralyzed right arm and hand. After three years of recovery, he used the G.I. Bill and returned to Kansas to get a **law degree** and was admitted to the bar. He ran for a **state legislative seat** and won. Several years later, he won a seat in the **House of Representatives**. After three years, he ran and was elected a Kansas **U.S. senator** in 1968. In 1972, he **divorced his wife** of 23 years, and two years later he met and **married Elizabeth Hanford**. President Ford selected Dole as his running mate in the 1976 election. Having lost the election, Dole returned to the **Senate** where he served until 1996 and remained active in politics.

It was believed Ford lost because of Vietnam issues, high unemployment, Cold War tensions, and the Nixon pardon. Also, as a president, Ford was "too nice." He had folksy charm but lacked the star quality of a Reagan. Lyndon Johnson did not have kind words about President Ford; LBJ stated, "The trouble with Jerry Ford is that he cannot walk and chew gum at the same time." And "Ford is a nice fellow, but he spent too much time playing football without a helmet." After the 1976 elections, the Democrats were still in control of Congress: Senate 61-38 and House 292-143.

Proud of not having a war during his tenure, Ford stated when leaving the presidency, "**There are no soldiers marching except in the inaugural parade**." On a statue of Ford in the Rotunda are words from his 1974 inaugural: "Our Constitution works; our great Republic is a government of laws and not of men. Here the people rule." Gerald Ford was awarded the **Presidential Medal of Freedom** in 1999 by Bill Clinton.

Ford died on December 26, 2006, at his Rancho Mirage, California home and was buried at the Gerald R. Ford Presidential Library & Museum in Grand Rapids, Michigan. No last words are known. Wife Betty died on July 8, 2011, at age 93 and was buried with her husband.

Most historians rate Ford's **performance as average**.

Key Events

Intel co-founder Gordon Moore coined "**Moore's Law,**" which stated that the speed of the computer would double every 18 months, thereby halving the cost of processing (1974); publishing heiress **Patricia Hearst** was kidnapped by the Symbionese Liberation Army (1974); Vice President Rockefeller took residence in the former **Naval Observatory**, which Congress had just made the **official residence** of the vice president (1974); the federal government released surplus gas to overcome a shortage (1974); the Strategic Arms Limitation Talks (SALT) treaty with Russia was approved (1974); the Chairman of the House Ways & Means Committee, **Wilber Mills**, was discovered cavorting with stripper **Fanne Foe**; facing enormous political pressure he resigned and joined Alcoholics Anonymous (1974); the **Financial Accounting Standards Board** (FASB) was formed after the demise of the Accounting Principles Board (1974); **boxer Muhammad Ali** introduced the "**rope-a-dope**" while defeating heavyweight champion George Foreman in Zaire's "**Rumble in the Jungle**" (1974); Atlanta Braves baseball player **Henry Aaron** hit his **715th homerun**, breaking Babe Ruth's record

(1974); the **inaugural Golf Hall of Fame** opened and added Walter Hagen, Ben Hogan, Bobby Jones, Byron Nelson, Jack Nicklaus, Francis Ouimet, Arnold Palmer, Gary Player, Gene Sarazen, Sam Snead, and Harry Vardon (1974); **Frank Sinatra** had a picture taken with Mafia bosses Carlo Gambino and Sam Giancana (1974); the **DJIA** closed at 616.24 at year end, down 27.6 percent (1974); **Microsoft** was created by Bill Gates and Paul Allen (1975); DEC introduced the **minicomputer** (1975); the **New York City financial crisis** curtailed essential services (1975); the **Jack Dempsey restaurant closed** in New York City (1975); TRW designed a **flexible benefits program** using after tax dollars to select life, medical, and AD&D insurance (1975); **Elvis Presley** received $60,000 for a one-night performance in Detroit, Michigan (1975); **CEO pay** was reportedly about **40 times** the average worker's pay (1975); *Newsweek* reported the median CEO pay was $1 million as opposed to $12,000 for all workers (1975); having begun in 1962, the **Vietnam War ended** (1975); reportedly, America and Russia reduced the number of their missiles to 25,000 and 22,000 respectively, thereby lowering the gap between the two countries (1975); a **bomb** exploded in a **LaGuardia Airport** baggage area, killing 14 people (1975); **women** were admitted to the **military academies** (1975); in the "**Thrilla in Manila**," Muhammad Ali defeated Joe Frazier (1975); Dr. Richard Raskind became **Dr. Renee Richards** following a sex reassignment operation (1975); Chicago mob boss **Sam Giancana** was killed in his kitchen (1975); teamster boss **Jimmy Hoffa** disappeared in a Detroit parking lot (1975); New York City, on the brink of bankruptcy because of unfunded commitments by **Mayor John Lindsay**, was saved with help from investment banker Felix Rohatyn (1975); coach **John Wooden** won the UCLA's tenth national championship and then retired (1975); the **Minnesota Vikings** lost their straight fourth Super

Bowl game (1975); the **DJIA** closed at 852.41 at year end, up 38.2 percent (1975); the **Windows on the World restaurant opened** on top of the World Trade Center (1976); **Drexel Burnham Lambert** was founded and focused on high-yield junk bonds (1976); Raymond Damadian received the patent for the **MRI scanner** (1976); the **video-cassette recorder** was introduced by JVC (1976); biotech company **Genentech** focused on creating insulin (1976); **Steve Jobs** and **Steve Wozniak** launched the **Apple I** in a garage (1976); John Bogle established the **Vanguard Group** index fund (1976); **Eastern Airlines** unions were forced to concede "**givebacks**" to avoid bankruptcy (1976); crime boss **Carlo Gambino died** of a heart attack (1976); a coast-to-coast **celebration of the bicentennial** took place (1976); the American Basketball Association **(ABA) was dissolved, but four teams** – the Denver Nuggets, the Indiana Pacers, New Jersey Nets, and the San Antonio Spurs – joined the **NBA** (1976); at an American Legion convention, 29 died due to **Legionnaires Disease** (1976); *Directors & Boards* began publication (1976); the **DJIA** closed at 1,004.65 at year end, up 17.9 percent (1976); the first commercial use of the **fiber optic telephone system** began (1977); Kresge became **Kmart** (1977); 3M created the **Post-it** (1977); and the first use of capital punishment since 1967 occurred when a firing squad was used on the murderer **Gary Gilmore** (1977).

Jimmy Carter
(39ᵀᴴ President)

January 20, 1977 – January 20, 1981

James Earl Carter Jr. was born on October 1, 1924, to James Earl Carter Sr. and Lillian Gordy Carter, in Plains, Georgia. He was the first president **born in a hospital** and was the oldest sibling of Billy, Gloria, and Ruth. His father nicknamed Jimmy "**hotshot**." Jimmy's job was to feed the pigs, milk the cows, and pick, boil, and sell the peanuts, earning a dollar a day. Jimmy later worked in his father's store. Jimmy's family history dated back to 1635, and one ancestor fought in the American Revolution. Jimmy had an uncle, Tom Gordy, who was in the U.S. Navy. The career appealed to Jimmy – adventure, travel, and a chance to leave the peanut farm. So, he set his sights on getting into the Naval Academy.

JIMMY CARTER (39TH PRESIDENT)

Jimmy's parents instilled in him strong **Christian values**, and his father insisted that Jimmy complete any task he started and do it to **perfection**. His farmer father was a strong **disciplinarian**; his mother was a nurse and a compassionate **supporter**. When not working or in school, Jimmy loved to read adventure stories, mysteries, and naval history. Jimmy attended schools in Plains and Archery, where he got good grades due in part to being able to read **over 2,000** words per minute with 90% retention. Unable to get into Annapolis upon graduation, he went to **Georgia Southwestern College** and **then Georgia Institute of Technology** before finally getting admitted to the **U.S. Naval Academy** in 1943. He went through a year of hazing before becoming a track star with good grades. He graduated 50th in his class of 810 in 1946, a class that produced 35 admirals and one president (Jimmy). Shortly after graduation, Jimmy married his long-time sweetheart, **Eleanor Rosalynn Smith**, on July 7, 1946. They would go on to have **four children:** Amy, Chip, Jack, and Jeff.

Eleanor Rosalynn Smith was born on August 18, 1927, in Plains, Georgia. Her mother was a seamstress and her father a farmer. Rosalynn knew Jimmy in high school (she graduated valedictorian), but they did not date until after her freshman year at **Georgia Southwestern College**, when he was a midshipman at the **U.S. Naval Academy**. Jimmy proposed marriage, but she turned him down because she wanted to finish school. When she graduated, he proposed again, and she accepted. And Jimmy made her his partner in decision-making.

Jimmy's first assignment as a **second lieutenant** was the dilapidated battleship, *USS Wyoming*. He then applied to the **submarine school**. As part of the two-hour interview, **Admiral Rickover** asked, "Did you always do your best?" His answer was "no." From that day forward, Jimmy believed he gave his very best every minute of his life. Carter graduated third in a class of fifty-two in 1952. He later said Rickover's influence on his life was second only to his parents'. And Jimmy's experience with the **nuclear reactor** was invaluable later in dealing with the accident at Three-Mile Island in 1979, while he was president.

In 1953, upon hearing of his father's death, Jimmy **resigned his commission** and returned to Plains to run the **Golden Peanut Company**. Rosalynn was not thrilled with this choice but reluctantly agreed and took over the accounting for the company as Jimmy traveled to political events. Because of **family debts**, they lived in subsidized housing until he got out of debt, making Jimmy the first president to have lived in a **public housing project**.

Carter became active in **local and state** politics and was elected to the **state senate** in 1962 and reelected in 1964. He, along with ten friends, claimed to have seen an unidentified flying object (UFO) in 1968. In 1970, Carter was elected governor of Georgia. Upon leaving the state capital in 1975, he positioned himself for the Democratic nomination for president, stating, "The time for racial discrimination is over." In a 1976 *Playboy* interview, he stated, "I've looked on many women with lust. I've committed adultery in my heart many times. God knows I will do this and forgives me."

During his campaign for president, his opponent **Ted Kennedy** said that Carter was **imprecise** and intentionally **indefinite**. Kennedy's followers also used the motto ABC (**Anybody but Carter**). But **Kennedy's** campaign was having **difficulty** overcoming his drinking problem, a failed marriage, and a Chappaquiddick fatality. Carter was also running against **Scoop**

Jackson and **Governor Wallace**, who charged that Carter was too liberal for conservatives and too conservative for liberals. But Carter's friendly and warm manner, coupled with a firm, determined style and a reminder that he was the only Washington-outsider, was key. He won the **nomination** at the Democratic convention in 1976 after fighting off a challenge by Senator Ted Kennedy. Minnesota U.S. Senator **Walter Mondale** was selected by Carter as a running mate from a list of some 4,000 possibilities and a rating system designed by strategist and friend **Ham Jordan**.

Walter Mondale was born on January 5, 1928, in Ceylon, Minnesota. His father was a Methodist minister. Walter grew up to be known as "**Fritz**" and was active in sports and school activities. He worked on Hubert Humphrey's senate campaign in 1948, and he graduated from the **University of Minnesota** in 1951. He was drafted into the **U.S. Army** to serve as an enlisted man in the Korean conflict. He returned to America to graduate from the University of Minnesota **Law School** in 1956. Shortly after, he was admitted to the Minnesota Bar and **married** his long-time sweetheart, **Joan Adams**. In 1960, Mondale was appointed **Minnesota attorney general**, and in 1964 he was appointed to the **U.S. Senate**, filling the vacancy created by Hubert Humphrey's election as vice president.

Given that past presidents had either gotten us into wars or extended those in existence, along with the Watergate fiasco, many Americans were **distrustful** of Washington "insiders." As an "**outsider**," when Jimmy said, "I will never lie to you," it seemed to many an appropriate change. This view swept Carter into the presidency, albeit by a narrow margin over President Ford. In the **1976 election**, **Jimmy Carter** and **Walter Mon-**

dale defeated President **Gerald Ford** and Senator **Robert Dole** 40,977,147 to 39,422,671 in the popular vote and 297 to 240 in the electoral vote. The negative fallout from Ford's pardon of President Nixon following the Watergate break-in was a major contribution to Carter's victory. Jimmy Carter was the first elected president from the South since Zachary Taylor in 1849.

Jack Watson was assigned by Carter to head the transition team into the White House. He was a Harvard law school graduate who worked for a white-shoe Atlanta law firm. The transition team (Jack Watson and Edwin Meese) and the election team (Hamilton Jordan, Robert Hammer, and Jody Powell) were immediately at odds. The election team thought the transition team was going to take over the election. The transition team all wore suits; the election team wore chinos and T-shirts. The transition team were polite and disciplined; the election team were crude and impolite.

Gerald Ford stated, "Teddy Roosevelt once said, speak softly and carry a big stick, and Jimmy Carter wants to speak loudly and carry a flyswatter." Carter and Ford didn't like each other, but at Carter's inaugural he recognized Ford and thanked him "for all he has done to heal our land." And he repeated those words at Ford's funeral.

Carter had a difficult time getting his programs implemented, in spite of a **Democratic Congress**. Carter wanted to do everything once; he refused to prioritize, and he had no one to help persuade him to do so. And he immersed himself in details. He not only read everything; he corrected grammatical errors. Before the end of his first year, Carter's **approval rating** was in the low 30s.

Carter came into office at a time of **high inflation** and **recession**. Inflation was nearing 20% as too much money was chasing too few goods, which required the Federal Reserve to raise interest rates to also near 20%. Carter also had to address public concerns about the development of the **neutron bomb**, with its ability to kill thousands with little structural damage. He upset the right by returning the **Panama Canal** to Panama, and he upset the left when he bailed out the Chrysler company debts and pardoned 50,000 draft dodgers.

Because Jordan was a **brilliant strategist**, Carter placed him "first among equals." But Jordan did not like to socialize, and he did not want to handle routine matters, so he became very unpopular with Congress.

Carter decided he would not have a chief of staff, which represented centralization of power. Carter wanted to be the one in charge. Not having a chief of staff meant no one was managing access to Carter and he was involved in trivial matters. Carter said he liked hearing different views, but he had no one to look after the day-to-day problems. Needing someone to organize his day, Carter reluctantly gave the **chief of staff position** to Hamilton. He did not want it, and he did a terrible job. So midway in his term, Carter appointed Jack Watson, his chief of staff and things improved dramatically.

Dick Cheney warned Carter of turf battles, and it happened. **Zbigniew Brzezinski** (Carter's national security advisor) and Secretary of State **Cyrus Vance** feuded constantly. They had a different view on virtually everything. In contrasting the two leaders, Carter said Zig was "too competitive" and Vance was "too easy." Mixed messages coming from the top two led to confusion as to American intent. But the biggest change in relative roles in the White House was that of the **vice president**. Carter not only gave Mondale an office in the West Wing (he was the first vice president to have one), Mondale was also included in all major decisions, along with Rosalynn. She and Jimmy had lunch every week to discuss policy matters and personal items. Carter used Mondale as a troubleshooter. He became an important part of Carter's team, shaping administration policies and cabinet appointments.

Rosalynn used her experience as a governor's wife to aid in the transition to first lady. She settled into the White House, creating the first office of the **First Lady** in the East Wing. Funds were created to maintain the area. The president called her "a very equal partner." Rosalynn sent her daughter, Amy, to a public school and brought her nanny to the White House.

Polls indicated that Americans liked Carter personally but considered him a bad micro-managing problem solver and not a big-picture motivator. Carter got elected because he was a Washington outsider, but once inside he failed to maintain voter appeal. His inauguration on January 20, 1977 marked the beginning of his single term as president of the United States.

Carter's initial **cabinet** included **Vice President** Walter Mondale, **Secretary of State** Cyrus Vance, **Secretary of the Treasury** Michael Blumenthal, **Attorney General** Griffen Bell, **Secretary of the Interior** Cecil Andrus, **Secretary of Agriculture** Robert Bergland, **Secretary of Labor** Ray Marshall, **Secretary of Commerce** Juanita Kreps, **Secretary of Defense** Harold Brown, **Secretary of Health, Education and Welfare** Joseph Califano, **Secretary of Housing and Urban Development** Patricia Harris, **Secretary of Transportation** Brockman Adams, **Secretary of Education** Shirley Hufstedler, and **Secretary of Energy** James Schlesinger. The **Department of Energy** was added by Carter when he saw the importance of not being dependent on others for oil. And the **Department of Education** was created because Carter saw the need for more focus on education. The

Department of Health, Education and Welfare was changed to the **Department of Health and Human Services** because education now had its own department. First Lady Rosalynn frequently attended cabinet meetings, but she never spoke until after the meeting, when she shared her thoughts with Jimmy.

In **Abood vs Detroit Board** (1977), the U.S. Supreme Court ruled that payments by nonunion members to the unions that negotiate their contracts are legal if not used to fund political activity infringing on free speech.

In 1977, **Congress** increased the pay of congressmen to $57,500 per annum (up from 1975's $44,600), that of the associate justices of the U.S. Supreme Court to $72,000 per annum (up from 1976's $66,000), and that of the chief justice to $75,000 per annum (up from 1976's $68,800).

The leaders of Carter's key staff were **Jody Powell** (press aide), **Hamilton Jordan** (political strategist), **Robert Hamer** (financial matters), **Jack Watson** (chief of staff), and best friend **Bert Lance**.

In **Regents of the University of California vs Bakke** (1978), the U.S. Supreme Court ruled that affirmative action was unfair if it led to reverse discrimination by the use of rigid quotas.

The **1978 Age Discrimination in Employment Act** raised the protected age to 70 (with exceptions); the **1978 Civil Service Reform Act** provided a merit pay system for certain managers in the GS and executive level positions; the **1978 Civil Rights Amendment** stipulated that pregnancy and childbirth be treated the same as other disabilities for benefit purposes; and the **1978 Revenue Act** made a number of changes, either adding or deleting taxable items.

President Carter was **not one for pageantry**. He carried his own briefcase, banned "hail to the chief" when he arrived, sold the presidential yacht (*Sequoia*), reduced the number of radios, and Carter brought the **first computers** into the White House. He declined the invitation to throw out a pitch at the 7th game of the World Series.

Jimmy Carter **dressed casually**, usually in a plaid shirt, blue jeans, and desert boots. When entertaining, he wore off-the-rack suits. Both Carters were light drinkers and did not serve hard liquor at social events. Conversely, **Jimmy's** brother was an alcoholic and a constant embarrassment. **White House dinners** showcased not only Southern cooking but also regional cooking from other parts of the country. Jimmy was a **good cook**, probably only second to President Eisenhower. With economizing, the cost of state dinners dropped to less than $5 a head. As time went on, the low-budget informality made the White House look **cheap and indecisive**.

The Carters' **breakfast** included country ham with redeye gravy, biscuits, and coffee; **lunch** included Brunswick stew, corn bread, and grits; and **dinner** included black-eyed peas with rice, candied apples, country ham with redeye gravy, collard or turnip greens, eggplant, fried chicken, fish, red beans and white rice, squash, tomatoes, turnips, zucchini, and grits. Jimmy Carter was partial to his version of **grits**: corn meal mixed with butter, salt, and water.

In 1978, Carter gave an impassioned speech on the country's confidence crisis. The country focused more on consumption than achievement. Believing his **cabinet** was part of the problem, he asked each member to submit their **resignation**. He accepted them from Adams, Bell, Blumenthal, Califano, and Schlesinger. Carter was also disappointed in **Andrew Young**, his highest-ranking Black employee, for making some inappropriate comments while serving as America's Ambassador to the United Nations.

Worried about the blood feud between Jews and Muslims, Carter got **Israeli Prime Minister** Menachem Begin and **Egyptian President** Anwar Sadat to meet with him at the **presidential retreat**, **Camp David**, built in the Maryland wilderness 60 miles from D.C. by FDR. He named it Shangri-la, but it was renamed Camp David by President Eisenhower after his father and grandson. The **Middle East** was still simmering from the Six-Day War in 1967, when Israel took the Gaza Strip, the Golan Heights, the Sinai Peninsula, and the West Bank, followed by the 1973 Yom Kippur War started by Egypt, with the Arab states forming OPEC to control oil prices following U.S. arms shipments to Israel. Begin, an orthodox Jew, Carter, a devout Baptist, and Sadat, a pious Muslim, met on September 5, 1978. After much discussion, a **peace settlement** was signed on September 17. The three returned together in a helicopter to the White House, where the Peace Accords were signed. Formal peace treaties were signed at the White House on March 26, 1979. The Carters hosted a dinner that night for over 1,300 people. Significantly, the **treaty is still in effect**. This treaty was clearly Carter's **greatest achievement**, but Carter did not receive a Nobel Peace Prize, while both Begin and Sadat did receive **Nobel Peace Prizes**. Begin died of a heart attack on March 9, 1992; Sadat was assassinated on October 6, 1981.

The **1979 Technical Corrections Act** created tax credit employee stock ownership plans, and the **1980 Miscellaneous Revenue Act** permitted employees to make three-way tradeoffs among cash, benefits, and deferred compensation. Also in 1979, **Congress** increased the pay of the congressmen to $60,653 annum (up from 1977's $57,500), that of the associate justices of the U.S. Supreme Court to $81,300 per annum (up from 1977's $66,000), and that of the chief justice to $84,700 per annum (up from 1977's $75,000).

Carter's judgement was called into question when he invited the **Shah of Iran** (who was dying of cancer) into the United States for medical treatment. This action incensed the Iranians and led to their November 4, 1979 take-over of the **U.S. Embassy** in Tehran and the taking of **90 hostages** (who would be held for 444 days). Carter vacillated over what to do, and finally, on April 24, 1980, he sent in a Delta force to rescue them. Several helicopters crashed, and eight rescuers were killed. **Operation Eagle Claw** was a failure, and the rescue debacle was a key grievance during Ronald Reagan's presidential campaign.

After the Russians invaded Afghanistan in 1979, Carter withdrew from the Strategic Arms Limitation Talks Treaty with the Soviet Union in 1980. The U.S. also withdrew from the summer Olympics in Russia. Carter stated, "We must adjust to changing times but hold to unchanging principles," and later added, "Our American values are not luxuries but necessities."

There was **one televised presidential debate** between Democratic President Jimmy Carter, Republican Ronald Reagan, and Independent John Anderson on September 21, 1980, in Baltimore, Maryland. There was a **second televised debate** between President Jimmy Carter and Ronald Reagan on October 28, 1980, in Cleveland, Ohio. The **vice presidential debate** between Democrat Walter Mondale and Republican George H.W. Bush, scheduled for October 2, 1980, was canceled.

In the **1980 election**, Democrats President **Jimmy Carter** and Vice President **Walter Mondale** were defeated by Republicans **Ronald Reagan** and **George Bush** for the presidency and vice presidency. Carter and Mondale lost the popular vote 35,483,883 to 43,904,153 and the electoral vote 40 to 483 in a landslide defeat. National Unity nominee **John Anderson** received 5,720,060 popular votes and no electoral votes. In 1980, the U.S. population was 230 million.

The **1980 Multiemployer Pension Plan Amendments Act** permitted the Secretary of Labor to treat severance plans as welfare, not pension plans, and the **1980 Depository Institutions Deregulation and Monetary Control Act** deregulated savings-account rates and enforced minimum bank capital requirements.

In 1980, Congress increased the pay of the associate justices of the U.S. Supreme Court to $88,700 per annum (up from 1979's $81,300), that of the chief justice to $92,400 per annum (up from 1979's $84,700), and that of the cabinet secretaries to $69,600 per annum (up from 1975's $63,000). Congress made no other pay changes during Carter's term of presidency.

Looking back on Carter's term of office, clearly his **greatest achievement** was the peace accord between Egypt and Israel. Since the signing in 1979, not a shot has been exchanged between the two countries. Second was the **pardoning of some 50,000 Vietnam War draft dodgers**. Other accomplishments included a comprehensive **energy policy** approval of the **Panama Canal Treaty**, saving the involvement of thousands of troops; the creation of **two new cabinet positions** (education and energy); **deregulation** of the airplane industry; the **election** of more Black people and women as federal judges than all previous presidents (but Carter had no Supreme Court openings); ending the unworkable two-China policy (establishing full-diplomatic relations with China); **expanding the national park system**; establishing strong **pollution controls**; fostering **human rights** in foreign countries; placing **defensive missiles** in Europe; reducing the **federal deficit**; and reestablishing **civil**

service reform. Carter had a difficult time getting his programs approved, usually only with significant compromises.

But Carter had several significant **domestic failures**: poor consumer protections, little healthcare improvement, no tax reform, few welfare changes, the inability to get the Iranian hostages released, and **OPEC** (Organization of Petroleum Exporting Countries) announcement of a 50% increase in the price of oil in response to the Camp David peace treaty. The result, a dramatic increase in the price of gasoline, resulted in very unhappy drivers. Additionally, Carter's **insiders** did not go out of their way to get approval and respect. And **unemployment rose to 15%, interest rates increased to 20%,** and **inflation rose to 10%.**

And Carter's **foreign** policy was far from a notable success. He gave back the **Panama Canal** (upsetting many), although it saved sending 100,000 troops to defend the Canal. He had no answer for the Russian invasion of **Afghanistan**. And inviting an ousted Shah to America led to a **takeover of the American Embassy** in Iran and the taking of a number of American hostages. Only after Reagan had been sworn in on January 21, 1981, did Iran release the hostages. The obvious appearance was that Carter could not get the hostages released. Unknown to the president, Rosalynn engaged Carter's brother, Billy, a registered foreign agent with Libya, to help free the hostages. But nothing came of it.

In their last night in the White House, the Carters listened to **Willie Nelson** sing "Georgia on My Mind." Upon leaving the White House, former president Carter stated, "Rosalynn was my equal partner in everything I accomplished. She gave me wise guidance and encouragement when I needed it."

After leaving the White House, **Jimmy returned to the peanut business**, lecturing at Emory University, and writing books.

JIMMY CARTER (39TH PRESIDENT)

Unlike most former presidents, Jimmy did not play golf. Jimmy and wife Rosalynn opened the **Carter Center** in 1982, a nonprofit organization that promoted advances in agriculture, democracy, human rights, and public health. Two years later, Jimmy and Rosalynn started the nonprofit organization **Habitat for Humanity International**. Their goal was to build new homes for the poor. Habitat was the world's largest not-for-profit homebuilder. Carter had become a person recognized for his involvement in improving conditions for the disadvantaged. Later, he teamed up with the U.S. Fish and Wildlife Service to help preserve the declining monarch butterfly population. In 2002, Jimmy Carter was awarded the **Nobel Peace Prize** for actively promoting social justice. Teddy Roosevelt and Woodrow Wilson had received the award earlier.

Reflecting on his life, **Jimmy noted he was content**. Among his accomplishments were serving in the U.S. Navy nuclear submarine program under Admiral Rickover, negotiating peace between Egypt and Israel, being a successful peanut farmer for many years, authoring 30 books, teaching Sunday School and Bible Class for over half his life, having a successful marriage with Rosalynn for over 70 years, building homes for **Habitat for Humanity** for 30 years, becoming governor of Georgia and president of the United States, and becoming the first Southern president since Zachary Taylor in 1848.

However, most historians consider Carter's presidential performance **somewhat below average**. His approval rating when he left office was 35%; only Nixon and Truman were lower. Americans liked Carter personally but not politically. But he led a full life. He fared much better after leaving the presidency at age 56 in 1981. The Carters moved back to Plains, Georgia, the only house they ever owned. They went to church, fished, and hiked. Jimmy learned to ski, climbed Mt. Fiji, and began writing his 32 books. In 1984, he and Rosalynn joined Habitat for Humanity committing to a week a year helping to build over 4,000 houses for the poor. In 1999, Carter received the **Presidential Medal of Freedom** from President Clinton. In 2002, Jimmy received the **Nobel Peace Prize.** Theodore Roosevelt, Woodrow Wilson, and Barack Obama received the awards during their presidency, Carter received his after leaving the office. He might have received it along with Mr. Begin and Mr. Sadat in 1978 for reaching a peace settlement between Egypt and Israel but Carter was not nominated in time.

Rosalynn died on November 19, 2023, at age 96 having been married to Jimmy for 77 years. To date only Bess Truman, age 97, outlived Rosalynn among First Ladies. Jimmy continued writing books as he fought off brain cancer. He spent the last two years of his life in a hospice and died on December 29, 2024, at the age of 100. He is the longest living former president in U.S. history. **Five** former presidents died in their **90's**: George H.W. Bush (94), Gerald Ford (93), Ronald Reagan (93), John Adams (90), and Herbert Hoover (90). The **five** who survived until their **80's** were Harry S. Truman (88), James Madison (85), Thomas Jefferson (83), Richard M. Nixon (81), and John Quincy Adams (80). The **ten** who did not die until into their **70's** were Martin Van Buren (79), Dwight D. Eisenhower (78), Andrew Jackson (78), James Buchanan (77), Millard Fillmore (74), James Monroe (73), William Howard Taft (73), John Tyler (71), Grover Cleveland (71), and Rutherford B. Hayes (70). The **twelve** who passed in their **60's** were William Henry Harrison (68), George Washington (67), Benjamin Harrison (67), Woodrow Wilson (67), Andrew Johnson (67), Zachary Taylor (65), Franklin Pierce (64), Lyndon B. Johnson (64), Ulysses S. Grant (63), Franklin D. Roosevelt (63), Calvin Coolidge (60), and Theodore Roosevelt (60).

Key Events

The Departments of Education and Energy were created (1977); severe winter weather caused a natural gas shortage (1977); the SEC created a safe harbor for stock appreciation rights (SARs), indicating that their exercise would not be a simultaneous purchase and sale and thereby not conflict with the six-month holding period in Section 16 required of corporate officers (1977); the FBI released 40,000 pages of secret files on the Kennedy Assassination (1977); oil began flowing through the **Alaska pipeline** (1977); **Perrier** introduced bottled water in the United States (1977); Lawrence Ellison founded **Oracle** (1977); the **Studio 54** discotheque opened in New York City (1977); **Kohlberg Kravis Roberts** pioneered the leveraged buyout (1977); automatic teller machines (**ATMs**) were introduced by Citibank (1977); the **Apple II** computer went on the market (1977); the **DJIA** closed at 831.17 at year-end, down 7.3 percent (1977); the SEC required that the proxy report pay for the highest five paid executive officers (it had been three) (1978); the Financial Accounting Standards Board issued **FAS Interpretation 28**, describing the treatment of stock appreciation rights and other variable stock plans under APB 25 (1978); the commercial airline industry was deregulated (1978); within months of being fired from Ford after 32 years (8 years as president), Lee Iacocca joined **Chrysler** as president with a $1.5 million sign-on bonus, as well as a $360,000 salary (1978); California voters set off a nationwide "**tax payers' revolt**" with Proposition 13 by reducing property taxes (1978); the **Jim Jones cult** resulted in over 900 killed in mass suicide in Guyana (1978); Mafia family boss **Joe Colombo** died of cardiac arrest at age 53 (1978); a New York City financial crisis was averted by **federal** loan guarantees (1978); George Lucas released the film *Star Wars* (1978); toxic wastes were found in the **Love Canal** near Niagara Falls, New York (1978); the **DJIA** closed at 805.01 at year-end, down 3.1 percent (1978); President Carter created the **Office of Personnel Management** to provide personnel services to the federal government (1979); President Carter endorsed a $1.5 billion loan to Chrysler (1979); President Carter outlined a 10-year, $140 billion program to reduce foreign oil dependency (1979); the United States resumed diplomatic relations with China (1979); the **Susan B. Anthony** dollar coin was introduced (1979); Sony introduced the cassette player **Walkman** (1979); voicemail was invented (1979); **ESPN** (Entertainment and Sports Programming Network) began operation, focusing on college and university sports (1979); the "**poison pill**" was created by Marty Lipton (1979); Johnson & Johnson put in the **first 401(k) plan** (1979); for the first time, all twenty-five executives in the annual *Business Week* report on pay made above $1,000,000 in total pay (1979); a partial meltdown of the nuclear plant at **Three Mile Island** was the worst nuclear disaster in the United States (1979); mob boss "**Carmine**" **Galante** was killed in New York City (1979); an **American Airlines** jet crashed following its takeoff in Chicago, killing 275 people (1979); the Bureau of Labor Statistics began the **Employee Benefits Survey** to collect specific information on paid leave, pensions, and the various insurance programs (1979); the **DJIA** closed at 838.74 at year-end, up 4.2 percent (1979); reportedly, America had over 24,000 missiles and Russia had over 30,000, giving Russia the first-time lead in the missile count (1980); the FASB issued **FAS 43**, stating that vested payments of future employee absences are an accrued liability (1980); the New York City ***Zagat*** restaurant guide was introduced (1980); gold was worth $839 an ounce (1980); Nike went public (1980); John Postel introduced the **Internet** (1980); Ted Turner launched **CNN**, a 24-hour TV news station (1980); Reginald Jones (GE), Thomas Murphy (GM), David Rockefeller (Chase Manhattan Bank), and Irving Shapiro (DuPont) all stepped down as CEOs (1980); **Michael Bloomberg** received a $10 million golden parachute from Salomon Brothers (1980); CEO pay was reportedly 40 times the average worker pay (1980); the U.S. boycotted the **Summer Olympics** in Moscow because of Russia's presence in Afghanistan (1980); in the **Winter Olympics**, the U.S. defeated the Russians in hockey on "a miracle on ice" (1980); Mark Chapman shot and killed former **Beatle John Lennon** in New York City (1980); the U.S. population rose to 226 million (1980); the **DJIA** closed at 963.99 at year-end, up 14.9 percent (1980); and Michael Bloomberg set up **Bloomberg Financial** (1981).

Ronald Reagan
(40ᵀᴴ President)

January 20, 1981 – January 20, 1989

Ronald Wilson Reagan was born on February 6, 1911, to John Edward Reagan and Nellie Wilson Reagan in an apartment above a general store in the farming town of Tampico, Illinois. He was the younger of the two Reagan sons; the elder son was John Neil Reagan. His father, Jack, looked at his ten-pound crying baby and asked, "How can such a little fat **Dutchman** make such a racket?" The nickname **Dutch** was born.

Father Jack was a Catholic and Reagan's mother, Nelle, a Protestant. The family fell on hard times and moved frequently. Dutch taught himself to read at age five. Born left-handed, he learned to write with his right hand. Jack was an alcoholic and a failed shoe salesman who worked for the Works Progress Administration during the **Great Depression**. Ronald learned the value of **ambition** and **hard work** from his father and the value of **dreams** and **prayers** from his mother. Ronald was a **voracious reader**. In school, he was a **drum major** for the band. Beginning at age 15, he was a **lifeguard** for seven years and saved over 75 lives before going on to the small **Eureka College**. There, he got a **football scholarship** and washed dishes for room and board. His interests were **acting** and **athletics**, and he began a daily diary that he continued until his death. He was an **average student** but actively engaged in **drama and football**, was captain of the **swimming team**, and was president of the **student council**.

Reagan graduated in 1932 and got a job as a **sports announcer** for a radio station in Davenport, Iowa. On a 1937 trip to Los Angeles to cover the Chicago Cubs, he met a movie agent who got him a **screen test** with **Warner Brothers**, who signed him for a **seven-year contract** at $200 a week.

When the **Japanese attacked Hawaii** on December 7, 1941, Reagan, who was in the Army Reserves as a first lieutenant, was called up to **active duty**. But because of poor eyesight and partial deafness, he was **rejected**. Instead, he was ordered to serve in the **Motion Picture Unit** of the military, where he made **patriotic and training films**. When the war ended, Reagan left the Army as a captain. In 1947, he joined the **Screen Actors Guild** and shortly thereafter was elected their **president**. In the capacity of the **Guild president**, Reagan testified in Washington before a House Committee **investigating communist activities** in the movie industry. It was there, in 1949, that he met his second wife-to-be, actress **Nancy Davis**. Both Ronald and Nancy made a number of feature films: Ronald 53 and Nancy 12, several of them together.

Ronald and Nancy got married on March 4, 1952, after Ronald divorced Jane Wyman, whom he had married on January 26, 1940. Ronald had two children with Jane Wyman: a daughter, Maureen, and a son, Michael. Nancy and Ronald had two children together, Patricia and Ronald Jr.

Nancy Reagan was born Anne Francis Robbins on July 6, 1921, in New York City. She was the daughter of salesman Kenneth Seymour Robbins and actress Edith Luckett Robbins. After graduating from **Smith College** in 1943, she started her **acting career** on Broadway but later switched to movies, signing a seven-year contract with Metro-Goldwyn-Mayer Studios in 1949 as **Nancy Davis**. She met Ronald Reagan in his capacity as president of the Screen Actors Guild. She went to him because she was being **charged as a communist**. He helped get her off the blacklist in 1952. He found her beautiful and outspoken. At 5ft 4 inches, Nancy was known as the **Iron Butterfly**. She was tenacious, with an eye for detail. The married couple appeared together in her last movie, *Hellcats of the Navy*, in 1957. She was at his side and played an **active role** in all of his campaigns. And she was an **influential advisor**. But Ronald did not always take her advice. Sometimes he would say, "That is enough, Nancy." At dinner, he would often turn off his hearing aid. Nonetheless, a longtime friend of both has stated, "Without Nancy, there would be no Governor Reagan, no President Reagan." In a note to Nancy Reagan, Richard Nixon said, "You will bring beauty, class and dignity to the White House." Some said Ronald and Nancy were **soulmates**.

In 1950, as his acting career was fading, Reagan got an invitation to host the *General Electric Theater* on weekly **television**. He did this for eight years. During this period, he visited all the GE plants and talked to over 200,000 GE workers. It gave him a good look at how government worked, and he concluded that **big government was not the solution to the country's issues, it was the problem**. In the early 60's, he was the TV host of *Death Valley Days*. By this time, the life-long Democrat had become a **Republican**, stating, "I didn't leave the Democratic Party; the Democratic Party left me!" Reagan added, "The Republican Party at its worst is better than the Democratic Party at its best." In a 1963 televised speech in support of Barry Goldwater's presidential campaign, Reagan stated, "We have a rendezvous with destiny, the last best hope of man on earth." The speech caught the attention of many. Reagan appealed to America's **patriotic spirit** as the Democratic Party was shifting to the left and the Republicans to the political right. Reagan was convinced you do not win by being angry and gloomy. You win with **enthusiastic optimism**.

Several millionaires convinced Reagan to run for California governor in 1966 against Pat Brown, who had defeated Richard Nixon by over 300,000 votes. Initially Reagan refused, saying he was an actor, not a politician, but eventually he decided to run for governor. Brown was a card-carrying liberal. Reagan was a proud conservative. He was a charming and effective speaker. On January 3, 1967, Ronald Reagan became **governor of California**, having defeated Pat Brown by over one million votes.

Reagan built a staff consisting of **William Clark, Michael Deaver, Edwin Meese, and Caspar Weinberger**. They focused on **domestic issues,** but Reagan also kept sight of **global matters**. In 1974, with his second term expiring, Reagan was exploring ways to stay in touch with the public. In a five-minute daily **radio** commentary on the news from 1975 to 1979, he delivered over 1,000 comments to over 20 million listeners. Unhappy with government appeasement of Russia, Reagan decided to run against President Ford in 1976. Ford had never been elected to office beyond the congressional levels, and he had never run a national campaign, much less gotten elected to national office.

Reagan lost the first five primaries but came from behind to win the North Carolina contest. At the **1976 Republican Convention**, Reagan came close, but **Ford was selected** to be the Republican candidate to face **Democrat Jimmy Carter**. Carter won. But on November 4, 1979, days before the election, 53 Americans were taken hostage in the American Embassy in Iran, and Reagan declared his candidacy for president. After bitter primaries, Reagan defeated **George H.W. Bush**.

The 1980s was a period of **unfriendly takeovers**, led by **Ted Forstmann**, **Henry Kravis**, and **Boone Pickens**, among others, who saw **undervalued assets** in a company, namely that their common stock price was less than their book value (especially after factoring in land at fair market value rather than the cost as carried on the balance sheet). They took out **massive loans to buy controlling interest**. After doing so, they **would sell off** parts of the business and cut back operations of the remainder to help retire the assumed debt. As the stock **market recovered**, these unfriendly takeovers became less prevalent, as they were no longer economically advantageous. Takeovers introduced golden parachute severance agreements.

In his **election campaign**, Reagan focused on several issues. First was the 1979 attack on the American Embassy in Iran and the taking of **52 hostages** who were still held captive. Second was the issue of a **stagnant economy** weighed down by high fuel prices. And third was the micro-management and **political incompetence** of President Carter.

Reagan promised that if elected president, he would **get the hostages released**, **stimulate the economy** with tax cuts, and

downsize the federal government while increasing military spending. Reagan won the nomination and picked his main opponent, George H.W. Bush, as his vice-presidential running mate.

In his **campaign**, a main Reagan question to voters was, "**When you go to vote, ask yourself, are you better off than you were four years ago?**" Because of his relaxed style, folksy charm, likeability, reassuring voice, and excellent speaking skills, he was named "**The Great Communicator.**" He dismissed this and said **he was not a great communicator; he communicated great ideas.** Nonetheless, he was a personable speaker, able to charm his audience, regardless of size. Without a doubt, he was an outstanding spokesman for the **conservatives**.

There was **one televised presidential debate** between Democratic President Jimmy Carter, Republican Ronald Reagan, and Independent John Anderson. It was held on September 21, 1980, in Baltimore, Maryland. There was **no vice presidential debate**.

In the **1980 election, Republicans Ronald Reagan** and **George H.W. Bush** defeated **Democrats** President **Jimmy Carter** and Vice President **Walter Mondale**, 43,904,153 to 35,483,883 in the popular vote and 489 to 49 in the electoral vote. Reagan and Bush won 44 of the 50 states. Independent Party candidate John Anderson received 5,720,060 popular votes but no electoral votes. At age 69, Reagan was the **oldest person elected president** to date.

George Herbert Walker Bush was born on June 12, 1924, to Prescott Bush and Dorothy Walker Bush in Milton, Massachusetts. Bush's father was a prominent, wealthy banker. George had **four siblings**: Jonathan, Nancy, Prescott Jr., and William. After attending private schools, Bush became the **Navy's youngest aviator** at the age of eighteen, flying over 50 missions and earning numerous medals. After military service, Bush went to **Yale University**, graduating with honors in under three years in 1948 but not before being the Yale captain of two college **World Series baseball champion**. Bush went to **Texas** and formed an oil company, becoming a very wealthy man. He then turned to politics and was voted into the **U.S. House of Representatives** in 1966. After several terms, he was appointed the **U.S. Ambassador to the United Nations** in 1971. He then became **Chair of the Republican National Committee**. This was followed by **envoy to China** and then **Director of the CIA**. In 1976, Bush decided to run for president of the United States but was defeated by Ronald Reagan in the primaries, who then chose Bush to be his vice-presidential nominee.

In his March 20, **1981, inaugural address**, Reagan focused on "an era of national renewal" and the announcement that the Iran hostages had been released. He further stated, "The business of our nation goes forward. These United States are confronted with an economic affliction of great proportions. **We must act today** to preserve tomorrow. And let there be no misunderstanding – we are going to begin to act, **beginning today**." Within minutes after Reagan was inaugurated, the **Americans** who had been held hostage for 444 days in Iran were **released**. Where Carter failed, Reagan succeeded.

In 1981, Reagan began his term of office with **unemployment** at 7.2%, annual **inflation** at 12%, and **interest rates** at 20%. In response to the economic downturn the country was facing, he said, "In this present crisis, government is not the solution to our problems, **government is the problem**," and "The most terrifying words in the English language are 'I am from the government and I'm here to help you.'" As the country was suffering from **high inflation**, **high interest rates**, and **high taxes**, Reagan signed the **1981 Economic Recovery Act**, which restored statutory stock options, extended IRA coverage, and lowered taxes.

Former Senator James Baker was not only a good friend of George H.W. Bush, he also ran Bush's campaign to be the Republican nominee for president. But they lost to Ronald Reagan, so Baker was surprised when Reagan asked Baker to be his **chief of staff**. Most thought that Reagan would select his good friend **Ed Meese**, who was his loyal confidant. But a friend of Reagan's said, "Meese could not organize a two-car funeral." Baker knew his way around Washington, unlike Meese and family friend Mike Deaver. The selling point was that **Nancy liked Baker's** self-possession and smooth manner. She was impressed with Baker and that was enough to convince her husband. Baker learned his job was to **control access** to the president, handle the **paperwork** (including speech writing), and **oversee** the White House staff. And to best **work with the first family**, Baker also made friends with long-time Reagan family friend, **Mike Deaver**. Baker knew his most difficult task was to bring **bad news** to the president or **disagree** with him on a course of action. Virtually everyone agreed Baker did the job very well.

Three men headed Reagan's White House staff and were called the **Troika.** They were **James Baker** (lawyer and George H.W. Bush's campaign manager), **Michael Deaver** (Reagan's California "spin doctor"), and **Ed Meese** (Reagan's campaign manager). Meese saw the press as the enemy, while Baker and Deaver saw the press as a source to be used to promote Reagan. All three had problems with Secretary of State **Alexander Haig**. And all three knew the first Sacramento Rule: "A **happy Nancy** means a **happy Ronald**."

President Reagan's initial **cabinet** included **Vice President** George H.W. Bush, **Secretary of State** Alexander Haig, **Secre-**

tary of the Treasury Donald Regan, **Attorney General** William Smith, **Secretary of the Interior** James Watt, **Secretary of Agriculture** John Block, **Secretary of Labor** Raymond Donovan, **Secretary of Commerce** Malcolm Baldridge, **Secretary of Defense** Caspar Weinberger, **Secretary of Housing and Urban Development** Samuel Pierce, **Secretary of Transportation** Andrew Lewis, **Secretary of Energy** James Edwards, **Secretary of Health and Human Services** Richard Schweiker, and **Secretary of Education** Terrell Bell.

Nixon said **Haig** was "the meanest, toughest, most ambitious son-of-a-bitch I ever knew. He'll make a great secretary of state."

Speechwriter Peter Robinson stated, "There was a lot more **infighting** going on in the Reagan White House than anybody was aware of because there were no such things as Tweeter, Twitter and Twotter in those days."

The special relationship between **Queen Elizabeth** and President Reagan was noted when she made him an honorary knight, enabling him to use the title "Sir."

In 1981, Congress increased the annual pay of the associate justices of the U.S. Supreme Court to $93,000 (up from 1980's $88,700) and the chief justice's pay to $96,800 (up from 1980's $92,400).

Two months after being inaugurated, **President Reagan was shot** and critically wounded. One bullet passed through a lung, and another missed his heart by an inch. **Press Secretary James Brady** was paralyzed from another shot, and a policeman and secret service agent were wounded. The shooter, **John Hinckley**, was captured and incarcerated. At the hospital, Reagan said to the doctor, "I hope you are a Republican." To Nancy, he quipped, "Honey, I forgot to duck."

Following up on a campaign promise to appoint a woman to the Supreme Court, Reagan nominated **Sandra Day O'Connor** to fill the vacancy created by the retirement of **Justice Potter Stewart**. She was approved by the Senate 99-0 on September 21, 1981, the **first woman** to serve on the U.S. Supreme Court. In **Gunther vs County of Washington** (1981), the U.S. Supreme Court ruled that dissimilar job pay differences may be illegal discrimination.

In spite of a Democratic controlled Congress, Reagan got the **1982 Tax Equity and Fiscal Responsibility Act** through Congress. It made changes in pension plans and made Medicare a secondary payer. In addition to lowering taxes, Reagan managed to cut federal spending and restore statutory stock options.

Reagan's **approval ratings** soared to 59% after he cut both income taxes and federal expenses, and as promised, Reagan **increased military sspending** significantly. This was the introduction of Reagan's economic policies, which were labeled **Reaganomics**: reduction in social programs and taxes and increases in defense spending. The **supply-side** economic policy meant a reduction in government involvement, and lowered taxes permitted the private sector, not the government, to expand the economy. By the end of 1981, the U.S. had Peacekeeper and Trident missiles and approval for the B-1 and Stealth bombers.

On May 22, 1982, Reagan spoke before England's **Parliament**, where he said, "Long term, the march of freedom and democracy will leave Marxism-Leninism on the **ash-heap of history**." A year later, he added to this statement, calling Russia the **evil empire**.

After the **1982 midterms**, the **GOP** controlled the Senate 54-46, but the **Democrats** retained control of the House 269-

166. Reportedly, Reagan once quipped, "I have left orders to be awakened at any time in case of a national emergency – even if I am in a cabinet meeting."

In 1982, Congress raised the pay of legislators to $69,800 per annum (up from 1979's $60,653), the pay of the associate justices of the U.S. Supreme Court to $96,700 per annum (up from 1981's $93,000) and the chief justice's pay to $100,700 per annum (up from 1981's $96,800).

In **Nixon vs Fitzgerald** (1982), the U.S. Supreme Court ruled that the president has absolute immunity from civil liability based on his official acts.

In April 1983, a bomb destroyed the American **Embassy in Beirut**, Lebanon, and six months later the Beirut Operations Center was bombed, killing 300 Marines. In October, Reagan ordered troops to the island of **Grenada** to stop a **left-wing coup** from taking place. That year, Reagan signed the **Martin Luther King Jr. holiday** (to be observed on January 20) into law and declared Times Beach, Missouri, a federal disaster area due to **toxic dioxin** in the soil. Also in 1983, Reagan stated, "Our **common enemies** are poverty, disease and above all, war." In 1983, Reagan got the **1983 Social Security Amendment** approved making payments partially taxable and phased in age 66 and 67 as retirement ages. He also passed the **1983 Technical Corrections Act,** which made pyramiding of stock-for-stock exercises disqualifying dispositions.

In 1983, Congress increased the annual pay of legislators to $69,800 (up from 1982's $60,653). It also raised the annual pay of cabinet secretaries to $82,900 (up from 1980's $69,600).

Later in 1983, the United States deployed cruise missiles in Europe and the **Strategic Defense Initiative** was on the drawing boards. It was designed to stop strategic nuclear weapons. But this combined with the increase in the trade deficit resulted in an increase in the **national debt**. To lessen the impact, Reagan cut federal social programs.

In **Arizona Governing Committee vs Norris** (1984), the U.S. Supreme Court ruled that an employee's sex cannot be a factor in determining their pension. In **Chevron vs National Resource Defense Council** (1984), the U.S. Supreme Court ruled that federal courts are to defer to agency legal interpretations when Congressional statutory language is ambiguous.

In 1984, Reagan signed three tax-related acts: the **1984 Deficit Reduction Act**, which lowered the long-term capital gains holding period to six months; the **1984 Tax Reform Act**, which essentially killed interest-free loans; and the **1984 Retirement Equity Act**, which established pre-retirement survivor benefits.

In 1984, Congress increased the annual pay of legislators to $72,600 (up from 1983's $69,800). It also increased the annual pay of the associate justices of the U.S. Supreme Court to $100,600 (up from 1982's $96,700) and the chief justice's pay to $104,700 (up from 1982's $100,700). And the cabinet secretaries' pay was increased to $86,200 (up from 1983's $82,900).

There were **two televised presidential debates** between Republican President Ronald Reagan and Democrat Walter Mondale. The first was on October 7, 1984, in Louisville, Kentucky. The second was on October 21, 1984, in Kansas City, Missouri. In the second debate, when asked about his advanced age, Reagan replied, "I will not exploit Mondale's youth and inexperience." There was **one vice presidential debate** between Republican Vice President George H.W. Bush and Democrat Geraldine Ferraro held on October 11, 1984, in Philadelphia, Pennsylvania.

WHAT YOU SHOULD KNOW ABOUT THE 47 U.S. PRESIDENTS

In the **1984 election**, Republicans **Ronald Reagan** and **George H.W. Bush** defeated Democrats **Walter Mondale** and **Geraldine Ferraro** 54,455,075 to 37,577,185 in the popular vote and 525 to 13 in the electoral vote. Ferraro was the **first woman** from a major party to run on a presidential ticket. The Republican victory was won by the largest margin in history. The **Republicans** held control of the Senate 53-46, and the **Democrats** still controlled the House 242-192, although the Republicans had gained some seats.

President Reagan's initial **cabinet** during his **second term** included **Vice President** George H.W. Bush, **Secretary of State** Alexander Haig, **Secretary of the Treasury** James Baker, **Attorney General** Edwin Meese, **Secretary of the Interior** Donald Hodel, **Secretary of Agriculture** John Block, **Secretary of Labor** William Block, **Secretary of Commerce** Malcolm Baldridge, **Secretary of Defense** Caspar Weinberger, **Secretary of Housing and Urban Development** Samuel Pierce, **Secretary of Transportation** Elizabeth Dole, **Secretary of Energy** James Herrington, **Secretary of Health and Human Services** Otis Bowen and **Secretary of Education** William Bennett.

Reagan's troika was now gone, **Baker** was Secretary of the Treasury, **Deaver** had become a lobbyist, and **Meese** was Attorney General.

In his January 20, **1985, inaugural address**, Reagan stated, "It is not my intention to do away with government. But **government is not the solution to your problems**, government is the problem," and "Peace is the highest aspiration of the American people."

Shortly after, he approved the **1985 Consolidated Budget Reconciliation Act (COBRA)**, which assured unemployed individuals access to health insurance for a limited period of time, and the **1985 Balanced Budget and Emergency Deficit Control Act**, which provided automatic spending cuts when the deficit exceeded the budget.

In **García vs San Antonio Metropolitan Transit Authority** (1985), the U.S. Supreme Court ruled that under the Commerce Clause, Congress is empowered to extend the minimum-wage and overtime requirements of the Fair Labor Standards Act to state and local governments. And in **New Jersey vs T.L.O.** (1985), the U.S. Supreme Court ruled that the Fourth Amendment's prohibition against unreasonable searches and seizures applies to searches conducted by public school officials in a school setting.

After **Iran** captured a high-ranking **CIA officer** in 1985, they offered him up in exchange for weapons. Reagan agreed, and **Colonel Oliver North** handled the exchange but diverted the proceeds of the weapons to support the anti-communist **Contra** insurgents in Nicaragua. This became the **Iran-Contra Affair**, and President Reagan appeared on TV and said the proceeds portion of the agreement was a mistake.

After setting the record of being in the chief of staff job for over four years, **Baker needed a change**. When Secretary of the Treasury **Donald Regan** suggested they switch jobs, Baker jumped at the opportunity. When the president agreed, it was done. And while Baker was a success in his new job, Regan had a difficult time. As the former Chair of Merrill Lynch, he was **accustomed to giving orders** rather than seeking consensus. And he could not hide his very large ego. He even had himself announced before entering a room. He was acting as if he were president. That was bad enough, but when **he hung up on the First Lady**, that was not simply a firing offense; Baker thought it a hanging offense. When the president learned of this, he asked for Regan's resignation and got it. They never spoke again. Regan was replaced with former Senate Majority Leader Howard Baker, the **great conciliator**. Like Jim Baker before him, Howard Baker knew that he could never substitute his judgement for that of the president.

Reagan's policies, labeled **Reaganomics,** were based on the economic theory of **supply-side economics** by Milton Friedman. The economy recovered and grew, until stocks were overpriced, and the stock market plummeted on October 19, 1987.

Reagan's style of management was **even-tempered and personable**. He enjoyed **listening** to vigorous debates on different opinions both inside and outside his cabinet meetings. Growing up during the **Great Depression**, Reagan was impressed with FDR's fireside chats, and when he became president, he took former President Nixon's advice and did daily **ten-minute radio** messages.

In 1985, Congress increased the annual pay of legislators to $75,100 (up from 1984's $72,600). The annual pay of associate justices of the U.S. Supreme Court was increased to $104,100 (up from 1984's $100,600), and the chief justice's annual pay was increased to $108,400 (up from 1984's $104,700).

For **breakfast**, the Reagans preferred bran cereal and melon or grapefruit. For **lunch**, Nancy preferred a salad, but the president liked either hot dogs or hamburgers and either navy or black bean soup. For **dinner**, both preferred Mexican cuisine (chili rellenos, enchiladas, guacamole, and refried beans). The president also liked steak and baked potato or meatloaf and mashed potatoes. Both liked sweet desserts. The president liked everything; Nancy was a picky eater. Reagan's **favorite snack** was the jellybean, the smaller in size the better. He substituted **jellybeans** for smoking. At **state dinners** (reportedly a total of 54), the menu favored the person being honored. Place settings typically ranged between twelve and twenty.

In 1986, Reagan signed **five pieces of legislation**: the **1986 Immigration Reform and Control Act**, which forbid the hiring of illegal aliens; the **1986 Age Discrimination Act**, which made mandatory retirement at any age illegal; the **1986 Federal Employer Retirement System Act**, which extended salary reduction plans to federal civilian employees; the **1986 Omnibus Budget Reconciliation Act**, which defined benefit funding; and the **1986 Tax Reform Act**, which made extensive changes to the definitions, forms, amounts, and timing of income and taxes.

In 1986, Congress increased the annual pay of the cabinet secretaries to $88,800 (up from 1984's $86,200).

In 1986, the **SEC** permitted tax withholding requirements to be met with shares of stock from an award or option if an irrevocable decision was made at least six months before the event. A year later they ruled that sales of shares acquired through stock option exercises were no longer required to be disclosed in the proxy. Also in 1986, Reagan elevated Supreme Court Associate **William Rehnquist** to **Chief Justice** following the resignation of Chief Justice Warren Burger. Following that action, Reagan nominated **Antonin Scalia** to the seat vacated by Rehnquist. Scalia was approved by the Senate 98-0 on September 17, 1986.

In the 1986 midterms, the **Democrats** took control of **both houses**, Senate 55-45 and House 258-164.

In a **1986** *Fortune* magazine article, Reagan explained his management style: "I believe you surround yourself with the **best people** you can find, **delegate** authority and **don't interfere** as long as the overall policy that you have decided upon is being carried out." Reagan's clarity of ideology allowed him to keep from micromanaging policy. Reagan once said, "When you can't make them see the light, **make them feel the heat.**"

On June 7, 1987, the 750th anniversary of Berlin's founding, Reagan stood by the Brandenburg Gate and proclaimed, "**Mr. Gorbachev, tear down this wall.**" Reagan added, "A nation could not survive without freedom, without human rights, without a religious spirit and with the force of its power directed at keeping its citizens under the gun."

Also in 1987, Congress increased the annual pay of legislators to $77,400 and later to $85,500 (up from 1985's $75,100). They also increased the annual pay of the associate justices of the U.S. Supreme Court to $107,200 and then to $110,000 (up from 1985's $104,100) and the chief justice's to $111,700 and then to $115,000 (up from 1985's $108,400). The pay of the cabinet secretaries was increased to $99,500 (up from 1986's $68,800). Congress made no other pay changes during Reagan's term of presidency.

At the end of 1987, Gorbachev and Reagan signed a treaty dismantling all American and Russian short-and intermediate-range missiles. In 1988, England's Prime Minister, Margaret Thatcher, stated Reagan, "won the Cold War without firing a shot." He provoked Russia to reform by demonstrating its inferiority.

In 1988, Reagan signed **two pieces of legislation**: the **1988 Insider Trading and Security Fraud Endorsement Act**, which increased the penalty for trading on inside information, and the **1988 Medicare Catastrophic Coverage Act**, which restructured covered benefits. And in **Hustler Magazine vs Falwell** (1988), the U.S. Supreme Court ruled that parodies of public figures and officials that do not contain defamatory false statements made with "actual malice," even those that inflict emotional distress, are protected by the First and Fourteenth Amendments against tort liability.

On January 22, 1989, Ronald Reagan stated in a **farewell address**, "The lesson of all this was, of course, that because we're a great nation, our challenges seem complex, it will always be this way. But as long as we remember our first principles and believe in ourselves, the future will always be ours." With that, he and Nancy boarded the plane. He had had the role of a lifetime, not bad for a movie actor. Flying over the White House, Reagan said to Nancy, "Look, dear, there is our little bungalow." They returned to their California home. The Reagan presidency was over. When Reagan left the presidency, his **Gallup approval rating** was at 64%, the highest at that point of any outgoing president except for FDR.

During his eight years in office, Reagan saw several changes in Soviet leadership:

- In November 1982, Leonid Brezhnev died, and former KGB head Yuri Andropov succeeded him.

- In February 1984, Yuri Andropov died, and Konstantin Cherenkov succeeded him.

- In March 1985, Konstantin Cherenkov died, and Mikhail Gorbachev succeeded him, and Foreign Minister Andrei Gromyko was fired and Eduard Shevardnadze replaced him.

Gorbachev led two reforms in Russia: **glasnost** (an increase in media freedom and an openness to diverse ideas) and **perestroika** (a shift from a centrally controlled economy to one that was market-based).

Gorbachev, like Reagan, had a simple, humble background. Both were also innovative and at times unpredictable. They agreed to four summits:

- **Geneva, Switzerland**, November 19, 1985 – Both agreed that a nuclear war could never be won and must never be fought, and America and the Soviets must reduce the mistrust and suspicion between them. This view followed the April 17, 1985 exposure of the nuclear power plant in Chernobyl, Ukraine.

- **Reykjavik, Iceland**, October 11, 1986 – Arms control and human rights were discussed, but little was accomplished. This was followed by Reagan's 1987 trip to Berlin where he shouted, "Mr. Gorbachev, tear down this wall."

- **Washington, D.C.**, December 8, 1987 – The Intermediate Range Nuclear Force (IRNF) Treaty was signed, eliminating all 859 missiles in America and 1,752 missiles in Russia. On the issue of whether the stated number of missiles had been eliminated, Reagan reminded everyone of his mantra: "trust but verify."

- **Moscow, Russia**, May 29-31, 1988 – Moderate progress on the Strategic Arms Reduction Treaty (START) was achieved, and Reagan announced that the **Evil Empire** no longer existed.

RONALD REAGAN (40TH PRESIDENT)

Gorbachev and Reagan liked each other very much. It was the basis of building **trust** in each other, and that achieved **progress**. Reagan's motto remained: **trust but verify**. Nancy told him his job was to trust. Her job was to verify.

A key factor in the Soviets' agreement to reduce the number of missiles were their concern over America's research into the **Strategic Defense Initiative**, a defense system to destroy incoming missiles. **Russia could not afford the expense** of developing a comparable system.

Reagan can be credited for the following during his eight years as president: on the domestic side, he **reduced government** and regulations, **lowered income taxes**, lowered **inflation**, and **restored economic growth**. On the foreign side: **he rescued the American hostages** held by Iran, established a **tough foreign policy** that achieved "peace through strength," and used "**trust but verify**" to create treaties and reduce nuclear arms, leading to the breakup of Russia and the end of the Cold War.

After leaving the office of the president in January 1989, to stay in shape, Reagan **exercised daily** – lifting weights, swimming, and taking long walks. While he probably **played golf** less than a dozen times while in the White House, he played several times a month once retired.

In May 1992, **Mikhail Gorbachev** visited Reagan in California to receive the first **Ronald Reagan Freedom Award**.

In 1994, Reagan published his **autobiography**, *An American Life*. During his life, he gave over 6,000 radio commentaries and penned over 10,000 letters. Ronald Reagan was the first living former president to be awarded the **Presidential Medal of Freedom** (by President Clinton). On November 5, 1994, Reagan announced he had **Alzheimer's**, and the Reagans founded the **Ronald and Nancy Reagan Research Institute** as a part of the National Alzheimer's Association.

Nancy cared for her husband until his **death from pneumonia** on June 5, 2004, at age 93. Nancy died on March 6, 2016, from **congestive heart failure** at age 94. Both were buried on the Reagan Presidential Library grounds in Simi Valley, California.

On Reagan's tomb, his words are inscribed: "I know in my heart that man is good, that what is right will always triumph, and that there is purpose and worth to each and every life."

Many historians consider him to be **one of the best presidents**. Of eight **Gallup polls** beginning in 1999 asking "Who was the **greatest President?**" surprisingly Ronald Reagan placed first in 2001, 2005, 2011, and 2012.

Key Events

Michael Bloomberg used his $10 million separation pay from Salomon Brothers to set up his own financial software service company (1981); John Gutfreund converted the private partnership firm of **Salomon Brothers** into Wall Street's first public finance corporation, thereby transferring the risks from themselves to their shareholders (1981); **Jack Welch** became the CEO of General Electric (1981); **Berkshire Hathaway** stock sold at $500 a share (1981); American Airlines introduced the **frequent flyer program** (1981); inflation dropped to a single digit for the first time in two years (1981); IBM introduced the **personal computer** (1981); after 19 years as TV's top anchorman, **Walter Cronkite** went off the air and was succeeded by Dan Rather (1981); singer **Diana Ross** left Motown Records and signed a $20 million contract with RCA Records (1981); 12,000 striking members of the **Professional Air Traffic Controllers Association** (founded in 1968) were fired by President Reagan (1981); *Columbia* completed the first successful space shuttle mission (1981); the U.S. Center for Disease Control reported the first case of **AIDS** (1981); the **DJIA** closed at 875.00 at year-end, down 9.2 percent (1981); Gerber introduced the Performance Accelerated Restricted Stock Award Plan (**PARSAP**), also known as a Time Accelerated Restricted Stock Award Plan (**TARSAP**) (1982); the performance-forgiveness loan was given to exercise stock options by **Digital Research** (1982); **Bendix** announced a change-of-control, the **double trigger** severance contract (1982); **NFL owners and players** settled a 57-day strike with a $1.6 billion settlement (1982); **David Packard** of HP was worth over $1 billion (1982); **unemployment** exceeded 10% for the first time since the Great Depression (1982); Eli Lilly produced **insulin** (1982); AT&T agreed to divest itself of the local Bell telephone system (the **Baby Bells**) in exchange for entering new business ventures while retaining long distance and equipment manufacturing operations (1982); American Telephone & Telegraph (**AT&T**) settled a 1974 anti-trust suit by spinning off 22 local and regional companies (1982); *USA Today* began publication (1982); **compact discs** appeared (1982); **Johnson & Johnson** removed all their Tylenol products from stores nationwide after a product-tampering incident killed seven people in Chicago (1982); **Dr. Barney Clark** became the first recipient of an artificial heart (1982); the **federal budget deficit** exceeded $100 billion for the first time (1982); Congress designated the third Monday in January as **Martin Luther King Jr. Day** (1982); *In Search of Excellence* was written by Thomas Peters and Robert Waterman (1982); many agreed that the **bull market** which began in August with the DJIA at 777 would run for almost 20 years (1982); the **DJIA** closed at 1,046.54 at year-end, up 19.6 percent (1982); Michael Milliken of Drexel Burnham Lambert fostered the use of **junk bonds** in takeovers (1983); **Berkshire Hathaway** stock sold at $1,000 a share (1983); **Chrysler** paid back the remainder of its federal loan (1983); the first cell phone was introduced by **Motorola** (1983); the **Internet** was born (1983); Reagan's executive order permitted civilian use of the Pentagon's GPS (**Global Positioning Service**) (1983); **Chrysler** introduced the mini-van (1983); Mafia head **Meyer Lansky** died of lung cancer at age 80 (1983); *The Change Masters* was written by Rosabeth Moss Kanter (1983); the **United States Football League** began playing with 12 teams, but it ended operations three years later (1983); in Chicago, Democrat Harold Washington became the nation's **first Black mayor** (1983); George H.W. Bush was the **first VP to act as president while a president was indisposed** - President Reagan underwent colon surgery (1983); 240 **United States Marines** were killed in Beirut by terrorists (1983); the U.S. invaded **Grenada** following a Marxist coup (1983); **Sally Ride** became the first American woman in space (1983); the **DJIA** closed at 1,258.64 at year-end, up 20.3 percent (1983); the United States dollar soared on the international market as inflation and unemployment both declined (1984); **Dell** became a public company (1984); the **Macintosh** computer from **Apple** was introduced (1984); Cincinnati Reds baseball player **Pete Rose** was banned for life from baseball for gambling (1984); during the night, Baltimore Colts owner **Robert Irsay** moved the team to Indianapolis (1984); Miami quarterback **Dan Marino** set a record of 48 TD passes in a season (1984); New York Ranger **Wayne Gretzky** surpassed **Gordie Howe** for career points with 1,072 (1984); the Federal Transportation Agency reduced funds to states that had **drinking ages under 21** (1984); the **DJIA** closed at 1,211.57 at year-end, down 3.7 percent (1984); **Steve Jobs** was pushed out of Apple by the board of directors (1985); **Bear Stearns** went public (1985); Sperry Rand and Burroughs merged to form **Unisys** (1985); the Navy Communication Specialist **John Walker** was arrested after 20 years of being a spy for Russia (1985); mob boss **Paul Castellano** was killed in front of Sparks Steakhouse in New York City by **John Gotti** who assumed the Gambino leadership (1985); **Palestinian terrorists** hijacked a cruise ship in the Mediterranean, killing one American (1985); *Competitive Advantage: Creating and Sustaining Superior Performance* was written by Michael Porter (1985); the **DJIA** closed at 1,546.67 at year-end, up 27.7 percent (1985); **private sector union** membership was at 14 percent of the workforce (1986); **Morgan Stanley** went public (1986); IBM outsourced microprocessors to **Intel** (1985) and operating systems to **Microsoft** (1986); Wall Streeter **Ivan Boesky** was fined $100 million by the SEC for illegal inside stock market trading and was sentenced to three years in prison (1986); the Jacob K. Javits **Convention Center** opened in New York City (1986); General Electric acquired **Kidder, Peabody** for $600 million and **RCA** for $6.4 billion (1986); **Zsa Zsa Gabor** married her ninth husband, Fredric Von Anhalt (1986); *The Transformational Leader* was written by Noel Tichy (1986); the **Walking Liberty** silver dollar was introduced (1986); space shuttle **Challenger** exploded in space, killing all seven on board (1986); the **DJIA** closed at 1,895.95 at year-end, up 22.6 percent (1986); the **stock market crashed**, but recovered by year-end (1987); the **DJIA** closed at 1,938.83 at year-end, up 2.3 percent (1987); **Betamax** lost virtually all of the video market to VHS (1988); Office Depot went public (1988); New York City's **Hell's Kitchen Westies** were all in jail or dead (1988); a terrorist bomb on a **Pan Am flight** killed all 259 on board over Scotland (1988); the play *Phantom of the Opera* opened on Broadway (1988);

Washington Redskins quarterback **Doug Williams** became the first African American to start and win a Super Bowl (1988); Surgeon General Koop declared that **smoking is addictive** (1988); **Snapple** bottled ice tea was introduced (1988); **Drexel Burnham Lambert** pleaded guilty to insider trading and paid $650 million in fines (1988); **Capital One** was founded (1988); the **DJIA** closed at 2,168.57 at year-end, up 11.9 percent (1988); RJR **Nabisco** was taken over by Kohlberg Kravis Roberts with $26 billion in junk bonds (1989); and Stern Stewart trademarked **EVA** (1989).

George H.W. Bush
(41ST President)

January 20, 1989 – January 20, 1993

George Herbert Walker Bush was born on June 12, 1924, to Prescott Bush and Dorothy Walker Bush in Milton, Massachusetts. He was **named after his grandfather**, George Herbert Walker, a prominent, wealthy investment banker. Bush's father, Prescott, was also a prominent, wealthy banker. And Prescott was a Republican **U.S. senator** from Connecticut from 1952 to 1963. Prescott was called "Pop" by GHW, so GHW became "Little Pop," which was shortened to **"Poppy"** when he went to college. He was called **Pop** by his children and later **Grampy** by his grandchildren. George grew up with three brothers, Prescott, Jonathan, and William, and a sister, Nancy. George's mother, Dorothy, was from a wealthy Missouri family. She believed in being humble and helping others – attributes she passed on to her children. She also taught them that "hatred corrodes the container it is carried in."

George attended private schools and at age 13 enrolled in **the Phillips Academy** in Andover, Massachusetts. There he was active in sports and graduated in 1942, and he then enlisted in the U.S. Navy. He graduated from the **Navy aviator** program before his 19th birthday, making him the youngest naval pilot on record. At age 20, on his **58th mission,** he bombed a Japanese radio station on the small island of Chichi Jima, some 700 miles south of Japan. While over the island, his plane was hit by gunfire, and he parachuted into the ocean. He drifted for over three hours before being rescued by the U.S. submarine *Finback*. Unfortunately, his two crew members drowned in the Pacific Ocean. George was awarded the **Distinguished Flying Cross** for bravery and returned to the U.S. and a Michigan naval base, where he met and **married Barbara Pierce**, daughter of a New York magazine publisher, in 1945. They would go on to have **six children: George** (later to become the 43rd president), John "**Jeb**" (later to become governor of Florida), **Neil** (later an investment banker), **Marvin, Dorothy** "Doro," and **Robin** (who died at age three). After his marriage, George enrolled in **Yale University**, where, like his father, he was a member of the prestigious **Skull and Bones Society**. He was also **captain of the baseball team** and played first base on a team that twice was the runner-up in the **College World Series**.

After graduation, Bush moved the family to **Odessa, Texas**, and founded an oil company. In 1966, Bush was elected to the **House of Representatives**, where he served two terms. After he lost an election for the U.S. Senate, President Nixon appointed him U.S. **Ambassador to the United Nations**. In 1971, he took over the

chairmanship of the Republican National Committee, and he was given the task of asking **President Nixon** to **resign in 1974**. He also served as **envoy to** China under President Ford and **director of the CIA** (also under President Ford), but Jimmy Carter chose to replace him in 1976, and Bush returned to Houston and the oil business. In 1979, Bush decided to run for president, but he was defeated by Ronald Reagan in the primaries, who then asked him to run as his vice president.

In the **1980 election**, Republicans **Ronald Reagan** and **George H.W. Bush** defeated Democrats President **Jimmy Carter** and Vice President **Walter Mondale** 43,904,153 to 35,483,883 in the popular vote and 383 to 49 in the electoral vote. John Anderson ran as part of the National Unity Party (without a vice president) and received 5,720,060 popular votes and no electoral votes.

In the **1984 election**, Republicans President **Ronald Reagan** and Vice President **George H.W. Bush** defeated Democrats **Walter Mondale** and **Geraldine Ferraro** 54,455,075 to 37,577,185 in the popular vote and 525 to 13 in the electoral vote. Ferraro was the first woman from a major party to be named on a national ticket.

Bush was the only vice president to serve as acting president. It was while President Reagan underwent colon surgery in 1985.

With Reagan ineligible to run again for president after having served the maximum of two terms, Bush decided to run for president in 1988. Bush had one of the longest government resumes of any president: House of Representatives; Chairman of the Republican National Committee; Director of the CIA; U.S. Liaison Office Head in China; U.S. Ambassador to the United Nations; and U.S. Vice President (for Ronald Reagan). Bush was well qualified to run for president. Bush once said, "I have strong opinions of my own, strong opinions, but I don't always agree with them."

Bush chose Indiana U.S. Senator **Daniel Quayle** as his running mate. **Daniel Danforth Quayle** was born on February 4, 1947, in Lebanon, Indiana. His father was an advertising manager and sportswriter for the local newspaper. Dan made the school **golf team** and then the varsity team at DePauw University in Greenville, Indiana, where he was also a member of the Kappa Epsilon fraternity. He worked waiting tables and doing kitchen chores. Upon graduation, he joined the **National Guard** and avoided being drafted. He later graduated **law school** at Purdue University, where he met his wife-to-be, Marilyn Tucker. In 1976, he was elected to the **U.S. House of Representatives**. He continued to find time for golf but was re-elected in 1978. In 1980, he defeated Democrat Birch Bayh for the **U.S. Senate**. The support of President Reagan led to Quayle's re-election. He then began making himself known to Vice President Bush and aligned himself with Bush's philosophy. Quayle's four years as vice president did little to enhance his image. Out of the office, he returned to the golf course. In 1999, he declared his candidacy for president, finishing eighth in an Iowa straw poll. Quayle dropped out of the race and virtually disappeared.

There were **two televised presidential debates** between Republican George H.W. Bush and Democrat Michael Dukakis. The first was held on September 25, 1988, in Winston-Salem, North Carolina. The second was held on October 13, 1988, in Los Angeles, California. Massachusetts Governor **Michael Dukakis** was labeled as "soft" on crime when he released convicted murderer Willie Horton, who went on to commit a rape. Michael Dukakis did not help his image when he was photographed aboard an army tank with a large helmet and sappy grin.

There was **one televised vice presidential debate** between Republican Daniel Quayle and Democrat Lloyd Bentsen. At the debate, Senator Dan Quayle defended his inexperience as similar to the late JFK's. Senator Bentsen turned to him and said, "I served with Jack Kennedy. I knew Jack Kennedy. Jack Kennedy was a friend of mine. **Senator, you are no Jack Kennedy.**"

In the **1988 election**, Republicans **George H.W. Bush** and **Dan Quayle** defeated Democrats **Michael Dukakis** and **Lloyd Bentsen** 48,886,097 to 41,809,074 in the popular vote and 426 to 111 in the electoral vote. George H.W. Bush was the fourteenth vice president to become president (John Adams, Thomas Jefferson, Martin Van Buren, John Tyler, Millard Fillmore, Andrew Johnson, Chester Arthur, Theodore Roosevelt, Calvin Coolidge, Harry Truman, Richard Nixon, Lyndon B. Johnson, and Gerald Ford preceded him). Only four vice presidents moved directly from that position to president via election (not death): John Adams, Thomas Jefferson, Martin Van Buren, and George H.W. Bush.

The initial **cabinet** of President Bush included **Vice President** Dan Quayle, **Secretary of State** James Baker, **Secretary of the Treasury** Nicholas Brady, **Attorney General** Richard Thornburgh, **Secretary of the Interior** Manuel Lujan, **Secretary of Agriculture** Clayton Yeutter, **Secretary of Labor** Elizabeth Dole, **Secretary of Commerce** Robert Mosbacher, **Secretary of Defense** Richard Cheney, **Secretary of Housing and Urban Development** Jack Kemp, **Secretary of Transportation** Samuel Skinner, **Secretary of Energy** James Watkins, **Secretary of Health and Human Services** Louis Sullivan, **Secretary of Education** Lauro Cavazos and **Secretary of Veterans Affairs** Edward Derwinski. Bush added the cabinet position of **veterans' affairs** due to the growth in the numbers of retired veterans; their healthcare issues were becoming a major issue.

In 1989, **Congress increased the annual pay** of the cabinet secretaries to $107,300 (up from 1987's $99,500). Also, Bush signed **three key acts** in **1989** into law: the **Worker Adjustment and Retraining Notification Act**, requiring a 60-day notice of a mass layoff or a plant closing; the **Deficit Reduction Reconciliation Act**, which modified Medicare reimbursement; and the **Omnibus Budget Reconciliation Act**, which added transitional rules for Medicare benefits.

In **Webster vs Reproductive Health Services** (1989), the U.S. Supreme Court ruled that a state statute that prohibited the use of public employees and facilities for non-lifesaving abortion services, and public funds, employees, and facilities for non-lifesaving abortion counseling services, and that mandated viability tests before performing abortions, was constitutional. And in **Texas vs Johnson** (1989), the U.S. Supreme Court ruled that the Due Process Clause of the Fourteenth Amendment does not forbid a state from requiring that evidence of an incompetent's wishes regarding the withdrawal of life-sustaining treatment be proven by "clear and convincing evidence."

Reportedly, **Bush had a 12-year affair** with his aide, Jennifer Fitzgerald, beginning when she joined his staff in 1974. The *Washington Post* said, "Fitzgerald has served the President-elect in a variety of positions."

Bush was 64 years old on the date of his inauguration. In his March 20, **1989, inaugural address**, Bush stated, "A new breeze is blowing. And a world refreshed by freedom seems reborn. The totalitarian era is passing." Bush added, "We know what works; freedom works. We know what's right: freedom is right." He also stated, "If anyone tells you that America's best days are behind her, they're looking the wrong way." But the Democrats still controlled Congress: Senate 55-45 and House 260-175. The 1990 midterms were the same: Senate 56-44 and House 267-167.

Bush famously said, **"Read my lips, no new taxes."** He would later regret these words when a new tax law was required, in order to reduce the deficit by $500 million and continue the Reagan policy of less government and more defense.

George liked to fish, hunt, and play golf and tennis. And he put a **horseshoe pit** on the South Lawn of the White House. He also created the **Daily Points of Light** recognizing someone in the White House each day for their volunteer work.

In 1990, **Congress increased the annual pay** of the associate justices of the U.S. Supreme Court to $118,600 (up from 1987's $110,000) and the pay of the chief justice to $124,000 (up from 1987's $115,000). The pay of the cabinet secretaries was increased to $138,900 (up from 1989's $107,300). And Congress increased the pay of the legislators twice, to $96,600 and $98,400 (up from 1987's $89,500).

Bush signed **five key acts** in **1990** into law: the **Clean Air Act** banned cancer-causing emissions and city pollution; the **Older Workers Protection Act** restored the equal benefit or equal cost principle and required that employee-signed waivers be voluntary; the **Americans with Disability Act** provided employment protections to mentally and physically challenged persons; the **Omnibus Budget Reconciliation Act** stated changes in tax definitions and rates; and the **Securities Enforcement Remedies and Penny Stock Reform Act** increased the power of the Securities and Exchange Commission and defined a penny stock.

While **Bush had a Reagan-like conservative philosophy**, he kept few of Reagan's staff. And unlike Reagan's troika, Bush had two key people: his campaign manager and former New Hampshire Governor **John Sununu**, and the Director of the Office of Management and Budget **Richard Darman**. Sununu was very bright and well organized. But many thought him abrasive, headstrong, and temperamental. He engaged in turf battles and wasn't well-liked. Sununu's major opponent was **Dick Darman**, who was also very bright and had a number of jobs under both Reagan and Ford. Like Sununu, Darman was not well liked, especially in his role as director of the Office of Management and Budget, a cabinet-level position. But Darman and Sununu joined forces and became the dominant voice in the Bush administration. Domestic policy was mainly controlled by Darman and Sununu, while **foreign policy** was the domain of Defense Secretary Dick Cheney, General Colin Powell, and Bush himself. Many historians agree that Bush's **foreign policy** was much better than his **domestic policy**.

In 1991, **Congress increased the annual pay** of the associate justices of the U.S. Supreme Court to $153,600 (up from 1990's $118,600) and the chief justice's pay to $160,600 (up from 1990's $124,000). The pay of the cabinet secretaries was increased to $143,800 (up from 1990's $138,900). And the pay of the legislators was increased twice, to $101,100 and then to $125,100 (up from 1990's $98,400).

Bush signed **three key acts** in **1991** into law: the **Securities Exchange Act** introduced Forms 3, 4, and 5; the **FDIC Improvement Act** required boards of directors to defend company practices; and the **Civil Rights Restoration Act** defined the rights of those whose civil rights had been violated.

Bush benefited from the **Reagan-Gorbachev** weakening of the Soviet Union that led to the **fall of the Berlin Wall** on

November 9, 1989, and the **implosion of the country** in December 1991. But before the collapse of Russia in 1991, the United States led a coalition of countries in an attack driving Iraq out of Kuwait in **1990's Operation Desert Shield,** and an invasion and victory in Iraq in 1991's **Operation Desert Storm**. Bush and Russian President Yeltsin announced the formal **end to the "cold war"** in 1992. Following these victories, **Bush's approval rating** soared to a historic 91%. But by late 1992, it had plummeted to 37%. The reasons for the drop included record unemployment, Bush having to reverse a promise of no tax increases due to federal deficits and widespread feelings that, after 12 years of Republican presidents, it was time for a change. Clinton's campaign manager, James Carville, kept shouting, "It's the economy, stupid."

In 1992, **Congress increased the annual pay** of the associate justices of the U.S. Supreme Court to $159,000 (up from 1991's $153,600) and the chief justice's pay to $166,200 (up from 1991's $160,600). The pay of the cabinet secretaries was increased to $148,400 (up from 1991's $143,800). And the pay of the legislators was increased to $129,500 (up from 1991's $125,100).

Bush signed **two key acts** in **1992** into law: the **Pension Portability Act** permitted lump sum transfers from pension payouts; and the **Unemployment Compensation Amendment Act** liberalized rollover rules between plans and IRAs, with a 20% tax withholding on non-IRA rollovers.

In **Planned Parenthood of Southeastern Pennsylvania vs Casey** (1992), the U.S. Supreme Court reaffirmed *Roe vs Wade* and a woman's right to have an abortion prior to fetal viability under the Due Process Clause of the Fourteenth Amendment but ruled that the standard of judicial review for evaluating State regulations on abortion should be less stringent.

Bush was known for making statements, including: "the undecided could go one way or the other," "I believe in both unions and non-unions," "I never apologize for America, regardless of the facts," "does everyone who has a job, want a job?", "some say I have no vision, I don't see that," and "war is a very dangerous place."

On May 7, 1992, the **27th Amendment to the U.S. Constitution** was ratified. It stated that no pay changes for a member of Congress shall take effect until the next election of the representatives.

There were **three televised presidential debates** between Democrat Bill Clinton, Republican President George H.W. Bush, and Independent Ross Perot. The first was held on October 11, 1992, in St. Louis, Missouri. The second was held on October 15, 1992, in Richmond, Virginia, and the third debate was held on October 19, 1992, in East Lansing, Michigan.

There was **one televised vice presidential debate** between Republican Vice President Dan Quayle, Democrat Al Gore, and Independent James Stockdale on October 13, 1992, in Atlanta, Georgia.

In the 1992 election, Democrats **Bill Clinton** and **Al Gore** defeated Republicans President **George Bush** and Vice President **Dan Quayle** 44,908,233 to 39,102,282 in the popular vote and 370 to 168 in the electoral vote. On the Independent ticket, **Ross Perot** and **James Stockdale** received 19,221,433 popular votes but no electoral votes. It was believed if Perot and Stockdale had not entered the election, Bush and Quayle would have been reelected. In 1992, Bush had a Gallup poll approval rating of 41.8%.

Following the defeat, **Bush was depressed** but nonetheless left the traditional letter of congratulations for Clinton on the presidential desk. The running for election of **governor of Florida** and **Texas** by his sons Jeb and George, respectively, helped heal the pain, but the rejection of the voters still hurt. To further ease the pain, George wrote down a **bucket list**. It began with more time with his wife, children, and grandchildren. This was followed by the completion of his president's library, setting up foundations for education and service-oriented programs, publishing a book containing letters he had written and received, the reenactment of his parachuting in the war, and a visit to the island of Chichi Jima that he had bombed to lay a wreath over his underwater plane and the bodies of his two crewmen. All these goals were accomplished. Also, Bush established the **George and Barbara Bush Foundation** that promoted education and public service and the George Bush **School of Government and Public Service**. He made **six parachute jumps**, the last at age 90. And although it was not on his bucket list, George and Bill Clinton became very **good friends**. Some believed that George became a father figure to Bill.

It took a **significant staff** to help George accomplish all of this, but his **energy**, sense of **humor,** and **pleasant manner** won over the needed volunteers. Few would believe the **amount** of mail he received and correspondence he created, not to mention his **extensive** travel and the various **projects** he created **after his retirement**.

Queen Elizabeth knighted George in 2009, but Barbara told George not to ever expect her to call him **Sir**. Bush was the second president to receive the award. **Reagan was the first**. Queen Elizbeth respected what H.W. had accomplished. President Obama gave Bush the **Presidential Medal of Freedom**, the country's highest civil award. George Bush's name was given to many things and places. Among his favorites were an aircraft carrier, the CIA Headquarters, and the Houston airport.

George had a number of medical problems, but that did not stop him from parachuting (with army assistance) on his 75th, 80th, and 85th birthdays. He had both hips replaced, one in 2000 and the other in 2007. He had back surgery in 2008. George came down with Parkinson's Disease in 2010. This led to a cane, followed by a walker, and finally a wheelchair. The disease also affected his speech. He had a blood clot in his lung in 2012 and food poisoning in 2018.

Wife Barbara suffered from a **defective heart** valve and **died** in April 2018 at the age of 93. She and George had been **married for 73 years**. George **died** after his wife on November 30, 2018 at the age of 94. Appropriately, George once stated, "The idea is to die young, as late as possible." He aged with dignity and never lost his sense of humor. After lying in state in the Rotunda of the Capitol Building, George joined Barbara in being buried in the Bush Library.

KEY EVENTS

Some 800 **insolvent savings and loan associations** were "bailed out" with $125 billion of federal money (1989); **Drexel Burnham Lambert** pleaded guilty to insider trading and paid some $650 million in fines (1989); **WorldCom** went public (1989); a seat on the **New York Stock Exchange** cost a record $625,000 (1989); the market price for a **New York taxicab medallion** was $136,000 vs. $10 in 1937 (1989); New York City required separating **smokers from non-smokers** in restaurants (1989); "Queen of Mean" hotel operator **Leona Helmsley** received a four-year prison sentence and a $7.1 million fine for income tax evasion; she bragged, "Only little people pay taxes." (1989); **Kohlberg Kravis Roberts bought** out **RJR Nabisco** for $25 billion (1989); **Panama** was invaded and its leader, Noriega was captured (1989); **Army General Colin Powell** became the first Black chairman of the Joint Chiefs of Staff (1989); **Douglas Wilder** (Virginia) was the nation's first Black governor (1989); Lieutenant Colonel Oliver North was found guilty on charges of creating the **Iran-Contra Scandal**, which was later overturned (1989); mismanagement in HUD and ethics violations among the Congressional leaders rocked the Capitol (1989); **Hurricane Hugo** caused $7 billion in damages (1989); the supertanker *Exxon Valdez* spilled millions of gallons of oil off the coast of Alaska (1989); a **San Francisco earthquake** before the World Series caused 63 deaths (1989); the **DJIA** closed at 2,753.20 at year-end, up 26.9 percent (1989); Russia was granted "**most favored nation**" status (1990); employee benefit changes were mainly addressed to shifting the rising cost of healthcare to employees through increased employee premiums and health maintenance organizations (HMOs) (1990); "junk bond" guru **Michael Milken** paid $500 million to settle SEC charges and was sent to prison for ten years (1990); Time Inc. and Warner Communications merged to form **Time Warner** (1990); investment bank **Drexel Burnham Lambert** collapsed in bankruptcy (1990); the **Professional Golfers Association Tour** announced it would not hold tournaments at golf clubs that held all-white memberships or showed any other signs of discrimination (1990); **Merrill Lynch** went public (1990); the **U.S. population** was close to 250 million (1990); **Frank Sinatra** performed his 1,000th concert (1990); the **DJIA** closed at 2,633.66 at year-end, down 4.3 percent (1990); the United States established diplomatic relations with former Soviet Republics as the U.S.S.R.

continued to collapse (1991); the New York automat **Horn & Hardart** closed (1991); **unemployment was at its highest** level in twenty years (1991); the Federal Reserve cut the **discount rate** to 3%, the lowest in almost thirty years (1991); **IBM** broke a lifetime employment pledge, announcing a layoff of thousands of workers (1991); **Eastern Airlines** went out of business after 68 years (1991); the **World Wide Web** was created (1991); Los Angeles policemen were indicted for beating Black motorist **Rodney King**; race riots followed (1991); **Ivana Trump** received a $25 million divorce settlement from Donald Trump (1991); the **DJIA** closed at 3,168.83 at year-end, up 20.3 percent (1991); Democrats held the White House and both houses of Congress, the first time either party did that since the Reconstruction Era (1992); Bush sent U.S. troops to **Somalia** (1992); Canada, Mexico, and the United States signed the **North American Free Trade Agreement** (1992); **Apple** introduced the **Newton** personal digital assistant (PDA) (1992); **Berkshire Hathaway** stock sold at $10,000 a share (1992); **Trans World Airlines** filed for bankruptcy (1992); pay innovations were essentially in executive compensation and were more in the way of design modification than in new forms of executive pay (1992); Disney CEO **Michael Eisner** earned almost $130 million from selling stock options (1992); changes in non-executive pay included greater use of broad-based stock options and cash incentives (1992); Mafia boss **John Gotti Sr.** was given a life sentence without parole (1992); *Tonight Show* host **Johnny Carson** retired and Jay Leno replaced him (1992); **Hurricane Andrew** caused over $25 billion in damages (1992); the **DJIA** closed at 3,301.11 at year-end, up 4.2 percent (1992); and Chicago Bulls's **Michael Jordan** scored 64 points, his second-highest-scoring game, in an upsetting 128-124 loss to the Orlando Magic (1993).

William J. Clinton
(42ᴺᴰ President)

January 20, 1993 – January 20, 2001

William Jefferson Blythe III was born on August 29, 1946, to William Jefferson Blythe Jr. and Virginia Blythe in Hope, Arkansas. His father, a **traveling salesman**, died three months after William's birth. Since his father had been married twice before marrying William's mother, William had a **half-brother**, **Roger**, and a **half-sister, Dorothy**. William was left with his **maternal grandparents** when his mother went to New Orleans to study nursing. Months later, she married **Roger Clinton** and returned to Hope, when William was four years old. Roger Clinton was an **alcoholic** and a **gambler**. He also abused his wife and William. But when William was 16 years old, Roger **adopted** William and gave him the Clinton name. His mother eventually got married five times.

In **high school**, Clinton was a very bright speed-reader who retained everything. He also wore glasses and played the **saxophone** in **a jazz trio** called the Three Blind Mice. After meeting **President Kennedy** during a Washington visit, Clinton decided to learn more about government. The following year, he interned for Arkansas **Senator William Fulbright**. Shortly after, he enrolled in **Georgetown University**. Following his graduation in 1968, Clinton won a **Rhodes Scholarship** (the first president to get one) and went on to **Oxford University** in England for three years. He returned to the United States and enrolled in **Yale University Law School**. Bill Clinton was the second president to graduate from Yale Law School in 1973; Gerald Ford was the first. While at Yale, he met **Hillary Rodham**.

Clinton's reputation as a **philanderer** had preceded him. He was handsome and personable. She was frumpy and had a superior attitude. Asked why he dated her, he said, "**She challenges me**, every moment of every day, intellectually. She makes me a better person. She gets me started, kicks my butt and makes me do the things I've got to do." **His charm and her methodology** would accomplish their mutual goal: the White House.

Hillary said she fell in love with Bill because he was "the first man who wasn't afraid of me." Later, she told a friend, "Bill Clinton is going to be president someday and I'm going to marry him." They both worked on George McGovern's presidential campaign in 1972, and both graduated from Yale in 1973. **Eligible to be drafted, Clinton** signed **a letter of intent** after graduation to join the Army Training Center, but he failed to follow through on the intention. Did this make him a draft dodger?

Bill and Hillary were married on October 11, 1975; he was 29 and she was 28. Their daughter, **Chelsea**, was born February 27, 1980. Bill Clinton grew up on an **unhealthy diet** of enchiladas, hamburgers, and fries, along with various snacks. But after **marrying Hillary**, he was put on a diet that included fruits and vegetables. While Clinton enjoyed a wide range of foods, he is the first president who **did not enjoy chocolate**; he is allergic to it.

Upon graduation, Hillary went to Washington, D.C. and joined the staff of the **House Judiciary Committee**. **Bill taught** law at the University of Arkansas in Little Rock. In 1974 he lost the race for a U.S. Senate seat, but in 1976, he was **elected attorney general** of Arkansas. And in 1978 he was elected **governor of Arkansas** at age 32, the youngest state governor. His political advisor, **Dick Morris**, was instrumental in getting Clinton elected governor and putting him on the right path for the presidency. In 1978, he began a multi-year affair with a nightclub performer, **Gennifer Flowers**. When he lost reelection in 1980, **Hillary made some changes**. She added "Clinton" to her name and dramatically improved her appearance, including makeup and clothing. Because **Clinton was reelected** in 1982, 1984, and 1986, he was nicknamed "**The Comeback Kid**."

Clinton's personal problems began with the **Whitewater scandal**, a 1978 real-estate transaction involving a bank failure, a government bailout, and illegal actions on a failed real estate agreement. This involved Bill and Hillary when Bill was governor of Arkansas. The investigation ended with no wrongdoing by the Clintons. He noted, "It's how you handle adversity, not how it affects you."

While governor, he set up a **testing program** for teachers which led to increased pay for those who passed the tests. Clinton also set up **basic skills tests** that students had to pass in order to enter high school. This led to the highest graduation rate in the nation. He also **improved healthcare programs** in the state. And he put in a **mandatory job-training program** for welfare recipients. These programs attracted the interest of companies who added some 200,000 jobs in the state. All of this helped make Clinton a candidate for national advancement in the Democratic Party. His rise was accelerated after he gave the **nomination address** at the 1988 Democratic National Convention for presidential candidate **Michael Dukakis**. Reportedly, Clinton slept with hundreds of women. But after **Gary Hart's** political meltdown over the publication of his sexual affair, Clinton had to clean up his act or he would not be elected president.

In 1990, Clinton headed up the **Democratic Leadership Council**, which gave him a platform to argue for government programs to solve national problems of inflation and slow the growth of unemployment. He met **Senator Al Gore** and the two promoted a business-oriented approach to national issues. In 1991, *Newsweek* magazine stated a poll of peers named Clinton the nation's **most effective governor**. And on October 3, 1991, Clinton announced he was running for president.

In February 1992, when lounge singer **Gennifer Flowers** announced her twelve-year affair with Clinton, Hillary led an attack on Flowers' character and veracity stating she was a liar **attempting blackmail**. And a procedure was put in place to respond to **bimbo eruptions**. Bill and Hillary decided to go on the attack together. They appeared on **"60 Minutes"** right after the 1992 Super Bowl. Bill denied the Flowers affair and **Hillary stood by her man** and asked if those with marital affairs should be stopped from running for elections to public office. An ABC

News poll said 80% of those surveyed stated Bill should not be prevented from running. And **Bill attacked President Bush** as being out of touch. While Bush advocated limited government involvement, Clinton chose to state the need for government involvement to stimulate the economy, using the phrase his campaign manager, **James Carville**, had coined: "**It's the economy, stupid**." Clinton also said he would take care of the **forgotten class, the lower-paid workers**.

In the 1992 election, Clinton chose another southerner for his vice president, **Senator Al Gore, Jr**. Clinton had worked with Gore when Clinton headed up the Democratic Leadership Council, and he liked Gore for his energy and leadership qualities. At the Democratic convention, Clinton and Gore were successful in getting the nomination. The two made up the youngest candidate ticket in history, with a combined age of 90 (Clinton 46 and Gore 44).

In his presidential campaign, Clinton faced three issues: his **extramarital affairs**, "forgetting" his Vietnam **draft induction notice**, and an 83% **approval rating for his opponent**, President George H.W. Bush. Also, the Democrats had lost their power base, having lost the 1980, 1984, 1988, and 1992 presidential elections. Clinton believed the Democrats lost because the Party had become **too liberal**.

There were **three televised presidential debates** between Republican President **George Bush**, Democrat **Bill Clinton**, and Independent **Ross Perot**. The first was held on October 11, 1992, in St. Louis, Missouri. The second was held on October 15, 1992, in Richmond, Virginia. And the third was held on October 19, 1992, in East Lansing, Michigan.

There was **one televised vice presidential debate** between Republican Vice President **Dan Quayle**, Democrat **Al Gore**, and Independent **James Stockdale** held on October 15, 1992, in Atlanta, Georgia.

In the **1992 presidential election,** Democrats **Bill Clinton** and **Al Gore** defeated Republicans President **George H.W. Bush** and Vice President **Dan Quayle** 44,908,233 to 39,102,282 for Independents **Ross Perot** and **James Stockdale** in the popular vote, and 370 to 168 in the electoral vote. Perot and Stockdale received no electoral votes.

Albert Arnold Gore Jr. was born on March 31, 1948. His mother was one of the first women to graduate from Vanderbilt University Law School. His father, Albert Gore, Sr., served 32 years in Congress – 14 as a representative and 18 as a senator. Al Gore, Jr. attended St. Albans School and then went on to graduate from **Harvard University** in 1969. He then enlisted in the U.S. Army and served in **Vietnam.** Following an honorable discharge, he worked as a **newspaper reporter** in Nashville before becoming a student at **Vanderbilt University.** After graduation, he **married his longtime girlfriend,** Mary Elizabeth "Tipper" Aitcheson, and they went on to have four children. He was elected to the **House of Representatives** in 1976 and won reelections in 1978, 1980, and 1982 before being elected to the **U.S. Senate** in 1984 and re-elected in 1990.

The Democrats controlled Congress: Senate 57-43 and House 276-258. In his January 20, **1993, inaugural address,** Clinton stated that government was neither the problem nor the solution. "We – the American people – we are the solution." Clinton hosted 14 inaugural balls where he played his saxophone. Their **Secret Service codes** were Eagle (Bill) and Evergreen (Hillary).

Clinton picked his good friend **Thomas "Mack" McLarty** as his first chief of staff. It was a poor choice; **Mack the Nice was a**

disorganized gatekeeper. There was no organization chart for the White House staff. The paperwork was a mess, and Clinton was late for everything. McLarty was replaced by OMB Director Leon Panetta. He was the **iron fist in a velvet glove**.

Clinton's initial **cabinet** during his first term in office included **Vice President** Al Gore, **Secretary of State** Warren Christopher, **Secretary of the Treasury** Lloyd Bentsen, **Secretary of Defense** Les Aspin, **Attorney General** Janet Reno, **Secretary of the Interior** Bruce Babbitt, **Secretary of Agriculture** Mike Espy, **Secretary of Commerce** Ronald Brown, **Secretary of Labor** Robert Reich, **Secretary of Health and Human Services** Donna Shalala, **Secretary of Housing and Urban Development** Henry Cisneros, **Secretary of Transportation** Frederico Peña, **Secretary of Energy** Hazel O'Leary, **Secretary of Education** Richard Riley, and **Secretary of Veterans Affairs** Jesse Brown. Janet Reno was the **first female attorney general**.

On the **international scene**, the United States sent air strikes against **Bosnian** troops who were engaged in "ethnic cleansing." And the U.S. joined England in **bombing Iraq** when that country violated the surrender terms of the **1991 Gulf War**. These actions were the result of international co-operation in response to acts of aggression. Clinton also successfully eliminated all the trade restrictions between Canada, Mexico, and the United States in the **1992 North American Free Trade Agreement** (NAFTA), quickly followed by the broader **General Agreement on Tariffs and Trade** (GATT), which included Asian nations. The U.S. Senate approved the Second Strategic Arms Reduction Treaty (START) with Russia and the Comprehensive Test Ban Treaty banning all nuclear weapons testing.

Clinton relied on his speed-reading skills to get through the details of the CIA prepared intelligence reports. They morphed into the **President's Intelligence checklist**: a simplified report. Asked what he thought about being president, Clinton responded, "Being president is like running a cemetery: you have a lot of people under you, but nobody is listening."

To address a federal budget deficit of close to $500 billion, one of the first actions Clinton took was to get the **1993 Revenue Reconciliation Act** approved, putting a $250 billion tax increase on the wealthy by introducing a number of changes in definitions and tax rules, the **1993 Family and Medical Leave Act** permitted people with medical problems or with newborn children to take up to 12 weeks of unpaid leave of absence. The **1993 Brady Act** required background checks on gun buyers.

In May 1993, Clinton committed "**Travelgate**." Reportedly, he fired office workers in the White House travel office in order to hire Hillary's friend, **Vince Foster**, who later apparently committed suicide over Foster's handling of Travelgate. Also in 1993, President Clinton signed the Oslo Accords with PLO leader **Yasser Arafat** and Israeli Prime Minister **Yitzhak Rabin** with the PLO recognizing Israel's right to exist. In December 1993, Clinton had to respond to "**Troopergate**," alleging he used Arkansas state troopers to meet sexual partners. He was cleared.

In 1993, Congress increased the annual pay of the legislators to $133,600 (up from 1992's $129,500). It also increased the pay of the associate justices of the U.S. Supreme Court to $164,100 (up from 1992's $159,000) and the chief justice's pay to $171,500 (up from 1991's 166,200).

Rather than take an 'up or down" stance on the issue of homosexuals in the military, he pushed a "**don't ask, don't tell**" policy in 1994, meaning military personnel were not required to answer questions about their sexual preferences. This approach did not settle the issue and was considered a failure. When asked if he ever used marijuana, he replied, "Yes, but I never inhaled."

Probably Bill's **biggest failure** was not being able to get his **national health insurance** plan accepted. He appointed his wife in charge of making it happen, just as she had done in Arkansas, but the health insurance industry responded with a heavy influx on TV and other media highlights, stating the proposed plan was too complicated and would put the government in charge of individual health.

The **1994 Uniformed Services Employment and Reemployment Rights Act** clarified and supplemented coverage of the **1974 Vietnam Era Veterans Reemployment Rights Act**, and the **1994 Retirement Protection Act** made a number of changes on cash out values, mortality tables, and underfunded pension plans.

A **state dinner** at the White House might include smoked shrimp, roast beef, various vegetables, some type of potato, salad, and sherbet, served with California wines. Regional specialties included apple pie, Florida key lime pie, Louisiana gumbo, and New York pizza topped with pineapple. But given a choice, President Clinton would choose fried chicken or grilled beef brisket with enchiladas.

In 1994, with Mexico facing international financial collapse, Clinton sent $12 billion in loans in exchange for Mexico's welcoming foreign investment. Mexico paid off most of the loan on schedule. Also, Clinton aided the agreement between Israel and Palestine and between England and Northern Ireland. But Clinton changed his position on **trade with China** because of the country's human rights violations. Later, he favored open trade, believing it would encourage China to promote a more favorable government position.

In May 1994, **Paula Jones** filed a suit of sexual harassment against Clinton for actions taken while he was Arkansas governor. The U.S. Supreme Court ruled that the charge against a sitting president could continue. On April 1, 1998, the case was dismissed by a district judge. Clinton and Jones agreed to an $850,000 settlement. Later in 1994, he provided federal money to the states, enabling them to hire 100,000 police officers.

Kenneth Starr was appointed to probe the **Whitewater** affair in 1994. Clinton suffered further personal setbacks when a grand jury indicted his **Whitewater** business partners for fraud in 1995.

The **1995 Consolidated Omnibus Budget Reconciliation Act** required continued medical coverage for terminated employees, and the **1995 Private Securities Litigation Act** made plaintiffs (not lawyers) responsible for directing class action lawsuits.

In 1995, when Clinton **refused to make major cuts to Medicare** and other programs demanded by the Gingrich budget, the **Republicans shut down the government**. It lasted for six weeks, and the Republicans lost the public trust. Later that year, Clinton proposed **balancing the budget** in ten years. The **Republicans again shut down the government,** but Clinton prevailed, and his plan passed. Clinton's first term of office ended with prolonged peacetime, economic growth, and low inflation and unemployment. **Clinton was successful** in reducing the number of government employees, balancing the federal budget, and reducing welfare expenses.

In **United States vs Lopez** (1995), the U.S. Supreme Court ruled that Congress exceeded its power to legislate under the

Commerce Clause in enacting the Gun-Free School Zones Act of 1990, which prohibits knowingly possessing a firearm in a school zone, as possession of a gun is not an economic activity that "substantially affects interstate commerce."

There were **two televised presidential debates** between Democratic President **Bill Clinton** and Republican **Bob Dole**. The first was held on October 6, 1996, in Hartford, Connecticut. The second was held on October 16, 1996, in San Diego, California.

And there was **one televised vice presidential** debate between Democratic Vice President **Al Gore** and Republican **Jack Kemp** held on October 9, 1996, in St. Petersburg, Florida.

In the **1996 presidential election**, Democrats President **Bill Clinton** and Vice President **Al Gore** won the presidency and vice presidency over Republicans **Robert Dole** and **Jack Kemp** 45,590,703 to 37,816,307 in the popular vote and 370 to 159 in the electoral vote. Reform candidates **Ross Perot** and **Pat Choate** received 7,866,284 popular votes but no electoral votes. Clinton was the first Democrat to win back-to-back elections since FDR. **Erskine Bowles** replaced Leon Panetta **as Clinton's chief of staff**. Because of a successful campaign by Congressman Newt Gingrich, the Republicans were able to regain control of both houses: Senate 52-48 and House 230-204, their first majority in both houses in four decades.

When Clinton's second term began, a story was leaked about his **affair** with **Monica Lewinsky**, a White House intern. Namely, that she gave him oral sex. Clinton denied the affair but then apologized to his cabinet about the allegation. The reaction in the White House was to "circle the wagons" and defend the president because losing to the Republicans would be worse. 1996 was the year Clinton's lowest Gallup poll approval rating was 53%.

Clinton's initial **cabinet** during his second term in office included **Vice President** Al Gore, **Secretary of State** Madeleine Albright, **Secretary of the Treasury** Robert Rubin, **Secretary of Defense** William Cohen, **Attorney General** Janet Reno, **Secretary of the Interior** Bruce Babbitt, **Secretary of Agriculture** Daniel Glickman, **Secretary of Commerce** William Daley, **Secretary of Labor** Alexis Herman, **Secretary of Health and Human Services** Donna Shalala, **Secretary of Housing and Urban Development** Andrew Cuomo, **Secretary of Transportation** Rodney Slater, **Secretary of Energy** Frederico Peña, **Secretary of Education** Richard Riley, and **Secretary of Veterans Affairs** Togo West. Madeleine Albright was the **first female Secretary of State**.

The **1996 Health Insurance Portability and Accountability Act** introduced a number of favorable improvements in health insurance, the **1996 Source Tax Act** prohibited states from taxing income earned in the state after moving to another state, the **1996 Congressional Accountability Act** required members of Congress to apply employment laws to their staff, the **1996 Private Securities Litigation Reform Act** reduced abusive litigation and coercive settlements, and the **1996 Taxpayer Bill of Rights Act** introduced the Savings Incentive Match Plan for employees of small companies and made other beneficial changes to insurance and pension plans.

Domestically, Clinton and Federal Chairman Alan Greenspan worked to achieve a return on prosperity. In 1997, the country reached a 30-year low in unemployment and the federal budget showed a surplus. The **1997 Taxpayer Relief Act** introduced a nondeductible (Roth) IRA and made a number of changes reducing taxes.

In 1997, Congress increased the annual pay of cabinet secretaries to $151,800 (up from 1992's $148,400).

On **January 26, 1998**, Bill Clinton looked into a **TV camera** and said, "**I did not have sexual relations** with that woman – Miss Lewinsky." But on **August 17, 1998**, before a **grand jury**, Clinton admitted he had "**inappropriate intimate physical contact**" with Monica Lewinsky. But he insisted it was non-sexual contact. In his view, oral sex was not sexual contact. **Impeachment proceedings** began in the Fall of 1998. Gerald Ford said, "Clinton has a sexual addiction," and that he was a very talented guy but had no conviction. But Jimmy Carter said, "Clinton is a man of integrity and honesty." Something had to be done, so Clinton reached out and got the pollster and political consultant who got him elected governor in Arkansas, **Dick Morris**. Clinton chose the code name "Charlie" for Morris and he went around **Chief of Staff Erskine Bowles**, reworking speeches and other policy statements. Clinton enjoyed the clandestine relationship. Eventually the rivalry resulted in Morris being pushed out. But he had gotten Clinton's presidency on track. When George Stephanopoulos' book, *All Too Human*, detailed the White House interactions, he was called "**a traitor**" by some.

The 1998 midterm elections showed little change: Senate 55-45 Republicans and House 223-211 Republicans.

In 1998, Congress increased the annual pay of the legislators to $136,700 (up from 1992's $133,600). It also increased the pay of the associate justices of the U.S. Supreme Court to $167,900 (up from 1992's $164,100) and the chief justice's pay to $175,400 (up from 1993's $171,500).

The **1998 IRS Restructuring and Reform Act** lowered the long-term capital tax holding period to 12 months (it had been 18) for the 20% rate. The **1998 Securities Litigation Uniform Standards Act** amended the Securities Act of 1933 and the Securities and Exchange Act of 1934, and declared that any class action brought in state court involving a "covered security" is removable to federal court.

In **United States vs Winslow Corporation** (1998), the U.S. Supreme Court ruled that the government is liable for damages for breach of contract as they had a contractual obligation to allow the thrifts to count goodwill and capital credits toward their regulatory capital reserve requirements, and both the "unmistakability doctrine" and the "sovereign act doctrine" cannot be used by the government as a defense to liability. In **Clinton vs City of New York** (1998), the U.S. Supreme Court ruled that the Line Item Veto Act violates Article I, Section 7's Presentment Clause, legislation that passes both Houses of Congress, before becoming law, must be presented to the president to be approved or vetoed; it grants no power to the president to unilaterally amend or repeal parts of the duly enacted laws.

On December 19, 1998, the House of Representatives **impeached Bill Clinton** on two crimes and misdemeanors, **perjury** and **obstruction of justice**. The Senate vote to convict and remove from office failed. On perjury, the vote was 54 not guilty and 45 guilty. On obstruction of justice, the vote was 50 not guilty and 50 guilty. A two-thirds majority (67 of 100 votes) is required to convict. The trial ended on February 6. **Clinton was the second president who faced impeachment** (President Andrew Johnson was the first). Clinton's Gallup poll was 73% during the week of his impeachment. Apparently, Clinton's sex life was unimportant compared with other issues, such as high inflation and unemployment. Was leadership more important than personal morality?

The **1999 Gramm-Leach-Bliley Act** repealed the 1993 Glass-Steagall Act, thereby allowing banks to sell insurance and stocks, and permitted insurance companies entry to banks. That year, Clinton also submitted the **first balanced budget** in 30 years in 1999.

In 1999, Congress increased the annual pay of cabinet secretaries to $157,000 (up from 1997's $151,800).

In 2000, Congress increased the annual pay of the legislators to $141,300 (up from 1998's $136,700). It also increased the pay of the associate justices of the U.S. Supreme Court to $173,600 (up from 1998's $167,900) and the chief justice's pay to $181,400 (up from 1998's $175,400). Also in 2000, Congress raised the annual pay of cabinet secretaries to $161,200 (up from 1999's $157,000). Congress made no other pay changes during Clinton's term of presidency.

The **2000 Senior Citizens' Freedom to Work Act** eliminated the Social Security earnings test for those over age 65, the **2000 Worker Economic Opportunity Act** excluded stock option earnings from overtime requirements, the **2000 Electronic Signatures in Global and National Commerce Act** declared electronic signatures legally binding, and the **2000 Commodity Futures Modernization Act** exempted OTC derivates from government oversight.

In **United States vs Morrison** (2000), the U.S. Supreme Court ruled that a provision of the Violence Against Women Act of 1994, 42 U.S. C. Section 13981, which provides a federal civil remedy for victims of gender-motivated violence, is unconstitutional as it exceeds Congress's authority under the Commerce Clause of Article 1, Section 8, and the Equal Protection Clause of the Fourteenth Amendment, as the Act does not regulate an activity that substantially affects interstate commerce and does not redress harm caused by the state.

Clinton's first term of office began with economic problems; his last term ended with an **annual surplus of $160 billion**, resulting in a projected total surplus of $5 trillion.

On his last day in office, in 2001, Clinton granted **140 pardons**. The view of many was that he made poor choices in his personal life but was likeable and had done a good job running the federal government. **His life was a mixture of good and bad**, but he was a very likeable and skillful politician. After leaving office, Clinton remained an **A-list celebrity**, earning large fees and endorsing political candidates.

Clinton published his memoirs in the book *My Life*. It sold over two million copies, for which he had received a $15 million dollar advance. And he campaigned for **Hillary in 2000 to be a U.S. senator from New York**. In 2000, Clinton stated. "I don't know whether the White House is the finest public housing in America or the crown jewel of prison life. It's a very isolating life." In 2002, Clinton finally apologized to Monica Lewinsky for the disruption in her personal life.

A 2006 **Gallup poll** showed Clinton with a 66% rating, the highest of any recent president. Most historians say Clinton did **a better job than most presidents**.

In 2013, President Obama gave Clinton the **Presidential Medal of Freedom**, the nation's highest civil honor. Al Gore went on to focus on global warming – his book *Climate Change* won a Pulitzer Prize.

Bush Sr. and Clinton became great friends – unusual for political enemies where one won and the other lost in face-to-face elections. Since leaving the government, Clinton has joined former President George H.W. Bush in forming a foundation for humanitarian matters: to ease poverty and improve people's health. The two bonded and **together raised hundreds of millions of dollars** for various charities during Clinton's term of office and beyond. At the dedication of Clinton's Library, George H.W. Bush stated, "Bill Clinton was one of the most gifted American political figures in modern times."

Key Events

Sears Roebuck ceased catalog sales (1993); Clinton appointed his wife Hillary Rodham Clinton in a failed attempt to overhaul the healthcare system (1993); Clinton signed the North American Free Trade Agreement **NAFTA** (1993); the FBI raid on **Branch Davidian** near Waco, Texas, resulted in 70 dead cult members (1993); **Ruth Bader Ginsburg's** nomination to the U.S. Supreme Court was confirmed by the Senate 96-3 (1993); a **$496 federal budget reduction** over five years was confirmed (1993); CEOs who left office included: **John Akers (IBM), Paul Lego (Westinghouse), John Sculley (Apple Computer), Robert Stempel (GM),** and **Kay Whitmore (Eastman Kodak)** (1993); the **Travelers Group** was created by a $1.1 billion acquisition of Travelers Insurance (1993); Lou Gerstner took over a top job at **IBM** (1993); the Apple board ousted **John Sculley** as it floundered on bankruptcy (1993); Pfizer introduced **Viagra** for erectile dysfunction (1993); a Central Park concert by **Luciano Pavarotti** drew 250,000 (1993); an agreement of 120 nations was reached to destroy all weapons of mass destruction within ten years (1993); a car bomb exploded in the parking garage of **the World Trade Center**, killing six people (1993); limits on gun purchases took effect (1993); **Deion Sanders** played for both the Atlanta Braves (baseball) and the Atlanta Falcons (football) on the same day (1993); a District Court ruled that **McDonnell Douglas** violated ERISA requirements when, upon closing a plant, terminated employees lost health insurance and pension accruals (1993); the **DJIA** closed at 3,754.09 at year end, up 13.7 percent (1993); House Ways and Means Chairman **Daniel (Rosty) Rostenkowski** was sent to prison for mail fraud and jury tampering (1994); CIA Agent **Aldrich Ames** pleaded guilty to spying for Russia and received a life sentence (1994); Macy's department stores were bought by **Federated Department Stores** (1994); the **web browser** was introduced (1994); AT&T bought **McCaw Cellular** and renamed it AT&T Wireless (1994); the **Federal Reserve** increased short-term rates to 6% (from 3%) in six steps (1994); *Built to Last* was written by James Collins and Jerry Porras (1994); *Inside the Boardroom* was written by William Bowen (1994); **Lehman** went public (1994); the first **credit default swap** transaction took place (1994); the TV show *Friends* aired (1994); a baseball players' strike cancelled the World Series (1994); a Los Angeles earthquake claimed 61 lives (1994); the online recruiting tool **The Monster Board** revolutionized job searches (1994); **DirecTV** began coverage of regional NFL games (1994); the **Buffalo Bills** lost their fourth straight Super Bowl game (1994); the **DJIA** closed at 3,834.44 at year end, up 2.1 percent (1994); more than 140 heads of state met to celebrate the **United Nations's** 50th anniversary (1995); diplomatic relations were restored between Vietnam and the U.S. (1995); the United States sent troops to **Bosnia for peacekeeping** (1995); **Newt Gingrich** was elected Speaker of the House of Representatives (1995); Walt Disney acquired **ABC** and **ESPN** for $19.5 billion (1995); **Chase Manhattan** and **Chemical Bank** merged (1995); **Netscape's** IPO set off a .com IPO buying frenzy (1995); **Sun Micro Systems** launched the software platform Java (1995); the **eBay** auction site opened (1995); **Berkshire Hathaway** stock sold above

$30,000 a share (1995); split-dollar life insurance was put in at **General Electric** (1995); a jury found **O.J. Simpson not guilty** in the murder of his wife and another man (1995); **Timothy McVeigh** and **Terry Nichols** were convicted of bombing a federal building in Oklahoma City, killing 168 people two years earlier (1995); New York replaced the electric chair with a **lethal injection** for capital punishment (1995); the **Dow-Jones Industrial Average** went above 4,000 for the first time and closed for the year above 5,000 (1995); a truck bomb in Saudi Arabia killed United States Marines in a housing complex (1996); **AT&T** announced a cutback of 50,000 jobs from a 300,000-person workforce (1996); the **Liggett Group** agreed to a class action tobacco settlement (1996); a major **Midwest drought** bankrupted thousands of farmers (1996); **AT&T Wireless** and **Lucent** spun off from AT&T (1996); **Time Warner** and **Turner Broadcasting** merged (1996); a record 864 companies went public (1996); **Al Dunlap** became CEO of Sunbeam after slashing costs at Scott Paper (1996); Sergey Brin and Larry Page joined to create **Google** (1996); the Institute of Shareholder Services (**ISS**) introduced the Equity Plan Scorecard (1996); Al Kaczynski was charged with being the **Unabomber** (1996); **TWA Flight 800** exploded in midair off New York, killing 230 people (1996); a pipe bomb exploded in **Atlanta during the Olympics**, killing one person (1996); the **Women's National Basketball Association** began with eight teams: the Charlotte Sting, Cleveland Rockers, Houston Comets, and New York Liberty in the Eastern Conference and the Los Angeles Sparks, Phoenix Mercury, Sacramento Monarchs, and Utah Starzz in the Western Conference (1996); Cleveland Browns owner Art Modell moved his team to Baltimore; Cleveland was left with its franchise but no players (1996); *The Balanced Scorecard* was published by Robert Kaplan and David Norton (1996); the **DJIA** closed at 6,448.27 at year end, up 26 percent (1996); a spacecraft arrived on Mars (1997); **Amazon.com** went public (1997); mergers included **Dean Witter** and **Morgan Stanley**, **WorldCom** and **MCI**, and **Lockheed Martin** and **Northrop Grumman** (1997); baseball player **Jackie Robinson's** number 42 was retired for all clubs (1997); the **DJIA** closed at 7,908.25 at year end, up 22.6 percent (1997); bombs exploded at United States Embassies in Africa and Osama bin Laden was charged as the mastermind (1998); mergers continued with **Bell Atlantic** and **GTE**, **Citicorp** and **Travelers Group**, **Bank America** and **NationsBank**, and **Banc One** and **First Chicago** (1998); Ram Charan published *Boards at Work* (1998); **Exxon** acquired **Mobil** (1998); developer **Donald Trump** acquired the General Motors building in New York City for $800 million (1998); the **camera phone** was introduced (1998); Apple introduced the personal computer **iMac** (1998); the **Hubble Space Telescope** showed planets outside of our solar system (1998); the largest uninterrupted stretch of federal deficits since 1970 ended with a federal budget surplus of $70 billion, a record (1998); the **DJIA** closed at 9,181.43 at year end, up 16.1 percent (1998); **Boris Yeltsin** left office completely after the collapse of Russia (1999); United States troops went to **Kosovo for peacekeeping** (1999); the last **cigarette billboards** came down in an agreement between 40 states and cigarette companies (1999); **BellSouth** and **SBC**, merged forming **Cingular** (1999); **Pfizer** acquired **Warner-Lambert** (1999); **Goldman Sachs** went public (1999); Microsoft founder **Bill Gates** was worth $100 billion and the Microsoft market cap exceeded $500 billion (1999); Bill Bain and Mitt Romney formed **Bain Capital** (1999); the TV show *The Sopranos* made its debut (1999); the House of Representatives barred Clinton from sending troops to Yugoslavia without its approval (1999); **John Kennedy, Jr.** and his wife died when a plane he piloted crashed (1999); the **DJIA** closed at 11,497.12 at year end, up 25.2 percent (1999); the **Bell Atlantic** and **GTE** merger completed, forming **Verizon Communications** (2000); the **NASDAQ** hit a high of 5,049 but closed the year at 2,471 (2000); Chase Manhattan purchased **J.P. Morgan** for $30 billion forming **JPMorgan Chase** (2000); the labor participation rate of 67.3% was at an all-time high (2000); **gold** fell to $255 an ounce (2000); Edward Lawler published *Rewarding Excellence* (2000); **AT&T** became the largest cable company with the acquisition of **Media One** (2000); Mark Cuban bought the **NBA Dallas Mavericks** for $285 million (2000); the **Y2K computer** problem in 2000 did not happen (2000); the U.S. population rose to over 280 million (2000); former New York Mets baseball player **Bobby Bonilla** received a $1.1 million yearly payout until 2035 in a contract buyout (2000); and the **DJIA** closed at 10,780.85 at year end, down 6.17 percent (2000). For the period 1992 through 2000, the DJIA rose 227%!

George W. Bush
(43ʳᴅ President)

January 20, 2001 – January 20, 2009

George Walker Bush was born on July 6, 1946, to George H.W. and Barbara Bush, in New Haven, Connecticut, where his father **George H.W. Bush** was attending **Yale University**, after serving as a Navy pilot in **World War II. G.H.W. Bush** graduated from Yale in 1948 and moved the family to Midland, Texas, where he took a job selling supplies to oil drilling companies. George had four surviving siblings (one died at age three): Dorothy, Jeb, Neil, and Marvin. **George** attended a **private prep school** in Houston, the same school wife-to-be Laura Welch attended, but he did not meet her. Later he went to the **Philips Academy** in Andover, Massachusetts. There George was very competitive in class and in sports. He was also the **head cheerleader**.

George W. received a bachelor's degree from **Yale University** in 1968, with a major in history and a grade average of C. He was also a member of the exclusive **Skull and Bones Society**. Bush returned to Texas and joined the **Texas Air National Guard**, where he flew **F-102 fighter jets**. He stayed at the same apartment complex as his wife-to-be, but again, they never met. Honorably discharged in 1974 from the service, he enrolled in **Harvard University**, where he received an MBA in 1975. He then returned to Houston to be an oilman. There he enjoyed attractive women and fast cars. In 1979, he met **Laura Welch** at a barbecue, and they immediately started dating. Three months later, on November 5, 1977, they were **married**. She was not only very attractive, she was also very likeable. Laura was a former librarian and elementary school teacher. She was also a champion of education and a strong proponent of denouncing the oppression of women. Later, when George was **governor of Texas**, she was asked about her role as wife of a politician. She replied, "I find it is really best not to give your mate a lot of advice as I don't want a lot of advice from him." George and Laura had **twin daughters**, Barbara and Jenna, in 1981. Barbara was named after George's mother, and Jenna was named after Laura's mother. George was the first president to have twins.

George was unsuccessful in his run for a seat in the U.S. House of Representatives in 1978. He ran for office because he believed the federal government was getting too involved in the natural gas industry and wanted to do something about it. After losing the election, George focused on his small company, **Bush Exploration**.

In 1983, George merged his company with another. Three years later, **Harken Energy** bought out George's company for $600,000 of Harken's company stock and a consulting contract. George liked his beer and bourbon, but in 1986, with urging from Laura, he **swore off alcohol** and joined Laura at the **Methodist Church**. With George's father running for president in 1988, the son moved his family to New York and became an advisor on George HW's campaign. Following his father's victory, George W moved his family back to Houston and the oil business.

In 1989, George W and a group of oilmen invested in the **Texas Rangers** baseball team. For his $800,000 investment, George got a two percent ownership, which he later sold for close to $15 million. In 1990, George W sold two-thirds of the Harken stock he owned for $850,000. He focused his time and energy on running a **volunteer organization** that concentrated on repairing the homes of the less fortunate. After four years, George decided to go back into politics. He chose to run for **governor of Texas**. With the help of wealthy friends and his father's campaign advisors, George W received over 53% of the votes cast and **defeated Governor Ann Richards**. Over 20,000 attended his inauguration, and within a year he had cut taxes, encouraged new businesses, put welfare recipients to work and improved education. In 1998, he **won re-election** with 68 percent of the vote. With the support of his family and friends, George W decided to run for president. Dan Quayle sought the Republican party's nomination for president in the 2000 election, but due to little interest he withdrew in September 1999 and joined the private sector. By January 2000, Bush was the front-runner out of a number of candidates. Three months later he had the endorsement of 27 governors, 175 congressmen and 41 U.S. senators. George W easily won the **Republican nomination for president** at the Party's 2006 convention.

At the convention, George W announced that he was a "**compassionate conservative**," believing in local over national control, improving education, putting welfare recipients to work, and encouraging new business to achieve better-paying jobs. He also announced that **Dick Cheney** would be his vice president. He added Dick Cheney because he would be a valuable partner in the Bush administration. Cheney had a distinguished political career and had the federal government experience that Bush needed.

Richard Bruce Cheney was born on January 30, 1941, in Lincoln, Nebraska, but his family moved to Casper, Wyoming, in 1945, where Dick became active in sports. In 1958, he received a full scholarship to **Yale University**, but he accumulated bad grades and disciplinary notices. In 1962, he was kicked out of school and returned to Wyoming, where he joined the International Brotherhood of Electrical Workers. But his bad habits continued, and his girlfriend, Lynne Vincent, told him she would not tolerate them, and he had to change. He did. He went to the **University of Wyoming** and graduated in 1964 with an **MA** in political science. They were married soon after. Dick received a fellowship at the **University of Wisconsin** while working on a **PhD** in 1968. He also started working for Wisconsin **Governor** Warren Knowles and **Congressman** William Steiger. In 1969, Cheney became **Chief of Staff** for President Gerald Ford. After Ford's loss to Jimmy Carter, Cheney returned to Wyoming and won the state's sole seat in the **House of Representatives** in 1978. Cheney won re-election five times and was the **House Minority whip** when President George H.W. Bush appointed Cheney Secretary of Defense. In 1990 and 1991 he oversaw U.S. involvement in the Gulf War, for which Bush awarded him the **Presidential Medal of Freedom**. When Bush lost the 1992 election, Cheney left government service and worked with the **American Enterprise Institute** and **the Council on Foreign**

Relations. Cheney then joined an oil field service company, **Halliburton**, as Chairman and Chief Executive, and remained there until 2000, when he left to run for vice president. Meanwhile, his wife Lynne served as Chair of the National Endowment for the Humanities from 1986 to 1993. Their **daughter**, Liz, won Cheney's **former Wyoming House** seat.

There were **three televised presidential debates** between Republican George Bush and Democrat Al Gore. The first was held on October 3, 2000, in Boston, Massachusetts. The second was held on October 11, 2000, in Winston-Salem, North Carolina, and the third was held on October 17, 2000, in St. Louis, Missouri. There was **one televised vice presidential debate** between Democrat Joseph Lieberman and Republican Dick Cheney on October 5, 2000, in Danville, Kentucky.

In the **2000 election**, Republicans **George W. Bush and Richard Cheney lost** the popular vote to Democrats **Albert Gore** and **Joseph Lieberman** 50,456,167 to 50,996,064, but **won** the electoral vote 271 to 266, and thereby the election. This was the **third** presidential election where the electoral vote winner had lost the popular vote. The predecessors were Hayes in 1876 and Harrison in 1888. But unlike these two, the popular vote in Florida, the 2000 election was so close, favoring Gore by only 1,784 votes, that Florida law mandated a recount. The U.S. Supreme Court ruled that the Florida Supreme Court's manual recount order violated the Equal Protection Clause. On November 26, the Florida recount gave Bush 2,912,790 votes to 2,912,253 for Gore, a margin of 537 votes. That recount gave Bush Florida's 25 electoral votes, for a total of 271 – one more than required to be elected. Bush was elected president and Cheney was elected vice president.

George W. Bush is only the second son of a president to become president. John Quincy Adams, son of John Adams, was the first. Because he and his father were both addressed as president, George decided their nicknames should be **George the 41st** and **George the 43rd**, reflecting their queue in the presidential order.

In his **2001 inaugural address**, George W., age 54, stated, "The peaceful transfer of authority is rare in history, yet common in this country. With a simple oath, we affirm old traditions and new beginnings." In 2001, the Senate was split 50-50, but the Republicans controlled the House 221-212.

The president and vice president received their first **pay increases** since 1969. In 2001, the president's pay was increased to $400,000 a year (up from $200,000) and the vice president's annual pay was increased to $175,400 (up from $171,000). The senators' and congressmen's pay were increased to $145,100 (up from 2000's $141,300). Also in 2001, the associate justices of the U.S. Supreme Court's pay were increased to $178,300 (up from 2000's $173,600), and the chief justice's pay was increased to $186,300 (up from 2000's $181,400). And cabinet secretaries' pay was increased to $166,700 (up from 2000's $161,200).

In 2002, congressional pay was increased to $150,000, and then again in 2003 to $154,700. Annual pay for the associate justices of the U.S. Supreme Court was increased to $184,400 in 2002, $190,100 in 2003, $194,300 in 2004, $199,200 in 2005, $203,000 in 2006, and $208,100 in 2008. And beginning in 2002, the chief justice received an annual pay increase to $192,600, then $198,600 in 2003, $203,000 in 2004, $208,100 in 2005, $212,100 in 2006, and $217,400 in 2008. Cabinet secretaries' pay was increased annually to $171,900 in 2002, $174,500 in 2003, $175,700 and $180,100 in 2004, $183,500 in 2005, $186,600 in 2006, $191,300 in 2007, and $196,700 in 2008. There were no other pay changes during Bush's term of presidency.

Bush's initial **cabinet** during his first term of office included **Vice President** Richard Cheney, **Secretary of State** Colin Powell, **Secretary of the Treasury** Paul O'Neil, **Secretary of Defense** Donald Rumsfeld, **Attorney General** John Ashcroft, **Secretary of the Interior** Gale Norton, **Secretary of Agriculture** Ann Veneman, **Secretary of Commerce** Donald Evans, **Secretary of Labor** Elaine Chao, **Secretary of Health and Human Services** Tommy Thompson, **Secretary of Housing and Urban Development** Melquiades Rafael Martinez, **Secretary of Transportation** Norman Mineta, **Secretary of Energy** Spencer Abraham, **Secretary of Education** Roderick Paige, **Secretary of Veterans Affairs** Anthony Principi, and **Secretary of Homeland Security** Tom Ridge. Tom Ridge was the first Secretary of Homeland Security, added after the 9/11 attack.

Andrew Card was George the 43rd's first chief of staff; he had been deputy chief of staff under the 41st. Card and the 43rd worked well together. Since Vice President Cheney had been a chief of staff under President Ford, he knew how to work with Card.

Bush signed **three key pieces of legislation** in **2001** into law: the **No Child Left Behind Act** focused on safe school settings and well-prepared teachers; the **Economic Growth and Tax Reconciliation Act** provided a 39.1% max tax on income over $297,350 for 2001-03; 37.6% on income over $280,350 for 2004-05; and 35% on income over $288,350 for 2006 and later, but returned to 2001 rates in 2011; and the **USA Patriot Act** required financial institutions to verify the identity of account holders. But other than the tax cut, George W. had a difficult first year. **Republican Jeffords switched** to being a Democrat, putting the Democrats in the majority in the Senate. After he stated Russian Vladimir **Putin was trustworthy**, the press labeled Bush naïve. Bush's tax energy proposals were seen as favoring big oil companies. And Bush was blocked on many of his other initiatives in Congress. By August, he was frustrated and took his family back to his ranch in Crawford, Texas. Bush led all other presidents in taking vacation days; **reportedly he took 533 days, but he worked hard to stay in shape. He even had a treadmill** on Air Force One.

Then, less than eight months into his presidency, nineteen terrorists attacked the United States on **September 11, 2001**. It would forever be known as "**9/11**." The terrorists had picked the code number for distress. **The first plane** hit the first of the Twin Towers in New York City at 8:46 am, and the **second plane** hit the other tower at 9:02 am. Shortly after, both towers were demolished and over 3,000 people were killed, versus 2,400 in Pearl Harbor. A **third plane** hit the Pentagon in Washington, D.C., killing several hundred, and a **fourth plane** was taken over by the passengers and crashed in Pennsylvania. Speculations were that it was headed either for the Capitol Building or the White House. There was worry over a second attack, possibly a nuclear bomb.

George the 43rd learned of the crashes while visiting a school in Sarasota, Florida. He was immediately **rushed onto Air Force One** and stayed in the air until the conditions stabilized. He then got on television and stated, "It is not enough to serve our enemies with legal papers. We will bring the terrorists to justice: we will **bring justice to the terrorists**. Either way justice will be done." Many interpreted "justice" as "**dead or alive**." Following his address, **Bush's approval rating soared**. Upon learning the former Saudi **Osama bin Laden** was the mastermind behind 9/11 and was hiding in **Afghanistan**, Bush ordered a paramilitary attack on the country, **Operation Enduring Freedom**.

The president would eat healthy, light meals with Laura, but when she was away, he would have steak and fried onion rings and/or anything Tex-Mex.

In the **midterms**, the Republicans gained control of both Houses: Senate 51-48 and House 229-204.

The **Help America Vote Act of 2002** established a program providing payments to improve the administration of elections.

Bush signed **two key acts** in **2002** into law: the **Revenue Act** liberalized some personal deductions; and the **Sarbanes-Oxley Act** prohibited executive loans, accelerated SEC reporting, required forfeiture of overpayments from restated earnings because of misconduct on non-compliance with disclosure requirements, created the Public Oversight Board, and prohibited retaliation against employee whistleblowers.

George liked inviting baseball stars to a White House luncheon and adding their autographs to his collection of over 250 signed balls. The Clintons had invited celebrities and dignitaries for conversation, not signed mementos.

Bush signed **three key acts** in **2003** into law: the **Tax Act** lowered the estate tax; the **Jobs Growth Tax Relief Reconciliation Act** lowered the max tax on dividends and long-term capital gains tax to 15% and put other earnings at a max tax of 35% on income over $311,950; and the **Medicare Act** introduced pretax health savings accounts permitted tax-free withdrawals to pay medical bills, and added a prescription drug benefit.

In **Grutter vs Bollinger** (2003), the U.S. Supreme Court ruled that ethnicity may be a consideration in reviewing candidates for law school. In **Nevada Department of Human Resources vs**

Hibbs (2003), the U.S. Supreme Court ruled that public employees have the right to take public sector employers to court for violations of the FMLA Act.

President Bush's White House was unlike any others. He himself was better prepared than most incoming presidents. The 43rd had worked with his father, "George the 41st," in the White House and saw the interactions of principals and associates. "George the 43rd" was also the **first president with an MBA**, from Harvard no less. And he employed the principles of Peter Drucker, the management organization guru – identify specific goals with measurable results. He had two specific areas of responsibility: domestic and foreign. The 43rd wanted to be known as **the decider**.

On the **domestic front** there was clarity, collegiality, loyalty, and uniformity on well-defined policies. And there were no leaks to the press. Essentially, the principals were inexperienced and not well known. Bush's first chief of staff, Andy Card, was the 41st's deputy chief of staff, and knew the workings of the White House. He was efficient, organized, and ran a well-organized staff. Chief of Staff James Baker was his role model.

The **foreign front** was totally different. Policies were more general, and the leaders were not only well experienced, but they were also well known. They had worked under earlier presidents and were all members of the National Security Council. The **backbiting** and **infighting** were the worst among Vice President Richard **Cheney**; Secretary of State Colin **Powell**; National Security Advisor Condoleezza **Rice**: Senator Chuck **Hagel**; and Secretary of State Donald **Rumsfeld**. Vice President Cheney was the primary voice on national security issues. He had been chief of staff for President Ford and acted as the chief of staff for the 43rd, and he could not be fired. Another exception to the team-approach was **Michael Gerson**, Bush's top speech writer. His cohorts saw him as a credit-grabber who advanced his reputation at the expense of others. The major issue of contention was **how to handle the September 11, 2001**, air attack on the Pentagon and the New York Twin Towers. A month later, worried about Iraq's weapons of mass destruction, Bush sent Secretary of State **Powell** to the United Nations in an effort to avoid war. The Security Council demanded **Hussein** turn over his weapons following Powell's statement, "We have firsthand knowledge of biological weapons on rails and wheels." When Hussein failed to comply, President Bush initiated **Operation Iraqi Freedom** in 2003 with congressional approval. It commenced with U.S. air strikes. Iraq's military forces, including the feared Republican Guard, were quickly overwhelmed, and many of the troops melted into the civilian population. There was no evidence of any chemical or biological weapons used by the Iraqis. Within days, **Iraq was defeated**. Career Ambassador **Paul Bremer** was put in charge of the coalition. But then, counter to what had been agreed to by Bush, Bremer disbanded Iraq and got rid of those running the country. Everything fell apart. There was domestic resistance to the **Abu Ghraib** treatment of prisoners. And the vice president's chief of staff Lewis "Scooter" **Libby**, was convicted of lying, ordered to pay a $250,000 fine, and sentenced to 30 months' imprisonment. Bush later **commuted** his sentence.

Bush signed **two key acts** in **2004** into law: the **Tax Act** lowered marginal and estate taxes; and the **American Jobs Creation Act** tightened requirements for tax deferred treatment.

Before the 2004 elections, **Andy Card** told President Bush he wanted to leave. He had been in the job for over five years. Bush agreed, thanked him for his service, and then appointed **Joshua**

Bolten, head of the Office of Management and Budget, as the new chief of staff. Bolten told the cabinet members that they had to give Bush better options on issues.

There were **three televised presidential debates** between Republican President George W. Bush and Democrat John Kerry. The first was held on September 30, 2004, in Coral Gables, Florida. The second was held on October 8, 2004, in St. Louis, Missouri. And the third was held on October 13, 2004, in Tempe, Arizona. There was **one televised vice presidential debate** between Republican Vice President Richard Cheney and Democrat John Edwards on October 4, 2004, in Cleveland, Ohio.

In the **2004 election**, despite concerns about the decision to **go to war with Iraq** and **significant unemployment**, voters turned out in record numbers. Republicans President **George W. Bush** and Vice President **Richard Cheney** defeated Democrats **John Kerry** and **John Edwards** 62,040,610 to 59,028,444 in the popular vote and 286 to 251 in the electoral vote. Bush was elected president and Cheney was elected vice president. But for many voters, Bush not only **lost their trust**, they charged him as incompetent. His approval rating fell to 24%. The **Republicans** controlled the **Senate** 51-48 and the **House** 229-204. In his March 20, **2005, inaugural address**, President Bush referenced Iraq by stating that, "The survival of liberty in our land increasingly depends on the success of liberty in other lands."

Bush's initial **cabinet** during his second term of office included **Vice President** Richard Cheney, **Secretary of State** Condoleezza Rice, **Secretary of the Treasury** John Snow, **Secretary of Defense** Donald Rumsfeld, **Attorney General** Alberto Gonzales, **Secretary of the Interior** Gale Norton, **Secretary of Agriculture** Mike Johanns, **Secretary of Commerce** Carlos

Gutierrez, **Secretary of Labor** Elaine Chao, **Secretary of Health and Human Services** Michael Leavitt, **Secretary of Housing and Urban Development** Alphonso Jackson, **Secretary of Transportation** Norman Mineta, **Secretary of Energy** Samuel Bodman, **Secretary of Education** Margaret Spellings, **Secretary of Veterans Affairs** Jim Nicholson, and **Secretary of Homeland Security** Michael Chertoff. Alberto Gonzales became the first Hispanic-American to be appointed **U.S. Attorney General**. Condoleezza **Rice** was the first African American **Secretary of State**.

In **Arthur Anderson LLP vs United States** (2005), the U.S. Supreme Court ruled that the obstruction of justice charge against the company was overturned because of flawed instructions in the lower court. In **Smith vs City of Jackson** (2005), the U.S. Supreme Court ruled that employment discrimination from disparate impact is a recoverable action under the Age Discrimination in Employment Act (ADEA). In **United States vs Booker** (2005), the U.S. Supreme Court ruled that the Federal Sentencing Guidelines that allow judges to enhance sentences based on facts other than those determined by a jury violate a defendant's Sixth Amendment right to jury trial. In **United States vs Olson** (2005), the U.S. Supreme Court ruled that under the Federal Tort Claims Act, the United States waives sovereign immunity "under circumstances" where local law would make a "private person" not a "state or municipal entity" liable in tort. In **Rousey vs Jacoway** (2005), the U.S. Supreme Court ruled that IRA assets are exempt from Chapter 7 bankruptcy claims if necessary for the support of the debtor and dependents.

Bush signed **two key acts** in **2005** into law: the **Bankruptcy Abuse Prevention and Consumer Protection Act** covered bankruptcy requirements; and the **Tax Act** reduced taxes to

47% from 48%. Also in **2005,** eight former **KPMG** partners were indicted for selling inappropriate tax shelters; WorldCom CEO **Bernie Ebbers** was sentenced to 25 years for $11 billion accounting fraud; Adelphia founder **Robert Rigas** was sentenced to 15 years for looting billions from his company; **Martha Stewart** was given five months in prison and five months in house confinement for an insider trade violation; Tyco CEO **Kozlowski** was sentenced to 8 to 15 years for looting the Tyco treasury and had to pay some $170 million in fines; **John Roberts** was sworn in as Supreme Court chief justice, replacing **William Rehnquist**, who died, and **Samuel Alito** was sworn in as a justice to replace retiring **Sandra Day O'Connor**.

The 2006 midterms gave the Democrats control of the **House** 233-202, and the **Senate** split 49-49. Bush vetoed a bill on **stem cell research** that year.

In **Burlington Northern & Santa Fe Railway Co. vs White** (2006), the U.S. Supreme Court ruled that materially adverse actions in response to complaints of unlawful discrimination or harassment may constitute unlawful retaliation under Title VII. In **United States vs Georgia** (2006), the U.S. Supreme Court ruled that Title II of the Americans with Disabilities Act of 1990 abrogates state sovereign immunity regarding Eighth Amendment violations and Congress has the authority to enforce Title II under section 5 of the Fourteenth Amendment. In **Zedner vs United States** (2006), the U.S. Supreme Court ruled that a defendant cannot prospectively waive their right to a speedy trial under the Speedy Trial Act of 1974 and is not stopped from challenging whether their signed waiver is excludable under the Act. In **United States vs Gonzalez-Lopez** (2006), the U.S. Supreme Court ruled that convictions must be reversed when a defendant is denied their Sixth Amendment right to paid counsel of their choice. In **United States vs Grubbs** (2006), the U.S. Supreme Court ruled that anticipatory warrants that do not describe the "triggering condition" do not violate the Fourth Amendment's particularity requirement. In **Salinas vs United States** (2006), the U.S. Supreme Court ruled that simple possession of a controlled substance does not constitute a "controlled substance offense" under the U.S. Sentencing Commission Guidelines Manual, as the guidelines require "intent to manufacture, import, export, distribute or dispense." In **Whitman vs Department of Transportation** (2006), the U.S. Supreme Court ruled that the Civil Service Reform Act, while it does not expressly confer jurisdiction, does not divest federal courts of the jurisdiction conferred by 28 U.S.C. §1331. In **Merrill Lynch vs Dabit** (2006), the U.S. Supreme Court ruled that if stockholders were misled into holding declining shares of stock, they are permitted to sue.

Bush signed **three key acts** in **2006** into law: the **Tax Act** lowered taxes on estates, dividends, and long-term capital gains; the **Pension Protection Act** changed definitions and eligibility; and the **Secure Fence Act** added 700 miles of southern border protection at a cost of $2.3 billion.

In **Hinck vs United States** (2007), the U.S. Supreme Court ruled that the Internal Revenue Code §6404(h) grants exclusive jurisdiction to the Tax Court to review interest abatement claims against the IRS. In **Rita vs United States** (2007), the U.S. Supreme Court ruled that the federal courts of appeals may apply "a presumption of reasonableness" to sentences that fall under the Federal Sentencing Guidelines. In **Logan vs United States** (2007), the U.S. Supreme Court ruled that where a defendant retains their civil rights at all times, the exemption contained in the Armed Career Criminal Act (ACCA) is not applicable. In

Beck et al. vs Pace Int'l Union et al. (2007), the U.S. Supreme Court ruled that a merger is not an acceptable reason for the termination of a single employer-defined benefit pension plan. In **Kennedy et al. vs Plan Administrator for DuPont Savings and Investment Plan et al.** (2007), the U.S. Supreme Court ruled that an ERISA plan administrator was right to pay Kennedy's ex-wife because Kennedy did not change the beneficiary form after his divorce. In **Ledbetter vs Goodyear Tire and Rubber** (2007), the U.S. Supreme Court ruled that certain sex discrimination claims are subject to a tight statute of limitations.

In 2007, Bush announced a **troop surge in Iraq**. At a press conference on Iraq, someone threw a shoe at Bush, he ducked, and it missed. He later said, "It was a size 10." The **Fair Minimum Wage Act** became law in **2007**. It increased the federal minimum wage to $5.85, $6.55, and $7.25 an hour in stages. The **2007 Tax Act** lowered the tax rate to 45 percent.

In **John R. Sand & Gravel Co. vs United States** (2008), the U.S. Supreme Court ruled that the six-year statute of limitations in the Tucker Act, an act that permits claims to be brought in the Court of Claims, requires "sua sponte" consideration of the timeliness of the lawsuit. In **Boulware vs United States** (2008), the U.S. Supreme Court ruled that a defendant accused of tax evasion does not need to show evidence of intent at the time of distribution that their distributions were a return of capital to claim return of capital treatment. In **United States vs Clintwood Elkhorn Mining Co.** (2008), the U.S. Supreme Court ruled that taxpayers seeking refunds of taxes that are unlawfully assessed in violation of the Export Clause must file a "timely administrative refund claim" before bringing a lawsuit against the government.

In an attempt to blunt the impact of high unemployment, a tumbling stock market, and a major recession, George W. signed **eight acts** into law in **2008**: the **Economic Stabilization Act** placed limitations on executive pay for companies under the Troubled Asset Relief Program (TARP); the **Emergency Economic Stabilization Act** put further restrictions on executive pay for TARP companies; the **Worker, Retiree, and Employer Recovery Act** liberalized funding of defined benefit plans and waived distribution requirements of pension plans; the **Americans with Disabilities Act** expanded eligibility requirements; the **War Supplemental Appropriations Act** added an additional 13 weeks of unemployment benefits; the **Housing and Economic Recovery Act** extended the survival of Fannie Mae and Freddie Mac, along with establishing a $300 billion fund for at-risk homeowners; the **Heroes Earnings Assistance and Relief Act** gave a tax credit to employers supplementing active duty pay and made provisions for economic payments to military families; and the **Genetic Information Non-Discrimination Act** prohibited employment and healthcare coverage discrimination due to genetic information.

Bush entered the office as a peacetime president, but he left it in a state of war. He entered office with a favorable balance of payments but left the country significantly in debt due to war costs. His approval rating averaged about 50% during his presidency, ranging from a high of 90 after 9/11 to a low of about 20% near the end of his term of office. The **Gulf War** had defined the presidency of **George the 41st**. The **Iraq War**, which led to the formation of **ISIS**, defined the presidency of **George the 43rd**. Tax cuts and program costs resulted in a three trillion dollar increase in the budget wiping out the half trillion left by President Clinton. A faltering economy, the war in Iraq, and his response to

9/11 were the major issues during Bush's second term in office. The last four years of Bush's term were marked by an increase of the DJIA to 13,265 in 2006, followed by a dramatic fall to 8,776 in 2008, making an excellent jumping off point for new stock option grants. The **Articles of Impeachment** were drawn up in the House but failed to draw enough interest to even get to a vote.

George and Laura attended the Obama inauguration on January 20, 2009, and then flew to Midland, Texas, where a "welcome home" party awaited, after which the two went to their ranch in Crawford. In retirement, the 43rd wrote a book, *Decision Points*, which focused on key decisions during his life. **It sold over two million copies.** He remained silent on his views of President Obama.

The **DJIA** was virtually unchanged for the four-year period of Bush's first term, (2000 closed at 10,787, and 2004 closed at 10,783). With a flat stock market, companies moved away from stock options into stock awards and cash plans.

Most historians consider Bush's performance as **somewhat below average**.

Key Events

The economy saw the **last of 12** U.S. government surpluses in 69 years (2001); **Hillary Rodham Clinton** took office as a U.S. senator in New York (2001); **Republicans** had a narrow edge in **both Houses of Congress** (2001); 20 United States **steelmakers filed for bankruptcy** (2001); Mafia bosses **Joseph Bonanno** and **John Gotti Sr.** both died of cancer (2001); the **Trump World Tower** opened at United Nations Plaza (2001); **Enron** filed for bankruptcy, the biggest in history (2001); the **General Electric** and **Honeywell** merger attempt failed (2001); following the International Accounting Standards Board's (IASB) requiring the **expensing of stock options,** the Financial Accounting Standards Board (FASB) announced it too would revisit the matter (2001); hundreds of **dot.com companies filed for bankruptcy** following falling stock prices (2001); *Business Driven Compensation Policies* was written by Herbert Heneman (2001); *Good to Great* was written by James Collins (2001); the federal **short term interest rate** had 10 decreases during the year, bringing it down to 1.75% (2001); an **American Airlines** flight crashed in New York City, killing 265 people (2001); war was declared on terrorist **Osama bin Laden** and the Afghanistan **Taliban** (2001); the Broadway play *The Producers* set a record of 12 Tony Awards (2001); the **DJIA** closed at 10,021.50 at year-end, down 7.1 percent (2001); a new Department of **Homeland Security** was created with over 100,000 employees from 22 merged agencies (2002); the Senate approved the **Strategic Offensive** reducing stockpiled nuclear weapons (2002); the former Secretary of State **Henry Kissinger** was named head of a federal commission to investigate the 9/11 attack (2002); the United States declared war against Iran (2002); the **Conference Board Commission** on Public Trust and Private Enterprise issued a **Blue Ribbon report** calling for tighter control of executive compensation (2002); a reduction in the federal **short term interest** rate lowered it to 1.25% (2002); the **Euro** became the common European currency (2002); AOL Time Warner and Xerox were among the companies that **restated earnings** (2002); **Hewlett Packard** acquired **Compaq** for $19 billion (2002); **Iraq** was taken over by United States and British troops for allegedly hiding weapons of mass destruction (2002); **Kmart** filed for bankruptcy (2002); **Pfizer** acquired Pharmacia for $60 billion and became the world's largest pharmaceutical company (2002); accounting firm **Arthur Anderson** virtually disappeared after its **Enron** involvement (2002); the telecom giant **WorldCom** imploded (2002); F.B.I. agent **Robert Hanssen** was arrested for spying for Russia (2002); the **DJIA** had a five year low of 7,286 during the year before starting a new bull market, closing at 8,341.63 at year-end, down 15.9 percent (2002); against the law, the *New York Times* revealed the name of CIA operative **Valerie Plame** (2003); California replaced Governor Gray Davis with **Arnold Schwarzenegger** on a recall vote (2003); **Saddam Hussein was captured and executed in Iraq** (2003); President Bush declared the end of major Iraq combat operations (2003); the spaceship *Columbia* burst into flames on reentry, killing the seven astronauts on board (2003); the **Delaware Court of Chancery** ruled that directors may be personally liable if they do not "act in good faith" (2003); the **National Association of Corporate Directors** (NACD) issued a Blue Ribbon Commission Report on Executive Compensation and the Role of the Compensation Committee (2003); the federal **short-term interest rate** was reduced from 1.25% to 1.0% (2003); Tyco CEO **Dennis Koslowski** was charged with plundering the company to support a lavish lifestyle (2003); former **Merrill Lynch** research internet analyst Henry Blodget agreed not to provide investment advice following a regulator investigation (2003); **Delta Airlines** CEO Leo Mullins gave back over $9 million in pay voluntarily following company losses (2003); **Campbell Soup** agreed to a $35 million settlement for allegedly boosting sales and profits (2003); the worst **blackout** in the nation's history paralyzed the Northeast for a day (2003); the supersonic **Concorde** made its last flight (2003); the **DJIA** closed at 10,453.92 at year-end, down 25.3 percent (2003); a **9/11 Commission Report** called for intelligence operations restructuring (2004); **George Bush** was reelected president, defeating John Kerry (2004); the **Boston Red Sox** won their first World Series since selling Babe Ruth to the New York Yankees (2004); the **U.S. Labor Department** made it easier to be exempted from **overtime premium pay** (2004); **WorldCom** emerged from bankruptcy (2004); the short-term **federal interest rate** increased .25% to 1.25%, later to 1.50%, and then 2.25% (2004); healthcare company **Johnson & Johnson** acquired the medical device company **Guidant** for $25 billion (2004); software maker **Oracle** acquired **PeopleSoft** for $10 billion (2004); **Kmart** acquired **Sears** for $11.5 billion (2004); **Hathaway stock** increased to over $90,000 a share (2004); business executive **Donald Trump** starred in reality TV show *The Apprentice* (2004); Harvard grad Mark Zuckerberg launched **Facebook** (2004); four **hurricanes** ripped through Florida and parts of the South during the summer (2004); a **tsunami** killed over 200,000 people in South Asia (2004); NBC anchor **Tom Brokaw** retired (2004); the **DJIA** closed at 10,783.01 at year-end, up 3.1 percent (2004); **House Majority Leader** Tom DeLay stepped down after being indicted and later convicted of money laundering (2005); oil costs exceeded $70 a barrel, up from $25 two years earlier (2005); eight former **KPMG** partners were indicted for inappropriate tax shelters (2005); **Delta Airlines** and **Northwest Air** filed for Chapter 11 bankruptcy (2005); Steve Wynn completed a $2.7 billion Las Vegas resort hotel, naming it the Wynn (2005); *Vanity Fair* article indicated Watergate's "**Deep Throat**" was former FBI agent W. Mark Felt (2005); rock star **Michael Jackson** was acquitted of child molestation charges (2005); the **DJIA** closed at 10,717.50 at year-end, down 0.6 percent (2005); former Republican lobbyist **Jack Abramoff** pleaded guilty to bribery and other charges (2006); Vice President **Dick Cheney** wounded a friend with a shotgun blast while hunting (2006); **Zacarias Moussaoui**, the only person tried for the 9/11 terror attack, pleaded guilty to conspiracy and was sentenced to six life terms in Virginia (2006); Secretary of Defense **Donald Rumsfeld** resigned and was succeeded by Robert Gates (2006); former Princeton professor **Ben Bernanke** became chair of the Federal Reserve (2006); **Henry Paulson** left Goldman Sachs and became Treasury Secretary (2006); the **Delaware Supreme Court** upheld their ruling for the Disney directors in a shareholder suit regarding the $190 million severance pay of **Michael Ovitz** (2006); regulators investigated more than 80 companies believed to have backdated executive stop options (2006); the **Delaware Court of Chancery** disallowed a director, in his capacity as such, the right to sue the company he served (2006); Massachusetts passed a healthcare bill with **individual mandated coverage**, a precursor to national legislation (2006); **AT&T** bought **BellSouth** Corporation for $67 billion (2006); the insurance giant **AIG** settled a SEC claim of $1.64 billion for deceiving investors and regulators (2006); **InBev** bought **Anheuser-Busch** for $52 billion (2006); the **Berkshire Hathaway stock price** went above $100,000 a share (2006); the New York Stock Exchange became **NYSE**, a publicly traded company (2006); the first tweet was sent by **Twitter** co-founder Jack Dorsey (2006); former Enron CEOs **Kenneth Lay** and **Jeffrey Skilling** were convicted of charges leading to the company's collapse (2006); **Democrats** won control of the House and Senate in the midterm elections (2006); proxy advisor **Glass Lewis & Co.** assigned grades ranging from "A" to "F" for CEO pay-for-performance packages (2006); over 1,200 companies **restated their financial statements** to correct errors (2006); heavy rains resulted in **severe flooding** in Mid-Atlantic states, forcing hundreds of thousands to leave their homes and causing over $1 billion in damages (2006); Roger Goodell succeeded Paul Tagliabue as **NFL Commissioner** (2006); the **DJIA** closed at 12,463.15 at year-end, up 16.3 percent (2006); Representative **Nancy Pelosi** became the first woman Speaker of the House (2007); President Bush announced he was sending 20,000 more troops to Iraq (2007); chief presidential political advisor **Karl Rove** resigned (2007); U.S. Attorney General **Alberto Gonzales** resigned after allegations of firing U.S. attorneys (2007); the vice president's chief of staff Lewis "**Scooter**" **Libby,** was found guilty of perjury and obstruction of justice (2007); the House Committee on **Oversight and Government Reform** investigated the relationship of consultants providing executive pay advice and providing other services (such as auditing) to companies (2007); President Bush stated that boards must step up to their responsibility and pay executives based on performance (2007); **ten Republicans** and **eight Democrats** announced their interest in being nominated for president of the United States (2007); **Robert Murdoch** paid $5 billion to buy the ***Wall Street Journal*** (2007); **Apple** introduced the **iPhone**, transforming the cell phone (2007); **Dewey Ballantine** LLP and **LeBoeuf Lamb, Green & Macrae** LLP merged to form Dewey & LeBouef LLP (2007); the **UAW** received a 55 percent stake in Chrysler in exchange for $6 billion debt in a healthcare account (2007); as sub-primes were defaulting in record numbers, by year-end more than one-third had defaulted (2007); **Hathaway stock sold** above $140,000 a share (2007); a deep recession began at year-end (2007); baseball player **Barry Bonds** was indicted on charges of perjury and obstruction of justice after becoming the all-time leader in home runs (2007); TV drama ***The Sopranos*** went off the air (2007); **Santa Ana winds** in California caused fires that consumed more than 400,000 acres and destroyed more than 2,000 homes (2007); after years of steady increases, house prices began to drop all over America (2007); for the first time in its history, Harvard named a woman, **Drew Gilpin Faust**, as president (2007); **U.S. Senator George Mitchell** released a report indicating 86 Major League players used performance-enhancing drugs (2007); the **DJIA** closed at 13,264.82 at year-end, up 6.4 percent (2007); **Timothy Geithner** was appointed Secretary of the Treasury (2008); **Hillary Clinton** was appointed Secretary of State (2008); Illinois Governor **Rod Blagojevich** was convicted of attempting to sell the state senate seat vacated by Barack Obama (2008); the Federal Reserve cut **interest rates** several times to spur the U.S. economy (2008); the Justice Department declassified a brief sanctioning the extreme **questioning of al-Qaeda** detainees (2008); the Federal Reserve set the **short term interest** rate to zero (2008); the Treasury announced plans to purchase up to $700 billion of **"toxic" mortgage-backed securities** (2008); the Federal Reserve granted **AIG an $85 billion** loan in exchange for 79.9% control of the company (2008); Alaska's U.S. Senator **Ted Stevens** was indicted on charges of corruption (2008); Massachusetts U.S. Senator **Ted Kennedy** learned he had brain cancer (2008); the collapse of the **mortgage market** caused the loss of some 900,000 jobs, and five million houses, and the stock market decline amounted to $35 trillion (2008); **Lehman Brothers** collapsed (2008); **Bear Stearns** merged with **JPMorgan Chase** (2008); with $55 billion in subprime losses, **Merrill Lynch** was sold to **Bank of America** for $50 billion (2008); **Citigroup** agreed to pay off its $45 billion in losses (2008); Bank of America, Chevron, and Kraft Foods were **added to the Dow Jones Industrial Average**, while

AIG, Altria, and Honeywell were removed (2008); mortgage leader **Washington Mutual** collapsed, the largest bank failure in U.S. history (2008); **Toyota** became America's number one car seller (2008); **Stephen Ross** bought the NFL **Miami Dolphins** for $1.1 billion (2008); **Visa** did an IPO for $17.9 billion (2008); the Federal Reserve put **Fannie Mae** and **Freddie Mac** under "conservatorship" (2008); Texas state authorities raided a **fundamentalist church**, taking into protective custody more than 400 children and charging the church officials with having sex with 12-year-olds (2008); heavy rains in the Midwest caused the **worst flooding** since 1993 (2008); **two trains** collided in California, killing 25 and injuring over 100 (2008); **oil peaked** at $147 a barrel (2008); swimmer **Michael Phelps** won a record eight Olympic gold medals (2008); and the **DJIA** closed at 8,776.39 at year-end, down 33.8 percent (2008). The **Consumer Price Index** rose an average of about 2.5% a year during Bush's presidency.

Barack Obama
(44th President)

January 20, 2009 – January 20, 2017

Barack Hussein Obama was born on August 4, 1961, to Barack Obama Sr. and Stanley Ann Obama, in Honolulu, Hawaii. He was the son of **Barack Obama Sr.**, who was Black and was born and raised in Kenya, Africa. After winning a scholarship to **Nairobi College,** he then went to the **University of Hawaii.** There he met **Stanley Ann Dunham**, who was born in Kansas and was white, fell in love, and got married in 1960. They produced one child, **Barack** (which means **Blessed** in Swahili). Obama had no full siblings, only half-siblings from his father's side: Auma, Bernard, David, George, Mark, Maya, and Roy. Barack Sr. went to **Harvard University**, leaving wife and child in Hawaii. The couple **divorced** when Barack Jr. (his nickname was

Barry), was two years old and Barack Sr. returned to Kenya. Ann met **Lolo Soetoro**, a student from **Indonesia**. They got married when he graduated from the University of Hawaii, when Barry was six years old, and moved to Indonesia. Lolo became an **anthropologist** in Jakarta. Barry learned the language, but he also took correspondence courses in English. Barry remembers his meals consisted of fermented soybean cake, fried rice, meatballs, roasted grasshoppers, and snake. The parents **divorced** in 1971. Ann, Barry, and Maya returned to Hawaii, where the two children went to a private college-preparatory school. While in high school, Barry's mixed-race led to **harassment**, and he quit the tennis team but continued with basketball. He then changed his name back to Barack and started reading Black authors and wearing his hair in an **afro**.

When Barack graduated from high school in 1979, Ann returned to Indonesia leaving the two children with her parents. Barack attended **Occidental College** in Los Angeles on a scholarship and then went to **Columbia University**. He graduated in 1983 with a bachelor's degree in political science and took a job as a research assistant before moving to Chicago and becoming a *community organizer* for $13,000 a year in 1985.

In 1985, he **flew to Kenya** to meet his extended family, his father had died. Upset with the poor living conditions of the family, Barack wrote *Dreams from my Father*. In 1988, Barack returned to the United States and entered **Harvard Law School**. He graduated in 1991, **magna cum laude** and was the **first African-American** to head the prestigious *Harvard Law Review*.

Michelle LaVaughn Robinson was born on January 17, 1964, in Chicago, Illinois. She graduated **cum laude** with a **bachelor's degree** from **Princeton University** in 1985 and enrolled in **Harvard Law School**, graduating with a J.D. in 1988 and joining the **law firm** Sidley & Austin, specializing in marketing and intellectual property rights. There **she met Barack**, who was a summer associate. He wanted to date her, but she had no interest. However, **he pursued** her, and finally she gave in. Barry enjoyed trying new foods and was labeled a "foodie." In Chicago, he enjoyed Italian food, soul food, and steak and eggs. He also enjoyed a hamburger with Grey Poupon mustard. He would later be called "**President Poupon**," "**First Eater**," and the "**Food President**."

Three years after meeting, Barack and Michelle **got married** on October 3, 1992. Michelle went to work for Chicago Mayor Richard Daley. After three years she became **associate dean of students** at the **University of Chicago**. Six years later, she was **executive director** for the University of Chicago's community affairs. In 2005, she was promoted to **vice president**. When Barack became the Democratic candidate for president in 2008, Michelle stepped down and joined the campaign. She was nicknamed "the closer" for her work. Their daughters, Malia Ann, and Sasha were born in 1998 and 2001.

When he had the time, Obama's personal interests included reading all the *Harry Potter* **books** to his daughters and *Spider-Man* for himself. On TV, he preferred **watching sports** (especially basketball) to news programs. Obama's daughters graduated from high school in Washington, D.C., Malia in 2016 and Sasha in 2019.

In 1997, Barack was elected a **state senator**, and in 2004 he was a keynote speaker at the Democratic Presidential Convention. This led to his election as a **U.S. senator** in 2004, followed by his being selected as the **Democratic candidate for president,** having fought off **Hillary Clinton** for the Democratic nomination for president. He was very complimentary of his opponent, and after the election he named her as his **Secretary of State**, believing that being the wife of former President Bill Clinton would be too much of a complication if she were vice president. Obama decided to choose **Delaware's Senator Joe Biden** as his running mate. Obama believed Biden not only had great **foreign policy** and **domestic experience** but would also give Obama the **unvarnished truth**, even if he was a little long-winded.

In his **presidential campaign**, Obama stated, "Change will not come if we wait for some other person or if we wait for some other time. We are the ones we have been waiting for. We are the change that we seek." Obama's **campaign slogan** was "Change we can believe in," and his promise was "yes, we can." On the campaign trail Obama tried to establish rapport with Iowa farmers, he said, "In Chicago, the main livestock is squirrels."

There were **three televised presidential debates** between Democrat Barack Obama and Republican John McCain. The first was held on September 26, 2008, in Oxford, Mississippi. The second was held on October 7, 2008, in Nashville, Tennessee. And the third was held on October 15, 2008, in Hempstead, New York. There was **one televised vice presidential debate** between Democrat Joe Biden and Republican Sarah Palin on October 2, 2008, in St. Louis Missouri.

In the 2008 election, Democrats **Barack Obama** and **Joseph Biden** defeated Republicans **John McCain** and **Sarah Palin** 66,882,230 to 58,343,671 in the popular vote and 365 to 173 in the electoral vote. Obama became the **first African-American president**. Biden became Obama's vice president.

Joseph Robinette Biden was **born on November 20, 1942**, in Scranton, Pennsylvania, and grew up in a **working-class, Cath-**

olic family. When Joe started speaking, he developed a stutter which plagued him for years. While in third grade, Joe worked on his stutter by speaking with marbles in his mouth. In 1960, the family moved to Wilmington, Delaware, where Joe went to a Catholic college-prep high school. There he was active in sports and was elected class president. He also became interested in politics as it was a dinnertime topic. After graduation, he went to the **University of Delaware** where he graduated in 1965 with a bachelor's degree. He then entered the **University of Syracuse Law School**, graduating in 1968 with a J.D. It was at Syracuse that he met and married Neilia Hunter in 1968. They went onto have three children: **Joseph** (Beau), **Robert Hunter**, and **Naomi Christina**. After being admitted to the Delaware bar, Joe became a **public defender**. Shortly thereafter, he was **drafted** into the army but **failed the physical** due to asthma. In 1972, he was **elected to the U.S. Senate** from Delaware. He would go on to be **elected for 36 years**. But shortly after his inauguration, his wife and daughter were killed in a car accident. Both sons were injured but survived. Joe married his second wife, **Jill Jacobs**, on June 17, 1977. Biden had been introduced to her by his brother, **Frank**. They went onto have one child, **Ashley Blazer**. Jill earned a **doctorate** in education and served as an **English professor**. Joe was unsuccessful in two attempts at gaining the Democratic nomination for the presidency, but in 2008 he was **Obama's running mate**.

Voter dissatisfaction with the economy and President Bush not only contributed to Obama's victory, but also increased the Democrats' control in the House of Representatives (254 to 173) and gave them control of the Senate (56 seats to 40 with 4 independents). More than 70 million people turned on their TV sets to watch (and listen) to **Obama's acceptance speech**. He stated, "The state of our economy calls for action, bold and swift." And we will act, not only to create jobs but to lay a foundation for growth."

On the day of his inauguration, Obama was 47 years old. He is the first president **born outside of the lower 48 states**. In his January 20, **2009, inaugural address**, Obama stated, "On this day we come to proclaim an end to the petty grievances of false promises, the recriminations and worn-out dogmas that for too long have strangled our politics." Obama also stated, "For too long, we've been blind to the way past injustices continues to shape the present."

The recession that began with the end of Clinton's presidency was in full force upon Obama's arrival. The problem had been caused by many Americans taking-on high-interest mortgages that they were unable to afford. The result was a large number of foreclosures and the loss of homes, followed by an unemployment rate of 7.8%, which would rise to 10% in October. And Obama was upset about executive pay. He stated, "What gets people upset, and rightfully so, is when executives get rewarded for failure." As a follow-up, Secretary of the Treasury Timothy Geithner, ordered that companies who had not repaid bailout money were to reduce executive pay by 50%.

Obama issued an executive order on January 22, 2009, restricting CIA interrogation practices and ordering the closure of the **Guantanamo Bay prison** in Cuba (but this was blocked by Congress). Thus, Obama failed on his 2007 campaign promise to close the Guantanamo Bay terrorist detention facility, but the number of prisoners declined to a little more than a hundred (from a high of close to 700) through releasing the detainees.

A number of former chiefs of staff met with Obama to give him counsel on who should be his **chief of staff**. Obama decided to take **Rahm Emanuel,** a former Clinton aide who was a brilliant hard charger in the House of Representatives. He put a sign on his desk that said, "Undersecretary for Go F*ck Yourself." He had a **big ego** and a **sharp** temper. Obama relied heavily on two typically different people: long-time friend **Valerie Jarrett** and Chief of Staff **Rahm Emanuel.** Valerie was soft-spoken. Rahm was famously profane. These two were the enforcers of the "No Drama Obama" rule.

The initial **cabinet** members during Obama's first term of office were: **Vice President** Joe Biden **Secretary of State** Hillary Clinton, **Secretary of the Treasury** Timothy Geithner, **Secretary of Defense** Robert Gates, **Attorney General** Eric Holder, **Secretary of the Interior** Ken Salazar, **Secretary of Agriculture** Thomas Vilsack, **Secretary of Commerce** Gary Locke, **Secretary of Labor** Hilda Solis, **Secretary of Health and Human Services** Kathleen Sebelius, **Secretary of Housing and Urban Development** Shaun Donovan, **Secretary of Transportation** Ray LaHood, **Secretary of Energy** Steven Chu, **Secretary of Education** Arne Duncan, **Secretary of Veterans Affairs** Eric Shinseki, and **Secretary of Homeland Security** Janet Napolitano.

Obama did not want the backstabbing, access jockeying, internal turmoil and leaks that prevailed with previous White House staff. He had a strong distaste for contentiousness and disagreement. He **wanted commitment, empowerment, inclusion,** and **loyalty.** There was no room for prima donnas. The rule was "stay within your lane." When balancing family and politics in the White House, Michelle called herself "Mom-in-Chief."

President Obama's first priority was to stimulate the economy. He got Congress to pass four laws. The **2009 American Recov-**

ery and Investment Act** provided $787 billion for construction projects, research, and social programs. It placed restrictions on companies receiving federal funds through TARP (Troubled Asset Relief Programs) including restrictions on executive pay. The **2009 Economic Stimulus Act** established a special master to oversee executive pay for TARP companies. The **2009 Ledbetter Act** revised a statute of limitations on pay discrimination issues. And the **2009 Tax Act** increased the tax exemption on estates to $3.5 million from $2 million. As a U.S. senator, Obama had promised **legislative transparency** and that, if elected president, he would post pending bills online for five days before signing. Shortly after taking the oath of office, he signed into law several acts that were passed only days earlier by Congress. Guess he forgot his pledge.

In **Nelson vs United States** (2009) the U.S. Supreme Court ruled that the United States Sentencing Guidelines are not mandatory for sentencing actions.

In 2009, Congress increased the pay of legislators to $174,000 (up from 2008's $169,000); associate justices of the Supreme Court's pay was increased to $213,900 (up from 2008's $208,100); and the chief justice's pay was increased to $223,500 (up from 2008's $217,400). Cabinet secretaries' pay was increased to $199,700 (up from 2008's $196,700).

Obama and **Secretary of the Treasury Geithner loaned money** to Citibank and other financial institutions suffering from the 2008 mortgage crisis, as well as, to auto companies: General Motors and Chrysler, who were not selling cars. The government gave $2 trillion to stabilize banking and the credit markets supported by stress tests for them. Republicans charged that Obama had presided over the largest **government expansion** in decades.

Shortly after the inauguration, President Obama's **approval ratings** were about 70%, but by the summer they had fallen to 50%. He was being criticized on a number of fronts. The Republicans were charging him with being responsible for the largest government in history. The **TEA** (Taxed Enough Already) party stated he was not doing enough on tax reform. And many did not agree with the government bailing out General Motors, calling it **Government Motors** because the government owned 603 of GM's shares. Also, many were concerned that, due to spending and tax cuts Obama had raised the **federal deficit** to a record $176.4 billion.

In **Crawford vs Nashville and Davidson County** (2009), the U.S. Supreme Court ruled that witnesses giving testimony are protected against retaliation under Section 704(1) of the 1964 Civil Rights Act. In **14 Penn Plaza LLC vs Pyett** (2009), the U.S. Supreme Court ruled that a collective bargaining agreement that requires mandatory arbitration by union members is enforceable. And in **Ysursa vs Pocatello Education Association** (2009), the U.S. Supreme Court ruled that the court cannot violate union First Amendment rights.

To reach out to the public with his messages, Obama liked the idea of FDR's fireside chat. He took advantage of the advancement in technology and put a video on the Internet every Saturday morning, and he also established a **YouTube Channel** at the White House.

President Obama received an average of 1,000 letters per day. He made it a practice to **read ten letters a day**. The letters ranged from despair to hope, from "thank you" to "you are doing a terrible job." Some he answered himself, some he passed on to another person, and some he ignored. He believed this was an important way to stay in touch with the people. Obama once said to his staff, "One voice can change a room." Some who had received a note from the president cited how important it was to them that their message had been heard.

On October 29, 2009, the **Gross Domestic Product** rose at a 3.5% annual, signaling the end of the recession. On December 10, 2009, Obama received the **Nobel Peace Prize** for "efforts to strengthen international diplomacy." Previous presidential winners were Theodore Roosevelt and Woodrow Wilson. President Obama stated, "You don't make peace with your friends. You make peace with your enemies and the best way to start is to break bread together."

Obama decided to let Congress write the healthcare law. Reflecting on the amount of detail in the package, House Speaker Nancy Pelosi said, "We have to pass the bill to find out what is in it," a classic case of putting the cart before the horse. In March 2010, Obama got the **Patient Protection and Affordable Care Act** approved by Congress without a single Republican vote. It extended eligibility and healthcare coverage to some 32 million Americans. It passed in the House 219 to 211 and the Senate by 60 to 39. Labeled Obama's greatest accomplishment, it succeeded where the Clintons' plan had failed. Obama had gotten a **federal national healthcare** program adopted. To comply with the cost of the plan, many companies found it necessary to let some people go. The *Wall Street Journal* reported that "President Obama has imposed the largest tax increase in history on the middle class," when the Supreme Court ruled that the individual mandate was a tax. It was said that Obamacare had eighteen new tax hikes of over $360 billion during his time in office. The Republicans tried repeatedly to get Obamacare repealed, but they failed. When the **U.S. Supreme Court ruled** the **Act was constitutional**, the game was over.

Early in **2010**, Obama created the **National Commission on Fiscal Responsibility** and appointed Erskine Bowles and Alan Simpson to head it up. They called for deep spending cuts. In 2010, Obama also signed the **Tax Relief and Unemployment Compensation Act**, an $18 billion act to stimulate job growth. Shortly after, he and Russian President Medvedev signed an arms reduction treaty, but some 50,000 U.S. troops remained in Iraq. Also in 2010, Obama signed the **Unemployment Compensation Extension Act**, which extended unemployment benefits for 20 weeks. That year, he also signed legislation which imposed some 400 regulations on the financial systems portion of the U.S. economy, described in 2,300 pages addressing many aspects of corporate governance. Obama also signed the **2010 Foreign Account Tax Compliance Act**, requiring the reporting of income received outside the United States. Obama said, "Focusing on making money is a lack of what's important. At some point, one has enough money." The **2010 Model Business Corporation Act** cited the business judgement rule and duty of loyalty of shareholders. The **2010 Tax Act** repealed the estate tax for one year. And the **2010 Pension Act** gave two alternatives to the seven-year amortization rule. Later, **pay czar Feinberg** held pay under $500,000 for executives at AIG, Chrysler, General Motors and AMAAC. He also identified 17 banks for making "ill advised" payments to their executives. Reportedly the **top 10% of earners** received 48% of all income vs 34% fifty years earlier. The Federal Reserve announced it would buy **$600 billion** in treasury securities to stimulate the economy.

In **Citizens United vs Federal Election Committee** (2010), the U.S. Supreme Court ruled that government is prohibited from restricting political expenditures of companies and unions.

When **Chicago Mayor Richard Daley** announced he would not run for reelection, it opened the door for Emanuel's dream job.

He resigned as chief of staff and was elected mayor of Chicago. **Bill Daley**, son of the former mayor, was the next chief of staff.

In **2010**, with the retirement of Associate Justice **John Paul Stevens** on August 5, 2010, the Senate confirmed Obama's choice, Solicitor General and former Dean of Harvard Law School **Elena Kagan**, who opposed the military's "don't ask, don't tell" policy.

In **the 2010 midterm elections**, the Republicans picked up six seats in the Senate (raising their total to 47) and 63 seats in the House (for a total of 236).

In **2011**, based on intelligence reports, Obama learned of the presence of Osama bin Laden in a compound in Pakistan. Obama then authorized **Operation Neptune Spear**, four helicopters and 24 SEALS to get Osama. The result was the **death of Osama bin Laden** on May 2, 2011. When Osama bin Laden was killed, countless documents were captured. But instead of deferring the announcement and acting on the information, Obama made a quick announcement of Osama bin Laden's death, which gave the insurgents time to react and cover their tracks. What followed was a number of individual attacks on the U.S. by radical Islamists.

Later in 2011, Obama signed legislation extending the **USA Patriot Act**, and the **Budget Control Act** which set the estate tax at 35 percent with a $5 million exemption and raised the debt ceiling of $2 trillion to $14.3 trillion. The result was the loss of America's AAA credit rating to AA+. In **AT&T Mobility vs Concepcion** (2011), the U.S. Supreme Court ruled that federal rules are favored over Californian arbitration rules. In late **December 2011**, Obama finally announced that the **war in Iraq was over**, and the last American troops had left the country.

Several years later, Obama sent military advisors to Iraq when Islamic extremists identified as **ISIS** moved into Iraq which was followed by **Operation Intent Resolve**, which launched 12,000 air strikes at 31,000 targets in Iraq. North Carolina Representative Walter Jones tried and failed to get Obama impeached for unauthorized use of drones in Afghanistan and Pakistan as an abuse of power.

In **Christopher vs SmithKline Beecham Corp** (2012), the U.S. Supreme Court ruled that pharmaceutical sales representatives are not eligible for overtime, as they are considered to be outside salespeople. In **Arizona vs United States** (2012), the U.S. Supreme Court overturned most of Arizona's tough immigration laws but left in place the police's ability to do roadside immigration checks. In **National Federation of Independent Business et al vs Sebelius, Secretary of Health and Human Services** (2012), the U.S. Supreme Court upheld the "2010 Patient Protection and Affordable Care Act." Also in **2012**, the **Middle-Class Tax Relief and Job Creation Act** extended the payroll tax holiday and unemployment compensation. Also in 2012, when Obama signed an executive order creating the **Deferred Action for Childhood Arrivals (DACA)**, he allowed illegal minor children to stay in the United States in renewable two-year periods. The result was over **100,000 unaccompanied minors** entering the U.S. between 2014 and 2015.

A year-end **government shutdown** was avoided with a $915 billion omnibus funding federal agencies through fiscal year 2012. **President Obama** a released copy of his **birth certificate** to dispel rumors of his being born outside of the U.S. When **Bill Daley resigned** in 2012, he was **replaced** with OMB Director **Jacob Lew,** who was the third OMB director to **take the job** (the others were Leon Panetta (President Clinton) and Joshua

Bolton (President George Bush), on the day Jacob Lew began as chief of staff in June.

In Obama's speech for the democratic nomination at the **2012 Democratic National Convention** in Charlotte, North Carolina, Obama took exception to President Reagan's view of the government. Obama stated, "We don't think government can solve all our problems, but we don't think that government is the source of all our problems." He also said, "Government works best when people can participate in that government."

In the **2012 Republican National Convention**, former Massachusetts Governor Mitt Romney was named the presidential nominee and Wisconsinite Paul Ryan was named his running mate.

On September 11, 2012, the under-protected **U.S. Embassy in Benghazi**, Libya, was attacked by Islamic terrorists, resulting in the death of the U.S. Ambassador and three others. This occurred two months before Obama's re-election. Obama and Secretary of State Hillary Clinton were questioned about the issue of adequate security.

There were **three televised presidential debates** between Democratic President Barack Obama and Republican Mitt Romney. The first was held on October 3, 2012, in Denver, Colorado. The second was held on October 16, 2012, in Hempstead, New York. And the third was held on October 22, 2012, in Boca Raton, Florida. There was **one televised vice presidential debate** between Democratic Vice President Joe Biden and Republican Paul Ryan held on October 11, 2012, in Danville, Kentucky.

In the **2012 election**, Democrats **Barack Obama** and **Joe Biden** defeated Republicans **Mitt Romney** and **Paul Ryan**, 65,455,010 to 60,771,703 in the popular vote and 332 to 206 in the electoral vote. Democrats maintained a Senate majority with 53 seats, but the Republicans held on to a House majority with 234 of the 425 seats. Former JPMorgan Chase executive **John Boehner** became Speaker of the House of Representatives.

In his **January 2013 State of the Union Address**, Obama stated a healthcare plan was important. Government spending consumed over 8% of GNP, compared with a little over 1% 10 years ago, but it was more important to fix the economy. The country was in a recession. Unemployment was close to 8%, the stock market was down, and banks were suffering from a mortgage crisis with people unable to meet interest payments. Obama called for government action to gain more manufacturing jobs and a millionaire's tax to increase revenue and achieve better net income balance.

At his **inaugural address** on January 20, **2013**, Obama used Lincoln's bible. It had not been used since Lincoln. Obama stated, "We are made for this moment, and we will seize it, so long as we seize it together." Democrats controlled both houses.

Obama's initial **cabinet** members during his second term of office included **Vice President** Joe Biden, **Secretary of State** John Kerry, **Secretary of the Treasury** Jack Lew, **Secretary of Defense** Chuck Hagel, **Attorney General** Eric Holder, **Secretary of the Interior** Sally Jewell, **Secretary of Agriculture** Thomas Vilsack, **Secretary of Commerce** Penny Pritzker, **Secretary of Labor** Thomas Perez, **Secretary of Health and Human Services** Sylvia Burwell, **Secretary of Housing and Urban Development** Shaun Donovan, **Secretary of Transportation** Anthony Fox, **Secretary of Energy** Ernest Montz, **Secretary of Education** Arne Duncan, **Secretary of Veterans Affairs** Eric Shinseki, and

Secretary of Homeland Security Jeh Johnson. Later, **Loretta Lynch** became the first Black woman to become the U.S. Attorney General.

Although Obama promised "an unprecedented level of openness in government," *New York Times* editor Margaret Sullivan reported Obama showed "an unprecedented attack on a free press" in 2013. Other reporters questioned receiving negative feedback after asking difficult questions. Was Obama unduly sensitive to questioning? Apparently, the Obama administration even evoked the **1917 Espionage Act** when seeking information leaks in his staff. Like several other past presidents, reportedly Obama had a bad temper, which occasionally led to hostile outbursts and vindictive actions.

In **Gabelli vs Securities Exchange Commission** (2013), the U.S. Supreme Court ruled that the Commission must act promptly in seeking civil penalties. In **Vanos vs Ball State** (2013), the U.S. Supreme Court ruled that a supervisor is defined as a person with authority to hire, fire, remote, promote, transfer, and discipline a worker. In October 2013, healthcare.gov, the government website for the Affordable Care Act crashed! The systems had not been tested.

In **2013, Congress, unable to agree to cuts** in the $16.4 trillion debt, triggered an automatic $85 billion reduction in federal programs or 2.4 percent of the $3.6 trillion federal budget. The **weekly jobless** rate fell to 346,000 or 7.2% of the workforce, the lowest in six years. Only 63.1 percent of the **labor force** was working or looking for work, the lowest level since 1978.

In **2013**, the **American Taxpayer Relief Act** increased the max tax to 39.6 percent (from 35 percent) and the capital gains tax to 20 percent (from 15 percent).

When **Tim Geithner** announced his resignation as Treasury Secretary, **Jack Lew** was appointed as his replacement, followed by Deputy National Security Advisor **Denis McDonough** as Lew's replacement. Lew learned from Jim Baker that "there's no accountability without clear responsibility."

In his **January 2014 State of the Union Address**, President Obama stated he would give Congress a voice in the **nuclear agreement** with Iran. In response to the question of how he would get Congress to act on his preferences, in 2014 President Obama said, "I've got a pen and a phone," implying he did not need Congress.

In **2014**, the *Wall Street Journal* announced that 52% of **Dodd-Frank laws** had been covered with 389 rules. Also in **2014, two key laws** were enacted. In the **Workforce Innovation and Opportunity Act,** job training programs were consolidated into a single funding program, and the **Veterans Access, Choice, and Accountability Act** allowed vets to receive treatment at non-VA facilities. And in 2014, the U.S. Supreme Court ruled on four cases. In **Harris vs Quinn** (2014), the U.S. Supreme Court ruled that nonunion workers are not required to pay union dues. In **Schuette vs Coalition to Defend Affirmative Action** (2014), the U.S. Supreme Court ruled that an applicant's race cannot be used for admission to a public university. In **United States vs Quality Stores** (2014), the U.S. Supreme Court ruled that severance payments are subject to Social Security and Medicare taxes. In **Integrity Staff vs Busk** (2014), the U.S. Supreme Court ruled that Amazon workers are not entitled to overtime when subjected to end-of-shift searches for theft. Also in 2014, Defense Secretary **Chuck Hagel** resigned and was succeeded by **Ashton Carter. Taxpayers paid $1.4 billion** in income taxes, an average of $4,400 a person. In the same year, almost half of the federal government expenditures went to **Social Security, Medicare,** and related programs.

In early **2015,** President Obama discussed **American-Cuban relations** with Cuban President Raul Castro at a meeting in Panama. Later, President **Obama removed Cuba** from a list of countries sponsoring **terrorism.** This was followed by both countries **reopening their embassies** and restoring diplomatic relations. He also stated, "The shadow crisis has passed. We have risen from the recession." Defining his doctrine underlying decisions to thaw relations with countries such as Iran and Cuba, President Obama stated that "we will engage but preserve all our capabilities."

It was reported that the **rise of ISIS** was largely overlooked until it became a real issue in 2015. Later in the year, the **Nigerian terrorist Boko Haram** kidnapped hundreds of schoolgirls that were sold into slavery. Their actions were largely ignored by the Obama administration.

U.S. Secretary of State **John Kerry** broke his leg in Geneva, Switzerland while meeting with Iran on nuclear talks. On June 14, **2015,** the Obama Administration secured a **nuclear deal** with six countries that got Iran to limit Iranian nuclear capability in exchange for lifting economic sanctions on Iran. In responding to the **nuclear treaty with Iran**, Obama stated, "We don't have diplomatic leverage to eliminate every vestige of a peaceful nuclear program in Iran. What we have is the leverage to make sure that they don't have a weapon now. That's exactly what we've done."

On August 3, **2015,** Obama announced the **Clean Power Plan,** imposing carbon dioxide limits on power plant emissions. The Supreme Court later ruled it unconstitutional. The U.S. and over

190 countries agreed to reduce **greenhouse gases**. The **U.S. and Cuba reopened embassies** in their countries. Also in **2015**, four laws were enacted. The **Clay Hunt Act** required an annual evaluation of veterans' mental health care and suicide prevention programs for veterans. The **Freedom Act** reined in government data collection. The **Equity in Government Compensation Act** suspended Fannie Mae and Freddie Mac CEO pay packages. And the **Veterans Entrepreneurship Act** increased capital access for veterans.

In **Rodriguez vs United States** (2015), the U.S. Supreme Court ruled that in the absence of reasonable suspicion, a police extension of a traffic stop in order to conduct a dog sniff violates the Constitution's shield against unreasonable seizure. In **Mach Mining vs EEOC** (2015), the U.S. Supreme Court ruled that it is limited to the EEOC's statutory obligation to give the employer notice and opportunity to achieve voluntary compliance. In **EEOC vs Abercrombie & Fitch Stores** (2015), the U.S. Supreme Court ruled that to prevail in a disparate treatment claim an applicant need show only that his need for an accommodation was a motivating factor in the employer's decision, not that the employer had knowledge of the need.

In **December 2015**, President Obama signed the **Paris Accord**, a voluntary, non-binding agreement with 195 countries to lower greenhouse gas emissions. Obama signed an executive order reducing these emissions by 15% below 2015 levels by 2025.

Associate Justice of the **U.S. Supreme Court Antonin Scalia died** on February 13, 2016. On March 16, 2016, Obama nominated **Merrick Garland** as his successor, but the Senate refused to confirm him, as it was too close to the end of Obama's term. Stating it would be reviewed after the 2016 election.

At the June **2016 Democratic Convention** in Philadelphia, Pennsylvania, former Secretary of State **Hillary Clinton** was nominated for president and U.S. Senator **Tim Kaine** was nominated for vice president. Although Obama thought **Biden would be an adequate president**, it is **believed he thought Hillary would be a better one**, remembering how effective she was in debating him. When questioned as to his presidential qualifications after ruling himself out of the race, **Vice President Joe Biden** replied, "I believe I would have been a very good president, but the timing is not right."

In **Hefferman vs Paterson NJ** (2016), the U.S. Supreme Court ruled that when an employer demotes an employee out of a desired position to prevent the employee from engaging in protected political activity, the employee is entitled to challenge that unlawful action under the First Amendment. In **Betterman vs Montana** (2016), the U.S. Supreme Court ruled that the Sixth Amendment's speedy trial guarantee does not apply once a defendant has been found guilty at trial or has pleaded guilty to criminal charges. In **Fisher vs University of Texas at Austin** (2016), the U.S. Supreme Court ruled that the race-conscious admissions program in use at the time of the petition application was lawful under the Fourth Amendment.

Bill and Hillary Clinton revealed receiving **$139 million** for the 2007-2014 period. Former Secretary of State **Hillary Clinton** admitted to deleting about 30,000 **personal emails**. The State Department Inspector and the FBI General criticized Hillary Clinton using her **private e-mail** while Secretary of State. Presidential candidate **Hillary Clinton** and her husband Bill defended the non-political nature of their **family foundation**.

Of the **17 Republican candidates** for president of the United States only Donald Trump remained going into the convention.

At the **August 2016 Republican Convention**, in Charlotte, North Carolina, **Donald Trump** was selected as the candidate for president and Indiana Governor **Michael Pence** was selected as his vice-presidential running partner. Commenting on Donald Trump's candidacy for president, President Obama stated, "This is not a reality show."

When presidential candidate **Donald Trump** was asked about his taxes, he replied, "It's none of your business." When queried about his flexibility on issues, he replied, "I am totally flexible on very, very many issues."

In **2016, three key laws** were enacted. The **Comprehensive Recovery Act** awarded grants to address opioid and heroin abuse. The **FOIA** provided provisions to improve the Freedom of Information Act. The **International Megan's Law** stated that registered sex offenders must provide advance notice of travel.

At the **White House Correspondents' Dinner** in 2016, President Obama said, "Taking a stand on behalf of what is true does not require you shredding your objectivity." Based on evidence, Russia hacked into Democratic Party records in an attempt to influence the presidential voting, President Obama shut down two Russian facilities in the U.S. and **expelled 35 Russian diplomats** for their actions.

Although presidential candidate Obama promised that, if elected, he would go through the federal budget line by line to eliminate waste, given the presence and amount of some questionable items, one wonders if he really did that. The budget was historically late in being finalized, namely by after the first Monday of February. And eight of the largest annual federal deficits were set by Obama up through his term of office; three exceeded one trillion dollars. It was almost as much as all the previous presidents had done in total.

In **2016**, the **Pew Research Center** reported that a majority of Americans, for the first time in some forty years, said we were no longer viewed as the world's peacekeeper. Some went on to state we should no longer have that responsibility.

A major issue during Obama's tenure as president was the **thousands of veterans** who died while awaiting care in veterans' hospitals. Also, evidence supports that the IRS targeted GOP supporters; the response by some was that this was not the first time that audit of persons not in political power occurred.

The Obama administration had more than its share of **fraud**. This included food stamps, Medicare and Medicaid, and unemployment compensation. Obama seemed to be surprised about **domestic scandals** and international actions. Didn't he have the CIA and FBI to keep him current?

Obama's **lack of foreign policy experience** led to some embarrassing comments and questionable actions. Among them were sending troops to Libya and Syria without congressional approval and that the "special relationship" with England was strained when Obama returned a bust of Winston Churchill to England that had been in the Oval Office since George Bush the 41st was president. And although America had supported **Israel** ever since it's 1948 origin, Obama seemed to align himself more with Israel's enemies than with Israel and its friends. One must question to what extent President Obama blamed the Republicans in general, and his predecessor President George Bush the 43rd in particular, for things that happened during Obama's term of office. Some believe that Obama did little other than show weakness to our enemies and brand us as unreliable to others.

The Obama administration did not receive good grades for helping American homeowners, whose **heavily mortgaged homes** had a fair value less than the outstanding mortgage. The **stagnation** continued past Obama's term of office. Records show that the **growth in employment** that Obama cited was overwhelmingly in part-time, not full-time jobs. While presidents have been known to reward generous donors with **political appointments**, given the limitations of the Pendleton Act, some have questioned Obama in his selections.

In his final **State of the Union Address**, President **Obama** defended his record, stating, "We recovered from the worst economic crisis in generations." During his eight years as President, the country recovered from the **Great Recession** of 2007-2009 left to him by President Bush. Obama left the country with bankruptcies down, home values increased, the stock market up, and unemployment down. Before leaving office, Obama gave out more **Medals of Freedom** to entertainers and big donors than all the previous presidents combined. He also signed a record number of some **145 executive orders creating new regulations**.

While most presidents granted a handful of or fewer **commutations** on their last day in office, President Obama handed out 330 commutations – setting a new record for the most commutations granted in a single day.

Was Obama a great president? It may be argued he did not enforce immigration laws; he waged war without a vote from Congress, and he made appointments without the advice and consent of the Senate. Given his work on Obamacare, he was more a chief legislator than a chief executive and he strengthened the view of those who believed he attempted to create an American elected monarch. But many historians would rate his performance more effective than most.

WHAT YOU SHOULD KNOW ABOUT THE 47 U.S. PRESIDENTS

KEY EVENTS

Senator Ted Kennedy died of brain cancer (2009); the U.S. Treasury ordered **seven companies** that had not repaid government bailout money **to cut top executive pay** by 50% (2009); **Fannie Mae** reported a loss of $72 billion after mortgage forfeitures (2009); the **Federal Reserve** announced the review of bank pay policies to ensure they were not based on excess risk (2009); Illinois Governor **Rod Blagojevich** was removed from office after being found guilty of corruption and attempting to sell Barack Obama's vacant U.S. Senate seat (2009); financier **Bernard Madoff** was found guilty of a massive Ponzi scheme and sentenced to a lifetime in prison (2009); retiring Associate Justice of the U.S. Supreme Court **David Souter** was replaced by **Sonia Sotomayor**, the court's first **Hispanic Justice** (2009); mark-to-market loss on **sub-prime mortgages** was put at $3 trillion (2009); **Pfizer** acquired **Wyeth** for $68 billion (2009); **General Electric** sold NBC to Comcast for $30 billion (2009); **Visa** raised almost $15 billion in an IPO (2009); Moody's and Standard & Poor's **stripped GE** of the AAA rating it had held for 42 years (2009); General Motors stopped producing **Oldsmobile and Pontiac** in an attempt to avoid bankruptcy (2009); **Chrysler** announced the closing of 800 of its 3,200 dealerships (2009); **General Motors** expected to close 6,000 of its dealerships by 2010 (2009); ten large banks repaid $68 billion in **TARP** bailouts (2009); the human resource consulting firms **Towers Perrin** and **Watson Wyatt** agreed to merge forming **Towers Watson** (2009); **GM** exited bankruptcy retaining Buick, Cadillac, and Chevrolet (2009); Goldman Sachs paid back the **$700 billion it had been loaned** from the U.S. government (2009); Cisco and Travelers replaced Citigroup and General Motors in the DJIA composite of 30 companies (2009); **Circuit City** went bankrupt (2009); a **swine flu** virus broke out in the U.S. (2009); some **8.4 million jobs** were lost since the beginning of the 2008 recession (2009); after a US Airways jet lost power when geese flew into the engines, **Captain Sullenberger** put the plane onto the Hudson River, saving the crew and all 155 passengers (2009); 36 hours after a concert rehearsal, **Michael Jackson** died (2009); late night TV host **David Letterman** confessed to sexual affairs when faced with blackmail (2009); **Ship Captain Richard Phillips** was saved from Somali pirates (2009); the **DJIA** closed at 10,428.05 at year end, up 18.8 percent (2009); the final landing of the space shuttle *Atlantis* ended the space shuttle program (2010); Democratic House Representative **Charles Rangel** was found guilty of 11 counts of ethics violations (2010); retiring U.S. Supreme Court Associate Justice, **John Paul Stevens** was replaced by **Elena Kagan** (2010); the **Simpson Bowles Commission** called for cuts in federal spending to lower the government debt (2010); the Ninth Circuit Court of Appeals ruled that in addition to the right to keep and bear arms, the **Second Amendment** protects the right to buy and sell arms (2010); a giant oil spill in the **Gulf** was blamed on **Halliburton** (2010); **America's debt** passed $14 trillion (2010); **Continental Airlines** and **United Airlines** agreed to a $3 billion merger (2010); **Merck** acquired **Schering** for $50 billion (2010); **Michael Jordan** was the first ex-basketball player to become the majority owner of an NBA team (the Charlotte Bobcats) (2010); **unemployment** ended the year at 8.5% and: the **DJIA** ended the year at 11,577.51, up 11.0 percent (2010); **Patrick Kennedy, Jr.**, left the House of Representatives, ending 64 consecutive years of a Kennedy serving as an elected official in Washington, D.C. (2011); the **Martin Luther King, Jr. Memorial** opened in Washington, D.C. (2011); Republican **John Boehner** was elected Speaker of the House (2011); a compromise **bill to raise the**

debt ceiling, along with $900 billion in spending cuts was enacted into law (2011); Representative **Gabrielle Giffords** was shot and wounded by a gunman in Tucson, Arizona (2011); entertainer Bill Cosby was accused of years of sexual misconduct (2011); the **city of Detroit** filed for bankruptcy (2011); the **Public Accounting Oversight Board** charged the accounting firm **Deloitte & Touche** with placing too much faith in companies they audited (2011); **equity trading** in the U.S. reached a new high of $24.9 trillion in March (2011); **Anthem** acquired Cigna Managed Care for $48 billion (2011); **Aetna** acquired **Humana** for $37 billion (2011); **Borders** bookstore filed for bankruptcy closing 200 stores (2011); **JPMorgan Chase** agreed to pay $154 billion for fraud charges stemming from misleading investors in subprime mortgages (2011); **McGraw-Hill** split into two companies: one focused on education and the other on business markets (2011); the grocer **A&P** filed for bankruptcy (2011); **ACE Ltd.** bought property and casualty company **Chubb** for $28.2 billion (2011); **CBS, Fox**, and **NBC** agreed to pay $27.9 billion for the TV rights to NFL games from 2014 through 2022 (2011); **Boeing** sold its first **787 Dreamliner** to **Nippon Airways** (2011); the price of **gold** reached an all-time high of over $1,930 an ounce (2011); **Hurricane Irene** resulted in costs upward of $10 billion (2011); a **tornado** considered the deadliest storm since 1947, with winds of 200 miles an hour, leveled Joplin, Missouri, killing 158 people and destroying 4,000 buildings (2011); the **housing market slump** began (2011); the **DJIA** at year end was 12,217.56, up 5.5 percent (2011); voters in Colorado and Washington legalized the recreational use of marijuana (2012); voters in Maine, Maryland and Washington States approved **same-sex marriage** (2012); the NASA craft *Curiosity* landed on Mars (2012); President Obama announced that no private citizen would be prosecuted for **paying a ransom** (2012); **Hostess Brands**, the maker of **Twinkies** and other snacks, closed its doors (2012); **McGraw-Hill** sold its education unit to **Apollo Global Management** for $25 billion (2012); *Newsweek* magazine went electronic, ending 92 years of print history (2012); **American Airlines** filed for bankruptcy (2012); **Facebook**'s IPO grossed over $100 billion with founder **Mark Zuckerberg** owning 20% of the shares (2012); **United Health Group** was added to the DJIA, replacing Kraft Foods (2012); **Eastman Kodak** filed for bankruptcy (2012); **Hurricane Sandy** hit New Jersey and New York, killing 200 and causing more than $80 billion in damages (2012); the **Chechen brothers** set off bombs at the Boston Marathon killing three and wounding over 200 (2012); for the first time in 25 years, **26,000 Chicago** teachers and support staff walked out on strike (2012); the worst **drought** in 50 years hit Midwest farmers (2012); the **U.S. women's gymnastics** team won the Olympic gold medal in London, as did the **men's basketball** team, the **women's soccer** team and the **women's volleyball** team (2012); the **DJIA** closed the year at 13,104.14, up 7.3 percent (2012); contractor **Edward Snowden** leaked NSA surveillance programs (2013); lacking funding, the **federal government was shut down** for the first time in 17 years (2013); **JPMorgan** and the **Justice Department** agreed to a $13 billion settlement by the company for mortgage bond issues (2013); a federal appeals court reinstated **minimum wage and overtime pay** for two million **homecare workers** (2013); the California Labor Commission ruled that **Uber car drivers** were employees not independent contractors (2013); **American Airlines** and **U.S. Airways** announced an $11 billion merger (2013); **Berkshire Hathaway** and **3G Capital** bought **Heinz** for $23 billion (2013); **Office Depot** and **Office Max** agreed to an $18.6

billion merger (2013); **Citigroup** paid $13 billion to settle mortgage security charges (2013); **JPMorgan Chase** settled mortgage back securities charges for $14 billion (2013); **Berkshire Hathaway** stock priced above $150,000 a share (2013); the Volker Rule, prohibiting banks from trading on their own using customer money, was approved by federal regulations (2013); the **jobless rate fell** to 5.7% at year-end (2013); during the year, there were over **40,000 acquisition and merger transactions** accounting for over $3.5 trillion and over 280 **IPOs** valued at over **$1 billion** (2013); the **DJIA** closed at year-end at 16,576.66, up 26.5% (2013); **Janet Yellen** was the first woman to be Chair of the Federal Reserve (2014); the National Labor Relations Board (NLRB) ruled **graduate students** at private universities were employees **eligible to join unions** (2014); the **Waldorf-Astoria Hotel** was sold to a Chinese group for $2 billion (2014); **Michael Dell** announced a plan to take his company private (2014); **AT&T** agreed to buy **Direct TV** for $48.5 billion (2014); **Berkshire Hathaway** stock was priced above $200,000 a share (2014); oil declined to less than $60 a barrel, half of its previous high (2014); a **New York City taxicab medallion** needed to operate a cab cost $1 million (2014); **Ebola virus** reached the U.S. and caused the first death (2014); a police choke-hold killed Black man **Eric Garner** in New York City, setting off protests (2014); some **50 policemen** were killed and 50,000 assaulted in the U.S. (2014); **Buffalo, New York**, received six feet of snow within several days as **Florida** celebrated nine consecutive years with no hurricanes (2014); the **U.S. population** was at 319 million (2014); **taxpayers paid $1.4 billion** in income taxes, an average of $4,400 a person (2014); the **DJIA** closed the year at 17,823.07, up 7.5% (2014); the Defense Department announced that **women were eligible** for combat positions (2015); federal regulators approved the **use of drones** by property insurance companies inspecting damaged property (2015); the Food and Drug Administration (**FDA**) ruled artery-clogging **artificial trans fats** were to be removed from food preparation (2015); South Carolina took down the **Confederate Flag** that had flown over the state capital for 54 years (2015); the **FDA** approved the Novartis drug **Entresto** for treating **heart failure** (2015); New York Governor **Andrew Cuomo** announced a $4 billion five year project to improve delay-plagued LaGuardia Airport (2015); the FDA reported **new Ebola virus vaccines** were 100% effective (2015); the SEC announced that effective January 1, 2017, companies must report to shareholders the **ratio of CEO median pay** to that of other company employees (2015); the **FDA** approved **Addyi** from Sprout Pharmaceuticals for the treatment of **low sex drive** in men and women (2015); the **NLRB** ruled that companies and their independent staffing companies were "**joint employers**" subject to employee unionization (2015); former President **Jimmy Carter** announced he was suffering from cancer in the brain and the liver (2015); President **Obama** issued an executive order stating that a federal contractor must provide a minimum of seven paid days of **sick leave** a year (2015); Ohio Republican House Speaker **John Boehner** announced he was stepping down as speaker and also was resigning from Congress; he was succeeded by Wisconsin's **Paul Ryan** (2015); the U.S. Supreme Court ruled the right to marry also applied to **same-sex couples** (2015); **Tesla** announced its lowest-price electric car would cost over $75,000 (2015); **Staples** acquired **Office Depot** for $6.3 billion (2015); reportedly, the top 50 U.S. companies were sitting on over $1 trillion in cash, much of it overseas (2015); **Charter Communications** bought **Time Warner Cable** for $55 billion (2015); market capitalization of the largest **coal companies** had fallen to $1.2 billion versus $22 billion in 2010 (2015); **CVS Health Group** acquired the pharmacy service provider **Omnicare** for $12.7 billion (2015); **Coty Inc.** bought 42 beauty brands from **Proctor & Gamble** for $12 billion (2015); **Google** created "**Alphabet**," a new holding company (2015); **Anheuser-Busch** acquired **SAB Miller** for $107 billion (2015); **oil** dropped below $40 a barrel, a seven-year low (2015); U.S. **home ownership** fell to 63.7%, the lowest rate since 1993 (2015); a **U.S. spaceship** carrying cargo to a space station exploded shortly after takeoff (2015); **Pope Francis** visited the U.S. and was the first Pontiff to address a Joint Session of Congress, address the United Nations, and visit a Philadelphia prison (2015); the 1935 copyright of the "**Happy Birthday to You**" song was challenged (2015); *Playboy* **magazine** announced it would no longer publish nude pictures of women (2015); after releasing sensitive information, CIA cyber spying analyst; **Edward Snowden** went into exile in Russia (2015); **acquisitions and mergers** of $4.6 trillion for the year set a record (it was $4.3 trillion in 2007) (2015); over 47,000 **Americans** died of a drug overdose (2015); the **DJIA** closed the year at 17,425.03, down 2.2% (2015); the **FDA** approved Merck's product of **Keytruda** for **lung cancer** (2016); GOP presidential candidate **Donald Trump** called CEO pay "a total and complete joke" (2016); Trump adopted the slogan "**Make America Great Again**" (MAGA) (2016); **Hillary Clinton** became the leading **Democratic** candidate for U.S. president following the first Democratic debate (2016); President **Obama commented** that ISIS's extreme ideology "is a real problem that Muslims must confront, without excuse" (2016); by year-end, there had been **two Democratic** and **four Republican** debates. For the **Democrats**, the key candidates were former Secretary of State Hillary

Clinton, Former Governor Martin O'Malley, and Senator Bernie Sanders. The **Republicans** featured Dr. Ben Carson, Carly Fiorina, Donald Trump, and Governors and Former Governors Jeb Bush, Chris Christie, Bobby Jindal, John Kasich, Mike Huckabee, and George Pataki, as well as current and former Senators Ted Cruz, Lindsey Graham, Rand Paul, Marco Rubio, and Rick Santorum (2016); the **U.S. Treasury redesigned** the $5, $10 and $20 **bills** adding nine women and civil rights leaders to join Lincoln, Hamilton and Jackson (2016); of the 17 initial **Republican candidates** for president of the United States, only Donald Trump remained by convention time; of the seven initial **Democratic candidates** for president of the United States, only Hillary Clinton remained, having survived a convention vote versus Senator Bernie Sanders (2016); President **Obama** lifted the embargo on **Cuba** and opened an embassy (2016); new **treasury regulations** reduced the tax advantages of **inversions** and relocations to lower tax countries (2016); the Federal Drug Administration (**FDA**) assumed responsibility for regulating **e-cigarettes** (2016); the Obama administration stated students should use bathroom facilities that match their **gender identity** (2016); Obama lifted the arms embargo on **Vietnam,** stating, "This change removes a lingering vestige of the Cold War." (2016); President Obama ordered background checks on **gun buyers** and the licensing of **gun sellers** (2016); **Draft Kings** and **Fan Duel** were ordered to stop business in NY state (2016); reportedly, presidential candidate **Donald Trump** had been involved in some 3,500 legal actions over 30 years (2016); to avoid a conflict of interest, President-Elect Donald Trump announced he would dissolve the **Donald Trump Foundation** (2016); the Delaware Court of Chancery ruled **compensation committee directors** who set their own pay can be sued by investors since they are not protected by a business-judgement rule (2016); former New York Assembly Speaker **Sheldon Silver** received a 12-year prison sentence for extortion and money laundering (2016); former Majority Leader of the New York Senate **Dean Skelos** received a five-year prison sentence for corruption charges (2016); former Speaker of the House **Dennis Hastert** received a 15 month prison sentence for sexual abuse (2016); **Xerox** announced the split of their service and hardware businesses (2016); the **price of oil,** below $27 a barrel, was the lowest price since 2007 (2016); **Peabody Energy**, the country's largest coal company, filed for bankruptcy protection due to low coal prices (2016); **Sun Edison**, the world's largest renewable energy developer, filed for bankruptcy (2016); **Charter** acquired **Time Warner Cable** for $55 billion (2016); **Abbott Laboratories** agreed to acquire **St. Jude Medical** for $25 billion, combining heart disease specialists (2016); **Microsoft** acquired social network service **LinkedIn** for $26 billion (2016); **Energy Transfer** and **Williams Companies** agreed to a $38 billion merger (2016); AT&T acquired Time Warner for over $80 billion (2016); all **three U.S. stock indices** achieved a new record on the same day: DJIA (18,613.52); Nasdaq (5,228.40); and the S&P 500 (2,185.79) (2016); **Dell** completed a $60 billion acquisition of EMC (2016); **Donald Trump** declared a $916 million business loss permitting him to avoid personal income taxes for 18 years (2016); the **S&P 500** created the 11th category by splitting off REITs (2016); almost 75% of **Fortune 500** companies avoided federal income tax with offshore subsidiaries (2016); the famed New York City **Carnegie Deli** closed after almost 80 years of service (2016); for the second time in ten years, the **Federal Reserve** raised short-term interest rates, this time to 0.63% (2016); **Bayer AG** was acquired by Monsanto for $66 billion (2016); business startups amounted to over $67 billion but that was down 15% from 2015 (2016); acquisitions and mergers exceeded $3.6 trillion in 2016, down close to 17% from 2015 (2016); Ringling Brothers and Barnum & Bailey circus shuts down after 146 years (2016); and the **DJIA** closed year end at 19,762.60, down 13.4% (2016). During Obama's eight-year presidency, the increase in the DJIA was 125.2%. Needless to say, **stock option gains were significant** during Obama's term of office.

Donald J. Trump
(45ᵀᴴ President)

January 20, 2017 – January 20, 2021

Donald John Trump was born on June 14, 1946, in Queens, New York City, to **Frederick** and **Mary Anne Trump**. Donald's father was a wealthy real estate developer whose focus was on modest housing in Queens. Fred was arrested in 1927 for joining 1,000 KKK members marching through Queens, NY. Donald's mother, Mary MacLeod, was born in Scotland and immigrated to New York. Donald had two brothers (Fred Jr. and Robert). Fred Sr. often took his children to work so they could learn property development. Fred Sr. was well-liked and very ambitious, striving to be a multi-millionaire. Donald patterned his life after his father's. At age 13, Donald was sent to the **New**

York Military Academy near West Point. There he learned discipline, how to promote himself, and the importance of achieving self-defined goals. Later, Donald attended **Fordham University** for two years and then transferred to the **Wharton School of Finance** at the **University of Pennsylvania**. Donald graduated in 1968 with a finance degree and then joined his father in business. In 1971, Fred Sr. signed the company over to Donald, who renamed it the **Trump Organization.** The company's focus was on building skyscrapers in Manhattan for businesses. In October 1973, the Department of Justice charged the Trump Organization with **discrimination against African Americans**, thereby violating the Fair Housing Act of 1968. Donald Trump denied the charges and signed a consent decree ending the issue without admitting guilt.

After years of dating beautiful women, the handsome, wealthy bachelor married **Ivana Zelnickova** in 1977, she was 28. They had three children: Donald Jr., Ivanka, and Eric. They were divorced in 1992.

In 1978, Trump bought the **Commodore Hotel** near Grand Central Terminal, refurbished it, and renamed it the **Grand Hyatt**. This was followed by **Trump Tower** and its luxury apartments on Fifth Avenue. As the country was **moving into a recession**, Trump used the opportunity in the early 1980s to **buy up property in Manhattan** and **New Jersey**.

In 1987, with help from a ghost writer, Trump wrote *The Art of the Deal*. Trump used insults and threats of lawsuits to bully opponents, and he bragged about his ability to make deals, stating, "You either created and exploited fear or you succumb," and "There are two kinds of people, those with killer instincts and those without it." Reportedly, he is brash, childish, deceitful, and irritable, but a marketing genius. Clearly, Trump was driven to be a success, not a loser. Trump continues to have a focus on his successes, and seemingly a penchant for impulsive actions. Some actions were more successful than others; some resulted in bankruptcy.

In 1988, he bought the **Plaza Hotel** and extensively refurbished it. This was followed by **three casinos** in Atlantic City, **Trump's Castle, Trump Plaza,** and **Trump Taj Mahal**, as well as golf courses and more resorts; all eventually failed. In December 1988, a Gallup poll ranked Trump America's tenth most admired person.

Trump created a publicly traded company in 1995. It was an initial success but the stock bottomed out in the pennies. He was also an owner of the short-lived **U.S. Football League** with the New Jersey Generals and the **Miss USA beauty pageant**. In 1993, Trump married model **Marla Maples** (age 35). They had one child, **Tiffany**. They divorced in 1999. In 1997, he published the book *The Art of the Comeback*, describing his business successes and sexual conquests.

Melania Knauss (age 35) met Trump in 2002 and began dating him; they were engaged in 2004 and were married the following year. They have one child, **Barron William**. As Donald got ready for his 2016 presidential campaign, Melania stated, "I am very political in private life. I have my own mind; I am my own person. I don't want to change him, and he doesn't want to change me." She was the second First Lady born outside of the United States; Louisa Adams, wife of John Quincy Adams, was the first.

In 2004, Trump created and hosted the television show *The Apprentice*, with the contestants competing for an opportunity to run one of Trump's companies within a one-year $250,000 contract. Those who failed were told by Trump, "**You're fired.**" He continued with the show until 2016, when he became a presidential candidate.

A number of women have indicated that Trump sexually violated them. There were two especially high-profile cases. **E. Jean Carroll** accused Trump of raping her in the mid-1990s in a Bergdorf Goodman dressing room. She went to court and was awarded $5 million in damages. The other situation was with the porn star **Stormy Daniels**, who had a one-night stand in 2006 with Trump in Lake Tahoe. She was paid $130,000 to sign a non-disclosure contract to buy her silence. Trump denied the event and Daniels sued him to break the NDA, writing a book stating there was no foreplay, only a terrible kiss followed by brief sex in the missionary position. There was also a 2006 encounter with 1998 **Playboy Playmate** of the Year **Karen McDougal**, which lasted for some time.

In 2007, Trump's funded ocean resort never got off the ground, and hundreds lost their invested money. Sometimes Trump got financial assistance from his father. Congressional documents revealed that the **Trump International Hotel** in Washington, D.C. lost $70 million while Trump was president.

On June 16, 2015, **Trump announced he was running for the presidency as a Republican**. His motto was, "**Make America Great Again**" (MAGA). He was one of seventeen major candidates, making this the largest primary in modern presidential history. Trump went into an attack mode centered around **MAGA**. Trump borrowed MAGA from President Reagan, who used, "Let's Make America Great Again" in his 1980 presidential campaign, but didn't trademark it. Trump seized the opportunity, removed "let's" from the slogan, and applied for, and won, the trademark on July 14, 2015.

Republican candidate for president Donald Trump announced he would cut the top tax rate to 25%, lower the corporate rate to 15%, and eliminate taxes for 75 million Americans at a cost of $10 trillion over ten years. He was criticized for making outlandish statements against Black people and women on Twitter. Accusations of crude comments about women did not derail Trump's campaign, and his proactive comments energized a band of supporters. Some said **Donald** was a blue-collar billionaire who liked **talking with** blue-collar workers, **rather than at** them. Trump stated, "Our country, our people, our laws, have to be our top priority again." But later, Trump stated, "**It is time for termination of all laws and regulations** that are inappropriate or no longer needed." Trump favored **strict immigration control**, (including building a wall on the Southern border with Mexico), reform of criminal justice policies, and the **lowering of prescription drug prices**. Trump also claimed that the cost of Obamacare was out of control and that he was looking at alternatives.

Later in 2015, **Vice President** Biden announced he would not run for president. Trump said, "Vice President Biden is a crazy S.O.B. who can't put two sentences together." Also in 2015, Hillary Clinton announced that she was entering the 2016 U.S. Presidential election as a Democrat and immediately became the favorite to win the party's nomination. For the **Democrats**, the key candidates were former Secretary of State **Hillary Clinton** and Senator **Bernie Sanders**.

The **Republican** candidates for president included **Dr. Ben Carson, Carly Fiorina, Donald Trump,** Governors and Former Governors **Jeb Bush, Chris Christie, Bobby Jindal,** John

Kasich, Mike Huckabee, and George Pataki, and current and former Senators Ted Cruz, Lindsey Graham, Rand Paul, Marco Rubio, and Rick Santorum.

In June 2016, Hillary Clinton won the nomination at the Democratic convention and selected Senator Tim Kaine as her vice-presidential running mate. In August 2016, the Republicans held their virtual convention in Charlotte, North Carolina, featuring the Trump family. Not surprisingly, Donald Trump and Mike Pence were nominated for president and vice president, respectively.

Michael Richard Pence was born on June 7, 1959, in Columbus, Indiana. He was one of six children born to Edward and Nancy Pence, who ran a convenience store. Michael helped in the family store until he left for Hanover College. After graduating in 1981 with a bachelor's degree in history, he went on to Indiana University School of Law, where he met his wife-to-be, Karen. They got married shortly after and had three children. After graduating and being admitted to the Indiana bar, Pence practiced law and created a syndicated talk radio and television show. In 2000, at the age of 40, Pence was elected to the U.S. House of Representatives, where he was re-elected five times. In 2013, Pence was elected governor of Indiana, where he continued his philosophy of limited government and low taxes. During his term of office, he reduced income taxes while making investments in roads, schools, and good-paying jobs. In June 2016, Pence joined Donald Trump as his vice-presidential candidate, stating he was a Christian, a conservative, and a Republican, in that order.

In his campaign speech, Trump called for the "complete shutdown of Muslims entering the United States." Trump's campaign motto was MAGA; "Make America Great Again." He stated that he would revive the economy, improve public health, and restore law and order. Clinton's slogan was "Strength you can count on."

Asked if he would accept the **voting results**, Trump indicated that he would need to know the circumstances of the election results before he would accept the results. Obama promised a smooth transition from his presidency to the next president.

There were **three televised presidential debates** between Democrat Hillary Clinton and Republican Donald Trump. The first was held on September 26, 2016, in West Hempstead, New York. The second was held on October 9, 2016, in St. Louis, Missouri. And the third was held on October 19, 2016, in Las Vegas, Nevada. There was **one televised vice presidential debate** between Democrat Tim Kaine and Republican Mike Pence, held on October 4, 2016, in Farmville, Virginia.

Political polls were unanimous in predicting a **Clinton victory** in the **2016 election**. In a stunning upset and repudiation of the status quo, Republican presidential nominee **Donald Trump** and vice presidential nominee former Indiana Governor **Mike Pence** defeated Democratic presidential nominee **Hillary Clinton** and her running mate, Virginia U.S. Senator **Tim Kaine**. Trump received 304 electoral votes to Clinton's 227, exceeding the 270 needed to win. **Donald Trump was elected president** and **Mike Pence was elected vice president**. But Clinton and Kaine won the popular vote 65,853,514 to 62,984,828, a total of close to 130 million votes for the two top candidates, the lowest since 1996. Nearly 100 million eligible to vote did not vote.

Republicans held the **governorship** and **both houses** in 24 states; the Democrats held six. Trump had the benefit of a Republican-controlled Congress. In the **Senate**, the **Republicans**, led by Majority Leader Mitch McConnell of Kentucky, **held 52 seats** (a loss of two) vs 46 for the Democrats (a gain of two) and two independents. In the **House of Representatives**, led by House Speaker Paul Ryan of Wisconsin, the **Republicans held 241 seats** (a loss of eight) vs. the **Democrats 194 seats** (a gain of eight). Given this Congressional advantage, it was surprising that Trump later was unsuccessful at controlling immigration, restructuring Obamacare (especially after the failure to pass a replacement bill early in his administration), and rebuilding transportation infrastructure.

The election went on record as being the **most expensive of all time** – it cost almost $3 billion, with presidential candidates spending over $1.3 billion, House of Representatives $1 billion, and some $700 million for the Senate.

In spite of winning the electoral vote, Trump stated the **electoral college** should be eliminated and replaced by the popular vote, even though Trump lost the **popular vote** to Clinton by 2,868,686 votes. **Trump is the fifth president who won the electoral vote but lost the popular vote.** The U.S. Constitution specifies that the president and vice president can only be elected to office by votes from the Electoral College. The Constitution makes no mention of popular **voting.** Those who won the electoral vote but lost the popular vote were: **John Quincy Adams** in 1824, who lost to **Andrew Jackson** by 44,804 votes (1824 was the first time popular votes were recorded); **Rutherford Hayes**, who in 1876 lost to James Tilden by 264,292 votes; **Benjamin Harrison,** who in 1889 lost to Grover Cleveland by 95,972 votes; and **George W. Bush**, who in 2000 lost to Albert Gore by 539,897 votes.

How can a person win a majority of electoral votes and not win a majority of popular votes? It happens when the candidate wins a state with a large number of electoral votes by a small margin of popular votes, while losing states with a small number of electoral votes by a large margin of popular votes.

In his **victory speech**, Trump stated that, "It is time for us to come together as one united people." He went on to add that "I will be president for all Americans." In her **concession address**, Clinton stated, "I know we still have not shattered that highest and hardest glass ceiling. But someone, someday will."

Trump became one of the first to be elected president without having been elected to any previous political office or having served in the military. At age 70, he is the oldest elected first-term president. He also entered office with the lowest approval rating of any previous U.S. president.

In his January 20, **2017, inaugural address**, President Trump stated, "Today we are taking the power of Washington, D.C. and giving it back to you, the American people. What truly matters is not which party controls our government, but whether our government is controlled by the people. We will no longer accept politicians who are all talk and no action. The time for empty talk is over. Together we will make America great again," and "From this moment on, it's going to be America first." Trump repeated his promises of strict immigration controls, aggressive border control (including building a wall on the Southern border with Mexico) and reforming the criminal justice system. Shortly after being inaugurated, he banned immigration from seven Muslim majority countries. The action was upheld by the U.S. Supreme Court. Thousands marched in response to his ban of Muslims. Trump came into office with an opportunity to reshape the U.S. Supreme Court. In addition to the seat vacated by Antonin Scalia, there were four aging justices: Ruth Bader Ginsburg (age 83), Anthony Kennedy (age 80), Stephen Breyer (age 78), and Clarence Thomas (age 69).

Trump did get a **tax bill** passed with major reductions in corporate taxes, but individuals lost most of the deductions for mortgage interests, real estate taxes, and sales taxes. Attempts to restructure **Obamacare** basically failed, as did reductions in immigration. The same can be said about improvements in the aging transportation infrastructure. Trump was more successful on the **international front** than on the **domestic front**. He met with Russian President **Putin** and North Korean Leader **Kim Jong Un**; withdrew some troops from **Afghanistan**; moved the American Embassy in Israel from **Tel Aviv** to Jerusalem; withdrew from a **nuclear treaty** with Iran; assisted **Saudi Arabia** in Yemen's civil war; and negotiated **trade agreements** with Canada, China, Japan, Mexico, and South Korea.

Within his first 30 days, Trump signed a flurry of **Executive orders** affecting Obama actions. These resulted in massive peaceful demonstrations across America and the world. After the election, Trump did not have security briefings; instead, he used Twitter, relying heavily on the social media platform.

Reince Priebus, the former Republican National Committee Chairman, was Trump's first **chief of staff**. When Priebus met with a dozen former chiefs of staff, they told him that he had to be empowered, or he would fail. Former President Obama added, "Every one of my chiefs at different times told me something that pissed me off. They weren't always right; sometimes I was. But they were right to do it. They knew they had to tell me what I needed to hear rather than what I wanted to hear." This was important because Trump had no knowledge of how Washington really worked. In his life, Trump had accomplished virtually everything by himself. He was the **alpha male**. Why would he accept advice from anyone? He feared no one. He feared nothing. Being his chief of staff was going to be difficult.

Priebus learned that Trump was not reading any of the voluminous **transition briefs** that had been prepared for him. Not surprisingly, Priebus left six months into the job. He was replaced by General **John Kelly**, former Director of Homeland Security, a four-star general who had headed up the Southern Command. Kelly quickly established that all contact with Trump went through him. Kelly knew that his job was to make certain Trump heard what he needed to know.

President Trump's **initial cabinet** included **Vice President** Mike Pence, **Secretary of State** Rex Tillerson, **Secretary of the Treasury** Steven Mnuchin, **Secretary of Defense** Jim Mattis, **Attorney General** Jeff Sessions, **Secretary of the Interior** Ryan Zinke, **Secretary of Agriculture** Sonny Perdue, **Secretary of Commerce** Wilbur Ross, **Secretary of Labor** Alexander Acosta, **Secretary of Health and Human Services** Tom Price, **Secretary of Housing and Urban Development** Ben Carson, **Secretary of Transportation** Elaine Chao, **Secretary of Energy** Rick Perry, **Secretary of Education** Betsy DeVos, **Secretary of Veterans Affairs** David Shulkin, and **Secretary of Homeland Security** John F. Kelly.

There were **five key laws** enacted during Trump's first year in office. The **2017 Tax Cuts and Jobs Act** lowered the top tax rate but also limited local and state tax deductions to $10,000 (previously had been unlimited). The **2017 Veterans Cost-of-Living Adjustment Act** increased veterans' compensation. The **2017 Rapid DNA Act** increased the number of DNA samples to be added to the FBI database. The **2017 Fair Access to Investment** and Research Act required the SEC to establish "safe harbor" provisions for brokers and dealers. The **2017 Veterans Educational Assistance Act** eliminated the 15-year time restriction for the use of educational benefits.

In 2017, the U.S. Supreme Court ruled on **six key cases**. In **McLane Co. vs Equal Employment Opportunity Commission**, the U.S. Supreme Court ruled that the appropriate standard of review for a district court's decision on an EEOC subpoena should be "abuse of discretion," and not "*de novo.*" In **Manrique vs United States**, the U.S. Supreme Court ruled that Appellate courts lack jurisdiction over an appeal of a restitution award when the judgment that awarded restitution was entered after the notice of appeal was filed. In **Kokesh vs Securities and Exchange Commission**, the U.S. Supreme Court ruled that "[A]ny claim for disgorgement in an SEC enforcement action must be commenced within five years of the date the claim accrued." In **National Labor Relations Board vs SW General Inc.**, the U.S. Supreme Court ruled that a person who has been nominated by the president of the United States for a position cannot hold the same job on an acting basis while awaiting Senate confirmation. In **Epic Systems vs Lewis**, the U.S. Supreme Court decided how two federal laws, the National Labor Relations Act and the Federal Arbitration Act, relate to whether employment contracts can legally bar employees from collective arbitration. Also, in **Cyan Inc vs Beaver County Employees Retirement Fund**, the U.S. Supreme Court ruled the Securities Litigation Uniform Standards Act of 1998 did not strip state courts of jurisdiction to adjudicate class actions alleging only 1933 Securities Act violations; nor did it authorize removing such suits from state to federal court.

On December 6, 2017, as a favor to Prime Minister Netanyahu, Trump recognized **Jerusalem** as the capital of Israel and moved the **American embassy** there from Tel Aviv.

In his **January 2018 State of the Union Address**, Trump explicated parts of the strong economy and listed his accomplishments before 45 million viewers. In February 2018, the **American Civil Liberties Union** sued the Trump administration for illegally separating children from their immigrant parents. Trump responded by instructing Homeland Security not to allow large groups of people into the United States.

Angry over illegal crossings, in June 2018 Trump tweeted, "We cannot allow all of these people to invade our Country." Asylum was denied for those persons who passed through a third country.

Trump restored **travel bans to Cuba** and announced **H-1B visas** would go to the most skilled or highest paid candidates, no longer through a lottery system. He announced plans to **defund** New York City, Portland, and other **places with police cuts and lawless protests**.

Following a North Korean nuclear bomb test, Trump told the United Nations that the U.S. **would destroy North Korea** if it threatened the U.S. Some believed that Trump was a **clear and present danger** of beginning a nuclear war.

Trump had issues among his key staff. Former National Security Advisor **Michael Flynn** admitted to lying about Moscow talks, and Health and Human Services Secretary **Tom Price** resigned after benefitting from private aircraft flights. Trump fired FBI Director **James Comey** on May 9, 2017, after he led an investigation into Russian influence on the presidential election. Former FBI Director **Robert Mueller** was appointed Special

Counsel to investigate the Russian influence matter, and he found there had been Russian interference. Later, Trump fired Secretary of the Navy **Richard Spencer**, for terminating a Navy Seal for having pictures of a dead jihadist. Trump fired Secretary of State **Rex Tillerson** following a disagreement and replaced him with CIA **Director Pompeo**, who in turn was replaced by CIA officer **Gina Haspel**. Trump asked for and received the resignation of Attorney General **Jeff Sessions**, who was replaced with **Matthew Whitaker**. In August 2018, a former Trump campaign advisor **Paul Manafort** was sentenced to 47 months for fraud and tax evasion. Later in August, former personal attorney to Trump, **Michael Cohen**, pleaded guilty to campaign finance violations, including paying hush money to cover Trump's sexual affairs, for which he was jailed, and published a book stating that Trump committed the same crimes as Cohen. In his book *Rage*, Bob Woodward stated that former Secretary of Defense **Jim Mattis** said, "Trump was unfit for the presidency." Former Vice President **Joe Biden** said Trump's performance was despicable, both in his handling of the Coronavirus and in leading the economy into a recession.

Two items that took up much of Trump's time were responding to "fake news" by the press and the ongoing investigation by Special Counsel, and former FBI Director Robert Mueller on the Russian involvement in the 2016 presidential election. **Steve Bannon** was credited by *Time* magazine with being Trump's brains and getting him support from white voters. Trump thought Bannon got too much credit and removed him from his staff.

There were **six key laws** enacted during **2018**. The **Jobs for Our Heroes Act** made it easier for veterans to apply for commercial driver's licenses. The **Law Enforcement Mental Health** and **Wellness Act** required the Justice Department to report practices that could be adopted to law enforcement agencies. The **National Flood Insurance Protection Act** authorized a new national program. The **Abolish Human Trafficking Act** provided program assistance to human trafficking survivors. The **Tax Reform Act** provided a number of changes in various deductions and exemptions. The **Criminal Justice Reform Act** reduced or eliminated mandatory minimum sentences for drug-related federal crimes.

In 2018, the U.S. Supreme Court ruled on **five key cases**. In **Class vs United States**, the U.S. Supreme Court ruled that a guilty plea alone does not waive a defendant's right to challenge the constitutionality of his conviction on direct appeal. In **Marinello vs United States**, the U.S. Supreme Court ruled that to convict for obstruction the Government must prove a defendant was "aware of a pending tax-related proceeding or could reasonably foresee that such a proceeding would commence." In **Wisconsin Central Ltd. vs United States**, the U.S. Supreme Court ruled that under the Railroad Retirement Tax Act of 1937, employee stock options are not taxable "compensation" because they are not "money remuneration." In **Trump vs Hawaii**, the U.S. Supreme Court ruled that President Donald Trump's proclamation restricting entry into the United States of individuals from countries that pose a safety or security threat did not violate the president's statutory authority. In **Lucia vs Securities and Exchange Commission**, the U.S. Supreme Court ruled administrative law judges of the Securities and Exchange Commission must be appointed through the president or another delegated officer of the United States, rather than hired.

After the **midterm elections** of 2018, the Republicans held 53 **Senate** seats (a gain of two) and the Democrats held 47 seats (a loss of two). It was a different story in the **House** of Representatives. The Democrats held 235 seats (a gain of 41), and the Republicans held 199, having lost 42 seats and giving the Democrats control of the House for the first time in eight years. **Nancy Pelosi** returned as Speaker of the House.

Unable to get **funding for his wall** across the southern border with Mexico, on December 20, 2018, Trump shut down the government. It did not re-open for 35 days, the longest shutdown on record.

When President Trump invited the **Clemson University** football team to the White House for winning the NCAA football championship in January 2019, he paid over $5,000 out of his own pocket. He had to because he had shut down the government, keeping thousands from their work, including his kitchen staff. Later in January 2019, Trump initiated a "remain in Mexico" policy for asylum seekers.

Following the re-opening of the government, Trump gave his **2019 State of the Union Address** to Congress. The hour and a half speech was **one of the longest on record**. He called for rebuilding the nation's infrastructure systems and the healthcare system. He reiterated the need for a southern wall to keep out convicts, drugs, and other illegal immigrants. He stated, "We must choose between greatness or gridlock, results or resistance, vision or vengeance, incredible progress, or pointless destruction. Tonight, I ask you to choose greatness."

Trump awarded the **Presidential Medal of Freedom** (America's highest award to non-military citizens) to **Babe Ruth** (baseball player), **Antonin Scalia** (Supreme Court Justice), **Elvis Presley** (entertainer), **Orrin Hatch** (U.S. Senator), and **Miriam Adelson** (GOP donor), bringing the total to date to 70 awardees.

There were **three key laws** enacted during **2019**. The **Consolidated Appropriations Act** provided $687.8 billion in discretionary funds to the Defense Department. The **National Defense Authorization Act** authorized the procurement of aircraft, weapons, and troop strengths. The **Veterans Compensation Cost-of-Living Adjustment Act** provided increased pay to veterans.

In 2019, the U.S. Supreme Court ruled on **seven key cases**. In **Henry Schein Inc. vs Archer and White Sales Inc.**, the U.S. Supreme Court ruled that the Federal Arbitration Act does not permit a court to resolve a question of arbitrability when parties to the contract at issue delegated such questions to an administrator. In **Yovino vs Rizo**, the U.S. Supreme Court ruled that the Ninth Circuit erred in counting a judge who had died and was no longer a judge when the en banc decision was filed as a member of the majority. In **Fourth Estate Public Benefit Corp. vs Street.com**, the U.S. Supreme Court ruled that registration of a copyright claim occurs when the Copyright Office registers the copyright, not when the application, copies of the work, and fee have been delivered. In **Lorenzo vs Securities and Exchange Commission**, the U.S. Supreme Court ruled that those who do not "make" false or misleading statements, but who disseminate them with the intent to defraud, can be found in violation of securities laws. In **Altitude Express vs Zarda**, the U.S. Supreme Court ruled that under Title VII of the Civil Rights Act of 1964, employees could not be discriminated against on the basis of sexual orientation or gender identity. In **Fort Bend County, Texas vs Davis**, the U.S. Supreme Court affirmed the ruling of the United States Court of Appeals for the 5th Circuit, holding a federal court can hear claims under Title VII of the Civil Rights Act of 1964 even if the plaintiff has not completed an administrative process required under Title VII. In **Franchise Tax Board of California vs Hyatt**, the U.S. Supreme Court determined that unless they consent, states have sovereign immunity from private suits filed against them in the courts of another state.

A federal appeals court ruled President Trump lacked the authority to require drug companies to disclose prices in TV commercials. But a different federal appeals court ruled that Trump could withhold funds from states who declared themselves **immigrant sanctuaries**.

In December 2019, **House Speaker Nancy Pelosi** initiated a formal **impeachment** inquiry of President Trump for abuse of power and obstruction of Congress. This led to a vote on **abuse of power**, 230 to 197, and **obstruction of Congress**, 229-198.

One of Trump's greatest achievements was reshaping the **U.S. Supreme Court**. After U.S. Supreme Court Associate Justice **Antonin Scalia** was found dead in March 2016, President Obama nominated Merrick Garland as Scalia's replacement, but Senate Majority Leader Mitch McConnell said the replacement should be chosen by the next president. President Trump nominated **Neil Gorsuch** (age 50), who was approved by the Senate on April 7, 2017. After a bitter battle in the Senate, on October 6, 2018, Trump managed to replace retiring U.S. Supreme Court Justice **Anthony Kennedy** (age 80) with **Brett Kavanaugh** (age 53). Later, U.S. Supreme Court Associate Justice **Ruth Bader Ginsburg** died on September 18, 2020, at age 87, having served 27 years on the court. Ginsburg was the first woman and first Jewish person to lie in state at the U.S. Capitol Building. Trump nominated **Amy Coney Barrett** (age 48) to fill the vacancy. She was confirmed by the Senate as the 115th Justice on October 26,

2020. Only the aging Stephen Breyer, born in 1938, and Clarence Thomas, born in 1948, remained candidates for replacement.

On January 21, 2020, a traveler from China became America's **first COVID-19** case. This was followed by a **travel ban** for those traveling from China because of COVID-19, and a travel ban was also placed on travelers from Europe. President Trump declared a COVID-19 emergency. This action was followed by the World Health Organization declaring a global pandemic, and the White House urged Americans to wear **face masks.** Trump signed an executive order, **Operation Warp Speed**, calling for the fast development and distribution of a COVID-19 vaccine.

On February 5, 2020, the Senate voted 52 to 48 to convict Trump on **abuse of power** and 53 to 47 to convict on **obstruction of Congress.** The impeachment failed, as both votes fell short of the two-thirds required majority. Romney was the only Republican who voted to convict on abuse of power.

Trump signed an executive order cutting the costs of **prescription drugs** for seniors. Later he refused to visit **a U.S. military graveyard** outside of Paris, stating the dead soldiers were all "losers." Earlier, he had called **Senator McCain** a loser for being captured.

In 2020, Trump announced a $25 billion bailout of the **airline industry**, but compelled meat-processing plants to stay open in spite of the COVID virus. Trump revoked or delayed 98 environment **fuel regulation changes** and lowered the Obama-imposed **auto-emission standard**, which made cars cheaper to buy. Trump also used the **Defense Production Act** to order General Motors to ramp up production of needed **ventilators** for Coronavirus patients, but this was overturned by Congress. Trump raged at the 3M company for selling needed **N95** masks to Canada and South America, and he stopped funding the **World Health Organization** for its poor handling of the Coronavirus outbreak. Using the Coronavirus and the U.S.'s high unemployment crisis as his basis, Trump signed an executive order stopping **immigration** into the United States.

When **Attorney General Barr** intervened to reduce the sentence of Trump's confidant, **Roger Stone**, more than 2,600 former officials and lawyers from the Justice Department signed a letter calling for Barr's resignation.

Trump later awarded the **Presidential Medal of Freedom** to **Jerry West** (a basketball player) and six Dayton, Ohio **policemen** who had stopped a mass shooter. The Patriots' Coach **Bill Belichick** declined to receive the medal from Trump, stating his values were more important than a medal.

There were **seven key laws** enacted during **2020**. The **Paycheck Protection Flexibility Act** provided small business loans. The **Never Again Education Act** required the Holocaust Museum to commit resources toward improving understanding of the Holocaust. The **Families First Coronavirus Response Act** provided benefit funding for Coronavirus patients. The **Coronavirus Air, Relief, and Economic Stability Act** authorized a $2.2 trillion stimulus package for businesses and individuals, in addition to $500 billion in forgivable loans. The **Setting Every Community Up for Retirement Enhancement Act** increased tax brackets but not tax rates. The **Healthcare Enhancement Act** provided a $484 billion Coronavirus relief package. The **COVID-19 Relief Act** provided $900 billion in additional relief for individuals and institutions.

In 2020, the U.S. Supreme Court ruled on **six key cases**. In **Intel Corp Investment Policy Committee vs Sulyma**, the U.S. Supreme Court ruled that ERISA's three-year statute of limitations for fiduciary breach requires the individual to be aware of the information. In **Babb vs Wilkie**, the U.S. Supreme Court ruled that the Age Discrimination in Employment Act "demands that personnel actions be untainted by any consideration of age." In **Trump vs Vance**, the U.S. Supreme Court ruled that "Article II and the Supremacy Clause do not categorically preclude, or require a heightened standard for, the issuance of a state criminal subpoena to a sitting President." In **Bostock vs Clayton County**, the U.S. Supreme Court ruled that Title VII of the Civil Rights Act of 1964 protects employees against discrimination because of sexuality. In **Guerrero-Lasprilla vs Barr**, the U.S. Supreme Court ruled that lower courts may review whether immigration agencies properly applied relevant laws to a given set of facts in such cases. In **Liu vs Securities Exchange Commission,** the U.S. Supreme Court ruled that disgorgement awards can be awarded by the courts as equitable relief under the Securities Act of 1933, but they are limited to the wrongdoer's net profits and must be awarded for victims.

There were **two televised presidential debates** between candidates Democrat Joe Biden and Republican Donald Trump. The first debate was held on September 29, 2020, in Cleveland, Ohio. The second debate was cancelled due to the COVID epidemic. The third debate was held on October 22, 2020, in Nashville, Tennessee. The **vice presidential debate** between candidates Democrat Kamala Harris and Republican Mike Pence was held on October 7, 2020, in Salt Lake City, Utah.

In the **2020 election**, on November 3, 2020, Democrats **Joseph Biden** and **Kamala Harris** received 81,283,485 popular votes vs

74,223,744 for Republicans **Donald Trump** and **Mike Pence**. And Biden and Harris won 306 electoral votes vs 232 for Trump and Pence. Joe Biden was elected president and Kamala Harris was elected vice president. Trump quickly charged that the election had been fixed. When **Attorney General William Barr** refused to act on Trump's claim, Trump threw his lunch at the dining room wall. The U.S. Supreme Court rejected Trump's request to overturn Biden's victory in Georgia, Michigan, Pennsylvania, Texas, and Wisconsin. Republicans filed over 50 lawsuits challenging the election results.

COVID-19 vaccines from Pfizer and Moderna were approved for Emergency Use Authorization (EUA) by the Food and Drug Administration in December 2020. By year end, there had been over **20 million COVID-19 cases** in America, which included **350,000 deaths**.

In Trump's January 6, 2021, **"Stop the Steal" speech**, Trump claimed that he had lost the presidential election due to voter fraud, specifically, that dead people and illegal immigrants had voted for Joe Biden. Trump urged the attending protestors to enter the Capitol Building. While Congress was counting the Electoral College votes, the **U.S. Capitol went into lockdown** amid hundreds of rioting **Trump protestors** seeking to overturn the Biden victory. The **Electoral College** confirmed **Joe Biden's presidential victory** by a vote of 306 to 232 over Donald Trump. Each state gets a number of electoral votes equal to the number of its representatives in Congress. Biden also won 81,281,502 popular votes vs 74,222,596 for Trump. Because President Trump claimed Biden stole the election, **Facebook** and **Twitter** locked him out of his accounts. Of those identified in the rioting, 900 were charged with a violent attack on the federal government. Of these, 390 pleaded guilty.

The IRS reported that the tax returns for former President Trump and his wife, Melania, reported negative income for four years of the six-year period between 2015 and 2020. And the IRS failed to audit President Trump's tax returns during his first two years in office in spite of the requirement to do so.

On January 13, 2021, by a vote of 232 to 197, the House of Representatives **impeached** President Trump for **incitement of insurrection** for the **January 6** attack on the U.S. Capitol Building by some 2,500 Trump supporters in a "Save America" rally. Included was the charge of attempting to negate the votes of millions of people in cities with large Black populations like Atlanta, Detroit, and Philadelphia, violating statutes from the 1870s aimed at the KKK's efforts to disenfranchise Black citizens. Trump is the **first U.S. president to have been impeached twice**. On February 13, 2021, the Senate voted 57 to convict and 43 not to convict on the charge of inciting an insurrection. Seven Republicans joined all 50 Democrats. The vote fell short of the two-thirds required to convict.

Before leaving the presidency, **Trump granted 143 pardons**, including to **Rod Blagojevich** (former Illinois Governor), **Eddie DeBartolo** (former San Francisco 49ers owner), **Michael Flynn** (former National Security Advisor), **Bernard Kerik** (former NYC Police Commissioner), **Michael Milken** (former Wall Streeter), and **Roger Stone** (former Trump Campaign Advisor). On January 19, 2021, Trump left the White House and **flew to Florida**, taking with him hundreds of classified documents.

On **January 20, 2021**, Biden and Harris were inaugurated. Trump did not attend the event. He and his wife were in Florida.

In mid-January 2022, the **FBI searched Trump's Florida residence** and left with fifteen boxes of classified documents. Federal law bars the removal of classified documents to unauthorized locations. Trump argued the documents were "all declassified" and he would have turned them over to the Justice Department if he had been asked.

In June of 2023, Trump was charged with 31-counts **of violating the Espionage Act** over classified documents found by the FBI in 10 boxes at Trump's Florida residence. In January, shortly after a federal appeals court ruled that former President Trump had **to provide tax returns** from 2015 to 2020, the U.S. Supreme Court ruled that Trump had to **release his financial records**. Trump's tax returns revealed he had **paid no taxes for 10 of the last 15 years**. Trump said, "I work very hard to pay as little income tax as possible." Trump's organization, but not Trump, was found guilty of **tax evasion** by the IRS. His chief financial officer, Allen Weisselberg, agreed to a plea bargain.

In early 2024, Trump had to appear in a New York court, where a jury ruled that Trump must pay **$83 million** to E. Jean Carroll for **defamation charges** following a sexual attack on her years earlier by Trump. He said that the ruling was "absolutely ridiculous" and that he would appeal the verdict.

New York State Attorney General Letitia James charged Donald Trump with inflating his property values in order to get better terms on insurance and loans. She asked that he be barred from doing business in New York State and pay a $370 million penalty. A New York judge ruled that Trump must pay a $355 million fine plus interest. Unable to get a $454 million bond, Trump went to an appeals court and got the amount reduced to $175 million. He got the bond. Then the judge imposed a gag order on Trump with a $1,000 fine for each violation.

In response to the charge that he instigated the January 6 riot in an attempt to overturn the presidential election results, Trump filed a claim that, as president, he had immunity. A U.S. District Court of Appeals rejected the claim, and Trump filed an appeal with the U.S. Supreme Court.

In **The People of the State of New York vs Donald Trump**, the prosecutors claimed that Trump paid **porn star Stormy Daniels $130,000** to keep her from saying anything about their brief sexual affair by signing a non-disclosure agreement. They also charged him with violating election rules in 2020 by stating the pay was for legal fees and convincing the former *National Enquirer* owner to silence any negative stories about him. Donald Trump pleaded not guilty to 34 felony counts of falsifying business records over "**hush money**" payments to porn star Stormy Daniels. Former Trump attorney **Michael Cohen** stated that Trump told him to pay Stormy $130,000 and have her sign a non-disclosure agreement. Stormy Daniels testified that their brief sexual encounter took place in Lake Tahoe and rebutted the allegation by Trump's attorney that she made it up just to get some money. Trump pleaded not guilty. The **hush money trial** lasted a few weeks, but it took only several hours for the jury to find Trump guilty on all 34 felony counts. After hearing the verdict, Trump responded, "The trial was a sham, it was rigged." President Biden's response was, "It's reckless. It's dangerous. It is irresponsible for anyone to say it is rigged. Just because someone does not like the verdict." Trump blasted Manhattan District Attorney Alvin Bragg and Judge Juan Merchan on his social media platform **Truth Social.** The judge hit Trump with a $9,000 fine for every time he broke the gag order. Later the judge deferred sentencing until after the November election.

Federal Judge Aileen Cannon dismissed the **Trump classified documents** case in a 93-page statement. She ruled that the special counsel was improper, as it was not based on a specific statute, and it was not made by the president or confirmed by the Senate. Special Counsel Jack Smith said he would appeal the ruling.

Who is Donald Trump? Most would agree he is a complex person. He has strong confidence in his own abilities, coupled with an unrelenting drive to be successful, which has made him a very wealthy man. But his overconfidence has led to some financial failures, and when he has not been successful, he has traditionally blamed others. While working in the real estate world, he was not shy about using the legal system either as a defendant or a plaintiff. Some have said he is brash. Given that criticism, how did Trump get elected president? Even his critics agree that he is a great campaigner. Also, he is a hardworking, self-motivated, gregarious person who enjoys talking with farmers and working-class people. And he also listens to what people have to say. And Trump gets things done. He generally delivers what he has promised. And unlike President Biden, Trump appears at funerals of the working class to give a sympathetic ear. Without a doubt, voters have overlooked Trump's legal problems and personal issues to elect him president.

Key Events

Trump and Pence were inaugurated as millions of women protesting Trump's election marched in cities around America (2017); Trump withdrew the U.S. from the **Trans-Pacific Trade Agreement** and issued **dozens of executive orders**, many overturning previous President Obama actions (2017); another

Trump action initiated the **building of a wall** separating the U.S. from Mexico and illegal immigrants (2017); Trump banned the **entry of travelers from certain Muslim countries** (2017); Trump ordered a **missile attack on Syria** after they initiated a chemical weapons attack in their country (2017); Trump ordered the **bombing of tunnels** in Afghanistan (2017); **Trump fired** FBI Director **James Comey** (2017); Trump imposed **economic sanctions** on Iran, North Korea, and Russia following a North Korean missile test (2017); coalition troops **captured Mosul**, Iraq, an ISIS stronghold (2017); twenty-two people were killed in El Paso, Texas, by a shooter (2017); **Representative Steve Scalise** was gravely wounded by a terrorist at baseball practice (2017); **Hurricane Maria** caused massive damage and over 3,000 deaths in Puerto Rico (2017); hundreds were injured and 58 were killed by a shooter at a Las Vegas concert (2017); eight bikers were killed by a truck in New York City (2017); at a Baptist church in Sutherland Springs, Texas, a shooter killed 26 people (2017); right-wing protestors held a violent protest in Charlottesville, Virginia, and were faced with counter demonstrators. Trump said there were "very fine people on both sides" (2017); the electronics firm **Foxconn** announced it would build a $10 billion plant in Wisconsin (2017); the **Fearless Girl** statue was placed in front of the **Charging Bull** on Wall Street (2017); **Pfizer** announced it would sell a generic version of **Viagra** for half price (2017); Ross Cellino and Steve Barnes split up the **Cellino and Barnes Law Firm** (2017); social network **Twitter** expanded to 280 characters, twice the original 140 (2017); **Netflix** membership hit an all-time high of 100 million members (2017); **Sinclair Broadcasting** acquired **Tribune Media** for $4 billion (2017); **Walmart** offered a discount to online buyers (2017); **Tesla** passed **General Motors** as the most valuable automobile company (2017); **Arby's Restaurant** acquired **Buffalo Wild Wings** for $2.4 billion (2017); **publisher Meredith** acquired **Time Inc.** for $2.8 billion (2017); **Ford Motors** recalled 1.3 million R-series pickups for door failure (2017); **CVS** acquired **Aetna** for $69 billion (2017); **Macy's** announced plans to close 100 stores (2017); **United Technologies** acquired **Rockwell Collins** for $30 billion (2017); **Lord & Taylor** sold its New York City store for $850 million (2017); **Uber** ordered 24,000 self-driving Volvo vehicles (2017); the **National Collegiate Athletic Association** broke the record for one billion in revenue (2017); the **DJIA** closed at 24,719.22, up 25.08% (2017); Robert Mueller's investigation led to **indictments** of Russian officials for their part in Trump's election (2018); the government announced a **one billion dollar fine against Wells Fargo** for improper financial actions (2018); Trump withdrew the U.S. from the **2015 Iran Nuclear Agreement** (2018); the Justice Department charged **12 Russian intelligence officers with hacking** in the 2016 presidential election (2018); New York Governor **Andrew Cuomo** announced the opening of the first new gates as part of **LaGuardia Airport's** modernization project (2018); former President **Jimmy Carter** announced he was anticipating his death from brain cancer (2018); Senator **John McCain** made it known he did not want Trump at his funeral (2018); New York City filed charges against Officer Pantaleo for his illegal chokehold on **Eric Garner** that caused his death in 2014 (2018); **Brett Kavanaugh's** nomination to the U.S. Supreme Court was confirmed by the U.S. Senate (2018); Democrat **Nancy Pelosi** reclaimed her position as Speaker of the House following the Democrat's taking control of the House in the November election (2018); **Nikki Haley** resigned as Ambassador to the United Nations (2018); a Michigan State University sports doctor, **Larry Nassar**, was sentenced to prison following decades of sexual abuse of women (2018); a shooter killed 17 students in Parkland, Florida (2018); comedian **Bill Cosby** was found guilty of indecent sexual assault (2018); National Football League owners ruled that athletes must either stand or stay in the locker room during the **National Anthem** (2018); package bombs addressed to CNN and prominent Democrats were intercepted (2018); a gunman killed 11 at a synagogue in Pittsburgh, Pennsylvania (2018); a wildfire in northern California wiped out the town of **Paradise** killing 85 people (2018); after five years of painful rehab from a car accident, golfer **Tiger Woods** won a tournament (2018); **Hurricane Michael** caused significant damage, as did a Hawaiian volcanic eruption (2018); **Sears** filed for bankruptcy (2018); **Facebook** lost $119 billion in market valuation, the largest one-day loss in history (2018); **Ford** recalled 1.4 million mid-size cars with steering wheel problems (2018); **H&R Block** closed 400 locations (2018); **American Airlines** signed a contract to buy 47 Dreamliners from Boeing for $12.3 billion (2018); the FDA approved Merck's lung cancer product, **Keytruda,** along with Novartis's heart failure drug, **Entresto** (2018); the FDA also reported that a new **Ebola** virus vaccine was 100% effective (2018); **Pfizer** announced its restructuring into consumer healthcare, innovative medicines, and established medicines (2018); Cigna acquired **Express Scripts** for $54 billon (2018); **Toys "R" Us** filed for bankruptcy (2018); two hundred year old gunmaker **Remington** filed for bankruptcy (2018); Alibaba founder Joseph Tsai acquired the **Brooklyn Nets** pro basketball team for $2.3 billion, and hedge fund head **Dave Tepper** acquired the NFL Carolina Panthers for the same amount (2018); **Fox TV** extended its Major League Baseball coverage in a new seven-year, $5.1 million contract (2018); **Barron's** and **Forbes** issued virtually identical reports stating that in the NFL, the Dallas Cowboys had the most valuable franchise at $5.5 billion, followed by the New England Patriots at $4.1 billion, and the New York Giants at $3.9 billion (2018); the **DJIA** closed at 23,327.46, down 5.63% (2018); Trump announced his "**Remain in Mexico**" policy for asylum seekers and then withdrew the U.S. from the 1987 **Intermediate-Range Missile Treaty** (2019); NASA announced **Mars Opportunity rover mission** terminated (2019); the Justice Department charged some 50 people for **cheating on college admissions** for their children (2019); the Federal Aviation Administration grounded the **Boeing 737** after two fatal crashes (2019); **White House security** was tightened following several incidents of individuals accessing the property without authorization (2019); following their record fourth **World Cup**, American women were honored by New York City with a **tickertape parade** (2019); President Trump announced a **bailout for farmers** affected by new tariff rules (2019); Senate Republicans abandoned plans to defeat the **Affordable Care Act** (2019); **Bernard Madoff** was sentenced to 120 to 150 years in prison after pleading guilty to a massive Ponzi scheme (2019); movie producer **Harvey Weinstein** was charged with multiple counts of sexual assault (2019); an **E. coli outbreak** was traced to romaine lettuce (2019); a gunman killed 12 people in Virginia Beach, Virginia (2019); the EPA ends the **Clean Power Plan** (2019); **financier Jeffrey Epstein** was charged with multiple counts of sexual abuse of women before allegedly hanging himself in prison (2019); a shooter killed 23 people in El Paso, Texas (2019); unemployment fell to 3.5%, a 50-year low (2019); **Harley-Davidson** recalled some 45,000 motorcycles for brake issues (2019); **Pacific Gas & Electric** filed for bankruptcy (2019); **Purdue Pharma** filed for bankruptcy over the opioid crisis (2019); automakers **Chrysler, Fiat,** and **Peugeot** agreed to merge, creating a $50 billion market value (2019); **ISIS leader Abu Bakr al-Baghdadi** was killed in Syria (2019); **Ford Motors** recalled some 320,000 vehicles for a variety of safety issues (2019); **General Motors** recalled 640,000 trucks due to faulty seat belts (2019); **Chrysler** and **General Motors** filed for bankruptcy (2019); milk company **Dean Foods** filed for bankruptcy (2019); **Playboy** closed its club in New York City, its last club (2019); **Bristol-Myers Squibb** acquired Celgene for $74 billion (2019); **Blockbuster Video** closed all but one of its 9,000 stores (2019); **Dick's Sporting Goods** stopped selling firearms in all 125 stores (2019); **Walmart** announced it would no longer sell assault rifles (2019); **Pier 1** closed all 145 stores (2019); **Occidental Petroleum** acquired Anadarko Petroleum for $38 billion (2019); coal company **Cloud Peak Energy** filed for bankruptcy (2019); **Gap** intended to reopen 800 Old Navy stores (2019); IBM acquired software company **Red Hat** for $34 billion (2019); **Disney** acquired film and television properties from 20th Century Fox for $71 billion (2019); the **DJIA** closed at 28,538.44, up 22.3% (2019); the CDC reported **1,282 cases of measles**, the highest since 1992 (2019); after the **first case of COVID-19**, President Trump **banned non-Americans from entry** to the U.S. after traveling in China (2020); after the death of Black man **George Floyd** by a Minneapolis policeman, widespread demonstrations in support of **Black Lives Matter** followed (2020); six people were indicted after their failed attempt to kidnap Michigan Governor **Gretchen Whitmer** (2020); Trump's signed legislation **added $7.8 trillion** to the federal deficit (2020); following the death of **Ruth Bader Ginsburg, Amy Coney Barrett** was confirmed as an Associate Justice of the U.S. Supreme Court (2020); Trump withdrew the U.S. from the **2014 Paris Climate Agreement** (2020); Russia launched a **massive cyberattack** on U.S. government installations (2020); the **U.S. women's soccer team** filed a $66 million lawsuit for gender discrimination, as they were paid less than the men's team (2020); by mid-year, there were 100,000 COVID-19 deaths (2020); former NBA star **Kobe Bryant**, his daughter, and seven others were killed in a California helicopter crash (2020); **Bayer,** which had acquired **Monsanto** and its herbicide **Roundup**, agreed to pay $10 billion to settle cancer-claim lawsuits (2020); companies that declared bankruptcy included **Borden Dairy, Briggs & Stratton, Boy Scouts, Brooks Brothers, Century 21, Fairway Markets, Hertz, J. Crew, Lord & Taylor, Neiman Marcus, JC Penney, and Pioneer Energy**. Companies that avoided bankruptcy but had partial shutdowns included **Bath & Body Works** (50 stores), **Dunkin' Donuts** (450 stores), **Estée Lauder** (150 stores), **General Motors** (2 plants), **Macy's** (125 stores), **Papyrus** (260 stores), **Pizza Hut** (300 stores), **Signet Jewelers** (400 stores), **Starbucks** (400 stores), and **Victoria's Secret** (450 stores) (2020); a 20% reduction in jobs at **AT&T** (thousands), **American Airlines** (19,000), **General Aviation** (13,000), **Toys "R" Us** (30,000), **Macy's** (130,000), **Marriott** (120,000), **Raytheon** (10,000), **United Airlines** (16,000), and **Walt Disney** (32,000) (2020); **Advanced Micro Systems** acquired chipmaker Xilinx for $35 billion (2020); **AstraZeneca** bought Alexion Pharmaceuticals for $39 billion (2020); **Salesforce** acquired Slack Technology for $27.7 billion (2020); **7-Eleven** acquired Marathon gas stations for $31 billion (2020); **T-Mobile** acquired competitor Sprint for $26 billion (2020); former New York City Mayor **Rudy Giuliani** stated that Donald Trump still owed him some $2 million for legal fees incurred while Giuliani was challenging the former president's election loss to Biden (2020); the **DJIA** closed at 30,606.48, up 7.3% (2020); during Trump's four years in office, the Dow Jones Industrial Average replaced Exxon Mobil, Pfizer, and Raytheon with Amgen, Honeywell, and Salesforce (2020); on January 6th, President Trump held a rally to stop the electoral college count (2021); and the U.S. House of Representatives decided to **impeach President Trump** a second time (2021).

Joseph R. Biden, Jr. (46ᵗʰ President)

January 20, 2021 - January 20, 2025

Joseph Robinette Biden, Jr. was born on November 20, 1942, in Scranton, Pennsylvania, to Joseph Biden Sr. and Catherine Eugenia Biden. **Joe was the first of four children**; the others were Valerie (born in 1945), James (born in 1949), and Frank (born in 1953). His father worked several jobs, while Joe's mother stayed home to care for Joe, his younger sister, and two younger brothers. Joe was active in sports and became interested in politics since it was a regular conversation over dinner. In 1954, the **family moved to Delaware**, where the father became a successful used car salesman. Joe went to a Catholic school, where he was active in the classroom and the football field. But **Joe was teased in class because he had a stutter**. He solved this over time by reciting passages from a book with a mouth full of marbles. He went on to **the University of Delaware**, where he became a lifeguard at age 20. He graduated 506th in a class of 688 in 1968. He said he had three degrees, but he really had two.

While on Spring break in 1963, Joe met his wife-to-be, **Neilia Hunter**, in Nassau. She was a graduate of Syracuse University and currently an English teacher in Syracuse, New York. After he graduated from Delaware in 1965, Joe enrolled in the **Syracuse University Law School** so he could be closer to Neilia. They got **married** on August 27, 1966. After he graduated in 1968, they moved to Wilmington, Delaware, where Joe got admitted to the bar and served on the New Castle County Board. They had **three children**: Beau (born in 1969), Hunter (born in 1970), and Naomi (born in 1972). After Naomi's birth, Joe decided to run for the **U.S. Senate** from Delaware. His election team consisted of his **sister Val**, a former University of Delaware homecoming queen, who served as campaign manager; **Val's husband**, who was in charge of finance; and Joe's **brother Frank**, who managed the campaign HQ. Joe was handsome, with a Kennedy-like charm, and went door-to-door to churches and schools asking for votes. Joe focused on the 18-19-20-year-olds, as they had just gotten the right to vote. Joe and the staff worked 18 hours a day, six days a week. To cover expenses, Joe took a **second mortgage** on his house. The **campaign was a success**; Joe unseated longtime Senator **J. Caleb Boggs** in 1972.

A little more than a month after the election, his wife **Neilia and the three children** were **hit by a tractor-trailer while Neilia was driving**. She had moved into the truck's lane. The truck driver was innocent. All four occupants were taken to the **hospital**, where **Neilia and Naomi** were pronounced **dead**, but Beau and Hunter survived. At the hospital, Joe was **sworn in to** the office of U.S. Senator. He was so distraught that he thought of resigning from the Senate, but his family convinced him to stay in the office. Joe's 30th birthday was **after** the election but **before** inauguration, making him the youngest senator in history. Joe believed that socializing was an important way to stay in touch with others.

Joe met **Jill Jacob** in March 1975 on a blind date set up by Joe's brother Frank. Jill divorced her husband, Bill Stevenson, in May 1975. Joe and Jill got married in the United Nations Chapel on June 17, 1977. Graduating from the University of Delaware in 1975, where she had been **Homecoming Queen** and on the **Dean's List**, Jill went on to get a Master of Education degree from West Chester State College in 1981. Her daughter, Ashley, was born on June 8, 1981. Pausing for two years to raise three children, she went on to get a **Master of Arts in English** from **Villanova University** in 1987. Joe almost died from a brain aneurysm in February 1988, but he fully recovered. In 2007, Jill received a **Doctor of Education** from the **University of Delaware**. She has been active in all of Joe's vice-presidential and presidential campaigns while continuing to teach. Later, Joe and Jill set up the Biden Cancer Initiative, the Biden Foundation, the Biden Center for Diplomacy, and the Biden Institute.

Substance abuse runs in Joe's family. His father was an alcoholic. While Joe did not drink alcohol, others in the family were social drinkers. Reportedly, Valerie, Frank, and Hunter used drugs.

As **Chair of the Senate Judiciary Committee**, Biden was successful in blocking Robert Bork from a seat on the U.S. Supreme Court and almost did the same for Clarence Thomas, given the testimony of Anita Hill on sexual harassment. Joe served as **Chairman of the Senate Foreign Relations Committee** for twelve years and was therefore knowledgeable about post-war issues, terrorism, and weapons of mass destruction. As ranking member of the **Senate Judiciary Committee** for sixteen years, he was a leader in discussions about sexual assault, especially violence against women. **Senator Biden's war votes were mixed**. He voted against the Gulf War and voted against virtually all of Reagan's military proposals. But later, Biden voted in favor of war with Iraq.

Altogether, Biden served **36 years** in the Senate, **commuting daily** by train to and from Wilmington and Washington, D.C. until 2009, when he was elected Obama's vice president. Biden had run for president in 1988 and 2008 but was unsuccessful. Joe ran again in 2008 but dropped out after coming in fifth in the Iowa Caucus. In January 2009, he was inaugurated as the **47th vice president of the United States**. Leaving the Senate after 36 years to join Barack Obama as his vice president, Biden was **one of history's longest serving senators**. Biden once called Obama "the first mainstream African-American who is articulate and bright and clean." What did he mean by "clean?"

Nicknames for Joe Biden included Amtrak Joe (for his Delaware-Washington commutes), Lunch Bucket Joe, Moral Man Joe, Middle Class Joe, and Ordinary Joe. Negative nicknames included Faux Family Man, Creepy Joe, Dopey Joe, Senile Joe, and Sleepy Joe.

In the **2008 election**, Democrats **Barack Obama** and **Joe Biden** defeated Republicans **John McCain** and **Sarah Palin**, 66,882,230 to 58,343,671 in popular votes and 365 to 173 in electoral votes, to become president and vice president, respectively. Obama became the first person of color to become president.

The vice president's **major responsibility** was to use his contacts and influence in Congress to get Obama's legislation passed. Biden was seen as a **consensus builder**. He was helpful, but he did not have an outstanding record. One of the first Obama assignments for Vice President Biden was to chair a **Middle-Class Task Force**. It went nowhere, probably because it had no middle-class members.

As vice president, Joe and his wife moved into the **Naval Observatory**, a 10,000 square foot house on Embassy Row. Jill taught at Northern Virginia Community College, making her the first First Lady to work full-time.

Although **Biden's children went to private schools**, in January 2020, he stated he supported the public school system, "When we divert public funds to private schools, we undermine the entire public education system."

In March 2010, Biden watched as Obama signed into law the **2010 Patient Protection and Affordable Care Act**. Obama succeeded where the Clintons had failed – establishing national health insurance. As Obama signed the act, Joe was heard to say, "This is a big f---ing deal." It was **one of Biden's biggest gaffes**. And President Biden repeatedly got caught **in misstatements**. Was it deliberate or was it simply advanced age causing cognitive problems? Reminds one of **Abe Lincoln's quote**, "No man's memory is good enough to be a successful liar." Biden too often put his foot in his mouth. President Obama once said, "Don't underestimate Joe's ability to f—k things up."

As for **food**, Biden liked peanut butter and jelly sandwiches (like George W. Bush); he liked the use of ketchup (like Clinton and Trump); he liked cottage cheese (like Gerald Ford); and he liked ice cream (like virtually every president, except Barack Obama, who lost his taste for it). Biden's favorite ice cream was one named after him by the Splendid Ice Cream Company – White House Chocolate Chip in a waffle cone.

Vice President **Biden advised President Obama not to seek and kill Osama bin Laden**, but Obama ignored the advice. On May 2, 2011, Obama sent SEAL Team 6 to Osama's Palestinian home, where they killed the terrorist.

Obama considered replacing Biden with Hillary Clinton for his second term, but Hillary decided not to accept, and Obama again went with Biden. Prior to the **2012 election**, Biden had one debate with the Republican vice-presidential candidate, Paul Ryan. Due to Biden's lengthy and sometimes confusing statements, Ryan was considered to have won the debate. In the **2012 election**, Democrats **Barack Obama** and **Joseph Biden** defeated Republicans **Mitt Romney** and **Paul Ryan** 65,455,010 to 60,771,703 in the popular vote and 332 to 206 in the electoral vote. **Obama and Biden had been re-elected president and vice president**. Upon reelection as vice president, Biden said he would work to **address violence against women, end cancer, raise middle-class standards,** and **reduce gun violence**.

Hunter Biden graduated from **Yale Law** in 1996, founded his own lobby, and found ways in which rich people from other countries gave money for apparently little received. Then Hunter **shifted from lobbying to consulting,** as it required little of the lobby disclosure requirement. At age 43, Hunter entered the **Navy Reserve**. In less than a year, he was **discharged for use of cocaine**.

With inflation on the rise, the hardest hit was those below the upper class. Increases in prices of basic items forced hard choices. Biden stated, "We have a decision. One way to fight inflation is to drive down wages and make Americans poorer. I think I have a better idea to fight inflation: companies should lower their costs, not your wages." But government borrowing put pressure on the value of the dollar, and that led to inflation.

After high school, Joe's son **Beau** went to the University of Pennsylvania. After graduation, he passed the Delaware bar and went on to become the **Attorney General of Delaware**. When Joe vacated his Senate seat, Beau hoped to be named his successor, but Beau's National Guard Unit was activated, and shortly after he came down with **brain cancer** and died on May 31, 2015, at age 46. Joe was devastated. **Hunter consoled Beau's wife Hallie and moved in with her**. Then he had an affair with a stripper and, as proved by DNA, was the father of her baby boy. But father **Joe refused to acknowledge Hunter's failures**. Of his first family, only Hunter remained. For these reasons, Joe decided not to run for president in 2016.

In February 2017, the University of Pennsylvania announced the opening of the **Penn Biden Center** for Diplomacy and Global Engagement led by Presidential Practice Professor Joe Biden. In December 2018, the University of Delaware announced it was renaming its public policy school the **University of Delaware Biden Institute**. With the announcement, money started flowing in, much of it from China, based on a research and academic agreement with China. Are both the Delaware and Pennsylvania institutions' financial structures going to benefit the Bidens for years to come?

In April 2019, **Hunter's laptop** was found in a repair shop in Delaware. After it was seized by the FBI, a copy of the contents went public in October 2020. On October 14, 2020 (just before the presidential election), the *New York Post* printed the first of several articles that would be labeled "Laptop from Hell," focusing on Hunter's dealings with businessmen in foreign countries, all leading to money going to Hunter for unknown reasons. One revealed a package between a Chinese energy company and the Biden family. Hunter Biden had done business with China, selling a realty firm to them in 2014. It was the first of a number of business deals. **What did Hunter have to offer**, other than access to the president of the United States? Joe Biden had played down the threat of China, in spite of polls that showed Americans did not trust China. And Joe Biden charged that the contents of the laptop were the result of a Russian plot to discredit Joe. Why would Hunter forget to pick up the laptop he left in the Delaware repair shop? Did he believe it would never be discovered, or did he want it to be discovered, and if so, for what reason? A 2017 message on Hunter's machine revealed a message to a Chinese equity fund that said, "I am sitting here with my father, and we would like to understand why the commitment made has not been fulfilled."

Always looking for money, **Hunter became an artist**. He even got publicity when the *New York Times* featured him. Reportedly asking for $500,000 for each painting, he sold several, totaling $4 million. Was the money for the art, or was it influence peddling?

Joe announced his candidacy for the Democratic nomination for president in May 2019. He stated his goal was to rebuild the middle class and reunite the nation. **Four months later**, he admitted he had engaged in **plagiarism** on works dating back to Syracuse Law School. Biden stated, "We choose truth over facts." An interesting statement, are not facts true?

Harris dropped out of the presidential race in December 2019, well before the Iowa caucus and the New Hampshire primary.

Vice President **Joe Biden saved her political career** when, in August 2020, he named her his vice-presidential candidate for the 2020 election.

In February 2020, Joe Biden claimed that he had been arrested trying to see Nelson Mandela. Reportedly, that never happened.

Early in 2020, **President Trump announced he and Vice President Mike Pence were running for re-election.** COVID's beginning in March 2020, race riots, and mass shootings meant less campaigning and increased attention on safety. Democratic presidential hopefuls participated in several debates, but with the **onset of the Coronavirus**, several gatherings were cancelled. Joe Biden, Pete Buttigieg, Amy Klobuchar, Bernie Sanders, and Elizabeth Warren participated in the last debate. Mike Bloomberg had dropped out, but not before his campaign cost more than the combined campaign cost of all the other Democratic candidates. While Trump and Pence did some campaigning, Joe Biden chose to be safe and stayed home until late summer.

During the primaries, Biden faced opposition from Senators **Bernie Sanders** and **Elizabeth Warren**. Sanders won New Hampshire and Nevada, but large wins for Biden in South Carolina and Alabama kept Biden in the race. On March 3rd, 2020, Super Tuesday, while Sanders won California, Biden won the other key states. Beginning with 30 candidates, the race had come down to Sanders and Biden. Shortly after Super Tuesday, Bernie Sanders suspended his campaign and warned President Putin not to interfere with the 2020 election, On April 13, 2020, Sanders then endorsed Biden for the presidency.

During his election campaigning, Biden stated, "If I am elected president, I will always choose to unite rather than divide." As for **immigration**, Biden announced in 2020, "All those people seeking asylum deserve to be heard, that's who we are, we're a nation that says if you are fleeing oppression, you should come here." Unsaid was that Biden probably believed that people who were let into the country would be grateful and probably would become Democratic voters.

Later in 2020, boasting about his record, Biden said, "I have a record second to none. The NAACP has endorsed me every time I've run." That would be impressive, except for the fact that the NAACP has stated it does not endorse political candidates.

The **2020 Democratic Convention** was held in July in Milwaukee, Wisconsin. It was held virtually, not physically, due to the COVID-19 crisis. Joe Biden and Kamala Harris received the nominations for president and vice president. Harris was the first **woman of color** chosen as a vice-presidential candidate.

The **2020 Republican Convention** was held in August in Charlotte, North Carolina. It also was held virtually and featured the Trump family. Not surprisingly, **Trump and Pence** were renominated. Trump praised his own performance, stating that he had delivered on all his promises and that, if reelected, he would revive the economy, improve public health, and reinstate law and order.

The summer of 2020 was a period of unrest, highlighted by the Minneapolis police killing of George Floyd followed by angry crowds of protestors shouting **Black Lives Matter**.

During his **presidential campaign**, Biden stated he would eliminate Trump's tax cuts, lower military spending, and spread the money among the lower classes. He would bring back "don't ask, don't tell." He would achieve a 100% clean energy economy by

2024. He would improve Obamacare with a more liberal **Bidencare**. He would give illegal immigrants government funded medical care. He would confiscate all guns held by Americans. He would ensure women would be at least maybe half of all judges he appointed. He would create programs for transgender people. He would expand the size of the federal government. During his campaign, Biden also stated, "This nation has to come together." But a number of women came forward to state that it was inappropriate for Joe Biden to put his hands on them or attempt to kiss them. Biden replied he was always a hands-on, friendly, affectionate person.

During his last week in office, President Obama awarded Biden the **Presidential Medal of Freedom** for over 50 years of government service. To the surprise of many, Obama did not endorse Biden as his successor. Presumably, his thought was that while Biden would be an adequate president, Hillary Clinton would be a better one. And she would have a better chance of standing up to Republican candidate Donald Trump in the debates. One has to assume Biden was disappointed, but was he really surprised? More importantly, Biden later obtained the Democratic nomination for president.

There were **three televised presidential debates scheduled** between candidates Democrat Joe Biden and Republican President Donald Trump. The first debate was held on September 29, 2020, in Cleveland, Ohio. The second debate was cancelled due to the COVID epidemic. The third debate was held on October 22, 2020, in Nashville, Tennessee. In the debates, Joe was **lengthy** and **vague** in his statements; Trump was very unpleasant, calling Biden "Sleepy Joe." Shortly after the last presidential debate, Trump caught COVID-19 and was hospitalized. There was **one vice presidential debate** between candidates Democrat Kamala Harris and Republican Mike Pence held on October 7, 2020, in Salt Lake City, Utah. Harris easily won her virtual debate with Pence.

In the 2020 election, Democrats Joe Biden and Kamala Harris received 306 electoral votes vs 222 for President Donald Trump and Vice President Michael Pence, and Biden and Harris received 81,271,502 popular votes vs 74,444,596 for Trump-Pence.

Kamala (meaning "lotus" in Sanskrit) **Harris** was born on October 20, 1964, in Oakland, California, to a father who had immigrated from Jamaica and a mother who had immigrated from India. Both had a doctorate, the father in economics and the mother in cancer research. When Kamala was twelve, her parents divorced, and she moved to Montreal with her mother, where Kamala attended high school. After graduation, she returned to the United States. After graduating from **Howard University** in 1986, she went to the **University of California's** Hastings College of Law, graduating in 1990 and subsequently being admitted to the California bar and practicing law. In 1990, Harris joined the Alameda County District Attorney's Office. Later, she served as managing attorney in the San Francisco City attorney's office and then was elected **California attorney general** in 2010. In 2014, she married attorney Douglas Emhoff, who had two children, Ella and Cole. In 2017, she was elected a **U.S. senator** from California. She served on the Senate Homeland Security and Governmental Affairs Committee and the Senate Select Committee on Intelligence, as well as the Senate Judiciary Committee. She announced her candidacy for vice president in mid-2020 and participated in a number of debates before being nominated as the vice president at the Democratic

Convention in Milwaukee, Wisconsin, joining presidential nominee Joe Biden.

Two-thirds of the popular votes were **mail-in ballots**. The great majority were cast Democrats. Republicans had been urged by Trump to appear physically to vote. Biden became the first president from Delaware and was the second **Catholic** to be elected president; John Kennedy was the first. The **U.S. Supreme Court rejected Trump's request** to overturn Biden's victory in Georgia, Michigan, Pennsylvania, Texas, and Wisconsin. Trump called it a **stolen victory for Biden**.

In a run-off election in Georgia, Democrats **Jon Ossoff** and **Rev. Raphael Warnock** defeated Republicans **David Perdue** and **Kelly Loeffler**, giving the **Democrats control of the Senate**. Therefore, Democratic **Senator Chuck Schumer** replaced Republican Mitch McConnell as **Majority Leader** of the Senate. The Democrats also held the majority in the House of Representatives.

While Congress was counting the **Electoral College votes**, President Donald Trump urged his supporters to stop the count. The U.S. Capitol went into **lockdown** amid thousands of **Trump supporters** storming the U.S. Capitol Building on January 6, 2021, seeking to **overturn** Biden's victory. But Congress confirmed the **electoral votes** were 306 for Biden and 222 for Trump, and the **popular votes** were 81,281,502 for Biden and 74,222,596 for Trump. Joe Biden was elected president and Kamala Harris was elected vice president. Following the January attack on the Capitol Building, more than 1,000 were arrested.

When Biden was sworn in as the **46th president** on the west side of the Capitol Building on January 20, 2021, it was ringed with federal troops to avoid another January 6, 2021-style riot. The Trumps declined to attend the inauguration, following three other presidents who failed to honor their successors: John Adams (1801), John Quincy Adams (1829), and Andrew Johnson (1869). The inauguration ball was cancelled due to fears of riots and spreading COVID; some half a million Americans were already dead from it.

At the time of **Biden's inauguration**, the **Congressional Budget Office** projected a $14.5 trillion budget deficit in ten years. Two years later, the CBO increased this amount by $6 trillion for the same period. Of this amount, $5 trillion was reportedly due to Biden's executive orders and legislation.

In his **inaugural address**, President Biden welcomed Vice President Kamala Harris, the first mixed-race woman elected to the White House. He also promised to be a "president for all Americans" and to usher in a period of "renewal and resolve." He also stated, "We must end the Civil War that exists between the reds and the blues. My whole soul is focused on being together. We can and will again be the leading force for good in the world."

Biden selected Jeff Zients to be his **chief of staff**. Biden's initial cabinet included **Vice President** Kamala Harris, **Secretary of State** Antony Blinken, **Secretary of the Treasury** Dr. Janet Yellen, **Secretary of Defense** Lloyd Austin, **Attorney General** Merrick Garland, **Secretary of the Interior** Deb Haaland, **Secretary of Agriculture** Tom Vilsack, **Secretary of Commerce** Gina Raimondo, **Secretary of Labor** Julie Su, **Secretary of Health and Human Services** Xavier Becerra, **Secretary of Housing and Urban Development** Marcia Fudge, **Secretary of Transportation** Pete Buttigieg, **Secretary of Energy** Jennifer Granholm, **Secretary of Education** Dr. Miguel Cardona, **Secretary of Veterans Affairs** Denis McDonough, and **Secretary of Homeland Security** Alejandro Mayorkas.

After defeating Trump for the presidency, Biden charged that Trump's presidential circus was over, and the adults were back in charge. **Where were the adults?** How reassuring was it that **Transportation Secretary Pete Buttigieg** repeatedly said that parenting twins was the most demanding job that he had ever had? Keeping people safe while travelling much easier? There was a major supply-chain crisis because imported supplies were left on West Coast docks awaiting trucks to move them into America. But apparently, Buttigieg was too busy changing diapers to take action. And why could **Energy Secretary Jennifer Granholm** not answer a reporter's question of how many barrels of oil the country consumed each day? The answer was 18 million and rising. And **Secretary of State Antony Blinken** had been warned by Senator McCain not to publish a date of withdrawal from Afghanistan, as it would lead to disaster. Blinken did so any way and it was a disaster.

In the first hours of his presidency, Biden signed a **multitude of executive orders** reversing many of Trump's decisions. This included rejoining the Paris Agreement on climate control and the World Health Organization. Biden also went on attack with COVID-19, telling people they should **wear a mask** for 100 days and pledging to distribute 100 million vaccine shots. **Mandatory vaccination** was the centerpiece of Biden's COVID-19 strategy. Biden mistakenly stated that if vaccinated, you would not get COVID. Biden should have said, "If you get vaccinated, you will probably not die from COVID-19." He started with the military and extended it to companies and healthcare workers.

In early January 2021, the House of Representatives impeached-President Trump a second time on a vote of 252 to 197, this time for **incitement of insurrection** on January 6, 2021. The Senate voted to convict on a vote of 57 to 43. Failing the needed two-thirds required to convict, the charges failed. Biden and Harris were inaugurated on January 20, 2021.

Biden ensured the broad distribution of **COVID-19 vaccines** and stated his goal was to vaccinate 70% of America by July 4th. But Biden failed to promote **Pfizer's Paxlovid**, which had proven effective in lessening the effect of COVID-19 once the person had been infected. Biden himself had taken it. The World Health Organization (WHO) was slow to recognize the growing impact of COVID-19. Biden also reversed a number of Trump's executive orders and, later that year, got a $1 billion infrastructure bill and a $3.5 billion dollar bill for social reforms adopted. He was an FDR-style social reformer. His **domestic goal** was to improve the economy. His **foreign policy** was to avoid risk.

In January 2021, President Biden signed an executive order stating a new **White House policy on ethics**. Its goal was to "restore and maintain public trust in government." In short, it was to reverse the actions of the Trump government of influence peddling. While it controlled lobbyists, it excluded consultants. In late **January 2021**, President Biden promised schools that had been closed due to COVID-19 that they would be reopened within 100 days. In late January, the Center for Disease Control and Prevention issued COVID-19 guidelines. The **American Federation of Teachers** objected to the way in-person teaching could be taught, arguing that in-person teaching increased the spread of the virus. Shortly after, Biden amended the 100-day pledge and stated that opening one day a week met the "open" requirement for those up to grade eight. Teachers did not want to be forced to return full-time. But the loss of in-person teaching resulted in lower math and science test scores. It would not be until early 2022 that the Biden administration would announce that 95% of public schools had returned to full-time in-person teaching.

A shortage of **baby formula** was created when an Abbott Laboratory plant was shut down due to contamination. In response, Biden activated the **Defense Production Act**, which enabled baby formula to be imported from other countries.

In May 2021, President Biden promised to alter **President Trump's harsh immigration rules**, which admitted only 15,000 people per year. Biden believed the annual cap should be 125,000. President Obama admitted 85,000 in his last year. Reportedly, in Biden's first year as president, over two million people came into the country illegally.

Biden sought to have **Saudi Arabia** postpone a decrease in its oil output; he even met with the Saudi King. The result, shortly after Biden left was that the Saudis cut oil production to a million barrels a day. So much for Biden's ability to influence a foreign leader.

Joe believed that the **decline of unions** was the reason the middle class was also in decline. He once stated, "History shows us that when the union movement is strong, the middle class is strong." Biden was the **first president to join a union strike rally**. Biden's support of unions was returned with support from the unions.

The **U.S. Supreme Court issued three key rulings** in 2021. In **AMG Capital Management, LLC vs Federal Trade Commission** (2021), the U.S. Supreme Court ruled that Federal Trade Commission Act Section 13(b) does not authorize the FTC "to seek, or a court to award, equitable monetary relief;" in **Van**

Buren vs United States (2021), the U.S. Supreme Court ruled that to exceed authorized access under the Computer Fraud and Abuse Act, an individual accesses a computer with authorization but obtains information in an area of the computer that is off-limits; and in **United States vs Arthrex, Inc.** (2021), the U.S. Supreme Court ruled that the "unreviewable authority wielded" by Administrative Patent Judges "during inter partes review is incompatible with their appointment by the Secretary of Commerce to an inferior office."

Congress passed the **2021 Infrastructure Investment and Jobs Act,** a $1.2 trillion bill, which Biden signed. Biden then signed the **2021 Juneteenth National Independence Day Act**, making **June 19th a federal holiday** commemorating the end of slavery. It was the first additional holiday since 1963, when Martin Luther King Jr. Day was added. There are now 14 federal holidays. And the **2021 American Rescue Plan Act** allocated $1.9 trillion to bolster a recovering economy hit by the COVID-19 pandemic. It quickly had an impact on inflation, which rose from a 40-year low of 1% to a 40-year high of over 9% by mid-2022.

Biden decided to end the **Afghanistan War,** which, since it began in 2001, had cost $2.5 trillion to date. But the August 15, 2021, complete **withdrawal** was a disaster. President Biden ignored advice to keep 2,500 marines at the Kabul airport to ensure an orderly withdrawal. Thousands stormed the Bagram Air Base (some 25 miles from Kabul, the capital). In an attempt to get on the aircraft, some got into the wheel openings, only to fall out as the plane rose. Reportedly, close to 125,000 people were evacuated, but more than 80,000 were left behind, including some 1,000 Americans. Also left behind was over $7 billion worth of military equipment, ranging from rifles to aircraft.

Within hours, the Taliban took over the country and the equipment. One is reminded of the words of President Obama about Vice President Joe Biden: "Don't underestimate Joe's ability to f- - k things up." And when the 13 bodies of dead Marines were received at the Dover Air Force Base, Biden looked at his watch and, in his words, chose to focus on the death six years earlier of his son Beau, who died of brain cancer, not from a military death. Where was Joe's empathy?

In 2021, **Congress set the pay** of the vice president at $235,100 per annum (up from 2018's $230,700), the cabinet secretaries' pay at $223,500 per annum (up from 2019's $221,400), the associate justices of the U.S. Supreme Court's pay at $268,300 per annum (up from 2020's $265,600), and the chief justice's pay at $280,500 per annum (up from 2020's $277,700).

In Biden's first year, **over 3 million illegal immigrants** entered America. How many were terrorists? The elected vice president, Harris, was **given the task of solving the immigration crisis** by President Biden. She did nothing to hinder the large number of illegal immigrants coming in daily. Under pressure to visit the area, she told NBC's Lester Holt she did not understand why visiting the border would be important. With that, **Harris's poll numbers** fell.

According to the Major Cities Chiefs Association major crime increased significantly since Joe Biden became the U.S. president. To paraphrase the words of the political strategist James Carville, "It is the immigration policy, stupid." The Chiefs also claimed that the **paradox of gun control** is that it has little effect on bad people getting guns; it only makes it difficult for law-abiding people to get weapons to protect themselves.

In his January 2022 **State of the Union Address**, Biden called for a ban on assault weapons, reiterating what he'd put forth in the **1994 Violent Crime Control and Law Enforcement Act**, that also gave billions to hire more police and to build more prisons.

In his second year in office as POTUS, Biden claimed **voter identification** was a hardship for lower-income voters. The national debt increased about $4 trillion in the first two years of Biden's term as president; it was close to $8 trillion for Trump's four years.

President Biden had promised to **cure cancer and stop COVID**. He also promised that the $5.5 trillion **Build Back Better** bill would not have a negative impact on the deficit. How did he expect to achieve that? Biden argued that increased federal spending somehow did not increase inflation or raise the national debt. Was this Biden-economics? Add the $2 trillion COVID Act to the $5.5 trillion **Build Back Better Act** (which did not get passed) and you will definitely have an increase in inflation and an increase in the total debt. Simply, "too many dollars chasing too few goods and services." The year 2022 began with inflation at a 40-year high. Reportedly, Biden enjoyed swimming nude in the White House pool while he contemplated the country's problems.

Joe was **inconsistent** at times. While a senator, he did not support the Vietnam war, but he also was against draft dodger amnesty. Biden voted against the Persian Gulf War in 1990 but voted for the Iraq War in 2020. Former Defense Secretary **Bob Gates** stated that Biden was wrong for over forty years on national security issues. Biden did not support racial segregation but was against desegregated busing. He initially supported

Robert Bork for the Supreme Court but later opposed him. Joe was on record supporting welfare reform but also supported tax cuts for the wealthy. Although a practicing Catholic, Biden's views on abortion and gay marriage are inconsistent with Catholic principles, leading some priests and bishops to say they would deny him confession. Biden admitted that his vote for the **1999 Gramm-Leach-Bliley Act** was wrong, as it repealed the **1933 Glass-Steagall Act**, which separated commercial and investment banking.

Russia invaded Ukraine on February 24, 2022. Biden called President Putin a "crazy S.O.B. for invading the Ukraine." Given that America was importing 600,000 barrels of Russian oil every day, an embargo was not possible. It would have been possible if Biden had not shut down the Keystone XL pipeline which would have brought 800,000 barrels a day into Texas. Russia had made it clear; Ukraine could not join NATO. That would mean American missiles in Ukraine would threaten Russia. Some said the best way to ensure that did not happen was to allow Russia to take over Ukraine. Some has claimed that Ukraine is a corrupt country, second only to Russia.

In March 2022, an **ABC poll** found a majority of Americans did not believe Biden had the mental sharpness to be president. Add to this, balance problems left 62% of those polled stated the 83-year-old president was too old to run for reelection. And 62% of the public also stated that Trump, age 77, was also too old to be reelected.

There were **three key laws** enacted in **2022**. The **Emmett Till Anti-Lynching Act** amended Title 18 of the United States Code designating lynching as a hate crime. The **Suspending Normal Relations with Russia and Belarus Act** suspended the most favored nation tariff rates on all imported items from Belarus and Russia. And the **Equal Pay for Teams USA Act** amended Title 36 of the United States Code, requiring all athletes to receive equal compensation and expense reimbursement regardless of gender.

On June 24, 2022, in **Dobbs vs Jackson Women's Health Organization**, the U.S. Supreme Court ruled to overturn the 1973 landmark **Roe vs Wade** constitutional right to an abortion, instead allowing states to determine whether or not an abortion should be allowed. In **Biden vs Missouri** (2022), the U.S. Supreme Court ruled that Secretary of Health and Human Services has the authority to require employees to be vaccinated against COVID-19. In **United States vs Washington** (2022), the U.S. Supreme Court ruled that state workers' compensation law that discriminates against the federal government and falls outside the scope of Congress' waiver is unconstitutional under the Supremacy Clause. In **Biden vs Texas** (2022), the U.S. Supreme Court ruled that the government's recission of Migrant Protection Protocols did not violate the Immigration and Nationality Act Section 1225.

It was alleged many Americans believed that Biden had slipped in energy and mental fitness from his peak years. And additionally, it was reported that President Biden had taken more personal days off than any of the previous seven presidents. A July 2022 *New York Times* poll showed 64% of Democrats did not want Biden to run for reelection. This was a major change from 2000, when **Biden** was considered by many **safer than Donald Trump**. Since then, Biden's record was more liberal than many thought would occur. That said, he did not seem to have much competition for 2024.

Reportedly, many say Biden was a **warm and friendly** person, but **White House staffers** reportedly feared the **temper** of President Biden, who cursed them on a frequent basis. This was quite the opposite of his public image of a **kind, folksy grandfather**. Some said it reminded them of the cursing LBJ. Allegedly, Biden said to White House staffers, "God dammit, how the f - -k don't you know this," "Don't f- - king bullshit me," "Get the f- -k out of here," and "Get the f - -k out of the car." How did Biden square this with what he told political appointees on Inauguration Day: "I'm not joking when I say this: 'If you're ever working with me and I hear you treat another colleague with disrespect, talk down to someone, I promise you, **I will fire you** on the spot.'"? Did he forget he said this?

President Biden had to face repeated **allegations** that his son, **Hunter**, had **inappropriate conversations with country leaders**, twisting their arm for money, using his father as a threat for noncompliance. A House Oversight Committee looked into these allegations. Hunter was charged with having a gun while a drug addict. That is a felony. The president's response: "My son, like a lot of people, had a drug problem. He's fixed it. I'm proud of him." Others had stated there was evidence that he had not solved his drug problem. **Abraham Lincoln** reportedly said, "You can fool some of the people all of the time. And all of the people some of the time. But you can't fool all of the people all of the time."

In the 2022 midterm elections, the Democrats received 51 Senate seats, and the Republicans received 49 seats. In the House of Representatives, the Democrats received 213 seats, and the Republicans received 222 seats.

In November 2022, **classified documents were found** in the Penn Biden Center. The documents dated back to when Biden was vice president. Later in December, additional classified documents were found in Joe Biden's garage. They also dated back to when Biden was vice president. Both of these events were too late to affect the midterm or January elections. It should be remembered that while presidents can declassify documents, vice presidents cannot.

In December 2022, America swapped **Victor Bout**, a Russian arms dealer, for the return of basketball star **Brittney Griner**, who had been arrested in Russia on drug charges in February 2022. Did not Biden send a message that we would trade to get captives returned, a policy that will ensure future abductions?

In 2022, **Congress increased the pay** of the associate justices of the U.S. Supreme Court to $274,200 per annum (up from 2021's $268,300) and the chief justice's pay to $286,700 per annum (up from 2021's $280,500). And the cabinet secretaries' pay was increased to $245,500 (up from 2021's ($203,500).

Deaths from opioids, led by **fentanyl**, continued to rise dramatically, with over 150,000 overdose deaths in 2022. The Biden administration talked about the issue, but there was little progress made in finding a solution.

Special Counsel Richard Hur was assigned to investigate whether or not President Biden should be charged with a crime for **mishandling the storage of confidential material** from his term as vice president under Barack Obama that was found in November 2022. In his 400-page report, Hur concluded Biden was careless and just too forgetful to be charged with a crime. A jury might conclude the careless handling of confidential material was accidental and had been forgotten. Facts would show Biden was simply **an elderly man with a poor memory**. The **Justice Department** stated it would not press criminal charges against Biden. Several doctors suggested Biden should take a cognitive test. The White House response was that Biden would not take a cognitive test. Trump said he took a cognitive test and "aced it."

In June of 2023, Hunter appeared before a federal jury, charged with lying on a federal form stating he was not a drug addict, using the form to **buy a gun**, and possessing that gun without a permit. The First Lady sat in the audience. Hunter's ex-wife and a former girlfriend testified that Hunter was constantly using drugs, usually cocaine. The jury found him **guilty on all counts**. He faced up to **25 years** in prison and a **$750,000** fine. His first wife sued Hunter for not paying his required **alimony**. And he reduced a $20,000 a month commitment to a former girlfriend to $5,000. **Hunter** also admitted he **had not paid taxes** of over one million dollars in both 2017 and 2018, which is a felony.

There were **two key laws** enacted in **2023**. The **COVID-19 Origin Act** required the Director of National Intelligence to declassify information relating to the origin of COVID-19. And the **Fiscal Responsibility Act** suspended the U.S. debt ceiling of $31.4 trillion.

In **United States vs Texas** (2023), the U.S. Supreme Court ruled that Texas and Louisiana lacked Article III standing to challenge the Guidelines for the Enforcement of Civil Immigration Laws. In **United States vs Hansen** (2023), the U.S. Supreme Court ruled that a federal statute on encouraging/inducing illegal immigration was not overbroad because it forbid only "purposeful solicitation and facilitation of specific acts known to violate federal law." In **Biden vs Nebraska** (2023), the U.S. Supreme Court ruled that the Secretary of Education did not have authority under the HEROES Act to "establish a student loan forgiveness program that will cancel about $430 billion in debt principal." In **Helix Energy Solutions Group Inc vs Hewitt** (2023), the U.S. Supreme Court ruled that a person paid exclusively on a day rate cannot satisfy the salary test of the **Fair Labor Standards Act**.

A September 2023 CNN poll revealed that 61% of Americans polled believed that President **Joe Biden was involved in his son Hunter's business dealings**. Hunter's misplaced laptop had incriminating data about arranged meetings with President Biden. Former Biden family business associate **Tony Bobulinski** testified before Congress, stating, "Joe Biden was an enabler for a foreign influence-peddling operation." Joe Biden was "the brand" being sold by the Biden family. Bobulinski added that international business transactions took place, with tens of millions of dollars flowing directly to the Biden family. Was it because Joe Biden was the U.S. president?

During 2023, **Congress increased the pay** of associate justices of the U.S. Supreme Court to $285,400 (up from 2022's $274,200) and the chief justice's annual pay to $298,500 (up from 2022's $286,700). And cabinet secretaries' annual pay was increased to $246,400 (up from 2022's $236,900). Congress made no other pay changes during Biden's term of presidency.

In his **2023 State of the Union Address**, President Biden urged the Republicans to work with him on raising taxes on the wealthy and expanding social services for the needy, noting that he had signed more than 300 pieces of legislation in the last two years.

Google reported that President Biden's **approval rating of 41%** at the end of his third year of office was less than any of the previous seven presidents. Obama's 43% was the second lowest. George the 43rd's 58% was the highest.

The year 2023 ended with 2.7 million jobs created versus 4.8 million in 2022. The average hourly wage was $34.27, up 4.1% over 2022. The Federal Reserve set the short-term interest rate at 5.23 to 5.27.

In an hour-long **State of the Union Address** on March 7, 2024, before a joint session of Congress, President Biden was fiercely energetic. Referring to his opponent, Donald Trump, Biden stated, "Not since President Lincoln and the Civil War has freedom and democracy been under assault at home as they are today."

On the subject of the recovery from the COVID crisis of two years ago, Biden added, "It doesn't make the news, but in thousands of cities and towns the American people are writing the greatest comeback story never told." On abortion, Biden noted, "Clearly those bragging about overturning Roe vs Wade have no clue about the power of a woman." Biden also promised a $5 trillion increase in taxes on companies and the highly paid, combined with a $7 trillion social services budget.

The **2024 American Privacy Rights Act** ensured that personal identification information was removed from vessel manifests.

Biden's **immigration policy** was a major issue. Republican businessmen saw immigrants as potential workers at low wages. **Biden seemed to favor illegal immigration** and has issued an executive order banning ICE from deporting illegal immigrants, even killers and rapists. Biden's view was they were not illegal immigrants; they were **undocumented entrants**. But an easy immigration policy, short of a completely open border, creates a strain on the nation's healthcare system and potential risks of bringing terrorists and criminals into the country, along with opioids and fentanyl. Texas responded by busing immigrants to sanctuary cities. The most popular were Chicago and New York City. Florida began flying them to Martha's Vineyard, where President Obama had a multi-million-dollar home.

President Biden **stopped funding a wall** separating Mexico from the U.S., and he ended the **Stay in Mexico** policy. Biden also gave responsibility for the southern border to his vice president, Kamala Harris, stating that those seeking asylum should seek it from the home country and not wait until crossing into America. Biden did adopt **Title 42**, which barred entry of a person coming from or through countries with communicable disease issues, it was later removed. In less than two years, some 4.2 million immigrants entered.

In spite of an earlier decision by the U.S. Supreme Court that the Biden administration lacked the authority to forgive college loans, Biden went on to forgive some 74,000 persons with some $5 billion in college loans. In 2024 at a Trump rally in New Jersey, Trump called President Biden **"a total moron"** and the country's worst president.

There were **five key laws** enacted in 2024. The **All-American Flag Act** required that the United States flag be domestically made. The **End Fentanyl Act** required the Commissioner of U.S. Customs and Border Protection to regularly review, and update policies and manuals related to inspecting ports of entry. The **Federal Pension Oversight Act** authorized the Inspector General of the Bureau of Prisons to inspect covered facilities on a schedule. The **Enhanced Presidential Securities Act** required the Director of the United States Secret Service to conduct a comprehensive review of the number of agents to protect the president, vice president, and major presidential and vice-presidential candidates. The **National Defense Authorization Act** specified the budget for national defense.

In **Trump vs United States** (2024), the U.S. Supreme Court ruled that former President Donald Trump was partially immune from prosecution charges that he plotted to subvert the 2020 election. The president may be prosecuted for private conduct but not official acts. In **Moyle vs United States** (2024), the U.S. Supreme Court ruled that emergency abortions were permitted if the woman's life was threatened. In **Fischer vs United States** (2024), the U.S. Supreme Court ruled that the U.S. Justice Department inaccurately charged those involved in the January 6, 2021, Capitol demonstration with obstruction charges. In **Loper Bright Enterprises vs Raimondo** (2024), the U.S. Supreme Court ruled that agencies have no special competence in resolving statutory ambiguities. In **Harrington vs Purdue Pharma L.P.** (2024), the U.S. Supreme Court ruled that a $6 billion opioid settlement could not be protected from civil lawsuits regarding Oxycontin misuse. In **United States vs Rabimi** (2024), the U.S. Supreme Court ruled that people under domestic violence restraining orders may be disarmed. In **SEC vs Jarkesy** (2024), the U.S. Supreme Court ruled that SEC use of administrative proceedings violated the Seventh Amendment right to a jury trial.

In 2024, **Congress increased the pay** of legislators to $174,000 (up from 2009's $169,300). The annual pay of associate justices of the U.S. Supreme Court was increased to $298,500 (up from 2023's $285,400), and the chief justice's pay was increased to $312,200 (up from 2023's $298,500). And the cabinet secretaries' pay was increased to $257,900 (up from 2023's $246,400). Congress made no other pay changes during Biden's term of presidency.

On April 27, 2024, President Biden and former President Trump engaged in their **first presidential debate of 2024** in Atlanta, Georgia. There was no audience, only two interviewers. Unexpectedly, Trump was professional, not belligerent as expected, but he reportedly uttered at least 30 lies, which went unchallenged by Biden, who stammered, stumbled, and had a faulty memory and a blank stare. **Trump ended his comments** by stating that **Biden was the worst U.S. president in history** and clearly should not be reelected: "Crooked Joe is not fit to run for President, and he is not fit to serve and never was." **After the debate**, calls started to come in for Biden to drop out of the presidential race. But Biden refused, stating only God could get him to quit. Defenders stated Biden simply had a "bad night," as did Reagan and Obama on their first debates. But future events would show it was not "just a bad night." Weeks after co-hosting a $30 million fundraiser for President Biden, actor George Clooney published an open letter in the *New York Times* asking Biden to withdraw from the race for reelection. Even the *New York Times* published a statement that it was time for President Biden to step aside. Reporter Carl Bernstein reported that he had noted between 15 and 20 occasions in recent years where President Biden had cognitive and physical issues.

Days after the debate, at a Biden rally in North Carolina, **Biden was a different man**. He was energetic, positive, and coherent. He stated, "I know I am not a young man and may not do debates very well, but I know how to tell the truth, and I will beat Trump. He is a one-man crime wave." Biden publicly stated, "I am firmly committed to staying in the race, running this race to the end." If Biden's refusal to step out of the presidential election race led to Donald Trump's victory, would Biden's legacy not be that of an aged, mentally failing, egocentric failure? More and more Democrats were saying, "Thanks for what you have done, but **it is time to step aside.**"

Several weeks after the Biden-Trump debate, **Biden held a press conference** at the NATO HQ in Washington, D.C., where about a dozen reporters raised questions that were reportedly planted so that Biden had a ready response on his teleprompter. But his **responses** were again in a **rambling, stumbling manner**, and he made a number of **mistakes**, including saying Putin when he meant President Zelensky and referring to Trump when he meant Vice President Harris. In short, **Biden did little to reassure voters that he was mentally capable** of being their president. More calls came in asking him to step down from the upcoming election. He again refused.

Not to be left out of the slander game, Harris called Trump a Hitler-like fascist. She also said, "Trump is unstable, obsessed with revenge, and out for unchecked power." Then she added, "We have to stop pointing fingers and start locking arms." Harris also stated, "It is important to choose between a country rooted in freedom and one ruled by chaos and division." Harris's key point was that the country had a need for hope and unity, now and in the days ahead.

Just before the November 5th election, Harris, like Trump, held rallies in the seven key states that would determine the election: Arizona, Georgia, Michigan, Nevada, North Carolina, Pennsylvania, and Wisconsin. Both candidates ended their comments with "get out and vote."

In addition to a significant decline in his cognitive and physical abilities, Biden led the nation to the highest inflation in some forty years. Many people had difficulty putting food on the table without going into debt. Inflation is the result of too much money chasing too little supply. Democrats favored increasing wages, but that increases inflation. Massive government spending for social programs was a major factor in the **loss of the nation's triple A credit rating** for only the second time (the first was during Obama's presidency).

Biden did not want to talk about high inflation, the worst illegal immigration crisis on record, and a record-high crime rate throughout the nation. After over three years, **Bidenomics** was less than a success. About the only positive results were low unemployment and significant growth in jobs. Climate and environmental justice were a key part of Biden's domestic policy before the worst changes in climate had taken place, little has changed. Biden was left with little to talk about except to attack Trump. Joe Biden's 39% Gallup poll rating was lower than his seven predecessors', most of them with scores in the 50's. Only Obama's (43) and Trump's (45) were lower than 50%.

Among increasing calls for the aged, mentally ailing President Biden to step aside, **Biden blamed President Obama, Nancy Pelosi, and Chuck Schumer for picking Hillary Clinton instead of him, which led to Donald Trump's victory in 2017.**

While the **Republican National Convention** was meeting in Milwaukee, Wisconsin, where they nominated Trump for president and Vance for vice president, Biden spoke before the **NACCP in Las Vegas** and gave another weak performance. He then went to a Hispanic meeting but never got to speak because he **came down with COVID** and left for his Delaware home. This was followed by more calls for him to leave the race.

On Sunday, July 21, 2024, in a letter addressed to "My Fellow Americans," President Biden wrote, "It has been the greatest honor of my life to serve as President. And while it has been my intention to seek reelection, I believe it is in the **best interest of my party and the country for me to stand down** and to focus solely on fulfilling my duties as president for the remainder of my term." That was not good enough for Republican vice-presidential nominee J.D. Vance, who stated, "If the President isn't fit to campaign, he cannot be trusted to remain in the White House and **he should resign.**"

Shortly after Biden dropped out of the race, he sent out the following announcement: "Today I want to offer **my full support and endorsement for Kamala to be the nominee** of our party this year – it's time to come together and beat Trump. Let's do this." Within hours of Biden's endorsement, Harris received $81 million in pledged contributions. She then had to determine how to get access to Biden's campaign funds.

Kamala Harris was the daughter of a Jamaican father and an Indian mother. She had a career in law enforcement: first as San Francisco's district attorney in 2004 and then as California's first Black woman attorney general. (Yet law enforcement shifted right to support Trump's campaign for a safe America.) In 2016, Harris was the second Black woman to be elected to the U.S. Senate. **Harris faced criticism** from some in her attempt to secure the 2020 Democratic nomination for president. She failed in that attempt. She dropped out of the race in December 2019, well before the Iowa caucus and the New Hampshire primary. **President Joe Biden rescued her political career** when in August 2020, he named her his vice-presidential candidate for the 2020 election. **Harris had to defend Biden's policies** that led to a poor withdrawal from Afghanistan, the millions of illegal aliens that were allowed to enter the country (when she was put in charge of the matter), an annual 8% inflation (marked with high prices for food and gasoline), the appeasement of Iran, and billions of dollars to Ukraine with no favorable end in sight. **She could not show evidence that she helped solve these issues.** And Republicans charged Harris with helping cover up President Biden's failing physical and mental abilities. Possible challengers to Harris for president included Andy Beshear (Kentucky governor), Pete Buttigieg (transportation secretary), Roy Cooper (North Carolina governor), J.B. Pritzker (Illinois governor), Josh Shapiro (Pennsylvania governor), Elizabeth Warren (Massachusetts senator) and Gretchen Whitmer (Michigan governor).

Days before the election, both Harris and Trump held rallies in Pennsylvania and Wisconsin. Trump called Harris "lazy and slow." Harris called Trump unhinged, a fascist, and a hater of women. Biden called Trump followers garbage. Trump got in a sanitation truck to take out the trash and manned the French fry grill at a McDonald's, mimicking Harris's comment that she had worked at a McDonald's. Billionaire Mark Cuban stated, "You have never seen Trump around strong, intelligent women," but numerous women vocally objected to his comment.

In June, Biden's campaign spent $59.4 million; Trump's campaign spent $9.9 million. Also in June, **Biden's campaign had $281 million** available, while **Trump's campaign had $237 million**. But hours after Biden had withdrawn from the campaign, his fund received $46.7 million.

The Democratic National Convention opened on August 19, 2024, in Chicago, Illinois. With Biden no longer a candidate for the 2025 presidency, the 896 delegates pledged to him were free to vote for whomever they wanted. But an open convention against Harris did not happen. In accepting the Democratic nomination for U.S. President, Kamala Harris covered three topics: her upbringing, her experience as the vice president, and her policy agenda. She was much more specific on the first two topics than on the third. She vowed to reduce the cost of everyday needs and implement a tax cut, but there were no specifics to back up her statements.

On the evening of August 19, 2024, before thousands of delegates at the National Democratic Convention in Chicago, Harris took the podium and said, "Joe, I thank you for your historic leadership, for your lifetime of service to our nation and all you will continue to do. We are forever grateful to you." After being introduced by his daughter, Ashley, President Biden opened his remarks with, "America, I Love You." The crowd responded with, "We love you too, Joe," along with applause. Joe replied, "I've got five months left of my presidency and I have a lot to do. I intend on getting it done. It has been the honor of my lifetime to serve as your president. I love my job, but I love my country more. And all this talk about how I'm angry at all those people who said I should step down, it's not true. Democracy must be preserved by electing Kamala Harris as president and Tim Walz as vice president. Republicans Donald Trump and J.D. Vance are losers. Trump has been convicted of 32 felonies."

Highlights of the Harris economic policy, estimated to cost $1.7 trillion, were: (1) a federal ban on "price gouging" (i.e. price controls). This would result in an increased demand for limited goods and thus higher inflation. (2) bringing back the $3,600 child tax credit, raising it to $6,000. The result would be a disincentive to work and increased inflation as parents spend the tax credit. (3) giving up to $25,000 to first-time homeowners, resulting in more inflation, and (4) setting up a $40 billion "innovation fund" to encourage builders and cities to build more affordable housing. But Harris did not state how she was going to pay for these changes. After receiving the Democratic nomination for president, Kamala Harris reversed some of her earlier positions, including "not charging anyone who crossed the border illegally, banning fracking for oil, and a mandatory buy-back guns policy.

Democratic presidential nominee Kamala Harris selected **Minnesota Governor Tim Walz as her vice-presidential candidate.** The plain-speaking, common man liberal made the Democratic candidates the **most far-left ticket in history.**

The **first televised presidential debate** between former President Donald Trump and Vice President Kamala Harris took place in Philadelphia on September 10, 2024. The only people present at the debate were the candidates and two ABC television newspersons. Trump attacked her liberal economic and immigration policies. She responded by challenging his tariffs and tax cuts for the rich. In their speeches, the *New York Times* reported Harris made two false statements and three misleading ones. Trump made ten false statements and five misleading ones. The consensus was that Harris had the better night, raising the question, would there be another debate?

The House GOP released a report stating that the Biden-Harris administration "imposed a historic $1.5 trillion in new federal regulatory costs to fundamentally change American life." The added red tape made it harder for businesses to operate at a profit.

In the **2024 election**, Democrats Kamala Harris and Tim Walz received 226 electoral votes (versus 306 for Joe Biden and Kamala Harris in 2020). Republicans Donald Trump and

JOSEPH R. BIDEN, JR. (46TH PRESIDENT)

J.D. Vance received 312 electoral votes (versus 222 for Donald Trump and Mike Pence in 2020). Receiving more than 270 votes, Donald Trump had been elected president and J.D. Vance had been elected vice president in 2024. Harris called Trump and congratulated him on his victory. In the 2024 election, Kamala Harris and Tim Walz received 74,404,730 popular votes (versus 81,284,666 for Joe Biden and Kamala Harris in 2020). Donald Trump and J.D. Vance received 75,889,045 popular votes (versus 74,224,319 for Donald Trump and Mike Pence in 2020).

Many have asked the questions why did Trump get elected? The possible answer is that he listens to people, regardless of their position. It was clear the Democrats did not listen in the 2024 election. The working class, which traditionally had been the backbone of the Democrats, believed they were too far left of center and that they did not listen to concerns about inflation and immigration.

There are some very positives of Donald Trump. He is a very hardworking, self-motivated, gregarious person who wants to be known for the great things he has accomplished. And he gets things done. Generally, he delivers what he has promised. He wants to be viewed as a great president. Without a doubt, these are the qualities that got him elected president twice. Voters have overlooked Trump's legal problems and personality issues. Voters believe in him.

In the U.S. Senate, the Democrats now held 47 seats, and the Republicans held 53 seats. In the House of Representatives, the Democrats held 209 seats, and the Republicans held 226 seats.

The Democrats not only lost the White House, but they also lost the U.S. Senate and the House of Representatives as well. The consensus was that the Democrats had lost the rural and working class to the Republicans. The question now is, what will the Republicans do with total control of the federal administration?

After each state finalized the vote count, the information was sent to the appropriate state's governor who then appointed the electors in the college. The total number of electors is equal to the number of senators and representatives for the state. On December 17th, the electors of each state met and cast their electoral votes for the president and the vice president. The sealed results were then sent to the U.S. Senate. It was to be received no later than the fourth Wednesday in December. Kamala Harris, as the President of the Senate, presided over the count of the Electoral College on January 6, 2025. Strange that Harris had to verify her own defeat, but that is how it reads in the U.S. Constitution. The framers of the Constitution never imagined the vice president would have run for president. If Trump had been defeated it would have been expected for him to object to this process. But he had not lost and on January 6, 2025, Harris announced that Trump become president, and Vance was elected vice president.

Trump's first personnel decision was to select his campaign co-director, Susie Wiles, known as the Iron Maiden, as his chief of staff. Susie has a long history of successfully getting people elected. She is the first woman to hold the position and is the daughter of former legendary player and broadcaster, Pat Summerall. Trump announced he is putting loyalty high on the required qualifications for a position in his administration. He also announced that he will not make the mistakes he made in his first presidency. He wants people who are loyal to him and in agreement with his policies' philosophies. He seeks harmony. Trump announced his number one priority is to fix the border crisis.

Shortly after the election, the Justice Department announced they had uncovered an Iranian plot to assassinate Donald Trump after the election, believing he would lose, and security would be easier to circumvent. This action is revenge for the drone, ordered by President Trump in 2020, that killed Iran's Quds Force leader. As a result of this discovery, President-elect's security has been significantly enhanced.

After the November 5th election, the popular votes were counted in each state. It takes days before the count is official. When the count was final, the state's governor formally appointed the state electors, equal in number to the total of representatives and senators for the state.

President Biden and President-elect Trump met in the Oval Office on November 13th along with their chief of staff to discuss domestic and international issues in a cordial two-hour meeting.

In his **farewell address**, President Biden warned, "Today an **oligarchy** is taking shape in America of extreme wealth, power, and influence that **threatens our entire democracy**, our basic rights, and freedom." Clearly, Biden was taking a shot at **billionaires** Elon Musk and Mark Zuckerberg. He went on to say, "**It is up to us to make our dreams come true.** We are the United States – there is nothing, nothing beyond our capacity when we do it together. Now it is your turn to stand guard. May you all beat and guard. May you all be keepers of the flame. Thank you for the great honor."

As **Joe Biden** left the presidency, the question is how historians will judge his **performance**. Given the issues of high inflation, loss of the Triple A credit rating due to mass spending, causing multimillions in increased interest charges and the millions of illegal immigrants allowed to enter the country, some may argue he may be one of the **worst presidents**, but few can argue he was a more effective senator than a president.

Key Events

During the U.S. **withdrawal from Afghanistan**, a number of people were killed by the Taliban (2021); the state of Georgia was the first of several states to impose restrictions on voting (2021); following charges of sexual harassment, **New York Governor Andrew Cuomo resigned** (2021); **California's recall election of Governor Gavin Newsom failed**, as 62% voted to retain him (2021); GOP House members voted to remove **Liz Cheney**, a Trump critic, from the White House Republican Conference (2021); in July, the **U.S. Supreme Court** reinstated two **discriminatory election laws** in Arizona (2021); Texas adopted a law **prohibiting abortions** after a fetal heartbeat was detected (2021); the Center for Disease Control reported that the rare **monkey pox disease** had spread to America (2022); the U.S. government reported that the **Family Medical Leave Act** did cover mental health treatment (2022); testimony before the House Committee investigating the **January 6th attack on the Capitol Building** revealed, that, while President Trump watched the event, he made no attempt to stop it (2022); the government announced that **more than one million undocumented immigrants had entered the United States** since Joe Biden became president (2022); the **federal deficit** was reduced by $1.7 trillion, but it was still higher than before Biden's election (2022); the **IRS failed to audit President Trump's tax returns** during his first two years in office in spite of the requirement to do so (2022); the IRS reported that **tax returns** for former **President Trump** and his wife **reported negative income** for four of the six yearly periods between 2015 and 2020 (2022); the **U.S.**

JOSEPH R. BIDEN, JR. (46TH PRESIDENT)

Supreme Court rejected a challenge to the U.S. Securities and Exchange Commission's power to place a **gag order** on parties who settle with this agency (2022); the **U.S. Supreme Court overturned** a New York State law that placed **strict limits on carrying guns** outside the home (2022); the **U.S. Supreme Court**, in a 6 to 3 ruling, **overturned** the 49-year-old ruling of **Roe vs Wade** that permitted abortions, allowing states to determine whether or not abortions should be permitted (2022); New York State passed a **law prohibiting** anyone under the age of 21 from buying a **fast-firing assault weapon** (2022); the **U.S. Supreme Court** ruled a person cannot be barred from **publicly exercising his faith** (2022); **Ketanji Brown Jackson** was sworn in as the **first Black woman** to serve as an **Associate Justice** of the U.S. Supreme Court (2022); the **U.S. Supreme Court** ruled that a Georgia **death row inmate** could die as he preferred, by firing squad, not lethal injection (2022); the **January 6** House subcommittee decided that the insurrection at the Capitol Building was a **planned uprising** triggered by President Trump, not a spontaneous action (2022); a U.S. Court of Appeals ruled that the **House Ways & Means Committee** was entitled to receive **six years of former President Trump's tax returns** (2015-2020) (2022); former President Trump's Chief Financial Officer, **Allen Weisselberg**, reached a **plea bargain** on charges of income tax evasion (2022); the U.S. Supreme Court **denied** former President **Trump's request to block acquisition of his tax returns** (2022); a federal district judge ruled that a federal law **preventing the purchase of guns is unconstitutional** (2022); with a federal judge striking down Title 42, it was estimated as many as **18,000 illegal immigrants would come in daily** (2022); the **Republicans regained control of the House** in the midterm elections (2022); given that in both the first and second quarter, the country had negative GDP numbers, the country was officially in a **recession** (2022); **embryos** frozen over 30 years prior were brought to life as twins (2022); the Center for Disease Control reported that there were **over 100,000 deaths** from drug overdoses and two-thirds were from fentanyl (2022); the **stock market** closed out the **worst** first **six months** since 2020 (2022); **Insurance Business America** reported that acquisitions and mergers in the first half of 2022 reached their highest level in ten years (2022); a **Stifel Financial** poll of corporate executives revealed 97% believed the economy was headed for a recession (2022); at a charity event, **Warren Buffett** was reportedly paid $19 million to have a personal lunch (2022); Big-Four accounting firm **Ernst & Young** announced it was splitting its auditing and consulting practices (2022); The *Wall Street Journal* reported that workers were returning to work as the COVID-19 infection rate continued to decline (2022); an armed man was stopped from killing U.S. **Supreme Court Associate Justice Brett Kavanaugh** (2022); **Nancy Pelosi's husband** was attacked by a right-wing terrorist with a hammer (2022); it was estimated that over $45 billion was lost through federal **unemployment compensation** claims during the pandemic (2022); **FTX founder Sam Bankman-Fried** was charged with stealing billions of dollars from his cryptocurrency exchange customers while misleading investors and lenders. Other **cryptocurrency failures** included Alameda, Celsius Network, and Voyager Network (2022); Reuters reported that the gap between average CEO pay ($2.5 million) and median worker pay ($23,698) was 670 to 1 the previous year (2022); the **Bloomberg Millionaire Index** reported that the 50 wealthiest persons in their study lost more than a half a trillion dollars (2022); **Equilar** reported that the **highest paid CEOs** were: Trader's Desk's Jeff Green ($850 million), Qualtrics's Zig Serafin ($550 million), Expedia's Peter Kern ($250 million), Coty's Sue

Nabi ($250 million), and Warner Brothers's David Zaslav ($249 million) (2022); due to high taxes, the **number of millionaires** in New York dropped from 55,100 to 54,370 year-to-year (2022); according to **Forbes**, the world's richest were Elon Musk ($198.5 billion), Bernard Arnault ($172.5 billion), Gautam Adani ($147.5 billion), Jeff Bezos ($124 billion), and Warren Buffett ($108.5 billion) (2022); **Bruce Ellig** published the fourth edition of the desk-top reference book *The Complete Guide to Executive Compensation* (2022); the **DJIA** closed at 33,147.25, down 9.12% (2022); after 15 votes, Republican **Kevin McCarthy** was elected Speaker of the House (2023); upon review, it was learned that Donald **Trump paid little or no taxes** for the years 2015, 2016, and 2017 because of hundreds of millions of dollars in tax deductions (2023); failures and financial distress in the **cryptocurrency** industry blocked a number of companies from going public (2023); **Chicago Mayor Lori Lightfoot** was not re-elected, reportedly due to voter anger over the rising crime rate (2023); Florida Governor **Ron DeSantis** announced he was running for president as a Republican (2023); **Guantanamo Bay prison** in Cuba still held 30 men without trial for more than 20 years (2023); the U.S. Senate ruled that anyone appearing on the **Senate floor** must be in a business suit (2023); House Speaker **McCarthy** was voted out of his job, the first speaker outed in 234 years, and **Mike Johnson** was voted in (2023); Republican **George Santos** was expelled from the House of Representatives for lies, misuse of campaign funds, and other wrongful behavior. He was the first person expelled without being convicted of an illegal act or supporting the confederacy (2023); an **IRS official** was charged with unlawfully releasing the 1961 and 1967 tax returns of Donald Trump (2023); the **third Republican presidential debate** included Chris Christie, Ron DeSantis, Nikki Haley, Tim Scott, and Vivek Ramaswamy (2023); in the

fourth Republican presidential debate, Chris Christie, Ron DeSantis, Nikki Haley, and Vivek Ramaswamy spent more time criticizing each other than commenting on the absent Donald Trump (2023); overwhelmed by the arrival of over **150,000 immigrants**, New York City offered free airline tickets costing less than one day of housing (2023); the Biden Administration announced that some **472,000 Venezuelan immigrants** would receive work permits and protection from deportation (2023); Oath-Keepers leader **Stewart Rhodes** was sentenced to 18 years in prison for his role in the January 6, 2021, attack on the U.S. Capitol Building (2023); the U.S. Supreme Court ruled that President Biden **did not have** the **authority to forgive some $400 billion** in loans to some 45 million former students (2023); the New York Supreme Court ruled that control of Trump's New York State property would be placed with a third party (2023); Ponzi schemer **Bernard Madoff's 40,000 clients** were 90% made whole with $4.2 billion in payments (2023); **FTX** founder Sam Bankman-Fried was found guilty of stealing $10 billion from his company (2023); **President Biden's son, Hunter**, was indicted on nine counts of felonies and misdemeanors that could lead to 17 years in prison (2023); a jury found attorney **Rudy Giuliani** guilty of falsely charging that Georgia election officials had rigged the 2022 presidential election and fined him $148 million (2023); Judge Arthur Engoron stated, "Donald **Trump inflated his wealth** to rip off banks, insurance firms, and New York State," reportedly for close to $170 million (2023); the **U.S. Supreme Court** unanimously agreed to a new code of ethics (2023); U.S. debt was **over $33 trillion** for the first time in history, and the federal budget was over **$63 billion** (2023); sixty-six million people were on **Medicare** (2023); some **3.2 million immigrants** entered the U.S. in 2023 vs 2.8 million in 2022 and 2.0 million in 2021 (2023); **mergers and acquisitions** fell to the lowest level in a decade, off 20% in a year or about $3 trillion (2023); **Stephen Schwarzman** of Blackstone headed the compensation package list with $253 million (2023); **Forbes** dropped **Donald Trump** from its list of 400 richest Americans with its $2.9 billion cutoff (2023); the AFL-CIO reported average CEO pay was $16 million a year (2023); 78,000 residents of **New York** left, with 58,000 going to Florida (2023); in December, over **225,000 illegal immigrants** entered the south border of the United States, creating a backlog of over three million cases (2023); the **DJIA** closed at 37,689.54, up 13.70% (2023); **opening his campaign**, President Biden chose to focus solely on the problems of Donald Trump as a president. Biden chose not to talk about his failures to control inflation, and illegal immigration, or the loss of the U.S.'s triple AAA credit rating (2024); the SEC ruled that the **Bitcoin** product was to be available to be traded like other investment products (2024); over **20 million people** had signed up for a healthcare plan provided under the Affordable Care Act (2024); Donald **Trump took over 50%** of the Iowa votes, Ron DeSantis was second, and Nikki Haley was third. Shortly after, Senator Tim Scott and Governor Ron DeSantis dropped out of the race and gave their support to Donald Trump (2024); in spite of an earlier U.S. Supreme Court decision voiding an extended forgiveness of college loans, President Biden forgave 74,000 persons of some **$5 billion in college loans** (2024); healthcare insurance companies were struggling with the costs of weight-control products such as **Ozempic**, forcing them to stop reimbursement (2024); presidential candidate Donald Trump charged that pending legislation to limit immigration was a failed attempt to solve a border control failure (2024); Alabama was the first state to **execute a killer** by use of nitrogen (2024); the only competition for the Democratic nomination President Biden saw was Robert Kennedy, Jr. (2024); reportedly, Donald Trump was worth three billion dollars, but much of it was in real estate (2024); former President Trump called **NATO obsolete** and remiss in enforcing the charter requirements that each member spend at least two percent of its GNP on the military. Since Trump believed Russia was a threat to Europe, not the United States, he said he saw no need to support NATO (2024); **Jennifer Crowley**, mother of troubled shooter son Ethan, was the first parent found guilty of manslaughter in Oxford, Michigan (2024); a U.S. District Court of Appeals unanimously rejected former President Donald Trump's immunity claims. Trump therefore could be tried for illegally attempting to overthrow the 2020 election results. He appealed the verdict. (2024); **Charles Littleton**, a former IRS contractor, received five years in prison for leaking Donald Trump's tax records (2024); the U.S. Supreme Court ruled that federal officials could **tear down the razor wire** put up by Texas Governor Greg Abbott to keep out immigrants. His reply: "I will put up more wire" (2024); **Cigna Group** sold its Medicare business to Health Care Service Corp for $3.3 billion (2024); the Justice Department stated it **would not press criminal charges** against President Biden for classified documents found in his garage from his time serving as vice president under Obama (2024); unhappy with **Delaware's incorporation** rules, several companies looked to Texas and Wyoming as an alternative (2024); presidential candidate Donald Trump stated he would not respond to a **Russian attack** on any NATO country not meeting the 2% of GDP for military defense (2024); by mid-year, 20 of the 30 **NATO countries** were setting aside 2% or more of their gross domestic product for their military (2024); the House of Representatives impeached Homeland Secretary Alejandro Mayorkas on a vote of 214-213 on a failed border security issue but the Senate failed to convict (2024); the Senate

JOSEPH R. BIDEN, JR. (46TH PRESIDENT)

approved a **$95 billion foreign aid** package for Israel and Ukraine (2024); Democrat **Tom Suozzi** defeated Republican Mazi Pilip in a special election for the House seat of ousted Republican George Santos, leaving the Republicans with only a one seat advantage (2024); **Amazon** replaced Walgreens on the Dow Jones Industrial Average (2024); the **Alabama Supreme Court** ruled that frozen embryos are children (2024); five states (California, Colorado, Massachusetts, New York, and Wisconsin) allowed the issuance of an **abortion pill** (2024); Senate Minority Leader **Mitch McConnell** announced he was stepping down from his leadership position following November's election (2024); **Truth Social** had a successful IPO, with Trump's reported worth over $4.5 billion (2024); it was estimated that by September 2024 over **8 million illegal immigrants** would have entered the United States, with a backlog of 3 million awaiting a decision on an asylum request (2024); dozens of Jewish students feared for their safety due to protests at **Columbia University** denouncing the war in Gaza (2024); the **Bureau of Alcohol, Tobacco and Firearms** issued a ruling that anyone selling firearms must be federally licensed (2024); the IRS charged Donald Trump with writing off tax deductions for the work on the **Trump International Hotel and Tower** in Chicago (2024); U.S. Supreme Court **Justice Thomas** was accused of accepting expensive gifts from billionaire friends (2024); Independent candidate for President **Robert Kennedy Jr**. reported that a worm got into his brain, leaving him with "cognitive struggles" (2024); West Virginia Democratic **Senator Joe Manchin** announced he was switching to an Independent (2024); the **Libertarian Party** selected Oliver Chase as its presidential candidate (2024); **California wildfires** destroyed over 300,000 acres (2024); a new blood test is able to **detect Alzheimer's** (2024); **Walmart** ended its relationship with Capital One for Walmart credit cards (2024); retailers reported they **would open more stores** than they shut for the year (2024); the Justice Department charged **Boeing Aircraft** with failing to comply with a 2021 agreement to make safety inspections on the 787 Dreamliner, which had several crashes (2024); **Tesla** recalled 125,000 vehicles for seatbelt problems (2024); **Chevon** acquired **Hess Oil** for $53 billion (2024); Merck acquired **Eyebiotech** for $1.3 billion (2024); after losing a proxy battle for Disney, investor **Nelson Peltz** sold all of his Disney shares (2024); President Biden released a **three phase proposal for peace between Israel and Hamas** that would last for a six week period: a full and complete cease-fire, a release of hostages and soldiers in captivity, and a binding peace agreement (2024); an Equilar survey found that **CEO pay rose** 12.6% to $16.3 million for 2023 (2024); **Waste Management** acquired Stericycle for $5.8 billion (2024); **Vermont** was the first state to pass a law requiring fossil fuel companies to pay for damages caused by climate change (2024); a Miami condo assessed **residents $30 million** to make building repairs, an average of $134,000 per resident (2024); President Biden **increased tariffs** on batteries, electric cars, and semiconductors from China (2024); **Chrysler recalled** over one million cars for rear-camera problems (2024); **chipmaker Nvidia's** market value of $3.34 trillion exceeded Microsoft's $3.32 and Apple's $3.29 (2024); President Biden announced that some 500,000 long-term **undocumented spouses** would not be deported (2024); the FDA reported a new pill for **continuous positive airway pressure** (CPAP) addressed sleep apnea (2024); **Pat Sajak** retired as host of Wheel of Fortune after 41 years (2024); the **number of tornadoes** during the month of June were among the most in the nation's history (2024); President Biden signed an executive order **closing the border** when more than 2,500 immigrants entered the southern U.S. per day. It was still estimated more than 1.8 million would enter the United States (2024); **Hunter Biden's first wife**, Kathleen Buhle, sued him for not paying alimony and other expenses (2024); scientists reported that persons with two copies of the **gene variant APOE4** would develop Alzheimer's (2024); U.S. Supreme Court Justice **Samuel Alito** refused to comment on the upside down American flag (sign of distress) on his property (2024); U.S. Supreme Court Associate Justice **Clarence Thomas** reported he took two vacations paid for by a millionaire (2024); California raised the **hourly minimum wage to $20** (2024); U.S. household wealth rose to **$160 trillion** by mid-year (2024); the **three market value largest publicly** traded companies were Microsoft ($3.15 trillion), Nvidia ($3.02 trillion), and Apple ($2.99 trillion) (2024); some 200 **D-Day veterans**, average age 100, returned to the beaches of Normandy for the **80th anniversary** of the 1944 allied landing (2024); the NBA signed an **eleven-year deal** with Amazon, ESPN, and NBC for $11 billion (2024); due to lower profits, Kroger cut CEO **Rodney McMullen's** pay by 18% to $15.7 million (2024); **Caterpillar** agreed to pay $800,000 to end hiring discrimination against Black applicants (2024); the Center for Disease Control announced a second person had contracted **bird flu** (2024); **tornadoes hit Iowa** and caused extensive damage (2024); the Labor Department issued a ruling that workers earning less than $1,128 a week must be paid time-and-a-half for hours worked in excess of 50 hours a week (2024); following a class action lawsuit, the **National Collegiate Athletic Association** stated schools could pay athletes for their participation in school programs (2024); Major League Baseball added the **Negro League statistics** to its record book, changing record leaders (2024); a U.S. District Judge blocked a Biden administration attempt to cap late credit card fees at $8 (2024); **Walmart** laid off hundreds of corporate jobs and asked remote workers to return to work (2024); restaurant chain **Red Lobster** filed for bankruptcy protection while negotiating with landlords on rent (2024); inflation core prices for April rose 3.6% annually, the least in a year (2024); Tesla shareholders approved **Elon Musk's** $45 billion pay package (2024); the U.S. Supreme Court rejected an effort to stop access to the abortion pill (2024); the DJIA, Nasdaq, and the S&P 500 all set new record highs during the month of June (2024); Tesla changed its business address from Delaware to Texas, not liking the Delaware rulings on Elon Musk's pay (2024); **Conoco Phillips and Marathon Oil** agreed on a $17 billion merger (2024); **Hurricane Beryl** was the earliest in the season to reach Category 5 status (2024); a federal judge blocked **SEC-proposed rules** requiring hedge funds and private equity firms to be more transparent (2024); health and life insurance provider **Prudential** announced a $2 billion stock buyback (2024); the **Boston Celtics** basketball team signed a record five-year $314 million contract with player Jason Tatum (2024); **Saks Fifth Avenue** acquired Neiman Marcus for $2.7 billion (2024); **Amazon.com joined** Alphabet, Apple, Microsoft, and Nvidia in the $2 trillion market-capitalization companies (2024); **Boeing** acquired Spirit AeroSystems for $4.7 billion (2024); **Cedar Fair and Six Flags** agreed to an $8 billion merger (2024); **Verizon** replaced the checkmark logo with the letter V (2024); former President Donald Trump's attorney **Rudolph Giuliani** was removed from his WABC radio program for continuing to challenge the 2020 presidential election results (2024); the **TGI Fridays** restaurant chain filed for bankruptcy (2024); and the **DJIA** closed at 42,544.22, up 12.88%.

Donald J. Trump
(47ᵀᴴ President)

January 20, 2025 – January 20, 2029

On **November 15, 2022, Donald J. Trump announced his campaign for a non-consecutive second presidential term** in a speech at Mar-a-Lago in Palm Beach, Florida.

Significant events during the year 2022 included: the **U.S. Supreme Court overturned** a New York State law that placed **strict limits on carrying guns** outside the home; the **U.S. Supreme Court**, in a 6 to 3 ruling, **overturned** the 49-year-old ruling of **Roe vs Wade** that permitted abortions, allowing states to determine whether or not abortions should be permitted; the **U.S. Supreme Court** ruled a person cannot be barred from **publicly exercising his faith**; the **U.S. Supreme Court** ruled that a

Georgia **death row inmate** could die as he preferred, by firing squad, not lethal injection; the House subcommittee decided that the insurrection on January 6th at the Capitol Building was a **planned uprising** triggered by President Trump, not a spontaneous action; a U.S. Court of Appeals ruled that the **House Ways & Means Committee** was entitled to receive **six years of former President Trump's tax returns** (2015-2020); former President Trump's Chief Financial Officer, **Allen Weisselberg**, reached a **plea bargain** on charges of income tax evasion; the U.S. Supreme Court **denied** former President **Trump's request to block acquisition of his tax returns**; a federal district judge ruled that a federal law **preventing the purchase of guns was unconstitutional**; the **Republicans regained control of the House** in the midterm elections; given that in both the first and second quarter the country had negative GDP numbers, the country was officially in a **recession**; Reuters reported that the gap between average CEO pay ($2.5 million) and median worker pay ($23,698) was 670 to 1; and the **DJIA** closed at 33,147.25, down 9.12%.

In 2023, there were **four primary televised debates** among the Republican candidates for president. The **first** was held on **August 23rd in Milwaukee, Wisconsin**. In attendance were Doug Burgum, Chris Christie, Nikki Haley, Ron DeSantis, Asa Hutchinson, Mike Pence, Vivek Ramaswamy, and Tim Scott. The **second** televised Republican presidential primary debate was held on **September 27th in Simi Valley, California**. The participants were Doug Burgum, Chris Christie, Ron DeSantis, Nikki Haley, Mike Pence, Vivek Ramaswamy, and Tim Scott. The **third** televised Republican presidential primary debate was held on **November 8th in Miami, Florida**. The participants were Chris Christie, Ron DeSantis, Nikki Haley, Vivek Ramaswamy, and Tim Scott. The **fourth** televised Republican presidential primary debate was held on **December 6th in Tuscaloosa, Alabama**. The participants were Chris Christie, Ron DeSantis, Nikki Haley, and Vivek Ramaswamy.

Significant events during the year 2023 included: after 15 ballots, Republican **Kevin McCarthy** was elected Speaker of the House with 216 votes; upon review, it was learned that Donald **Trump paid little or no taxes** for the years 2015, 2016, and 2017; the U.S. Senate ruled that anyone appearing on the **Senate floor** must be in a business suit; House Speaker **Kevin McCarthy** was voted out of his job, the first speaker outed in 234 years, and **Mike Johnson** was voted in; Republican **George Santos** was expelled from the House of Representatives for lies, misuse of campaign funds, and other wrongful behavior. He was the first person expelled without being convicted of an illegal act or supporting the confederacy; overwhelmed by the arrival of over **150,000 immigrants**, New York City offered free airline tickets costing less than one day of housing; the Biden administration announced that some **472,000 Venezuelan immigrants** would receive work permits and protection from deportation; Oath-Keepers leader **Stewart Rhodes** was sentenced to 18 years in prison for his role in the January 6, 2021, attack on the U.S. Capitol Building; the U.S. Supreme Court ruled that President Biden **did not have** the **authority to forgive some $400 billion** in loans to some 45 million former students; the New York Supreme Court ruled that control of Trump's New York State property would be placed with a third party; Ponzi schemer **Bernard Madoff's 40,000 clients** had been 90% made whole with $4.2 billion in payments; **FTX** founder Sam Bankman-Fried stole $10 billion from his company; **President Biden's son, Hunter,** was indicted on nine counts of felonies and misdemeanors that could lead to 17 years in prison; a jury found attorney **Rudy Giuliani** guilty for the slander that Georgia election officials had rigged the 2020 presidential election and sentenced him to pay $148 million; Judge Arthur Engoron stated, "Donald **Trump inflated his wealth** to rip off banks, insurance firms, and New York State," reportedly by close to $170 million; the **U.S. Supreme Court** unanimously agreed to a new code of ethics; the U.S. debt was **over $33 trillion** for the first time in history, and the federal budget was over **$63 billion**; sixty-six million people were on **Medicare**; some **3.2 million immigrants** entered the U.S. in 2023 vs 2.8 million in 2022 and 2.0 million in 2021; the AFL-CIO reported the average **CEO pay** for 2022 was $16 million; Forbes dropped **Donald Trump** from its list of the 400 richest Americans with its $2.9 billion cutoff; and the **DJIA** closed at 37,689.54, up 13.70%.

A **fifth** Republican presidential televised primary debate was held on **January 10th, 2024, in Des Moines, Iowa**. The participants were Ron DeSantis and Nikki Haley.

The **first voting** Republican presidential primary was held on **January 15, 2024, in Iowa**. Donald Trump took over 51% of the votes cast and 20 delegates. Ron DeSantis received 21% of the votes and 9 delegates, Nikki Haley received 19% of the votes and 8 delegates, and Vivek Ramaswamy received 8% of the votes and 3 delegates. After the votes were counted, DeSantis and Ramaswamy dropped out of the race and gave their support to Donald Trump. The **second voting** Republican presidential primary was held on **January 23, 2024, in New Hampshire**, where Trump received 54% of the votes and 13 delegates. Nikki Haley received 43% of the votes and 9 delegates, and the remaining 3% went to other candidates. The **third voting** Republican presidential primary was scheduled to be held on **February 6,**

2024, in Nevada, but was boycotted by the Republican Party. The **fourth voting** Republican presidential caucus was held on **February 6, 2024, in Nevada**. Donald Trump received over 99% of the votes and 26 delegates. The **fifth voting** Republican presidential caucus was held on **February 9, 2024, in the Virgin Islands**. Trump received over 74% of the votes and 20 delegates, and Haley received over 25% of the votes but no delegates. The **sixth voting** Republican presidential primary was held on **February 24, 2024, in South Carolina**. Trump received 60% of the votes and 47 delegates. Receiving 40% of the votes (and three delegates) in her home state, Haley withdrew from the race, leaving Trump the de facto Republican candidate.

At a February rally, Trump announced that he would encourage Putin to invade a NATO country that had not invested the required 2% of their GDP in their military. President Biden stated, "President Putin is a crazy S.O.B. for invading the Ukraine." While he was staying at a Trump Hotel in Las Vegas, a waitress complained to Trump that it was **unfair to have to pay taxes on tips**. Trump thought it was a good idea and added it to his campaign platform.

On June 27, 2024, President Joe Biden and former President Donald Trump engaged in a **pre-election debate**. Trump was energetic but held back any emotional outbursts. Instead, he repeatedly ignored the interviewer's questions to make his own points about Biden's failings. Reportedly, Trump misspoke thirty times on issues when making his points. He even called Biden a moron and the worst president in history. Biden never challenged Trump on his lies. On the issue of nine million illegal immigrants entering the country in the past three years, Trump added that Biden would bankrupt Medicare by giving immigrants medical coverage. **Biden's performance was pathetic.**

He mumbled and stumbled in a weak voice. Trump challenged Biden to take a **cognitive test**. Trump claimed he had taken one and was told he probably had the highest score of any president. Trump ended with, "He's not equipped to be president. You know it and I know it. I will Make America Great Again!" Clearly, **Trump had won the evening**, and shortly after the debate, **calls started coming in for Biden to withdraw from the election**. Even the *New York Times* printed the statement, "The President should end his quest for a second term." The view of many was that Biden's mental and physical abilities no longer could meet the demands of being the president. Biden's response: "I am in to win." After the debate, Trump stated he was in a very good physical and mental state.

In **Trump vs United States** (2024), the U.S. Supreme Court granted **immunity** to U.S. presidents for actions that are official acts. The court ruled that evidence related to official acts cannot be used to prove charges against unofficial acts. The three dissenters in the 6 to 3 decision stated that the court had made the president king. He can do no wrong. This in spite of the fact that the **constitution makes no mention of presidential immunity**.

On July 13, 2024, at a rally in Butler, Pennsylvania, **Thomas Matthew Crooks** shot at Trump several times with his AR-15-style rifle **from a nearby rooftop**, only **hitting his ear**. The **assassin was shot and killed** by the Secret Service. Trump was quickly covered by five Secret Service agents and wrestled off the stage, with Trump raising his right arm in a clenched fist. Rushed to a nearby hospital, Trump was treated and released. One attendee, Corey Comperatore, was killed as he shielded his wife and child. Two other attendees were wounded and released from the hospital. Trump's first words were, "By luck or by God I'm still here." Some said it changed his belligerent style. He said he **threw out**

his tough presidential acceptance speech and focused on uniting the country.

On July 15, 2024, within minutes of their arrival at the **National Republican Convention** in Milwaukee, Wisconsin, delegates revealed the Trump-endorsed Republican Party platform. It was a shortened version of the 2020 Republican platform. It was approved with a vote of 84 to 18. At the convention, former President Donald Trump received the Republican nomination for president. He read his hour-long **acceptance speech**, opening with, "I stand before you this evening with a message of confidence, strength, and hope. Together, we will launch a new era of safety, prosperity, and freedom for citizens of every race, religion, color, and creed. The discord and division in our society must be healed. As Americans we are bound together by a single fate and a shared destiny. We rise together or we fall apart. I am running to be president for all of America – not half of America because there is no victory in winning for half. The discord and division in our society must be healed." This toned-down appeal for unity was a major departure from the normal Trump rhetoric of slandering Biden. Trump then went on to describe the **assassination attempt**, stating, "If I had not moved my head, the assassin's bullet would have perfectly hit its mark, and I would not be here tonight. None of us knows God's plan, or where life's adventure will take us. But if the event of last Saturday makes anything clear, it is every single moment we have on earth is a gift from God. We have to make the most of every day, for the people and country we love."

Trump then went on to review his successes as the 45th president (which included a number of misstatements). Then he described what he would do as the 47th president, with special emphasis on solving **crime** and **immigration issues**. All of this was in a rambling, repetitive series of statements. Trump was neither humble nor modest. At the end of his speech, former President Trump stated, "I am proud to accept the nomination for president of the United States. **The past is over; it is time to unite."** Trump named **Ohio Senator J.D. Vance** as his vice presidential running mate.

On July 21, 2024, President Biden announced he would not seek re-election and Vice President Kamala Harris had his full support.

At an August 1, 2024, rally, J.D. Vance, Donald Trump's vice-presidential candidate, labeled Kamala Harris "**a sociopathic childless cat-lady who is miserable in her own life**."

On September 10, 2024, former President Donald Trump and Vice President Kamala Harris engaged in their **first presidential televised debate**. It took place in Philadelphia, Pennsylvania in a room that was empty except for two ABC interviewers. Harris attacked Trump's tax cuts for the rich and his extensive tariff philosophy. Trump responded with comments on Harris's immigration position and liberal economic policies, but he failed to attack her price control position and flip-flops on health insurance and fracking. Harris was poised; Trump was combative. **Most agreed that Harris had the better night**. The *New York Times* reported that Trump made ten false statements and six misleading ones. Harris made two false statements and three misleading ones.

On September 15, 2024, **Ryan Wesley Routh** was detained for an **attempted assassination** of former President **Donald Trump** at Trump's golf course in West Palm Beach, Florida.

In response to **Harris's** earlier **comment** that she had **worked at McDonald's** when she was young, **Trump** donned an apron and **handled the French fry station at a McDonald's**. Later, he appeared at a **rally in New York City's Madison Square Garden**. He opened his comments with, "I am thrilled to be back in the city I love." But one of the warm-up comedians made the inappropriate comment that "the floating **garbage** in the Atlantic Ocean is **called Puerto Rico**." Not a great way to get the Puerto Rican vote. When President Biden heard about the comment, he stated, "**The only garbage are Trump supporters.**" Trump's response? He got into a **sanitation truck** to send the message he was picking up the garbage.

Meanwhile, **millionaire Mark Cuban claimed**, "I have never seen Trump with strong, intelligent women." Cuban backed off from the comment when a number of strong, intelligent women told him they were offended by it.

Just before the election, **Trump, like Harris, campaigned in the seven key states that would determine the election:** Arizona, Georgia, Michigan, Nevada, North Carolina, Pennsylvania, and Wisconsin. Trump's message was that the country was on the brink of ruin because of rising prices and uncontrolled immigration. He then urged the crowd to get out and vote.

In the **2024 election**, Republicans Donald **Trump** and J.D. **Vance** received **312 electoral votes** (more than the required minimum of 270) **versus 226 electoral votes** for Democrats Kamala **Harris** and Tim **Walz. Trump was the elected president, and Vance was the elected vice president. Trump and Vance** also received **77,237,942 popular votes** vs **74,940,837** for **Harris and Walz.**

With his election in 2016 and 2024, Donald Trump was the second person to be elected president to two non-consecutive terms of office. Grover Cleveland did it in 1884 and 1892. Thus, there were only 45 men who were presidents.

Trump announced that he would not make the mistakes he made in his first presidency. **He wanted only people who were loyal to him and in agreement with his policies.** One assumes they were also qualified for the position offered. He indicated his first priority was to select a chief of staff. Trump quickly selected Susie Wiles, who had been so effective in running his election campaign, then turned his attention to his cabinet secretaries and the other key positions. All would begin their new jobs at noon on January 20, 2025.

Shortly after the election, the **Justice Department** announced they had uncovered an **Iranian plot to assassinate Donald Trump** after the election, in the belief that he would lose, and security would be easier to circumvent. This action was revenge for the drone strike ordered by President Trump in 2020, that killed Iran's Quds Force leader. As a result of this discovery, the President-elect's security was significantly enhanced.

Comparing the 2024 election with the 2020 election, Donald **Trump** and J.D. **Vance** received **roughly 3 million more popular votes in 2024** than Donald **Trump** and Mike **Pence in 2020**. And Kamala **Harris** and Tim **Walz** received **roughly 6.25 million fewer votes in 2024** than Joe **Biden** and Kamala **Harris received in 2020**.

In the **U.S. Senate, 53 Republicans** were voted into office (a gain of four) versus **47 for the Democrats** (a loss of four), including 2 Independents. In the **U.S. House of Representatives, 220 Republicans** were voted into office versus **215 Democrats**. The Republicans had control of Congress until at least the 2026 midterm elections.

Special Counsel Jack Smith decided to **drop all federal criminal charges** against president-elect Donald Trump, including attempting to overthrow the 2020 presidential election and unlawfully retaining classified documents. The reason for this decision was that **Justice Department policy prohibited the prosecution of a sitting president**, even though Trump was president-elect and was not a sitting president until he was inaugurated on January 20th.

After each state finalized the presidential vote count, the information was sent to the **appropriate state's governor, who then appointed the electors in the college**. The total number of electors is equal to the number of senators and representatives for the state. On December 17th, the **electors of each state met and cast their electoral votes** for the president and the vice president. The **voting results**, along with an electoral certificate, were **sent to the U.S. Senate** in a ceremonial mahogany box. It had been received prior to the fourth Wednesday in December in accordance with the U.S. Constitution.

The newly elected Democratic representatives held 215 seats, and the Republicans held 220 seats. In the Senate, the Republicans held 53 seats, and the Democrats held 47 seats. All took office at noon on January 3, 2025, because in accordance with the 20th Amendment to the U.S. Constitution, the terms of outgoing Senators and Representatives ended at noon on the 3rd day of January 2025. Republican **Speaker of the House Mike Johnson** and Republican **Majority Leader of the Senate John Thune** also took office at that time.

Significant events during the year 2024 included: Trump **began his campaign**; In President Biden's campaign, he chose to focus solely on the problems of Donald Trump as a president and chose not to talk about his failure to control inflation and illegal immigration or the loss of the U.S. triple A credit rating; in spite of an earlier U.S. Supreme Court decision voiding an extended forgiveness of college loans, President Biden forgave 74,000 persons some **$5 billion in college loans**; the

Justice Department stated it **would not press criminal charges** against President Biden for classified documents found in his garage from his time serving as vice president under Obama; unhappy with **Delaware's incorporation** rules, several companies looked to Texas and Wyoming as alternatives; the **Alabama Supreme Court** ruled that frozen embryos were children; five states (California, Colorado, Massachusetts, New York, and Wisconsin) allowed the issuance of an **abortion pill**; **Truth Social** had a successful IPO, with Trump's reported worth over $4.5 billion; the Federal Reserve reduced the short-term interest rate for the third time in the year to a new range of 4.25 to 5.0 percent; the U.S. population was estimated to be 340 million, up 3.4 million, with 2.7 million due to immigration; a U.S. District Court of Appeals unanimously rejected immunity claims by former president Donald Trump; **Charles Littleton**, a former IRS contractor, received five years in prison for leaking Donald Trump's tax records; the U.S. Supreme Court ruled that federal officials could **tear down the razor wire** put up by Texas Governor Greg Abbott to keep out immigrants. His reply: "I will put up more wire"; **Amazon** replaced Walgreens on the Dow Jones Industrial Average; Senate Minority Leader **Mitch McConnell** announced he was stepping down from his leadership position following November's election; Independent candidate for president **Robert Kennedy Jr**. reported that a worm got into his brain, leaving him with "cognitive struggles"; Tesla shareholders approved **Elon Musk's** $45 billion pay package; the DJIA, Nasdaq, and the S&P 500 all set new record highs; **Amazon.com joined** Alphabet, Apple, Microsoft, and Nvidia in the $2 trillion market-capitalization companies; former President Donald Trump's attorney **Rudolph Giuliani** was removed from his WABC radio program for continuing to challenge the 2020 presidential election results; President Biden **pardoned his son Hunter** of gun and tax charges; Jimmy Carter died at age 100, making him the longest living former president; and the **DJIA** closed at 42,544.22, up 12.88%.

On January 6, 2025, in accordance with the U.S. Constitution, Kamala Harris, as vice president of the United States and president of the Senate, presided over a **joint session of Congress** to determine the outcome of the electoral voting for the president of the United States; Harris was joined by Speaker of the House Mike Johnson.

The **electoral vote count** was reported for each state (taken in alphabetical order) by **two senators**, Democrat Amy Klobuchar from Minnesota and Republican Deb Fischer from Nebraska, and **two representatives**, Democrat Joe Morelle from New York and Republican Bryan Steil from Wisconsin. They read the electoral voting results in a scripted manner.

The Republicans rose and applauded when Trump won the state, and the Democrats rose and applauded when Harris won the state. The final outcome was Trump with 312 votes and Harris with 226 votes. Donald Trump had been elected president and J.D. Vance had been elected vice president. With that, Harris reported the results on the record; Congress had certified the election of Trump and Vance. Both would be sworn into office on January 20th, 2025, in Washington, D.C. Unlike January 6, 2021, there were no protests over the election; it was a peaceful transfer of power.

Harris was not the first sitting vice president who had presided over a vote count over her defeat as a presidential candidate; Richard Nixon did it in 1961 (he lost to John Kennedy), and Al Gore did it in 2001 (he lost to George Bush). Mike Pence was precluded from doing so in 2021 due to the riot at the Capitol Building.

Why did the framers of the Constitution not anticipate this issue? The Constitution was adopted in 1788, and John Adams was the first vice president to run for president and (in 1797) be elected president. A simple solution would have been for the Constitution to have stated that if the seated vice president ran for president, the president pro tem of the Senate, not the president of the Senate, would preside over a joint session of Congress to validate the electoral voting results.

Trump's proposed initial **cabinet** included **Vice President** J.D. Vance, **Secretary of State** Marco Rubio, **Secretary of the Treasury** Scott Bessent, **Secretary of Defense** Pete Hegseth, **Attorney General** Pam Bondi, **Secretary of the Interior** Doug Burgum, **Secretary of Agriculture** Brooke Rollins, **Secretary of Commerce** Howard Lutnick, **Secretary of Labor** Lori Chavez-DeRemer, **Secretary of Health and Human Services** Robert F. Kennedy Jr., **Secretary of Housing and Urban Development** Scott Turner, **Secretary of Transportation** Sean Duffy, **Secretary of Energy** Chris Wright, **Secretary of Education** Linda McMahon, **Secretary of Veterans Affairs** Doug Collins, and **Secretary of Homeland Security** Kristi Noem.

According to Forbes, Trump's cabinet would have at least five billionaires and president-elect Donald Trump's net worth was believed to be $5.5 billion.

Key **Trump** appointments included **Chief of Staff** Susie Wiles, **Ambassador to Israel** Mike Huckabee, **Ambassador to the United Nations** Elise Stefanik, **Border Czar** Tom Homan, **Director of the CIA** John Ratcliffe, **Director of the FBI** Kash Patel, **Director of Communications** Steven Cheung, **Director of the Federal Trade Commission** Andrew Ferguson, **Director of the Office of Management & Budget** Russell Vought, **Department of Government Efficiency Heads** Elon Musk and Vivek Ramaswamy (both having since departed), **Director of** the Securities and Exchange Commission Paul Atkins, **Domestic Policy Advisor** Stephen Miller, **Federal Communications Commission Chairman** Brendan Carr, **Medicare & Medicaid Director** Dr. Mehmet Oz, **National Intelligence Director** Tulsi Gabbard, **National Security Advisor** Michael Waltz, **Press Secretary** Karoline Leavitt, **Surgeon General** Dr. Janette Nesheiwat, and **White House Counsel** William McGinley.

Trump appointed a **transition team** to assist in his assuming the presidency. They were **Susie Wiles** (incoming chief of staff), **Pam Bondi** (attorney general nominee), and **Boris Epshteyn** (legal advisor). Shortly after their appointment, they signed an agreement with the Justice Department allowing the FBI to do background checks on Trump's appointees.

On the morning of January 20, 2025, the outgoing president, Joe Biden, and his wife, Jill, hosted the traditional breakfast for incoming President Donald Trump and his wife, Melania. Following the event, the four went to the Capitol Building for the inauguration.

Due to the weather, Trump's inauguration was held inside the Capitol Building's Rotunda; the unstated reason may have been for increased security due to two assassination attempts on Trump's life. The last time the inauguration was held in the Capitol Building was in 1985, when bad weather forced the inauguration of Ronald Reagan inside. Among the hundreds of attendees were past Presidents Bill Clinton, George Bush, and Barack Obama, and soon to be former President Joe Biden.

At noon on Monday, January 20, 2025, James David Vance accompanied by his wife and child, took the oath of office as vice president from **Chief Justice of the U.S. Supreme Court John Roberts**. This was followed by Donald J. Trump, accompanied by his wife Melania, who took the oath of office as president from **Chief Justice John Roberts**. These oaths were the same as those taken by George Washington and John Adams. Donald Trump was then the 47th president of the United States, and J.D. Vance was then the 56th vice president of the United States. Reportedly, Trump was the first convicted felon to be president of the United States. Obviously, a majority of voters were less impressed with what he had done than with what he promised to do if elected.

Trump gave his inauguration address. Realizing that January 20th was also Martin Luther King Jr. Day, Trump stated he was confident this administration would make King's dream come true; America would be great again. Because if we work together, there is nothing that we cannot achieve. He vowed that he would stop U.S. decline and create an America that would be the envy of all. He went on to state the Gulf of Mexico would be renamed the Gulf of America, we would take back the Panama Canal given to Panama by President Carter, and he would rename Mount Denali, so named by President Obama, to Mount McKinley. He focused on solving the immigration crisis and lowering inflation.

The inauguration ended shortly after noon with a 21-cannon salute, prayers by religious leaders, and songs celebrating "America." Following the inauguration, Joe and Jill Biden returned to their Delaware home and Donald and Melania went to the White House, along with honored guests. Then Trump signed 36 executive orders.

Among the executive orders Trump signed were the following: the 1,600 people arrested in the January 6th uprising at the Capitol Building were pardoned, protection was revoked for transgender troops, a national emergency at the southern border was declared, designated drug cartels were named as terrorist organizations, federal employees were ordered back to work for a 5-day week, Biden's order removing Cuba from the terrorist list was revoked, Biden's order that at least 50% of the cars sold in the U.S. must be electric was also revoked, the Department of Government Efficiency was established, the U.S. was withdrawn from the Global Minimum Tax arrangement, U.S. membership from the World Health Organization was also withdrawn, the Gulf of Mexico was renamed the Gulf of America, and Mount Denali was renamed Mount McKinley.

The Trumps and Vances then joined a group of dignitaries for an inauguration luncheon. That evening, there were several inaugural balls where the Trumps and Vances made appearances. By midnight, Inauguration Day was over.

The following day, President Trump and his administration went to work. Trump had accomplished quite a bit during his first term in office, but during the 2024 presidential campaign he acknowledged there was still work to be done to make America great again.

Does Donald Trump want to be remembered as one of America's greatest presidents? Of course he does!

With that in mind, Trump has set out a comprehensive and detailed set of goals. Deport criminal illegal immigrants. Keep other illegals from entering the country. Keep inflation under control. Restore full employment. Get lower Fed interest rates. Achieve peace with Hamas and the Ukraine. Help maintain peace elsewhere in the world.

If President Trump achieves all of that, without doubt he will rank as one of America's greatest presidents, and receive a Nobel Peace Prize as well.

APPENDIX A

DECLARATION OF INDEPENDENCE

IN CONGRESS, JULY 4, 1776.
THE UNANIMOUS DECLARATION OF THE THIRTEEN UNITED STATES OF AMERICA.

When, in the Course of human events, it becomes necessary for one people to dissolve the political bands which have connected them with another, and to assume among the powers of the earth, the separate and equal station to which the Laws of Nature and of Nature's God entitle them, a decent respect to the opinions of mankind requires that they should declare the causes which impel them to the separation.*

We hold these truths to be self-evident, that all men are created equal, that they are endowed by their Creator with certain unalienable Rights, that among these are Life, Liberty and the pursuit of Happiness.

That to secure these rights, Governments are instituted among Men, deriving their just powers from the consent of the governed,

That whenever any Form of Government becomes destructive of these ends, it is the Right of the People to alter or to abolish it, and to institute new Government, laying its foundation on such principles and organizing its powers in such form, as to them shall seem most likely to effect their Safety and Happiness. Prudence, indeed, will dictate that Governments long established should not be changed for light and transient causes; and accordingly all experience hath shewn, that mankind are more disposed to suffer, while evils are sufferable, than to right themselves by abolishing the forms to which they are accustomed. But when a long train of abuses and usurpations, pursuing invariably the same Object evinces a design to reduce them under absolute Despotism, it is their right, it is their duty, to throw off such Government, and to provide new Guards for their future security.

Such has been the patient sufferance of these Colonies; and such is now the necessity which constrains them to alter their former Systems of Government. The history of the present King of Great Britain is a history of repeated injuries and usurpations, all having in direct object the establishment of an absolute Tyranny over these States. To prove this, let Facts be submitted to a candid world.

He has refused his Assent to Laws, the most wholesome and necessary for the public good.

He has forbidden his Governors to pass Laws of immediate and pressing importance, unless suspended in their operation till his Assent should be obtained; and when so suspended, he has utterly neglected to attend to them.

He has refused to pass other Laws for the accommodation of large districts of people, unless those people would relinquish the right of Representation in the Legislature, a right inestimable to them and formidable to tyrants only.

He has called together legislative bodies at places unusual, uncomfortable, and distant from the depository of their public Records, for the sole purpose of fatiguing them into compliance with his measures.

He has dissolved Representative Houses repeatedly, for opposing with manly firmness his invasions on the rights of the people.

He has refused for a long time, after such dissolutions, to cause others to be elected; whereby the Legislative powers, incapable of Annihilation, have returned to the People at large for their exercise; the State remaining in the mean time exposed to all the dangers of invasion from without, and convulsions within.

He has endeavoured to prevent the population of these States; for that purpose obstructing the Laws for Naturalization of Foreigners; refusing to pass others to encourage their migrations hither, and raising the conditions of new Appropriations of Lands.

He has obstructed the Administration of Justice, by refusing his Assent to Laws for establishing Judiciary powers.

He has made Judges dependent on his Will alone, for the tenure of their offices, and the amount and payment of their salaries.

He has erected a multitude of New Offices, and sent hither swarms of Officers to harrass our people, and eat out their substance.

He has kept among us, in times of peace, Standing Armies without the Consent of our legislatures.

He has affected to render the Military independent of and superior to the Civil power.

He has combined with others to subject us to a jurisdiction foreign to our constitution, and unacknowledged by our laws; giving his Assent to their Acts of pretended Legislation:

For Quartering large bodies of armed troops among us:

For protecting them, by a mock Trial, from punishment for any Murders which they should commit on the Inhabitants of these States:

For cutting off our Trade with all parts of the world:

For imposing Taxes on us without our Consent:

For depriving us in many cases, of the benefits of Trial by Jury:

For transporting us beyond Seas to be tried for pretended offences:

For abolishing the free System of English Laws in a neighbouring Province, establishing therein an Arbitrary government, and enlarging its Boundaries so as to render it at once an example and fit instrument for introducing the same absolute rule into these Colonies:

For taking away our Charters, abolishing our most valuable Laws, and altering fundamentally the Forms of our Governments:

For suspending our own Legislatures, and declaring themselves invested with power to legislate for us in all cases whatsoever.

He has abdicated Government here, by declaring us out of his Protection and waging War against us.

He has plundered our seas, ravaged our Coasts, burnt our towns, and destroyed the lives of our people.

He is at this time transporting large Armies of foreign Mercenaries to compleat the works of death, desolation and tyranny, already begun with circumstances of Cruelty & perfidy scarcely paralleled in the most barbarous ages, and totally unworthy the Head of a civilized nation.

He has constrained our fellow Citizens taken Captive on the high Seas to bear Arms against their Country, to become the executioners of their friends and Brethren, or to fall themselves by their Hands.

He has excited domestic insurrections amongst us, and has endeavoured to bring on the inhabitants of our frontiers, the merciless Indian Savages, whose known rule of warfare, is an undistinguished destruction of all ages, sexes and conditions.

In every stage of these Oppressions We have Petitioned for Redress in the most humble terms: Our repeated Petitions have been answered only by repeated injury. A Prince whose character is thus marked by every act which may define a Tyrant, is unfit to be the ruler of a free people.

Nor have We been wanting in attentions to our British brethren. We have warned them from time to time of attempts by their legislature to extend an unwarrantable jurisdiction over us. We have reminded them of the circumstances of our emigration and settlement here. We have appealed to their native justice and magnanimity, and we have conjured them by the ties of our common kindred to disavow these usurpations, which, would inevitably interrupt our connections and correspondence. They too have been deaf to the voice of justice and of consanguinity. We must, therefore, acquiesce in the necessity, which denounces our Separation, and hold them, as we hold the rest of mankind, Enemies in War, in Peace Friends.

We, therefore, the Representatives of the united States of America, in General Congress, Assembled, appealing to the Supreme Judge of the world for the rectitude of our intentions, do, in the Name, and by Authority of the good People of these Colonies, solemnly publish and declare, That these United Colonies are, and of Right ought to be Free and Independent States; that they are Absolved from all Allegiance to the British Crown, and that all political connection between them and the State of Great Britain, is and ought to be totally dissolved; and that as Free and Independent States, they have full Power to levy War, conclude Peace, contract Alliances, establish Commerce, and to do all other Acts and Things which Independent States may of right do.

And for the support of this Declaration, with a firm reliance on the protection of divine Providence, we mutually pledge to each other our Lives, our Fortunes and our sacred Honor.

— John Hancock

Georgia:	Button Gwinnett
	Lyman Hall
	George Walton
North Carolina:	William Hooper
	Joseph Hewes
	John Penn
South Carolina:	Edward Rutledge
	Thomas Heyward, Jr.
	Thomas Lynch, Jr.
	Arthur Middleton
Maryland:	Samuel Chase
	William Paca
	Thomas Stone
	Charles Carroll of Carrollton
Virginia:	George Wythe
	Richard Henry Lee
	Thomas Jefferson
	Benjamin Harrison
	Thomas Nelson, Jr.
	Francis Lightfoot Lee
	Carter Braxton
Pennsylvania:	Robert Morris
	Benjamin Rush
	Benjamin Franklin
	John Morton
	George Clymer
	James Smith
	George Taylor

APPENDIX A

	James Wilson
	George Ross
Delaware:	Caesar Rodney
	George Read
	Thomas McKean
New York:	William Floyd
	Philip Livingston
	Francis Lewis
	Lewis Morris
New Jersey:	Richard Stockton
	John Witherspoon
	Francis Hopkinson
	John Hart
	Abraham Clark
New Hampshire:	Josiah Bartlett
	William Whipple
	Matthew Thornton
Massachusetts:	**John Hancock**
	Samuel Adams
	John Adams
	Robert Treat Paine
	Elbridge Gerry
Rhode Island:	Stephen Hopkins
	William Ellery
Connecticut:	Roger Sherman
	Samuel Huntington
	William Williams
	Oliver Wolcott

§

Note: While every attempt was made to be accurate, you should not rely on the contents of this appendix without independently verifying their accuracy. This author apologizes for any inaccuracies.

APPENDIX B

THE CONSTITUTION OF THE UNITED STATES

WE THE PEOPLE of the United States, in Order to form a more perfect Union, establish Justice, insure domestic Tranquility, provide for the common defence, promote the general Welfare, and secure the Blessings of Liberty to ourselves and our Posterity, do ordain and establish this Constitution for the United States of America.

Article. I.

Section. 1. All legislative Powers herein granted shall be vested in a Congress of the United States, which shall consist of a Senate and House of Representatives.

Section. 2. The House of Representatives shall be composed of Members chosen every second Year by the People of the several States, and the Electors in each State shall have the Qualifications requisite for Electors of the most numerous Branch of the State Legislature.

No Person shall be a Representative who shall not have attained to the Age of twenty five Years, and been seven Years a Citizen of the United States, and who shall not, when elected, be an Inhabitant of that State in which he shall be chosen.

[Representatives and direct Taxes shall be apportioned among the several States which may be included within this Union, according to their respective Numbers, which shall be determined by adding to the whole Number of free Persons, including those bound to Service for a Term of Years, and excluding Indians not taxed, three fifths of all other Persons.] The actual Enumeration shall be made within three Years after the first Meeting of the Congress of the United States, and within every subsequent Term of ten Years, in such Manner as they shall by Law direct. The Number of Representatives shall not exceed one for every thirty Thousand, but each State shall have at Least one Representative; and until such enumeration shall be made, the State of New Hampshire shall be entitled to chuse three, Massachusetts eight, Rhode-Island and Providence Plantations one, Connecticut five, New-York six, New Jersey four, Pennsylvania eight, Delaware one, Maryland six, Virginia ten, North Carolina five, South Carolina five, and Georgia three.

When vacancies happen in the Representation from any State, the Executive Authority thereof shall issue Writs of Election to fill such Vacancies.

The House of Representatives shall chuse their Speaker and other Officers; and shall have the sole Power of Impeachment.

Section. 3. The Senate of the United States shall be composed of two Senators from each State, [chosen by the Legislature] thereof for six Years; and each Senator shall have one Vote.

Immediately after they shall be assembled in Consequence of the first Election, they shall be divided as equally as may be into three Classes. The Seats of the Senators of the first Class shall be vacated at the Expiration of the second Year, of the second Class at the Expiration of the fourth Year, and of the third Class at the Expiration of the sixth Year, so that one third may be chosen every second Year; [and if Vacancies happen by Resignation, or otherwise, during the Recess of the Legislature of any State, the Executive thereof may make temporary Appointments until the next Meeting of the Legislature, which shall then fill such Vacancies.]

No Person shall be a Senator who shall not have attained to the Age of thirty Years, and been nine Years a Citizen of the United States, and who shall not, when elected, be an Inhabitant of that State for which he shall be chosen.

The Vice President of the United States shall be President of the Senate, but shall have no Vote, unless they be equally divided.

The Senate shall chuse their other Officers, and also a President pro tempore, in the Absence of the Vice President, or when he shall exercise the Office of President of the United States.

The Senate shall have the sole Power to try all Impeachments. When sitting for that Purpose, they shall be on Oath or Affirmation. When the President of the United States is tried, the Chief Justice shall preside: And no Person shall be convicted without the Concurrence of two thirds of the Members present.

Judgment in Cases of Impeachment shall not extend further than to removal from Office, and disqualification to hold and enjoy any Office of honor, Trust or Profit under the United States: but the Party convicted shall nevertheless be liable and subject to Indictment, Trial, Judgment and Punishment, according to Law.

Section. 4. The Times, Places and Manner of holding Elections for Senators and Representatives, shall be prescribed in each State by the Legislature thereof; but the Congress may at any time by Law make or alter such Regulations, except as to the Places of chusing Senators.

The Congress shall assemble at least once in every Year, and such Meeting shall be [on the first Monday in December,] unless they shall by Law appoint a different Day.

Section. 5. Each House shall be the Judge of the Elections, Returns and Qualifications of its own Members, and a Majority of each shall constitute a Quorum to do Business; but a smaller Number may adjourn from day to day, and may be authorized to compel the Attendance of absent Members, in such Manner, and under such Penalties as each House may provide.

Each House may determine the Rules of its Proceedings, punish its Members for disorderly Behaviour, and, with the Concurrence of two thirds, expel a Member.

Each House shall keep a Journal of its Proceedings, and from time to time publish the same, excepting such Parts as may in their Judgment require Secrecy; and the Yeas and Nays of the Members of either House on any question shall, at the Desire of one fifth of those Present, be entered on the Journal.

Neither House, during the Session of Congress, shall, without the Consent of the other, adjourn for more than three days, nor to any other Place than that in which the two Houses shall be sitting.

Section. 6. The Senators and Representatives shall receive a Compensation for their Services, to be ascertained by Law, and paid out of the Treasury of the United States. They shall in all Cases, except Treason, Felony and Breach of the Peace, be privileged from Arrest during their Attendance at the Session of their respective Houses, and in going to and returning from the same; and for any Speech or Debate in either House, they shall not be questioned in any other Place.

No Senator or Representative shall, during the Time for which he was elected, be appointed to any civil Office under the Authority of the United States, which shall have been created, or the Emoluments whereof shall have been encreased during such time; and no Person holding any Office under the United States, shall be a Member of either House during his Continuance in Office.

Section. 7. All Bills for raising Revenue shall originate in the House of Representatives; but the Senate may propose or concur with Amendments as on other Bills.

Every Bill which shall have passed the House of Representatives and the Senate, shall, before it become a Law, be presented to the President of the United States; If he approve he shall sign it, but if not he shall return it, with his Objections to that House in which it shall have originated, who shall enter the Objections at large on their Journal, and proceed to reconsider it. If after such Reconsideration two thirds of that House shall agree to pass the Bill, it shall be sent, together with the Objections, to the other House, by which it shall likewise be reconsidered, and if approved by two thirds of that House, it shall become a Law. But in all such Cases the Votes of both Houses shall be determined by Yeas and Nays, and the Names of the Persons voting for and against the Bill shall be entered on the Journal of each House respectively, If any Bill shall not be returned by the President within ten Days (Sundays excepted) after it shall have been presented to him, the Same shall be a Law, in like Manner as if he had signed it, unless the Congress by their Adjournment prevent its Return, in which Case it shall not be a Law.

Every Order, Resolution, or Vote to which the Concurrence of the Senate and House of Representatives may be necessary (except on a question of Adjournment) shall be presented to the President of the United States; and before the Same shall take Effect, shall be approved by him, or being disapproved by him, shall be repassed by two thirds of the Senate and House of Representatives, according to the Rules and Limitations prescribed in the Case of a Bill.

Section. 8. The Congress shall have Power To lay and collect Taxes, Duties, Imposts and Excises, to pay the Debts and provide for the common Defence and general Welfare of the United States; but all Duties, Imposts and Excises shall be uniform throughout the United States;

To borrow Money on the credit of the United States;

To regulate Commerce with foreign Nations, and among the several States, and with the Indian Tribes;

To establish an uniform Rule of Naturalization, and uniform Laws on the subject of Bankruptcies throughout the United States;

To coin Money, regulate the Value thereof, and of foreign Coin, and fix the Standard of Weights and Measures;

To provide for the Punishment of counterfeiting the Securities and current Coin of the United States;

To establish Post Offices and post Roads;

To promote the Progress of Science and useful Arts, by securing for limited Times to Authors and Inventors the exclusive Right to their respective Writings and Discoveries;

To constitute Tribunals inferior to the supreme Court;

To define and punish Piracies and Felonies committed on the high Seas, and Offenses against the Law of Nations;

To declare War, grant Letters of Marque and Reprisal, and make Rules concerning Captures on Land and Water;

To raise and support Armies, but no Appropriation of Money to that Use shall be for a longer Term than two Years;

To provide and maintain a Navy;

To make Rules for the Government and Regulation of the land and naval Forces;

To provide for calling forth the Militia to execute the Laws of the Union, suppress Insurrections and repel Invasions;

To provide for organizing, arming, and disciplining, the Militia, and for governing such Part of them as may be employed in the Service of the United States, reserving to the States respectively, the Appointment of the Officers, and the Authority of training the Militia according to the discipline prescribed by Congress;

To exercise exclusive Legislation in all Cases whatsoever, over such District (not exceeding ten Miles square) as may, by Cession of particular States, and the Acceptance of Congress, become the Seat of the Government of the United States, and to exercise like Authority over all Places purchased by the Consent of the Legislature of the State in which the Same shall be, for the Erection of Forts, Magazines, Arsenals, dock-Yards and other needful Buildings; -And

To make all Laws which shall be necessary and proper for carrying into Execution the foregoing Powers, and all other Powers vested by this Constitution in the Government of the United States, or in any Department or Officer thereof.

Section. 9. The Migration or Importation of such Persons as any of the States now existing shall think proper to admit, shall not be prohibited by the Congress prior to the Year one thousand eight hundred and eight, but a Tax or duty may be imposed on such Importation, not exceeding ten dollars for each Person.

The Privilege of the Writ of Habeas Corpus shall not be suspended, unless when in Cases of Rebellion or Invasion the public Safety may require it.

No Bill of Attainder or ex post facto Law shall be passed.

No Capitation, or other direct, Tax shall be laid, [unless in Proportion to the Census or Enumeration herein before directed to be taken.]

No Tax or Duty shall be laid on Articles exported from any State.

No Preference shall be given by any Regulation of Commerce or Revenue to the Ports of one State over those of another: nor shall Vessels bound to, or from, one State, be obliged to enter, clear, or pay Duties in another.

No Money shall be drawn from the Treasury, but in Consequence of Appropriations made by Law; and a regular Statement and Account of the Receipts and Expenditures of all public Money shall be published from time to time.

No Title of Nobility shall be granted by the United States: And no Person holding any Office of Profit or Trust under them, shall, without the Consent of the Congress, accept of any present, Emolument, Office, or Title, of any kind whatever, from any King, Prince, or foreign State.

Section. 10. No State shall enter into any Treaty, Alliance, or Confederation; grant Letters of Marque and Reprisal; coin Money; emit Bills of Credit; make any Thing but gold and silver Coin a Tender in Payment of Debts; pass any Bill of Attainder, ex post facto Law, or Law impairing the Obligation of Contracts, or grant any Title of Nobility.

No State shall, without the Consent of the Congress, lay any Imposts or Duties on Imports or Exports, except what may be absolutely necessary for executing it's inspection Laws: and the net Produce of all Duties and Imposts, laid by any State on Imports or Exports, shall be for the Use of the Treasury of the United States; and all such Laws shall be subject to the Revision and Controul of the Congress.

No State shall, without the Consent of Congress, lay any Duty of Tonnage, keep Troops, or Ships of War in time of Peace, enter into any Agreement or Compact with another State, or with a foreign Power, or engage in War, unless actually invaded, or in such imminent Danger as will not admit of delay.

ARTICLE. II.

Section. 1. The executive Power shall be vested in a President of the United States of America. He shall hold his Office during the Term of four Years, and, together with the Vice President, chosen for the same Term, be elected, as follows:

Each State shall appoint, in such Manner as the Legislature thereof may direct, a Number of Electors, equal to the whole Number of Senators and Representatives to which the State may be entitled in the Congress: but no Senator or Representative, or Person holding an Office of Trust or Profit under the United States, shall be appointed an Elector.

[The Electors shall meet in their respective States, and vote by Ballot for two Persons, of whom one at least shall not be an Inhabitant of the same State with themselves. And they shall make a List of all the Persons voted for, and of the Number of Votes for each; which List they shall sign and certify, and transmit sealed to the Seat of the Government of the United States, directed to the President of the Senate. The President of the Senate shall, in the Presence of the Senate and House of Representatives, open all the Certificates, and the Votes shall then be counted. The Person having the greatest Number of Votes shall be the President, if such Number be a Majority of the whole Number of Electors appointed; and if there be more than one who have such Majority, and have an equal Number of Votes, then the House of Representatives shall immediately chuse by Ballot one of them for President; and if no Person have a Majority, then from the five highest on the List the said House shall in like Manner chuse the President. But in chusing the President, the Votes shall be taken by States, the Representation from each State having one Vote; A quorum for this Purpose shall consist of a Member or Members from two thirds of the States, and a Majority of all the States shall be necessary to a Choice. In every Case, after the Choice of the President, the Person having the greatest Number of Votes of the Electors shall be the Vice President. But if there should remain two or more who have equal Votes, the Senate shall chuse from them by Ballot the Vice President.]

The Congress may determine the Time of chusing the Electors, and the Day on which they shall give their Votes; which Day shall be the same throughout the United States.

No Person except a natural born Citizen, or a Citizen of the United States, at the time of the Adoption of this Constitution, shall be eligible to the Office of President; neither shall any person be eligible to that Office who shall not have attained to the Age of thirty five Years, and been fourteen Years a Resident within the United States.

[In Case of the Removal of the President from Office, or of his Death, Resignation, or Inability to discharge the Powers and Duties of the said Office, the Same shall devolve on the Vice President, and the Congress may by Law provide for the Case of Removal, Death, Resignation or Inability, both of the President and Vice President, declaring what Officer shall then act as President, and such Officer shall act accordingly, until the Disability be removed, or a President shall be elected.]

The President shall, at stated Times, receive for his Services, a Compensation, which shall neither be increased nor diminished during the Period for which he shall have been elected, and he shall not receive within that Period any other Emolument from the United States, or any of them.

Before he enter on the Execution of his Office, he shall take the following Oath or Affirmation:- "I do solemnly swear (or affirm) that I will faithfully execute the Office of President of the United States, and will to the best of my Ability, preserve, protect and defend the Constitution of the United States."

Section. 2. The President shall be Commander in Chief of the Army and Navy of the United States, and of the Militia of the several States, when called into the actual Service of the United States; he may require the Opinion, in writing, of the principal Officer in each of the executive Departments, upon any Subject relating to the Duties of their respective Offices, and he shall have Power to grant Reprieves and Pardons for Offenses against the United States, except in Cases of Impeachment.

He shall have Power, by and with the Advice and Consent of the Senate, to make Treaties, provided two thirds of the Senators present concur; and he shall nominate, and by and with the Advice and Consent of the Senate, shall appoint Ambassadors, other public Ministers and Consuls, Judges of the supreme Court, and all other Officers of the United States, whose Appointments are not herein otherwise provided for, and which shall be established by Law: but the Congress may by Law vest the Appointment of such inferior Officers, as they think proper, in the President alone, in the Courts of Law, or in the Heads of Departments.

The President shall have Power to fill up all Vacancies that may happen during the Recess of the Senate, by granting Commissions which shall expire at the End of their next Session.

Section. 3. He shall from time to time give to the Congress Information of the State of the Union, and recommend to their Consideration such Measures as he shall judge necessary and expedient; he may, on extraordinary Occasions, convene both Houses, or either of them, and in Case of Disagreement between them, with Respect to the Time of Adjournment, he may adjourn them to such Time as he shall think proper; he shall receive Ambassadors and other public Ministers; he shall take Care that the Laws be faithfully executed, and shall Commission all the Officers of the United States.

Section. 4. The President, Vice President and all civil Officers of the United States, shall be removed from Office on Impeachment for, and Conviction of, Treason, Bribery, or other high Crimes and Misdemeanors.

Article. III.

Section. 1. The judicial Power of the United States, shall be vested in one supreme Court, and in such inferior Courts as the Congress may from time to time ordain and establish. The Judges, both of the supreme and inferior Courts, shall hold their Offices during good Behaviour, and shall at stated Times, receive for their Services, a Compensation, which shall not be diminished during their Continuance in Office.

Section. 2. The judicial Power shall extend to all Cases, in Law and Equity, arising under this Constitution, the Laws of the United States, and Treaties made, or which shall be made, under their Authority; - to all Cases affecting Ambassadors, other public Ministers and Consuls; - to all Cases of admiralty and maritime Jurisdiction; - to Controversies to which the United States shall be a Party; - to Controversies between two or more States; - [between a State and Citizens of another State;] between Citizens of different States, - between Citizens of the same State claiming Lands under Grants of different States, [and between a State, or the Citizens thereof;- and foreign States, Citizens or Subjects.]

In all Cases affecting Ambassadors, other public Ministers and Consuls, and those in which a State shall be Party, the supreme Court shall have original Jurisdiction. In all the other Cases before mentioned, the supreme Court shall have appellate Jurisdiction, both as to Law and Fact, with such Exceptions, and under such Regulations as the Congress shall make.

The Trial of all Crimes, except in Cases of Impeachment; shall be by Jury; and such Trial shall be held in the State where the said Crimes shall have been committed; but when not committed within any State, the Trial shall be at such Place or Places as the Congress may by Law have directed.

Section. 3. Treason against the United States, shall consist only in levying War against them, or in adhering to their Enemies, giving them Aid and Comfort. No Person shall be convicted of Treason unless on the Testimony of two Witnesses to the same overt Act, or on Confession in open Court.

The Congress shall have Power to declare the Punishment of Treason, but no Attainder of Treason shall work Corruption of Blood, or Forfeiture except during the Life of the Person attainted.

Article. IV.

Section. 1. Full Faith and Credit shall be given in each State to the public Acts, Records, and judicial Proceedings of every other State. And the Congress may by general Laws prescribe the Manner in which such Acts, Records and Proceedings shall be proved, and the Effect thereof.

Section. 2. The Citizens of each State shall be entitled to all Privileges and Immunities of Citizens in the several States.

A Person charged in any State with Treason, Felony, or other Crime, who shall flee from Justice, and be found in another State, shall on Demand of the executive Authority of the State from which he fled, be delivered up, to be removed to the State having Jurisdiction of the Crime.

[No Person held to Service or Labour in one State, under the Laws thereof, escaping into another, shall, in Consequence of any Law or Regulation therein, be discharged from such Service or Labour, but shall be delivered up on Claim of the Party to whom such Service or Labour may be due.]

Section. 3. New States may be admitted by the Congress into this Union; but no new State shall be formed or erected within the Jurisdiction of any other State; nor any State be formed by the Junction of two or more States, or Parts of States, without the Consent of the Legislatures of the States concerned as well as of the Congress.

The Congress shall have Power to dispose of and make all needful Rules and Regulations respecting the Territory or other Property belonging to the United States; and nothing in this Constitution shall be so construed as to Prejudice any Claims of the United States, or of any particular State.

Section. 4. The United States shall guarantee to every State in this Union a Republican Form of Government, and shall protect each of them against Invasion; and on Application of the Legislature, or of the Executive (when the Legislature cannot be convened) against domestic Violence.

ARTICLE. V.

The Congress, whenever two thirds of both Houses shall deem it necessary, shall propose Amendments to this Constitution, or, on the Application of the Legislatures of two thirds of the several States, shall call a Convention for proposing Amendments, which in either Case, shall be valid to all Intents and Purposes, as Part of this Constitution, when ratified by the Legislatures of three-fourths of the several States, or by Conventions in three fourths thereof, as the one or the other Mode of Ratification may be proposed by the Congress; Provided that no Amendment which may be made prior to the Year One thousand eight hundred and eight shall in any Manner affect the first and fourth Clauses in the Ninth Section of the first Article; and that no State, without its Consent, shall be deprived of its equal Suffrage in the Senate.

Article. VI.

All Debts contracted and Engagements entered into, before the Adoption of this Constitution, shall be as valid against the United States under this Constitution, as under the Confederation.

This Constitution, and the Laws of the United States which shall be made in Pursuance thereof; and all Treaties made, or which shall be made, under the Authority of the United States, shall be the supreme Law of the Land; and the Judges in every State shall be bound thereby, any Thing in the Constitution or Laws of any State to the Contrary notwithstanding.

The Senators and Representatives before mentioned, and the Members of the several State Legislatures, and all executive and judicial Officers, both of the United States and of the several States, shall be bound by Oath or Affirmation, to support this Constitution; but no religious Test shall ever be required as a Qualification to any Office or public Trust under the United States.

Article. VII.

The Ratification of the Conventions of nine States, shall be sufficient for the Establishment of this Constitution between the States so ratifying the Same.

Done in Convention by the Unanimous Consent of the States present the Seventeenth Day of September in the Year of our Lord one thousand seven hundred and Eighty seven and of the Independence of the United States of America the Twelfth In witness whereof We have hereunto subscribed our Names,

G°. Washington -- Presidt and deputy from Virginia

Delaware	Geo: Read
	Gunning Bedford jun
	John Dickinson
	Richard Bassett
	Jaco: Broom
Maryland	James McHenry
	Dan of St. Thos. Jenifer
	Danl Carroll
Virginia	John Blair
	James Madison Jr.
North Carolina	Wm. Blount
	Richd. Dobbs Spaight
	Hu Williamson
South Carolina	J. Rutledge
	Charles Cotesworth Pinckney
	Charles Pinckney
	Pierce Butler

Georgia	William Few
	Abr Baldwin
New Hampshire	John Langdon
	Nicholas Gilman
Massachusetts	Nathaniel Gorham
	Rufus King
Connecticut	Wm. Saml. Johnson
	Roger Sherman
New York	Alexander Hamilton
New Jersey	Wil: Livingston
	David Brearley
	Wm. Paterson
	Jona: Dayton
Pennsylvania	B Franklin
	Thomas Mifflin
	Robt. Morris
	James Wilson
	Geo. Clymer
	Thos. FitzSimons
	Jared Ingersoll
	Gouv Morris

§

Note: While every attempt was made to be accurate, you should not rely on the contents of this appendix without independently verifying their accuracy. This author apologizes for any inaccuracies.

APPENDIX C

AMENDMENTS TO THE CONSTITUTION OF THE UNITED STATES

Amendment I

Congress shall make no law respecting an establishment of religion, or prohibiting the free exercise thereof; or abridging the freedom of speech, or of the press; or the right of the people peaceably to assemble, and to petition the Government for a redress of grievances.

Amendment II

A well regulated Militia, being necessary to the security of a free State, the right of the people to keep and bear Arms, shall not be infringed.

Amendment III

No Soldier shall, in time of peace be quartered in any house, without the consent of the Owner, nor in time of war, but in a manner to be prescribed by law.

Amendment IV

The right of the people to be secure in their persons, houses, papers, and effects, against unreasonable searches and seizures, shall not be violated, and no Warrants shall issue, but upon probable cause, supported by Oath or affirmation, and particularly describing the place to be searched, and the persons or things to be seized.

Amendment V

No person shall be held to answer for a capital, or otherwise infamous crime, unless on a presentment or indictment of a Grand Jury, except in cases arising in the land or naval forces, or in the Militia, when in actual service in time of War or public danger; nor shall any person be subject for the same offence to be twice put in jeopardy of life or limb; nor shall be compelled in any criminal case to be a witness against himself, nor be deprived of life, liberty, or property, without due process of law; nor shall private property be taken for public use, without just compensation.

Amendment VI

In all criminal prosecutions, the accused shall enjoy the right to a speedy and public trial, by an impartial jury of the State and district wherein the crime shall have been committed, which district shall have been previously ascertained by law, and to be informed of the nature and cause of the accusation; to be confronted with the witnesses against him; to have compulsory process for obtaining witnesses in his favor, and to have the Assistance of Counsel for his defence.

Amendment VII

In Suits at common law, where the value in controversy shall exceed twenty dollars, the right of trial by jury shall be preserved, and no fact tried by a jury, shall be otherwise reexamined in any Court of the United States, than according to the rules of the common law.

Amendment VIII

Excessive bail shall not be required, nor excessive fines imposed, nor cruel and unusual punishments inflicted.

Amendment IX

The enumeration in the Constitution, of certain rights, shall not be construed to deny or disparage others retained by the people.

Amendment X

The powers not delegated to the United States by the Constitution, nor prohibited by it to the States, are reserved to the States respectively, or to the people.

The first ten Amendments (Bill of Rights) were ratified effective December 15, 1791.

AMENDMENT XI

The Judicial power of the United States shall not be construed to extend to any suit in law or equity, commenced or prosecuted against one of the United States by Citizens of another State, or by Citizens or Subjects of any Foreign State.

The Eleventh Amendment was ratified February 7, 1795.

AMENDMENT XII

The Electors shall meet in their respective states and vote by ballot for President and Vice-President, one of whom, at least, shall not be an inhabitant of the same state with themselves; they shall name in their ballots the person voted for as President, and in distinct ballots the person voted for as Vice-President, and they shall make distinct lists of all persons voted for as President, and of all persons voted for as Vice-President, and of the number of votes for each, which lists they shall sign and certify, and transmit sealed to the seat of the government of the United States, directed to the President of the Senate; -- the President of the Senate shall, in the presence of the Senate and House of Representatives, open all the certificates and the votes shall then be counted; -- The person having the greatest number of votes for President, shall be the President, if such number be a majority of the whole number of Electors appointed; and if no person have such majority, then from the persons having the highest numbers not exceeding three on the list of those voted for as President, the House of Representatives shall choose immediately, by ballot, the President. But in choosing the President, the votes shall be taken by states, the representation from each state having one vote; a quorum for this purpose shall consist of a member or members from two-thirds of the states, and a majority of all the states shall be necessary to a choice. [And if the House of Representatives shall not choose a President whenever the right of choice shall devolve upon them, before the fourth day of March next following, then the Vice-President shall act as President, as in case of the death or other constitutional disability of the President.] The person having the greatest number of votes as Vice-President, shall be the Vice-President, if such number be a majority of the whole number of Electors appointed, and if no person have a majority, then from the two highest numbers on the list, the Senate shall choose the Vice-President; a quorum for the purpose shall consist of two-thirds of the whole number of Senators, and a majority of the whole number shall be necessary to a choice. But no person constitutionally ineligible to the office of President shall be eligible to that of Vice-President of the United States.

The Twelfth Amendment was ratified June 15, 1804.

Superseded by section 3 of the Twentieth Amendment.

Amendment XIII

Section. 1. Neither slavery nor involuntary servitude, except as a punishment for crime whereof the party shall have been duly convicted, shall exist within the United States, or any place subject to their jurisdiction.

Section. 2. Congress shall have power to enforce this article by appropriate legislation.

The Thirteenth Amendment was ratified December 6, 1865.

Amendment XIV

Section. 1. All persons born or naturalized in the United States, and subject to the jurisdiction thereof, are citizens of the United States and of the State wherein they reside. No State shall make or enforce any law which shall abridge the privileges or immunities of citizens of the United States; nor shall any State deprive any person of life, liberty, or property, without due process of law; nor deny to any person within its jurisdiction the equal protection of the laws.

Section. 2. Representatives shall be apportioned among the several States according to their respective numbers, counting the whole number of persons in each State, excluding Indians not taxed. But when the right to vote at any election for the choice of electors for President and Vice-President of the United States, Representatives in Congress, the Executive and Judicial officers of a State, or the members of the Legislature thereof, is denied to any of the male inhabitants of such State, being twenty-one years of age, and citizens of the United States, or in any way abridged, except for participation in rebellion, or other crime, the basis of representation therein shall be reduced in the proportion which the number of such male citizens shall bear to the whole number of male citizens twenty-one years of age in such State.

Section. 3. No person shall be a Senator or Representative in Congress, or elector of President and Vice-President, or hold any office, civil or military, under the United States, or under any State, who, having previously taken an oath, as a member of Congress, or as an officer of the United States, or as a member of any State legislature, or as an executive or judicial officer of any State, to support the Constitution of the United States, shall have engaged in insurrection or rebellion against the same, or given aid or comfort to the enemies thereof. But Congress may by a vote of two-thirds of each House, remove such disability.

Section. 4. The validity of the public debt of the United States, authorized by law, including debts incurred for payment of pensions and bounties for services in suppressing insurrection or rebellion, shall not be questioned. But neither the United States nor any State shall assume or pay any debt or obligation incurred in aid of insurrection or rebellion against the United States, or any claim for the loss or emancipation of any slave; but all such debts, obligations and claims shall be held illegal and void.

Section. 5. The Congress shall have the power to enforce, by appropriate legislation, the provisions of this article.

The Fourteenth Amendment was ratified July 9, 1868.

Changed by section 1 of the Twenty-Sixth Amendment.

Amendment XV

Section. 1. The right of citizens of the United States to vote shall not be denied or abridged by the United States or by any State on account of race, color, or previous condition of servitude.

Section. 2. The Congress shall have the power to enforce this article by appropriate legislation.

The Fifteenth Amendment was ratified February 3, 1870.

Amendment XVI

The Congress shall have power to lay and collect taxes on incomes, from whatever source derived, without apportionment among the several States, and without regard to any census or enumeration.

The Sixteenth Amendment was ratified February 3, 1913.

Amendment XVII

The Senate of the United States shall be composed of two Senators from each State, elected by the people thereof, for six years; and each Senator shall have one vote. The electors in each State shall have the qualifications requisite for electors of the most numerous branch of the State legislatures.

When vacancies happen in the representation of any State in the Senate, the executive authority of such State shall issue writs of election to fill such vacancies: *Provided*, That the legislature of any State may empower the executive thereof to make temporary appointments until the people fill the vacancies by election as the legislature may direct.

This amendment shall not be so construed as to affect the election or term of any Senator chosen before it becomes valid as part of the Constitution.

The Seventeenth Amendment was ratified April 8, 1913.

Amendment XVIII

Section. 1. After one year from the ratification of this article the manufacture, sale, or transportation of intoxicating liquors within, the importation thereof into, or the exportation thereof from the United States and all territory subject to the jurisdiction thereof for beverage purposes is hereby prohibited.

Section. 2. The Congress and the several States shall have concurrent power to enforce this article by appropriate legislation.

Section. 3. This article shall be inoperative unless it shall have been ratified as an amendment to the Constitution by the legislatures of the several States, as provided in the Constitution, within seven years from the date of the submission hereof to the States by the Congress.

The Eighteenth Amendment was ratified January 16, 1919.

It was repealed by the Twenty-First Amendment December 5, 1933.

Amendment XIX

The right of citizens of the United States to vote shall not be denied or abridged by the United States or by any State on account of sex.

Congress shall have power to enforce this article by appropriate legislation.

The Nineteenth Amendment was ratified August 18, 1920.

Amendment XX

Section. 1. The terms of the President and the Vice President shall end at noon on the 20th day of January, and the terms of Senators and Representatives at noon on the 3d day of January, of the years in which such terms would have ended if this article had not been ratified; and the terms of their successors shall then begin.

Section. 2. The Congress shall assemble at least once in every year, and such meeting shall begin at noon on the 3d day of January, unless they shall by law appoint a different day.

Section. 3. If, at the time fixed for the beginning of the term of the President, the President elect shall have died, the Vice President elect shall become President. If a President shall not have been chosen before the time fixed for the beginning of his term, or if the President elect shall have failed to qualify, then the Vice President elect shall act as President until a President shall have qualified; and the Congress may by law provide for the case wherein neither a President elect nor a Vice President shall have qualified, declaring who shall then act as President, or the manner in which one who is to act shall be selected, and such person shall act accordingly until a President or Vice President shall have qualified.

Section. 4. The Congress may by law provide for the case of the death of any of the persons from whom the House of Representatives may choose a President whenever the right of choice shall have devolved upon them, and for the case of the death of any of the persons from whom the Senate may choose a Vice President whenever the right of choice shall have devolved upon them.

Section. 5. Sections 1 and 2 shall take effect on the 15th day of October following the ratification of this article.

Section. 6. This article shall be inoperative unless it shall have been ratified as an amendment to the Constitution by the legislatures of three-fourths of the several States within seven years from the date of its submission.

The Twentieth Amendment was ratified January 23, 1933.

AMENDMENT XXI

Section. 1. The eighteenth article of amendment to the Constitution of the United States is hereby repealed.

Section. 2. The transportation or importation into any State, Territory, or Possession of the United States for delivery or use therein of intoxicating liquors, in violation of the laws thereof, is hereby prohibited.

Section. 3. This article shall be inoperative unless it shall have been ratified as an amendment to the Constitution by conventions in the several States, as provided in the Constitution, within seven years from the date of the submission hereof to the States by the Congress.

The Twenty-First Amendment was ratified December 5, 1933.

AMENDMENT XXII

Section. 1. No person shall be elected to the office of the President more than twice, and no person who has held the office of President, or acted as President, for more than two years of a term to which some other person was elected President shall be elected to the office of President more than once. But this Article shall not apply to any person holding the office of President when this Article was proposed by Congress, and shall not prevent any person who may be holding the office of President, or acting as President, during the term within which this Article becomes operative from holding the office of President or acting as President during the remainder of such term.

Section. 2. This article shall be inoperative unless it shall have been ratified as an amendment to the Constitution by the legislatures of three-fourths of the several States within seven years from the date of its submission to the States by the Congress.

The Twenty-Second Amendment was ratified February 27, 1951.

Amendment XXIII

Section. 1. The District constituting the seat of Government of the United States shall appoint in such manner as Congress may direct:

A number of electors of President and Vice President equal to the whole number of Senators and Representatives in Congress to which the District would be entitled if it were a State, but in no event more than the least populous State; they shall be in addition to those appointed by the States, but they shall be considered, for the purposes of the election of President and Vice President, to be electors appointed by a State; and they shall meet in the District and perform such duties as provided by the twelfth article of amendment.

Section. 2. The Congress shall have power to enforce this article by appropriate legislation.

The Twenty-Third Amendment was ratified March 29, 1961.

Amendment XXIV

Section. 1. The right of citizens of the United States to vote in any primary or other election for President or Vice President, for electors for President or Vice President, or for Senator or Representative in Congress, shall not be denied or abridged by the United States or any State by reason of failure to pay poll tax or other tax.

Section. 2. The Congress shall have power to enforce this article by appropriate legislation.

The Twenty-Fourth Amendment was ratified January 23, 1964.

Amendment XXV

Section. 1. In case of the removal of the President from office or of his death or resignation, the Vice President shall become President.

Section. 2. Whenever there is a vacancy in the office of the Vice President, the President shall nominate a Vice President who shall take office upon confirmation by a majority vote of both Houses of Congress.

Section. 3. Whenever the President transmits to the President pro tempore of the Senate and the Speaker of the House of Representatives his written declaration that he is unable to discharge the powers and duties of his office, and until he transmits to them a written declaration to the contrary, such powers and duties shall be discharged by the Vice President as Acting President.

Section. 4. Whenever the Vice President and a majority of either the principal officers of the executive departments or of such other body as Congress may by law provide, transmit to the President pro tempore of the Senate and the Speaker of the House of Representatives their written declaration that the President is unable to discharge the powers and duties of his office, the Vice President shall immediately assume the powers and duties of the office as Acting President.

Thereafter, when the President transmits to the President pro tempore of the Senate and the Speaker of the House of Representatives his written declaration that no inability exists, he shall resume the powers and duties of his office unless the Vice President and a majority of either the principal officers of the executive department or of such other body as Congress may by law provide, transmit within four days to the President pro tempore of the Senate and the Speaker of the House of Representatives their written declaration that the President is unable to discharge the powers and duties of his office. Thereupon Congress shall decide the issue, assembling within forty-eight hours for that purpose if not in session. If the Congress, within twenty-one days after receipt of the latter written declaration, or, if Congress is not in session, within twenty-one days after Congress is required to assemble, determines by two-thirds vote of both Houses that the President is unable to discharge the powers and duties of his office, the Vice President shall continue to discharge the same as Acting President; otherwise, the President shall resume the powers and duties of his office.

The Twenty-Fifth Amendment was ratified February 10, 1967.

Amendment XXVI

Section. 1. The right of citizens of the United States, who are eighteen years of age or older, to vote shall not be denied or abridged by the United States or by any State on account of age.

Section. 2. The Congress shall have power to enforce this article by appropriate legislation.

The Twenty-Sixth Amendment was ratified July 1, 1971.

Amendment XXVII

No law, varying the compensation for the services of the Senators and Representatives, shall take effect, until an election of representatives shall have intervened.

The Twenty-Seventh Amendment was ratified May 7, 1992.

AMENDMENT RATIFICATION DATES

☞ The first ten Amendments (Bill of Rights) were ratified effective December 15, 1791.

☞ The Eleventh Amendment was ratified February 7, 1795.

☞ The Twelfth Amendment was ratified June 15, 1804. *Superseded by section 3 of the Twentieth Amendment.*

☞ The Thirteenth Amendment was ratified December 6, 1865.

☞ The Fourteenth Amendment was ratified July 9, 1868. *Changed by section 1 of the Twenty-Sixth Amendment.*

☞ The Fifteenth Amendment was ratified February 3, 1870.

☞ The Sixteenth Amendment was ratified February 3, 1913.

☞ The Seventeenth Amendment was ratified April 8, 1913.

☞ The Eighteenth Amendment was ratified January 16, 1919. *Repealed by the Twenty-First Amendment December 5, 1933.*

☞ The Nineteenth Amendment was ratified August 18, 1920.

☞ The Twentieth Amendment was ratified January 23, 1933.

☞ The Twenty-First Amendment was ratified December 5, 1933.

☞ The Twenty-Second Amendment was ratified February 27, 1951.

☞ The Twenty-Third Amendment was ratified March 29, 1961.

☞ The Twenty-Fourth Amendment was ratified January 23, 1964.

☞ The Twenty-Fifth Amendment was ratified February 10, 1967.

☞ The Twenty-Sixth Amendment was ratified July 1, 1971.

☞ The Twenty-Seventh Amendment was ratified May 7, 1992.

§

Note: While every attempt was made to be accurate, you should not rely on the contents of this appendix without independently verifying their accuracy. This author apologizes for any inaccuracies.

APPENDIX D

PRESIDENTS AND VICE PRESIDENTS OF THE UNITED STATES

This is a chronological listing of the presidents and vice presidents of the United States.

To be elected president, a person must receive at least 270 of the 538 electoral votes from the **Electoral College**. Each state's number of electors is equal to the number in the U.S. Senate and persons in the House of Representatives. The person receiving the most popular votes in a state receives all or a portion of the state's total electors. When the position of president is vacant, the vice president becomes the president.

The president is head of the **executive branch**; it is responsible for carrying out laws made by the **legislative branch**, consisting of the Senate and the House of Representatives, who are responsible for making the laws. The third branch of the federal government is the **judicial branch**, headed by the U.S. Supreme Court, which evaluates if the laws are consistent with the U.S. Constitution.

Beginning with **John Adams**, the president has taken residence in the **White House**, located at 1600 Pennsylvania Avenue, NW, Washington, D.C. 20500. It has 132 rooms with 28 fireplaces. The president's office is in the West Wing, and the private residence is upstairs. The building was initially called the **Executive Mansion**, but after Theodore Roosevelt had it painted white in 1901, he officially named it the **White House.**

The current pay for the president is $400,000 a year plus a $50,000 expense account, and for the vice president it is $235,100 with no expense account. George Washington received $25,000 a year, and Vice President John Adams received $5,000. Neither had an expense account.

§

1789 Federalist **George Washington** took office as the 1st president; defeating Federalist **John Adams**, who was vice president

1792 Federalist **George Washington** was re-elected president; Federalist **John Adams** was re-elected vice president

1796 Federalist **John Adams** was elected as the 2nd president; defeating Democratic-Republican **Thomas Jefferson**, who was vice president

1800 Democratic-Republican **Thomas Jefferson** was elected as the 3rd president, defeating Federalist John Adams; **Aaron Burr** was vice president

1804   Democratic-Republican **Thomas Jefferson** was re-elected president, defeating Federalist Charles Pinckney; **George Clinton** was vice president

1808   Democratic-Republican **James Madison** was elected as the 4th president, defeating Federalist Rufus King; **George Clinton** was vice president

1812   Democratic-Republican **James Madison** was re-elected president, defeating Federalist DeWitt Clinton; **Elbridge Gerry** was vice president

1816   Democratic-Republican **James Monroe** was elected as the 5th president, defeating Federalist Rufus King; **Daniel D. Tompkins** was vice president

1820   Democratic-Republican **James Monroe** was re-elected president, defeating Federalist John Quincy Adams; **Daniel D. Tompkins** was vice president

1824   Democratic-Republican **John Quincy Adams** was elected as the 6th president, defeating Democratic-Republican Andrew Jackson; **John C. Calhoun** was vice president

1828   Democrat **Andrew Jackson** was elected as the 7th president, defeating National Republican John Quincy Adams; **John C. Calhoun** was vice president

1832   Democrat **Andrew Jackson** was re-elected president, defeating National Republican Henry Clay; **Martin Van Buren** was vice president

APPENDIX D

1836   Democrat **Martin Van Buren** was elected as the 8th president, defeating Whig William Henry Harrison; **Richard M. Johnson** was vice president

1840   Whig **William Henry Harrison** was elected as the 9th president, defeating Democrat Martin Van Buren; **John Tyler** was vice president

1841   Whig **John Tyler** took office as the 10th president following the death of William Henry Harrison; there was no vice president

1844   Democrat **James K. Polk** was elected as the 11th president, defeating Whig Henry Clay; **George M. Dallas** was vice president

1848   Whig **Zachary Taylor** was elected as the 12th president, defeating Democrat Lewis Cass; **Millard Fillmore** was vice president

1850   Whig **Millard Fillmore** took office as the 13th president following the death of Zachary Taylor; there was no vice president

1852   Democrat **Franklin Pierce** was elected as the 14th president, defeating Whig Winfield Scott; **William R. King** was vice president

1856   Democrat **James Buchanan** was elected as the 15th president, defeating Republican John C. Frémont; **John C. Breckinridge** was vice president

1860   Republican **Abraham Lincoln** was elected as the 16th president, defeating Democrat Stephen Douglas; **Hannibal Hamlin** was vice president

1864 Republican **Abraham Lincoln** was re-elected president, defeating Democrat George McClellan; **Andrew Johnson** was vice president

1865 Democrat **Andrew Johnson** took office as the 17th president following Abraham Lincoln's assassination; there was no vice president

1868 Republican **Ulysses S. Grant** was elected as the 18th president, defeating Democrat Horatio Seymour; **Schuyler Colfax** was vice president

1872 Republican **Ulysses S. Grant** was re-elected president, defeating Democrat Horace Greeley; **Henry Wilson** was vice president

1876 Republican **Rutherford B. Hayes** was elected as the 19th president, defeating Democrat Samuel Tilden; **William A. Wheeler** was vice president

1880 Republican **James A. Garfield** was elected as the 20th president, defeating Democrat Winfield Scott Hancock; **Chester A. Arthur** was vice president

1881 Republican **Chester A. Arthur** took office as the 21st president following Republican James A. Garfield's assassination; there was no vice president

1884 Democrat **Grover Cleveland** was elected as the 22nd president, defeating Republican James Blaine; **Thomas A. Hendricks** was vice president

1888 Republican **Benjamin Harrison** was elected as the 23rd president, defeating Democrat Grover Cleveland; **Levi P. Morton** was vice president

APPENDIX D

1892 Democrat **Grover Cleveland** was elected as the 24th president, defeating Republican Benjamin Harrison; **Adlai E. Stevenson** was vice president

1896 Republican **William McKinley** was elected as the 25th president, defeating Democrat William Jennings Bryan; **Garret Hobart** was vice president

1900 Republican **William McKinley** was re-elected president, defeating Democrat William Jennings Bryan; **Theodore Roosevelt** was vice president

1901 Republican **Theodore Roosevelt** took office as the 26th president upon the death of Republican William McKinley; there was no vice president

1904 Republican **Theodore Roosevelt** was elected president, defeating Democrat Alton Parker; **Charles W. Fairbanks** was vice president

1908 Republican **William Howard Taft** was elected as the 27th president, defeating Democrat William Jennings Bryan; **James S. Sherman** was vice president

1912 Democrat **Woodrow Wilson** was elected as the 28th president, defeating Republican William Howard Taft; **Thomas R. Marshall** was vice president

1916 Democrat **Woodrow Wilson** was re-elected president, defeating Republican Charles Hughes; **Thomas R. Marshall** was vice president

1920 Republican **Warren G. Harding** was elected as the 29th president, defeating Democrat James Cox; **Calvin Coolidge** was vice president

1923 Republican **Calvin Coolidge** took office as the 30th president following the death of Republican Warren Harding; there was no vice president

1924 Republican **Calvin Coolidge** was elected president, defeating Democrat John W. Davis; **Charles G. Dawes** was vice president

1928 Republican **Herbert Hoover** was elected as the 31st president, defeating Democrat Al Smith; **Charles Curtis** was vice president

1932 Democrat **Franklin D. Roosevelt** was elected as the 32nd president, defeating Republican Herbert Hoover; **John N. Garner** was vice president

1936 Democrat **Franklin D. Roosevelt** was re-elected president, defeating Republican Alfred Landon; **John N. Garner** was vice president

1940 Democrat **Franklin D. Roosevelt** was re-elected president, defeating Republican Wendell Willkie; **Henry A. Wallace** was vice president

1944 Democrat **Franklin D. Roosevelt** was re-elected president, defeating Republican Thomas Dewey; **Harry S. Truman** was vice president

1945 Democrat **Harry S. Truman** took office as the 33rd president following the death of Democrat Franklin D. Roosevelt; there was no vice president

1948 Democrat **Harry S. Truman** was elected president, defeating Republican Thomas Dewey; **Alben W. Barkley** was vice president

APPENDIX D

1952 Republican **Dwight D. Eisenhower** was elected as the 34th president, defeating Democrat Adlai Stevenson; **Richard M. Nixon** was vice president

1956 Republican **Dwight D. Eisenhower** was re-elected president, defeating Democrat Adlai Stevenson; **Richard M. Nixon** was vice president

1960 Democrat **John F. Kennedy** was elected as the 35th president, defeating Republican Richard Nixon; **Lyndon B. Johnson** was vice president

1963 Democrat **Lyndon B. Johnson** took office as the 36th president following John F. Kennedy's assassination; there was no vice president

1964 Democrat **Lyndon B. Johnson** was elected president, defeating Republican Barry Goldwater; **Hubert H. Humphrey** was vice president

1968 Republican **Richard M. Nixon** was elected as the 37th president, defeating Democrat Hubert Humphrey; **Spiro T. Agnew** was vice president

1972 Republican **Richard M. Nixon** was re-elected president, defeating Democrat George McGovern; **Spiro T. Agnew** was vice president

1974 Republican **Gerald R. Ford** took office as the 38th president following Nixon's resignation; **Nelson A. Rockefeller** was vice president

1976 Democrat **Jimmy Carter** was elected as the 39th president, defeating Republican Gerald Ford; **Walter F. Mondale** was vice president

1980 Republican **Ronald Reagan** was elected as the 40th president, defeating Democrat Jimmy Carter; **George H.W. Bush** was vice president

1984 Republican **Ronald Reagan** was re-elected president, defeating Democrat Walter Mondale; **George H.W. Bush** was vice president

1988 Republican **George H.W. Bush** was elected as the 41st president, defeating Democrat Michael Dukakis; **Dan Quayle** was vice president

1992 Democrat **William J. Clinton** was elected as the 42nd president, defeating Republican George H.W. Bush; **Al Gore** was vice president

1996 Democrat **William J. Clinton** was re-elected president, defeating Republican Bob Dole; **Al Gore** was vice president

2000 Republican **George W. Bush** was elected as the 43rd president, defeating Democrat Al Gore; **Dick Cheney** was vice president

2004 Republican **George W. Bush** was re-elected president, defeating Democrat John Kerry; **Dick Cheney** was vice president

2008 Democrat **Barack Obama** was elected as the 44th president, defeating Republican John McCain; **Joe Biden** was vice president

2012 Democrat **Barack Obama** was re-elected president, defeating Republican Mitt Romney; **Joe Biden** was vice president

APPENDIX D

2016 Republican **Donald J. Trump** was elected as the 45th president, defeating Democrat Hillary Clinton; **Mike Pence** was vice president

2020 Democrat **Joseph R. Biden, Jr.** was elected as the 46th president, defeating Republican Donald Trump; **Kamala Harris** was vice president

2024 Republican **Donald J. Trump** was elected as the 47th president, defeating Democrat Kamala Harris; **J.D. Vance** was vice president

§

Note: While every attempt was made to be accurate, you should not rely on the contents of this appendix without independently verifying their accuracy. This author apologizes for any inaccuracies.

APPENDIX E

PRESIDENTIAL HIGHLIGHTS

GEORGE WASHINGTON *(1ST PRESIDENT) 1789-1797*

Washington was born on February 22, 1732, to Augustine and Mary Ball Washington on their 1,000-acre farm in Westmoreland County, Virginia. George was the oldest of six children. He also had a half-sister and three half-brothers, one who died in infancy. George had an elementary education through tutoring, and he memorized all 110 sayings of the *Rules of Civility and Decent Behavior in Company and Conversation* and quoted them throughout his life. When George's father and mother died, he was raised by one of his stepbrothers. He lost all his teeth except for one by the age of 19 and wore ill-fitting dentures made of ivory and slaves' teeth. For the rest of his life, George lived on soft foods and took laudanum (a combination of alcohol and opium) for the pain. In 1752, George was commissioned as a lieutenant in the Virginia militia. Shortly after, he came down with smallpox. In 1755, George was commissioned as a colonel in the Virginia Regiment. In 1759, George married the wealthy Martha Dandridge Custis. They had no children, but George adopted her two children from a previous marriage. On June 4, 1776, Congress approved the Declaration of Independence from England. A year later, Congress approved the stars and stripes of the American flag. Following a number of battles, General Cornwallis surrendered his troops in 1781 in Yorktown. The war was effectively over. In 1782, England agreed to recognize America's independence. A peace treaty was signed in 1783. Shortly after, Washington resigned his commission, and Congress ordered the army to be disbanded. Before the end of the year, Washington said goodbye to his officers at the Fraunces Tavern in New York City and returned to his farm until he was elected president in 1789. Washington's farewell address as president warned against permanent alliances with foreign peers. It was published in 1796. He then left for his farm. George's military career resulted in his being put in charge of the Continental Army. He was the first president who won an election in 1789 and reelection in 1792, unanimously. Washington was the first president to serve under the new U.S. Constitution adopted in 1788. At 6'4", he was one of the tallest presidents. He formed the first cabinet, consisting of Vice President John Adams, Secretary of State Thomas Jefferson, Secretary of the Treasury Alexander Hamilton, Secretary of War Henry Knox, Attorney General Edmund Randolph, and Postmaster General Samuel Osgood. Washington's annual pay was $25,000. He declined a third term as president and retired to his 21-room mansion, 8,000-acre farm, and wealthy wife. He died in 1799 at age 68. His facial image is engraved on Mount Rushmore in the Black Hills of South Dakota. His image is also on the U.S. dollar bill.

The nation's capital was named in his honor, as well as a state, and a monument also bearing his name was erected in Washington, D.C.

JOHN ADAMS *(2ND PRESIDENT) 1797-1801*

Adams was born on October 30, 1735, in Braintree, Massachusetts, to John Adams and Susanna Boylston Adams. John had two younger brothers. The three children grew up in a strictly disciplined Puritan household. Although John hated school, he enjoyed studying government and the classical languages. At age 15, he entered Harvard University. After graduation, he studied law and became a successful attorney. In 1764, John married Abigail Smith. They would have five children together. John Quincy grew up to become America's sixth president. John and Abigail had a good marriage and John relied heavily on her advice and counsel. Six years into the marriage, John defended British troops who fired into a crowd, killing five people. It was called the Boston Massacre. That said, Adams was a very vocal spokesperson for American independence from England. He worked with Thomas Jefferson on the Declaration of Independence, and the two became great friends. In 1774, Adams was delegated to the First Continental Congress and the Second a year later. The focus was independence. The Declaration of Independence was approved by Congress on July 4, 1776. Shortly after, Congress created the Continental Army by combining state militias and they appointed George Washington Commander of the Army. After years of fighting, Adams worked out a treaty, the Treaty of Paris, which was signed by England in 1783. Also in 1783, Adams went to England as America's ambassador, and Jefferson went to France as America's ambassador. The French Revolution caused a major split between the two. For years, they would not speak to each other. In June 1788, Congress adopted the U.S. Constitution. John ran for president in both 1789 and 1793. Both times, he came in second to George Washington. The newly adopted U.S. Constitution said that the person who came in second in the count of electoral votes would be the president's vice president. The position paid $5,000 a year.

Both Adams and Jefferson ran for the presidency in 1796. Adams received 71 electoral votes; Jefferson received 68. Adams was elected president and Jefferson was elected vice president. Adams was the first president to live in the newly built Executive Mansion. But Adams spent more time in Massachusetts than in Washington. So, he was defeated in the 1800 election by his own vice president. Jefferson and Aaron Burr each received 73 electoral votes, while Adams received only 65. Congress voted and decided Jefferson was president and Burr was his vice president. When Adams lost the 1800 election for president, he and wife Abigail left the Executive Mansion at 4:00am so they did not have to see Jefferson take residence. Over the years, Adams and Jefferson repaired their friendship, and both died on July 4, 1826, the 50th anniversary of the birth of the nation. Adams died at age 90; Jefferson was 83.

THOMAS JEFFERSON (3ʀᴅ ᴘʀᴇsɪᴅᴇɴᴛ) *1801-1809*

Jefferson was born on April 13, 1743, in Albemarle County, Virginia, to Peter and Jane Jefferson. Thomas had nine siblings. He began receiving private tutoring in classical languages and science at age five. In 1762, Thomas graduated from the College of William & Mary and went on to practice law. He was elected to the Virginia House of Burgess in 1769. He married his third cousin, Martha Wayles Skelton, in 1772. They would have six children together. Martha was a widow with wealth that Jefferson lacked. He used some of the money to build a house on the thousand-plus acres he inherited from his father. Jefferson named the house Monticello, or "little mountain" in Italian. Delegates from seven states met in New York for the Continental Congress to discuss the human rights that were being outlawed by the British. Later, Jefferson met John Adams, and they worked on a declaration of independence from England. Thomas turned the draft into a final document that was approved by the Continental Congress on July 4, 1776. Jefferson would be known as the father of the Declaration of Independence. He and Adams became close friends in their mutual fight for independence. Jefferson was also known as the Sage of Monticello. He served as governor of Virginia from 1779 to 1781. Jefferson was devastated when Martha died in 1782. Before she died, Thomas promised her that he would never remarry. But he soon took up with Sally Hemings, one of his biracial slaves. They went on to have four children together. Jefferson then focused on improving Monticello and inventing various items. He also became an accomplished architect, educator, lawyer, musician, and writer. In 1785, he went to Paris as America's minister to France. While there, he supported the French Revolution, to the dismay of John Adams, who was serving as America's minister to England. The two friends became enemies. In 1790, Jefferson returned to America to become secretary of state to President Washington. In 1793, Thomas Jefferson and James Madison formed the Democratic-Republican Party in opposition to the Federalist Party favored by John Adams and Alexander Hamilton. Jefferson believed the federalists gave the executive branch more power than intended in the U.S. Constitution. Jefferson was an advocate of states' rights rather than federal government power. In 1796, Jefferson was elected vice president, coming in second to John Adams, who was elected president. But in the 1800 election, Thomas Jefferson, and Aaron Burr each received 73 electoral votes, defeating John Adams, who received 65 votes. The House voted 36 times to decide the split, ending with Thomas Jefferson as president and Aaron Burr as vice president. In 1801, Jefferson installed the first indoor bathroom in the Executive Mansion. His most significant appointment was John Marshall as chief justice of the U.S. Supreme Court in 1801. Marshall would serve in that capacity for 34 years. By far, Jefferson's greatest accomplishment was the Louisiana Purchase in 1803. For $18 million, the United States purchased 827,000 square miles of land, virtually doubling the size of the country. In 1819, Jefferson founded the University of Virginia. On July 4, 1826, at age 83, he, like John Adams at age 90, died. Like Washington, Jefferson has his facial image engraved on Mount Rushmore, in the Black Hills of South Dakota. His image also appears on the American nickel and the two-dollar bill.

JAMES MADISON (4ᵀᴴ PRESIDENT) 1809-1817

Madison was born on March 16, 1751, in Port Conway, Virginia, to James and Eleanor Rose Conway Madison. James was the oldest of twelve offspring. The family lived on a 5,000-acre tobacco farm called Montpelier. James was schooled at home before going to the College of New Jersey (later named Princeton University). After graduation in 1771, James became a lawyer and a colonel in Virginia's Orange County Militia. In 1797, he was elected to the Continental Congress. There he worked on improving the Articles of Confederation, which provided strong rights to the states but little to the central government. Madison knew other countries would not consider America seriously if it functioned as thirteen separate entities instead of one nation. So, he went to work on converting the Articles into a new constitution. It was adopted by Congress in 1787, but it had to be ratified by at least nine of the thirteen states. Knowing that would not happen unless the states were convinced it needed to be done, Alexander Hamilton, James Madison, and John Jay wrote eighty-five articles explaining why and how the power of the federal government had to be changed. Together these articles were called the Federalist Papers and was published in 1787. The U.S. Constitution was ratified by the required nine states on September 17, 1787; the remaining four states followed. The Constitution was adopted by Congress on March 4, 1789. Madison would be called the Father of the Constitution, as he had written most of it, as well as the first ten amendments to the Constitution, which were called the Bill of Rights. These amendments were ratified by Congress, effective December 15, 1791. Madison served eight years in the U.S. House of Representatives. In 1794, Madison married Dolley Payne Todd. He had one stepson. In 1801, Madison became Secretary of State for President Jefferson. In the 1808 election, Democratic-Republicans James Madison and George Clinton defeated Federalists Charles Pinckney and Rufus King for the presidency and vice presidency of the United States. An 1810 census reported the U.S. population was 7,239,988 and 1,191,364 were slaves. At the time of the election, Madison was 5'4" and weighed 100 pounds. He was the first president to wear full-length pants rather than knee breeches. He was also the first president to show his own hair rather than wear a powdered wig. Dolley Madison created the role of official hostess for the Executive Mansion. She also created the role now known as the First Lady. She was a charismatic extrovert; Madison was a shy introvert. Madison started the War of 1812 by declaring war on England for harassing American ships. This happened on June 18, 1812. Following the

War of 1812, the nation began to shift away from an agricultural society as the industrial revolution began to take place, shaping tariff policy. In the 1812 election, Democratic-Republicans James Madison and Elbridge Gerry defeated Federalists DeWitt Clinton and Jared Ingersoll for the offices of president and vice president. On April 24, 1814, British troops landed in Maryland. Francis Scott Key wrote the **Star-Spangled Banner** as he watched the British attack Fort McHenry in Baltimore, and they proceeded to Washington, D.C. and set fire to the Executive Mansion. This was the first time since the Revolutionary War that foreign troops were in America. They proceeded to the Capitol Building and set it on fire. Then they moved to the Executive Mansion, where they feasted on food and wine, then set it on fire, and left on December 24, 1814. **The Treaty of Ghent** ended the war between England and the United States. But the British attacked New Orleans after the first of January 1815 and were repelled by Andrew Jackson's troops. Like Jefferson, Madison was an ineffective public speaker but a great writer, and more is said about his writing the Constitution and Bill of Rights than his eight years as president. Madison died on June 28, 1836, at age 85.

JAMES MONROE *(5ᵀᴴ PRESIDENT) 1817-1825*

Monroe was born on April 28, 1758, in Westmoreland, Virginia, to Spence and Elizabeth Monroe on a small family farm. Monroe had four siblings and initially was home-schooled. Later he went to Campbelltown Academy and then to the College of William & Mary. After graduation in 1774, he went to fight in the Revolutionary War as a lieutenant in the Third Virginia Infantry. Monroe later transferred to the Continental Army as a captain. He left the army as a colonel and was the first president wounded in the war. From 1780 to 1783, Monroe studied law under Thomas Jefferson. He then set up a practice in Fredericksburg, Virginia. While a delegate to the Continental Congress, he married Elizabeth Kortright in 1786. They had three children together. In 1790, Monroe became the first person to serve as a U.S. senator before becoming president. Later, he served as Secretary of State for President Madison and later as Secretary of War. Monroe was the first president who previously held two cabinet positions simultaneously. In the 1816 election, Democratic-Republicans James Monroe and D.D. Tompkins defeated Federalists Rufus King and John Howard for the positions of president and vice president. The result was that four of the first five presidents came from Virginia. Monroe was the last president to wear buckled shoes, knee breeches, long white stockings, and a powdered wig. Monroe decreed that the American flag could only have thirteen stripes (honoring the original thirteen colonies) and the number of stars was to equal the number of states. Monroe's daughter was the first president's daughter to be married in the Executive Mansion. The Missouri Compromise of 1820 stated that states north of the Mason-Dixon line would be admitted as free states and those south of the line would be admitted as slave states. In 1820, the U.S. population was 9.6 million, 60,000 of whom were in New York City. In the 1820 election, Democratic-Republicans James Monroe and Daniel Tompkins essentially ran unopposed, as the Federalist Party had collapsed. Democratic-Republicans John Quincy Adams and Richard Stockton received one electoral vote from a New Hampshire elector, who wanted only Washington to be elected unanimously. The most significant event during Monroe's term was his announcement of the Monroe Doctrine in his 1823 Annual Address. It stated that any attempt to colonize the Western Hemisphere would be considered a direct threat to the

United States. Wanting to send Black Americans back to Africa, Monroe authorized the purchase of land in Liberia, Africa. In his honor, its capital was named Monrovia. It was the first time a U.S. president's name was used for a capital in a foreign country. Monroe left the presidency in significant debt. He was the third president to die on July 4th (it was in 1831). John Adams and Thomas Jefferson were the previous two. Monroe was 73 at the time of his death.

JOHN QUINCY ADAMS (6TH PRESIDENT) 1825-1829

Adams was born on July 11, 1767, in Braintree, Massachusetts, to John and Abigail Adams. John Quincy was named after his great-grandfather and was the son of former President John Adams. John Quincy had four siblings. He was home-taught, and at the age of eleven, he accompanied his father to France, two years later to the Netherlands, then to Russia, and finally back to America, where he entered Harvard University, following his father. John Quincy graduated second in his class from Harvard in 1787 and went on to practice law in Boston. In 1797, he married Louisa Catherine Johnson. They went on to have four children together. In 1814, he was a negotiator in the Treaty of Ghent, which ended the War of 1812. That year, he was appointed Secretary of State under President Monroe and wrote the Monroe Doctrine for the president. In the 1824 election, John Quincy Adams, Henry Clay, William Crawford, and Andrew Jackson all ran as Democratic-Republicans. John Calhoun ran unopposed for vice president. This election was the first when popular votes were counted. Henry Clay supported the electoral vote for Adams, making him the electoral winner and the president. Adams was the first president elected without winning the popular vote. In 1828, the Democratic Party was founded. Born in England, Louisa was the first foreign born First Lady. In 1830, Adams was the first former president elected to the House of Representatives, where he served for nine terms. In 1836, over opposition by Adams, the House passed the gag rule, which limited debate in Congress. In 1841, Adams successfully defended slaves who rioted on the ship *Amistad*. Adams died at the age of 80, in 1848, in the House of Representatives.

ANDREW JACKSON (7ᵀᴴ PRESIDENT) 1829-1837

Jackson was born on March 15, 1767, in Waxhaw, South Carolina, to Andrew and Elizabeth Hutchinson Jackson. Both parents arrived years earlier from Ireland. His father died before Andrew was born. Andrew had two older brothers. Andrew learned to read and write from frontier schools. At age 11, Andrew read newspaper articles to his neighbors. At age 13, he joined the South Carolina militia and fought in the American Revolution. His mother died when Andrew was age 14. After his release from the militia, he studied law and became a public prosecutor and then a judge. In 1791, Jackson married Rachel Robards. They had no children but adopted Rachel's cousin. Five years later, Jackson was elected to the U.S. House of Representatives. In 1814, he was commissioned a major general in the Tennessee militia. He took 2,500 volunteers to defend New Orleans against the British. After defeating them, Jackson defeated the Seminole Indians in Florida. That led to him being elected governor of Florida, and later he was elected to the U.S. Senate. In the 1824 election, Jackson won the popular vote but lost the electoral vote to John Quincy Adams following a vote in the House of Representatives. In the 1828 election, Democrats Andrew Jackson and John Calhoun defeated

National Republicans John Quincy Adams and Richard Rush in both the electoral and popular votes. Calhoun was the first person to serve as a vice president under two different presidents (John Quincy Adams and Andrew Jackson). Over 30,000 people came to Jackson's inaugural party. Shortly after, he brought running water to the Executive Mansion. The U.S. population was almost 13 million in 1830. Following Jackson's signing the 1830 Indian Removal Act, some 13,000 Cherokees were forced out of Georgia and sent to Oklahoma. Some 6,000 died on the Trail of Tears before reaching Oklahoma. In the 1832 election, Democrats Andrew Jackson and Martin Van Buren defeated National Republicans Henry Clay and John Sergeant. Jackson vetoed the Second Bank of the United States, moving many into state banks. Jackson vetoed more Congressional actions than the six previous presidents combined. He was also the first president censured. In 1835, Jackson narrowly missed being shot and killed. In 1836, 180 men at the Alamo fought off Santa Anna's army of 10,000 for several days before giving up. The Financial Panic of 1837 occurred during Jackson's last year in office. Jackson died at age 78, in 1845.

MARTIN VAN BUREN *(8*TH *PRESIDENT) 1837-1841*

Van Buren was born on December 5, 1782, in Old Kinderhook, New York, to Dutch parents, Abraham and Maria Hoes Van Buren. Martin had seven siblings, four full and three half. Maria's marriage to Abraham was her second marriage. Martin was the first president born an American citizen; the previous seven were born British citizens. Martin was the first president whose second language was English; his first was Dutch. Initially, he went to a one-room schoolhouse, and later he attended the Kinderbrook Academy. Then he worked in a law office for five years before becoming a lawyer. He signed all of his memos "OK," short for old Kinderbrook. He thus introduced "OK" into the English lexicon. In 1807, he married Hannah Hoes. They went on to have five children. In 1821, Martin was elected a U.S. senator, and in 1828, he was elected governor of New York. In 1829, he was appointed secretary of state for President Jackson. Since Van Buren's wife had died in 1819, Martin moved in with Senator Rufus King. A year later, Martin helped set up the Democratic party. In the 1832 election, Democrats Andrew Jackson and Martin Van Buren defeated National Republicans Henry Clay and John Sergeant in both the electoral and popular votes. In the 1836 election, Democrats Martin Van Buren and Richard Johnson defeated Whigs William Henry Harrison and Francis Granger in both the electoral and popular votes. The Financial Panic of 1837 followed a period of inflation, bank failures, thousands of bankruptcies, and an unemployment rate of 25%. This resulted in a five-year period of depression that doomed Van Buren's chance of being re-elected. In 1839, Van Buren set up an independent banking system that would be the model for the Federal Reserve adopted by President Wilson. In 1840, the U.S. population was 17 million. Van Buren died on July 24, 1862, at age 79.

WILLIAM HENRY HARRISON *(9ᵀᴴ PRESIDENT) 1841-1841*

Harrison was born on February 9, 1773, in Berkeley Plantation, Virginia, to Benjamin Harrison V and Elizabeth Bassett Harrison. Benjamin served as a member of the Second Constitutional Congress, where he signed the Declaration of Independence. And Benjamin's great-grandson, also named Benjamin, was elected the 23rd U.S. president in 1888. William had private tutors before attending Berkeley Plantation and then medical school. He then joined the First Infantry Regiment, serving under General Anthony Wayne. In 1794, William was cited for bravery in the Battle of Fallen Timbers. In 1795, William married Anna Symmes. They would have ten children together, 48 grandchildren, and 106 great-grandchildren. William was prolific if not profound. He served as a territorial delegate to Congress from 1798 to 1801, and then for ten years he served as governor of Territorial Indiana. He was forever called "Old Tippecanoe" for defeating Shawnee Chief Tecumseh in the Battle of Tippecanoe in 1811. And William defeated the British in the 1813 Battle of the Thames River. Three years later, he was elected to the U.S. House of Representatives. In 1819, he was elected an Ohio state senator, and in 1825, he was elected a U.S. senator from Ohio. In the 1840 election, Whigs William Henry Harrison and John Tyler defeated Democrats President Martin Van Buren and Vice President Richard Johnson in both the electoral and popular votes. Harrison caught a cold during his one hour and 40-minute, 8,445-word inaugural speech. He spoke in the cold, driving rain without a hat or an overcoat. He died at age 68 on April 4, 1841, having been in office only 32 days. He was the first president who died in office. It was the shortest period on record for a presidency. John Tyler was named president. Congress decided to give the widow Harrison a pension – a lump sum of $25,000.

JOHN TYLER *(10ᵀᴴ PRESIDENT) 1841-1845*

Tyler Jr. was born on March 29, 1790, on his family's plantation in Charles City, Virginia, to John Tyler Sr. and Mary Armstead Tyler. His father was a former governor of Virginia and a Federal District Court Judge. John had six siblings. He attended local schools and the College of William & Mary, graduating in 1807 to practice law and enter state politics. He then commanded a local militia in the War of 1812 and married Letitia Christian in 1813. They had eight children together. Three years later, Tyler was elected to the U.S. House of Representatives and then served as governor of Virginia for two years. In 1827, he was elected to the U.S. Senate from Virginia. But he resigned in 1836, when he refused to overturn a Senate censure of President Jackson. Three years later, he failed to get reelected as Virginia's governor. Tyler was an early supporter of the Whig Party, who then endorsed him as Harrison's vice president. His recognition in the South complemented Harrison's popularity in the North. Tyler was the young, handsome statesman, complementing Harrison's grandfatherly image. When Harrison died, there was a debate as to whether Tyler was to be the president or only to act as one until a special election was held. Tyler did not wait. He quickly had himself sworn in as the tenth president. This infuriated many. Nonetheless, he was the first man to be elected to the four federal offices: representative, senator, vice president, and president. The year 1841 was the first year of three presidents: Van Buren, Harrison, and Tyler. When Congress passed a national bank bill over Tyler's veto, his cabinet resigned. He appointed a new one in two days. After Letitia died in 1842, it was only two years before Tyler met and married actress Julia Gardiner. He was the first president to get married while in office. They had two daughters and five sons together. In 1844, Samuel Morse used Morse code to send the first telegraph message, "What Hath God Wrought." Tyler died on January 18, 1862, at age 71 and was buried in a Confederate flag-draped coffin.

JAMES K. POLK *(11ᵀᴴ PRESIDENT) 1845-1849*

Polk was born on November 2, 1795, in Pineville, North Carolina, to Samuel and Jane Knox Polk. James was the oldest of ten children. He suffered from poor health and initially could not attend school. After a kidney stone operation at age 16, he went to a school in Mt. Zion, Tennessee. James did well academically and entered the University of North Carolina. After graduation in 1818, he went on to study law. He then served in a local militia, rising to the rank of colonel. In 1822, James was elected to the Tennessee House of Representatives. In 1824, James married Sarah Childress. They would have no children. The following year, he was elected to the U.S. House of Representatives, and in 1835 he became Speaker of the House. He was elected governor of Tennessee in 1839. In the 1844 election, Democrats James Polk and George Dallas defeated Whigs Henry Clay and Theodore Frelinghuysen in both electoral and popular votes. But Polk was the first elected president who did not carry his own state. And he was the first former speaker of the House of Representatives to be elected president. The U.S. Naval Academy was established in 1845. Polk believed in Manifest Destiny, the supposed God-given right of white Americans to take over land not already in their control. Following border disputes with Mexico, Congress declared war on Mexico in 1846. Following America's victory, Mexico ceded several states, including Arizona, California, New Mexico, and Texas, to the United States for $15 million. Adhesive postage stamps were approved by Congress in 1847. Polk worked hard but did not trust others. That included banks: he carried his money in a suitcase. He also introduced gas lighting to the Executive Mansion. Polk laid the Washington Monument cornerstone in 1848, the same year that gold was discovered in California. Polk died at age 53 on June 15, 1849.

ZACHARY TAYLOR *(12TH PRESIDENT) 1849-1850*

Taylor was born on November 24, 1786, in Orange County, Virginia, to Richard and Sarah Taylor. Zachary had seven siblings. He received an education through private tutors and then joined the Kentucky militia. Zachary married Margaret Mackall Smith in 1810. They would go on to have six children. As a captain, he helped defend Fort Harrison from an Indian attack during the War of 1812. As a major, he fought in the Black Hawk War and the Seminole War. As a general, Taylor drove the Mexican army out of Texas and then defeated Santa Anna's army in the Mexican War of 1847. Because he wore old, ragged clothes and was always ready to fight, he was nicknamed, "Old Rough and Ready." In the election of 1848, Whigs Zachary Taylor and Millard Fillmore defeated Democrats Lewis Cass and William Butler in both the electoral and popular votes. The winners met for the first time only days before the election. They were victorious because the newly formed Free-Soil Party, headed by former President Van Buren, took away votes from Cass and Butler. At his inauguration, Taylor stated, "For more than half a century, during which kingdoms and empires have fallen, this Union has stood unshaken." Polk was the first president whose party lacked a majority in both houses during his term of office. He was also the first president to not have been previously elected to any office, and he had never voted. Following the discovery of gold in California, the dollar and twenty-dollar gold pieces were minted. The 1850 census put the U.S. population at 23 million, which included 2.5 million immigrants. Taylor died at age 65 in 1850. Abraham Lincoln delivered the eulogy.

MILLARD FILLMORE *(13TH PRESIDENT) 1850-1853*

Fillmore was born on January 7, 1800, in Locke, New York, to Nathaniel and Phoebe Fillmore. He had eight siblings. Millard was home-taught and then attended New Hope Academy. After graduating in 1818, he studied law and began a law practice in Buffalo, New York. In 1826, he married Abigail Powers, one of his New Hope Academy teachers. They went on to have two children. He was elected to the New York State Assembly in 1828 and five years later was elected to the U.S. House of Representatives. In 1844, he was unsuccessful in running for governor of New York, but in 1848, he was elected Zachary Taylor's vice president. Shortly after, Fillmore turned down an honorary degree from Oxford University, saying he was not worthy. With Taylor's death, Fillmore became president on July 9, 1850. Fillmore was the fifth vice president to become president (John Adams, Thomas Jefferson, Martin Van Buren, and John Tyler preceded him). And Fillmore was the second vice president to become president upon the death of his president (John Tyler was the first). In 1852, the **New York Times** began publication. That same year, Harriet Beecher Stowe published **Uncle Tom's Cabin** and Lynn, Massachusetts, became the shoemaking capital of the country. In the 1850s, the slavery issue tore apart the Whig Party, resulting in the southerners joining the Democratic Party and the northerners joining the Republican Party. Fillmore then retired to Buffalo, where he founded the University of Buffalo and then served as its first chancellor. In 1856, Fillmore was the presidential candidate for the Know Nothing Party. Fillmore was soundly defeated by James Buchanan. Before leaving the presidency, Fillmore acquired the first stove for the Executive Mansion, ending the practice of preparing food over an open fire. Fillmore married Catherine McIntosh in 1858 (Abigail having died in 1853). They would have no children. Fillmore died on March 8, 1874, at age 74.

FRANKLIN PIERCE *(14ᵀᴴ PRESIDENT) 1853-1857*

Pierce was born on November 23, 1804, in Hillsborough, New Hampshire, to Benjamin Sr. and Anna Pierce. Franklin had four siblings. After years in a schoolhouse, Franklin went to Hancock Academy and then Francistown Academy. He graduated from Bowdoin College in 1824 and went on to study law. In 1829, Pierce was elected to the New Hampshire House of Representatives and soon after became speaker of the house. Five years later, Pierce was elected to the U.S. House of Representatives. In 1834, Franklin married Jane Appleton. They would go on to have three children. Two years later, Pierce was elected to the U.S. Senate. After serving one term, Pierce returned to New Hampshire to resume his law practice. In 1847, after declining President Polk's invitation to be his attorney general, Pierce enlisted in the U.S. Army, where he rose to the rank of brigadier general. After leaving the army in 1851, he was elected a "dark horse" candidate at the Democratic Convention. Pierce's campaign slogan was "We Polked you in '44 and we shall Pierce you in '52." In the 1852 election, Democrats Franklin Pierce and William King defeated Whigs Winfield Scott and William Graham in both the electoral and popular votes. Pierce delivered his inaugural address completely without notes, having memorized the 3,319-word document, and went on to state, "I believe that involuntary servitude as it exists in different states of the Confederacy is recognized by the Constitution." In 1853, Pierce was the first president to have a full-time bodyguard and put up a Christmas tree in the Executive Mansion. In 1854, the Republican Party was founded in Ripon, Wisconsin, by northern Whigs who had left the Democratic Party. The Bessemer process for converting iron to steel in open blast furnaces was developed in 1855. In 1856, abolitionist John Brown led anti-slavery protests in Lawrence, Kansas, and Isaac Singer developed the affordable sewing machine. Pierce died at age 65 on October 8, 1869.

JAMES BUCHANAN (15ᵀᴴ PRESIDENT) 1857-1861

Buchanan was born on April 23, 1791, in Cove Gap, Pennsylvania, to James and Elizabeth Buchanan. James had nine siblings. He attended the Old Stone Academy and then went to Dickinson College, where he studied law, graduating in two years in 1809. He practiced law in Lancaster, Pennsylvania. He fought with the Pennsylvania militia during the War of 1812. But he was the first president who served in the military without becoming a commissioned officer. He served a two-year term with the Pennsylvania state legislature and then returned to his law practice. In 1819, James was briefly engaged to Anne Coleman, but their engagement broke off, and he remained single for the rest of his life. In 1821, Buchanan was elected to the U.S. House of Representatives. After serving five terms, he was appointed U.S. Minister to Russia for three years and was then elected to the U.S. Senate in 1834. In 1845, he was appointed Secretary of State under President Polk for four years. In 1853, he was appointed U.S. Minister to Great Britain for three years. In the 1856 election, Democrats James Buchanan and John Breckinridge defeated Republicans John C. Frémont and William Dayton in both the electoral and popular votes. In his inaugural address, Buchanan stated that the slavery issue should be settled in the courts or by the states. Two days after the speech, the U.S. Supreme Court issued the Dred Scott decision that slavery was permitted in all U.S. territories. Buchanan had to deal with three major issues: the financial panic of 1857, the fallout of the Dred Scott decision, and fighting over slavery after the repeal of the 1820 Missouri Compromise Act. In 1857, Congress gave Buchanan $25,000 to buy a portrait of five presidents for the Executive Mansion. Buchanan was the first, and only lifelong, bachelor president, and as such his niece served as the Executive Mansion hostess. Buchanan lived with Rufus King, another bachelor, for some twenty years. In 1858, the Republicans nominated Abraham Lincoln for a seat in the U.S. Senate. The U.S. senatorial debate drew 30,000 attendees. In Buchanan's 1860 State of the Union Address, he stated that neither Congress nor the president had the power to prevent a state from leaving the Union. Two weeks later, South Carolina seceded from the Union. The 1860 census reported the U.S. population at 31 million. Buchanan died at age 77 on June 1, 1868.

ABRAHAM LINCOLN (16ᵀᴴ PRESIDENT) 1861-1865

Lincoln was born on February 12, 1809, in Hodgenville, Kentucky, to Thomas and Nancy Lincoln. He was the first president born outside of the original 13 colonies. Abraham had a sister, born before him, and a younger brother, who died in infancy. The family moved from their one-room cabin to a larger log cabin in Spencer County, Indiana, in 1816. Both children were home-schooled. In 1818, Abraham's mother died during childbirth, as did the child. Several years after Nancy's death, Thomas married Sarah Bush. They would go on to have three children together. In 1830, the family moved to Macon County, Illinois. Although he had no formal education, Abraham liked to read and went on to become a lawyer and was admitted to the Illinois bar in 1837. Before that happened, he had been a blacksmith, a rail splitter, a store clerk, a bartender, a ferryboat captain, a surveyor, and a postmaster. Lincoln was despondent for several years when his first love died in 1835. But in 1842, he married Mary Todd. Amid a stormy relationship, Lincoln said, "I fell in love with her and what is more, I have never fallen out." They went on to have four children. Lincoln served in both the Illinois state legislature and the U.S. House of Representatives. Lincoln switched from the Whig Party to the Republican Party, which was formed in Ripon. In 1858, the Republicans nominated Lincoln for the Illinois seat held by Democrat Stephen Douglas. The outcome was important because of the 31 states, 15 were slaves and 16 were free states. Lincoln and Douglas engaged in seven three-hour debates before crowds numbering as many as 15,000. The two candidates were in sharp contrast to each other. Douglas was 5'4" and Lincoln was 6'4." And the fiery words of Douglas contrasted with the quiet words of Lincoln, who often quoted from the Bible, including, "A house divided cannot stand," referring to the slavery issue. Douglas was chosen as the senator because the decision was made by the state legislature, controlled by the Democrats. In the 1860 election, Republican candidates Abraham Lincoln and Hannibal Hamlin defeated three Democrats, Stephen Douglas, John Bell, and John Breckinridge. The slavery issue had split the Democratic Party, ensuring a Lincoln victory. Lincoln-Hamlin were not on the ballot of ten southern states, but they still took 180 of the 303 electoral votes. However, Lincoln-Hamlin only received about one-third of the popular vote. Unhappy with the abolitionist Lincoln's election, a number of groups were formed to assassinate him. Private detective Allan Pinkerton learned of one planned attempt in Baltimore. Lincoln would be killed as he changed train stations on his way to Washington, D.C. for his inauguration. The plot was foiled when Lincoln changed his plans and arrived in Baltimore a day early. A crowd of 10,000 expecting to see Lincoln killed were disappointed to discover that he was already in the nation's capital. On April 12, 1861, Jefferson Davis, president of the seven states that left the Union, ordered troops to fire on the Union's Fort Sumter in Charleston, South Carolina. The Civil War had begun. Lincoln called for 75,000 volunteers to serve in the Union Army. There were a number of famous battles between the North and the South from 1861 until the South's surrender in 1865. Lincoln took two significant actions before the war ended: the January 1, 1863 Emancipation Proclamation, freeing all slaves, and the November 19, 1863 Gettysburg Address, given at the site of a union cemetery, commemorating the dead. In the 1864 election, Lincoln replaced Hamlin with Andrew Johnson, the only southern senator who supported the Union. Lincoln and Johnson defeated Democrats George McClellan and George Pendelton in both the electoral and popular votes by wide margins. With the end of the war on April 9, 1865, steel mills replaced iron factories, breweries emerged in Milwaukee and St. Louis because of the German population, and meat packing expanded in Chicago. On April 14, 1865, at age 56, President Lincoln was shot and killed by actor John Wilkes Booth while watching a play in the nation's capital. Lincoln died the following day. He was the first assassinated president. Booth was shot and killed in Maryland, and his four co-conspirators were hanged. After lying in state in the Capitol Building, Lincoln's body was placed on an eight-coach train for burial in Springfield, Illinois. In 1865, the famed Hatfield and McCoy feud began with the murder of a Union McCoy by a Confederate Hatfield. Lincoln's image is on the penny and the dollar bill. The Lincoln Memorial in the nation's capital features a seated Lincoln. In the White House, there is a Lincoln sitting room and a Lincoln bedroom. In 1941, the facial features of Washington, Jefferson, Roosevelt, and Lincoln were engraved on Mount Rushmore in South Dakota. Many cities bear his name.

ANDREW JOHNSON *(17ᵀᴴ PRESIDENT) 1865-1869*

Johnson was born on December 29, 1808, in Raleigh, North Carolina, to Jacob and Mary Johnson. Andrew had one older brother. His father died when Andrew was three years old. He grew up in poverty and never attended school. He worked as a tailor's apprentice, moved to Greeneville, and served as a tailor. Andrew met and married Eliza McCardle in 1827. She tutored him in reading and writing. They went on to have five children. His political career included becoming mayor of Greeneville and then a state legislator, serving in the U.S. House of Representatives from 1843 to 1853, in the U.S. Senate from 1857 to 1862, and as military governor of Tennessee from 1862 until 1864, when he was elected Abraham Lincoln's vice president. Johnson disagreed with seceding from the Union and was the only southern senator to remain in the Senate when the Confederacy was formed. Johnson served only six weeks as vice president before Lincoln was assassinated. Johnson was inaugurated president on April 15, 1865. Johnson was the third vice president to assume the presidency upon the death of his president (John Tyler and Millard Fillmore preceded him). He was the sixth vice president to become president (John Adams, Thomas Jefferson, Martin Van Buren, John Tyler, and Millard Fillmore preceded Johnson). And Johnson was the second person to be elected to the four key federal offices: representative, senator, vice president, and president (John Tyler preceded Johnson). Johnson was the first president who had not been in the military or served as a lawyer. Johnson served his term without a vice president. He was a heavy drinker and frequently drunk. The 13th Amendment to the U.S. Constitution removed involuntary servitude from the United States. It was ratified on December 6, 1865. The 1866 Civil Rights Act declared all persons born in the United States (except Native Americans) were citizens of the United States. The Act also gave ex-slaves the right to own property and enforce contracts. In 1866, the Ku Klux Klan was formed by former Confederate soldiers. That same year, Congress authorized the five-cent coin, calling it a nickel due to its nickel content. In 1867, Alaska was purchased from Russia for $7.2 million, about 2¢ an acre. In February 1868, Johnson was impeached by the House for firing their Secretary of War Edwin Stanton without Senate approval. He was not convicted because the required two-thirds majority fell one vote short. The 14th Amendment to the U.S. Constitution was ratified on July 9, 1868. It stated that persons born in the United States are citizens and cannot be deprived of life, liberty, or property without due process of law. Johnson died on January 15, 1876, at age 65. Many historians believe that Johnson was second only to James Buchanan as the worst president of the United States.

ULYSSES S. GRANT (18TH PRESIDENT) 1869-1877

Grant was born Hiram Ulysses Grant on April 27, 1822, in Point Pleasant, Ohio, to Jesse Root and Hannah Simpson Grant. He was named Hiram after his maternal grandfather. Grant had five siblings. He excelled at riding and training horses on the family farm. He attended local schools until entering the Presbyterian Academy, graduating at age 17. In 1839, Grant was admitted to the U.S. Military Academy at West Point, New York, upon the recommendation of Congressman Thomas Hamer. He was an unimposing man of 5'7" and weighed 175 pounds. Unfortunately, Hamer misidentified Grant, naming him Ulysses Simpson Grant, a name that Grant adopted. Grant graduated in 1843, the twenty-first in his class of thirty-nine cadets, and he was commissioned a second lieutenant in the Fourth U.S. Infantry. While stationed in Missouri, he spent time with the family of his West Point roommate Frederick Dent. Grant spent even more time with Frederick's sister Julia. Grant went off to fight in the Mexican-American War, where he was cited for bravery and promoted to first lieutenant. Grant returned to Missouri and married Julia in 1848. After six years of various assignments in the United States, with a wife and four children, Grant resigned from the army, and for the next seven years he went from job to job. When the Civil War began in 1861, Grant accepted command of an Illinois company of volunteers and rose to the rank of brigadier general when the unit was merged into the U.S. Army. After several significant victories, Lincoln promoted Grant to major general. In 1862, he suffered heavy losses in the Battle of Shiloh, but he followed that action with key victories in the Battle of Vicksburg and the Battle of Chattanooga. In 1864, Lincoln promoted Grant to lieutenant general in charge of the Union Army. In April 1865, Grant accepted the surrender of General Lee and the Confederate Army. Six days later, President Lincoln was shot and killed by John Wilkes Booth, and Vice President Andrew Johnson was sworn in as president. When President Johnson fired Secretary of War Edwin Stanton without the approval of Congress, Johnson was impeached. But he survived the impeachment by one vote in the U.S. Senate. President Johnson then appointed Grant as Stanton's replacement. After serving one year, Grant quit and in 1868 was named the Republican candidate for president. In the 1868 election, Grant and his vice-presidential candidate, Schuyler, defeated Democrats Horatio Seymour and Francis Blair in both the electoral and popular votes. Grant was the first president to have graduated from West Point. The Executive Mansion was in such bad condition that Julia refused to move in until it was repaired. It was the first renovation since it was burned by the British in the War of 1812. Grant's first mistake was appointing friends rather than qualified candidates to his cabinet. Wall Street spectators drove down the value of government money not backed by gold, and the stock market crashed in September 1869. The 1869 Judiciary Act increased the number of associate justices in the U.S. Supreme Court to eight from its current six. In 1869, Wyoming was the first state to give women the right to vote. The 15th Amendment to the U.S. Constitution was ratified on February 3, 1870, and stated the right to vote could not be denied on account of race, color, or previous servitude. The 1870 Enforcement Act authorized federal troops to enforce the 15th Amendment. In 1870, the U.S. population was close to 40 million, led by New York City's one million. The 1871 Civil Rights Act outlawed the Ku Klux Klan. The Great Chicago Fire killed over 300 people, left some 100,000 homeless, and destroyed over 17,000 buildings in 1871. The 1872 Revenue Act terminated the personal income tax. In the 1872 election, Republicans Ulysses Grant and Henry Wilson defeated Democrats Horace Greeley and Benjamin Brown in both the electoral and popular votes. Following the election, Congress increased the president's pay to $50,000 a year, up from Washington's $25,000, and the vice president's pay was increased to $10,000 a year, up from $5,000. The 1875 Bland Act restored the silver dollar to legal currency, and the 1875 Specie Resumption Act returned America to the gold standard. Government scandals plagued the Grant administration fueled by patronage, although Grant himself was guilty only of appointing incompetents. In 1876, Alexander Graham Bell invented the telephone. After leaving office, Grant turned all of his money over to his son for investment. Unfortunately, the son lost all the money. Grant turned to writing his memoirs. He finished the book a month before he died from cancer of the mouth from smoking on July 23, 1885, at the age of 63. Sales of the book paid off all of his debts.

RUTHERFORD B. HAYES *(19TH PRESIDENT) 1877-1881*

Hayes was born on October 4, 1822, in Delaware, Ohio, to Sophia and Rutherford Hayes. His father died two months before Rutherford was born. Hayes was the second president to be born after his father died, Andrew Jackson was the first. Rutherford had two siblings. Due to a wealthy uncle, Rutherford attended private schools before going to Kenyon College. He graduated in 1842 and went to Harvard Law School, graduating in 1845. John Adams was the first president to graduate from Harvard, and his son John Quincy Adams was the second. After Harvard, Rutherford set up a law practice in Cincinnati. In 1852, Rutherford married Lucy Ware Webb. They went on to have eight children. Rutherford enlisted in the Ohio Volunteer Infantry. He served throughout the Civil War (one of seven presidents to do so), rising to the rank of major general. Hayes was wounded five times in the war. Hayes was elected to the U.S. House of Representatives in 1864, but did not take his seat until the war was over. Beginning in 1868, Hayes served three terms as governor of Ohio. In the 1876 election, Republicans Rutherford Hayes and William Wheeler defeated Democrats Samuel Tilden and Thomas Hendricks by one electoral vote. But he was the second president to win the election but lose the popular vote. John Quincy Adams was the first. One of Hayes's first actions was to remove federal troops from the South, ending Reconstruction. In 1877, Hayes had Alexander Graham Bell install the first telephone in the Executive Mansion. Also in 1877, Thomas Edison invented the phonograph. In 1879, St. Patrick's Cathedral opened. In 1880, Hayes installed indoor plumbing and put in the first typewriter in the Mansion. In 1880, the U.S. population exceeded 50 million. Also in 1880, Queen Victoria sent Hayes the Resolute Desk, carved from the timbers of the British warship H.M.S. *Resolute*. The desk is still in the Oval Office today. In 1881, the Earp brothers fought rustlers at the O.K. Corral. Hayes died on January 17, 1893, at the age of 70.

JAMES A. GARFIELD (20ᵀᴴ PRESIDENT) 1881-1881

Garfield was born on November 19, 1831, near Cleveland, Ohio, to Abram and Eliza Garfield. James had four siblings. His father died when James was two years old, leaving his mother to support the family. She married Alfred Belden several years after Abram's death. The children divided their time between work and school. As a teenager, James worked on barges and tugboats until he contracted malaria. He later attended and graduated from Hiram College in 1854 and Williams College in 1856. James then served as a classics professor at Hiram College and taught both Greek and Latin. He also served as president of the college. He then became a traveling preacher for the Disciples of Christ for several years, making him the first ordained preacher to become president. In 1858, James married schoolteacher Lucretia Rudolph. They went on to have seven children. In 1859, Garfield was elected an Ohio state senator, during which time he studied law. He then joined the Union Army and was quickly promoted to colonel. He fought in both Shiloh and Chickamauga and had been promoted to general when President Lincoln persuaded him to take a seat in the U.S. House of Representatives while still in the army. As chair of the Military

Affairs Committee, he proposed legislation to establish the precursor to the Reserve Officer Training Corps (ROTC) on college campuses. He went on to become House Majority Leader before leaving after serving eighteen years. He became a U.S. senator from Ohio and then was nominated by the Republican Party for president. Garfield was chosen on the 36th ballot when candidate James Blaine gave his votes to him. Chester Arthur was chosen for the vice president position. In the 1880 election, Republicans James Garfield and Chester Arthur defeated Democrats Winfield Hancock and William English in both the electoral and popular votes. The difference was Arthur's home state of New York. Garfield's nickname was the "Preacher President." His saying was, "Pluck is better than luck." He did not have much of the latter. Garfield was shot by Charles Guiteau in the Washington, D.C. train station on July 2, 1881. Guiteau believed Garfield had denied him a political appointment. Garfield was taken to his bedroom in the Executive Mansion. The July Fourth celebration was canceled for the first time. For weeks, Garfield seemed to be recovering, but he died on September 19, 1881, at age 49. His death was caused by several surgeries without sterilizing the surgical instruments. He was the second president to be assassinated; Abraham Lincoln was the first. Guiteau was hanged for his crime. Garfield was in office only 199 days, second fewest to William Henry Harrison's 32 days. Congress awarded Garfield's widow, Lucretia, and all living presidential widows a $5,000 annual pension.

CHESTER A. ARTHUR *(21ST PRESIDENT) 1881-1885*

Arthur was born on October 5, 1829, in Fairfield, Vermont, to Malvina and Reverend William Arthur. Chester was the fifth of eight children. He was homeschooled before attending school in Schenectady. After high school, he enrolled in the Lyceum College in the city. But after a year, he switched to the men-only Union College. He opted for a classical curriculum, was president of the debating society. and edited the school newspaper. He graduated Phi Beta Kappa in 1851, and in 1859, he married Ellen Herndon. They went on to have three children. And in 1859, he joined the New York State Militia. During the Civil War, Arthur served as quartermaster general of New York, rising to the rank of brigadier general. In 1871, President Grant appointed Arthur customs collector of the Port of New York. Receiving a percentage of all collected customs by 1873, Arthur's salary exceeded $50,000 per annum. The customs house collected over 75% of the country's import taxes. The president of the United States was paid $25,000 a year until it was raised to $50,000 in 1873. President Hayes removed Arthur from the job in an attempt to curb the spoils system in 1877, and Arthur went back to his law practice. Wife Ellen died in 1880 at the age of 42. Shortly after her death, Arthur was selected by the Republican Party to be James Garfield's vice president in the 1880 election. The two defeated Democrats Winfield Scott Hancock and William H. English in both the electoral and popular votes. Garfield was elected president and Arthur was elected vice president. In mid-1881, Julie Sand sent Arthur a letter stating, "The hours of Garfield's life are numbered, and you are his successor." Garfield was assassinated on September 19, 1881, and Arthur became president. He was the fourth vice president to assume the presidency upon the death of the president (Tyler, Fillmore, and Johnson preceded him). Believing the Executive Mansion was shabby, Arthur refused to move in until all 132 rooms had been renovated. This included the installation of an elevator, a new bathroom, and a new set of china for 14-course state dinners. Known as "elegant Arthur," he spent considerable money on clothes and changed his attire several times during the day. In 1882, Julia Sand resumed sending Arthur letters, giving him unsolicited advice on what to do. He generally agreed with her suggestions. He managed to get the 1883 Pendleton Act approved. It required competitive examinations for federal civil service jobs. And Arthur reportedly stated, "I may be president of the United States, but my private life is nobody's damned business." That privacy would last until JFK's presidency. Plagued with Bright's Disease, Arthur died at age 59 on November 18, 1886.

GROVER CLEVELAND (22ND PRESIDENT) 1885-1889

Cleveland was born on March 18, 1837, in Caldwell, New Jersey, to Ann and Richard Cleveland. Grover had eight siblings. Grover was home-taught. When his father died in 1853, Grover was sixteen and his plans for college evaporated. He went to work to support the family. But he also studied law and set up a practice in Buffalo, New York in 1859. When the Civil War broke out, Grover paid an immigrant $150 to take his place in the military draft. In 1870, he served as sheriff in Erie County, New York. In 1874, he met and allegedly raped Maria Halpin. She got pregnant, but he refused to marry her. The baby was put in the Buffalo Orphan Asylum, and he committed Maria to an insane asylum. Grover was elected mayor of Buffalo, and two years later, he was elected governor of New York. In 1883, the Democrats chose Cleveland to be their presidential candidate. In the 1884 election, Democrats Grover Cleveland and Thomas Hendricks defeated Republicans James Blaine and John Logan, winning both the electoral and popular votes. Given Cleveland's illegitimate child, he might have been defeated if women were able to vote. In his inaugural speech, Grover stated, "Though the people support the government, the government should not support the people." In 1886, Grover married Frances Folsom, whom he had met twelve years earlier when she was nine years old. Grover was the first, and only, president to be married in the Executive Mansion, although John Tyler was the first to marry while in office. That same year, Cleveland dedicated the Statue of Liberty in New York Harbor. Cleveland added the Secretary of Agriculture to his cabinet due to the importance of food to the economy and the fact that farmers were struggling to survive. Cleveland liked to eat and drink good bourbon. He also liked to smoke, resulting in a malignant tumor in his mouth requiring the removal of a portion of his upper jaw in 1893. He personally answered the telephone in the Executive Mansion and vetoed 414 pieces of legislation, a total greater than his twenty-one predecessors combined. He lost to Republican Benjamin Harrison in the 1888 election. He returned to Buffalo and his law practice.

BENJAMIN HARRISON (23RD PRESIDENT) 1889-1893

Harrison was born on August 20, 1833, in North Bend, Ohio, to John Scott and Elizabeth Irwin Harrison. Harrison had twelve siblings and worked on his father's farm. He was homeschooled and then went to Miami University after a brief period at Farmers College. In 1852, Harrison graduated third in his class and went on to become a lawyer. In 1853, Benjamin married Carolina Scott. They met while he was taking a mathematics course from her father at Miami University. They went on to have three children. In 1863, Harrison formed a company of voluntary infantry to fight in the Civil War. He quickly was commissioned a colonel and left a brigadier general when the war ended. He returned to his law practice in Indianapolis and became a Republican. In 1876, he ran for governor of Indiana but lost. However, he won a seat in the U.S. Senate in 1880. In the 1888 election, Republicans Benjamin Harrison and Levi Morton defeated Democrats President Grover Cleveland and Allen Thurman in the electoral vote, although they lost the popular vote. Harrison was the last bearded president. In his inaugural speech, Harrison stated, "The decent and manly examination of the acts of government should not only be tolerated but encouraged." Shortly after the inauguration, the Capitol was flooded from the Johnstown flood. And electric lights were installed in the Executive Mansion in 1889. Also in 1889, the *Wall Street Journal* began publication. In 1890, Harrison gave 140 speeches, Yosemite National Park was created, and the U.S. population almost reached 63 million. In 1892, John L. Sullivan became the world's first heavyweight boxing champion. In the 1892 election, Republicans Benjamin Harrison and Whitelaw Reid lost both the electoral and the popular vote to Democrats Grover Cleveland and Adlai Stevenson. Harrison had been defeated, and Cleveland was re-elected president. Harrison returned to his law practice in Indianapolis and wrote several books. He died at age 67 on March 13, 1901.

GROVER CLEVELAND *(24ᵀᴴ PRESIDENT) 1893-1897*

Following Cleveland's defeat in 1888, Grover's wife said, "We'll be back in four years so keep everything in good shape." The Clevelands returned to New York City. They returned to the Executive Mansion four years later. In the 1892 election, Democrats Grover Cleveland and Adlai Stevenson defeated Republicans President Benjamin Harrison and Vice President Whitelaw Reid in both the electoral and popular votes. Cleveland became the first president to win two non-consecutive terms of office. In his inaugural address, he stated, "Above all tell the truth." Also in 1893, he repealed the Sherman Silver Purchase Act that put America on a silver standard with the issuance of certificates rather than coins. This act led to the Panic of 1893, set off by a stock market crash throwing the country into a major depression, resulting in a 20% unemployment rate and hundreds of failed banks. One of Cleveland's greatest achievements was breaking the Pullman Strike in 1894. And Cleveland stated that the first Monday in September would be Labor Day, a national holiday. In 1896, Charles Dow and Edward Jones created the Dow Jones Industrial Average using the price of twelve stocks to measure the performance of the stock market. Cleveland sought a third term in the 1896 election, but the Democratic Party selected William Jennings Bryan. Also in 1896, Mount Denali in Alaska was renamed Mt. McKinley. Cleveland died at the age of 71 on June 24, 1908.

WILLIAM MCKINLEY *(25ᵀᴴ PRESIDENT) 1897-1901*

McKinley was born on January 29, 1843, in Niles, Ohio, to William and Nancy Allison McKinley. William was the seventh of nine children. William was home-schooled and responsible for the care of the family cattle. He later attended the Poland Academy, where he overcame his shyness and excelled in the school's debate team. When the Civil War broke out, William enlisted in the Ohio Voluntary Regiment under the future President Rutherford B. Hayes. By the end of the war, McKinley had risen to the rank of major. He then enrolled in Albany Law School. He passed the Ohio bar exam (aided by a photographic memory) and practiced law in Canton, Ohio. In 1871, he married Ida Saxton, whom he had met at his bank. They went on to have two daughters together. In 1877, he was elected to the U.S. House of Representatives. After fourteen years, he was elected governor of Ohio and served two terms before being nominated for president at the Republican convention. Garret Hobart, whom he had never met, was picked for the vice president slot. Their favorite campaign slogan was, "Four more years of the full dinner pail." McKinley did little travel; instead, he ran his campaign from his front porch. Hobart convinced McKinley to defend the gold standard. In the 1896 election, Republicans William McKinley and Garrett Hobart defeated Democrats William Jennings Bryan and Arthur Sewall in both the electoral and popular votes. Defending the gold standard was a major reason for the McKinley-Hobart victory after Bryan made his famous speech at the Democratic convention, "We will answer their demands for a gold standard by saying to them: You shall not press down upon the brow of labor this crown of thorns; you shall not crucify mankind upon a cross of gold." McKinley was the first president to ride in a car to his inauguration. When McKinley took the oath of office, the economic depression that followed the Panic of 1893 had passed and the country was on the path to prosperity in a period called the Gilded Age. Hobart's wife assisted in many Executive Mansion events because McKinley's wife suffered from epilepsy. The defining event of McKinley's presidency was the sinking of the U.S. battleship *Maine* on February 15, 1898, in Cuba's Havana Harbor. Believing Spain was responsible, the U.S. declared war on Spain and sent to Cuba the First Volunteer Cavalry headed by Theodore Roosevelt who took San Juan Hill and Commodore Dewey who destroyed six

Spanish warships in Manila Bay. The Treaty of Paris ended the war, and the United States took possession of Cuba, Guam, the Philippines, Puerto Rico, and Wake Island. The five boroughs of New York City were created in 1898. In 1899, McKinley sent troops into China to quell the Boxer Rebellion, and he acquired the Samoan Islands from England and Germany that same year. The 1900 Gold Standard Act declared gold was the only backing of the U.S. dollar. In the 1900 election, Republicans President William McKinley and Vice President Theodore Roosevelt defeated Democrats William Jennings Bryan and Adlai Stevenson. Roosevelt succeeded Hobart, who had died fifteen months before the end of his term in office. McKinley was shot on September 6, 1901, by anarchist Leon Czolgosz at the Pan-American Exposition in Buffalo, New York. McKinley died on September 14, 1901, at age 58, six months into his second presidency. Roosevelt became the third vice president to become president following a president's assassination (Abraham Lincoln and James Garfield were the first two assassinated).

THEODORE ROOSEVELT (26TH PRESIDENT) 1901-1909

Roosevelt was born on October 27, 1858, in New York City, New York, to Theodore and Martha Bulloch Roosevelt. Theodore had three siblings. The wealthy family lived in New York City, where he was home-schooled by tutors. He loved physical exercise and grew into a strong and athletic man as his asthma attacks became less frequent. But he also suffered from a weak heart and was nearsighted. He was known as Ted to family, TR to friends, but Teddy to no one (he loathed that nickname). In 1876, TR left for Harvard with these words from his father; "Take care of your morals first, then your health and finally your studies." Ted's father died during TR's second year at Harvard. By that time, TR had published his first of 30 books, as well as, countless articles, letters, and speeches. He was also a voracious reader, reading a book a day. Aided by a photographic memory and his father's admonition, TR graduated in 1880. Within months, he married Alice Hathaway Lee. They had one child together. In 1882, TR was elected a New York State assemblyman. On February 14, 1884, both TR's wife and his mother died. Two years later, he married Edith Carow. They honeymooned in England and then returned to New York City. They had five children together. Beginning in 1889, TR spent four years on the U.S. Civil Service Commission and then became New York City's police commissioner for two years. In 1897, he was appointed an Assistant Secretary to the Navy, and in 1898, he volunteered to fight in the Spanish American War. Serving as a lieutenant colonel, TR formed the Rough Riders. Later, TR served as governor of New York, and in 1900, he was elected McKinley's vice president because former Vice President Hobart had died. As vice president, TR said the following about foreign policy: "Speak softly and carry a big stick." And used the bully pulpit to state his views. Within six months of his election to vice president, McKinley was assassinated, and TR became president at the age of 42. As he took office, the country was changing: people were leaving their farms and moving to cities to work in factories. He was the fifth vice president to become president upon the death of the president (Tyler, Fillmore, Johnson, and Arthur preceded him). Upon his becoming president, TR's wife renovated the Executive Mansion, making the upstairs for family and the downstairs for business. In 1901, TR officially changed the name of the Executive Mansion to the White House after painting it white. Shortly after, he added the position of Secretary of Commerce and Labor to his cabinet due to the importance of the interaction of business and labor. TR was an avid hunter. On one of his hunts, he refused to shoot a small bear. A small stuffed bear was sent to him, and TR's daughter named it a Teddy bear. TR was also a sports enthusiast and enjoyed skinny dipping in the Potomac River. TR's greatest accomplishment was the purchase of the French-abandoned rights to the Panama Canal property from Colombia in 1903 for $40 million. In the 1904 election, Republicans Theodore Roosevelt and Charles Fairbanks defeated Democrats Alton Parker and Henry G. Davis in both the electoral and popular votes. In 1906, TR was the first president to win the Nobel Peace Prize (for his role in ending the Russo-Japanese War). Also in 1906, TR used the Sherman Antitrust Act of 1890 to break up some 44 companies. A year later, he sent the Great White Fleet around the world. Second only to the Panama Canal, TR's greatest accomplishment was that not one shot was fired from or to a foreign country during TR's seven years in office. TR died on January 6, 1919, at age 60. In 1941, the facial features of Washington, Jefferson, Theodore Roosevelt, and Lincoln were engraved on Mount Rushmore in South Dakota.

WILLIAM HOWARD TAFT (27ᵀᴴ PRESIDENT) 1909-1913

Taft was born on September 15, 1857, in Cincinnati, Ohio, to Alphonso and Louisa Torrey Taft. Alphonso had been President Grant's Secretary of War. William had five siblings, two half-brothers and three full siblings. William was always overweight. His nicknames were Big Bill and Big Lub. After attending public school, he went to Yale University. Graduating second in his class of 132 in 1878, he went on to practice law. In 1887, he became a judge in the Supreme Court of Ohio. Then he went on to become solicitor general, governor of the Philippines, and Secretary of War under Theodore Roosevelt. In 1886, William married Helen Herron. They went on to have three children. Taft's goal was to get on the U.S. Supreme Court, but he was convinced he would get the Republican nomination for president. He got it. In the 1908 election, Republicans William Howard Taft and James Sherman defeated Democrats William Jennings Bryan and John Kern in both the electoral and popular votes. Upon his election, Congress increased the pay of the president to $75,000 a year, up from $50,000 in 1873 for President Grant. In 1909, W.E.B. DuBois formed the National Association for the Advancement of Colored People (NAACP). Taft was the first president to throw out the first pitch to begin the baseball season. He was also credited with initiating the seventh inning stretch. At a game in that inning, he got up to stretch, and everyone seeing it did the same out of respect for the president. In 1910, powerful bankers laid the foundation for what would become the Federal Reserve System, making it appear to be part of the federal government, which it was not. Also in 1910, Taft put the Interstate Commerce Commission in charge of the emerging telephone and telegraph industry. And in 1910, the U.S. population almost reached 12 million. Unhappy with large companies, in 1911 Taft got the U.S. Supreme Court to rule that Rockefeller's Standard Oil of New Jersey had an unreasonable monopoly and ordered its breakup. Also in 1911, IBM began as the Computing Tabulating and Recording Company. In 1912, the ocean liner the *Titanic* sank, killing 1,500 people. Also in 1912, Ford announced the eight-hour day and five-day workweek. Taft loved to eat, evidenced by his weighing over 350 pounds. His wife installed the first White House housekeeper and planted 3,000 cherry trees donated by Japan. Taft was defeated by Woodrow Wilson in the 1912 election. Following his defeat, Taft became a law professor at Yale University. And in 1921, he was appointed Chief Justice of the United States of the Supreme Court by President Harding. Taft considered this more important than being president of the United States. He was the first person to have been president and U.S. Supreme Court Chief Justice. He served in the latter capacity until his death on March 8, 1930, at age 73.

WOODROW WILSON (28TH PRESIDENT) 1913-1921

Wilson was born on December 28, 1856, in Staunton, Virginia, to Janet and Joseph Wilson. Joseph was a Presbyterian minister. Woodrow had three siblings. When the Civil War broke out, Joseph served the Confederacy as a minister. During his childhood, Woodrow had a difficult time learning how to read, as he suffered from dyslexia. He also had difficulty breathing and poor blood circulation. After being home-schooled, Woodrow entered the College of New Jersey (later to become Princeton University). After graduating in 1879, he briefly practiced law before entering Johns Hopkins University focusing on history and political science. After returning from Johns Hopkins with a PhD, Woodrow married Ellen Louise Axson in 1885. They went on to have three children. He went to teach at Wesleyan College in 1888 and then to Princeton as a professor. Two years later, he was president of Princeton University. In 1911, Woodrow was elected governor of New Jersey. In the 1912 election, Democrats Woodrow Wilson and Thomas Marshall defeated Progressive Party candidates Theodore Roosevelt and Hiram Johnson in both the electoral and popular votes. Wilson was the first president to have a PhD. In his cabinet, he separated the positions of Labor and Commerce, believing each department should be represented by separate secretaries. On April 8, 1913, the 17th Amendment to the U.S. Constitution was ratified, defining the terms and conditions of U.S. senators. That year,

Wilson also signed the Underwood Simmons Tariff Act, which introduced an estate tax and a graduated personal income tax. On March 1, 1914, some 358,000 Americans filed tax returns for the first time. Months later, Ellen died of Bright's disease. World War I began in June of 1914 with the assassination of the Archduke of Austria-Hungary. In 1916, General Motors was formed, having acquired 22 companies. In 1918, Wilson married Edith Bolling. They had no children together. Following the sinking of the ship *Lusitania* by a German submarine, the U.S. declared war on Germany on April 6, 1917. The war ended on November 11, 1918, after more than eight million lost their lives. In the 1918 election, Democrats Woodrow Wilson and Thomas Marshall defeated Republicans Charles Hughes and Charles Fairbanks in both the electoral and popular votes. Wilson was elected president and Marshall was elected vice president. Republican Jeannette Rankin was the first woman elected to the U.S. House of Representatives. In 1918, the Ford Model T car sold for $450, equal to a factory worker's yearly pay and the *New York Times* received the first Pulitzer Prize for journalism. The 18th Amendment was ratified on January 16, 1919, banning intoxicating liquors, marking the start of Prohibition. During that year, Wilson was paralyzed following several strokes. Wife Edith represented her husband without telling anyone that he was ill. In 1920, Charles Ponzi promised investors a 50 percent return in 90 days. That same year, Charles Darrow and William Jennings Bryan faced off in the famed Scopes evolution trial. On August 18, 1920, the 19th Amendment to the U.S. Constitution was ratified, stating that the right to vote did not depend on a person's sex, thereby giving women the right to vote. In 1921, Congress established a quote system for immigration. After Wilson's term of office ended, he set up a law practice in Washington, D.C. Wilson died at age 67 on February 3, 1924.

WARREN G. HARDING *(29ᵀᴴ PRESIDENT) 1921-1923*

Harding was born on November 2, 1865, near Blooming Grove, Ohio, to George and Phoebe Elizabeth Harding. Warren had seven siblings. His father was a farmer, and his mother was a midwife. Warren's nickname was Big Foot because he wore a size 14 shoe. His mother nicknamed him Winnie because she had wanted his name to be Winfield, but her husband had said no. Warren went to a one-room schoolhouse and later graduated from Ohio Central College in 1882. He went on to be a reporter, editor, and publisher of the *Marion Daily Star*, which he bought in 1884 for $300. He married his piano teacher, Florence King, in 1891, but they had no children. Depressed after several nervous breakdowns, he admitted himself to the Battle Creek Sanitarium run by Dr. Kellogg, the inventor of corn flakes, who believed his cereal could cure depression. He liked having sex with other women, but Florence stayed with him even though she knew about his many affairs. Beginning in 1899, he spent four years in the Ohio State Senate, he then served a term as lieutenant governor of Ohio, and he was elected a U.S. senator in 1915. In the 1920 Republican Convention, he was chosen as the nominee for president. In the 1920 election, Republicans Warren Harding and Calvin Coolidge defeated Democrats James Cox and Franklin Roosevelt in both the electoral and popular votes. Harding was the first person elected president while still serving in the U.S. Senate. For some reason, Harding let his dog sit in a chair in the Cabinet room. In 1921, eight Chicago White Sox baseball players were banned from baseball for conspiring with gamblers to change the outcome of the World Series. Not surprising, Harding's markedly racist views resulted in his being believed to have been inducted into the Ku Klux Klan in a White House ceremony in 1922. Also in 1922, Georgia resident Rebecca Felton became the first woman elected to the U.S. Senate. Harding's administration was rocked by scandal, ranging from philandering to government officials taking bribes. Probably the worst was when Interior Secretary Albert Fall took $400,000 in bribes in 1923 for illegally leasing the oil reserves from the Teapot Dome. In 1923, Alfred Sloan introduced decentralization, as opposed to Ford's centralization control. Harding died on August 2, 1923, at age 57, while traveling to Alaska. Many historians consider Harding one of the worst performing of all presidents. He is joined by James Buchanan (the 15th president) and Andrew Johnson (the 17th president).

CALVIN COOLIDGE *(30TH PRESIDENT) 1923-1929*

Coolidge was born on July 4, 1872, in Plymouth, Vermont, to John and Victoria Coolidge. Calvin was the first president born on the Fourth of July. Calvin was sickly and suffered from asthma. He was devastated when his mother died when he was 12 years old. He had only one sibling, and she died when he was 18 years old. His schooling consisted of elementary school followed by the Black River Academy, St. Johnsbury Academy, and Amherst. After graduating in 1893, he went on to practice law. In 1905, Calvin married Grace Goodhue. They went on to have two children. In 1907, he was elected to the Massachusetts House of Representatives. This was followed by his being mayor of Northampton. In 1911, he began four years as a state senator. Coolidge served as President Harding's vice president. When Harding died on August 2, 1923, Coolidge became the 30th president. This happened when Coolidge was vacationing in Vermont with his notary public father, who swore his son into office. This was the first time a president was not sworn in by a U.S.

Supreme Court Justice. Coolidge was the sixth vice president to become president due to his president's death (Tyler, Fillmore, Johnson, Arthur, and Roosevelt preceded him). In the 1924 presidential campaign, Coolidge's campaign slogan was, "Keep cool and keep Coolidge." In the 1924 election, Republicans Calvin Coolidge and his running mate Charles Dawes defeated Democrats John Davis and Charles W. Bryan in both the electoral and popular votes. Progressive Party candidates Robert La Follette and his running mate Burton Wheeler were a distant third. Coolidge was elected president and Dawes was elected vice president. In a January speech, Coolidge stated, "The chief business of the American people is business." Coolidge quickly restored faith in a government shaken by scandal and graft by cleaning house of corrupt officials. He stated, "Nothing is easier than spending public money; nothing is harder than to resist doing it." Coolidge was known as Silent Cal, a man of few words. Once, told by a woman that she had bet $50 that she could get him to say more than two words, he replied, "You lose." Calvin and Grace were very different. He was aloof, and she was outgoing and charming. Calvin declined to run for a second full term in 1928. Months later, the stock market crashed. Coolidge died at age 60 on January 5, 1933.

HERBERT HOOVER *(31ST PRESIDENT) 1929-1933*

Hoover was born on August 10, 1874, in West Branch, Iowa, to Quakers Jesse Clark and Huldah Randall Hoover. Herbert had two siblings. Herbert's father died when he was six years old; his mother died when he was nine years old. An uncle then took Herbert to Oregon, where he was paid $1 for every 100 bags of potatoes he packed. In 1885, Hoover attended Friends Pacific Academy. In 1891, Hoover was the first student to enroll in

Stanford University. Four years later, he graduated with a degree in geology and went to work as a mining engineer. He used his knowledge to locate gold mines around the world. In 1898, he married Lou Henry (her father had wanted a boy), also a geology student at Stanford. They went on to have two children. Lou and Herbert traveled extensively. While in China during the Boxer Rebellion, both learned to speak Chinese. Herbert was a millionaire by age 40. During World War I, Hoover headed the U.S. Food Administration. His work earned him a place on a list of the ten greatest living Americans published by the *New York Times*. From 1921 to 1923, Hoover served as Secretary of Commerce under President Coolidge. When Coolidge decided not to run in the 1928 election, Herbert Hoover expressed interest in the job. Before the Republican presidential convention even opened, Hoover had 476 of the 545 delegates. He accepted the nomination by telegram. In the 1928 election, Republicans Herbert Hoover and Charles Curtis defeated Alfred Smith and Joseph Robinson by a wide margin in both the electoral and popular votes. The four-time New York governor Smith was the first person of the Catholic faith to be nominated for president. Hoover was sworn in as president by former president and current Chief Justice of the U.S. Supreme Court, William Taft. All plans for economic growth disappeared with the 1929 stock market crashes on October 24th and October 25th. Within weeks, the market lost over $25 billion, some 1,300 banks had closed, and millions of people had lost their jobs. The Great Depression followed the stock market crash. In 1930, Babe Ruth was asked how he could justify an $80,000 annual salary while President Hoover received $5,000 less. Ruth's reply: "I had a better year." In the 1932 election, Democrats Franklin Roosevelt and John Nance Garner defeated Republicans President Herbert Hoover and Vice President Charles Curtis by a wide margin in both the electoral and popular votes. Roosevelt and Garner had been elected president and vice president. And the Democrats took over Congress. Hoover failed in his attempt to secure the Republican nominations for president in 1936, 1940, and 1944. In a 1951 Gallup poll, Hoover was rated the fifth most admired man in the country. Asked why, Hoover stated, "I outlived my critics." Hoover died at age 90 on October 20, 1964.

FRANKLIN D. ROOSEVELT *(32ND PRESIDENT) 1933-1945*

Roosevelt was born on January 30, 1882, in Hyde Park, New York, to James and Sara Delano Roosevelt. Franklin had a half-brother from his father's first marriage. His mother came from a wealthy family, and his father headed a successful coal company. President Theodore Roosevelt was a fifth cousin. Franklin went to private schools and started collecting stamps. He graduated from both Harvard and Columbia Law Schools. He met and married Anna Eleanor Roosevelt (daughter of Theodore's brother) in 1905. They would go on to have six children. Franklin quickly picked up the nickname FDR when he practiced law. To help him with correspondence, FDR hired Missy Leland. In the 1920 election, FDR was the running mate of Democrat James Cox. They were defeated, and FDR returned to his law practice. In 1921, he was stricken with polio, and he was unable to walk for the rest of his life. In 1928, he was elected governor of New York and began a lifelong affair with Lucy Mercer, Eleanor's private secretary. In 1932, the Democrats nominated FDR for president with John Nance Garner as his vice president. FDR and Garner defeated Republicans President Herbert Hoover and Vice President Charles Curtis in both the electoral and popular votes. Months into the vice-president's job, Garner said the job "was not worth a bucket of warm piss," adding, "It was the worst damn fool mistake I ever made." In FDR's first 100 days, he focused on government intervention to put the 12 million unemployed to work, to aid the sick and elderly, and to assist in the recovery of banking, business, and farming. To meet these goals, he created an alphabet of government agencies. To reduce the time between election and inauguration, FDR was able to get the 20th Amendment to the U.S. Constitution ratified on January 23, 1933, which stated the terms of the president and vice president shall end on the 20th day of January. Previously they ended on March 4th. The election would still be in November. FDR put a heated swimming pool in the White House, which he used daily. In 1933, FDR banned private ownership of gold, and in the same year, about half of the workforce had no jobs. On December 5, 1933, the XXI Amendment repealed the XVIII Amendment, ending prohibition. Bill Wilson created Alcoholics Anonymous in 1934. In 1935, FDR established Social Security and prohibited employers from intervening with unionization of their employees. In the 1936 election, Democrats President FDR and Vice President John Nance Garner defeated Republicans Alfred Landon and Frank Knox in both the electoral and popular votes. The Democrats continued their control of both the House and the Senate. The 1939 Fair Labor Standards Act established overtime pay and a minimum hourly wage. In 1940, the U.S. population exceeded 131 million. In 1940, FDR wanted an unprecedented third term. In the 1940 election, President FDR and his Vice President Henry Wallace easily defeated Republicans Wendell Wilkie and Charles McNary in both the electoral and popular votes. And the Democrats continued their control of Congress. On December 8, 1941, Japan attacked American ships by air in Pearl Harbor, Hawaii. That same day, Congress declared war on Japan, and on December 11, 1941, following Germany and Italy's declaration of war on America,

Congress declared war on both countries. The turning point in the war was the 1942 naval victories over Japan, followed by America taking over Japanese-held islands in the Pacific. In 1944, allied troops landed on the beaches of Normandy to begin an assault on German troops. The 1945 Yalta Conference of Churchill, Roosevelt, and Stalin decided occupational issues. FDR decided to go for a fourth term and was convinced Harry Truman would be a better running mate than Henry Wallace. In the 1944 election, Democrats FDR and Harry Truman defeated Republicans Thomas E. Dewey and John Bricker in both the electoral and popular votes. FDR was the only person to have been elected president four times. The Democrats controlled Congress. In his twelve years as president, FDR had appointed eight associate U.S. Supreme Court justices. On April 12, 1945, FDR died at age 63 in Warm Springs with Lucy at his side. Many historians consider FDR one of the best presidents due to his leading the country out of the Great Depression and winning the war against Germany and Japan. In 1941, the facial features of George Washington, Thomas Jefferson, Theodore Roosevelt, and Abraham Lincoln were engraved on Mount Rushmore in South Dakota.

HARRY S. TRUMAN *(33RD PRESIDENT) **1945-1953***

Truman was born on May 8, 1884, in Lamar, Missouri, to John and Martha Truman. Harry had two siblings and worked on his father's farm. He attended the University of Missouri and Kansas City Law School but graduated from neither. He was the first 20th century president without a college degree. Truman served as captain of an artillery unit in World War I. In 1919, he married his longtime friend Elizabeth "Bess" Wallace. They would go on to have one child. In 1922, Truman served as supervisor

APPENDIX E

of buildings and roads in Jackson County. Working his way up, he was elected to the U.S. Senate in 1934. Before the 1944 election, President FDR decided Vice President Henry Wallace had to be dropped from the ticket, and he selected Senator Harry Truman. They defeated Republicans Thomas Dewey and John Bricker in both the electoral and popular votes. In 1945, following a meeting of FDR, Churchill, and Stalin in Yalta to discuss the Allied countries' occupation of Germany, FDR went to Warm Springs, Georgia to relax. There, on April 12, 1945, FDR died from a stroke. Truman got a phone call telling him to go the White House. There he was told of FDR's death and his own presidency. He had only met FDR twice. On May 7, 1945, Germany surrendered. But Japan fought on, so Truman was briefed on the plan to attack Japan. When he learned some 100,000 Americans would lose their lives in a land invasion, Truman ordered the use of the atomic bomb. On August 6, 1945, it was dropped on Hiroshima. When Japan failed to surrender, a second atomic bomb was dropped, this time on Nagasaki. On September 2, 1945, Japan surrendered on the battleship *Missouri*. General Douglas MacArthur was put in charge of the Japanese government. Truman knew he needed someone to give him honest advice on various issues, so he selected John Steelman, whom he had worked with in the Senate. Steelman took the job on December 12, 1946, and held it until Truman left office on January 20, 1953. This job was later named Chief of Staff. In late January 1945, after a four-week strike, some 750,000 steel workers settled for more pay after Truman seized the steel mills. Later the U.S. Supreme Court ruled that Truman was wrong in taking over the steel mills, and some 440,000 coal miners involuntarily settled a strike in two months for more pay. The 1948 Democratic Convention settled on Harry Truman rather than Henry Wallace or Strom Thurmond for president. In the 1948 election, Truman and Barkley defeated Republicans Thomas Dewey and Earl Warren in both the electoral and popular votes. Their victory was viewed as an upsetting surprise. Before the official announcement, the *Chicago Tribune* published a paper with the headline, "Dewey Defeats Truman." Truman waived the erroneous headline to the public. Truman had been elected president and Barkley had been elected vice president. The Democrats had regained control of the Senate and the House. In 1949, Congress increased the annual pay of the president to $100,000 from 1909's $75,000, and the pay of the vice president was increased to $30,000 from 1909's $20,000. Following his 1949 inauguration, Truman left the White House and moved across the street to the Blair House in order to have the White House renovated. The 62 rooms were expanded to 132 at a cost of $6 million over two years. On November 1, 1950, two Puerto Rican nationalists were unsuccessful in assassinating President Truman. That same year, Senator McCarthy began his attack on the State Department, reporting they hired communists. The Korean War began on June 25, 1950, as 90,000 North Korean troops invaded South Korea. Calling it a "police action," not a war, American troops started their advance only to have Chinese troops enter the action on October 25, 1950. In 1950, the U.S. population exceeded 150 million. The 22nd Amendment to the U.S. Constitution was ratified on February 7, 1951. It limited presidents to two four-year terms of office. Truman could have run for another term because he was grandfathered by the 22nd Amendment, but he chose to retire on January 20, 1953, when his term of office ended. He died on December 26, 1972, at the age of 88.

DWIGHT D. EISENHOWER *(34ᵀᴴ PRESIDENT) 1953-1961*

Eisenhower was born on October 14, 1890, in Denison, Texas, to David and Ida Eisenhower. He grew up in Abilene, Kansas, with five brothers, and all attended local schools. He quickly was given the nickname Ike. To help his mother, he learned how to be a good cook. He also helped his father in his general store. A sports injury in his freshman year in high school required him to repeat his freshman year. Seeing a military academy was a way to get a free college education, he applied to and was accepted into West Point. Ike graduated 61st in a class of 1,264 in 1915. World War I had ended, so he was assigned to a fort in Texas. There he met and married Mamie Doud in 1916. They would go on to have two sons, but one died at the age of three. After several years, Ike got a spot in the general staff school. After graduation, he worked several years under General John Pershing before being assigned Chief of Staff for General Douglas MacArthur in 1939. His next assignment was Chief of Staff for Army Five-Star General George Marshall, who assigned Ike the task of developing a strategy to defeat the Japanese after they bombed Pearl Harbor in 1941. Ike was then promoted to a two-star general and put in charge of planning Operation Overlord, the landing of troops in Europe. He was given a personal driver, former model Kay Summersby. Working long hours together led to love. With his success in Europe, Ike was promoted to a five-star general and put in charge of European troops. When the war was over, he wanted to bring Kay to America and divorce Mamie. But Marshall told Ike if he did, they would be booted out of the army. So, in 1950, he returned to America without Kay and became president of Columbia University. In 1952, Ike accepted the Republican nomination for president with Richard Nixon as his vice president. In the 1952 election, the two defeated Democrats

Adlai Stevenson and John Sparkman in both the electoral and popular votes. Following his army experience, Ike formally created the position of Chief of Staff to the president. He selected New Hampshire Governor Sherman Adams. In his first term of office, Ike is credited with being the first president to create the position of Chief of Staff. Ike added a new Secretary of Health, Education, and Welfare to his cabinet. Ike enjoyed cooking and was probably the all-time best president cook. Grilling was his specialty. And he played golf whenever he could. He was the first president to have a hole in one. Since his work schedule limited his golf time, he installed a putting green behind the White House. And he spent his vacation time at the master's course in Atlanta. He also renamed the president's retreat Camp David. FDR had named it Shangri-la. In 1953, Ralph Ellison won a National Book Award for *Invisible Man*. And in 1954, Ike added "one nation under God" to the Pledge of Allegiance and "In God We Trust" to U.S. currency and Elvis Presley launched a singing career. In 1955, Disneyland opened in Anaheim, California. In the 1956 election, Republicans President Dwight D. Eisenhower and Vice President Richard Nixon defeated Democrats Adlai E. Stevenson and Estes Kefauver in both the electoral and popular votes. In 1959, Xerox introduced the 914 Copier, called that because it copied on nine-inch by fourteen-inch paper. In 1960, the Russians shot down Gary Powers's U-2 spy plane, leading to the cancellation of a Paris Summit. Powers was later released in exchange for a captured Russian spy. In 1960, the U.S. population approached 180 million. Ike was disappointed when John F. Kennedy defeated Richard Nixon in the 1960 election. Ike and Mamie left for their farm near Gettysburg. Following his leaving the White House, Gallup polls identified Ike as being admired and respected for his military career and presidency. He died at age 78 on March 28, 1969.

JOHN F. KENNEDY *(35ᵀᴴ PRESIDENT) 1961-1963*

Kennedy was born on May 29, 1917, in Brookline, Massachusetts, to Joseph and Rose Kennedy. John, known to his friends as either Jack or JFK, was the second of nine children. Among the mantras of his father were, "Win at all costs," "Complaining is strictly prohibited," and "To whom much is given, much is expected." The family moved around Boston until settling in **Hyannis Port** on Cape Cod, Massachusetts. JFK was educated in private schools before entering Harvard. A football injury at Harvard gave him back pain for the rest of his life. A speed reader, JFK graduated from Harvard in 1940. In 1938, the family moved to England, where his father was appointed U.S. Ambassador to the country. JFK's older brother, Joe Jr., was a pilot and was killed at the beginning of World War II. Jack entered the Navy Reserve and was called up and put in charge of the patrol boat PT-109 in the Pacific. In 1943, his boat was cut in half by a Japanese destroyer. He was rescued and was the first president-to-be to receive a "Purple Heart." In 1946, JFK was elected to the U.S. House of Representatives. After serving three terms, he met Jacqueline Bouvier, and they were married in 1953. They went on to have three children. In 1951, Jack was elected to the U.S. Senate. In 1957, JFK became the first president-to-be to receive a Pulitzer Prize. It was for the book *Profiles in Courage* which he wrote while recovering from an operation. It is the story of risks taken by eight senators. In the 1960 Democratic Convention, Kennedy was nominated for president and Senate Majority Leader Lyndon Johnson was named his running mate. In the 1960 election, the two defeated Republicans Richard Nixon and Henry Cabot Lodge in both the electoral and popular votes. Kennedy had been elected president and Johnson had been elected vice president. The election had been preceded by four televised debates which the poised and articulate JFK had won. JFK was the first Roman Catholic president and, at age 43, was the youngest elected president and the first president born in the 20th century. Kennedy deleted the Postmaster General position from his cabinet because U.S. mail no longer had a monopoly on mail delivery. President Eisenhower and President Kennedy were very different. Eisenhower was a highly organized extrovert. Kennedy was a disorganized, indecisive introvert. In his inaugural speech, Kennedy challenged America, stating, "Ask not what your country can do for you, ask what you can do for your country." Kennedy had an active travel schedule. In 1961 in Germany, he stated, "Ich bin ein Berliner," not knowing he had said he was a pastry. In 1962, astronaut John Glenn made three orbits around Earth. Soon after, JFK announced that before the end of the decade, we would land on the moon. Later in the year, JFK learned that the Russians were building nuclear missile sites in Cuba. He invoked the Monroe Doctrine and ordered the dismantling of the sites. Six days later, the missiles were on their way back to Russia. On November 22, 1963, JFK and Jackie rode with Texas Governor Connally and his wife in a Dallas motorcade when three shots rang out and JFK was mortally wounded. He died 25 minutes later in a Dallas hospital. Former Marine sniper Lee Harvey Oswald was arrested and then shot and killed by night club owner Jack Ruby. JFK's body and Jackie were put on Air Force One, where Vice President Johnson was sworn in as the 36th president. It was the second time a president was not sworn in by a U.S. Supreme Court Chief Justice. The first time was Calvin Coolidge in 1923. JFK's body was taken to the Capitol Building to lie on the Lincoln catafalque. Representatives from 92 countries and thousands of people paid their respects as they passed the closed casket. After the viewing, the body was taken to Arlington National Cemetery, where Jackie lit an eternal flame as fifty planes flew overhead, missing the lead plane, and riflemen fired a 21-gun salute as a bugler played "Taps." On September 24, 1964, the Warren Commission, named after U.S. Supreme Court Justice Earl Warren, having interviewed 900 persons, reported that Lee Harvey Oswald was the lone assassin. Three shots, six seconds, and one gunman? Not everyone believed that conclusion. But JFK was the first to receive the Presidential Medal of Freedom, posthumously. In 1968, Jackie married billionaire Aristotle Onassis. She died at age 64 on May 19, 1994.

LYNDON B. JOHNSON (36TH PRESIDENT) 1963-1969

Johnson was born on August 27, 1908, in a farmhouse in Stonewall, Texas, to Samuel and Rebekah Baines Johnson. Lyndon had four siblings and was known by his initials, LBJ. His grandparents were early Texas settlers and had built a large cattle ranch. LBJ grew up on that ranch. He was home-schooled until he entered high school. After graduation in 1924, LBJ went through a number of jobs before going to Texas State Teachers College. After graduation in 1930, he took classes at Georgetown University Law School in 1934. That same year married Claudia "Lady Bird" Taylor. LBJ called her "the steel magnolia" because she was ambitious, determined, and focused. JFK called the two "Uncle Capone and his little Pork Chop." They went on to have two daughters. She recorded everything she did in a daily diary. After graduation, LBJ served as the director of the National Youth Administration. In 1937, he was elected to the House of Representatives and Lady Bird went with him to Washington, D.C. Following the attack on Pearl Harbor, LBJ enlisted in the U.S. Navy. After the war, he returned to his House seat and then was elected to the U.S. Senate from 1949-1960.

The last of those five years, he was the majority leader. Then he was asked to be Jack Kennedy's vice-presidential candidate. They won the 1960 election, defeating Republicans Richard Nixon and Henry Cabot Lodge. Johnson assumed the presidency with the death of President Kennedy on November 22, 1963. He was sworn in on Air Force One with the widowed Jacqueline Kennedy on board. LBJ was sworn in by District Judge Sarah Hughes, as no U.S. Supreme Court Justice was available. Hughes is the only woman to have sworn in a president. LBJ was the fourth president to come into office following the assassination of a president (Lincoln, Garfield, and McKinley preceded him). He was the third president to have served in the four key elected federal offices, namely representative, senator, vice president, and president (John Tyler and Andrew Johnson preceded him). LBJ went through five chiefs of staff: Walter Jenkins, Bill Moyers, Jack Valenti, Marvin Watson, and James Jones. In 1963, LBJ appointed Arthur Goldberg to the U.S. Supreme Court. LBJ fought a war on poverty and established a Great Society featuring both civil and voting rights. He was also very promiscuous, having sex with a number of women in many places, including the White House. For the 1964 election, LBJ chose Senator Hubert Humphrey as his vice president. Avoiding having to explain why he did not choose Attorney General Bobby Kennedy, LBJ announced cabinet members were not reliable for the vice-presidential position. In the election, Democrats Lyndon Johnson and Hubert Humphrey easily defeated Republicans Barry Goldwater and William Miller in both the electoral and popular votes. In Miranda vs Arizona, the U.S. Supreme Court ruled in 1966 that criminal suspects must be informed of their rights before being questioned by the police. In the 1966 midterms, the Democrats held control of the Senate 64-36 and the House 247-187. In March 1968, LBJ announced on television he would not seek reelection that year. He left office on January 20, 1969, and returned to his ranch with his wife. LBJ died at age 64 on January 22, 1973. LBJ received the Presidential Medal of Freedom posthumously in 1980 from President Carter.

RICHARD M. NIXON *(37ᵀᴴ PRESIDENT) 1969-1974*

Nixon was born on January 9, 1913, in Yorba Linda, California, to Frank and Hannah Nixon. Richard had four siblings and was raised in a poor, devout Quaker household. Nixon did well in school, graduating first in high school. After school, Richard worked on a roadside farm stand and at a gas station. He was an accomplished piano and violin player. After high school, he was accepted into Harvard, but the family did not have enough money for his tuition, so Richard went to nearby Whittier College and paid his tuition and other expenses by working while attending school. He graduated second in a class of eighty-five in 1934. He received a scholarship to go to Duke University Law School, graduating third in a class of twenty-five in 1937, and then opened a law practice. In 1940, he married former model Thelma "Patricia" Ryan. They went on to have two daughters. In 1942, Nixon joined the U.S. Navy, rising to the rank of lieutenant commander before leaving the service at the end of the war. He was then elected to the U.S. House of Representatives. As a member of the House of Un-American Activities Committee he led the investigation into State Department official Alger Hiss and writer Whittaker Chambers. This work gave Nixon national recognition, leading to a 1950 U.S. Senate seat. When it was revealed, he had received the gift of a dog named Checkers (which he gave to one of his daughters), only an impassioned speech by him kept him on as the vice-presidential candidate of Dwight Eisenhower. In the 1952 election, Dwight Eisenhower and Richard Nixon defeated Democrats Adlai Stevenson and Estes Kefauver in both the electoral and popular votes. Unable to seek a third term, Eisenhower was replaced with Nixon in the 1960 election. Henry Cabot Lodge was Nixon's running mate. They were defeated by Democrats John Kennedy and Lyndon Johnson in both the electoral and popular votes. Then Nixon moved to New York City to set up a law practice. Because of Nixon's views on the need for law and order, he received the Republican nomination for president in the 1968 election. He chose Maryland Governor Spiro Agnew as his running mate. In the 1968 election, Republicans Richard Nixon and Spiro Agnew defeated Democrats Hubert Humphrey and Edmund Muskie in both the electoral and popular votes. Independent Party candidates George Wallace and Curtis LeMay ran a distant third. The Democrats still controlled Congress. Upon his being elected president, Congress increased Nixon's annual salary to $200,000 (up from 1949's $100,000) and Agnew's annual salary to $62,500 (up from 1964's $43,000). In 1969, Neil Armstrong and Buzz Aldrin were the first Americans to walk on the moon. The AFL and NFL merger took effect, forming the National Football League in 1969. New York City's One World Trade Center opened in 1970. Monday Night Football started in 1970 with Howard Cosell, Keith Jackson, and Don Meredith. Among the laws Nixon signed was the 1970 Economic Stabilization Act, which gave the president the authority to establish price and wage controls. In 1971, President Nixon commuted the prison sentence of teamster boss Jimmy Hoffa. Also in 1971, Steve Jobs and Steve Wozniak were introduced to one another. In the 1972 election, Republicans Richard Nixon and Spiro Agnew defeated Democrats George McGovern and Sargent Shriver in both the electoral and popular votes. After being elected, Nixon installed a one-lane bowling alley in the White House. Concerned about White House leaks of information, Nixon created a plumber's unit to find leakers and stop the leaks. The plumbers broke into the Democratic Headquarters in the Watergate Hotel on June 17, 1972, and they were caught. Special prosecutor Archibald Cox was assigned to investigate the break-in. Presidential aide Butterfield announced that there was a taping system in the White House. Nixon said the tapes were under executive privilege. Attorney General Richard Kleindienst resigned when Nixon asked him to fire Cox. Elliott Richardson took Kleindienst's place, but when Nixon asked him to fire Cox, Elliott also resigned and Acting Attorney General Robert Bork did fire Cox. Nixon appointed Leon Jaworski to replace Cox. It was the "Saturday Night Massacre" covered by *Washington Post* writers Carl Bernstein and Robert Woodward in their book *All the President's Men*. In 1972, *The Godfather* gave new meaning to the word "family." In January 1973, a peace treaty ended the war in Vietnam. It also ended the military draft. In April 1973, aides John Ehrlichman, H.R. Haldeman, and Charles Colson resigned, and White House counsel John Dean was fired by Nixon. Also in 1973, the U.S. Supreme Court in Roe vs Wade ruled that women had the right to an abortion. In October 1973, on the Jewish holiday of Yom Kippur, Egyptian and Syrian forces attacked Israel. The war was over in three weeks; Israel had won with U.S. help. On October 10, 1973, Spiro Agnew was charged with tax evasion, and he resigned his vice-presidency. Nixon appointed long-time Congressman Gerald Ford. In "Battle of the Sexes" in 1973, Billie Jean King defeated Bobby Riggs in tennis. In United States vs Nixon, the U.S. Supreme Court on July 24, 1974, ordered Nixon to turn over the audio tapes. Faced with being the first president removed from office by impeachment, Nixon decided to resign and did so on August 8, 1974. The family flew to Yorba Linda. Upon Nixon's resignation, Gerald Ford became the 38th president. He was the first man to be named the vice president and the president without being elected to either office. Nixon returned to his law practice and wrote eight books before dying in New York City on April 22, 1994, at the age of 81.

GERALD R. FORD *(38*TH *PRESIDENT) 1974-1977*

Ford was born on July 14, 1913, in Omaha, Nebraska, to Leslie Lynch and Dororthy Gardiner King. At birth, Ford's name was Leslie Lynch King, but his mother divorced her husband that year, and in 1919 she married Gerald Rudolph Ford. Leslie was given his new father's name. He had three younger half-brothers. Ford enjoyed sports and was a boy scout in 1921 and the first eagle scout to become president. He attended local schools and then went to the University of Michigan, where he was the center and a linebacker on the university's undefeated football team in 1932 and 1933. After graduation in 1935, Ford went to Yale University Law School. He graduated in 1941 and tried out for several pro-football teams. But he chose to do male modeling instead and was on the cover of *Cosmopolitan* magazine. At the beginning of World War II, Ford enlisted in the U.S. Navy as an officer. After the war, Ford went to Grand Rapids, Michigan, to practice law. He met and married Elizabeth "Betty" Bloomer Warren in 1948. They went on to have four children. Following surgery, Betty developed alcohol and drug dependencies and entered a rehab facility. In 1949, Ford was elected to the U.S. House of Representatives as a Republican and was re-elected 12 times. He was known to be a consensus builder. While serving as minority leader in the House, Ford was selected by Richard Nixon to replace the departing Spiro Agnew as Nixon's vice president. With Nixon's resignation on August 8, 1974, Ford became the 38th president. Ford was the first person to serve as both the vice president and the president without being elected to either position. On September 8, 1974, Ford pardoned Nixon for any federal crimes he committed. In April 1975, the Vietnam War ended. In November 1975, Ford approved the Halloween Massacre as six key people changed jobs. Steve Jobs and Steve Wozniak launched Apple I in 1976. And in the 1976 election, Republicans Gerald Ford and Robert Dole were defeated by Democrats Jimmy Carter and Walter Mondale. It was believed Ford's pardon of Nixon was a key factor in his defeat. In 1999, Ford received the Presidential Medal of Freedom from President Clinton. Ford died on December 26, 2006, at the age of 93.

JIMMY CARTER *(39TH PRESIDENT) 1977-1981*

Carter was born on October 1, 1924, in Plains, Georgia, to James and Lillian Carter. Jimmy was the first president born in a hospital. He is the oldest of three siblings. His job was to feed the pigs, milk the cows, and pick the peanuts. His dad was the disciplinarian, and his mother was the friendly supporter. Jimmy attended local schools and got good grades, partially because of being able to read 2,000 words a minute. He went to the U.S. Naval Academy in 1943 and graduated 50th in a class of 810 in 1945. Also in 1945, he married his longtime sweetheart, Eleanor Rosalynn Smith. They went on to have four children. Carter then went to submarine school, where he graduated 3rd in a class of 52 in 1952. A year later, he resigned his commission due to his father's death. Jimmy returned to Plains, Georgia, and took over his father's peanut business. He became active in local and state politics and in 1970 was elected governor of Georgia. Later, he won the Democratic nomination for president with Walter Mondale as his vice president. In the 1976 election, Democrats

Jimmy Carter and Walter Mondale defeated Republicans Gerald Ford and Robert Dole in both the electoral and popular votes. Jimmy Carter was the second person to walk from the inauguration to the White House, Thomas Jefferson was the first. The key staff in Carter's administration were press aide Jody Powell, political strategist Hamilton Jordon, Chief of Staff Jack Watson, best friend Bert Lance, and wife Rosalynn. Carter deleted the cabinet position of Health, Education, and Welfare. He added the Secretary of Health and Human Services, the Secretary of Education, and the Secretary of Energy. Jimmy's biggest achievement was getting Israeli Prime Minister Menachem Begin and Egyptian President Anwar Sadat to sign a peace treaty in 1979, after a war between both nations. Jimmy's biggest failure was not getting 52 hostages released from Iran. In the 1980 election, Democrats Jimmy Carter and Walter Mondale were defeated by Republicans Ronald Reagan and George Bush in both the electoral and popular votes. Polls showed that the public liked Jimmy personally but not politically because he was a micro-manager. After leaving the White House, Jimmy and Rosalynn started Habitat for Humanity. In 1999, Carter received the Presidential Medal of Freedom from President Clinton. In 2002, he received the Nobel Peace Prize for promoting social justice. Jimmy Carter was the longest-living former president in United States history dying on December 29, 2024, at the age of 100. Rosalynn died on November 19, 2023, at age 96 having been married to Jimmy for 77 years.

RONALD REAGAN *(40*TH *PRESIDENT) 1981-1989*

Reagan was born on February 6, 1911, in Tampico, Illinois, to John and Nellie Wilson Reagan. Ronald had an older brother. Ronald taught himself to read. He learned the value of ambition and hard work from his father and the value of dreams and prayers from his mother. Ronald was a voracious reader. He went to high school and was a drum major for the school band. He was also a lifeguard and over seven years saved over 75 lives before going on to the small Eureka College. Reagan's interests were acting and athletics. He played football and was captain of the swimming team. He was also president of the student council. Reagan graduated in 1932 and got a job as a radio sports announcer in Davenport, Iowa. He met a movie agent who got him a screen test with Warner Brothers, who signed him to a seven-year contract for $200 a week. In 1940, he married actress Jane Wyman. They went on to have two children. When the war started in 1941, he made training films for the army. In 1947, he joined the Screen Actors Guild and soon became president of the Guild, testifying before Congress on communist infiltration into the movie industry. There he met actress Nancy Davis. After Reagan divorced Wyman, he and Nancy were married. They appeared together in several movies. They had two children together. In 1950, Ronald switched from movies to television, doing the *General Electric Theater* for eight years. In the early 1960s, he was the host on *Death Valley Days*. By then, he had switched from being a Democrat to being a Republican. Friends convinced him to go into politics, and he became governor of California in 1967. He then did a five-minute daily radio program from 1975 to 1979. Also in 1979, days before the election, 52 Americans were taken hostage in the American Embassy in Iran, and Reagan declared his candidacy for president. In 1980, he won the Republican endorsement for president. In the 1980 election, Republicans Ronald Reagan and George H.W. Bush defeated Democrats Jimmy Carter and Walter Mondale in both the electoral and popular votes. Within minutes of his inaugural address, Iran released the hostages.

Three men headed Reagan's staff: James Baker, Michael Deaver, and Ed Meese. Wife Nancy was also a valuable asset. In 1981, Reagan fulfilled a campaign promise and appointed a woman to the U.S. Supreme Court, Sandra Day O'Connor. Also in 1981, the American Embassy in Beirut, Lebanon was bombed. In the 1984 election, Republicans President Ronald Reagan and Vice President George H.W. Bush defeated Democrats Walter Mondale and Geraldine Ferraro in both the electoral and popular votes. Ferraro was the first woman from a major party to run on a presidential ticket. In 1987, Reagan stood by the Brandenburg Gate in Berlin and shouted, "Mr. Gorbachev, tear down this wall." Because of their trusting relationship, Gorbachev and Reagan were able to dramatically reduce the number of missiles in their countries. Reagan followed the advice of wife Nancy: "trust but verify." In 1994, Reagan announced he had Alzheimer's and retired from public life. He died on June 5, 2004, at the age of 93. When George Bush the 43rd president gave Reagan the Presidential Medal of Freedom in 1993, he was the first living former president to receive the award.

GEORGE H.W. BUSH *(41ST PRESIDENT) 1989-1993*

George Herbert Walker Bush was born on June 12, 1924, in Milton, Massachusetts, to Prescott and Dorothy Walker Bush. HW was named after his grandfather, a prominent, wealthy investment banker. Father Prescott was also a prominent wealthy person and a Republican U.S. senator for over ten years. HW was known as "Pop" to his children and "Grampy" to his grandchildren. HW had four siblings and went to private schools until he enlisted in the U.S. Navy in 1942. Before his 19th birthday, he graduated from the Navy aviator program, making him the youngest to do so. On his 58th mission, his plane was shot down by the Japanese. HW was rescued but his two companions were not. In 1945, HW married Barbara Pierce. They would go on to have six children, including the future 43rd president. HW then enrolled in Yale University and was captain of the school's baseball team which won the college world series twice. After graduation, HW moved the family to Odessa, Texas, where he founded an oil company. In 1966, he was elected to the U.S. House of Representatives and later served as Ambassador to the United Nations, Chairman of the Republican Party, Envoy to China, and Director of the CIA. In the 1980 election, HW was elected Ronald Reagan's vice president and HW was re-elected vice president in the 1984 election. In the 1988 election, HW was elected president along with Dan Quayle as his vice president. HW added the position of Veteran Affairs to his cabinet. In 1989, he stated, "Read my lips. No new taxes." Regrettably, he later had to pass a new tax law in order to reduce the federal deficit. The Berlin Wall fell in 1989. In 1990, the U.S. led a coalition of countries to drive Iraq out of Kuwait and in 1991, got a victory in Iraq. The Cold War ended in 1992. In the 1992 election, Democrats Bill Clinton and Al Gore defeated Republicans President George H.W. Bush and Vice President Dan Quayle in both the electoral and popular votes. Many said the defeat was due to the "Read my lips" statement. Queen Elizabeth knighted HW in 2009. Bush received the Presidential Medal of Freedom in 2011 from President Obama. After leaving office, HW made six parachute jumps, the last at age 90. After years of medical problems, he died at age 93, in April 2018.

WILLIAM J. CLINTON *(42ND PRESIDENT) 1993-2001*

Clinton was born William Jefferson Blythe on August 29, 1946, in Hope, Arkansas, to William and Virginia Blythe. William's father died three months after he was born. Since his father had been married prior to Virginia, William had a half-brother and half-sister. William's mother left him with his grandparents. Later, she married Roger Clinton when William was four years old. At age 16, he was formally adopted by Roger, giving William the name Clinton. In high school, William did well, as he was a speed reader with high retention. Deciding to learn more about government, Clinton interned for Senator William Fulbright. Following a degree from Georgetown University, Clinton won a Rhodes Scholarship and went to Oxford University. After three years, he returned to the United States and enrolled in Yale Law School, where he met Hillary Rodham. Both graduated, and they were married in 1975. He enjoyed a wide variety of foods but was unable to eat chocolate because he was allergic to it. He taught law at the University of Arkansas before becoming governor of the state in 1978. That same year, he began a multi-year affair with nightclub performer Gennifer Flowers. But he had to clean up his act in order to be successful in politics. In 1992, Bill and Hillary appeared on the *60 Minutes* TV show, where he denied the Flowers affair. In the 1992 election, Democrats Bill Clinton and Al Gore defeated Republicans George H.W. Bush and Dan Quayle in both the electoral and popular votes. In 1994, Paula Jones filed a sexual harassment suit against Clinton for actions taken while he was the Arkansas governor. He also had to respond to the Travelgate investigation. In the 1996 election, Democrats President Bill Clinton and Vice President Al Gore defeated Republicans Robert Dole and Jack Kemp in both the electoral and popular votes. As his second term began, a story was leaked about Clinton's affair with White House intern Monica Lewinsky. In January 1998, Clinton looked into a TV camera and said, "I did not have sexual relations with that woman." In his view, oral sex was not sexual contact. The U.S. House of Representatives impeached Clinton in December 1998 on charges of perjury and obstruction of justice. But the Senate failed to find him guilty. Clinton was the second president to face impeachment. Andrew Johnson was the first. The 1933 Glass-Steagall Act was repealed, allowing banks to buy and sell insurance and stocks. It also permitted insurance companies' entry into banks. Clinton's last year in office ended with an annual surplus of $160 billion, resulting in a projected total surplus of $5 trillion. After leaving office, he went on to publish his memoirs and campaign for wife Hillary in her political endeavors. Clinton received the Presidential Medal of Freedom in 2013 from President Obama.

GEORGE W. BUSH *(43ʳᴰ PRESIDENT) 2001-2009*

Bush was born on July 6, 1946, in New Haven, Connecticut, to George H.W. Bush. His father was attending Yale University when his son was born, having served as a Navy pilot during World War II. G.H.W. graduated from Yale in 1948 and moved his family to Midland, Texas, where he took a job selling supplies to oil drilling companies. Son George had four siblings. He attended a private school in Houston, then the Philips Academy in Andover, Massachusetts, and then went to Yale University. Graduating in 1968, he returned to Texas and joined the Texas Air National Guard, where he flew fighter jets. Honorably discharged in 1974, he enrolled at Harvard University and received an MBA in 1975. He returned to Houston, where he enjoyed attractive women and fast cars. He met schoolteacher Laura Welch. After dating for three months, they were married in 1977. They went on to have twin daughters. George was the first president to have twins. George focused on his oil supply company until 1988, when he became an advisor to his father, who was running for president. Following his father's victory,

George returned to his company in Houston and invested in the Texas Rangers baseball team. In 1994, he was elected governor of Texas and served until 2000, when he was nominated as the presidential candidate by the Republican Party for the 2000 election. In that election, he and running mate Richard Cheney defeated Democrats Albert Gore and Joseph Lieberman in the electoral vote, but lost to them in the popular vote, with a difference of only five electoral votes between Bush and Gore, the victory was contested until it was finally confirmed five weeks after the election. Entering the White House with a $500 billion surplus, Bush quickly pushed through a massive tax cut favoring the wealthy. But the richest two percent, who earned 21 percent of total income, were paying 27.5% of all federal income taxes. On September 11, 2001, terrorists crashed two planes into the Twin Towers in New York City, another crashed in the Pentagon, and a fourth, taken over by passengers, crashed in Pennsylvania, over 3,000 were killed. Bush was in Florida when the crashes occurred, but he flew back to the White House for a televised speech. assuring Americans that he would conduct a war on terrorism. He followed it with an appearance at Ground Zero in New York. His popularity ratings soared. He identified Al-Qaeda head Osama bin Laden as the leader of the attack on America. Believing Osama was hiding in Afghanistan, Bush sent in troops and aircrafts crushing the Taliban extremists hiding Osama. In a 2002 State of the Union Address, Bush identified Iran, Iraq, and North Korea as the "Axis of Evil" and began building a case to overthrow Iraq's Saddam Hussein. In his 2003 State of the Union Address, Bush stated, "The British government has learned that Saddam Hussein recently sought significant quantities of uranium from Africa." This led to an invasion of Iraq and the capture of Hussein in December 2003. He was executed by hanging. In the election of 2004, President George

Bush and Vice President Richard Cheney defeated Democrats John Kerry and John Edwards in both the electoral and popular votes. Bush and Cheney had been reelected. Shortly after, Bush signed statements that America would fund the wars in Afghanistan and Iraq until he left the presidency. This would raise the total spending for Afghanistan to $200 billion and Iraq to $650 billion. Bush left office with a deficit of close to $400 billion, having inherited a surplus of some $500 billion. Because both he and his father had been president, the son identified his father as George the 41st and himself as George the 43rd, reflecting their queue in the presidential order. Key laws enacted during the 43rd's terms were the 2002 Sarbanes-Oxley Act, which tightened the financial reporting of companies, the 2003 Medicare Act, which introduced prescription drug benefits, and the 2007 Fair Minimum Wage Act, which increased the federal minimum wage. In retirement at his ranch in Texas, George the 43rd wrote *Decision Points*, which focused on key decisions he made during his life. It sold over two million copies.

BARACK OBAMA *(44*TH *PRESIDENT) 2009-2017*

Obama was born on August 4, 1961, in Honolulu, Hawaii, to Barack Sr. and Stanley Ann Obama. His father was born and raised in Kenya, Africa, and graduated from Nairobi College and the University of Hawaii. The son had one half sibling from his father's earlier marriage. His parents got divorced, and his mother remarried Lolo Soetoro, a student from Indonesia. After the marriage, the family moved to Indonesia, where Barack learned the language while also taking a correspondence course in English. The parents divorced in 1971, Ann and the two children returned to Hawaii. When Barack graduated from high school in 1979, Ann returned to Indonesia and left the two children with her parents. Barack went to Occidental College in Los Angeles and Columbia University in New York City. He graduated in 1983 with a bachelor's degree and moved to Chicago to become a community organizer. After a brief return to Kenya, Barack entered Harvard Law School. Graduating magna cum laude in 1991, he was the first African American to head the prestigious Harvard Law Review. He returned to Chicago and joined the law firm of Sidley & Austin. There he met Michelle Robinson, also a graduate of Harvard Law School. They got married in 1992 and went on to have two children. In 1997, Barack was elected a state senator in Illinois. In 2004, he was a keynote speaker at the Democratic Presidential Convention. This led to his election as a U.S. senator from Illinois, followed by being selected as the Democratic candidate for president in the 2008 election. Obama chose Delaware Senator Joe Biden for his running mate. In the 2008 election, Democrats Barack Obama and Joe Biden defeated Republicans John McCain and Sarah Palin in both the electoral and popular votes. Obama became the first African American president. He was also the first president born outside of the lower 48 states. President Obama's first priority was to stimulate the economy. He got Congress to pass several key acts, which he signed. He also got money for loans to automakers and financial institutions to aid in their recovery. Obama also presided over the largest government expansion in decades. His actions led to his being criticized on a number of fronts. In 2009, he was the fourth president to receive the Nobel Peace Prize for his efforts to strengthen international diplomacy, Theodore Roosevelt, Woodrow Wilson, and Jimmy Carter were earlier recipients. In 2010, Obama signed the landmark Dodd-Frank Wall Street Reform and Consumer Protection Act, which in 2,300 pages imposed some 400 regulations on the financial systems of the U.S. economy. The other notable law in 2010 was the March 23rd signing of the Patient Protection and Affordable Care Act, which introduced the long-awaited national health insurance coverage of phased in medical benefits. On May 2, 2011, the terrorist leader Osama bin Laden was found and killed in a compound in Pakistan by 24 Navy Seals. Later in 2011, Obama announced the war in Iraq was over. The under-protected U.S. Embassy in Benghazi, Libya, was attacked by Islamic terrorists on September 11, 2012. In the 2012 election, Democrats President Barack Obama and Vice President Joe Biden defeated Republicans Mitt Romney and Paul Ryan in both the electoral and popular votes. In his January 2013 State of the Union Address, it was important to fix the economy; the country was in a recession. In 2015, Cuba and the United States reestablished formal relations. Also in 2015, a nuclear treaty was signed with Iran and the Paris Accord was signed by 190 countries to lower greenhouse gas emissions. At the Democratic Convention in 2016, former Secretary of State Hillary Clinton and U.S. Senator Tim Kaine were nominated to be the presidential and vice-presidential candidates. At the Republican Convention, Donald Trump and Michael Pence were nominated to be the presidential and vice-presidential candidates. During his two terms of office, President Obama signed 145 executive orders creating new regulations, and eight of the largest federal deficits occurred, America lost its AAA credit rating for the first time in history. Thousands of veterans died awaiting care in veteran hospitals. A lack of foreign policy experience led to some questionable Obama actions, (such as returning to England a bust of Winston Churchill that had been in the Oval Office), and on his final day in office he gave out 330 commutations (setting the record for the most in a single day), for a total of 1,715 during his presidency (more than all of his predecessors).

DONALD J. TRUMP *(45ᵀᴴ PRESIDENT) 2017-2021*

Trump was born on June 14, 1946, in Queens, New York City, to Frederick and Anne Trump. Donald's father was a wealthy real estate developer whose focus was on modest housing in Queens. Donald had two brothers. His father often took his three sons to work so they could learn about property development. After public school, Donald was sent to the New York Military Academy near West Point. There he learned discipline, how to promote himself, and the importance of achieving self-defined goals. Later, he attended Fordham University for two years before going to the Wharton School of Finance at the University of Pennsylvania. He graduated in 1968 and joined his father in business. In 1971, his father signed the business over to Donald. He renamed it the Trump Organization and focused on building skyscrapers in Manhattan for business companies. In 1973, the Department of Justice charged the Trump Organization with discriminating against African Americans, thereby violating the Fair Housing Act of 1968. Trump denied the charges and signed a consent decree ending the issue without admitting guilt. After years of dating beautiful women, Trump married Ivana Zelnickova in 1977. They went on to have three children. In 1978, Donald bought the Commodore Hotel, refurbished it, and renamed it the Grand Hyatt. He then built the Trump Tower with its luxury apartments. As the country was moving into a recession, Donald used the opportunity to buy up property in Manhattan and New Jersey. In 1987, with help from a ghost writer, Trump wrote *The Art of the Deal*. In 1988, he bought and refurbished the Plaza Hotel, followed by three casinos in Atlantic City. Having divorced Ivana in 1992, he married Marla Maples in 1993. They would have one daughter. In 1997, he published *The Art of the Comeback*. Having divorced Marla in 1999, Trump married Melania Knauss in 2004. They would have one son together. Also in 2004, Trump began hosting the TV show *The Apprentice*. Trump had two high-profile sex lawsuits. First, E. Jean Carroll accused Trump of raping her and was awarded $5 million. The second arose from a one-night stand with porn star Stormy Daniels. She was paid $130,000. In 2015, Trump announced he was running for president. He was one of seventeen Republican candidates. He built his campaign around "Make America Great Again." He borrowed President Reagan's "Let's Make America Great Again" and removed "let's." In 2016, the Democrats nominated Hillary Clinton and Tim Kaine for president and vice president. The Republicans nominated Donald Trump and Mike Pence for president and vice president. In the 2016 election, Trump and Pence defeated Clinton and Kaine in the electoral vote but lost to them in the popular vote. Nearly 100 million did not vote. Trump became one of the few elected presidents without serving in the military or being elected to any prior public office. The Republicans had control in both the U.S. Senate and in the House. In his first 30 days, Trump signed a flurry of executive orders reversing Obama's actions. Former Republican National Committee Chair Reince Priebus was Trump's first chief of staff. He was soon replaced by former general John Kelly. In the midterm elections, the Republicans increased their control of the Senate but lost the House. One of Trump's greatest achievements was reshaping the U.S. Supreme Court. He placed Neil Gorsuch, Brett Kavanaugh, and Amy Coney Barrett on the court, replacing retiring or dying justices. In January 2020, the first COVID-19 case was diagnosed in a person who had traveled to China. In December 2019, the House formally impeached President Trump for abuse of power and obstruction of Congress. The vote was 230 to 197 on abuse of power and 229 to 198 on obstruction. The impeachment papers were forwarded to the Senate to either convict or not. On February 5, 2020, the Senate voted 48 to 52 to convict on abuse of power and 47 to 53 to convict on obstruction of Congress. The impeachment fell short of the two-thirds required majority. Republican Mitt Romney was the only Republican who voted to convict on abuse of power. Later in 2020, Trump announced a $25 billion bailout of the airline industry. The Republican Party nominated Donald Trump and Mike Pence to be returned to the president and vice president positions. The Democratic Party nominated Joe Biden and Kamala Harris for the two positions. In the 2020 election, Biden and Harris defeated Trump and Pence in both the electoral and popular votes. Biden and Harris had been elected president and vice president, but the votes had to be verified by the Electoral College. President Trump stated the election had been stolen from him and asked his attorney general to contact the states he had lost and challenge the results. The U.S. Supreme Court took no action, but Trump did. He spoke before a rally and told attendees to go to the Capitol Building and stop the verification process. The result was that a crowd broke into the Capitol Building, but they were not successful in stopping the Electoral College count, and the election results were validated. Trump claimed Biden stole the election. But on January 13, 2021, with a vote of 232 to 197, the House of Representatives impeached President Trump for incitement of insurrection for the January 6th attack on the Capitol Building. Trump was the first U.S. president to be impeached twice. On February 13, 2021, the Senate voted 57 to convict and 43 not to convict. The vote fell short of the required two-thirds to convict. Upon leaving the presidency, Trump granted 143 pardons. Not staying for the inauguration, the Trumps flew to their Florida home, taking hundreds of classified documents with them. Later in the month, the FBI entered the Trump house and

APPENDIX E

left with fifteen boxes of classified material. On November 14, 2022, Trump announced he would run for a second non-consecutive presidential term. In June of 2023, Trump was charged with 31 counts of violating the Espionage Act. New York filed a charge that the payment to Stormy Daniels violated the election rules, and a jury found him guilty on 34 felony counts. The judge deferred sentencing until after the election. On June 27, 2024, Donald Trump and President Biden held a debate. Trump was energetic, while Biden was lethargic and never challenged Trump on his 30 misstatements. The debate was in an empty arena; there was no audience, only two interviewers. Not surprisingly, many wanted Biden to step down as president. Finally, he did and stated that his vice president, Kamala Harris, should be the Democratic candidate for the 47th president. She was the Democratic nominee, along with Tim Walz as her running mate. Trump went to Butler, Pennsylvania, and narrowly missed being assassinated by young Thomas Crooks, who shot at Trump several times from a nearby rooftop. One shot nicked Trump's ear. He went to the Republican Convention and received their nomination for president. J.D. Vance received the nomination for vice president. In September, the Secret Service captured a man with a rifle on Trump's golf course in West Palm Beach, Florida. Security increased after those assassination attempts as Trump continued on the campaign trail, emphasizing Harris's role in inflation problems and the unchecked flood of illegal immigrants. In the 2024 election, Republicans Donald Trump and J.D. Vance defeated Democrats Kamala Harris and Tim Walz to be elected president and vice president. They were victorious in both the electoral and popular vote. They were inaugurated on January 20, 2025.

JOSEPH R. BIDEN, JR. *(46ᵀᴴ PRESIDENT) 2021-2025*

Biden was born on November 20, 1942, in Scranton, Pennsylvania, to Joseph and Catherine Eugenia Biden. Joe was the oldest of four children. In 1954, the family moved to Delaware, where Joe went to a Catholic school and was active in class and on the football field. But he was teased because of a stutter. Over time, he solved this problem by reciting passages from a book with a mouthful of marbles. He graduated 506th in a class of 688 at the University of Delaware. Joe met teacher Neilia Hunter while on spring break in Nassau. When he discovered she was a teacher in Syracuse, New York, he enrolled in Syracuse University Law School. They got married in 1966 and moved to Wilmington, Delaware, where he practiced law, and had three children together. Joe was elected to the U.S. Senate in 1972. About a month after the election, Neilia and the three children were hit by a tractor trailer while Neilia was driving. She and their daughter Naomi were killed, but sons Beau and Hunter survived. Joe's 30th birthday was after the election but before inauguration, making him the youngest senator in history. Joe met Jill Jacobs in 1975, and they got married in the United Nations Chapel in 1977. Jill was a graduate of the University of Delaware and had a Master of Education degree from West Chester State College in 1981, the same year her daughter, Ashley, was born. She also received a Master of Arts in English from Villanova University in 1987 and then a Doctorate of Education from the University of Delaware in 2007. She was by far the best-educated First Lady when Joe became president. Joe served 36 years in the Senate, commuting daily by train to and from Wilmington and Washington. In the 2008 election, Democrats Barack Obama and Joe Biden defeated Republicans John McCain and Sarah Palin in both the electoral and popular votes. Biden was a consensus builder and was helpful in using his Senate contacts to get Obama's legislation through the Senate. He and Jill moved to the Naval Observatory, the official residence of the vice president. In March 2010, Biden watched while Obama signed into law the 2010 Patient Protection and Affordable Care Act – national health insurance. Obama succeeded where the Clintons had failed. As Obama was signing the Act into law, Biden was heard saying, "This is a big f—king deal." Biden very often put his foot in his mouth. President Obama once said, "Don't underestimate Joe's ability to f—k things up." And Obama did not always take Biden's advice. He advised the president not to seek and kill Osama bin Laden. On May 2, 2011, the president sent in several SEAL Team 6's to Osama's Pakistani compound, where they killed him. In the 2012 election, Democrats President Barack Obama and Vice President Joe Biden defeated Republicans Mitt Romney and Paul Ryan in both the electoral and popular votes. Son Hunter graduated from Yale University's Law School and went into lobbying and the Navy Reserve. In less than a year, he was discharged for cocaine use. Son Beau graduated from the University of Pennsylvania and went on to become attorney general of Delaware, but he came down with brain cancer and died in 2015. Only Hunter was left from Joe's first marriage. In 2017, Biden received the Medal of Freedom from President Obama. Biden was the first president to receive the award before becoming the president. In 2019, Hunter's laptop was found in a repair shop. It was seized by the FBI, and a copy of the contents became public. Hunter had financial dealings with foreign governments and was receiving money from them. What did he have to offer other than access to his father, the president? Hunter also became an artist, receiving sizable sums for his work. In early 2020, President Trump announced he and Pence were running for reelection. And Vice President Biden announced he sought the Democratic nomination for president and wanted Kamala Harris as his vice president. At the 2020 Democratic Convention, they were unanimously approved for president and vice president. In 2024, Kamala Harris received the Democratic presidential nomination, and Tim Walz received the vice-presidential nomination. At the 2024 Democratic Convention, Kamala Harris accepted the Democratic nomination for president of the United States. She covered three topics: her upbringing, her experience as vice president, and her policy agenda, which included reducing the everyday cost of everyone's needs and a meaningful tax cut. On August 24, 2024, the U.S. House of Representatives released a report from the Oversight and Ways and Means Committee that stated, "Overwhelming evidence demonstrates that President Biden participated in a conspiracy to monetize his office of public trust to enrich his family. The Biden family and their business associates received tens of millions of dollars from foreign interests, leading those interests to believe that such payments would provide access to influence with President Biden." The allegations were backed up by bank records, documents, and testimony. Contrast this report with the praise Biden received at the Democratic National Convention, where he was singled out as their greatest president of all time. From that point on, Biden was kept in the background by Harris in her campaign. Leading up to the election, Harris flip-flopped on energy, fracking, private health insurance, illegal border crossings, and price controls. On October 1, 2024, Republican Senator and Republican vice-presidential candidate J.D. Vance met Democratic Governor and Democratic vice-presidential candidate Tim Walz in a televised debate in New York City. The prime focus was differences on abortion and immigration. The view on who won the debate was mixed. But many believed Vance won, as Walz missed opportunities to correct Vance on his mistakes. General Mark Milley, whom Trump had picked to head up the Joint Chiefs of Staff, stated that Trump was "fascist to the core." The ultra conservative Heritage Foundation issued a 920-page document labeled Project 2025, in which Trump would reshape the federal government, eliminating personal freedom. On October 22nd, Trump's former Chief of Staff, John Kelly, said he believed Trump was a fascist. It should be remembered that Trump fired Kelly. Harris picked up on Kelly's remarks and said, "Donald Trump is out for unchecked power. He is an Adolf Hitler like person, loyal to himself, not our Constitution. He is unhinged, unstable, and given a second term there would be no one to stop him from pursuing his worst impulses." National polls going into the November 5th election showed Harris and Trump virtually tied. In the 2024 election, Democrats Kamala Harris and Tim Walz were defeated by Republicans Donald Trump and J.D. Vance in both the electoral and popular votes. Trump was elected president and Vance was elected vice president.

DONALD J. TRUMP *(47TH PRESIDENT) 2025-2029*

Following his defeat to Joe Biden in the 2020 election, Donald and his family returned to their home in Florida, taking with them cartons of classified information, assumedly for help in writing a book. The house was raided by the FBI and the documents taken.

On November 15, 2022, Trump announced he was running for president in 2024. There were two unsuccessful attempts on his life. In the 2024 election, Republicans Donald Trump and J.D. Vance received 312 electoral votes (more than the required minimum of 270) and roughly 77,000,000 popular votes versus 226 electoral votes and roughly 75,000,000 popular votes for Democrats Kamala Harris and Tim Walz. Trump was the elected president, and Vance was the elected vice president. But it was not official.

Special Counsel Jack Smith decided to drop all federal criminal charges against President-elect Donald Trump, including attempting to overthrow the 2020 presidential election and unlawfully retaining classified documents. The reason for the decision was that Justice Department policy prohibited the prosecution of a sitting president, even though Trump was president-elect and was not a sitting president until he was inaugurated on January 20th.

Comparing the 2024 election with the 2020 election, Donald Trump and J.D. Vance received 3 million more votes in 2024 than Donald Trump and Mike Pence in 2020. But Kamala Harris received 6.25 million fewer votes in 2024 than Joe Biden and Kamala Harris received in 2020.

After each state finalized the vote count, the information was sent to the appropriate state's governor, who then appointed the electors to the college. The total number of electors was equal to the number of senators and representatives for the state. On December 17th, the electors of each state met and cast their electoral votes for the president and the vice president. The sealed results were then sent to the U.S. Senate. It was to be received no later than the fourth Wednesday in December.

In accordance with the 20th Amendment to the U.S. Constitution, the terms of the senators and representatives ended at noon on the 3rd day of January 2025.

Kamala Harris, as the president of the Senate, presided over the count of the Electoral College on January 6, 2025. Strange that

APPENDIX E

Harris had to verify her own defeat, but that is how it reads in the U.S. Constitution. The framers of the Constitution never imagined the vice president would have run for president. If Trump had been defeated it would have been expected for him to object to this process. But he had not lost and on January 6, 2025, Harris announced that, having received 312 electoral votes, Donald Trump had become the 47th president of the United States, and J.D. Vance had become vice president.

When Republican Donald Trump defeated Democratic Vice President Kamala Harris in the 2024 election, Trump became the second president to serve two nonconsecutive terms. Grover Cleveland did it in 1884 and 1892.

Trump quickly identified his cabinet candidates and other key appointees. Some went through extensive questioning at Senate confidential hearings as Trump awaited Senate actions.

Trump's January 20, 2025 inauguration was held indoors reportedly due to bad weather. Security might also have been a factor, since there were earlier attempts on his life.

Trump announced that he would not make the mistakes he made in his first presidency. He also stated he wanted only people who were loyal to him and in agreement with his policies. One assumes they were also qualified for the position offered. He indicated his first priority was to select his cabinet secretaries and other key positions.

On the morning of January 20, 2025, President Trump and his wife Melania went to the White House for the traditional breakfast on the date of the inauguration between the outgoing president and his wife and the incoming president and his wife. Upon its conclusion, they left for the inauguration at the Capitol Building. Chief Justice John Roberts first swore James David

Vance into the oath of vice president. Roberts then administered the oath of office to Donald Trump.

Trump then delivered his presidential speech, focusing on how he would make America great again. When his speech ended, the Trumps and Vances, along with other key people, went to the White House. The Bidens left for their home in Delaware. At the White House, Trump signed a number of executive orders before joining the guests for an inauguration luncheon. That evening, the Trumps and Vances hosted several inauguration balls, and then the day ended, and the inauguration was over, and work on his second term begins.

If he achieves all he has set out to do, he should rank as one of America's greatest presidents and receive a Nobel Peace Prize as well.

§

Note: While every attempt was made to be accurate, you should not rely on the contents of this appendix without independently verifying their accuracy. This author apologizes for any inaccuracies.

APPENDIX F

ABOUT THE AUTHOR

Bruce Ellig was born on October 15, 1936, to Robert and Lucille Ellig in Manitowoc, Wisconsin. He is an only child. Ellig retired after more than 35 years of human resources experience with Pfizer, Inc. For the last 11 of those years, he served as corporate vice president with worldwide responsibility for the human resources function, reporting to the chairman and CEO of the company. During that period, he was also responsible for the company's executive compensation program, and served as secretary to the executive compensation committee of the board of directors. Drawing on over 50 years of executive compensation experience, Ellig is recognized as a noted author and speaker on the subject.

Ellig has authored 134 articles and 12 books. Although he has written extensively about various forms of pay, two of his books – *Evolution of Employee Pay and Benefits* and *American History's Impact on Employee Pay and Benefits* – place pay development within the framework of the U.S. presidents.

As a speaker, Ellig has addressed more than 400 organizations on human resources and compensation issues. He has been widely quoted on human resources matters in general, and on executive compensation issues in particular, throughout the world. Additionally, he has been interviewed on national radio and television programs.

Ellig served on several boards of directors and their compensation committees, both for-profit and not-for-profit, in addition to having served on several editorial review boards. He has also been a member of a long list of premier HR organizations and has assumed leadership positions in many of them, including serving as the Chairman of the National Board of Directors for the Society for Human Resource Management.

Ellig has received numerous honors (including several "Man of the Year" awards), as well as cherished lifetime achievement awards from WorldatWork (formerly the American Compensation Association) and the Society for Human Resource Management. He was also among the first to be elected to the National Academy of Human Resources.

He received the Distinguished Business Alumni Award from the University of Wisconsin, where he earned his BBA and MBA and was elected to the Beta Gamma Sigma and Phi Beta Kappa academic honor societies. Since graduating from the Business School, he has established two scholarship programs, a professorship, and a Distinguished Chair at the university.

Ellig has been listed in the prestigious *Marquis Who's Who in the East, Who's Who in Finance and Industry, Who's Who in America,* and *Who's Who in the World*. In 2024, *Who's Who* also identified him as the top distinguished professional among the over more than 500 named.

Index

#

9/11 *508, 509, 512, 518, 519, 520, 522, 523, 782*
49ers *108, 582*

A

abolitionist *124, 129, 136, 164, 733, 735*
Abu Ghraib *512*
Adams, Abigail *29, 66, 723*
Adams, Charles *110, 276*
Adams, Daniel *132*
Adams, John *iii, 4, 5, 6, 8, 12, 14, 16, 19, 25, 27, 28, 30, 31, 32, 36, 37, 40, 45, 64, 66, 68, 71, 115, 153, 172, 185, 223, 246, 264, 310, 333, 371, 394, 413, 438, 471, 506, 606, 656, 658, 667, 705, 715, 716, 718, 719, 723, 731, 737, 741*
  Birth
    October 30, 1735 *14*
  Cabinet
    Habersham, Joseph (Postmaster General) *30*
    Jefferson, Thomas (Vice President) *30*
    Lee, Charles (Attorney General) *30*
    McHenry, James (Secretary of War) *30*
    Pickering, Timothy (Secretary of State) *30*
    Stoddert, Benjamin (Secretary of the Navy) *30*
    Wolcott, Oliver (Secretary of the Treasury) *30*
  Career
    Ambassador, U.S. representative to England *26*
    Continental Congress, First, delegate to *26*
    Declaration of Independence, drafting and adoption *26*
    Law practice, early American lawyers *26*
    Vice presidency, first to become president *27*
  Death
    July 4, 1826 *32*
  Elections
    1796 Presidential Election (Elected President) *31*
  Family
    Adams, Abigail, John Quincy, Susanna, Charles, and Thomas (Children) *26*
    Adams John and Susanna Boylston (Parents) *14*
    Adams, Samuel (Cousin) *25*
    Elihu and Peter (Brothers) *14*
  Inauguration
    1797, inaugural address *28*
  Key Events
    Bank of Manhattan, formation of *33*
    France, attacks on American ships *32*
    Frigates, launch of USS United States and USS Constitution (Old Ironsides) *32*
    Marshall, John, appointment as Chief Justice *33*
    Marshall, John, recognized as Father of the American justice system *33*
    Pennsylvania Academy of the Fine Arts, founding of *33*
    Sedition Act *30*
    XYZ Affair *32*
  Laws
    1765 Stamp Act *26*
    Alien Act *29*
    Alien Enemies Act *30*
    Naturalization Act *30*
    Punishment of Certain Crimes Act *29*
    Revenue Act *30*
    Sedition Act *30*
    Slave Trade Act of 1800 *31*
  Marriage
    Smith, Abigail (Wife) *26*
  U.S. Supreme Court Rulings
    Bingham vs Cabot *29*
    Fowler vs Lindsey *30*
    Hollingsworth vs Virginia *29*
    Mossman vs Higginson *30*

Adams, John Quincy *iii*, *61*, *62*, *63*, *66*, *67*, *68*, *69*, *70*, *74*, *75*, *76*, *82*, *86*, *171*, *225*, *378*, *438*, *506*, *562*, *567*, *606*, *706*, *722*, *723*, *724*, *725*, *741*
  Birth
    July 11, 1767 *66*
  Cabinet
    Barbour, James (Secretary of War) *69*
    Calhoun, John (Vice President) *69*
    Clay, Henry (Secretary of State) *69*
    McLean, John (Postmaster General) *69*
    Rush, Richard (Secretary of the Treasury) *69*
    Southard, Samuel (Secretary of the Navy) *69*
    Wirt, William (Attorney General) *69*
  Career
    Law practice, in Boston *67*
    Minister to Russia, service as *67*
    Secretary of State, appointment under President Monroe *67*
    Transcontinental Treaty of 1819, negotiation of *67*
    Treaty of 1818, assistance with *67*
    Treaty of Ghent, negotiation of *67*
    U.S. Senate, service in *67*
    U.S. Senator, service as *67*
  Death
    February 23, 1848 *71*
  Elections
    1824 election (Elected President) *68*
  Family
    Abigail, Susanna, Charles, and Thomas (Siblings) *66*
    Adams, John and Abigail (Parents) *66*
    Quincy, John (Great Grandfather) *66*
  Inauguration
    1825, inaugural address *69*
  Key Events
    Baltimore and Ohio Railroad, construction of *72*
    Cooper, Fenimore, publication of The Last of the Mohicans *71*
    Democratic Party, formation of *72*
    Erie Canal, opening linking Hudson River with Lake Erie *71*
    New York City, abolition of slavery *71*
    Passenger railroad, first in the U.S., establishment of *72*
    Smithsonian Institution, opening of *71*
    U.S. and England, joint occupation of Pacific Northwest *71*
  Webster, Noah, publication of American Dictionary of the English Language *72*
  Laws
    Judiciary Act *69*
    Tarrif Act *69*
  Marriage
    Johnson, Louisa Catherine (Wife) *67*
  U.S. Supreme Court Rulings
    Ogden vs Saunders *69*
    United States vs The Antelope *68*
Adams, Samuel *25*, *667*
Adams, Sherman *312*, *331*, *337*, *766*
Admiral Howe *5*
Adventures of Tom Sawyer, The *169*
Afghanistan *434*, *436*, *441*, *509*, *520*, *539*, *569*, *586*, *607*, *610*, *625*, *632*, *782*, *783*
Agnew, Spiro Theodore *393*
agricultural drought *277*
Air Force One *322*, *364*, *371*, *405*, *509*, *768*, *770*
Alamo *81*, *725*
Ali, Muhammad *383*, *385*, *409*, *421*, *422*
American Civil Liberties Union *254*, *572*
American-Cuban relations *544*
American Party *118*, *127*
American Revolution *42*, *60*, *73*, *424*, *724*
Amistad *71*, *93*, *724*
Anderson, John *434*, *435*, *447*, *469*
Anheuser-Busch *169*, *523*, *556*
annual pay *61*, *77*, *123*, *163*, *226*, *229*, *275*, *334*, *395*, *417*, *450*, *452*, *453*, *456*, *457*, *458*, *472*, *473*, *474*, *475*, *488*, *492*, *493*, *495*, *507*, *618*, *621*, *715*, *764*
Antebellum *141*
Apache *169*, *196*
Appomattox *148*, *149*, *159*
Arafat, Yasser *488*
Arlington National Cemetery *239*, *261*, *768*
Arnold, Benedict *8*
Arthur, Chester A. *iv*, *178*, *179*, *180*, *181*, *183*, *184*, *185*, *186*, *187*, *188*, *189*, *218*, *219*, *223*, *264*, *310*, *371*, *394*, *405*, *413*, *471*, *708*, *743*, *744*, *745*, *751*, *758*
  Birth
    October 5, 1829 *183*
  Cabinet
    Blaine, James (Secretary of State) *185*
    Hunt, William (Secretary of the Navy) *185*
    James, Thomas (Postmaster General) *185*

INDEX

Kirkwood, Samuel (Secretary of the Interior) *185*
Lincoln, Robert Todd (Secretary of War) *185*
MacVeagh, Isaac Wayne (Attorney General) *185*
Windom, William (Secretary of the Treasury) *185*
Career
  Customs Collector, Port of New York appointment *184*
  Law practice, involvement in *184*
  New York State militia, enlistment in *184*
  New York State, service as Quartermaster General and Brigadier General *184*
  Teaching *184*
Death
  November 18, 1886 *189*
Elections
  1880 Presidential Election (Elected President) *185*
Family
  Ann Eliza, Jane, Malvina, Mary, Regina, and William (Siblings) *183*
  Arthur, Malvina and Reverend William (Parents) *183*
  Ellen, William, and Chester Jr. (Children) *184*
Inauguration
  1881, inaugural address *185*
Key Events
  Brooklyn Bridge, opening of *190*
  Dakota apartment building, opening in New York *190*
  Electric fan, invention of *190*
  Electric power station, first introduced in New York City *190*
  Financial markets, crash of *190*
  Geronimo, defeat of the Chiricahua Apaches led by *190*
  Immigration, annual arrivals tripled to 800,000 *190*
  Motorcycle, introduction by Daimler *190*
  Northern Pacific Railroad, beginning of operations *190*
  Pen, patent of self-inking design *190*
  Ringling Brothers Circus, first performance *190*
  Standard Oil Company, control of 90% of petroleum industry *189*
  Telephone service, inauguration between Chicago and New York *190*
  Telephone service, start between New York and Boston *190*

Time zones, establishment of standard in U.S. *190*
U.S. Mint, opening in Carson City, Nevada *190*
Laws
  1883 Mongrel Tariff Act *187*
  1883 Pendleton Act *187*
  Chinese Exclusion Act *186*
Marriage
  Herndon, Ellen (Wife) *184*
U.S. Supreme Court Rulings
  Ex parte Yarbrough *188*
  United States vs Harris *187*
Articles of Confederation *7, 8, 9, 48, 719*
Astor, John Jacob *46, 82, 240*
Atlantic City Boardwalk *167*
atomic bomb *310, 323, 340, 763*
AT&T *240, 252, 463, 498, 499, 501, 523, 538, 554, 558, 591*

B

B-29 Enola Gay *310*
Baker, James *449, 454, 471, 511, 778*
Bank of America *169, 232, 271, 525*
Bank of the United States *17, 52, 53, 55, 57, 80, 81, 104, 725*
Bannon, Steve *573*
Barbary pirates *42*
Barkley, Alben *266, 313, 314, 316*
Barrett, Amy Coney *577, 590, 787*
Barrow, Clyde *302*
Battle Creek Sanitarium *257, 756*
Battle of Antietam *142*
Battle of Appomattox Court House *148*
Battle of Brandywine *7*
Battle of Bull Run *142*
Battle of Bunker Hill *66, 120*
Battle of Chattanooga *159, 739*
Battle of Fallen Timbers *91, 727*
Battle of Gettysburg *144*
Battle of Lake Erie *54*
Battle of Mobile *143*
Battle of Saratoga *7*
Battle of Shiloh *142, 159, 739*
Battle of Thames River *91*
Battle of the Bulge *299, 393*
Battle of the Revolution *37*
Battle of the Thames *54, 86, 727*
Battle of Tippecanoe *91, 727*
Battle of Trenton *6*
Battle of Vicksburg *143, 159, 739*

battleship Maine *215, 749*
Bay of Pigs *357, 360, 361*
Beirut *452, 464, 778*
Bell, Alexander Graham *169, 174, 181, 740, 741*
Bell, John *93, 97, 131, 136, 735*
Bernbach, Doyle Dane *322*
Bernhardt, Sarah *176*
Biden, Hunter *531, 594, 595, 598, 599, 600, 615, 617, 618, 636, 641, 645, 654, 790, 796*
Biden, Joseph R. *iv, 530, 531, 533, 540, 541, 546, 564, 573, 580, 581, 582, 584, 585, 591, 592, 593, 594, 595, 596, 597, 598, 599, 600, 601, 602, 603, 604, 605, 606, 607, 608, 609, 610, 611, 612, 613, 614, 615, 616, 617, 618, 619, 620, 621, 622, 623, 624, 625, 626, 627, 628, 629, 631, 632, 636, 637, 638, 640, 641, 645, 647, 648, 649, 650, 651, 652, 653, 654, 657, 658, 659, 712, 713, 784, 785, 788, 789, 790, 791, 792, 793, 794, 796*
   Birth
      November 20, 1942 *593*
   Cabinet
      Austin, Lloyd (Secretary of Defense) *606*
      Becerra, Xavier (Secretary of Health and Human Services) *606*
      Blinken, Antony (Secretary of State) *606*
      Buttigieg, Pete (Secretary of Transportation) *606*
      Cardona, Dr. Miguel (Secretary of Education) *606*
      Fudge, Marcia (Secretary of Housing and Urban Development) *606*
      Garland, Merrick (Attorney General) *606*
      Granholm, Jennifer (Secretary of Energy) *606*
      Haaland, Deb (Secretary of the Interior) *606*
      Harris, Kamala (Vice President) *606*
      Mayorkas, Alejandro (Secretary of Homeland Security) *607*
      McDonough, Denis (Secretary of Veterans Affairs) *607*
      Raimondo, Gina (Secretary of Commerce) *606*
      Su, Julie (Secretary of Labor) *606*
      Vilsack, Tom (Secretary of Agriculture) *606*
      Yellen, Dr. Janet (Secretary of the Treasury) *606*
   Career
      Elected to U.S. Senate *594*
      Served on the New Castle County Board *594*
   Elections
      2020 presidential election (elected president) *604*
   Family
      With Jill: Ashley (Child) *595*
      With Neilia: Beau, Hunter, and Naomi (Children) *594*
      Biden, Joseph Sr. and Catherine Eugenia (Parents) *593*
      Valerie, James, and Frank (Siblings) *593*
   Inauguration
      2021, inaugural address *606*
   Key Events
      Afghanistan withdrawal, Taliban killings during *632*
      Amazon.com, entry into $2 trillion market capitalization club alongside Alphabet, Apple, Microsoft, and Nvidia *642*
      Arizona election laws, Supreme Court reinstatement of discriminatory provisions *632*
      Biden, Hunter, conviction on federal tax charges *636*
      Bitcoin ETFs, SEC approval for trading on U.S. exchanges *637*
      California wildfires, 2024 season burns over 1 million acres statewide *639*
      Columbia University, Jewish students' safety concerns amid Gaza war protests *639*
      COVID-19, return to work amid declining infection rates *634*
      Cryptocurrency industry, major fraud and collapse events *634*
      Cuomo, Andrew, resignation following sexual harassment charges *632*
      Ellig, Bruce R., publication of The Complete Guide to Executive Compensation, fourth edition *635*
      Foreign aid, Senate approval of $95 billion package for Ukraine and Israel *638, 639*
      Israel-Hamas, ceasefire proposal *640*
      Musk, Elon, Tesla shareholders approve $45 billion compensation package *642*
      NCAA, policy change allowing schools to compensate athletes following class-action settlement *641*
      Razor wire removal, Supreme Court permits federal agents to dismantle Texas border barriers *638*
      Recession, 2022 U.S. GDP contraction and NBER criteria *633, 634*
      Roe v. Wade, overturning of by Supreme Court in 2022 *633*

INDEX

SEC gag order, Supreme Court rejection of challenge *632, 633*
Student loan forgiveness, $5 billion relief for 74,000 borrowers despite Supreme Court ruling *637*
Student loan forgiveness, Supreme Court ruling on *636*
Title 42, judicial ruling and projected migrant influx *633*
Trump, Donald, IRS failure to audit tax returns during first two years in office *632*
Trump, Donald, January 6 House subcommittee findings on Capitol insurrection *633*
Trump, Donald, statement on NATO defense obligations and response to Russian aggression *638*
U.S. national debt, surpassing $33 trillion milestone *636*
Venezuelan immigrants, Biden administration grants work permits and deportation protection *636*
Weight-control drugs, insurance reimbursement limits for Ozempic *637*
Laws
  2021 American Rescue Plan Act *610*
  2021 Infrastructure Investment and Jobs Act *610*
  2021 Juneteenth National Independence Day Act *610*
  2024 American Privacy Rights Act *619*
  All-American Flag Act *620*
  Anti-Lynching Act *613*
  COVID-19 Origin Act *617*
  End Fentanyl Act *620*
  Enhanced Presidential Securities Act *620*
  Equal Pay for Teams USA Act *614*
  Federal Pension Oversight Act *620*
  Fiscal Responsibility Act *617*
  National Defense Authorization Act *621*
  Suspending Normal Relations with Russia and Belarus Act *613, 614*
Marriage
  Hunter, Neilia (Wife) *594*
  Jacob, Jill (Second Wife) *595*
U.S. Supreme Court Rulings
  AMG Capital Management, LLC vs Federal Trade Commission *609*
  Biden vs Missouri *614*
  Biden vs Nebraska *617*
  Biden vs Texas *614*
  Dobbs vs Jackson Women's Health Organization *614*
  Fischer vs United States *621*
  Harrington vs Purdue Pharma L.P. *621*
  Helix Energy Solutions Group Inc vs Hewitt *618*
  Loper Bright Enterprises vs Raimondo *621*
  Moyle vs United States *621*
  SEC vs Jarkesy *621*
  Trump vs United States *621*
  United States vs Arthrex, Inc. *610*
  United States vs Hansen *617*
  United States vs Rabimi *621*
  United States vs Texas *617*
  United States vs Washington *614*
  Van Buren vs United States *609, 610*
Bidenomics *624*
Big Boy *311*
Big Three *298, 301*
Billingsley, Sherman *281*
Bill of Rights *17, 27, 49, 56, 78, 299, 330, 492, 690, 702, 720, 721*
Billy the Kid *189*
bin Laden, Osama *500, 509, 520, 538, 598, 782, 785, 791*
Bitcoin *637*
Black Friday *162, 167*
Black Hawk War *109, 730*
Black Lives Matter *590, 602*
Blagojevich, Rod *525, 550, 582*
Blaine, James *178, 180, 181, 185, 188, 192, 200, 708, 743, 745*
Blair, Francis *80, 160, 739*
Blair House *316, 317, 764*
Blinken, Antony *606, 607*
Bloomberg, Michael *441, 462*
Boehner, John *541, 551, 555*
Boggs, J. Caleb *594*
Boko Haram *544*
Booth, John Wilkes *149, 160, 736, 739*
Bork, Robert *401, 595, 613, 773*
Boston Gaiety Theatre *190*
Boston Massacre *4, 26, 716*
Boston Tea Party *4*
Bout, Victor *616*
Boxer Rebellion *216, 274, 750, 759*
Braddock, Edward *2*
Brady, James *450*
Brady, Mathew *142*
Breakers Hotel *220*
Breckinridge, John *127, 128, 130, 131, 136, 733, 735*

breeches *3, 51, 60, 720, 722*
Bricker, John *299, 762, 763*
British *2, 3, 4, 5, 6, 7, 8, 15, 18, 23, 26, 44, 46, 54, 55, 73, 74, 80, 83, 84, 91, 106, 161, 174, 246, 274, 299, 311, 367, 416, 520, 664, 665, 716, 718, 721, 724, 725, 727, 740, 742, 782*
Brown, Benjamin *164, 740*
Brown, John (abolitionist) *124, 129, 733*
Brown vs Board of Education Topeka *389*
Bryan, Charles W. *265, 758*
Bryan, William Jennings *206, 208, 212, 213, 216, 235, 245, 254, 709, 748, 749, 750, 753, 755*
Brzezinski, Zbigniew *429*
Buchanan, James *iii, vii, 106, 126, 127, 128, 261, 438, 707, 733, 738, 757*
  Birth
    April 23, 1791 *126*
  Cabinet
    Black, Jeremiah (Attorney General) *128*
    Breckinridge, John (Vice President) *128*
    Brown, Aaron (Postmaster General) *128*
    Cass, Lewis (Secretary of State) *128*
    Cobb, Howell (Secretary of the Treasury) *128*
    Floyd, John (Secretary of War) *128*
    Thompson, Jacob (Secretary of the Interior) *128*
    Toucey, Isaac (Secretary of the Navy) *128*
  Career
    Law, practice of *126*
    Pennsylvania militia, service as soldier in *126*
    Pennsylvania state legislature, two-year term in *126*
    Secretary of State, service under President Polk *127*
    U.S. House of Representatives, election to *127*
    U.S. Minister to England *127*
    U.S. Minister to Russia, three-year service as *127*
    U.S. Senate, election to *127*
  Death
    June 1, 1868 *132*
  Elections
    1856 Presidential Elections (Elected President) *127*
  Engagement
    Coleman, Anne (Did Not Marry) *127*
  Family
    Buchanan, James and Elizabeth (Parents) *126*
    Edward, George, John, William, Elizabeth, Elizabeth Jane, Maria, Mary, Sarah, and Harriet (Siblings) *126*
  Inauguration
    1857, inaugural address *128*
  Key Events
    Adams, Daniel, codification of baseball rules *132*
    Atlantic cable, completion of first *132*
    Combine harvester, introduction of *132*
    First commercial oil well, commencement of operation *132*
    Gold discovery, Pike's Peak, Colorado *132*
    Lincoln-Douglas debates, occurrence of *132*
    Minnesota, Oregon, and Kansas, admission to the Union *132*
    National Association of Baseball Players, formation of *132*
    Pony Express, commencement of business *132*
    Pullman, George, conversion of sleeping cars *132*
    U.S. population, reach of 31 million *132*
  Laws
    1820 Missouri Compromise Act *129*
    1854 Kansas-Nebraska Act *129*
    1857 Tariff Act *128*
    Pacific Telegraph Act of 1860 *130*
  U.S. Supreme Court Rulings
    Abelman vs Booth *129*
    Dred Scott vs Sandford *128*
    Land Warrant Titles *129*
Buffalo Bill Cody *156, 190, 203, 241*
Build Back Better *612*
Bunker Hill *4, 66, 120*
Burr, Aaron *19, 27, 31, 36, 37, 38, 40, 42, 43, 49, 705, 717, 719*
Bush, George H.W. *iv, 68, 85, 418, 434, 438, 446, 447, 449, 453, 454, 464, 467, 468, 469, 470, 471, 472, 473, 474, 475, 476, 477, 478, 480, 485, 486, 496, 497, 502, 505, 712, 777, 778, 779, 780, 781*
  Birth
    June 12, 1924 *467*
  Cabinet
    Baker, James (Secretary of State) *471*
    Brady, Nicholas (Secretary of the Treasury) *471*
    Cavazos, Lauro (Secretary of Education) *471*

INDEX

Cheney, Richard (Secretary of Defense) *471*
Derwinski, Edward (Secretary of Veterans Affairs) *471*
Dole, Elizabeth (Secretary of Labor) *471*
Kemp, Jack (Secretary of Housing and Urban Development) *471*
Lujan, Manuel (Secretary of the Interior) *471*
Mosbacher, Robert (Secretary of Commerce) *471*
Quayle, Dan (Vice President) *471*
Skinner, Samuel (Secretary of Transportation) *471*
Sullivan, Louis (Secretary of Health and Human Services) *471*
Thornburgh, Richard (Attorney General) *471*
Watkins, James (Secretary of Energy) *471*
Yeutter, Clayton (Secretary of Agriculture) *471*
Career
  China, appointment as U.S. envoy to *469*
  CIA, appointment as director of *469*
  House of Representatives, election to *468*
  Naval service, pilot duty in *468*
  Oil company, founding of *468*
  Republican National Committee, chairmanship of *469*
  U.S. Ambassador to United Nations, appointment of *468*
Death
  November 30, 2018 *478*
Elections
  1988 Presidential Election (Elected President) *471*
Family
  Bush, Prescott and Dorothy Walker Bush (Parents) *467*
  George, John "Jeb", Neil, Marvin, Dorotyh, and Robin (Children) *468*
Inauguration
  1989, inaugural address *472*
Key Events
  Exxon Valdez, oil spill incident *479*
  Hurricane Andrew, damages exceeding $25 billion *480*
  Hurricane Hugo, $7 billion in damages *479*
  King, Rodney, race riots following incident *480*
  New York City, restaurant smoking restrictions established *478*
  North American Free Trade Agreement (NAFTA), implementation of *480*
  Panama, U.S. invasion and capture of Noriega *479*
  Powell, Colin, first Black chairman of Joint Chiefs of Staff *479*
  San Francisco, earthquake in *479*
  Time Warner, formation of *479*
  Unemployment, highest level in twenty years *480*
  U.S. population, approaching 250 million *479*
  WorldCom, initial public offering *478*
  World Wide Web, creation of *480*
Laws
  27th Amendment to the U.S. Constitution ratified *476*
  Americans with Disability Act *473*
  Civil Rights Restoration Act *474*
  Clean Air Act *473*
  Deficit Reduction Reconciliation Act *472*
  FDIC Improvement Act *474*
  Older Workers Protection Act *473*
  Omnibus Budget Reconciliation Act *472, 473*
  Pension Portability Act *475*
  Securities Enforcement Remedies and Penny Stock Reform Act *473*
  Securities Exchange Act *474*
  Unemployment Compensation Amendment Act *475*
  Worker Adjustment and Retraining Notification Act *472*
Marriage
  Pierce, Barbara (Wife) *468*
U.S. Supreme Court Rulings
  Planned Parenthood of Southeastern Pennsylvania vs Casey *475*
  Texas vs Johnson *472*
  Webster vs Reproductive Health Services *472*
Bush, George W. *iv, 68, 468, 502, 503, 504, 505, 506, 507, 508, 509, 510, 511, 512, 513, 514, 515, 516, 517, 518, 519, 521, 522, 524, 526, 531, 540, 548, 549, 567, 597, 655, 657, 712, 778, 781, 782, 783*
Birth
  July 6, 1946 *502*
Cabinet
  Abraham, Spencer (Secretary of Energy) *508*
  Ashcroft, John (Attorney General) *508*
  Chao, Elaine (Secretary of Labor) *508*
  Cheney, Richard (Vice President) *508*

Evans, Donald (Secretary of Commerce) *508*
Martinez, Rafael (Secretary of Housing and Urban Development Melquiades) *508*
Mineta, Norman (Secretary of Transportation) *508*
Norton, Gale (Secretary of the Interior) *508*
O'Neil, Paul (Secretary of the Treasury) *508*
Paige, Roderick (Secretary of Education) *508*
Powell, Colin (Secretary of State) *508*
Principi, Anthony (Secretary of Veterans Affairs) *508*
Ridge, Tom (Secretary of Homeland Security) *508*
Rumsfeld, Donald (Secretary of Defense) *508*
Thompson, Tommy (Secretary of Health and Human Services) *508*
Veneman, Ann (Secretary of Agriculture) *508*
Cabinet - second term
Bodman, Samuel (Secretary of Energy) *514*
Chao, Elaine (Secretary of Labor) *514*
Cheney, Richard (Vice President) *513*
Chertoff, Michael (Secretary of Homeland Security) *514*
Gonzales, Alberto (Attorney General) *513*
Gutierrez, Carlos (Secretary of Commerce) *513*
Jackson, Alphonso (Secretary of Housing and Urban Development) *514*
Johanns, Mike (Secretary of Agriculture) *513*
Leavitt, Michael (Secretary of Health and Human Services) *514*
Mineta, Norman (Secretary of Transportation) *514*
Nicholson, Jim (Secretary of Veterans Affairs) *514*
Norton, Gale (Secretary of the Interior) *513*
Rice, Condoleezza (Secretary of State) *513*
Rumsfeld, Donald (Secretary of Defense) *513*
Snow, John (Secretary of the Treasury) *513*

Spellings, Margaret (Secretary of Education) *514*
Career
Oil exploration, involvement in *503*
Texas Air National Guard, enlistment in *503*
Texas, governorship of *504*
Texas Rangers, minority ownership in *504*
Volunteer organization, leadership in *504*
Elections
2000 Presidential Election (Elected President) *506*
2004 Presidential Election (Elected President) *513*
Family
Barbara and Jenna (Children) *503*
Bush, George H.W. and Barbara (Parents) *502*
Dorothy, Jeb, Neil, and Marvin (Siblings) *502*
Inauguration
2001, inaugural address *507*
2005, inaugural address *513*
Key Events
Airlines, Delta and Northwest file for Chapter 11 bankruptcy *522*
American Airlines, flight crash in New York City *520*
Cheney, Dick, hunting accident involving shotgun *523*
Clinton, Hillary, appointment as Secretary of State *525*
Clinton, Hillary Rodham, took office as U.S. senator *519*
Concorde, final flight of *521*
Dot-com companies, wave of bankruptcies *520*
Euro, adoption as common European currency *520*
Fannie Mae and Freddie Mac, placed under federal conservatorship *526*
General Electric and Honeywell, failed merger attempt *520*
Homeland Security, creation of *520*
Hussein, Saddam, capture and execution in Iraq *521*
Iraq, takeover by U.S. and British troops *520*
Lehman Brothers, collapse of *525*
Massachusetts, healthcare bill with individual mandate *523*
Mitchell Report, performance-enhancing drug use in Major League Baseball *525*

Northeast, regional blackout **521**
Phelps, Michael wins record eight Olympic gold medals **526**
Schwarzenegger, Arnold elected on a recall vote **521**
Steel industry, bankruptcy filings by major companies **519**
Stevens, Ted, indictment on corruption charges **525**
Strategic Offensive, creation of **520**
Trump World Tower, opening of **519**
Tsunami, South Asia disaster killing over 200,000 **522**
Washington Mutual, collapse and largest bank failure in U.S. history **526**
WorldCom, emergence from bankruptcy **522**
Laws
  2006 Tax Act **516**
  2007 Tax Act **517**
  American Jobs Creation Act **512**
  Americans with Disabilities Act **518**
  Economic Growth and Tax Reconciliation Act **508**
  Economic Stabilization Act **518**
  Emergency Economic Stabilization Act **518**
  Fair Minimum Wage Act **517**
  Genetic Information Non-Discrimination Act **518**
  Help America Vote Act of 2002 **510**
  Heroes Earnings Assistance and Relief Act **518**
  Housing and Economic Recovery Act **518**
  Jobs Growth Tax Relief Reconciliation Act **510**
  Medicare Act **510**
  No Child Left Behind Act **508**
  Pension Protection Act **516**
  Revenue Act **510**
  Sarbanes-Oxley Act **510**
  Secure Fence Act **516**
  Tax Act **510**, ***512***, ***514***
  USA Patriot Act **508**
  War Supplemental Appropriations Act **518**
  Worker, Retiree, and Employer Recovery Act **518**
Marriage
  Welch, Laura (Wife) **503**
U.S. Supreme Court Rulings
  Arthur Anderson LLP vs United States **514**
  Bankruptcy Abuse Prevention and Consumer Protection Act **514**
  Beck et al. vs Pace Int'l Union et al. **517**
  Boulware vs United States **517**
  Burlington Northern & Santa Fe Railway Co. vs White **515**
  Grutter vs Bollinger **510**
  Hinck vs United States **516**
  John R. Sand & Gravel Co. vs United States **517**
  Kennedy et al. vs Plan Administrator for DuPont Savings and Investment Plan et al. **517**
  Ledbetter vs Goodyear Tire and Rubber **517**
  Logan vs United States **516**
  Merrill Lynch vs Dabit **516**
  Nevada Department of Human Resources vs Hibbs **510**
  Rita vs United States **516**
  Rousey vs Jacoway **514**
  Salinas vs United States **516**
  Smith vs City of Jackson **514**
  United States vs Booker **514**
  United States vs Clintwood Elkhorn Mining Co. **517**
  United States vs Georgia **515**
  United States vs Gonzalez-Lopez **515**
  United States vs Grubbs **516**
  United States vs Olson **514**
  Whitman vs Department of Transportation **516**
  Zedner vs United States **515**
Bush, Jeb **468**, ***477***, ***502***, ***557***, ***564***
Butler, William **110**, ***730***
Buttonwood Agreement **23**

C

Calamity Jane **231**
Calhoun, John **61**, ***63***, ***68***, ***69***, ***70***, ***76***, ***77***, ***723***, ***724***
California Klondike Alaska gold **219**
Campbelltown Academy **58**, ***721***
Camp David **333**, ***433***, ***436***, ***766***
Capone, Al **253**, ***270***, ***271***, ***281***, ***282***, ***305***
Caraway, Hattie Wyatt **283**
Card, Andrew **508**
Carnegie, Andrew **132**, ***141***, ***169***, ***175***, ***204***, ***210***, ***230***, ***232***, ***252***, ***253***

carpetbaggers *148, 164*
Carson, Ben *557, 564, 570*
Carter Center *437*
Carter, Jimmy *iv, 91, 381, 404, 406, 418, 419, 424, 425, 426, 427, 428, 429, 430, 431, 432, 433, 434, 435, 436, 437, 438, 440, 446, 447, 448, 469, 493, 505, 555, 587, 654, 655, 658, 711, 712, 771, 775, 776, 777, 784*
  Birth
    October 1, 1924 *424*
  Cabinet
    Adams, Brockman (Secretary of Transportation) *430*
    Andrus, Cecil (Secretary of the Interior) *430*
    Bell, Griffen (Attorney General) *430*
    Bergland, Robert (Secretary of Agriculture) *430*
    Blumenthal, Michael (Secretary of the Treasury) *430*
    Brown, Harold (Secretary of Defense) *430*
    Califano, Joseph (Secretary of Health, Education and Welfare) *430*
    Harris, Patricia (Secretary of Housing and Urban Development) *430*
    Hufstedler, Shirley (Secretary of Education) *430*
    Kreps, Juanita (Secretary of Commerce) *430*
    Marshall, Ray (Secretary of Labor) *430*
    Mondale, Walter (Vice President) *430*
    Schlesinger, James (Secretary of Energy) *430*
    Vance, Cyrus (Secretary of State) *430*
  Career
    admitted to the U.S. Naval Academy eventually becoming second lieutenant *425*
    elected to the state senate *426*
    midshipman at the U.S. Naval Academy *425*
    ran the Golden Peanut Company *426*
  Death
    December 29, 2024 *438*
  Elections
    1976 election (Elected President) *427*
    1976 Presidential Election (Elected President) *427*
  Family
    Amy, Chip, Jack, and Jeff (Children) *425*
    Billy, Gloria, and Ruth (Siblings) *424*
    Carter, James Earl and Lillian Gordy (Parents) *424*
  Inauguration
    1977, inaugural address *430*
  Key Events
    Alaska pipeline completed *439*
    Automatic Teller Machines (ATMs) were introduced *439*
    CNN, launched by Ted Turner *441*
    Departments of Education and Energy were created *439*
    Ellison, Lawrence, founded Oracle *439*
    FASB issued FAS 43 *440*
    Internet introduced by John Postel *441*
    Jim Jones cult resulted in over 900 killed *439*
    Johnson & Johnson put in the first 401(k) plan *440*
    Office of Personnel Management created *440*
    Partial meltdown of the nuclear plant at Three Mile Island *440*
    Sony introduced the cassette player Walkman *440*
    Tax payers' revolt *439*
    U.S. population rose to 226 million *441*
  Laws
    1978 Age Discrimination in Employment Act *431*
    1978 Civil Rights Amendment *431*
    1978 Civil Service Reform Act *431*
    1978 Revenue Act *431*
    1979 Technical Corrections Act *433*
    1980 Depository Institutions Deregulation and Monetary Control Act *435*
    1980 Miscellaneous Revenue Act *433*
    1980 Multiemployer Pension Plan Amendments Act *435*
    Panama Canal Treaty *435*
  Marriage
    Smith, Eleanor Rosalynn (Wife) *425*
  U.S. Supreme Court Rulings
    Abood vs Detroit Board *431*
    Regents of the University of California vs Bakke *431*
Cartwright, Alexander *132*
Carver, George Washington *219*
Cassidy, Butch *210, 231*
Cass, Lewis *78, 80, 110, 112, 128, 707, 730*
Central Intelligence Group *313*
Chambers, Whittaker *315, 388, 771*
Cheney, Dick *418, 429, 471, 474, 505, 506, 508, 511, 513, 523, 712, 782, 783*
Chicago Tribune *315, 764*
Chickamauga *131, 178, 742*

INDEX

Chiricahua Apaches *190*
Chisholm, Shirley *385*
Christie, Chris *557, 564, 635, 636, 644, 645*
Churchill, Winston *297, 298, 301, 311, 315, 335, 368, 548, 762, 763, 785*
Church of Latter Day Saints *203*
Citigroup *57, 525, 550, 554*
Civil Rights Act *54, 154, 163, 335, 336, 362, 376, 377, 381, 397, 431, 474, 535, 576, 580, 737, 738, 740*
Civil Service Commission *162, 222, 751*
civil war *123, 130, 145, 303, 569, 606*
Civil War, the *117, 122, 131, 139, 140, 141, 147, 148, 150, 159, 160, 162, 171, 172, 179, 184, 191, 199, 200, 211, 213, 214, 242, 265, 398, 619, 736, 739, 741, 744, 745, 746, 748, 754*
Clanton, Billy *189*
Clark, William *38, 445*
Clay, Henry *67, 68, 69, 75, 79, 85, 103, 706, 707, 723, 725, 729*
Clean Power Plan *544*
Cleveland, Grover *iv, 188, 189, 191, 192, 193, 194, 195, 196, 197, 199, 201, 202, 205, 206, 207, 208, 209, 394, 438, 567, 651, 708, 709, 745, 746, 747, 748, 795*
  Birth
    March 18, 1837 *191*
  Cabinet
    Bayard, Thomas (Secretary of State) *193*
    Colman, Norman (Secretary of Agriculture) *194*
    Endicott, William (Secretary of War) *193*
    Garland, Augustus (Attorney General) *194*
    Hendricks, Thomas (Vice President) *193*
    Lamar, Lucius (Secretary of the Interior) *194*
    Manning, Daniel (Secretary of the Treasury) *193*
    Vilas, William (Postmaster General) *194*
    Whitney, William (Secretary of the Navy) *194*
  Cabinet - second term
    Bissel, Wilson (Postmaster General) *207*
    Carlisle, John (Secretary of the Treasury) *207*
    Grisham, Walter (Secretary of State) *207*
    Herbert, Hilary (Secretary of the Navy) *207*
    Lamont, Daniel (Secretary of War) *207*
    Morton, Julius (Secretary of Agriculture) *207*
    Olney, Richard (Attorney General) *207*
    Smith, Hoke (Secretary of the Interior) *207*
    Stevenson, Adlai (Vice President) *207*
  Career
    Buffalo, mayor of *192*
    Law, practice of *192*
    Sheriff, served as *191*
  Death
    June 24, 1908 *209*
  Elections
    1884 Presidential Election (Elected President) *192*
    1888 Presidential Election (Elected President) *195, 205*
  Family
    Cleveland, Richard Falley and Ann (Parents) *191*
    Esther, Francis Grover, Marion, Richard, and Ruth (Children) *194*
    Lewis, Richard, William, Ann, Mary, Margaret, Susan, and Rose (Siblings) *191*
  Inauguration
    1885, inaugural speech *193*
  Key Events
    Abbott Laboratories, formation of *197*
    American Telephone and Telegraph, formation as Bell Telephone subsidiary *196*
    Avon, formation of cosmetics company *196*
    Bristol-Myers Squibb, founding of *196*
    Business leaders, Carnegie, Morgan, and Rockefeller *210*
    Coca-Cola, founding of *196*
    Eastman, George, introduction of Kodak camera and founding of Eastman Kodak Company *197*
    Edison General Electric Company, formation of *197*
    Electric trolley, introduction of *196*
    Ford builds first automobile *209*
    France sends the Statue of Liberty for the New York Harbor *196*
    Geronimo, capture of Apache leader *196*
    Gold discovery, major find in Alaska *210*
    Great Blizzard, impact on Eastern United States *196, 197*
    Hershey Chocolate Company, founding of *209*
    Home Insurance Company, recognized as first skyscraper *196*

Honeywell, founding of **196**
Hydroelectric generator, first produced **210**
Johnson & Johnson, founding of **196**
Kellogg, introduction of cold cereal flakes **209**
Linotype machine, invention of **196**
Morgan, J.P., bailout of U.S. Treasury **209**
Mormon Temple, dedication in Salt Lake City **209**
Motion picture film, development of **196**
National Cash Register Company, founding of **196**
National Geographic Society, formation of **197**
New York City, first tickertape parade **196**
Philip Morris, founding of **196**
Punxsutawney Phil, first appearance of **196**
Sears, Roebuck, and Co., formation of **209**
United States Golf Association, formation of **209**
Utah, admission as 45th state **210**
Wireless telegraph and radio, invention of **209**
Zipper, patenting of **209**
Laws
  1886 Presidential Succession Act **195**
  1887 Dawes Act **195**
  1887 Interstate Commerce Act **195**
  1890 Sherman Antitrust Act **208**
  1890 Sherman Silver Purchase Act **207**
  1894 Revenue Act **208**
  1894 Tax Act **208**
Marriage
  Folsom, Frances (Wife) **194**
U.S. Supreme Court Rulings
  Kidd vs Pearson **195**
  Plessy vs Fergusson **208**
  Pollock vs Farmers Loan & Trust **208**
  Santa Clara County vs Southern Pacific Railroad Co. **195**
  United States vs E.C. Knight Co **208**
Clifford, Clark **338, 354, 355, 373**
Clinton, George **19, 27, 41, 42, 43, 50, 51, 52, 706, 720**
Clinton, Hillary **482, 483, 484, 486, 488, 496, 497, 519, 525, 529, 533, 540, 546, 556, 557, 564, 565, 566, 598, 603, 624, 713, 780, 781, 785, 787**

Clinton, William J. *iv, 170, 215, 222, 373, 406, 421, 438, 461, 475, 476, 477, 481, 482, 483, 484, 485, 486, 487, 488, 489, 490, 491, 492, 493, 494, 495, 496, 497, 501, 510, 518, 530, 532, 533, 536, 539, 546, 597, 657, 712, 775, 776, 779, 780, 781, 791*
Birth
  August 29, 1946 **481**
Cabinet
  Aspin, Les (Secretary of Defense). **487**
  Babbitt, Bruce (Secretary of the Interior) **487**
  Bentsen, Lloyd (Secretary of the Treasury) **487**
  Brown, Jesse (Secretary of Veterans Affairs) **487**
  Brown, Ronald (Secretary of Commerce) **487**
  Christopher, Warren (Secretary of State) **487**
  Cisneros, Henry (Secretary of Housing and Urban Development) **487**
  Espy, Mike (Secretary of Agriculture) **487**
  Gore, Al (Vice President) **487**
  O'Leary, Hazel (Secretary of Energy) **487**
  Peña, Frederico (Secretary of Transportation) **487**
  Reich, Robert (Secretary of Labor) **487**
  Reno, Janet (Attorney General) **487**
  Riley, Richard (Secretary of Education) **487**
  Shalala, Donna (Secretary of Health and Human Services) **487**
Cabinet - second term
  Albright, Madeleine (Secretary of State) **492**
  Babbitt, Bruce (Secretary of the Interior) **492**
  Cohen, William (Secretary of Defense) **492**
  Cuomo, Andrew (Secretary of Housing and Urban Development) **492**
  Daley, William (Secretary of Commerce) **492**
  Glickman, Daniel (Secretary of Agriculture) **492**
  Gore, Al (Vice President) **492**
  Herman, Alexis (Secretary of Labor) **492**

Peña, Frederico (Secretary of Energy) *492*
Reno, Janet (Attorney General) *492*
Riley, Richard (Secretary of Education) *492*
Rubin, Robert (Secretary of the Treasury) *492*
Shalala, Donna (Secretary of Health and Human Services) *492*
Slater, Rodney (Secretary of Transportation) .*492*
West, Togo (Secretary of Veterans Affairs) *492*
Career
 Attorney General of Arkansas, elected *483*
 Governor of Arkansas, elected *483*
 Law, teaching of *483*
Elections
 1992 Presidential Election (Elected President) .*486*
 1996 Presidential Election (Elected President) .*491*
Family
 Blythe, William Jefferson and Virginia (Parents) *481*
 Chelsea (Child) .*483*
 Roger and Dorthy (Half-Siblings) *481*
Inauguration
 1993, inaugural address *486*
Key Events
 Ames, Aldrich, guilty plea for spying for Russia *498*
 Bosnia, U.S. troops sent for peacekeeping *498*
 Brin, Sergey, and Page, Larry, creation of Google *499*
 Camera phone, introduction of *500*
 Dow-Jones Industrial Average, first time above 4,000 *499*
 eBay, launch of auction site *498*
 Gingrich, Newt, election as Speaker of the House *498*
 Kaczynski, Al, charges of being the Unabomber *499*
 Kennedy, John Jr., death in plane crash *501*
 McVeigh, Timothy, and Nichols, Terry, conviction for federal building bombing *499*
 North American Free Trade Agreement, signing of *497*
 Simpson, O.J., acquittal in murder trial *499*
 TWA Flight 800 exploded in midair off New York *499*
 United Nations' 50th anniversary celebrated *498*
 U.S. population, rise to over 280 million *501*
 Web browser, introduction of *498*
 World Trade Center, car bomb explosion in parking garage *497*
Laws
 1974 Vietnam Era Veterans Reemployment Rights Act *489*
 1992 North American Free Trade Agreement *487*
 1993 Brady Act *488*
 1993 Family and Medical Leave Act *488*
 1993 Revenue Reconciliation Act *488*
 1994 Retirement Protection Act *489*
 1994 Uniformed Services Employment and Reemployment Rights Act *489*
 1995 Consolidated Omnibus Budget Reconciliation Act *490*
 1995 Private Securities Litigation Act *490*
 1996 Congressional Accountability Act *492*
 1996 Health Insurance Portability and Accountability Act *492*
 1996 Private Securities Litigation Reform Act *492*
 1996 Source Tax Act *492*
 1996 Taxpayer Bill of Rights Act *492*
 1997 Taxpayer Relief Act *492*
 1998 IRS Restructuring and Reform Act *493*
 1998 Securities Litigation Uniform Standards Act *493*
 1999 Gramm-Leach-Bliley Act *494*
 2000 Commodity Futures Modernization Act *495*
 2000 Electronic Signatures in Global and National Commerce Act *495*
 2000 Senior Citizens' Freedom to Work Act *495*
 2000 Worker Economic Opportunity Act *495*
 General Agreement on Tariffs and Trade *487*
Marriage
 Rodham, Hillary (Wife) *483*
U.S. Supreme Court Rulings
 Clinton vs City of New York *494*
 United States vs Lopez *490*
 United States vs Morrison *495*
 United States vs Winslow Corporation *494*
Cochise *142*
Coffin, Charles *203*

Cold War *315, 321, 361, 417, 418, 420, 458, 461, 475, 557, 779*
Coleman, Lee *322*
Colfax, Schuyler *160, 161, 708*
College of William & Mary *23, 28, 34, 58, 92, 95, 717, 721, 727*
Colonel Jimmy Doolittle *297*
Colt, Samuel *81*
Columbia University *60, 271, 328, 528, 639, 765, 784*
Columbus, Christopher *18, 29*
Comanches *82*
Commissioner vs LoBue *335, 389*
Committee of Five *5*
Commodore Dewey *215, 749*
Common Sense *5, 14*
communist *316, 317, 330, 341, 388, 418, 443, 444, 455, 777*
Compromise of 1850 *112, 116, 117*
Concord *4, 124*
Coney Island Amusement Park *89*
Confederate *100, 130, 131, 140, 142, 143, 145, 147, 148, 149, 150, 151, 154, 156, 159, 167, 287, 409, 555, 728, 736, 738, 739*
Confederate Army *131, 159, 739*
Confederate Congress *100*
Congressional Gold Medal *315, 377*
Connecticut *6, 10, 64, 175, 295, 467, 491, 502, 667, 670, 686, 781*
Constitution *9, 10, 11, 13, 14, 15, 17, 20, 26, 27, 28, 36, 40, 41, 48, 49, 51, 56, 59, 67, 69, 81, 93, 96, 98, 118, 121, 122, 129, 130, 144, 154, 155, 161, 162, 163, 179, 188, 215, 223, 238, 244, 247, 250, 251, 254, 260, 269, 277, 280, 289, 290, 293, 312, 318, 319, 336, 357, 375, 379, 397, 400, 402, 404, 413, 476, 545, 567, 630, 653, 655, 656, 663, 669, 676, 679, 681, 683, 684, 690, 693, 695, 696, 697, 698, 705, 715, 717, 718, 720, 721, 732, 737, 738, 740, 754, 755, 761, 764, 793, 794, 795*
Continental Army *3, 5, 6, 11, 17, 22, 58, 715, 716, 721*
Continental Congress *4, 5, 6, 7, 9, 12, 25, 26, 42, 48, 50, 54, 59, 716, 718, 719, 722*
Coolidge, Calvin *iv, 258, 259, 261, 263, 265, 275, 286, 295, 310, 364, 372, 394, 413, 438, 471, 709, 710, 756, 758, 768*
 Birth
  July 4, 1872 *263*
 Cabinet
  Daugherty, Harry (Attorney General) *266*
  Davis, James (Secretary of Labor) *264*
  Denby, Edwin (Secretary of the Navy) *264*
  Hoover, Herbert (Secretary of Commerce) *264*
  Hughes, Charles (Secretary of State) *264*
  Mellon, Andrew (Secretary of the Treasury) *264*
  New, Harry (Postmaster General) *264*
  Wallace, Henry (Secretary of Agriculture) *264*
  Weeks, John (Secretary of War) *266*
  Work, Hubert (Secretary of the Interior) *264*
 Cabinet - second term
  Davis, James (Secretary of Labor) *266*
  Dawes, Charles (Vice President) *266*
  Hoover, Herbert (Secretary of Commerce) *266*
  Jardine, William (Secretary of Agriculture) *266*
  Kellogg, Frank (Secretary of State) *266*
  Mellon, Andrew (Secretary of the Treasury) *266*
  New, Harry (Postmaster General) *266*
  Wilbur, Curtis (Secretary of the Navy) *266*
  Work, Hubert (Secretary of the Interior) *266*
 Career
  Law, practice of *263*
  Lieutenant Governor of Massachusetts, position held *264*
  Massachusetts statehouse, service in *264*
  Mayor of Northampton, position held *264*
  State senator, election to *264*
 Death
  January 5, 1933 *269*
 Elections
  1924 Presidential Election (Elected President) *265*
 Family
  Abigail (Sibling) *263*
  Coolidge, John and Victoria (Parents) *263*
  John and Calvin Jr. (Children) *263*
 Inauguration
  1924, inaugural address *266*
 Key Events
  Bell Laboratories, founding of *270*
  Birdseye, Charles, invention of frozen foods *270*

INDEX

Bootleg liquor sales, exceeding $3.5 billion a year *271*
Capone, Al, war with Irish O'Bannion Mob *270*
Chrysler, Walter, founding of Chrysler automotive company *270*
Columbia Broadcasting System (CBS), founding of *272*
Columbia Presbyterian Hospital, creation of *271*
Disney Company, formation of *270*
Earhart, Amelia, first woman to fly across the Atlantic Ocean *272*
Electric chair, replacement of hangman's noose *271*
Hoover, Edgar, appointment as head of the FBI *270*
Ku Klux Klan, march on Washington, D.C. *270*
Liquid fuel rocket, creation of first *271*
Metro-Goldwyn-Mayer, founding of *270*
Mickey Mouse, creation by Walt Disney *272*
Mississippi Great Flood, displacement of 100,000 people *272*
National Broadcasting System (NBC), founding of *271*
New Yorker magazine, beginning of publication *270*
Pan American World Airways, creation of *271*
Radar, invention of *271*
Smith, Elinor, first licensed female airplane pilot *270*
Television, introduction of *271*
Time Magazine, first appearance on newsstands *270*
Laws
  1924 Immigration Act *267*
  1925 Certiorari Act *267*
  Air Commerce Act *267*
  Railway Act *267*
  Revenue Act *267*
Marriage
  Goodhue, Grace (Wife) *263*
U.S. Supreme Court Rulings
  Barnes vs Andrews *267*
  Myers vs United States *267*
  Nixon vs Herndon *267*
  Olmstead vs United States *267*
corporate income tax *236, 279, 282*
Cosa Nostra *203, 368*

Cotton Club *270, 307*
COVID-19 *578, 579, 581, 590, 591, 602, 603, 607, 608, 610, 614, 617, 634, 787*
Cox, Archibald *400, 401, 773*
Crawford, William *61, 63, 67, 75, 723*
Crédit Mobilier *161, 163*
Creek Nation *54, 71*
Creek War *74*
Crocket, Davy *82*
Crooks, George *142*
Crooks, Thomas Matthew *648, 789*
Crowninshield, Benjamin *61*
Cruz, Ted *557, 565*
Cuba *215, 217, 231, 240, 339, 344, 345, 357, 360, 361, 532, 544, 545, 557, 572, 635, 659, 749, 750, 768, 785*
Cuomo, Andrew *492, 555, 587, 632*
Currency Act *4*
Curtis, Charles *275, 276, 279, 287, 710, 759, 760*
Curtis, Martha Dandridge *3, 715*
Custer, George *169*
Czolgosz, Leon *218, 750*

D

Daily Points of Light *473*
Daley, Bill *538, 539*
Daley, Richard *537*
Dallas, George Mifflin *104*
Darman, Dick *474*
Darman, Richard *474*
Davis, Henry G. *226, 752*
Davis, Jefferson *110, 122, 131, 139, 140, 150, 736*
Davis, John *265, 758*
Dawes, Charles Gates *265*
Dayton, William *127, 733*
Dean, John *401, 403, 773*
Deaver, Michael *445, 449, 778*
Declaration of Independence *6, 7, 25, 26, 28, 30, 35, 46, 49, 54, 55, 90, 198, 229, 715, 716, 718, 726*
Deere, John *82*
Defense Production Act *317, 578, 609*
Deferred Action for Childhood Arrivals (DACA) *539*
Delaware *6, 10, 12, 170, 219, 521, 523, 530, 531, 557, 593, 594, 595, 596, 599, 600, 605, 624, 638, 642, 654, 658, 667, 670, 685, 741, 784, 790, 791, 796*
Democratic Leadership Council *484, 485*
Democratic mascot *76*

813

Democratic Party *20, 37, 50, 72, 82, 85, 87,
  98, 104, 117, 124, 135, 136, 139,
  184, 244, 267, 274, 309, 350, 445,
  484, 547, 723, 726, 731, 733, 735,
  748, 788*
Democrats *36, 70, 76, 79, 85, 92, 96, 103, 110,
  121, 127, 135, 136, 146, 160, 164,
  171, 172, 179, 185, 192, 195, 199,
  201, 205, 206, 208, 213, 216, 226,
  235, 237, 243, 246, 247, 248, 265,
  275, 279, 286, 287, 291, 293, 295,
  298, 299, 300, 314, 316, 318, 329,
  335, 337, 351, 352, 361, 377, 378,
  379, 389, 390, 391, 392, 393, 394,
  398, 418, 419, 420, 434, 447, 451,
  454, 457, 469, 471, 472, 476, 480,
  485, 486, 491, 506, 508, 513, 515,
  523, 524, 530, 531, 540, 541, 556,
  564, 566, 567, 574, 575, 580, 582,
  588, 596, 598, 604, 605, 614, 615,
  623, 624, 628, 629, 651, 652, 653,
  655, 724, 725, 726, 727, 729, 730,
  732, 733, 735, 736, 739, 740, 741,
  743, 744, 745, 747, 749, 750, 752,
  753, 754, 755, 756, 758, 759, 760,
  761, 762, 764, 765, 766, 770, 772,
  775, 776, 777, 778, 779, 780, 782,
  783, 784, 785, 787, 789, 790, 791,
  793, 794*
Dent, Frederick *159, 399, 414, 739*
Department of Energy *430*
Department of Health and Human Services
  431
Dewey, Thomas E. *299, 314, 710, 762, 763,
  764*
Dickinson, Emily *203*
Dinner Table Bargain *16*
Disney, Walt *270, 272*
District of Columbia *22, 173, 357*
Dodd-Frank laws *543*
Dole, Bob *415, 418, 419, 491, 712*
Donner, George *108*
doughboys *248*
Douglas, Stephen *130, 135, 136, 244, 707, 735*
Douglass, Frederick *108, 118, 173*
Dow, Charles *208, 748*
Dow Jones Industrial Average (DJIA) *208,
  210, 219, 220, 231, 232, 233, 239,
  240, 241, 252, 253, 254, 262, 270,
  271, 272, 281, 282, 283, 302, 303,
  304, 305, 306, 307, 320, 321, 322,
  323, 324, 340, 341, 342, 343, 344,
  345, 367, 382, 383, 384, 385, 386,
  407, 408, 409, 410, 422, 423, 439,
  440, 441, 463, 464, 465, 466, 479,
  480, 498, 500, 501, 519, 520, 521,
  522, 524, 525, 526, 550, 551, 552,
  553, 554, 556, 558, 559, 587, 589,
  590, 592, 635, 637, 639, 642, 644,
  646, 654, 655, 748*
Drucker, Peter *321, 511*

E

Eagleton, Thomas *398*
Easter Egg Hunt *174*
Ebbets Field *251, 305, 344*
Economist *100*
Edison, Thomas *168, 175, 190, 197, 209, 231,
  233, 742*
Edwards, John *513, 783*
Eisenhower Doctrine *332*
Eisenhower, Dwight D. *iv, 207, 312, 325, 326,
  329, 330, 331, 332, 333, 334, 335,
  337, 340, 342, 350, 353, 354, 355,
  365, 388, 389, 390, 408, 432, 433,
  438, 711, 765, 766, 768, 771, 772*
  Birth
    October 14, 1890 *325*
  Cabinet
    Benson, Ezra (Secretary of Agriculture)
      331
    Brownell, Herbert (Attorney General)
      331
    Dulles, John (Secretary of State) *331*
    Durkin, Martin (Secretary of Labor) *331*
    George, Humphrey (Secretary of the
      Treasury) *331*
    Hobby, Oveta Culp (Secretary of Health,
      Education and Welfare) *331*
    Humphrey, George (Secretary of the
      Treasury) *331*
    McKay, Douglas (Secretary of the Interior)
      331
    Nixon, Richard (Vice President) *331*
    Summerfield, Arthur (Postmaster General)
      331
    Weeks, Sinclair (Secretary of Commerce)
      331
    Wilson, Charles (Secretary of Defense)
      331
  Cabinet - second term
    Benson, Ezra (Secretary of Agriculture)
      335
    Brownell, Herbert (Attorney General) *335*
    Dulles, John (Secretary of State) *335*
    Folsom, Marion (Secretary of Health,
      Education and Welfare) *335*

INDEX

Humphrey, George (Secretary of the Treasury) *335*
Mitchell, Jane (Secretary of Labor) *335*
Mueller, Frederick (Secretary of Commerce) *335*
Nixon, Richard (Vice President) *335*
Seaton, Frederick (Secretary of the Interior) *335*
Summerfield, Arthur (Postmaster General) *335*
Wilson, Charles (Secretary of Defense) *335*
Career
  Chief of Staff of the Army, appointment to *328*
  Columbia University, presidency of *328*
  NATO, command of *328*
  Supreme Commander *327, 337*
  Third Army, Chief of Staff and promotion to two-star general *327*
Elections
  1952 Presidential Election (Elected President) *329*
  1956 Presidential Election (Elected President) *335*
Family
  Arthur, Earl, Edgar, Milton, Roy, and Paul (Siblings) *325*
  Doud Dwight, John (Children) *326*
  Eisenhower, David and Ida (Parents) *325*
Inauguration
  1953, inaugural address *330*
  1957, inaugural address *335*
Key Events
  Alaska, admission as 49th state *344*
  American Express, introduction of credit cards *343*
  American Football League, start of *345*
  Chase Manhattan Bank, creation of *341*
  Container ship, first launch of *342*
  Cuba, U.S. trade embargo on *344*
  Disneyland, opening in Anaheim, California *341*
  Ellison, Ralph, won National Book Award *340*
  Microchip, development of first *342*
  New York Curb Exchange, transformation into American Stock Exchange (AMEX) *341*
  Parks, Rosa, arrest in Montgomery, Alabama *342*
  Polio, discovery of cure for *342*
  Rosenberg, Julius and Ethel, execution for espionage *340*
  U.S. population, approaching 180 million *344*

USS Nautilus, first U.S. nuclear submarine *341*
Laws
  1953 Refugee Relief Act *332*
  1956 Federal Highway Act *335*
  1957 Civil Rights Act *336*
  1958 Former Presidents Act *336*
  1958 National Aeronautics and Space Act *336*
  1959 Labor-Management Reporting and Disclosure Act *336*
  1960 Pension Act *337*
  Civil Rights Act *335*
  Landrum-Griffin Act *337*
  Revenue Act *332*
  The Food for Peace Act *334*
Marriage
  Doud, Mary "Mamie" (Wife) *326*
U.S. Supreme Court Rulings
  Brown vs Board of Education of Topeka *333*
  Cooper vs Aaron *336*
  Commissioner vs Duberstein *337*
  Commissioner vs LoBue *335*
  Reid vs Covert *336*
  United States vs Reynolds *331*
Eisenhower, Mamie *330*
electoral college *11, 12, 75, 171, 206, 216, 275, 352, 357, 567, 581, 592, 605, 630, 704, 788, 794*
electoral votes *19, 27, 31, 36, 42, 50, 53, 59, 62, 67, 75, 76, 79, 85, 87, 88, 91, 96, 103, 110, 118, 121, 127, 130, 131, 136, 147, 160, 164, 171, 179, 192, 199, 201, 206, 213, 226, 238, 243, 248, 265, 291, 295, 299, 314, 351, 377, 389, 390, 393, 398, 419, 435, 447, 469, 476, 486, 491, 506, 566, 567, 581, 596, 604, 605, 628, 629, 630, 651, 653, 704, 717, 719, 735, 782, 793, 794, 795*
Ellis Island *204, 283, 341, 389*
Emancipation Proclamation *144, 145, 736*
Emanuel, Rahm *533*
Embargo Act *43, 50*
England *2, 3, 4, 5, 6, 8, 15, 21, 26, 29, 32, 51, 52, 53, 55, 59, 67, 70, 71, 72, 96, 118, 127, 131, 156, 157, 199, 215, 216, 222, 246, 294, 306, 311, 327, 347, 348, 358, 361, 368, 416, 451, 458, 482, 487, 489, 548, 715, 716, 718, 720, 721, 724, 750, 751, 767, 785*

815

English, William *179, 185, 743, 744*
Equal Employment Opportunity Commission *362, 397, 545, 571*
Espionage Act *249, 542, 583, 789*
Executive Mansion *16, 18, 29, 38, 55, 60, 61, 70, 77, 78, 85, 87, 98, 99, 105, 106, 117, 122, 129, 138, 140, 153, 161, 165, 166, 172, 173, 174, 180, 186, 192, 194, 195, 201, 205, 214, 218, 223, 236, 237, 705, 717, 719, 720, 721, 722, 725, 729, 731, 732, 734, 739, 742, 743, 744, 746, 747, 749, 751*

F

Facebook *522, 553, 581, 588*
Fairbanks, Charles *226, 227, 247, 752, 755*
Fair Deal *330, 374*
Fairfax, Sally *3*
Fair Labor Standards Act *293, 455, 618, 761*
Farnsworth, Philo *271, 282*
Farragut, David *143*
Fat Man *311*
Federal Customs Act *9*
Federalist *10, 20, 27, 28, 31, 36, 37, 40, 48, 57, 62, 127, 705, 706, 718, 720, 722*
Federalist Papers *10, 48, 720*
Federalist Party *36, 57, 62, 718, 722*
Federal Reserve *87, 208, 239, 240, 245, 290, 302, 429, 480, 498, 523, 525, 526, 537, 550, 554, 558, 619, 654, 726, 753*
Fenway Park *241*
Ferraro, Geraldine *453, 454, 469, 778*
Fifth Amendment *144, 260, 701, 702*
Fillmore, Abigail *116*
Fillmore, Millard *iii, 110, 111, 112, 114, 115, 118, 126, 127, 153, 185, 223, 264, 310, 371, 394, 413, 438, 471, 707, 730, 737*
  Birth
    January 7, 1800 *114*
  Cabinet
    Collamer, Jacob (Postmaster General) *115*
    Crawford, John (Secretary of War) *115*
    Ewing, Thomas (Secretary of the Interior) *115*
    Johnson, Reverdy (Attorney General) *115*
    Meredith, William (Secretary of the Treasury) *115*
    Preston, William (Secretary of the Navy) *115*
    Webster, Daniel (Secretary of State) *115*
  Career
    Law, practice of *114*
    New York State Assembly, election to *114*
    U.S. House of Representatives, election to *115*
  Death
    March 8, 1874 *118*
  Elections
    1852 Presidential Election (Elected Vice President) *117*
  Family
    Fillmore, Nathaniel and Phoebe (Parents) *114*
    Julia, Olive, Phoebe, Almon, Calvin, Charles, Cyrus, and Darius (Siblings) *114*
    Millard Jr. and Mary (Children) *114*
  Inauguration
    1851, inaugural address *115*
  Key Events
    Douglass, Frederick, wrote *The Heroic Slave* *118*
    Geronimo, leadership of the Apaches in the lower Southwest *119*
    Liberty Bell, delivery to Philadelphia *118*
    Melville, Herman, published *Moby Dick* *118*
    Morris, Robert, first Black judge in America *118*
    New York Times, founding of *118*
    Pinkerton Detective Agency set up *118*
    Stowe, Harriet Beecher, publication of Uncle Tom's Cabin with Simon Legree *118*
    Wells Fargo and Company, use of stagecoaches for banking and mail services *118*
    Y.M.C.A. of the USA, founding of *118*
  Laws
    Fugitive Slave Act of 1850 *116*
    Compromise of 1850 *116, 117*
  Marriage
    Powers, Abigail (Wife) *114*
  U.S. Supreme Court Rulings
    Cooley vs Board of Wardens *117*
    United States vs Guillem *117*
    United States vs Reid *117*
Financial Crisis of 1837 *92*
financial panic of 1857 *128, 734*
fireside chats *288, 301, 456*

INDEX

First Bank *16*, *17*
first Congressional action *99*
First Continental Congress *4*, *12*, *26*, *716*
first ten amendments *17*, *27*, *49*, *720*
Five Points *82*, *132*
Flowers, Gennifer *483*, *484*, *780*
Floyd, Charles (Pretty Boy) *302*
Flynn, Michael *572*, *582*
FOIA *547*
Folsom, Frances *194*, *746*
Ford, Bob *190*
Ford, Gerald R. *iv*, *22*, *372*, *399*, *402*, *403*, *405*, *411*, *412*, *413*, *414*, *415*, *416*, *417*, *418*, *419*, *420*, *421*, *427*, *428*, *438*, *446*, *469*, *471*, *474*, *482*, *493*, *505*, *508*, *511*, *597*, *711*, *773*, *774*, *775*, *776*
- Birth
  - July 14, 1913 *411*
- Cabinet
  - Brennan, Paul (Secretary of Labor) *414*
  - Brinegar, Claude (Secretary of Transportation) *415*
  - Butz, Earl (Secretary of Agriculture) *414*
  - Dent, Frederick (Secretary of Commerce) *414*
  - Flynn, James (Secretary of Housing and Urban Development) *415*
  - Kissinger, Henry (Secretary of State) *414*
  - Morton, Rogers (Secretary of the Interior) *414*
  - Rockefeller, Nelson (Vice President) *414*
  - Saxbe, William (Attorney General) *414*
  - Schlesinger, James (Secretary of Defense) *415*
  - Simon, William (Secretary of the Treasury) *414*
  - Weinberger, Caspar (Secretary of Health, Education and Welfare) *415*
- Career
  - House of Representatives, elected to, ascended to Minority Leader *412*
  - U.S. Navy, enlisted in *412*
- Death
  - December 26, 2006 *421*
- Elections
  - President without having been elected following Nixon's resignation *413*
- Family
  - Half-brothers James, Richard, and Thomas (Siblings) *411*
  - King, Leslie Lynch Sr. and Dorothy Gardner (Parents) *411*
  - Michael, John, Steven, and Susan (Children) *412*
- Inauguration
  - 1974, inaugural address *413*
- Key Events
  - 3M Post-it, created *423*
  - Apple I, launched by Steve Jobs and Steve Wozniak in garage *423*
  - Capital punishment, resumed after 1967 *423*
  - CEO pay, reported as 40 times average worker's salary *422*
  - DEC introduced the minicomputer *422*
  - Felix Rohatyn, instrumental in New York City's financial rescue *422*
  - Financial Accounting Standards Board, established as accounting rulemaker *421*
  - Kresge became Kmart *423*
  - LaGuardia Airport, bombing in baggage area killing 14 *422*
  - Microsoft, founded by Bill Gates and Paul Allen *422*
  - New York City, financial crisis *422*
  - U.S. military academies, women admitted to *422*
  - Video-cassette recorder, introduced to market *423*
  - Vietnam War, ended *422*
- Laws
  - 1972 War Powers Act *415*
  - 1974 Commodity Futures Trading Commission Act *416*
  - 1974 Employee Retirement Income Security Act *416*
  - 1974 Gold Act *416*
  - 1974 Reform Act *416*
  - 1974 Vietnam Era Veterans Reemployment Act *416*
  - 1975 Security Act Amendments *417*
  - 1975 Tax Reduction Act *417*
  - 1976 Tax Reform Act *419*
- Marriage
  - Warren, Elizabeth "Betty" Bloomer (Wife) *412*
- U.S. Supreme Court Rulings
  - Goss vs Lopez *418*
  - Gregg vs State of Georgia *419*
  - Taylor vs Louisiana *418*

Ford, Henry *230*, *270*, *271*
formal censure *80*

Fort Detroit *91*
Fort Harrison *109, 730*
Fort McHenry *55, 721*
Fort Ticonderoga *7*
Fourier, Charles *100*
Franklin, Benjamin *5, 6, 8, 22, 23, 28, 108, 666*
Fraunces Tavern *8, 715*
Free Soil Party *110*
Frelinghuysen, Theodore *103, 729*
Frémont, John C. *127, 707, 733*
French and Indian War *2, 42, 50*
French Navy *8*
French Revolution *17, 27, 716, 718*
Fromme, Lynette "Squeaky" *417*

G

Gallup poll *280, 291, 303, 314, 340, 400, 403, 459, 462, 476, 491, 494, 496, 562, 624, 760, 766*
Garfield, James A. *iii, 162, 177, 178, 179, 180, 181, 182, 185, 218, 227, 363, 371, 708, 742, 743, 744, 750, 770*
  Birth
    November 19, 1831 *177*
  Cabinet
    Arthur, Chester (Vice President) *180*
    Blaine, James (Secretary of State) *180*
    Hunt, William (Secretary of the Navy) *180*
    James, Thomas (Postmaster General) *180*
    Kirkwood, Samuel (Secretary of the Interior) *180*
    Lincoln, Robert Todd (Secretary of War) *180*
    MacVeagh, Isaac Wayne (Attorney General) *180*
    Windom, William (Secretary of the Treasury) *180*
  Career
    Barges and tugboats, work on *177*
    Colonel and eventually Major General in the Union Army *178*
    Congress, eighteen years of service in *178*
    Disciples of Christ, service as traveling preacher *177*
    Hiram College, professor and president *177*
    Law, practice of *178*
    Ohio State Senate, election to *178*
  Death
    September 9, 1881 *181*
  Elections
    1880 Presidential Election (Elected President) *179*
  Family
    Abram, Edward, Harry, Irvin, James, Eliza and Mary (Children) *178*
    Garfield, Abram and Eliza (Parents) *177*
    James, Mehetable, Thomas, and Mary (Siblings) *177*
  Inauguration
    1881, inaugural address *179*
  Key Events
    Barnum & Bailey Circus, formation of *182*
    Marshall Field's, founding of department stores *182*
    Red Cross, founding of *182*
  Laws
    1883 Pendleton Civil Service Reform Act *180*
  Marriage
    Rudolph, Lucretia (Wife) *178*
Garland, Merrick *545, 577, 606*
Garner, John Nance *279, 286, 287, 291, 292, 759, 760, 761*
Garrett, Pat *189*
gas lighting *106, 107, 729*
Gates, Horatio *7*
Gehrig, Lou *295, 305*
General Motors *219, 233, 253, 262, 271, 281, 303, 306, 321, 322, 341, 344, 368, 381, 407, 500, 534, 535, 537, 550, 578, 586, 590, 591, 755*
Georgia *10, 12, 20, 71, 78, 141, 146, 242, 262, 286, 409, 418, 419, 424, 425, 426, 436, 437, 476, 486, 515, 581, 605, 622, 623, 632, 633, 636, 644, 646, 651, 666, 670, 686, 725, 756, 763, 775*
Germany *216, 246, 248, 296, 298, 299, 301, 310, 340, 347, 348, 358, 362, 393, 750, 755, 761, 762, 763, 768*
Geronimo *119, 142, 190, 196*
Gerry, Elbridge *9, 53, 54, 57, 667, 706*
Gettysburg Address *145, 736*
Gilded Age *168, 214, 749*
Ginsburg, Ruth Bader *497, 568, 577, 590*
Giuliani, Rudolph *591, 592, 636, 642, 646, 654*
glasnost *460*
Glenn, John *359, 768*
God We Trust *333, 766*
Goldwater, Barry *377, 445, 711, 770*
Gonzales, Alberto *513, 514, 524*
Google *499, 556, 618*
GOP *224, 227, 229, 235, 237, 248, 249, 275, 278, 329, 451, 548, 556, 575, 628, 632*

INDEX

Gore, Al *476, 484, 485, 486, 487, 491, 492, 496, 506, 567, 655, 712, 779, 780, 782*
Gould, Jay *132, 162, 167, 190*
Government Motors *535*
Graham, Lindsey *557, 565*
Graham, William *121, 732*
Grand Ole Opry *271*
Granger, Francis *85, 93, 97, 726*
Grant, Hiram Ulysses *158, 738*
Grant, Ulysses S. *iii, 142, 143, 145, 146, 148, 149, 158, 159, 160, 161, 162, 163,164, 165, 166, 167, 172, 173, 178, 179, 184, 234, 236, 329, 438, 708, 738, 739, 740, 741, 744, 752, 753*
  Birth
    April 27, 1822 *158*
  Cabinet
    Borie, Adolph (Secretary of the Navy) *162*
    Colfax, Schuyler (Vice President) *161*
    Cox, Jacob (Secretary of the Interior) *162*
    Creswell, John (Postmaster General) *162*
    Hoar, Ebenezer (Attorney General) *162*
    Rawlins, John (Secretary of War) *162*
    Stewart, Alexander (Secretary of the Treasury) *162*
    Washburne, Elihu (Secretary of State) *162*
  Cabinet - second term
    Belknap, William (Secretary of War) *165*
    Creswell, John (Postmaster General) *165*
    Delano, Columbus (Secretary of the Interior) *165*
    Fish, Hamilton (Secretary of State) *165*
    Richardson, William (Secretary of the Treasury) *165*
    Robeson, George (Secretary of the Navy) *165*
    Williams, George (Attorney General) *165*
    Wilson, Henry (Vice President) *165*
  Career
    Brigadier General of the Illinois company of volunteers *159*
    Fourth U.S. Infantry, rose from second to first lieutenant *159*
    Union armies, appointed lieutenant general of all *159*
  Death
    July 23, 1885 *166*
  Elections
    1868 Presidential Election (Elected President) *160*
    1872 Presidential Election (Elected President) *164*
  Family
    Ellen, Frederick, Jesse, and Ulysses Jr. (Children) *159*

Grant, Jesse Root and Hannah Simpson (Parents) *158*
  Samuel, Orvil, Clara, Mary, and Virginia (Siblings) *158*
Inauguration
  1869, inaugural address *161*
  1873, inaugural address *165*
Key Events
  Atlantic City Boardwalk was completed in New Jersey *167*
  Avondale coal mine, collapse killed 179 miners *167*
  Bank of America, began operation *169*
  Bell, Alexander Graham, invention of telephone *169*
  Black Friday, financial panic *167*
  Central Pacific and Union Pacific railroads, linked East and West *167*
  Chewing gum and vacuum cleaners, patented *167*
  Colorado, admitted as a state *169*
  Custer and 7th Cavalry, massacred *169*
  Edison, Thomas, invented the electric typewriter *168*
  Goldman Sachs, founded *167*
  Heinz Ketchup, introduced *169*
  James, Jesse and gang, began operations *168*
  Library of Congress was given responsibility for copyrights *168*
  Metropolitan Museum of Art, opened in New York City *168*
  National Rifle Association, founded *168*
  Revels, Hiram, first African American U.S. senator *168*
  Rockefeller, John D., founded Standard Oil of Ohio *168*
  San Francisco, devastated by earthquake *167*
  U.S. population, near 40 million *167*
  U.S. Weather Bureau, founded *168*
  Vanderbilt, Cornelius, stopped Wall Street panic with stock purchase *167*
  Westinghouse, George, introduced air brakes *167*
  Wright, Jonathan, first Black judge on state Supreme Court *167*
  Wyoming, granted women vote *167*
  Yellowstone National Park, established *168*
Laws
  15th Amendment to the U.S. Constitution ratified *163*

1869 Judiciary Act *162*
1870 Civil Rights Act *163*
1870 Enforcement Act *163*
1871 Civil Rights Act *163*
1872 Amnesty Act *164*
1872 Revenue Act *163*
1873 Coinage Act *165*
1875 Bland Silver Act *166*
1875 Specie Resumption Act *166*
Marriage
   Dent, Julia (Wife) *159*
U.S. Supreme Court Rulings
   Collector vs Day *163*
   Ex Parte McCardle *162*
   Munn vs Illinois *166*
   Texas vs White *162*
Great Britain *4, 12, 15, 104, 106, 266, 296, 347, 661, 665, 733*
Great Depression *274, 278, 289, 301, 305, 306, 443, 456, 463, 759, 762*
Greater Caribbean *63, 224*
Great Railroad Strike *173*
Great Recession *549*
Great White Fleet *229, 752*
Greece *312*
Greeley, Horace *132, 161, 164, 708, 740*
greenbacks *143, 162*
Grenada *452, 464*
Griner, Brittney *616*
Guantanamo Bay *532, 635*
Guiteau, Charles *180, 743*
Gulf War *487, 505, 518, 596, 612*

H

Habitat for Humanity International *437*
Haig, Alexander *414, 449, 450, 454*
Haldeman, J.R. *392*
Hale, Nathan *6*
Halloween Massacre *418, 775*
Hamilton, Alexander *9, 10, 11, 15, 16, 17, 19, 20, 40, 41, 42, 46, 48, 165, 235, 400, 428, 429, 431, 557, 686, 715, 718, 720, 776*
Hamlin, Hannibal *131, 136, 140, 707, 735*
Hancock, John *6, 665, 667*
Hancock, Winfield Scott *179, 185, 708, 743, 744*
Hanson, John *14*
Harding, Warren G. *vii, 239, 256, 258, 286, 295, 371, 710, 756*

Birth
   November 2, 1865 *256*
Cabinet
   Coolidge, Calvin (Vice President) *259*
   Daugherty, Harry (Attorney General) *259*
   Davis, James (Secretary of Labor) *259*
   Denby, Edwin (Secretary of the Navy) *259*
   Fall, Albert (Secretary of the Interior) *259*
   Hays, William (Postmaster General) *259*
   Hoover, Herbert (Secretary of Commerce) *259*
   Hughes, Charles (Secretary of State) *259*
   Mellon, Andrew (Secretary of the Treasury) *259*
   Wallace, Henry (Secretary of Agriculture) *259*
   Weeks, John (Secretary of War) *259*
Career
   Marion Daily Star Newspaper, purchased *257*
   Newspaper, reporter, editor, and publisher *257*
   Ohio, lieutenant governor *258*
   Ohio State Senate, served four years *257*
   U.S. Senate, elected to *258*
Death
   August 2, 1923 *261*
Elections
   1920 Presidential Election (Elected President) *258*
Family
   Abigail, Charity, George, Mary, Phoebe, Eleanor, and Charles (Siblings) *256*
   Harding, George Tryon and Phoebe Elizabeth (Parents) *256*
Inauguration
   1921, inaugural address *258*
Key Events
   Coal strike, nationwide *262*
   Congress, resolution favoring Jewish homeland in Palestine *262*
   Filene, founding of first credit union *262*
   International treaties, establishment to promote peace and reduce tensions *262*
   Johnson & Johnson, introduction of Band-Aids *262*
   Port Authority of New York, formation by New Jersey and New York *261*
   Reader's Digest, beginning of publication *262*

INDEX

Recession, beginning of two-year period *262*
Rosenthal, Ida, introduction of Maidenform Bra *262*
Supreme Court, hiring of first law clerk at $3,600 *262*
Thompson, John, development of .45-caliber machine gun *262*
Laws
  1921 Revenue Act *259*
  Cable Act *260*
Marriage
  King, Florence (Wife) *257*
U.S. Supreme Court Rulings
  Adkins vs Children's Hospital of D.C. *260*
  Leser vs Garnett *259*
Harper's Ferry Virginia *129*
Harris, Kamala *580, 581, 602, 604, 605, 606, 611, 620, 623, 625, 627, 628, 629, 630, 650, 651, 652, 655, 713, 788, 789, 792, 793, 794, 795*
Harrison, Benjamin *iv, 195, 198, 199, 200, 201, 202, 204, 205, 206, 394, 438, 506, 567, 708, 709, 746, 747, 748*
  Birth
    August 20, 1833 *198*
  Cabinet
    Blaine, James (Secretary of State) *200*
    Miller, William (Attorney General) *200*
    Morton, Levi (Vice President) *200*
    Noble, John (Secretary of the Interior) *200*
    Proctor, Redfield (Secretary of War) *200*
    Rusk, Jeremiah (Secretary of Agriculture) *200*
    Tracy, Benjamin (Secretary of the Navy) *200*
    Wanamaker, John (Postmaster General) *200*
    Windom, William (Secretary of the Treasury) *200*
  Career
    Army, commission as colonel and promotion to brigadier general at the end of the war *199*
    Harrison, Benjamin, formation of company of volunteer infantrymen for Civil War *199*
    Law, practice of *199*
    U.S. Senate, elected to *199*
  Elections
    1888 Presidential Election (Elected President) *199*
    1892 Presidential Election (Lost Election) *201*
  Family
    Harrison, John Scott and Elizabeth Irwin (Parents) *198*
    Russell, Mary, and one who died at birth (Children) *199*
    Twelve, unnamed (Siblings) *198*
  Inauguration
    1889, inaugural address *200*
  Key Events
    American Tobacco and Caterpillar, formation of *203*
    Berkshire Hathaway, formation of *202*
    Carnegie Music Hall, opening of *204*
    Carrier, Willis, invention of air conditioning *203*
    Corbett, James, first heavyweight boxing champion *204*
    Ellis Island, opening of *204*
    Gas-powered automobile, invention of *203*
    General Electric, founding of *203*
    Immigration, impact on population increase by 50% since 1880 *203*
    Madison Square Garden, opening as a sports arena in New York City *203*
    Merck Company and Wm. Wrigley, founding of *203*
    Naismith, James, invention of basketball in Springfield, Massachusetts *203*
    Panic of 1893, caused by declining stock market *204*
    Peanut butter, development of *203*
    People's Party, formation of *202*
    Six states, admission to the Union *202*
    Tower Building, first true skyscraper in New York City *202*
    Unemployment, rise to 4 million nationwide *204*
    U.S. population, reach of almost 63 million *203*
    Yosemite National Park, creation of *203*
  Laws
    Dependent Pension Act *201*
    McKinley Act *201*
    National Reserve Act *201*
    Sherman Anti-Trust Act *201*
  Marriage
    Dimmick, Mary (Second Wife) *202*
    Scott, Caroline (First Wife) *198*

U.S. Supreme Court Rulings
  Davis vs Beacon **201**
Harrison, William Henry *iii, 54, 56, 85, 87, 90, 91, 92, 93, 96, 371, 438, 707, 726, 727, 743*
  Birth
    February 9, 1773 **90**
  Cabinet
    Badger, George (Secretary of the Navy) **93**
    Bell, John (Secretary of War) **93**
    Crittenden, John (Attorney General) **93**
    Ewing, Thomas (Secretary of the Treasury) **93**
    Granger, Francis (Postmaster General) **93**
    Tyler, John (Vice President) **93**
    Webster, Daniel (Secretary of State) **93**
  Career
    Brigadier General **91**
    Congress, territorial delegate **91**
    First Infantry Regiment, joined **90**
    Medical school, attended **90**
    Ohio state, senator **91**
    Territorial Indiana, governor **91**
    U.S. House of Representatives, elected to **91**
  Death
    April 4, 1841 **93**
  Elections
    1836 Presidential Election (Lost Election) **91**
    1840 Presidential Election (Elected President) **92**
  Family
    Anna, Elizabeth, Lucy, Mary, Benjamin, Carter, James, John Cleves, John Scott, and William (Children) **91**
    Harrison, Benjamin V and Elizabeth Bassett (Parents) **90**
    Six, unnamed (Siblings) **90**
  Inauguration
    1841, inaugural address **92**
  Key Events
    Nothing of interest **94**
  Marriage
    Symme, Anna (Wife) **91**
  U.S. Supreme Court Rulings
    United States vs The Amistad **93**
Harvard *12, 25, 27, 54, 67, 74, 170, 171, 217, 221, 222, 285, 307, 329, 347, 387, 396, 428, 486, 503, 511, 522, 525, 527, 528, 538, 716, 723, 741, 750, 760, 767, 771, 781, 784*

Hawaii *165, 214, 216, 333, 344, 443, 527, 528, 574, 761, 783*
Hayes, Rutherford B. *iii, 170, 171, 172, 173, 174, 175, 179, 184, 212, 334, 438, 506, 567, 708, 741, 742, 744, 748*
  Birth
    October 4, 1822 **170**
  Cabinet
    Devens, Charles (Attorney General) **173**
    Evarts, William (Secretary of State) **173**
    Key, David (Postmaster General) **173**
    McCrary, George W. (Secretary of War) **173**
    Schurz, Carl (Secretary of the Interior) **173**
    Sherman, John (Secretary of the Treasury) **173**
    Thompson, Richard (Secretary of the Navy) **173**
    Wheeler, William (Vice President) **173**
  Career
    Governor of Ohio, elected to **171**
    Law, practice of **170**
    Major General, promotion to **171**
    Ohio Volunteer Infantry, commission as major in the 23rd **171**
    U.S. House of Representatives, elected to **171**
  Death
    January 17, 1893 **175**
  Elections
    1876 Presidential Elections (Elected President) **171**
  Family
    Francis, James, Joseph, George, Manning, Rutherford Jr., Sardis, and Scott. Joseph, George, and Manning (Children) **171**
    Hayes, Sophia and Rutherford (Parents) **170**
    Lorenzo and Fanny (Siblings) **170**
  Inauguration
    1877, inaugural address **172**
  Key Events
    Bell Telephone Company, formation of **175**
    Edison, Thomas, demonstration of the phonograph invention **175**
    Edison, Thomas, invention of incandescent light bulb **175**
    Irish gangs, presence in lower New York City **176**
    Madison Square Garden, construction in New York City **175**
    Molly Maguires, breakup of terrorist mining group **175**

INDEX

Procter & Gamble, formation of *175*
Salvation Army, founding of *176*
St. Patrick's Cathedral, opening in New York City *175*
U.S. population, first exceedance of 50 million *176*
Vanderbilt, Cornelius, prominent in railroads and steamships *175*
Washington, Booker T., appointment to head Tuskegee Institute *176*
Yellow fever epidemic *175*
Laws
  Bland-Allison Act *174*
  National Quarantine Act *174*
  Posse Comitatus Act of 1878 *174*
Marriage
  Webb, Lucy Ware (Wife) *170*
U.S. Supreme Court Rulings
  Munn vs Illinois *173*
  Reynolds vs United States *174*
  United States vs Fox *173*
Hemings, Sally *35*, *718*
Hemingway, Ernest *271*
Hendricks, Thomas *171*, *192*, *193*, *741*, *745*
Henry, Patrick *4*
Hickok, Lorena *288*
Hicks, Whitehead *6*
Hinckley, John *450*
Hiroshima *311*, *763*
Hiss, Alger *316*, *330*, *388*, *771*
Hobart, Garret *212*, *213*, *214*, *709*, *749*
Holliday, Doc *190*, *196*
Holmes, Oliver Wendell *224*
Hoover Dam *280*
Hoover, Herbert *iv*, *249*, *259*, *264*, *266*, *269*, *273*, *275*, *278*, *279*, *280*, *286*, *438*, *710*, *759*, *760*
  Birth
    August 10, 1874 *273*
  Cabinet
    Adams, Charles (Secretary of the Navy) *276*
    Brown, Walter (Postmaster General) *276*
    Curtis, Charles (Vice President) *276*
    Davis, James (Secretary of Labor) *276*
    Good, James W. (Secretary of War) *276*
    Hyde, Arthur (Secretary of Agriculture) *276*
    Lamont, Robert (Secretary of Commerce) *276*
    Mellon, Andrew (Secretary of the Treasury) *276*
    Mitchell, William (Attorney General) *276*
    Stimson, Henry (Secretary of State) *276*
    Wilbur, Ray Lyman (Secretary of the Interior) *276*
  Career
    Mining engineer *274*
    Secretary of Commerce, served as *274*
    U.S. Food Administration, headed *274*
  Death
    October 20, 1964 *280*
  Elections
    1928 Presidential Election (Elected President) *275*
  Family
    Allen and Herbert Jr. (Children) *274*
    Hoover, Jesse Clark and Huldah Randall (Parents) *273*
    Mary and Theodore (Siblings) *273*
  Inauguration
    1929, inaugural address *276*
  Key Events
    Caraway, Hattie Wyatt, first woman elected to U.S. Senate *283*
    Chase Manhattan Bank, formed *282*
    Chrysler Building, opened in New York City *282*
    Corporate income tax, set at 1.75 percent *282*
    du Pont, Pierre, financed Prohibition repeal *283*
    Empire State Building, opened *282*
    Fall, Albert, convicted of accepting bribes *281*
    Flight simulator, introduced *281*
    Goldman Sachs, became private partnership *281*
    Kohler Plumbing, opened *282*
    Model A station wagon, introduced *281*
    Museum of Modern Art, opened in New York City *281*
    Polaroid strips, invented *281*
    Prohibition, in effect *281*
    Radio City Music Hall, opened in New York City *283*
    St. Valentine's Day, massacre *281*
    Waldorf-Astoria, opened *282*
  Laws
    1930 Smoot-Hawley Tariff Act *278*
    1931 Davis-Bacon Act *279*
    1931 Revenue Act *279*
    1932 Federal Kidnapping Act *279*
  Marriage
    Henry, Lou (Wife) *274*
  U.S. Supreme Court Rulings
    Near vs Minnesota *279*
    Powell vs Alabama *279*

The Pocket Veto Case *277*
Hoover, J. Edgar *254, 270, 354*
Hornet *298*
House of Representatives *10, 36, 48, 49, 54, 60, 67, 68, 69, 70, 71, 74, 75, 82, 86, 91, 92, 96, 103, 111, 115, 120, 121, 127, 134, 136, 147, 153, 155, 168, 171, 178, 193, 206, 212, 235, 248, 257, 265, 287, 315, 330, 348, 352, 370, 382, 385, 388, 392, 403, 412, 413, 420, 448, 468, 469, 470, 486, 494, 498, 500, 503, 505, 531, 533, 541, 551, 565, 567, 575, 582, 592, 605, 607, 615, 629, 635, 638, 645, 652, 669, 670, 673, 674, 678, 691, 692, 697, 700, 701, 704, 720, 724, 727, 728, 729, 731, 732, 733, 735, 737, 741, 742, 749, 755, 757, 767, 769, 771, 774, 779, 788, 792*
House Ways and Means Committee *11, 421, 498, 633, 644*
Houston, Sam *81, 326*
Howard, John *59, 722*
Howe, Elias *101*
Hubble Space Telescope *500*
Huckabee, Mike *557, 565, 656*
Hughes, Charles *247, 259, 264, 709, 755*
Humphrey, Hubert *376, 377, 378, 392, 393, 427, 711, 770, 772*
hush money *573, 584*

I

IBM *252, 302, 342, 344, 366, 368, 382, 408, 462, 465, 480, 497, 590, 753*
impeached *154, 155, 404, 414, 494, 539, 582, 607, 638, 738, 739, 781, 787, 788*
impeachment *10, 160, 403, 413, 493, 494, 519, 577, 578, 670, 671, 680, 681, 739, 773, 781, 787, 788*
inaugural address *14, 28, 37, 42, 51, 53, 59, 62, 69, 77, 79, 85, 92, 97, 104, 111, 115, 121, 128, 138, 139, 147, 165, 172, 179, 185, 200, 206, 214, 217, 227, 235, 244, 248, 258, 266, 276, 287, 295, 300, 316, 330, 335, 378, 398, 448, 454, 472, 486, 507, 513, 532, 541, 568, 606, 732, 733, 748, 777*
Indianapolis 500 *240*
Indian Nations *173*
Indians *2, 4, 10, 75, 78, 89, 154, 190, 670, 693, 724*
International Megan's Law *547*
Iran *298, 434, 436, 446, 448, 455, 461, 479, 520, 543, 544, 569, 586, 587, 626, 631, 652, 776, 777, 782, 785*

Iran-Contra Affair *455*
Iraq *475, 487, 512, 513, 517, 518, 520, 521, 524, 537, 538, 539, 586, 596, 612, 779, 782, 783, 785*
Irish Brigade *141*
Irish Potato Famine *107*
ISIS *518, 539, 544, 556, 586, 590*
Israel *314, 321, 401, 410, 433, 435, 437, 438, 488, 489, 548, 569, 572, 639, 640, 656, 773*

J

Jackson, Andrew *iii, 54, 55, 67, 68, 69, 70, 73, 74, 75, 76, 77, 78, 79, 80, 81, 84, 85, 96, 103, 129, 131, 170, 438, 557, 567, 706, 721, 723, 724, 725, 726, 728, 741*
Birth
March 15, 1767 *73*
Cabinet
Berrien, John (Attorney General) *77*
Branch, John (Secretary of the Navy) *77*
Calhoun, John (Vice President) *77*
Eaton, John (Secretary of War) *77*
Ingham, Samuel (Secretary of the Treasury) *77*
McLean, John (Postmaster General) *77*
Van Buren, Martin (Secretary of State) *77*
Cabinet - second term
Butler, Benjamin (Attorney General) *80*
Cass, Lewis (Secretary of War) *80*
Kendall, Amos (Postmaster General) *80*
McLane, Louis (Secretary of State) *79*
Taney, Roger (Secretary of the Treasury) *79*
Van Buren, Martin (Vice President) *79*
Woodbury, Levi (Secretary of the Navy) *80*
Cabinet - unofficial
Donaldson, Andrew (Nephew) *80*
Kendall, Amos (Newspaper editor) *80*
Lewis, William (General Jackson's former quartermaster) *80*
Overton, John (Friend and former business partner) *80*
Taney, Roger (Attorney General) *80*
Van Buren, Martin (Former secretary of state and vice president) *80*
Career
Florida, governor *75*
Law, practice of *74*
Public prosecutor, later judge *74*

INDEX

Tennessee militia, promoted to major general *74*
Tennessee Supreme Court, appointed to *74*
U.S. Senate (Tennessee), elected to *74*
Death
  June 8, 1845 *81*
Elections
  1824 Presidential Election (Lost Election) *75*
  1828 Presidential Election (Elected President) *76*
  1832 Presidential Election (Reelected second term) *79*
Family
  Hugh and Robert (Siblings) *73*
  Jackson, Andrew and Elizabeth Hutchinson (Parents) *73*
Inauguration
  1829, inaugural address *77*
  1833, inaugural address *79*
Key Events
  Adams, John Quincy, elected to U.S. House of Representatives after presidency *82*
  Baltimore and Ohio Railroad, began service *82*
  Deere, John, non-sticking steel plow introduced *82*
  Mormon Church, established by Joseph Smith *82*
  New York City, cholera epidemic *82*
  New York City Working Man's Party, founded *82*
  Oberlin College, first co-educational institution *82*
  South Texas, ruled by 20,000 Comanches *82*
  Texas Rangers, formed to protect Mexican border *82*
  Turner, Nat, led armed slave revolt *82*
Laws
  1828 Tariff Act *79*
  1830 Indian Removal Act *78*
  1832 Nullification Act *79*
Marriage
  Robards, Rachel (Wife) *74*
U.S. Supreme Court Rulings
  Barron vs Baltimore *78*
  Cherokee Nation vs Georgia *78*
  Indian Removal Act of 1830 *78*
  Worcester vs Georgia *78*

Jackson, Scoop *426*
Jacob, Jill *595*
James, Jesse *151, 168, 190*
Japan *122, 123, 216, 238, 296, 297, 299, 301, 310, 341, 468, 569, 753, 761, 762, 763*
Jay, John *8, 9, 14, 27, 31, 36, 48, 720*
Jefferson, Thomas *iii, vii, 6, 9, 16, 17, 19, 20, 22, 26, 27, 28, 30, 31, 34, 36, 37, 38, 42, 44, 46, 50, 59, 64, 71, 84, 89, 115, 150, 153, 185, 223, 230, 264, 310, 359, 371, 394, 413, 438, 471, 666, 705, 706, 715, 716, 718, 719, 722, 723, 731, 737, 762, 776*
Birth
  April 13, 1743 *34*
Cabinet
  Burr, Aaron (Vice President) *38*
  Dearborn, Henry (Secretary of War) *38*
  Dexter, Samuel (Secretary of the Treasury) *38*
  Habersham, Joseph (Postmaster General) *38*
  Lincoln, Levi (Attorney General) *38*
  Madison, James (Secretary of State) *38*
  Stoddert, Benjamin (Secretary of the Navy) *38*
Cabinet - second term
  Breckinridge, John (Attorney General) *43*
  Clinton, George (Vice President) *43*
  Dearborn, Henry (Secretary of War) *43*
  Gallatin, Albert (Secretary of the Treasury) *43*
  Granger, Gideon (Postmaster General) *43*
  Madison, James (Secretary of State) *43*
  Smith, Robert (Secretary of the Navy) *43*
Career
  Declaration of Independence, majority written by *35*
  Democratic-Republican Party, formed *36*
  France, minister to *35*
  Law, practice of *34*
  Secretary of State *35*
  Virginia, governor *35*
Death
  July 4, 1826 *45*
Elections
  1800 Presidential Election (Elected President) *36*
  1804 Presidential Election (Elected President) *41*

Family
  Jefferson, Peter and Jane (Parents) **34**
  Nine, unnamed (Siblings) **34**
  With Martha Wayles Skelton: Elizabeth, Jane, Lucy, Mary, Martha, and a boy who died at birth (Children) **35**
  With Sally Hemings: at least six (Children) **35**
Inauguration
  1801, inaugural address **37**
  1805, inaugural address **42**
Key Events
  Fulton, Robert, launched Clermont steamboat on Hudson River **46**
  Hamilton, Alexander, mistakenly credited with founding New York Times **46**
  HMS Leopard, demanded search of USS Chesapeake for deserters **46**
  Jefferson, ordered 200 gunboats to protect American coast **46**
  Jefferson, reduced public debt to $45 million **46**
  New York Post, founded **46**
  Pike, Zebulon, hired to map Louisiana Purchase **46**
  West Point Military Academy, established **46**
Laws
  1801 Judiciary Act **38**
  1802 Judiciary Act **38**
  1807 Embargo Act **43**
  1807 Judiciary Act **43**
Marriage
  Skelton, Martha Wayles (Wife) **35**
U.S. Supreme Court Rulings
  Faw vs Marsteller **41**
  Marbury vs Madison **40**
  United States vs Burr **43**
  United States vs Fisher **42**
Jenkins, Walter **373, 770**
Jerusalem **569, 572**
Jindal, Bobby **557, 564**
Johns Hopkins University **243, 393**
Johnson, Andrew *iii, vii,* **146, 147, 148, 152, 153, 154, 155, 156, 160, 185, 218, 219, 223, 261, 264, 289, 310, 371, 372, 394, 405, 413, 438, 471, 494, 606, 708, 736, 737, 738, 739, 744, 751, 757, 758, 770, 781**
Birth
  December 29, 1808 **152**
Cabinet
  Dennison, William (Postmaster General) **153**
  McCulloch, Hugh (Secretary of the Treasury) **153**
  Seward, William (Secretary of State) **153**
  Speed, James (Attorney General) **153**
  Stanton, Edwin (Secretary of War) **153**
  Usher, John (Secretary of the Interior) **153**
  Welles, Gideon (Secretary of the Navy) **153**
Career
  Greeneville, mayor of **152**
  Military governor of Tennessee, appointment to **153**
  Tailor, work as **152**
  U.S. House of Representatives, service in **153**
  U.S. Senate, service in **153**
Death
  July 31, 1875 **155**
Family
  Andrew, Charles, Martha, Mary, and Robert (Children) **152**
  Jacob and Mary Johnson (Parents) **152**
  William (Sibling) **152**
Inauguration
  1865, inaugural address **153**
Key Events
  Alaska, purchase from Russia for $7.2 million **156**
  Amnesty, for Confederate rebels declaring allegiance to the Union **156**
  Barbed wire, invention of **157**
  Coca-Cola, introduction of **156**
  Cody, Buffalo Bill, name origin after killing buffalo **156**
  Coffee percolator, invention of **156**
  Ku Klux Klan, formation of **156**
  Memphis, racial rampage by whites **156**
  Nebraska, admission to the Union **156**
  Race riot **156**
  Telegraph cable, linking of the United States and England **156**
  Tobacco, introduction of **157**
  World Almanac, first appearance of **157**
Laws
  13th Amendment to the U.S. Constitution ratified in 1865 **154**
  14th Amendment to the U.S. Constitution ratified **155**
  1866 Civil Rights Act vetoed by Johnson but veto overridden by Congress **154**
  Expatriation Act of 1868 **154**
  Judicial Circuits Act **154**
  Reconstruction Act **154**

Marriage
   McCardle, Eliza (Wife) *152*
   U.S. Supreme Court Rulings
      Ex parte Milligan *154*
      Mississippi vs Johnson *154*
Johnson & Johnson *196, 262, 440, 463, 522*
Johnson, Lyndon B. *iv, 330, 350, 351, 352, 353, 364, 365, 369, 370, 371, 372, 373, 374, 375, 376, 377, 378, 379, 380, 381, 383, 391, 394, 405, 412, 413, 420, 438, 471, 615, 711, 767, 768, 769, 770, 771, 772*
   Birth
      August 27, 1908 *369*
   Cabinet
      Celebrezze, Anthony (Secretary of Health, Education and Welfare) *372*
      Dillon, Douglas (Secretary of the Treasury) *372*
      Freeman, Orville (Secretary of Agriculture) *372*
      Hodges, Luther (Secretary of Commerce) *372*
      Kennedy, Robert (Attorney General) *372*
      McNamara, Robert (Secretary of Defense) *372*
      Rusk, Dean (Secretary of State) *372*
      Udall, Stewart (Secretary of the Interior) *372*
      Wirtz, Willard (Secretary of Labor) *372*
   Cabinet - second term
      Boyd, Alan (Secretary of Transportation) *378*
      Connor, John (Secretary of Commerce) *378*
      Fowler, Henry (Secretary of the Treasury) *378*
      Freeman, Orville (Secretary of Agriculture) *378*
      Gardner, John (Secretary of Health, Education and Welfare) *378*
      Humphrey, Hubert (Vice President) *378*
      Katzenbach, Nicholas (Attorney General) *378*
      McNamara, Robert (Secretary of Defense) *378*
      O'Brien, Lawrence (Postmaster General) *378*
      Rusk, Dean (Secretary of State) *378*
      Udall, Stewart (Secretary of the Interior) *378*
      Weaver, Robert (Secretary of Housing and Urban Development) *378*
      Wirtz, William (Secretary of Labor) *378*
   Career
      House of Representatives, election to *370*
      Military duty, enlistment for *370*
      Naval officer, service as *370*
      U.S. Senate, elected to *370*
   Death
      January 22, 1973 *381*
   Elections
      1964 Presidential Election (Elected President) *377*
   Family
      Four, unnamed (Siblings) *369*
      Johnson, Samuel and Rebekah Baines (Parents) *369*
      Lynda Bird and Luci Baines (Children) *370*
   Inauguration
      1965, inaugural address *378*
   Key Events
      Aldrin, Buzz, and Armstrong, Neil, moon landing *386*
      Ali, Muhammad, rise of *383*
      Anti-war demonstration, 300,000 march to the United Nations *384*
      Apollo 1, fire and death of three astronauts *385*
      Brooke, Edward, first elected Black U.S. Senator *384*
      Chavez, Cesar, leadership of strike against California wine growers *384*
      Evers, Medgar, assassination of *381*
      Gulf of Tonkin Resolution, allowance for Vietnam escalation *382*
      Hong Kong flu, death of 100,000 people in U.S. *385*
      Idlewild International Airport, renaming to John F. Kennedy International Airport *382*
      Intel, founding of *385*
      Kennedy, Joseph, death from stroke *386*
      King, Martin Luther Jr., assassination in Memphis *386*
      King, Martin Luther Jr., role in Equal Rights March on Washington *381*
      Malcolm X, assassination of *383*
      March for Civil Rights *381*
      National Organization for Women (NOW), formation of *384*
      New York Lottery, introduction of *384*
      Posthumous award of Presidential Medal of Freedom *383*

Power blackout, majority in Northeast *383*
U.S. troops, landing in Vietnam *384*
Verrazano-Narrows Bridge, opening of *382*
Laws
   25th Amendment to the U.S. Constitution ratified *379*
   1963 Transition Act *373*
   1964 Civil Rights Act *377*
   1964 Revenue Act *377*
   1965 Immigration and Nationality Act *379*
   1965 Medicare and Medicaid Act *379*
   1965 Tax Reform Act *379*
   1965 Voting Rights Act *379*
   1967 Age Discrimination in Employment Act *379*
   1968 Civil Rights Act *381*
   1968 Omnibus Crime Control Act *381*
   1968 Revenue & Expenditure Act *381*
   1968 Williams Act *381*
Marriage
   Taylor, Claudia "Lady Bird" (Wife) *370*
U.S. Supreme Court Rulings
   J.I. Case vs Borak *377*
   Loving vs Virginia *379*
   Miranda vs Arizona *379*
   New York Times vs Sullivan *377*
Johnson, Richard *85*, *86*, *87*, *92*, *96*, *726*, *727*
Johnstown Flood *200*
Joint Chiefs of Staff *313*, *479*, *793*
joint resolution *80*
Jones, Alfred Winslow *323*
Jones, Edward *208*, *748*
Jones, James *373*, *770*
Jones, Paula *490*, *780*
JPMorgan *141*, *175*, *189*, *197*, *200*, *203*, *207*, *209*, *210*, *224*, *230*, *232*, *254*, *303*, *501*, *554*
JP Morgan Chase *65*, *501*, *525*, *541*, *552*, *553*
Jungle, The *228*

K

Kaine, Tim *546*, *565*, *566*, *785*, *787*
Kansas-Nebraska Act of 1854 *134*
Kaw Reservation *275*
Kefauver, Estes *319*, *323*, *335*, *390*, *766*, *772*
Keller, Helen *268*

Kellogg *209*, *257*, *266*, *756*
Kemp, Jack *471*, *491*, *780*
Kennedy Doctrine *356*
Kennedy, Joe *344*, *347*, *348*, *350*, *356*, *361*, *407*
Kennedy, John F. *iv*, *44*, *188*, *223*, *278*, *303*, *320*, *328*, *338*, *339*, *340*, *344*, *346*, *347*, *348*, *349*, *350*, *351*, *352*, *353*, *354*, *355*, *356*, *357*, *358*, *359*, *360*, *361*, *362*, *363*, *364*, *365*, *366*, *367*, *368*, *371*, *372*, *375*, *377*, *378*, *380*, *383*, *386*, *390*, *391*, *393*, *394*, *398*, *407*, *412*, *439*, *471*, *482*, *594*, *605*, *655*, *711*, *745*, *766*, *767*, *768*, *769*, *770*, *772*
Birth
   May 29, 1917 *346*
Cabinet
   Day, Edward (Postmaster General) *353*
   Dillon, Douglas (Secretary of the Treasury) *353*
   Freeman, Orville (Secretary of Agriculture) *353*
   Goldberg, Arthur (Secretary of Labor) *353*
   Hodges, Luther (Secretary of Commerce) *353*
   Johnson, Lyndon B. (Vice President) *353*
   Kennedy, Robert (Attorney General) *353*
   McNamara, Robert (Secretary of Defense) *353*
   Ribicoff, Abraham (Secretary of Health, Education and Welfare) *354*
   Rusk, Dean (Secretary of State) *353*
   Udall, Stewart (Secretary of the Interior) *353*
Career
   Naval Reserve, joining and command of PT-109 *348*
   U.S. House of Representatives, elected to *348*
   U.S. Senate, election to and rise to majority leader *349*
Death
   November 22, 1963 *362*
Elections
   1960 Presidential Election (Elected President) *351*
Family
   Caroline, John Jr., and Patrick (Children) *349*

INDEX

Edward, Joseph Jr., Robert, Eunice, Jean, Kathleen, Patricia, and Rosemary (Siblings) *346*
Kennedy, Joseph and Rose (Parents) *346*
Inauguration
  1961, inaugural address *356*
Key Events
  Alliance for Progress, introduction to aid Latin American countries *367*
  Churchill, Winston, was made an honorary U.S. citizen *368*
  Electric typewriter, introduction of *366*
  Gagarin, Yuri, first man to circle the Earth *366*
  Goldberg, Arthur, first Jewish appointee to U.S. Supreme Court as Associate Justice *367*
  Hurricane Donna, devastation of the East Coast *367*
  Idlewild Airport, renaming to JFK Airport *368*
  Indian Point, opening of nuclear-powered plant *367*
  Kennedy, Ted, election to U.S. Senate *367*
  Nike, beginning of operations *367*
  Peace Corps, creation of *366*
  Powers, Francis Gary, exchange for Soviet spy Rudolph Abel *367*
  Shepard, Alan, first American in space *366*
  Throgs Neck Bridge, opening of *366*
  U.S. population, exceedance of 200 million *368*
  U.S. withdrawal of support from South Vietnam *368*
  Walton, Sam, opening of first discount store, later Walmart *367*
  Weight Watchers, incorporation of *368*
Laws
  1962 Manpower Development and Training Act *359*
  1962 Self-Employed Individuals Tax Retirement Act *359*
  1963 Equal Pay Act *361*
  1963 Transition Act *365*
  1964 Civil Rights Act *362*
Marriage
  Bouvier, Jacqueline (Wife) *348*
U.S. Supreme Court Rulings
  Baker vs Carr *360*
  Gideon vs Wainwright *362*
  Mapp vs Ohio *357*
Kennedy, Joseph *290, 303, 346, 347, 386*

Kennedy, Robert F. *341, 352, 353, 364, 368, 372, 373, 375, 380, 382, 383, 385, 386, 392, 770*
Kennedy Jr., Robert F. *637, 638, 639, 654, 656*
Kennedy, Ted *386, 399, 426, 427, 525, 550*
Kentucky Militia *109*
Kerik, Bernard *582*
Kern, John *235, 753*
Kerry, John *513, 522, 541, 544, 712, 783*
Key, Francis Scott *55, 721*
Khrushchev, Nikita *337, 344*
Kim, Jong Un *569*
King George VI *294*
King, Martin Luther Jr. *362, 380, 381, 383, 386, 392, 452, 463, 551, 610, 658*
King, Rufus *42, 50, 59, 84, 129, 686, 706, 720, 722, 726, 734*
King, William *121, 122, 732*
Kissinger, Henry *396, 399, 414, 520*
Kleindienst, Richard *397, 401, 773*
Knights of the Golden Circle *136*
Know Nothing Party *118, 731*
Knox, Henry *7, 16, 19, 715*
Korean War *318, 334, 335, 394, 764*
Kosygin, Alexei *380*
KPMG *515, 522*
Ku Klux Klan *156, 163, 260, 383, 738, 740, 756*

L

Labor Day *207, 748*
La Follette, Robert *240, 265, 758*
Lane, Harriet *129*
LASER *359*
laudanum *2, 714*
League of Nations *250*
Lee, Robert E. *146, 148, 159, 739*
LeMay, Curtis *393, 772*
L'Enfant, Pierre *17*
Lewinsky, Monica *491, 493, 496, 780*
Lewis, Meriwether *38*
Lewis, Sinclair *245, 255, 262, 271, 281, 282*
Lexington *4, 127, 128, 131*
Liberia *63, 723*
Liberty Bell *82, 118*
Lieberman, Joseph *506, 782*
Lincoln, Abraham *iii, vii, 22, 45, 46, 106, 113, 127, 131, 132, 133, 134, 135, 136, 137, 138, 139, 140, 141, 142, 143, 144, 145, 146, 147, 148, 149, 150, 153, 155, 159, 160, 172, 178, 180, 181, 184, 218, 219, 230, 244, 289, 302, 305, 319, 340, 362, 363, 364, 365, 371, 392, 397, 402, 541,*

*557, 597, 615, 619, 707, 708, 730,
734, 735, 736, 737, 739, 742, 743,
750, 752, 762, 768, 770*
Birth
  February 12, 1809 *133*
Cabinet
  Bates, Edward (Attorney General) *140*
  Cameron, Simon (Secretary of War) *140*
  Chase, Salmon (Secretary of the Treasury) *140*
  Hamlin, Hannibal (Vice President) *140*
  King, Horatio (Postmaster General) *140*
  Seward, William (Secretary of State) *140*
  Smith, Caleb (Secretary of the Interior) *140*
  Welles, Gideon (Secretary of the Navy) *140*
Cabinet - second term
  Dennison, William (Postmaster General) *148*
  Johnson, Andrew (Vice President) *148*
  McCulloch, Hugh (Secretary of the Treasury) *148*
  Speed, James (Attorney General) *148*
  Stanton, Edwin (Secretary of War) *148*
  Usher, John (Secretary of the Interior) *148*
Career
  Blacksmith, rail splitter, store clerk, bartender, ferryboat captain, surveyor, and postmaster, roles held prior to practicing law *134*
  Illinois state legislature, service in *134*
  Law, practice of *134*
Elections
  1860 Presidential Election (Elected President) *136*
  1864 Presidential Election (Elected President) *146*
Family
  Lincoln, Thomas and Nancy (Parents) *133*
  Robert Todd, Edward Baker, William Wallace, and Thomas Todd (Children) *134*
  Sarah, Thomas, and half-siblings John, Matilda, and Elizabeth (Siblings) *133, 134*
Inauguration
  1861, inaugural address *138*
  1865, inaugural address *147*
Key Events
  Breweries, emergence of *151*
  Civil War *150*
  Confederate States of America, formation of *150*
  Elevated railways, replacement of horse-drawn vehicles *151*
  James, Jesse, death by shooting after bank robbery *151*
  Otis, Elisha, patent for lifting device (elevator) *150*
  Pullman, George, introduction of swing-down upper and lower sleeping berths *151*
  Rockefeller, John D., entry into the kerosene business *150*
  Steel mills, replacement of iron factories *151*
  Trains, replacement of stagecoaches *151*
Laws
  Conscription Act *140, 141*
  Homestead Act *144*
  Legal Tender Act *143*
  National Banking Act *140*
  Railway Act *143*
  Revenue Act *140, 143, 146*
Marriage
  Todd, Mary (Wife) *134*
U.S. Supreme Court Rulings
  Ex Parte Vallandigham *146*
  United States vs Jackalow *142*
  United States vs Knight's Administrator *142*
  United States vs The Schooner Brilliante *144*
Lincoln-Douglas *132*
Lincoln, Robert Todd *180, 185*
Lindbergh Law *279*
Little Big Horn River *169*
Livingston, Philip *6, 667*
Lodge, Henry Cabot *250, 349, 351, 391, 767, 770, 772*
Logan, John *192, 745*
Louisiana Purchase *40, 41, 46, 59, 67, 719*
Luciano, Lucky *281*
Lusitania *246, 248, 755*
Lynchburg *131*

M

MacArthur, Douglas *299, 311, 318, 327, 763, 765*
Madison, Dolley *52, 105, 720*
Madison, James *iii, 7, 9, 17, 26, 38, 43, 47, 48, 50, 53, 64, 104, 438, 685, 706, 718, 720, 721*
  Birth
    March 16, 1751 *47*
  Cabinet
    Clinton, George (Vice President) *51*
    Eustis, William (Secretary of War) *51*
    Gallatin, Albert (Secretary of the Treasury) *51*

INDEX

Granger, Gideon (Postmaster General) *51*
Hamilton, Paul (Secretary of the Navy) *51*
Monroe, James (Secretary of State) *51*
Rodney, Caesar (Attorney General) *51*
Smith, Robert (Secretary of State) *51*
Cabinet - second term
   Armstrong, John (Secretary of War) *54*
   Gallatin, Albert (Secretary of the Treasury) *54*
   Gerry, Elbridge (Vice President) *54*
   Granger, Gideon (Postmaster General) *54*
   Jones, William (Secretary of the Navy) *54*
   Monroe, James (Secretary of State) *54*
   Pinkney, William (Attorney General) *54*
Career
   Bill of Rights, writing of *49*
   Continental Congress, elected to *48*
   House of Representatives, elected to *49*
   Law, practice of *47*
   Orange County Militia (Virginia), commissioned colonel in *48*
   Secretary of State *50*
   Virginia Constitutional Convention, member of *47*
Death
   June 28, 1836 *56*
Elections
   1808 Presidential Election (Elected President) *50*
   1812 Presidential Election (Elected President) *53*
Family
   Eleven, unnamed (Siblings) *47*
   Madison, James and Eleanor Rose Conway (Parents) *47*
   Payne, John (Stepson) *49*
Inauguration
   1809, inaugural address *51*
   1813, inaugural address *53*
Key Events
   Boston's Provident Institute for Savings, became probably the first savings bank *57*
   Chief Tecumseh and his tribe, defeated by William Henry Harrison's forces at Tippecanoe *56*
   Fulton, Robert, launched larger version of his first steamboat to traverse the Ohio and Mississippi Rivers *57*
   importation of slaves, prohibited in U.S. *56*
   Louisiana, Indiana, and Mississippi joined the Union *57*
   Providence, Rhode Island had more than 170 small factories *57*
   Stevens, John, first to be given a state charter to build a railroad in New Jersey *57*
   The Hartford Convention, ended the Federalist Party *57*
Laws
   1809 Intercourse Act *52*
   1812 Tariff Act *53*
   1813 Civil Rights Act *54*
   1816 Bank Legislation Act *55*
   1816 Tariff Act *55*
   Fletcher vs Peck *52*
Marriage
   Todd, Dolley Payne (Wife) *49*
U.S. Supreme Court Rulings
   Martin vs Hunter's Lessee *55*
   United States vs Peters *51*
Madison's War *53*
malaria *89, 170, 177, 182, 348, 742*
Mandelbaum, Fredericka *209*
Manifest Destiny *106, 112, 729*
Marbury vs Madison *40, 336*
Marine Corps *5, 43, 348*
Marine Corps Hymn *43*
Marquis de Lafayette *6*
Marshall, George C. *327*
Marshall, John *31, 33, 38, 43, 82, 719*
Marshall Plan *313, 334, 367*
Marshall, Thomas *238, 243, 244, 245, 247, 248, 754, 755*
Marxism *232, 451*
Maryland *10, 12, 54, 61, 82, 107, 142, 149, 231, 320, 392, 393, 394, 402, 433, 434, 447, 552, 666, 670, 685, 721, 736, 772*
Mason, George *6, 9, 35*
Massachusetts *4, 5, 9, 10, 12, 19, 25, 26, 29, 31, 32, 53, 54, 57, 58, 65, 66, 71, 72, 118, 136, 164, 203, 219, 258, 263, 264, 343, 346, 347, 361, 367, 398, 447, 467, 468, 470, 502, 506, 523, 525, 540, 626, 639, 654, 667, 670, 686, 716, 717, 723, 731, 757, 767, 778, 781*
Massachusetts minutemen *4*
Mayflower *269*
McCain, John *530, 578, 587, 596, 607, 712, 784, 790*
McCarthy, Joseph *317, 323, 341, 389*
McClellan, George *142, 146, 708, 736*
McCormick, Cyrus *82, 108*

831

WHAT YOU SHOULD KNOW ABOUT THE 47 U.S. PRESIDENTS

McIntosh, Catherine **118, 731**
McKinley, William **iv, 207, 211, 213, 222, 223, 227, 265, 371, 709, 749, 750**
  Birth
    January 29, 1843 **211**
  Cabinet
    Alger, Russell (Secretary of War) **214**
    Bliss, Cornelius (Secretary of the Interior) **214**
    Gage, Lyman (Secretary of the Treasury) **214**
    Gary, James (Postmaster General) **214 218**
    Hobart, Garret (Vice President) **214**
    Long, John (Secretary of the Navy) **214**
    McKenna, Joseph (Attorney General) **214**
    Sherman, John (Secretary of State) **214**
    Wilson, James (Secretary of Agriculture) **214**
  Cabinet - second term
    Gage, Lyman (Secretary of the Treasury) **217**
    Hay, John (Secretary of State) **217**
    Hitchcock, Ethan (Secretary of the Interior) **218**
    Knox, Philander (Attorney General) **217**
    Long, John (Secretary of the Navy) **218**
    Roosevelt, Theodore (Vice President) **217**
    Root, Elihu (Secretary of War) **217**
    Smith, Charles (Postmaster General) **218**
    Wilson, James (Secretary of Agriculture) **218**
  Career
    Governor of Ohio, elected **212**
    Law, practice of **212**
    Union Army, served as private **211**
    U.S. House of Representatives, served in **212**
  Death
    September 6, 1901 **218**
  Elections
    1896 Presidential Election (Elected President) **213**
    1900 Presidential Election (Elected President) **216**
  Family
    Abner, David, James, Abigail, Anna, Helen, Mary, and Sarah (Siblings) **211**
    Katherine and Ida (Children) **212**
    McKinley, William Sr. and Nancy Allison (Parents) **211**
  Inauguration
    1897, inaugural address **214**
    1901, inaugural address **217**
  Key Events
    Boston, first subway service in America **219**
    Electric trolleys, replaced horsecars **219**
    Galveston, Texas, hurricane killed over 2,000 **219**
    General Motors, opened **219**
    Kresge, first store opened **219**
    New York City, five boroughs established **219**
    Oil well, first major discovery in Spindletop **220**
    Pay phone, first appeared in New York City **219**
    U.S., 300,000 saloons **220**
    U.S. population, exceeded 75 million **220**
  Laws
    1897 Revenue Act **214**
    1898 Volunteer Army Act **215**
    1900 Gold Standards Act **216**
    Olney-Pauncefote Treaty **215**
    Treaty of Paris **215**
  Marriage
    Saxton, Ida (Wife) **212**
  U.S. Supreme Court Rulings
    Paquete Habana **216**
    United States vs Trans-Missouri Freight Association **214**
    United States vs Wong Kim Ark **215**
McLarty, Thomas "Mack" **486**
McLaury brothers **189, 190**
McNary, Charles **295, 761**
Meade, George **148**
Medal of Honor **143, 215, 222**
Medicaid **379, 548, 657**
Medicare **378, 379, 451, 459, 472, 490, 510, 543, 544, 548, 636, 638, 646, 647, 657, 783**
Meese, Ed **449, 778**
Meigs Jr., R. Jonathan **61**
Mellon, James **141**
Memorial Day **398**
Merrimac **143**
Mexican-American War **121, 128, 159**
Mexican War **109, 730, 739**
Middle East **401, 433**
midterms **237, 246, 249, 278, 293, 379, 394, 451, 457, 473, 510, 515, 770**
Mississippi Great Flood **272**

Missouri *62, 64, 100, 103, 123, 129, 143, 151, 159, 214, 299, 300, 308, 309, 319, 452, 453, 467, 476, 485, 506, 513, 530, 552, 566, 614, 722, 734, 739, 762,*
Missouri Compromise, The *62, 103, 123, 129, 722, 734*
Mitchell, John *395, 396, 397, 403*
Moby Dick *118*
Molly Maguires *151, 169, 175*
Mondale, Walter *419, 427, 430, 434, 447, 453, 454, 469, 712, 775, 776, 777, 778*
Monitor *143*
Monroe Doctrine *51, 63, 67, 71, 224, 360, 722, 723, 768*
Monroe, James *iii, 51, 54, 56, 58, 59, 60, 61, 62, 63, 64, 67, 68, 71, 76, 224, 341, 342, 360, 438, 706, 721, 722, 723, 768*
  Birth
    April 28, 1758 *58*
  Cabinet
    Adams, John Quincy (Secretary of State) *61*
    Calhoun, John (Secretary of War) *61*
    Crawford, William (Secretary of the Treasury) *61*
    Crowninshield, Benjamin (Secretary of the Navy) *61*
    Meigs Jr., R. Jonathan (Postmaster General) *61*
    Rush, Richard (Attorney General) *61*
    Tompkins, Daniel (Vice President) *61*
  Cabinet - second term
    Adams, John Quincy (Secretary of State) *63*
    Calhoun, John (Secretary of War) *63*
    Crawford, William (Secretary of the Treasury) *63*
    Meigs, Jonathan (Postmaster General) *63*
    Thompson, Smith (Secretary of the Navy) *63*
    Tompkins, Daniel (Vice President) *63*
    Wirt, William (Attorney General) *63*
  Career
    Continental Congress, delegate *59*
    France, served as minister to *59*
    Jefferson, Thomas, mentored in law by *59*
    Secretary of State, served under President Madison *59*
    Secretary of War, served under President Madison *59*
    Third Virginia Infantry, served as lieutenant in Revolutionary War *58*
    Transferred to the Continental Army as a captain. *58*
    U.S. Senate, first to serve before presidency *59*
    Virginia, governor of *59*
  Death
    July 4, 1831 *64*
  Elections
    1816 Presidential Election (Elected President) *59*
    1820 Presidential Election (Elected President) *62*
  Family
    Eliza, James, and Maria (Children) *59*
    Elizabeth, Andre, Joseph and Spence Jr. (Siblings) *58*
    Spence and Elizabeth Monroe (Parents) *58*
  Inauguration
    1817, inaugural address *59*
    1821, inaugural address *62*
  Key Events
    Alabama, Illinois, Maine, and Missouri joined the Union *64*
    Connecticut, first free school for the deaf established in *64*
    Depression, first major impact in South and West *64*
    First organized immigration of Black Americans from the U.S. departed for Sierra Leone *65*
    New York Times, first Pulitzer Prize for Journalism *64*
    Pensions approved for war veterans *64*
    Ricardo, David, wrote Principles of Political Economy *64*
    Troy Female Seminary, first women's college *65*
    Yale College, banned playing of football as too violent *65*
  Laws
    Land Act *62*
  Marriage
    Kortright, Elizabeth (Wife) *59*
  U.S. Supreme Court Rulings
    Cohens vs Virginia *62*
    Dartmouth College vs Woodward *61*
    Gibbons vs Ogden *64*
    McCulloch vs Maryland *61*
Monrovia *63, 723*
Monticello *19, 35, 39, 44, 45, 46, 718*
Montpelier *47, 56, 719*

Moore, Sara Jane *417*
Morgan, J.P. *141, 175, 189, 197, 200, 203, 207, 209, 210, 224, 230, 232, 303*
Morgan Stanley *303, 465, 500*
Morris, Dick *483, 493*
Morse, Samuel *100, 728*
Morton, Levi *195, 199, 200, 205, 747*
Mount Rushmore *22, 45, 150, 230, 715, 719, 736, 752, 762*
Mount Vernon *2, 3, 8, 19, 21*
Moyers, Bill *373, 770*
Muskie, Edmund *393, 772*

N

N95 *579*
Nagasaki *311, 763*
national anthem *55, 282*
National Commission on Fiscal Responsibility *537*
National Guard *308, 342, 368, 381, 385, 390, 470, 503, 599, 781*
National Press *309*
National Republicans *20, 70, 76, 79, 85, 725, 726*
National Rifle Association *168*
National Security Council *313, 396, 511*
National Volunteers *136*
National Youth Administration *370, 769*
Nation, Carrie *220, 240*
Nelson, George (Baby Face) *302*
Ness, Eliot *281*
New Deal *288, 289, 299, 301, 303, 306, 330, 374*
New Hampshire *10, 12, 62, 120, 121, 124, 164, 307, 319, 331, 474, 600, 601, 625, 646, 667, 670, 686, 722, 732, 766*
New Jersey *10, 12, 37, 41, 47, 57, 108, 167, 191, 208, 209, 213, 237, 243, 254, 261, 282, 304, 341, 380, 423, 455, 553, 561, 562, 620, 667, 670, 686, 719, 745, 753, 754, 786*
New Orleans *3, 23, 40, 43, 55, 74, 105, 365, 481, 721, 724*
New York City *6, 8, 10, 11, 13, 18, 41, 46, 48, 50, 60, 65, 71, 82, 119, 132, 141, 146, 160, 166, 167, 168, 175, 176, 184, 185, 189, 190, 196, 202, 203, 204, 205, 209, 217, 219, 221, 222, 230, 231, 232, 233, 239, 240, 241, 251, 252, 254, 255, 262, 271, 281, 282, 283, 290, 302, 305, 306,* *321, 322, 323, 324, 328, 343, 344, 351, 366, 367, 382, 385, 390, 391, 405, 406, 407, 408, 409, 418, 422, 439, 440, 441, 444, 465, 478, 500, 509, 520, 554, 558, 560, 572, 586, 587, 589, 590, 591, 620, 636, 645, 651, 715, 722, 740, 747, 750, 751, 772, 774, 782, 784, 786, 792*
New York Post *46, 599*
New York State Assembly *50, 114, 731*
New York Stock Exchange *23, 64, 478, 523*
New York Times *118, 189, 210, 232, 253, 274, 357, 377, 397, 408, 521, 542, 600, 614, 622, 628, 648, 650, 731, 755, 759*
New York Yankees *231, 281, 341, 342, 410, 522*
Nixon Doctrine *395*
Nixon, Richard M. *iv, 316, 328, 329, 330, 331, 335, 337, 338, 339, 348, 350, 351, 352, 355, 372, 376, 387, 388, 389, 390, 391, 392, 393, 394, 395, 396, 397, 398, 399, 400, 401, 402, 403, 404, 405, 406, 408, 409, 413, 414, 418, 420, 428, 437, 438, 444, 445, 450, 452, 456, 468, 469, 471, 655, 711, 765, 766, 767, 770, 771, 772, 773, 774, 775*
  Birth
    January 9, 1913 *387*
  Cabinet
    Agnew, Spiro (Vice President) *395*
    Blount, Winton (Postmaster General) *395*
    Finch, Robert (Secretary of Health, Education and Welfare) *395*
    Hardin, Clifford (Secretary of Agriculture) *395*
    Hickel, Walter (Secretary of the Interior) *395*
    Kennedy, David (Secretary of the Treasury) *395*
    Laird, George Melvin (Secretary of Defense) *395*
    Mitchell, John (Attorney General) *395*
    Rogers, William (Secretary of State) *395*
    Romney, George (Secretary of Housing and Urban Development) *395*
    Schultz, George (Secretary of Labor) *395*
    Stans, Maurice (Secretary of Commerce) *395*
    Volpe, John (Secretary of Transportation) *395*
  Cabinet - second term
    Agnew, Spiro (Vice President) *399*

INDEX

Blount, Winton (Postmaster General) *399*
Brennan, Peter (Secretary of Labor) *399*
Brinegar, Charles (Secretary of Transportation) *400*
Dent, Frederick (Secretary of Commerce) *399*
Hickel, Walter (Secretary of the Interior) *399*
Kissinger, Henry (Secretary of State) *399*
Lynn, James (Secretary of Housing and Urban Development) *400*
Morton, Rogers (Secretary of Agriculture) *399*
Richardson, Elliot (Attorney General) *399*
Schlesinger, James (Secretary of Defense) *399*
Schultz, George (Secretary of the Treasury) *399*
Weinberger, Caspar (Secretary of Health, Education and Welfare) *399*
Career
  House Un-American Activities Committee, member *388*
  Law, practice of *388*, *391*
  U.S. House of Representatives, elected to *388*
  U.S. Navy, served as lieutenant commander *388*
Death
  April 22, 1994 *406*
Elections
  1968 Presidential Election (Elected President) *393*
  1972 Presidential Election (Elected President) *398*
Family
  Arthur, Edward, Francis, and Harold (Siblings) *387*
  Nixon, Frank and Hannah (Parents) *387*
  Tricia and Julie (Children) *388*
Inauguration
  1969, inaugural address *394*
  1973, inaugural address *398*
Key Events
  Apollo 11, moon landing *407*
  Apollo 13, moon mission and return *408*
  Apple Computer founders Steve Jobs and Steve Wozniak introduced *408*
  Armstrong, Neil, and Aldrin, Buzz, first to walk on moon *407*
  Cellular telephone, introduced *410*
  Chicago Board Options Exchange (CBOE), opened *410*
  Concorde, first supersonic transport plane introduced *407*
  Corning, developed optical fibers *407*
  Lockheed Aircraft, received $250 million in federal loans *408*
  National Football League, created *407*
  Oil, priced at $2 per barrel *407*
  Over-the-Counter Market, became NASDAQ *408*
  U.S. mortgages, securitization began *407*
  Vietnam War, escalation *408*
  Walt Disney World, opened in Florida *409*
Laws
  26th Amendment to the U.S. Constitution ratified *397*
  1969 Personal Income Tax Act *395*
  1969 Tax Reform Act *395*
  1970 Clean Air Act *396*
  1970 Economic Stabilization Act *396*, *397*
  1970 Federal Pay Comparability Act *396*
  1970 Occupational Safety and Health Act *396*
  1970 Securities Investor Protection Act *396*
  1972 Civil Rights Act *397*
  1972 Clean Air Act *397*
  1973 Health Maintenance Organization Act *401*
  1973 War Powers Act *401*
  1974 Employee Retirement Income Security Act *404*
  1974 Gold Act *404*
  1974 Vietnam Veterans Reemployment Rights Act *404*
  Anti-Ballistic Missile (ABM) Treaty *398*
  Strategic Arms Limitation Talks *398*
Marriage
  Ryan, Thelma "Patricia" (Wife) *388*
U.S. Supreme Court Rulings
  New York Times Company vs United States *397*
  Roe vs Wade *400*
  Tinker vs Des Moines *395*
  United States vs Nixon *403*
  United States vs United States District Court *397*
Nobel Peace Prize *229*, *250*, *265*, *433*, *437*, *438*, *536*, *659*, *752*, *776*, *784*, *796*
Normandy *299*, *641*, *762*
Northeast Ordinance Act *9*
nuclear arms *338*, *461*

Nuclear Test Ban *361*
nuclear treaty *544, 569, 785*

O

Oakley, Annie *203*
oath of office *13, 139, 185, 188, 213, 413, 534, 657, 749, 796*
Obama, Barack *iv, 438, 477, 496, 519, 525, 527, 528, 529, 530, 531, 532, 533, 534, 535, 536, 537, 538, 539, 540, 541, 542, 543, 544, 545, 546, 547, 548, 549, 550, 552, 555, 556, 557, 559, 566, 569, 577, 578, 585, 596, 597, 598, 603, 609, 611, 616, 618, 620, 622, 624, 638, 654, 657, 658, 712, 779, 781, 783, 784, 785, 787, 790, 791*
  Birth
    August 4, 1961 *527*
  Cabinet
    Biden, Joe (Vice President) *533*
    Chu, Steven (Secretary of Energy) *533*
    Clinton, Hillary (Secretary of State) *533*
    Donovan, Shaun (Secretary of Housing and Urban Development) *533*
    Duncan, Arne (Secretary of Education) *533*
    Gates, Robert (Secretary of Defense) *533*
    Geithner, Timothy (Secretary of the Treasury) *533*
    Holder, Eric (Attorney General) *533*
    LaHood, Ray (Secretary of Transportation) *533*
    Locke, Gary (Secretary of Commerce) *533*
    Napolitano, Janet (Secretary of Homeland Security) *533*
    Salazar, Ken (Secretary of the Interior) *533*
    Sebelius, Kathleen (Secretary of Health and Human Services) *533*
    Shinseki, Eric (Secretary of Veterans Affairs) *533*
    Solis, Hilda (Secretary of Labor) *533*
    Vilsack, Thomas (Secretary of Agriculture) *533*
  Cabinet - second term
    Biden, Joe (Vice President) *541*
    Burwell, Sylvia (Secretary of Health and Human Services) *541*
    Donovan, Shaun (Secretary of Housing and Urban Development) *541*
    Duncan, Arne (Secretary of Education) *541*
    Fox, Anthony (Secretary of Transportation) *541*
    Hagel, Chuck (Secretary of Defense) *541*
    Holder, Eric (Attorney General) *541*
    Jewell, Sally (Secretary of the Interior) *541*
    Johnson, Jeh (Secretary of Homeland Security) *542*
    Kerry, John (Secretary of State) *541*
    Lew, Jack (Secretary of the Treasury) *541*
    Montz, Ernest (Secretary of Energy) *541*
    Perez, Thomas (Secretary of Labor) *541*
    Pritzker, Penny (Secretary of Commerce) *541*
    Shinseki, Eric (Secretary of Veterans Affairs) *541*
    Vilsack, Thomas (Secretary of Agriculture) *541*
  Career
    Community organizer *528*
    Illinois State Senate, elected to *529*
    Research Assistant *528*
    U.S. Senate, elected to *529*
  Elections
    2008 Presidential Election (Elected President) *530*
    2012 Presidential Election (Elected President) *540*
  Family
    Auma, Bernard, David, George, Mark, Maya, and Roy (Half-Siblings) *527*
    Malia Ann and Sasha (Children) *529*
    Obama, Barack Sr. and Stanley Ann (Parents) *527*
  Inauguration
    2009, inaugural address *532*
    2013, inaugural address *541*
  Key Events
    Boston Marathon, bombing by Chechen brothers *553*
    Cuba embargo lifted, U.S. embassy reopened *557*
    Detroit, filed for bankruptcy *552*
    Facebook, IPO grosses over $100 billion; Zuckerberg retains 20% *553*
    Federal Reserve, reviewed bank pay policies for excess risk *550*
    Fortune 500, used offshore subsidiaries to avoid tax *558*
    Housing market, slump begins *552*
    Hurricane Irene, caused over $10 billion in damages *552*

INDEX

Hurricane Sandy, New Jersey and New York; 200 killed, $80 billion damages 553
Kennedy, Ted, died of brain cancer 550
Madoff, Bernard, convicted of Ponzi scheme 550
Mergers and IPOs, $3.5 trillion total; 280+ over $1 billion 554
Pope Francis, addressed Congress and UN; visited U.S. 556
Recession of 2008, 8.4 million jobs lost 551
Simpson-Bowles, recommended spending cuts 551
Snowden, Edward leaks NSA surveillance programs 553
South Carolina, removed Confederate flag from capitol 555
Sullenberger, Chesley, landed plane on Hudson River; all 155 saved 551
Swine flu, U.S. outbreak 551
Trump, Donald, involved in 3,500 legal actions 557
U.S. equity trading, record $24.9 trillion 552
U.S. home ownership, dropped to 63.7% 556
U.S. national debt, surpassed $14 trillion 551
U.S. population, reached 319 million 554
U.S. stock indices, all reached record highs on same day 558
U.S. Supreme Court, ruled same-sex marriage legal 555
Volcker Rule, approved to ban proprietary trading with customer funds 554
Laws
 2009 American Recovery and Investment Act 533
 2009 Economic Stimulus Act 534
 2009 Ledbetter Act 534
 2009 Tax Act 534
 2010 Foreign Account Tax Compliance Act 537
 2010 Model Business Corporation Act 537
 2010 Pension Act 537
 2010 Tax Act 537
 American Taxpayer Relief Act 542
 Budget Control Act 538
 Clay Hunt Act 545
 Comprehensive Recovery Act 547
 Equity in Government Compensation Act 545
 Freedom Act 545
 Middle-Class Tax Relief and Job Creation Act 539
 Patient Protection and Affordable Care Act 536
 Tax Relief and Unemployment Compensation Act 537
 Unemployment Compensation Extension Act 537
 USA Patriot Act 538
 Veterans Access, Choice, and Accountability Act 543
 Veterans Entrepreneurship Act 545
 Workforce Innovation and Opportunity Act 543
Marriage
 Robinson, Michelle LaVaughn (Wife) 528
U.S. Supreme Court Rulings
 14 Penn Plaza LLC vs Pyett 535
 Arizona vs United States 539
 AT&T Mobility vs Concepcion 538
 Betterman vs Montana 546
 Christopher vs SmithKline Beecham Corp 539
 Citizens United vs Federal Election Committee 537
 Crawford vs Nashville and Davidson County 535
 EEOC vs Abercrombie & Fitch Stores 545
 Fisher vs University of Texas at Austin 546
 Gabelli vs Securities Exchange Commission 542
 Harris vs Quinn 543
 Heffernan vs Paterson NJ 546
 Integrity Staff vs Busk 543
 Mach Mining vs EEOC 545
 National Federation of Independent Business et al vs Sebelius, Secretary of Health and Human Services 539
 Rodriguez vs United States 545
 United States vs Quality Stores 543
 Vanos vs Ball State 542
 Ysursa vs Pocatello Education Association 535
Obamacare 536, 549, 564, 567, 569, 603
O'Brien, Larry 356
O'Connor, Sandra Day 451, 515, 778
O'Donnell, Kenneth 354, 356
Office of Strategic Services 297, 313, 321
O.K. Corral 176, 742
Old Hickory 75
One Nation Under God 333

OPEC 433, 436
Operation Desert Shield 475
Operation Desert Storm 475
Operation Eagle Claw 434
Operation Enduring Freedom 509
Operation Freedom Wind 418
Operation Intent Resolve 539
Operation Iraqi Freedom 512
Operation Neptune Spear 538
Operation Nickel 401
Operation Overlord 299, 327, 765
Operation Paperclip 320
Operation Rolling Thunder 379
Operation Torch 327
Operation Warp Speed 578
Oregon Territory 106
Oswald, Lee Harvey 363, 365, 375, 768, 769
Otis, Elisha 124, 150

P

Pabst and Schlitz 168
Palin, Sarah 530, 596, 784, 790
Palmetto Group 136
Panama Canal 226, 229, 252, 326, 429, 435, 436, 658, 752
Panic of 1837 81, 86, 725, 726
Panic of 1893 204, 207, 208, 214, 265, 748, 749
Paris Accord 545, 785
Paris Peace Treaty 8
Parker, Alton 226, 709, 752
Parker, Bonnie 302
Parsons, Wilton 338, 354, 355
patronage 162, 173, 174, 180, 202, 740
Paul, Rand 557, 565
pay 5, 14, 16, 17, 18, 29, 31, 40, 44, 45, 49, 55, 60, 61, 64, 70, 77, 81, 94, 99, 107, 110, 112, 117, 123, 130, 148, 154, 163, 164, 165, 173, 174, 181, 188, 189, 196, 202, 204, 208, 218, 219, 226, 229, 236, 238, 249, 251, 253, 261, 262, 267, 273, 275, 279, 289, 290, 293, 298, 311, 312, 317, 334, 340, 348, 350, 356, 358, 362, 364, 377, 387, 394, 395, 397, 402, 417, 419, 422, 431, 434, 435, 439, 440, 441, 450, 451, 452, 453, 456, 457, 458, 462, 472, 473, 474, 475, 476, 479, 480, 483, 488, 492, 493, 495, 507, 510, 512, 515, 517, 518, 521, 522, 523, 524, 525, 532, 534, 537, 543, 545, 550, 553, 555, 556, 557, 576, 611, 614, 616, 618, 621, 634, 637, 640, 641, 642, 644, 646, 654, 705, 715, 740, 753, 755, 761, 763, 764, 797
Pelosi, Nancy 524, 536, 575, 577, 587, 624, 634
Pence, Mike 547, 565, 566, 570, 580, 581, 585, 601, 602, 604, 629, 644, 652, 655, 713, 785, 787, 788, 791, 794
Pendleton, George 146
Penn Biden Center 599, 615
Pennsylvania 6, 10, 12, 20, 23, 33, 98, 104, 126, 132, 144, 145, 169, 175, 193, 281, 419, 453, 475, 509, 530, 546, 561, 581, 588, 593, 599, 605, 623, 626, 648, 650, 651, 666, 670, 686, 705, 733, 782, 786, 789, 790, 791
Pentagon 298, 333, 408, 464, 509, 512, 782
People's Department 143
People's Party 202
perestroika 460
Perot, Ross 476, 485, 486, 491
Pershing, John 22, 240, 249, 253, 254, 274, 327, 765
Personal Memoirs of U.S. Grant, The 166
Persons, Wilson 337
Pew Research Center 548
Pfizer's Paxlovid 608
Phi Beta Kappa 23, 184, 744, 798
Pickett, George 148
Pierce, Franklin iii, 117, 120, 121, 438, 707, 732
 Birth
  November 23, 1804 120
 Cabinet
  Campbell, James (Postmaster General) 122
  Cushing, Caleb (Attorney General) 122
  Davis, Jefferson (Secretary of War) 122
  Dobbin, Jame (Secretary of the Navy) 122
  Guthrie, James (Secretary of the Treasury) 122
  King, William (Vice President) 122
  Marcy, William (Secretary of State) 122
  McClelland, Robert (Secretary of the Interior) 122
 Career
  Brigadier General, Mexican American War 121
  Law, practice of 120
  New Hampshire House of Representatives, elected to 120

INDEX

Speaker of the House *120*
U.S. Army, enlisted in *121*
U.S. House of Representatives, elected to *121*
U.S. Senate, elected to *121*
Death
  October 8, 1869 *124*
Elections
  1852 Presidential Election (Elected President) *121*
Family
  Benjamin, Franklin Jr., and Frank (Children) *121*
  Pierce, Benjamin Sr. and Anna (Parents) *120*
Inauguration
  1853, inaugural address *121*
Key Events
  Adding machine, invented by John Burroughs *124*
  Bessemer process, developed *124*
  Brown, John, led anti-slavery protests *124*
  Kindergarten, first opened *124*
  Mississippi River, first railroad crossing *124*
  Rail service, began from New York to St. Louis *125*
  Republican Party, founded *124*
  Safety elevator, invented *124*
  Singer, Isaac, patented affordable sewing machine *125*
  Whitman, Walt, published Leaves of Grass *124*
  Young, Brigham, defied federal laws *124*
Laws
  1854 Gadsden Purchase *123*
  1854 Kansas-Nebraska Act *123*
  1857 Tariff Act *123*
Marriage
  Appleton, Jane (Wife) *121*
U.S. Supreme Court Rulings
  United States vs Booth *123*
  United States vs Fremont *123*
  United States vs Le Baron *123*
Pike's Peak *46, 132*
Pinckney, Charles *31, 36, 42, 50, 685, 706, 720*
Pinckney, Thomas *27*
Pinkerton, Allan *118, 137, 138, 139, 141, 172, 735*
Pinkerton Detective Agency *118, 141*
Plumbers Unit *400*
Poe, Edgar Allan *100, 101*

Polk, James K. *iii, 81, 88, 99, 102, 103, 104, 105, 106, 107, 108, 110, 121, 127, 707, 729, 730, 732, 733*
Birth
  November 2, 1795 *102*
Cabinet
  Bancroft, George (Secretary of the Navy) *106*
  Buchanan, James (Secretary of State) *106*
  Dallas, George (Vice President) *106*
  Johnson, Cave (Postmaster General) *106*
  Marcy, Robert (Secretary of War) *106*
  Mason, John (Attorney General) *106*
  Walker, Robert (Secretary of the Treasury) *106*
Career
  Law, practice of *102*
  Speaker of the House *103*
  Tennessee, governor *103*
  Tennessee House of Representatives, served in *103*
  U.S. House of Representatives, served in *103*
Death
  June 15, 1849 *107*
Elections
  1844 Presidential Election (Elected President) *103*
Family
  Franklin, John, Marshall, Samuel, William, Jane, Lydia, Naomi, and Ophelia (Siblings) *102*
  Polk, Samuel and Jane Knox (Parents) *102*
Inauguration
  1845, inaugural address *104*
Key Events
  Baseball, first game played in Hoboken *108*
  Boston and New York, millions immigrated to *107*
  California, gold discovered *108*
  Chicago–New York telegraph line, completed *108*
  Florida, Texas, Iowa, and Wisconsin, entered Union *108*
  Mexican-American War, sparked by Texas statehood *108*
  Pfizer, began as small chemical firm *108*
  Postage stamps, adhesive type approved *108*
  Salt Lake City, founded by Mormons *108*
  Smithsonian Institution, opened *108*

Texas Rangers arrested 300 cattle rustlers *107*
U.S. Naval Academy *107*
Washington Monument, plans initiated by Polk *108*
Women, demanded right to vote *108*
Laws
   1848 Treaty of Guadalupe Hidalgo *106*
   Drug Importation Act of 1848 *105*
   Independent Treasury Act of 1848 *105*
Marriage
   Sarah Childress (Wife) *103*
U.S. Supreme Court Rulings
   United States vs Briggs *105*
   United States vs Rogers *105*
   United States vs Yates *106*
Polk, Sarah *105*
Ponzi, Charles *254, 755*
popular vote *12, 19, 27, 42, 50, 53, 59, 62, 68, 70, 75, 76, 79, 85, 87, 88, 91, 92, 96, 103, 110, 118, 121, 127, 130, 131, 136, 146, 160, 164, 171, 179, 185, 192, 195, 199, 201, 205, 206, 213, 216, 226, 235, 238, 243, 247, 258, 265, 275, 279, 287, 291, 295, 299, 314, 329, 335, 351, 377, 389, 390, 391, 393, 398, 419, 428, 435, 447, 454, 469, 471, 476, 486, 491, 506, 513, 530, 541, 566, 567, 580, 581, 596, 598, 604, 605, 629, 631, 651, 652, 704, 723, 724, 725, 726, 727, 729, 730, 732, 733, 735, 736, 739, 740, 741, 743, 744, 745, 747, 748, 749, 752, 753, 754, 755, 756, 758, 759, 760, 761, 762, 763, 764, 766, 767, 770, 772, 776, 777, 778, 779, 780, 782, 783, 784, 785, 787, 788, 789, 790, 791, 793, 794*
postmaster general *5, 16, 19, 30, 38, 43, 51, 54, 61, 63, 69, 77, 78, 80, 86, 93, 97, 106, 112, 115, 122, 128, 140, 148, 153, 162, 165, 173, 180, 185, 194, 200, 207, 214, 218, 224, 227, 236, 245, 248, 259, 264, 266, 276, 288, 292, 296, 300, 331, 335, 353, 354, 373, 378, 395, 399, 715, 768*
Potsdam Conference *310*
Powell, Adam Clayton *344*
Powell, Colin *474, 479, 508, 511*
Powell, Jody *428, 431, 776*
Powell vs Alabama *279*
Powers, David *356*
Powers, Gary *337, 367, 766*
Presidential Medal of Freedom *361, 365, 377, 381, 383, 415, 421, 438, 461, 477, 496, 505, 575, 579, 603, 769, 771, 775, 776, 778, 779, 781, 791*
President's Daily Briefing *294, 375*
President's Day *22, 397*
Priebus, Reince *569, 787*
Proclamation *144, 145, 736*
Profiles in Courage *349, 350, 359, 767*
Progressive Bull Moose Party *238*
Pulitzer, Joseph *190, 219*
Pulitzer Prize *253, 304, 350, 366, 496, 755, 767*
Purple Heart *348, 767*
Putin, Vladimir *508, 569, 601, 613, 623, 647*

Q

Quaker *104, 273, 329, 387, 771*
Quartering Act *4*
Quayle, Dan *470, 471, 476, 485, 486, 504, 712, 779, 780*
Queen Elizabeth *294, 363, 416, 450, 477, 779*

R

Rabin, Yitzhak *488*
Rainey, Joseph *168*
Randolph, Edmund *9, 16, 19, 715*
Reagan, Nancy *444*
Reagan, Ronald *iv, 85, 92, 406, 418, 420, 434, 436, 438, 442, 443, 444, 445, 446, 447, 448, 449, 450, 451, 452, 453, 454, 455, 456, 457, 458, 459, 460, 461, 462, 463, 464, 469, 470, 473, 474, 477, 540, 563, 596, 622, 657, 712, 776, 777, 778, 779, 787*
Birth
   February 6, 1911 *442*
Cabinet
   Baldridge, Malcolm (Secretary of Commerce) *450*
   Bell, Terrell (Secretary of Education) *450*
   Block, John (Secretary of Agriculture) *450*
   Bush, George H.W. (Vice President) *449*
   Donovan, Raymond (Secretary of Labor) *450*
   Edwards, James (Secretary of Energy) *450*
   Haig, Alexander (Secretary of State) *449*
   Lewis, Andrew (Secretary of Transportation) *450*
   Pierce, Samuel (Secretary of Housing and Urban Development) *450*
   Regan, Donald (Secretary of the Treasury) *450*
   Schweiker, Richard (Secretary of Health and Human Services) *450*
   Smith, William (Attorney General) *450*

INDEX

Watt, James (Secretary of the Interior) *450*
Weinberger, Caspar (Secretary of Defense) *450*
Cabinet - second term
  Baker, James (Secretary of the Treasury) *454*
  Baldridge, Malcolm (Secretary of Commerce) *454*
  Bennett, William (Secretary of Education) *454*
  Block, John (Secretary of Agriculture) *454*
  Block, William (Secretary of Labor) *454*
  Bowen, Otis (Secretary of Health and Human Services) *454*
  Bush, George H.W. (Vice President) *454*
  Dole, Elizabeth (Secretary of Transportation) *454*
  Haig, Alexander (Secretary of State) *454*
  Herrington, James (Secretary of Energy) *454*
  Hodel, Donald (Secretary of the Interior) *454*
  Meese, Edwin (Attorney General) *454*
  Pierce, Samuel (Secretary of Housing and Urban Development) *454*
  Weinberger, Caspar (Secretary of Defense) *454*
Career
  Actor and TV host *445*
  California, governor *445*
  Screen Actors Guild, president *444*
Death
  June 5, 2004 *462*
Elections
  1980 Presidential Election (Elected President) *447*
  1984 Presidential Election (Elected President) *454*
Family
  Maureen, Michael, Patricia, Ronald Jr. (Children) *444*
  Reagan, John Edward and Nellie Wilson (Parents) *442*
  Reagan, John Neil (Sibling) *442*
Inauguration
  1981, inaugural address *448*
  1985, inaugural address *454*
Key Events
  AIDS, first case reported *463*
  American Airlines introduced the frequent flyer program *462*
  Berkshire Hathaway stock sold at $500 a share *462*
  Bush, George H.W., first VP to act as president while a president was indisposed *464*
  Capital One was founded *466*
  Cell phone, first introduced by Motorola *464*
  Columbia completed the first successful space shuttle mission *463*
  Dr. Barney Clark became the first recipient of an artificial heart *463*
  Federal budget deficit exceeded $100 billion for the first time *463*
  Internet, invention of *464*
  Macintosh computer from Apple was introduced *464*
  Morgan Stanley went public *465*
  Professional Air Traffic Controllers Association went on strike *463*
  Ride, Sally, first American woman in space *464*
  Space shuttle Challenger exploded in space *465*
  Stock market crashed *465*
  Terrorist bomb on a Pan Am flight killed all 259 on board *465*
  Unemployment exceeded 10% for the first time since the Great Depression *463*
  U.S. invaded Grenada *464*
  Walker, John arrested for spying for Russia *465*
  Washington, Harold, nation's first Black mayor *464*
Laws
  1981 Economic Recovery Act *449*
  1982 Tax Equity and Fiscal Responsibility Act *451*
  1983 Social Security Amendment *452*
  1983 Technical Corrections Act *452*
  1984 Deficit Reduction Act *453*
  1984 Retirement Equity Act *453*
  1984 Tax Reform Act *453*
  1985 Balanced Budget and Emergency Deficit Control Act *455*
  1985 Consolidated Budget Reconciliation Act (COBRA) *454*
  1986 Age Discrimination Act *457*
  1986 Federal Employer Retirement System Act *457*
  1986 Immigration Reform and Control Act *457*
  1986 Omnibus Budget Reconciliation Act *457*

1986 Tax Reform Act *457*
1988 Insider Trading and Security Fraud Endorsement Act *458*
1988 Medicare Catastrophic Coverage Act *459*
Marriage
   Reagan, Nancy (Second Wife) *444*
   Wyman, Jane (First Wife) *444*
U.S. Supreme Court Rulings
   Arizona Governing Committee vs Norris *453*
   Chevron vs National Resource Defense Council *453*
   García vs San Antonio Metropolitan Transit Authority *455*
   Gunther vs County of Washington *451*
   Hustler Magazine vs Falwell *459*
   New Jersey vs T.L.O. *455*
   Nixon vs Fitzgerald *452*
Reaganomics *451, 456*
Reb, Johnny *142*
recession *208, 262, 418, 428, 518, 524, 532, 536, 541, 544, 549, 551, 561, 573, 634, 644, 785, 786*
Reconstruction *148, 154, 163, 164, 172, 281, 290, 480, 741*
Red Cross *182, 285*
Rehnquist, William *457, 515*
Reid, Whitelaw *201, 206, 747, 748*
Republican Party *20, 50, 85, 117, 124, 134, 136, 178, 185, 188, 200, 247, 391, 445, 504, 647, 649, 718, 731, 732, 735, 743, 744, 779, 782, 788*
Republicans *20, 31, 36, 42, 50, 53, 59, 62, 67, 70, 75, 76, 79, 85, 127, 131, 135, 160, 164, 171, 179, 192, 195, 199, 201, 205, 206, 213, 214, 217, 226, 227, 235, 258, 260, 265, 275, 279, 286, 295, 299, 312, 314, 329, 335, 351, 377, 389, 390, 391, 393, 398, 419, 435, 445, 447, 454, 469, 471, 476, 486, 490, 491, 493, 506, 507, 510, 513, 519, 524, 530, 534, 535, 536, 538, 540, 541, 548, 557, 565, 566, 567, 574, 575, 581, 582, 589, 596, 598, 605, 615, 618, 626, 627, 628, 629, 630, 633, 639, 644, 651, 652, 653, 655, 720, 721, 722, 723, 725, 726, 733, 734, 735, 740, 741, 743, 745, 747, 749, 750, 752, 753, 755, 756, 758, 759, 760, 761, 762, 763, 764, 766, 767, 770, 772, 775, 776, 777, 778, 779, 780, 784, 785, 787, 789, 790, 791, 793*

Resolute Desk *174, 334, 742*
Revels, Hiram *168*
Revere, Paul *4*
Revolutionary War *8, 16, 17, 48, 54, 58, 59, 73, 109, 721*
Rice, Condoleezza *511, 513, 514*
Richardson, Elliott *401, 773*
Rigas, Robert *515*
Robinson, Joseph *275, 759*
Rockefeller, John D. *141, 150, 168, 189, 204, 210, 224, 231, 232, 237, 304, 415*
Rockefeller, Nelson *405, 414, 415, 418*
Rodgers, William *396*
Roe vs Wade *400, 412, 475, 614, 619, 633, 643, 773*
Romney, Mitt *500, 540, 578, 598, 712, 785, 788, 791*
Ronald and Nancy Reagan Research Institute *462*
Roosevelt Corollary *224*
Roosevelt, Franklin D. *iv, 235, 255, 258, 274, 279, 284, 285, 286, 287, 288, 289, 290, 291, 292, 293, 294, 295, 296, 297, 298, 299, 300, 301, 302, 303, 306, 307, 309, 310, 316, 319, 330, 333, 340, 347, 371, 374, 386, 433, 438, 456, 459, 491, 535, 608, 710, 756, 759, 760, 761, 762, 763, 766*
Birth
   January 30, 1882 *284*
Cabinet - first term
   Cummings, Homer (Attorney General) *288*
   Dern, George (Secretary of War) *288*
   Farley, James (Postmaster General) *288*
   Garner, John Nance (Vice President) *287*
   Hull, Cordell (Secretary of State) *287*
   Ickes, Harold (Secretary of the Interior) *288*
   Perkins, Frances (Secretary of Labor) *288*
   Roper, Daniel (Secretary of Commerce) *288*
   Swanson, Claude (Secretary of the Navy) *288*
   Wallace, Henry (Secretary of Agriculture) *288*
   Woodin, William (Secretary of the Treasury) *287*
Cabinet - second term
   Cummings, Homer (Attorney General) *292*
   Farley, James (Postmaster General) *292*
   Garner, John Nance (Vice President) *292*
   Hull, Cordell (Secretary of State) *292*

INDEX

Ickes, Harold (Secretary of the Interior) *292*
Morgenthau, Henry (Secretary of the Treasury) *292*
Perkins, Frances (Secretary of Labor) *292*
Roper, Daniel (Secretary of Commerce) *292*
Swanson, Claude (Secretary of the Navy) *292*
Wallace, Henry (Secretary of Agriculture) *292*
Woodring, Harry (Secretary of War) *292*
Cabinet - third term
   Biddle, Francis (Attorney General) *296*
   Ickes, Harold (Secretary of the Interior) *296*
   Jones, Jesse (Secretary of Commerce) *296*
   Knox, William (Secretary of the Navy) *296*
   Morgenthau, Henry (Secretary of the Treasury) *296*
   Perkins, Frances (Secretary of Labor) *296*
   Stettinius, Edward (Secretary of State) *296*
   Stimson, Henry (Secretary of War) *296*
   Walker, Francis (Postmaster General) *296*
   Wallace, Henry (Vice President) *296*
   Wickard, Claude (Secretary of Agriculture) *296*
Cabinet - fourth term
   Biddle, Francis (Attorney General) *300*
   Forrestal, James (Secretary of the Navy) *300*
   Holmes, Jesse (Secretary of Commerce) *300*
   Ickes, Harold (Secretary of the Interior) *300*
   Morgenthau, Henry (Secretary of the Treasury) *300*
   Perkins, Frances (Secretary of Labor) *300*
   Stettinius, Edward (Secretary of State) *300*
   Stimson, Henry (Secretary of War) *300*
   Truman, Harry (Vice President) *300*
   Walker, Francis (Postmaster General) *300*
   Wickard, Claude (Secretary of Agriculture) *300*
Career
   Law, practice of *285*
   New York, governor *286*
   New York State Senate, elected to *285*
   U.S. Navy, Assistant Secretary *285*
Death
   April 12, 1945 *301*

Elections
   1932 Presidential Election (Elected President) *286*
   1936 Presidential Election (Elected President) *291*
   1940 Presidential Election (Elected President) *294*
   1944 Presidential Election (Elected President) *299*
Family
   Anna, Elliott, Franklin Jr., James, John, one unnamed who died in infancy (Children) *285*
   Half-brother, unnamed (Sibling) *284*
   Roosevelt, James and Sara Delano (Parents) *284*
Inauguration
   1933, inaugural address *287*
   1941, inaugural address *295*
   1944, inaugural address *300*
Key Events
   Alcoholics Anonymous, created *303*
   American Bantam Car, introduced Jeep to U.S. Army *305*
   American Institute of Accountants, formed *303*
   Bronx-Whitestone Bridge, opened *305*
   DuPont, chemist created nylon *303*
   DuPont, introduced Teflon *304*
   Earhart, Amelia, disappeared in Pacific Ocean *304*
   Federal Bureau of Investigation (FBI), created *303*
   Federal Deposit Insurance Corporation (FDIC), formed *302*
   Federal Security Agency, created *305*
   Gallup poll, first conducted *303*
   Hewlett-Packard, formed *304*
   IBM, entered typewriter business *302*
   International Longshoremen's Association, went on strike *303*
   International Monetary Fund was created *307*
   LaGuardia, Fiorello, began 12-year term as New York City mayor *302*
   Life magazine, began publication *304*
   Lincoln Tunnel, opening of *304*
   Merrill Lynch, formation of *305*
   National Bank Notes, replaced by Federal Reserve Notes *302*
   National Basketball League, established *304*

843

NFL, first televised game *305*
Pfizer, first to mass produce penicillin *306*
Queens Midtown Tunnel, opened *305*
Rockefeller Center, first Christmas tree displayed *302*
Rockefeller, John D., and Mellon, Andrew, died *304*
Rubber, vulcanization invented *305*
Social Security, first checks mailed *303*
Television, invented *303*
Triborough Bridge, opened *304*
Unemployment, reached 25% *302*
U.S., banned private gold ownership *302*
U.S., declared neutrality in Spanish Civil War *303*
USS Akron, crashed into Atlantic Ocean *302*
Laws
  1933 Glass-Steagall Act *289*
  1933 National Industrial Recovery Act *289*
  1933 Revenue Act *289*
  1933 Securities Act *289*
  1934 Copeland Act *290*
  1934 Gold Reserve Act *290*
  1934 National Housing Act *290*
  1934 Revenue Act *290*
  1934 Securities Exchange Act *290*
  1935 Banking Act *290*
  1935 Federal Insurance Contribution Act *290*
  1935 National Labor Relations Act *291*
  1935 Social Security Act *291*
  1936 Walsh-Healey Workers Contract Act *292*
  1937 Bankhead-Jones Farm Tenant Act *292*
  1938 Fair Labor Standards Act *293*
  1938 Revenue Act *293*
  1939 Hatch Act *293*
  1939 Revenue Act *293*
  1940 Investment Advisors Act *296*
  1940 Investment Company Act *295*
  1940 Selection Service Act *296*
  1940 Smith Act *296*
  1942 Revenue Act *297*
  1942 Victory Tax *297*
  1942 Wage Stabilization Act *297*
  1943 Current Tax Payment Act *298*
  1943 Lend Lease Act *298*
  1944 G.I. Bill of Rights *299*
  1944 Victory Tax Act *299*

Twenty-First Amendment to the U.S. Constitution, ratified *290*
Marriage
  Roosevelt, Anna Eleanor (Wife) *285*
U.S. Supreme Court Rulings
  A.L.A. Schechter Poultry Corp. vs United States *291*
  Ashwander vs Tennessee Valley Authority *292*
  Betts vs Brady *297*
  Erie Railroad Co. vs Tompkins *293*
  Korematsu vs United States *297*
  National Labor Relations Board vs Fansteel Metallurgical Corp. *293*
  National Labor Relations Board vs Laughlin Steel Corp. *292*
  Rogers vs Hill *288*
Roosevelt, Theodore *iv, 22, 45, 207, 215, 216, 217, 218, 221, 223, 226, 230, 235, 238, 243, 250, 264, 284, 285, 310, 319, 340, 371, 394, 438, 471, 536, 705, 709, 749, 750, 752, 754, 760, 762, 784*
Birth
  October 27, 1858 *221*
Cabinet
  Cortelyou, George (Secretary of Commerce and Labor) *224*
  Gage, Lyman (Secretary of the Treasury) *224*
  Hay, John (Secretary of State) *224*
  Hitchcock, Ethan (Secretary of the Interior) *224*
  Knox, Philander (Attorney General) *224*
  Long, John (Secretary of the Navy) *224*
  Root, Elihu (Secretary of War) *224*
  Smith, Charles (Postmaster General) *224*
  Wilson, James (Secretary of Agriculture) *224*
Cabinet - second term
  Fairbanks, Charles (Vice President) *227*
  Garfield, James (Secretary of the Interior) *227*
  Moody, William (Attorney General) *227*
  Morton, Paul (Secretary of the Navy) *227*
  Root, Elihu (Secretary of State) *227*
  Shaw, Leslie (Secretary of the Treasury) *227*
  Straus, Oscar (Secretary of Commerce and Labor) *227*
  Taft, William (Secretary of War) *227*
  Wilson, James (Secretary of Agriculture) *227*
  Wynne, Robert (Postmaster General) *227*

INDEX

Career
  New York City, police commissioner *222*
  New York State Assembly, member *222*
  New York State, governor of *222*
  Spanish-American War, served as lieutenant colonel *222*
  U.S. Civil Service Commission, served on *222*
  U.S. Navy, assistant secretary *222*
Death
  January 6, 1919 *230*
Elections
  1904 Presidential Election (Elected President) *226*
Family
  Roosevelt, Theodore Sr. and Martha Bulloch (Parents) *221*
  Three, unnamed (Siblings) *221*
Inauguration
  1905, inaugural address *227*
Key Events
  Automat, invented *231*
  Bureau of the Census, established *231*
  Carnegie, Andrew, sold steel company to J.P. Morgan *230*
  Edison, Thomas, invented the battery *231*
  Einstein, Albert, described theory of relativity *232*
  Flagler's railroad, damaged by hurricane in Florida *233*
  Flatiron Building, 21-story structure opened *231*
  Ford, Henry, patented motor carriages *230*
  Ford Model T, produced *233*
  Ford Motor Company and International Harvester, established *231*
  JCPenney, first store opened *231*
  Long Acre Square, renamed Times Square *232*
  Maryland, first state with workers' compensation plan *231*
  Motion Picture Patents Company, created by Thomas Edison *233*
  National Collegiate Athletic Association (NCAA), formed *232*
  New York City, first subway system opened *232*
  New York City, recognized as nation's financial capital *230*
  New York City, taximeter cabs replaced hansom cabs *233*
  Oklahoma, admitted as 46th state *232*
  Rotary Club, founded *232*
  San Francisco, major earthquake *232*
  Standard of living, rising *230*
  Texas, oil boom *231*
  United Parcel Service, begins operation *233*
  Walgreens, opened first drug store *230*
  Wright, Wilbur and Orville, flew motorized glider in Kitty Hawk *231*
Laws
  1906 Meat Inspection Act *228*
  1906 Pure Food and Drug Act *228*
  Hepburn Act *228*
  Immigration Act *229*
  Railroad Regulation Act *228*
  Sherman Antitrust Act of 1890 *228*
Marriage
  Carow, Edith (Second Wife) *222*
  Lee, Alice Hathaway (First Wife) *222*
U.S. Supreme Court Rulings
  Adair vs United States *229*
  Lone Wolf vs Hitchcock *226*
  Northern Securities vs United States *227*
  Swift & Co. vs United States *228*
Rough Riders *215, 217, 222, 751*
Routh, Ryan Wesley *650*
Rubio, Marco *557, 565, 656*
Ruckelshaus, William *401*
Rules of Civility and Decent Behavior in Company and Conversation *1, 714*
Rumsfeld, Donald *414, 418, 508, 511, 513, 523*
Rush, Richard *61, 69, 70, 76, 725*
Rutgers University *213*
Ruth, Babe *196, 278, 366, 421, 522, 575, 759*
Ryan, Paul *540, 555, 567, 598, 785, 791*

S

Samoan Islands *216, 750*
Sanders, Bernie *557, 564, 601*
Santorum, Rick *557, 565*
Saturday Night Massacre *401, 773*
Saudi Arabia *401, 499, 569, 609*
Scalia, Antonin *457, 545, 568, 575, 577*
Schultz, Dutch *302, 314*
Scott, Dred *128, 733, 734*
Scott, Winfield *117, 121, 142, 707, 732*
Sears, Roebuck, and Co. *209, 497, 522, 588*
SEC *290, 296, 303, 312, 377, 381, 386, 409, 439, 457, 465, 479, 510, 523, 555, 571, 621, 637, 642*
Secret Service *149, 172, 220, 336, 365, 399, 417, 450, 486, 620, 648, 789*

Seminole Indians *75, 724*
Seminole War *100, 109, 730*
Senate *10, 13, 14, 15, 19, 37, 40, 48, 59, 67, 68, 74, 76, 79, 80, 84, 86, 92, 96, 121, 122, 127, 131, 135, 136, 147, 153, 154, 155, 160, 164, 168, 172, 179, 193, 199, 213, 214, 217, 224, 227, 229, 235, 237, 243, 244, 246, 248, 249, 250, 257, 258, 260, 262, 265, 267, 275, 276, 278, 279, 283, 285, 287, 291, 293, 295, 298, 299, 300, 309, 312, 313, 315, 316, 318, 319, 329, 330, 337, 341, 349, 350, 352, 361, 367, 368, 370, 376, 377, 378, 379, 382, 388, 390, 392, 394, 398, 400, 401, 403, 415, 420, 427, 451, 454, 456, 457, 468, 470, 473, 483, 486, 487, 491, 493, 494, 497, 507, 508, 510, 513, 515, 520, 523, 531, 536, 538, 541, 545, 549, 550, 558, 566, 567, 571, 574, 577, 578, 582, 585, 587, 589, 594, 595, 596, 599, 604, 605, 608, 615, 625, 629, 630, 635, 638, 639, 645, 652, 653, 654, 655, 656, 669, 670, 671, 673, 674, 678, 680, 684, 691, 692, 695, 697, 700, 704, 724, 728, 732, 733, 734, 737, 738, 739, 747, 756, 757, 761, 763, 764, 767, 769, 770, 771, 781, 787, 788, 790, 791, 794, 795*
Sergeant, John *79, 85, 725, 726*
Sewall, Arthur *213, 749*
Seymour, Horatio *160, 708, 739*
Shah of Iran *434*
Shangri-La *333*
Shawnee Chief Tecumseh *86, 91, 727*
Shays, Daniel *9*
Sherman, Roger *6, 667, 686*
Sherman, Tecumseh *146*
Shiloh *131, 142, 159, 178, 739, 742*
Skelton, Martha Wayles *28, 35, 717*
slavery abolishment *129*
Sloan, Alfred *262, 271, 320, 323, 368, 381, 757*
smallpox *2, 5, 73, 74, 89, 168, 715*
Smith, Alfred *275, 759*
Smith, Eleanor Rosalynn *425, 775*
Smith, Jack *585, 652, 794*
Sorenson, Ted *354, 366*
South Carolina *10, 12, 21, 22, 68, 73, 76, 79, 130, 141, 150, 168, 171, 242, 555, 601, 647, 666, 670, 685, 724, 734, 736*
Spanish American War *217, 222, 751*
Spanish fleet *215*

Sparkman, John J. *329, 389*
spoils system *78, 162, 184, 744*
square deal *228*
Stalin, Joseph *298, 301, 334, 337, 762, 763*
Stamp Act *26*
Star Route *180*
Star-Spangled Banner, The *55*
State Senate *164, 257, 756*
Statue of Liberty *194, 196, 746*
St Clair, James *404*
Steelman, John *312, 763*
Stevenson, Adlai *201, 206, 207, 216, 329, 335, 349, 389, 390, 709, 711, 747, 750, 766, 772*
Stewart, Martha *515*
Stockdale, James *476, 486*
stock market crash *207, 277, 278, 286, 748, 759*
St. Patrick's Cathedral *175, 742*
Strategic Defense Initiative *452, 461*
Sugar Act *4*
Summersby, Kay *327, 331, 765*
Sundance Kid *210, 231*
Sununu, John *474*
supply-side economics *456*
supremacy clause *49*
Swamp Fox *8*

T

Taft, Robert *314, 328*
Taft, William H. *iv, 227, 234, 235, 236, 237, 238, 239, 240, 243, 258, 276, 313, 314, 328, 333, 438, 709, 752, 753, 759*
Birth
September 15, 1857 *234*
Cabinet
Ballinger, Richard (Secretary of the Interior) *236*
Dickinson, Jacob (Secretary of War) *236*
Hitchcock, Frank (Postmaster General) *236*
Knox, Philander (Secretary of State) *236*
MacVeagh, Franklin (Secretary of the Treasury) *236*
Meyer, George (Secretary of the Navy) *236*
Nagel, Charles (Secretary of Commerce and Labor) *236*
Sherman, James (Vice President) *236*
Wickersham, George (Attorney General) *236*
Wilson, James (Secretary of Agriculture) *236*

INDEX

Career
  Law, Practice of *234*
  Philippines, civil governor *235*
  Post presidency
    Chief Justice of the United States Supreme Court *239*
    law professor at Yale *239*
    Solicitor General *235*
    Supreme Court of Ohio, judge *234*
Death
  May 22, 1943 *239*
Elections
  1908 Presidential Election (Elected President) *235*
Family
  Charles, Helen, and Robert (Children) *235*
  Frances, Henry, Horace, and half-brothers, Charles and Peter (Siblings) *234*
  Taft, Alphonso and Louisa Maria Torrey (Parents) *234*
Inauguration
  1909, inaugural address *235*
Key Events
  American Stock Exchange, opened *240*
  Amundsen, Ronald, discovered South Pole *240*
  Boy Scouts and Girl Scouts, founded *240*
  Electric washing machine, invented *240*
  Federal Reserve System, foundation laid *239*
  First transcontinental airplane flight, took 82 hours *240*
  Grand Central Terminal, opened in New York City *241*
  McGraw-Hill, book publishing company formed *239*
  National Association for the Advancement of Colored People (NAACP), founded *239*
  New York State, passed 1912 Sullivan Act *240*
  Peary, Robert, planted American flag at North Pole *239*
  U.S. Chamber of Commerce, formed *240*
  Villa, Pancho, invaded Texas *240*
Laws
  16th Amendment to the U.S. Constitution ratified *238*
  17th Amendment to the U.S. Constitution ratified *238*
  1909 Payne-Aldrich Tariff Act *236*
  1910 Mann-Elkins Act *236*
Marriage
  Herro, Helen "Nellie" (Wife) *235*

U.S. Supreme Court Rulings
  Standard Oil of New Jersey vs United States *237*
  United States vs American Tobacco Company *237*
Taliban *520*, *611*, *632*, *782*
Tappan, Lewis *101*
taxation authority *16*
Taylor, Frederick *209*
Taylor, Zachary *iii*, *106*, *109*, *110*, *115*, *371*, *428*, *437*, *438*, *707*, *730*, *731*
  Birth
    November 24, 1784 *109*
  Cabinet
    Clayton, John (Secretary of State) *111*
    Collamer, Jacob (Postmaster General) *112*
    Crawford, George (Secretary of War) *111*
    Ewing, Thomas (Secretary of the Interior) *112*
    Fillmore, Millard (Vice President) *111*
    Johnson, Reverdy (Attorney General) *111*
    Meredith, William (Secretary of the Treasury) *111*
    Preston, William (Secretary of the Navy) *112*
  Career
    Black Hawk War, served as major *109*
    Kentucky Militia *109*
    Mexican War, served as general *109*
  Death
    July 9, 1850 *112*
  Elections
    1848 Presidential Election (Elected President) *110*
  Family
    George, Hancock, Joseph, William, Elizabeth, Emily, and Sarah (Siblings) *109*
    Taylor, Richard and Sarah (Parents) *109*
  Inauguration
    1849, inaugural address *111*
  Key Events
    California, stagecoaches after Gold Rush *113*
    Gold Rush of 1849 *113*
    Hawthorne, Nathaniel, published The Scarlet Letter *113*
    U.S. population, reached 23 million *113*
  Marriage
    Smith, Margaret Mackall (Wife) *110*

U.S. Supreme Court Rulings
  Sheldon vs Sill *112*
  United States vs Staats *112*
TEA *535*
Tea Act *4*
Teapot Dome *260, 261, 281, 757*
Tehran *298, 434*
Tel Aviv *569, 572*
Tennessee Supreme Court *74*
Texas Rangers *82, 107, 409, 504, 782*
Third Kentucky Infantry Regiment *128*
Thoreau, Henry David *89, 124*
Thurman, Allen *192, 195, 199, 205, 747*
Thurmond, Strom *314, 763*
Tilden, Samuel *171, 708, 741*
Tippecanoe *57, 91, 727*
Title 42 *620, 633*
Todd, Dolley Payne *49, 720*
Todd, Mary *131, 134, 139, 140, 150, 735*
Tompkins, Daniel *59, 60, 61, 62, 63, 706, 722*
Tower Building *202*
toxic dioxin *452*
Trail of Tears *89, 725*
Transcontinental Treaty of 1819 *67*
travel ban *572, 578*
Treaty of 1818 *67*
Treaty of Ghent *55, 67, 721, 723*
Treaty of Versailles *250*
Tripoli *43*
Trippe, Juan *271, 282*
Troika *449*
Truman Doctrine *313*
Truman, Harry S. *iv, 299, 300, 308, 309, 310, 314, 372, 394, 413, 438, 471, 710, 762, 763*
  Birth
    May 8, 1884 *308*
  Cabinet
    Biddle, Francis (Attorney General) *310*
    Forrestal, James (Secretary of the Navy) *310*
    Ickes, Harold (Secretary of the Interior) *310*
    Morgenthau, Henry (Secretary of the Treasury) *310*
    Perkins, Francis (Secretary of Labor) *310*
    Stettinius, Edward (Secretary of State) *310*
    Stimson, Henry (Secretary of War) *310*
    Wallce, Henry (Secretary of Commerce) *310*
    Wickard, Claude (Secretary of Agriculture) *310*
  Cabinet - second term
    Acheson, Dean (Secretary of State) *316*
    Barkley, Alben (Vice President) *316*
    Brannan, Charles (Secretary of Agriculture) *316*
    Chapman, Oscar (Secretary of the Interior) *316*
    Forrestal, James (Secretary of Defense) *316*
    McGrath, James (Attorney General) *316*
    Sawyer, Charles (Secretary of Commerce) *316*
    Snyder, John (Secretary of the Treasury) *316*
    Tobin, Maurice (Secretary of Labor) *316*
  Career
    Haberdashery business, failed *309*
    National Guard, served as lieutenant *309*
    Supervisor of buildings and roads *309*
    U.S. Senate, elected to *309*
  Death
    December 26, 1972 *319*
  Elections
    1948 Presidential Election (Elected President) *314*
  Family
    Margaret (Child) *309*
    Truman, John and Martha (Parents) *308*
  Inauguration
    1949, inaugural address *316*
  Key Events
    Air Force One, introduction of *322*
    Atomic Energy Commission, creation of *320*
    Bell Labs, invented transistor *321*
    Central Intelligence Agency (CIA), created *321*
    Cold War, began with Russia *321*
    Conglomerate companies, beginning *324*
    Direct dial long distance service, introduced *323*
    Federal budget deficit, rose to 30% of GDP *320*
    Idlewild Airport, opened (later became JFK) *322*
    Israel, recognition as state *321*
    JFK was elected to two House terms *320*
    Lauder, Estée, launched cosmetic company *321*
    Malcolm X, joined U.S. Black Muslim leader Elijah Muhammad *324*
    McDonald's, first location opened *322*
    Microwave oven, invented *321*

INDEX

MIT Sloan School of Management, created *323*
Mobile telephone, went into service *320*
National Basketball Association (NBA), formed *323*
Pledge of Allegiance, recognized by Congress *320*
Polaroid, instant camera created *322*
Puerto Rico, became a U.S. commonwealth *323*
Reynolds, ballpoint pen, went on sale *320*
Robinson, Jackie, integrated professional baseball *321*
Sloan-Kettering Cancer Research Center, established *320*
Teflon, first products commercially sold *320*
Unemployment benefits, introduced *322*
United Nations, established *320*
U.S. Army bomber, struck Empire State Building *320*
U.S. Naval Academy, established *320*
Wage and price controls, lifted *320*
Laws
  1945 Employment Act *311*
  1947 National Security Act *313*
  1947 Portal-to-Portal Act *313*
  1947 Taft-Hartley Labor Act *313*
  1948 Revenue Act *314*
  1950 McCarthy Act *317*
  Presidential Succession Act *313*
Marriage
  Wallace, Elizabeth "Bess" (Wife) *309*
U.S. Supreme Court Rulings
  Inland Steel vs United Steel Workers *317*
  Morgan vs Virginia *311*
  United States vs Silk *312*
  Youngstown Sheet & Tube Company vs Sawyer *317*
Trump, Donald J. *iv, 480, 500, 519, 522, 546, 547, 556, 557, 558, 560, 561, 562, 563, 564, 565, 566, 567, 568, 569, 570, 572, 573, 574, 575, 577, 578, 579, 580, 581, 582, 583, 584, 585, 586, 587, 589, 590, 591, 592, 597, 601, 602, 603, 604, 605, 606, 607, 608, 609, 612, 613, 614, 617, 619, 620, 621, 622, 623, 624, 625, 626, 627, 628, 629, 630, 631, 632, 633, 635, 636, 637, 638, 639, 642, 643, 644, 645, 646, 647, 648, 649, 650, 651, 652, 653, 654, 655, 656, 657, 658, 659, 713, 785, 786, 787, 788, 789, 791, 793, 794, 795, 796*

Birth
  June 14, 1946 *560*
Cabinet
  Acosta, Alexander (Secretary of Labor) *570*
  Carson, Ben (Secretary of Housing and Urban Development) *570*
  Chao, Elaine (Secretary of Transportation) *570*
  DeVos, Betsy (Secretary of Education) *570*
  Kelly, John F. (Secretary of Homeland Security) *570*
  Mattis, Jim (Secretary of Defense) *570*
  Mnuchin, Steven (Secretary of the Treasury) *570*
  Pence, Mike (Vice President) *570*
  Perdue, Sonny (Secretary of Agriculture) *570*
  Perry, Rick (Secretary of Energy) *570*
  Price, Tom (Secretary of Health and Human Services) *570*
  Ross, Wilbur (Secretary of Commerce) *570*
  Sessions, Jeff (Attorney General) *570*
  Shulkin, David (Secretary of Veterans Affairs) *570*
  Tillerson, Rex (Secretary of State) *570*
  Zinke, Ryan (Secretary of the Interior) *570*
Cabinet - second term
  Bessent, Scott (Secretary of the Treasury) *656*
  Bondi, Pam (Attorney General) *656*
  Burgum, Doug (Secretary of the Interior) *656*
  Chavez-DeRemer, Lori (Secretary of Labor) *656*
  Collins, Doug (Secretary of Veterans Affairs) *656*
  Duffy, Sean (Secretary of Transportation) *656*
  Hegseth, Pete (Secretary of Defense) *656*
  Kennedy Jr., Robert F. (Secretary of Health and Human Services) *656*
  Lutnick, Howard (Secretary of Commerce) *656*
  McMahon, Linda (Secretary of Education) *656*
  Noem, Kristi (Secretary of Homeland Security) *656*
  Rollins, Brooke (Secretary of Agriculture) *656*
  Rubio, Marco (Secretary of State) *656*
  Turner, Scott (Secretary of Housing and Urban Development) *656*

Vance, J.D. (Vice President) *656*
Wright, Chris (Secretary of Energy) *656*
Career
    Plaza Hotel purchase; Atlantic City casinos; golf resorts *562*
    Real estate development: Grand Hyatt, Trump Tower, Manhattan and New Jersey acquisitions *561*
    Trump Organization *561*
Elections
    2016 Presidential Election (Elected President) *566*
    2024 Presidential Election (Elected President) *651*
Family
    Fred Jr. and Robert (Siblings) *560*
    Trump, Frederick and Mary Anne (Parents) *560*
    With Ivana: Donald Jr., Ivanka, and Eric (Children) *561*
    With Marla: Tiffany (Child) *562*
    With Melania: Barron (Child) *562*
Inauguration
    2017, inaugural address *568*
    2025, inaugural address *658*
Key Events
    COVID-19, ban on entry of non-Americans traveling from China after first U.S. case *590*
    COVID-19 death toll in U.S. reaches 100,000 by mid 2020 *591*
    Epstein, Jeffrey, charged with sexual abuse and dies by alleged suicide in prison *589*
    FDA reports new Ebola vaccine is 100% effective *588*
    Floyd, George, death by Minneapolis police sparks nationwide Black Lives Matter demonstrations *590*
    Hurricane Maria devastates Puerto Rico; over 3,000 deaths *586*
    Hurricane Michael and Hawaiian volcanic eruption cause widespread damage *588*
    Missile strike on Syria, ordered in response to chemical weapons attack *586*
    Muslim ban, entry restricted from select Muslim-majority countries *586*
    Russia launches major cyberattack on U.S. government systems *591*
    Senate Republicans abandon efforts to repeal the Affordable Care Act *589*
    Tesla surpasses General Motors as most valuable U.S. automobile company *586*
    Trans-Pacific Partnership, withdrawal from *585*
    Trump impeached a second time by U.S. House of Representatives *592*
    Uber orders 24,000 self-driving Volvo vehicles *587*
    U.S.–Mexico border wall construction begins, targeting unauthorized immigration *585, 586*
    U.S. withdraws from 1987 Intermediate-Range Missile Treaty *589*
    U.S. withdraws from 2015 Iran Nuclear Agreement *587*
    Women's March, millions march in protest in cities around America to the election of Trump and Pence *585*
Laws
    2017 Fair Access to Investment and Research Act *570, 571*
    2017 Rapid DNA Act *570*
    2017 Tax Cuts and Jobs Act *570*
    2017 Veterans Cost-of-Living Adjustment Act *570*
    2017 Veterans Educational Assistance Act *571*
    Abolish Human Trafficking Act *574*
    Consolidated Appropriations Act *576*
    Coronavirus Air, Relief, and Economic Stability Act *579*
    COVID-19 Relief Act *579*
    Criminal Justice Reform Act *574*
    Families First Coronavirus Response Act *579*
    Healthcare Enhancement Act *579*
    Jobs for Our Heroes Act *573*
    Law Enforcement Mental Health and Wellness Act *573, 574*
    National Defense Authorization Act *576*
    National Flood Insurance Protection Act *574*
    Never Again Education Act *579*
    Paycheck Protection Flexibility Act *579*
    Setting Every Community Up for Retirement Enhancement Act *579*
    Tax Reform Act *574*
    Veterans Compensation Cost-of-Living Adjustment Act *576*
Marriage
    Knauss, Melania (Third Wife) *562*
    Maples, Marla (Second Wife) *562*
    Zelnickova, Ivana (First Wife) *561*
U.S. Supreme Court Rulings
    Altitude Express vs Zarda *576*

INDEX

Babb vs Wilkie *580*
Bostock vs Clayton County *580*
Class vs United States *574*
Cyan Inc vs Beaver County Employees Retirement Fund *571*
Epic Systems vs Lewis *571*
Fort Bend County, Texas vs Davis *576, 577*
Fourth Estate Public Benefit Corp. vs Street.com *576*
Franchise Tax Board of California vs Hyatt *577*
Guerrero-Lasprilla vs Barr *580*
Henry Schein Inc. vs Archer and White Sales Inc. *576*
Intel Corp Investment Policy Committee vs Sulyma *580*
Kokesh vs Securities and Exchange Commission *571*
Liu vs Securities Exchange Commission *580*
Lorenzo vs Securities and Exchange Commission *576*
Lucia vs Securities and Exchange Commission *574*
Manrique vs United States *571*
Marinello vs United States *574*
McLane Co. vs Equal Employment Opportunity Commission *571*
National Labor Relations Board vs SW General Inc. *571*
Trump vs Hawaii *574*
Trump vs Vance *580*
Wisconsin Central Ltd. vs United States *574*
Yovino vs Rizo *576*
Trump protestors *581*
Truth Social *584, 639, 654*
Tryon, William *6*
Turkey *312*
Tweed, William *146*
Twelfth Amendment *96, 692, 702*
Twitter *450, 523, 564, 569, 581, 586*
Tyler, John *iii, 91, 92, 93, 95, 96, 97, 99, 115, 153, 185, 194, 223, 264, 310, 371, 372, 394, 413, 438, 471, 707, 727, 731, 737, 746, 770*
  Birth
    March 29, 1790 *95*
  Cabinet
    Badger, George (Secretary of the Navy) *97*
    Bell, John (Secretary of War) *97*
    Crittenden, John (Attorney General) *97*
    Ewing, Thomas (Secretary of the Treasury) *97*
    Granger, Francis (Postmaster General) *97*
    None (Vice President) *97*
    Webster, Daniel (Secretary of State) *97*
  Career
    House of Representatives, elected to *96*
    Law, practice of *95*
    U.S. Senate, elected to *96*
    Virginia, governor of *96*
  Elections
    1840 Presidential Election (Elected Vice President) *96*
  Family
    With Letitia: Alice, Ann, Elizabeth, Letitia, Mary, John, Robert, and Tazewell (Children) *95*
    With Julia: David, John, Julia, Lachlan, Lyon, Robert, and Pearl (Children) *99*
    Tyler, John Sr. and Mary Armstead (Parents) *95*
  Inauguration
    1841, inaugural address *97*
  Key Events
    Ether gas, first used as anesthetic *100*
    Florida and Texas, admitted to the Union *101*
    Fourier, Charles, established collectives *100*
    Free-Soil Party, formed *100*
    Morse, Samuel, sent first telegraph message *100*
    Poe, Edgar Allan, published The Murders in the Rue Morgue *100*
    Second Seminole War, ended *100*
    USS Princeton, deck gun explosion killed Ewing and Badger *100*
  Laws
    1841 Preemption Act *98*
    1842 Webster-Ashburton Treaty *98*
    1845 Tariff Act *99*
  Marriage
    Christian, Letitia (First Wife) *95*
    Gardiner, Julia (Second Wife) *98*
  U.S. Supreme Court Rulings
    Prigg vs Pennsylvania *98*
    United States vs Freeman *99*
    Winston vs United States *98*
typhoid fever *32, 112*

U

Ukraine 460, 613, 626, 639, 647, 659
Uncle Sam Grant 143
Uncle Tom's Cabin 116, 118, 141, 731
Underground Railroad 78, 116
Union Army 131, 142, 178, 211, 736, 739, 742
United States of America 8, 11, 296, 660, 669, 677, 685
University of Buffalo 117, 731
Untouchables 281
Up From Slavery, published 220, 223
U.S. Army 5, 121, 252, 305, 320, 331, 385, 393, 427, 486, 732, 739
U.S. Constitution 9, 10, 11, 13, 14, 15, 17, 20, 26, 27, 28, 36, 40, 41, 48, 49, 56, 69, 118, 122, 154, 155, 163, 179, 238, 244, 250, 251, 254, 280, 289, 290, 318, 319, 357, 375, 379, 397, 400, 402, 413, 476, 567, 630, 653, 655, 705, 715, 717, 718, 720, 737, 738, 740, 754, 755, 761, 764, 794, 795
U.S. Embassy 434, 540, 785
U.S. Grant 143, 166
U.S. Marine Corps 5
U.S. Military Academy 158, 159, 738
U.S. Naval Academy 320, 425, 775
U.S. Navy 5, 285, 330, 361, 388, 402, 412, 424, 437, 468, 769, 771, 774, 778
U.S. population 23, 31, 65, 78, 89, 113, 132, 167, 203, 240, 282, 306, 318, 344, 368, 435, 441, 479, 501, 554, 654, 720, 722, 725, 726, 730, 734, 740, 742, 747, 753, 761, 764, 766
U.S. Senate 67, 68, 74, 76, 79, 86, 92, 96, 121, 122, 127, 131, 135, 136, 147, 153, 155, 164, 168, 172, 193, 199, 227, 244, 258, 262, 265, 276, 283, 285, 309, 315, 330, 341, 349, 350, 361, 367, 370, 382, 427, 468, 470, 483, 486, 487, 531, 550, 587, 594, 625, 629, 630, 635, 645, 652, 653, 704, 724, 728, 732, 733, 734, 737, 739, 747, 756, 757, 763, 767, 769, 771, 787, 790, 794
U.S. senator 59, 75, 84, 91, 180, 300, 315, 341, 376, 420, 427, 467, 470, 496, 504, 519, 525, 529, 534, 546, 566, 575, 595, 604, 722, 726, 727, 743, 754, 756, 778, 784, 785
USS Akron 302
USS Arizona 296
USS Chesapeake 46
USS Constitution 32, 55
USS John F. Kennedy 380
USS Philadelphia 43
USS Princeton 100
USS Pueblo 385
USS United States 32

V

Valenti, Jack 373, 770
Valley Forge 7
Van Buren, Martin *iii*, 77, 78, 79, 80, 81, 83, 84, 85, 87, 91, 92, 96, 103, 104, 110, 115, 153, 185, 223, 264, 310, 371, 394, 413, 438, 471, 706, 707, 725, 726, 727, 731, 737
 Birth
  December 5, 1782 83
 Cabinet
  Butler, Benjamin (Attorney General) 86
  Dickerson, Mahlon (Secretary of the Navy) 86
  Forsyth, John (Secretary of State) 86
  Johnson, Richard (Vice President) 86
  Kendall, Amos (Postmaster General) 86
  Poinsett, Joel (Secretary of War) 86
  Woodbury, Levi (Secretary of Treasury) 86
 Career
  Jefferson, Thomas, campaigned for 84
  Law, practice of 84
  New York, attorney general 84
  New York, governor of 84
  New York Senate, elected to 84
  U.S. senator 84
 Death
  July 24, 1862 88
 Elections
  1836 Presidential Election (Elected President) 85
 Family
  Abraham, John, Martin, Winfield, and Smith Thompson (Children) 84
  Four, and three half-siblings, unnamed (Siblings) 83
  Van Buren, Abraham and Maria Hoes (Parents) 83
 Inauguration
  1836, inaugural address 85
 Key Events
  American Medical Association, formed 89
  Depression, lengthy 88

INDEX

Doubleday, Abner, set down rules of baseball *89*
Escalator, introduced at Coney Island Amusement Park *89*
Gag rule, prevented slavery debate in Congress *89*
Goodyear, Charles, patented workable rubber production *89*
Procter & Gamble, formed *88*
Topeka and Santa Fe Railway, private dining cars introduced *89*
Trail of Tears, thousands of Indians died on journey to Oklahoma *89*
Laws
    Independent Treasury Act of 1840 *87*
    The Neutrality Act of 1838 *87*
Marriage
    Hoes, Hannah (Wife) *84*
U.S. Supreme Court Rulings
    Sarchet vs United States *86*
    United States vs Morris *87*
Vanderbilt, Cornelius *82, 167, 175, 189*
Victorio *142, 169*
Vietnam *323, 368, 373, 374, 378, 379, 380, 382, 384, 385, 386, 399, 400, 404, 408, 416, 417, 419, 420, 422, 435, 485, 486, 489, 498, 557, 612, 773, 775*
Virginia *1, 2, 3, 4, 6, 9, 10, 11, 12, 16, 18, 23, 28, 29, 34, 35, 41, 43, 45, 46, 47, 48, 51, 54, 56, 58, 59, 60, 62, 64, 82, 90, 92, 95, 96, 99, 100, 109, 129, 139, 142, 146, 148, 158, 159, 174, 196, 242, 300, 311, 315, 338, 350, 379, 380, 419, 476, 479, 481, 485, 523, 566, 586, 589, 597, 639, 666, 670, 685, 714, 715, 717, 718, 719, 721, 722, 726, 727, 728, 730, 754, 779, 780*
Virginia militia *2, 3, 47, 715*

W

Wagner Act *291*
Wallace, George *368, 381, 393, 409, 772*
Wallace, Henry A. *295*
Wall Street Journal *202, 524, 536, 543, 634, 747*
Wall Street speculators *162*
Walz, Tim *627, 628, 629, 651, 652, 789, 792, 793, 794*
War bonds *297*
Ward, Montgomery *168*
War of 1812 *53, 55, 60, 67, 74, 86, 92, 95, 104, 109, 126, 720, 721, 723, 728, 730, 733, 740*
War Production Board *298*
Warren, Earl *314, 324, 328, 334, 355, 365, 375, 764, 769*
Warren, Elizabeth *601, 626*
Washington, Booker T. *176, 220, 223*
Washington, George *iii, vii, 1, 2, 3, 4, 5, 6, 7, 8, 9, 11, 12, 13, 14, 15, 16, 17, 18, 19, 20, 21, 22, 23, 27, 28, 29, 30, 32, 35, 37, 38, 40, 42, 44, 45, 46, 50, 55, 62, 108, 111, 150, 160, 164, 185, 200, 230, 269, 282, 289, 294, 300, 302, 319, 340, 348, 349, 354, 398, 400, 438, 658, 685, 705, 714, 715, 716, 717, 718, 719, 722, 736, 740, 752, 762*
Birth
    February 22, 1732 *1*
Cabinet
    Adams, John (Vice President) *16*
    Hamilton, Alexander (Secretary of the Treasury) *16*
    Jefferson, Thomas (Secretary of State) *16*
    Knox, Henry (Secretary of War) *16*
    Osgood, Samuel (Postmaster General) *16*
    Randolph, Edmund (Attorney General) *16*
Cabinet - second term
    Adams, John (Vice President) *19*
    Bradford, William (Attorney General) *19*
    Hamilton, Alexander (Secretary of the Treasury) *19*
    Knox, Henry (Secretary of War) *19*
    Pickering, Timothy (Postmaster General) *19*
    Randolph, Edmund (Secretary of State) *19*
Career
    Aid to General Edward Braddock *2*
    Lieutenant Colonel *2*
    Supreme Commander *5*
    Virginia Legislature, member of *3*
    Virginia Regiment, full colonel *3*
Death
    December 14, 1799 *21*
Elections
    1789 Presidential Elections (Elected President) *12*
    1792 Presidential Elections (Elected President) *19*
Family
    Ann, Lawrence and Augustine Jr. (Siblings) *1*
    John and Martha (Adopted Children) *3*
    Lawrence (Stepbrother) *2*
    Washington, Augustine and Mary Ball (Parents) *1*

Inauguration
   1789, inaugural address *13*, *14*
   1793, inaugural address *19*
Key Events
   Coast Guard, establishment of U.S. *23*
   Duer, William, involvement in financial crash *23*
   Flag, creation of American *23*
   Franklin, Benjamin, invention of lightning rod *22*
   Liberty Head gold coin, first $5 gold coin *24*
   Marshals Service, establishment of U.S. *23*
   Patent Office, establishment of U.S. *23*
   Pennsylvania Evening Post, first daily newspaper *23*
   Rhode Island, outlawing of slave importation *22*
   Smith, Adam, publication of The Wealth of Nations *23*
   Stock exchange, first in U.S. *23*
Laws
   1789 An Act to Regulate the Time and Manner of Administering Certain Oaths *9*
   1789 Federal Customs Act *9*
   1789 Revenue Act *16*
   1790 Federal Patent Act *16*
   1790 Funding Act *16*
   1790 Residence Act *16*
   1790 Tonnage Act *16*
   1791 Revenue Act *17*
   1792 Neutrality Act *18*
   1792 Presidential Succession Act *18*
   1794 Revenue Act *20*
   1795 Residence Act *20*
   Coinage Act *18*
   Legislation Act *17*
Marriage
   Curtis, Martha Dandridge (Wife) *3*
U.S. Supreme Court Rulings
   Talbot vs Janson *20*
   Ware vs Hylton *21*
   West vs Barnes *15*
Washington Monument *108*, *189*, *225*, *729*
Washington Post *331*, *401*, *472*, *773*
Watergate *400*, *401*, *403*, *404*, *405*, *406*, *409*, *427*, *428*, *522*, *773*
Watson, Jack *428*, *429*, *431*, *776*
Watson, Marvin *373*, *770*
Watson, Thomas *252*, *368*
West Point *8*, *46*, *158*, *159*, *161*, *166*, *300*, *308*, *326*, *329*, *561*, *738*, *739*, *765*, *786*

Wheeler, William *171*, *172*, *173*, *741*
Whig Party *80*, *85*, *87*, *91*, *93*, *96*, *110*, *111*, *115*, *116*, *117*, *134*, *707*, *728*, *731*, *735*
Whig presidential campaign *96*
Whip Inflation Now *417*
Whiskey Rebellion *20*
White House *29*, *39*, *44*, *77*, *116*, *147*, *150*, *165*, *181*, *188*, *223*, *224*, *225*, *229*, *238*, *239*, *246*, *248*, *259*, *260*, *268*, *278*, *279*, *288*, *290*, *293*, *309*, *313*, *316*, *330*, *337*, *339*, *354*, *355*, *356*, *357*, *358*, *359*, *364*, *370*, *372*, *375*, *378*, *382*, *383*, *389*, *396*, *399*, *401*, *402*, *403*, *406*, *412*, *428*, *429*, *430*, *432*, *433*, *436*, *437*, *444*, *449*, *450*, *459*, *461*, *473*, *480*, *482*, *487*, *488*, *489*, *491*, *493*, *496*, *509*, *510*, *511*, *533*, *535*, *547*, *575*, *578*, *582*, *589*, *598*, *606*, *608*, *612*, *615*, *617*, *625*, *629*, *632*, *657*, *658*, *705*, *736*, *751*, *753*, *756*, *761*, *763*, *764*, *766*, *770*, *772*, *773*, *776*, *780*, *782*, *795*, *796*
Whitewater *483*, *490*
Whitney, Eli *23*
Willkie, Wendell *295*, *710*
Wilson, Woodrow *iv*, *44*, *87*, *238*, *239*, *242*, *243*, *244*, *247*, *258*, *260*, *278*, *285*, *437*, *438*, *536*, *709*, *753*, *754*, *755*, *784*
   Birth
      December 28, 1856 *242*
   Cabinet
      Bryan, William Jennings (Secretary of State) *245*
      Burleson, Albert (Postmaster General) *245*
      Daniels, Josephus (Secretary of the Navy) *245*
      Garrison, Lindley (Secretary of War) *245*
      Houston, David (Secretary of Agriculture) *245*
      Lane, Franklin (Secretary of the Interior) *245*
      Marshall, Thomas (Vice President) *245*
      McAdoo, William (Secretary of the Treasury) *245*
      McReynolds, James (Attorney General) *245*
      Redford, William (Secretary of Comerce) *245*
      Wilson, William (Secretary of Labor) *245*
   Cabinet - second term
      Baker, Newton (Secretary of War) *248*
      Burleson, Albert (Postmaster General) *248*

INDEX

Daniels, Josephus (Secretary of the Navy) **248**
Gregory, Thomas (Attorney General) **248**
Houston, David (Secretary of Agriculture) **248**
Lane, Franklin (Secretary of the Interior) **248**
Lansing, Robert (Secretary of State) **248**
Marshall, Thomas (Vice President) **248**
McAdoo, William (Secretary of the Treasury) **248**
Redford, William (Secretary of Comerce) **248**
Wilson, William (Secretary of Labor) **248**
Career
   New Jersey, governor of **243**
   Princeton University, professor, administrator, and president **243**
Death
   February 3, 1924 **251**
Elections
   1912 Presidential Election (Elected President) **243**
   1916 Presidential Election (Elected President) **247**
Family
   Ann, Joseph, and Marion (Siblings) **242**
   Wilson, Joseph and Janet (Parents) **242**
Inauguration
   1913, inaugural address **244**
   1971, inaugural address **248**
Key Events
   Actors Equity Association, formed **251**
   Aero Products, later became Boeing Company, founded **252**
   American Civil Liberties Union, founded **254**
   American Tobacco Company, introduced Lucky Strike cigarettes **253**
   Barnes & Noble, opened first retail book store **253**
   Boston police strike, first by government employees **254**
   Consumer Price Index, created **252**
   Daylight savings time, established **253**
   Frigidaire Company, formed **253**
   Grand Canyon National Park, opened **254**
   Lions Club, formed **253**
   Merrill Lynch, brokerage **251**
   National quota system, created for immigration **255**
   Panama Canal, opened connecting Atlantic and Pacific Oceans **252**
   Prentice-Hall, began publications **251**
   Spanish Flu, killed 700,000 **253**
   Tulsa Massacre, hundreds killed **255**
   Wall Street, anarchists planted bombs, exploded at noon **254**
   Woolworth Building, first skyscraper in New York City **251**
   Wrigley Field, opened for Chicago Cubs **252**
Laws
   17th Amendment to the U.S. Constitution ratified **244**
   18th Amendment to the U.S. Constitution ratified **250**
   19th Amendment to the U.S. Constitution ratified **251**
   1914 Clayton Anti-Trust Act **246**
   Brushaber vs Union Pacific Railroad **247**
   Conscription Act **249**
   Espionage Act **249**
   Federal Reserve Act **245**
   Pittman Act **249**
   Revenue Act **249**
   Sedition Act **249**
   Selective Service Act **249**
   Underwood-Simmons Tariff Act **244**
   Volstead Act **251**
   War Risk Act **249**
   Webb-Kenyon Interstate Liquor Shipments Act **245**
Marriage
   Axson, Ellen Louise (First Wife) **243**
   Bolling, Edith (Second Wife) **247**
U.S. Supreme Court Rulings
   Dodge vs Ford Motor Company **250**
   Schenck vs United States **250**
   United States vs United States Steel Corp **250**
   Weeks vs United States **245**
women weavers' strike **65**
Works Progress Administration **290, 443**
World Health Organization **578, 579, 607, 608, 659**
World's Fair **119, 169, 204, 252, 305, 382**
World War I **246, 755**
World War II **285, 296, 298, 314, 322, 333, 352, 370, 393, 412, 502, 767, 774, 781**
Wounded Knee **203, 410**
Wright, Fielding **314**
Wright, Jonathan **167**
Wright, Wilbur and Orville **231**

X

XYZ Affair *32*

Y

Yale University *68, 76, 402, 412, 448, 468, 482, 502, 503, 505, 752, 753, 774, 779, 781, 791*
Yalta *301, 762, 763*
Yank, Billy *142*
Yom Kippur *401, 433, 773*
Yorktown *8, 297, 715*
Young, Andrew *432*

Z

Zangara, Giuseppe *287*
Zapruder, Abraham *363*

www.ingramcontent.com/pod-product-compliance
Lightning Source LLC
Chambersburg PA
CBHW040236110526
44582CB00022B/213/J